Studies in Church History

40

RETRIBUTION, REPENTANCE, AND RECONCILIATION

RETRIBUTION, REPENTANCE, AND RECONCILIATION

PAPERS READ AT
THE 2002 SUMMER MEETING AND
THE 2003 WINTER MEETING OF
THE ECCLESIASTICAL HISTORY SOCIETY

EDITED BY

KATE COOPER
and
JEREMY GREGORY

PUBLISHED FOR
THE ECCLESIASTICAL HISTORY SOCIETY
BY
THE BOYDELL PRESS
2004

First published 2004

A publication of the Ecclesiastical History Society
in association with The Boydell Press
an imprint of Boydell & Brewer Ltd
PO Box 9, Woodbridge, Suffolk IP12 3DF, UK
and of Boydell & Brewer Inc.
668 Mt. Hope Avenue, Rochester, NY 14620, USA
website: www.boydellandbrewer.com

ISBN 0 9529733 9 1

ISSN 0424-2084

A catalogue record for this book is available
from the British Library

Library of Congress Cataloging-in-Publication Data
Ecclesiastical History Society. Summer Meeting (2002 : Leeds, England)
Retribution, repentance, and reconciliation : papers read at the 2002 Summer Meeting and
the 2003 Winter Meeting of the Ecclesiastical History Society / edited by Kate Cooper,
Jeremy Gregory.
p. cm. – (Studies in church history, ISSN 0424-2084 ; 40)
Includes bibliographical references.
ISBN 0-9529733-9-1
1. Repentance – Christianity – History of doctrines – Congresses. 2. Retribution – Religious
aspects – Christianity – History of doctrines – Congresses. 3. Reconciliation – Religious aspects –
Christianity – History of doctrines – Congresses. I. Cooper, Catherine Fales, 1960– II. Gregory,
Jeremy. III. Ecclesiastical History Society. Winter Meeting (2003 : London, England)
IV. Title. V. Series.
BR141.S84 vol. 40
[BT800]
270 s–dc22   2003025129

Details of previous volumes are available from Boydell & Brewer Ltd

This book is printed on acid-free paper

Typeset by Pru Harrison, Woodbridge, Suffolk
Printed in Great Britain by
Antony Rowe Ltd, Chippenham, Wiltshire

CONTENTS

PREFACE

'Retribution, Repentance, and Reconciliation' was the theme chosen by Professor Hugh McLeod for his Presidency of the Ecclesiastical History Society in 2002–3. In a world marked by the repercussions of the events of 11 September 2001, and with religious and political tensions in so many parts of the globe, the theme was highly pertinent. The contents of the present volume comprise the seven main papers delivered at the summer conference of 2002 and the January meeting in 2003, and a selection of the communications offered in the summer. We are grateful to the members of the Society who lent their time and expertise to the peer review of submissions, and to the authors for their timely and productive response to the resulting queries and requests for revision.

The Society wishes to thank the University of Leeds, and especially the staff at Devonshire Hall for their co-operation at the summer conference, and is particularly indebted to Professor Claire Cross and Dr Krista Cowman for organizing the outings. Thanks are also due to the Institute for Historical Research in London and its staff for accommodating the January meeting.

As the incoming editors, we would like to thank Robert Swanson both for his sage counsel in our first year, and for his sterling work as editor of *Studies in Church History* for the last eight years. He has been single-handedly responsible for volumes 32 to 39. Perhaps only we can appreciate the huge amount of work he has done on the Society's behalf, and how any one in a full-time lecturing post, with all the pressures placed on the modern academic, can manage to take on this role without any assistance, and still remain sane, eludes us. We are thus grateful to the Society and to the University of Manchester for funding Dr Barbara Crostini as Editorial Fellow in Church History. The post was designed to assist us in our editorial task, in addition to supporting her own research in the history of Byzantine Christianity. As the authors in this volume will know, Barbara has gone beyond the call of duty, and her painstaking attention to detail, her hard work, and her unflagging sense of humour has made our task much easier and much more fun than we ever imagined.

Kate Cooper
Jeremy Gregory

CONTRIBUTORS

David BAGCHI
Lecturer in Theology, University of Hull

John BOSSY
Emeritus Professor of History, University of York

Andrew CAMBERS
Stipendiary Lecturer in History, Keble College, Oxford

William H. CAMPBELL
Research Student, Department of Mediaeval History, University of St Andrews

Eric Josef CARLSON
Professor of History, Gustavus Adolphus College, St Peter, Minnesota

Allan K. DAVIDSON
Lecturer in Church History, St John's College, Auckland, and Director of Postgraduate Studies, School of Theology, University of Auckland, New Zealand

John W. de GRUCHY
Robert Selby Taylor Professor of Christian Studies at the University of Cape Town, South Africa

Sarah HAMILTON
Lecturer, Department of History, University of Exeter

Margaret HARVEY
Senior Lecturer in History, now retired, University of Durham

Andrew HOLMES
Research Student, The Queen's University, Belfast

W. M. JACOB
Archdeacon of Charing Cross, London

Andrew JOTISCHKY
Senior Lecturer in History, Lancaster University

Tim MACQUIBAN
Principal of Sarum College, Salisbury

Hugh MCLEOD (*President*)
Professor of Church History, Department of Theology,
University of Birmingham

Peter MARSHALL
Senior Lecturer, Department of History, University of Warwick

Mary Clare MARTIN
Senior Lecturer in the School of Education and Training,
University of Greenwich

Graeme MURDOCK
Senior Lecturer, Department of History, University of
Birmingham

M. A. OVERELL
Research Associate and Associate Lecturer, The Open University

Irina PAERT
Lecturer in History, Department of History & Welsh History,
University of Wales, Bangor

Richard PRICE
Lecturer in the History of Christianity, Heythrop College,
London

Christopher M. SCARGILL
Vicar of Ipstones, Staffordshire

Michael SNAPE
Lecturer in Church History, Department of Theology,
University of Birmingham

Christine TREVETT
Professor, Department of Religious and Theological Studies,
Cardiff University

Peter VAN ROODEN
Reader, Research Centre for Religion and Society, University of
Amsterdam

Vincent VIAENE
Post-doctoral Fellow, Fonds Wetenschappelijk Onderzoek –
Vlaanderen / Catholic University of Leuven

Michelle WOLFE
Research Student, Department of History, Ohio State University

John WOLFFE
Senior Lecturer in Religious Studies, The Open University

ABBREVIATIONS

AHR	*American Historical Review* (New York, 1895–)
CathHR	*Catholic Historical Review* (Washington, DC., 1915–)
CChr.CM	Corpus Christianorum, continuatio medievalis (Turnhout, 1966–)
DNB	*Dictionary of National Biography* (London, 1885–)
EHR	*English Historical Review* (London, 1886–)
JBS	*Journal of British Studies* (Hartford, CT, 1961–)
JEH	*Journal of Ecclesiastical History* (Cambridge, 1950–)
JThS	*Journal of Theological Studies* (London, 1899–)
GCS	*Die Griechischen christlichen Schriftsteller* (Leipzig, Berlin, 1897–)
HistJ	*Historical Journal* (Cambridge, 1958–)
HMC	*Historical Manuscripts Commission*
HThR	*Harvard Theological Review* (New York and Cambridge, MA, 1908–)
MGH	*Monumenta Germaniae Historica inde ab a. c. 500 usque ad a. 1500*, ed. G. H. Pertz et al. (Hanover, Berlin, etc., 1826–)
ns	new series
os	old series
PG	*Patrologia Graeca*, ed. J. P. Migne, 161 vols + 4 index vols (Paris, 1857–66)
PL	*Patrologia Latina*, ed. J. P. Migne, 217 vols + 4 index vols (Paris, 1841–61)
PO	*Patrologia Orientalis*, ed. R. Graffin and F. Nau (Paris, 1907–)
PS	Parker Society (Cambridge, 1841–55)
RS	Rerum brittanicarum medii aevi scriptores, 99 vols (London, 1858–1981) = Rolls Series
SCH	Studies in Church History (London, Oxford, Woodbridge, 1964–)
SCH.S	Studies in Church History: Subsidia (Oxford, Woodbridge, 1978–)
STC	A. W. Pollard and G. R. Redgrave, *A Short Title Catalogue*

| | *of Books Printed in England, Scotland and Ireland and of English Books Printed Abroad 1475–1640*, 3 vols (2nd edn, London, 1976–91) |
| *TRHS* | *Transactions of the Royal Historical Society* (London, Cambridge, 1871–) |

INTRODUCTION

Recently the Archbishop of Canterbury, addressing the General Synod of the Church of England, called for an end to the civil war over homosexuality, and urged the need for 'repentance' and 'reconciliation'. In doing so he touched on two words that have been of central concern to Christians throughout their history. He did not mention what might befall those who failed to heed his appeal. Western Christians speak much more readily nowadays of forgiveness than of retribution, though the concept remains very much alive in other parts of the world – and indeed in some other areas of contemporary western culture. In Britain, for instance, while Christian ministers concentrate their efforts on trying to reclaim notorious criminals, the tabloid press gleefully announces that they will go to hell. In the second century, as Christine Trevett shows, some Christian rigorists so emphasized the threat of retribution that they tried to limit the possibilities of repentance by, for instance, confidently defining the sin against the Holy Ghost, for which there is no forgiveness. Such rigorism seems to have been especially persuasive in times of persecution, as is also shown by M. A. Overell's account of 'anti-Nicodemist' Protestants in the mid-sixteenth century. But for most of their history, Christians have held the principles of retribution, repentance and reconciliation in balance, insisting on the possibility of reconciliation between God and humanity and between human beings, on repentance as a necessary precondition, and the inevitability of retribution if there is no repentance and reconciliation. As Tim Macquiban argues, even those who preached most explicitly about the danger of hell generally held open the possibility of forgiveness for the truly repentant – the dying thief on the cross being the supreme example. While some of those who warned of hell may have enjoyed terrifying their audiences, just as some people nowadays enjoy predicting environmental disasters or nuclear winters, then as now most such prophets of doom were motivated primarily by humane concern, and a sense of responsibility towards those who could be saved if the escape route were pointed out sufficiently clearly.

A considerable number of the papers collected here are concerned with the processes by which churches disciplined their members, drawing up rules of permissible behaviour, punishments for those who deviated, and procedures by which they could show repentance and be reintegrated into the Christian community. In sectarian communities, whether in pre-Constantinian times, in modern pluralist societies, or in groups like the priestless Old Believers of Tsarist Russia, these rules only affected those who had chosen to belong, and thereby to separate themselves from the majority of their neighbours. But even here, as with the Old Believers, described by Irina Paert, the official rules might be so strict as to threaten the community's survival, and compromise might thus be necessary in practice. In the long centuries of Christendom, when nearly everyone was born into the Christian community, and had little option but to live and die in it, the church played a crucial part in defining rules for the whole of society. Yet, in practice, compromise was necessary here too. Other elites, with their own agendas, rivalled the clergy; values which had little connection with Christianity competed with those prescribed by the Church. One side of the coin can be seen in Ulster in the eighteenth and early nineteenth century, where, as Andrew Holmes shows, the many Presbyterians whose sexual mores did not conform with the norms defined by their church were nonetheless generally ready to appear before the church session and to show repentance. The other side is seen in the repeated attempts by the Reformed authorities in various parts of sixteenth- and seventeenth-century Europe to impose new restrictions on acceptable clothing. As Graeme Murdock contends, the frequency of such decrees suggested that a large part of the people had failed to internalize the values preached from the pulpit.

Within societies claiming to be Christian, the Church has had an essential role both within the system of justice generally, and specifically in the machinery for resolving disputes, as many contributions to the volume show. One function of human justice has commonly been seen as the bringing of sinners to repentance, so that they may escape divine punishment in the next life. But Christians have also commonly believed that God intervenes directly in the present life to punish individuals, communities and nations. Disasters of all kinds, personal and collective, have been interpreted in such terms. In the first half of the nineteenth century, the subject of John Wolffe's essay, wars, famines and cholera epidemics were understood in this light by many British evangelicals, though, by about 1860, Christians, as much as religious sceptics, were tending to question such arguments. These ideas have not died out entirely, even in western Europe, as is shown by recent claims that AIDS is a judgement of God on homosexuality, or on sexual promiscuity more generally.

These papers range widely though unevenly across Christian history. They include both detailed local studies and ambitious reinterpretations of long-term change, which identify major watersheds variously in the eleventh century, the sixteenth, the eighteenth or the nineteenth. The emphasis is mainly, though not exclusively, on western Europe, and especially on the early modern period. Many regions of the world and Christian traditions, and some relevant topics, are considered sparingly or not at all. Tyrannicide is one form of retribution that is not discussed. The motives of those who assassinated Henri III and IV of France, or who plotted unsuccessfully to kill James I or Hitler would have been worth considering here. There is also surprisingly little discussion of beliefs about hell and purgatory, or of the intense debates which have surrounded these doctrines. Providential judgements on individuals are only mentioned in passing. It is fitting, however, that the volume should end with John de Gruchy's paper, which includes discussion of South Africa's Truth and Reconciliation Commission: however bitterly Christians may disagree, as de Gruchy himself shows, about the preconditions for reconciliation and the means by which it may be achieved, reconciliation must surely be their ultimate objective.

Hugh McLeod
Birmingham, 15 July 2003

'I HAVE HEARD FROM SOME TEACHERS': THE SECOND-CENTURY STRUGGLE FOR FORGIVENESS AND RECONCILIATION

by CHRISTINE TREVETT

IN the close-knit valleys communities of South Wales where I was brought up, some fingers are still pointed at 'the scab', the miner who, for whatever reason, did not show solidarity in the strike of 1984–5, cement the definition between 'them' and 'us'.[1] In trouble-torn Palestine of the twenty-first century, or among the paramilitary groups of Northern Ireland today, suspected informers are summarily assassinated. In South Africa, the *Truth and Reconciliation Committee* continues its work in the post-apartheid era.[2] In second-century Rome and elsewhere, the 'brothers' and 'sisters' who made up the fictive kinship groups – the churches – in the growing but illicit cult of the Christians were conscious both of their own vulnerability to outside opinion and of their failures in relation to their co-religionists. The questions which they asked, too, were questions about reconciliation and/or (spiritual) death.

This was an age which was coming to recognize that the Church would indeed continue, alongside some writers' recognition that 'these are the last times'.[3] It was not so much the end of the cosmos as the fate of the individual which was beginning to engage even those well-versed in the language of apocalyptic.[4] What was to be done about failure, lack of loyalty, compromise and even criminal wrong-doing among Christians?

---

[1] Subsequent generations remain tainted by association, as in 'her father was a scab'.

[2] See below, John W. de Gruchy, 'From Resistance to National Reconciliation: the Response and Role of the Ecumenical Church in South Africa', 369–84.

[3] Ignatius, *Ephesians*, 11.1 [hereafter *Eph*]. All Apostolic Fathers' writings referred to, i.e. Ignatius's Letters, *1 Clement*, *2 Clement*, Polycarp's *Philippians*, *Martyrdom of Polycarp*, Hermas's *The Shepherd*, *Didache* and *The Epistle of Barnabas*, are accessible in *The Apostolic Fathers*, ed. and transl. Kirsopp Lake, Loeb Classical Library, 2 vols (London, 1972). The *Epistula Apostolorum* even sets a date. On this latter document see D. G. Müller, 'Epistula Apostolorum', in *New Testament Apocrypha* I, ed. W. Schneemelcher and R. McL. Wilson, 2 vols (revised edn, Cambridge, 1991), 249–84; Charles E. Hill, 'The *Epistula Apostolorum*: an Asian Tract from the Time of Polycarp', *Journal of Early Christian Studies* 7 (1999), 1–53 and the literature there.

[4] See e.g. Hermas's treatment of the Beast in *Vision* 4 of *The Shepherd*. This work is in three parts: Visions [hereafter *Vis*], Mandates [hereafter *Man*] and Similitudes [hereafter *Sim*].

In the second century there were of course the sins of adultery,[5] straying into dangerous theological company[6] and compromise through conformity with the social expectations of the world of the Roman empire. Implicit in these are two of 'The Big Three' sins,[7] which match also the concerns of the so-called 'Apostolic Decree' in Acts 15 – *viz.* adultery, idolatry and blood(shed). Adultery matched the Decree's 'fornication'; for New Testament writers, idolatry included 'food sacrificed to idols' and consumed in the shared meals of voluntary associations and trade guilds. In the second century, this concept included willingness, when challenged, to offer the libation before the image of the emperor or otherwise to deny Christ. I do not know of a second-century source dealing with an example of the last sin, if 'blood' is interpreted as bloodshed – but absence of evidence (of a church's response to such wrongdoing) is not evidence of absence. It is too early in the history of penitential discipline for the casuistry we see in the later Councils, in which a female Christian slave-owner might be accorded penance for bloodshed, in respect of having beaten her maidservant to death.[8]

The 'Big Three' apart, a recurring term in the literature of the Apostolic Fathers (from the first half of the century) was *dipsychia* – 'double-mindedness'.[9] This single concept might embrace a multitude of sins and accommodations,[10] and along with grave wrongs it raised questions about who was or was not to be associated with, and whether and how repentance might be publicly manifested and acknowledged. Such

---

[5] E.g. Hermas, *Man* 4.1.

[6] Seen in the Ignatian letters which are discussed below. Cf. *Sancti Irenaei Episcopi Lugdunensis, Adversus omnes Haereses*, ed. W. W. Harvey (Cambridge, 1857, repr. Ridgewood, NJ, 1965), 1.13.5 [hereafter Irenaeus, *AH*]: the wife of an Asiatic deacon, defiled theologically and physically by the Gnostic Marcus, was weaned back to the fold and spent all her time in public confession and weeping over her lapse.

[7] I borrow the phrase 'Big Three' from Everett Ferguson, 'Early Church Penance', *Restoration Quarterly* 36 (1994), 81–100. Adultery, idolatry and homicide become unpardonable sins for Tertullian in the early third century.

[8] Canon 5 of the early fourth-century Council of Elvira. For a discussion of its severities and inconsistencies, see James Dallen, *The Reconciling Community: the Rite of Penance* (Collegeville, MN, 1991), 58–62.

[9] The word and related forms occur in *1 Clement* 11.2; 23.2–3; *2 Clement* 11.2 and 5; 19.2; *Didache* 4.4; *Barnabas* 19.5; but especially in *The Shepherd: Vis* 2.2.4; 3.2.2; 3.3.4; 3.4.3; 3.7.1; 3.10.9; 3.11.2; 4.1.4 and 7; 4.2.4 and 6; *Man* 5.2.1; 9.1; 9.5–12; 10.1.1; 10.2.2 and 4; 11.1; 11.2.4; 11.13; 12.4.2; *Sim* 1.3; 2.2.7; 6.1.2; 8.7.1–2; 8.8.3 and 5; 8.9.4; 8.10.2; 8.11.3; 9.4; 9.18.3; 9.21.1–3; 10.2.

[10] In *The Shepherd*, for example, business affairs, riches and friendships with heathens, *Man* 10.1.4–5.

debates were compounded by the regular drama and tragedy born of external hostility towards Christians.

We should not think in terms of systematic persecution in the second century but rather localized outbreaks of hostility and harassment. This phenomenon left behind believers who were devastated by the group having been betrayed or deeply sorry that they had been among the betrayers. The slave of the Christian household – usually first to be rounded up when information was needed – may have been pressured under interrogation and torture into telling who worshipped and where, into denying personal association with Christians or loyalty to their beliefs, even into assenting to the kinds of accusations which were commonly made against Christians. Documents of the second century such as Pliny's letter to Trajan,[11] from his consular province of Pontus-Bithynia, and the martyrological sources from Smyrna and Gaul[12] tell of just such happenings. Yet the slave, she or he, would subsequently have to live in the ambit of Christians. Would this be in a state of reconciliation with individuals and Church?[13] What was to be done with the person of good standing, with *honour* in the eyes of the wider Greek or Roman community, who came broken and guilt-ridden to the Church after some local hostility in which he, a closet Christian among his pagan associates, had remained unscathed? Others well-known to him had not.

* * *

The difficulties of the third century and beyond were present in the second also, but we have few details.[14] Instead the sources give us all-too-brief glimpses of churches wrestling with the troublesome realities of failure and forgiveness at a time when the straight and narrow were

[11] Pliny (*Ep* 10.96), 112 CE, had tortured two female household servants (*ancillae*) who were *ministrae* (deacons) for evidence about the new religion.

[12] *Martyrdom of Polycarp*, 6.1 records the arrest of two 'lads' (male slaves). Under torture one revealed Polycarp's whereabouts. The letter from the churches of Lyon and Vienne, in Eusebius, *Historia Ecclesiastica*, ed. and transl. H. J. Lawlor and J. E. L. Oulton, Loeb Classical Library, 2 vols (London, 1973), 5.1.14 [hereafter *HE*], told of non-Christian slaves who succumbed to fear of suffering as they saw the Christians doing. When prompted they provided the accusations of incest and cannibalism of children which the authorities were looking for. On slaves accusing Christians of immorality, see too Justin Martyr, *Iustini Martyris Apologiae pro Christianis*, ed. Miroslav Marcovich, Patristische Texte und Studien 38 (Berlin and New York, 1994), 2.12.4.

[13] Hermas, *Sim* 9.26, tells of those who denied (under duress?) in time past and who had not returned to God and their church but were 'living alone'. For such, provided that they had not 'denied from their hearts', there was opportunity for repentance.

[14] Frances Young puts matters simply: 'Reconstructing exactly what was going on is not

still being defined, and variously defined by different kinds of Christians. 'Isms' took form in this century: Marcionism and Gnosticism, Encratism and Montanism. These movements prodded the Church into greater self-definition, that impacted upon its understanding of its own boundaries. Nevertheless, we have no liturgy of reconciliation, no picture of grovelling rites of *exomologesis*[15] – the humiliating confession as a prelude to restoration –, no treatises on binding and loosing, unless Melito of Sardis's writing on *The Key* (now lost) had been one such.[16] We know of no carefully-devised gradations of sins and sanctions, no Order of Penitents. There was as yet not even a canon of Scripture, no creed, no assured orthodoxy defined over against heresy. For much of the century, Jewish Christianity had not been squeezed so much by both sides, Jews and Christians, that it was wholly irrelevant. There were still not only judaizing Christians but Torah-observant Christians also.[17]

It would be good to have something akin to the treatises of Tertullian on penitence or purity but we are still in the wrong century, albeit only just.[18] His admirer Cyprian penned *De lapsis* decades afterwards (*c.*251). In second-century Christian writings, which sometimes only hint at problems and proposed solutions, we have to dig for the as-yet-unpolished nuggets on this subject. Yet there is enough to show us that at various points, and in various areas, different kinds of second-century Christians were either bound, on the one hand, to a rigidity which feared pollution, which stressed the purity and exclusivity of the group and was unforgiving or, on the other hand, did offer a more accommodating recognition of human weakness, the possibility of forgiveness and reconciliation. Middle ways were being forged between leaving unchallenged the pollution of Christian communities and regarding the imperfect and the failed as enemies/*echthroi*.[19]

---

easy', 'The Greek Fathers', in Ian Hazlett, ed., *Early Christianity: Origins and Evolution to AD 600: in Honour of W. H. C. Frend* (London, 1991), 135–47, 139.

[15] Cf. Tertullian, *de Paenitentia* 7–11 and *de Pudicitia* 13.18 [hereafter *de Paen* and *de Pud*]: all the works of Tertullian are edited in *Tertulliani Opera*, CChr.SL 1–2 (Turnhout, 1953–4); Origen, *Contra Celsum*, ed. Henry Chadwick (Cambridge, 1980), 6.15; Eusebius, *HE* 5.28.10–12. Irenaeus told of those who were ashamed to make public confession, lost hope of a Christian life and fell away or lived lives of vacillation (*AH* 1.13.7).

[16] Eusebius, *HE* 4.26.2.

[17] Iustini Martyris, *Dialogus cum Tryphone*, ed. Miroslav Marcovich, Patristische Texte und Studien 47 (Berlin and New York, 1997), 8 and 38.1; 112.4 [hereafter Justin, *Dial*].

[18] The earliest of Tertullian's Christian writings date from the final few years of the second century.

[19] For a review of the earliest evidence, see the introductory observations of Dallen, *The*

The Roman Christian called Hermas was author of the work entitled *The Shepherd*. He was once described memorably by B. H. Streeter as the White Rabbit among the Apostolic Fathers. He was timid and fussy, a 'kindly, incompetent middle-aged freedman, delightfully naïve', whose writing, said Streeter, showed his 'pottering mediocrity'.[20] Certainly there are things about this long document, *The Shepherd*, which do suggest 'Hermas in Wonderland'. Like the story of Alice, it is about change and the change is often signalled by extraordinary meetings with other-worldly or representative figures: Rhoda, the woman Church, angels including the Shepherd himself, and so on. The sweep of *change* is an important element in this work – change in a multi-faceted Church which was still being built, tested and perfected, and change in Hermas himself.

Today *The Shepherd* is not a writing with a large (scholarly) fan-club, but in the second, third and fourth centuries it was regarded in many churches as a writing with authority. We find it, for reasons unclear, bound, like the *Epistle of Barnabas*, with the canonical material in the pages of *Aleph*, Codex Sinaiticus, preserved in the British Library, London. By the time of Tertullian, however, in the early third century, there were those who had cause to disapprove of *The Shepherd*. This book – the nearest thing we have to a second-century document devoted to repentance and reconciliation– was too lax for the rigorists, too forgiving of even the worst of sins. As Tertullian slipped sideways into the New Prophecy (Montanism),[21] he, never liberal in sentiments,

Reconciling Community, 5–24 and the useful overview by Ferguson, 'Early Church Penance' (see n. 6). Other and some 'classic' studies include O. D. Watkins, *A History of Penance*, 2 vols (London, 1920), I; R. S. T. Haslehurst, *Some Account of the Penitential Discipline of the Early Church in the First Four Centuries* (London, 1921); Josef Hoh, *Die kirchliche Busse im II. Jahrhundert: eine Untersuchung der patristischen Busszeugnisse von Clemens Romanus bis Clemens Alexandrinus* (Breslau, 1932); Bernhard Poschmann, *Poenitentia Secunda. Die kirchliche Busse im ältesten Christentum bis Cyprian und Origenes. Eine dogmengeschichtliche Untersuchung* (Bonn, 1940), with texts, and, in English, his *Penance and the Anointing of the Sick* (London, 1964); W. Telfer, *The Forgiveness of Sins: an Essay in the History of Christian Doctrine and Practice* (London, 1959); F. van der Paverd, 'Disciplinarian Procedures in the Early Church', *Augustinianum* 21 (1981), 175–213; Karl Rahner, *Theological Investigations: vol. XV. Penance in the Early Church* (London, 1983); Ingrid Goldhahn-Müller, *Die Grenze der Gemeinde: Studien zum Problem der zweiten Busse im Neuen Testament unter Berücksichtigung der Entwicklung im 2. Jahrhundert bis Tertullien* (Göttingen, 1989).

[20] B. H. Streeter, *The Primitive Church* (London, 1929), 203.

[21] The term *Montanism* does not emerge until Cyril of Jerusalem in the fourth century. Tertullian, even when a Montanist, was always a Catholic, a view which is not peculiar to me. Christine Trevett, *Montanism: Gender, Authority and the New Prophecy* (Cambridge, 1996),

frothed about *The Shepherd*'s teaching on repentance. The fact that Tertullian labelled it '*The Shepherd* of adulterers' tends to be one of the very few things people know about Hermas's work.[22]

It is to Hermas, sometime in the early decades of the second century,[23] that we owe the phrase which forms my title, 'I have heard from some teachers', and those words lead us into the field of debate about forgiveness in different kinds of Christian communities. The debate is one we cannot follow with clarity because the sources which tell us of it are few and diverse geographically and in genre. Study of the second century is like that. Nevertheless, *The Shepherd* from Rome has to be the starting point[24] and, significantly, it has also been described by Carolyn Osiek as representing the Christianity of 'ordinary' Romans.[25]

This document, which came down on the side of forgiveness, was not from the circle of the educated elite. The circle around the Roman author of *1 Clement* (*To the Corinthians*), which identified with the values of the honour-seeking classes and *Pax Romana*, was different from that of Hermas[26] and different again from the philosophy and apologetics of Justin Martyr and his associates when in Rome. 'Ordinary' Roman Christians like Hermas,[27] who were neither intellectuals nor in receipt

66–76 and 114–16 on forgiveness; arguing similarly, David Rankin, *Tertullian and the Church* (Cambridge, 1995).

22 Tertullian, *de Pud* 20.

23 *The Shepherd* has been variously dated between 60–160 CE. Many writers now assume its evolution over several decades. A few assume multiple authorship (which I do not). I take it to date from around 90–120 CE and to have been created over an extended period.

24 It proved to be probably the most widely-read document of the first five Christian centuries, outside of (now) canonical writings.

25 Carolyn Osiek's work on *The Shepherd* includes *Rich and Poor in the Shepherd of Hermas: an Exegetical-Social Investigation* (Washington, DC, 1983); 'The Genre and Function of *The Shepherd* of Hermas', in Adela Yarbro Collins, ed., *Early Christian Apocalypticism: Genre and Social Setting, Semeia* 36 (1986), 113–21; 'The Early Second Century Through the Eyes of Hermas: Continuity and Change', *Biblical Theology Bulletin* 20 (1990), 116–22 and *The Shepherd of Hermas: a Commentary*, Hermeneia Commentary Series (Minneapolis, MN, 1999).

26 Most writers on first- and early second-century Rome (Lampe, Brändle and Stegemann, Jeffers, Maier among them) acknowledge the existence of a number of different house churches in Paul's time and later. Harry O. Maier has drawn attention to the differences between Clement's circle and that of Hermas: *The Social Setting of the Ministry as Reflected in the Writings of Hermas, Clement and Ignatius* (Waterloo, Ont., 1991). Cf. also Christine Trevett, 'Charisma and Office in a Changing Church', in Alan Kreider, ed., *The Origins of Christendom in the West* (Edinburgh, 2001), 179–203.

27 Some writers have been dismissive of Hermas's intelligence. Martin Dibelius, *Der Hirt des Hermas* (Tübingen, 1923), 423, thought he lacked any theology, while others have called him 'blundering' and 'careless'. See J. Christian Wilson, *Toward a Reassessment of the Shepherd of Hermas: Its Date and Pneumatology* (Lewiston, N.Y., and Lampeter, 1993), 1–4 and William Jerome Wilson, 'The Career of the Prophet Hermas', *HThR* 20 (1927), 21–62, 35: 'If men

of much, if any, of that *honour* which was so highly prized, raised the issues which *The Shepherd* addressed. Failure, repentance and reconciliation were among their concerns, as Hermas, for one, envisaged storm clouds looming.

Hermas the *threptos* (*Vis* 1.1) – a foundling, an exposed infant raised in slavery – had become a freedman whose fortunes had variously risen and fallen. This fussy White Rabbit was a sensitive if generally cheerful soul.[28] Perhaps he had been rather too laid-back in times past but now he was troubled (so his visions indicated) by the direction some Christians in Rome were taking. This was the Rome of Pliny the Younger's letters, of Tacitus and acid-penned satirist Juvenal and of the epigrams of Martial. Some were of the opinion that all the dregs settled there. In its teeming streets and insanitary tenements[29] lived also the Christians who made up the house-churches. Hermas's picture was of their factionalism, the breakdown of cohesion in churches. Matters of status, honour, what we might call 'class', real poverty and mutual mistrust were in the mix.[30] *The Shepherd* was recalling Christians to a single-minded loyalty to the parallel society which was the Church in the churches.

The rhetoric of this apocalyptic writing may lead us to think that the Roman churches were in more dire a state than they actually were,[31] yet as Hermas presented matters, 'The Great Tribulation' was yet to

such as Hermas had become the real leaders of Christianity, if such books as his had made up the New Testament, the church could hardly have survived. For the intellectual quality of its leadership has been one large secret of Christianity's success'.

Carolyn Osiek, 'The Oral World of Early Christianity in Rome: the Case of Hermas', in Karl P. Donfried and Peter Richardson, eds, *Judaism and Christianity in First-Century Rome* (Grand Rapids, MI, and Cambridge, 1998), 151–72, 152 on 'ordinary' Christians.

28 Hermas, *Vis* 1.2.3. He had also been over-indulgent as a parent and unassertive.

29 See the survey article on the city by J. B. Patterson, 'The City of Rome from Republic to Empire', *Journal of Roman Studies* 82 (1992), 186–215; James S. Jeffers, 'Jewish and Christian Families in First-Century Rome', in Donfried and Richardson, eds, *Judaism and Christianity*, 128–50, 132, states: 'The majority of Jews and Christians of necessity would have lived either in tiny apartments several stories above ground floor, in the homes of their masters or former masters, or in *tabernae* where their shops were located.' See too idem, *Conflict at Rome: Social Order and Hierarchy in Early Christianity* (Minneapolis, MN, 1991), ch. 1, for a vivid picture of the life of the lower classes in the *insulae* tenements and the ground-floor *tabernae*.

30 I consider all such matters in my forthcoming book from University of Wales Press, *Christian Women and the Time of the Apostolic Fathers (pre-160 CE): Corinth, Rome and Asia Minor*, Part Two.

31 Writers have noted that Hermas's picture of the churches in Rome suggests the same kinds of problems which are found in much later documents. See e.g. W. H. C. Frend, *Martyrdom and Persecution in the Early Church: a Study of a Conflict from the Maccabees to Donatus* (Oxford, 1965), 181.

come.[32] Failures of pastoral care were all too apparent and the tendency of those who had some honour in the world was to cling to it rather than be loyal to their co-religionists when the going got tough.[33] With his own children embroiled in something unacceptable but undescribed,[34] how could he *not* be troubled by matters of punishment, penitence and reconciliation? Robin Lane Fox described *The Shepherd* as a document showing 'the print-out of Christianity's impact on a sensitive Christian soul'.[35]

Hermas, now reforming and instructed to live celibately within marriage,[36] envisaged the pitiless *Shepherd of Punishment* shepherding onto precipices and thorny entrapments those of the flock who had fallen prey to luxury and the lusts of this world, and who looked cheerful and well-fed.[37] The vision frightened him, who once had been prone to easy cheerfulness and love of success.

The Shepherd from Rome was not the only document to be dealing with the matter of the fate of the failing. In the *Apocalypse of Peter*, from Asia Minor or Egypt, perhaps,[38] paraenesis was also couched in Apocalypse form and as the message of the pre-ascension Jesus. It was reminding Christians of what judgement day and hell would be like, with brief references to paradise also. Here, from pre-150 CE, is the earliest Christian vision of hell to have survived.[39] Its punishments

[32] *The Shepherd* has many elements of an Apocalypse in it but is not a true one. On Great Tribulation, see R. J. Bauckham, 'The Great Tribulation in the Shepherd of Hermas', *JThS* NS 25 (1974), 27–40.

[33] Failure in the face of persecution was a special case. Cf. Hermas, *Vis* 3.2–4; *Sim* 6.2.2–4 and especially *Sim* 9.19.1. Hermas, though not guiltless, had never gone so far (*Vis* 3.2). In *Vis* 3.3 one Maximus, who had formerly denied the faith, was challenged about the coming persecution.

[34] I am not here discussing the extent to which the biographical details of Hermas and his family may be literary devices.

[35] Robin Lane Fox, *Pagans and Christians* (London, 1986), 388–9.

[36] Hermas, *Vis* 2.2.1–4. See too *Man* 4.4 on post-widowhood continence and the remission of sins. Lifelong continence became a requirement in some later penances.

[37] Hermas, *Vis* 6.2.4–7. Luxury was broadly defined in terms of all acts (such as the satisfying of a bad temper) done with pleasure (*Sim* 6.5.5). Useful, life-giving luxuriating (including enjoyment of doing good) was distinguished from the unrepentant, harmful, death-bringing sort.

[38] R. J. Bauckham, 'The Apocalypse of Peter: an Account of Research', in *Aufstieg und Niedergang der römischen Welt* II.25.6 (Berlin and New York, 1988), 4712–50 [hereafter ANRW]; idem, 'Jews and Christians in the Land of Israel at the time of the Bar Kochba War, with Special Reference to the *Apocalypse of Peter*', in Graham N. Stanton and Guy G. Stroumsa, eds, *Tolerance and Intolerance in Early Judaism and Christianity* (Cambridge, 1998), 228–38; D. G. Müller, 'Apocalypse of Peter', in *New Testament Apocrypha*, 2: 620–38 [hereafter *Ap Pet*].

[39] Richard Bauckham, *The Fate of the Dead: Studies on the Jewish and Christian Apocalypses*,

reflected the *lex talionis* principle. It offered, among the castigations of the disobedient children, erring slaves, homosexuals and betrayers of the faith and the faithful, vivid images of accusatory offspring, formerly aborted or exposed, the mothers punished neck-high in excretions, guilty males hung by feet or thighs, both well-attested euphemisms for penis.[40]

Angels of punishment and Petrine apocalyptists would not have made for stress-free Christian living. The perils of hell coloured some Christians' thinking.[41] In Rome in the 150s, Justin Martyr knew of an anxious Christian woman who had taken to warning her pagan husband of the perils of hell. Perhaps she was familiar with *The Shepherd*'s promise that the heathen, like unrepentant sinners generally, would burn (*Sim* 4.4).[42] Her husband ensured that her catechist was put to death.[43]

So was the woman or man who strayed after baptismal remission of sins lost to hell? Were their cases hopeless, even if they sought repentance and reconciliation? Did the *kind* of sin make a difference? There was no single or simple second-century answer. In his contact with other Christians in Rome, Hermas too had encountered different perspectives on the matter of post-baptismal sin.

'I have heard from some teachers', he reported, saying 'that there is no second repentance beyond the one given when we went down into the water and received remission of our former sins.'[44] The angelic

---

Supplements to Novum Testamentum 93 (Leiden, 1998); Martha Himmelfarb, *Tours of Hell: an Apocalyptic Form in Jewish and Christian Literature* (Philadelphia, PA, 1983). This Apocalypse was also considered authoritative by some. See e.g. the Muratorian Canon, ll. 71–4, and Clement of Alexandria according to Eusebius, *HE* 6.14.1 The text is considered in Dennis D. Buchholz, *Your Eyes Will Be Opened: a Study of the Greek (Ethiopic) Apocalypse of Peter* (Atlanta, GA, 1988), 19–42 on early witnesses to its use and 43ff. on secondary ones.

[40] P. Gray, 'Abortion, Infanticide, and the Social Rhetoric of the *Apocalypse of Peter*', *Journal of Early Christian Studies* 9 (2001), 313–37.

[41] The Greek Rainer Fragment of the *Ap Pet* offers the 'curious doctrine', subsequently edited out (Buchholz, *Your Eyes Will Be Opened*, 348, comparing *Epistula Apostolorum* and *Sib Orac* 2. 330–38), of universal salvation, in that any of the saved may request others' release from punishment. See his *Supplement* on this issue, 348–51.

[42] Repentance was open to such people until the last day, however: Hermas, *Vis* 2.2.4–5.

[43] Justin, *2 Apol* 2. See Margaret Y. Macdonald, *Early Christian Women and Pagan Opinion: the Power of the Hysterical Woman* (Cambridge, 1996), 205–13; P. Lampe, *Die Stadtrömischen Christen in den ersten beiden Jahrhunderten: Untersuchungen zur Sozialgeschichte* (Tübingen, 1987), 200–3.

[44] Hermas, *Man* 4.3.1; *Man* 4.3.3–5 seems to imply a separation, like that made later by Clement of Alexandria, between baptismal 'remission' of sin and penitential 'purgation': Clemens Alexandrinus, *Stromata* Buch I–IV, ed. Otto Stählin, revised edn Ludwig Früchtel, Die griechischen christlichen Schriftsteller 52.15 (Berlin, 1985), 2.13; 4.24 [hereafter *Strom*

intermediary said that he had heard correctly. This was Hermas's starting point but it was not the final picture which *The Shepherd* produced.

What Hermas had 'heard' was probably an understanding of matters found also in the Roman circle around the author of the Epistle to the Hebrews.[45] That too had been uncompromising:

> For it is impossible to restore again to repentance those who have once been enlightened, who have tasted the heavenly gift, and have become partakers of the Holy Spirit. . . if they then commit apostasy, since they crucify the Son of God on their own account and hold him up to contempt. . . for if we sin deliberately after receiving the knowledge of the truth, there no longer remains a sacrifice for sins but a fearful prospect of judgement, and a fury of fire. . .[46]

Here and in Hebrews 6:8, by analogy with cultivated land which proves worthless, the end is to be burnt.[47]

In both *The Shepherd* and in Hebrews scholars have found language and ideas which may be paralleled in the writings from Qumran.[48] Evidently Hebrews was interpreted by some Christians as signaling that there was no repentance for apostasy, at least.[49] In the case of *The Shepherd*, however, as the work progressed and particularly in the section

---

and GCS]. Cf. also Eusebius, *HE* 5.28.12. It witnesses to a Church wrestling with the dangers of inconsistency and hypocrisy. See Rahner, *Penance*, 77; Poschmann, *Poenitentia Secunda*, 159–68; idem, *Penance*, 28–9; Graydon F. Snyder, *The Shepherd of Hermas*, The Apostolic Fathers 6 (Camden, NJ, 1969), 36, 69–72; Ferguson, 'Early Church Penance', 94; Osiek, *Shepherd of Hermas*, 114–15.

[45] Heb. 13: 24: 'They who are of Italy'. There are parallels between passages in Hebrews and the Roman Clement's Letter to Corinth (36, 1–6) also. Useful sources are F. F. Bruce, 'To the Hebrews: a Document of Roman Christianity', *ANRW* II.25.4, 3496–3601; Harold W. Attridge, *The Epistle to the Hebrews*, Hermeneia Commentary Series (Philadelphia, PA, 1989); William L. Lane, *Hebrews*, Word Biblical Commentary 47, 2 vols (Dallas, TX, 1991), 1: Hebrews 1–8.

[46] Heb. 6: 4–6; 10: 26–27 (RSV).

[47] Once enlightened (Hebrews makes no mention of water or baptism, cf. 10: 32) but straying, a fresh start, or renewal (*anakainizein*), in repentance was impossible. Cf. also Heb. 10: 28–31; 12: 16–17 on the fate of Esau who desired repentance.

[48] Characterized by sharp boundary definitions, careful scrutiny pre-membership, rites of discipline and graded periods of exclusion. See Göran Forkman, *The Limits of the Religious Community: Expulsion from the Religious Community within the Qumran Sect, within Rabbinic Judaism and within Primitive Christianity* (Lund, 1972).

[49] Second-century reservations about the authority of this document may be related not just to its anonymity and the distinctive nature of its exegesis, but also to its uncompromising stance.

known as the *Mandates*, that rigorous ideal was being tamed in ways fitting to pastoral reality.[50] Hence in due course Tertullian would sneer at '*The Shepherd* of adulterers', given its teaching that properly penitent adulterers, like even properly penitent deniers of the faith, might enjoy reconciliation.[51] Tertullian turned to believing that murder, the idolatry which was lapsing from Christianity and adultery/fornication, could never be forgiven on earth,[52] though he too had once allowed that the rites of *exomologesis* would extinguish hell for the publicly penitent.[53]

Without specifying procedures for *acts* of repentance or rites of reconciliation, *The Shepherd* stressed prompt and sincere conversion (*metanoia*). Repeated acts of repentance, he said – for which some Roman churches may have had provision –,[54] followed by reversion to

---

50   Another point of contact between Hebrews and *The Shepherd* is the use of the unusual (for early Christians) term *hegoumenoi* for leaders (Heb. 13: 7. 17 and 24; Hermas, *Vis* 2.26; 3.9.7f). Ecclus 30: 18 (cf. 17: 17; 4: 17) may lie behind both and the term occurs also in *1 Clement* 1.3 (cf. 21.6). Whether and to what extent Hermas was associated with the circles which produced or received Hebrews is not easy to establish. He shows no knowledge of the kind of quotation and exegesis of Scripture which Hebrews contains and quotes only a (lost) non-canonical writing, *The Book of Eldad and Modat* (*Vis* 2.3.4). The words 'The Lord is near those that turn to him' may suggest that the work contained teaching on forgiveness.

51   In *The Shepherd*, the *truly* repentant sinner might be received back (*Man* 4.1.8–9) and not even the adulterer, the teacher of false doctrine and the apostate were wholly beyond the pale (*Sim* 8).

52   There should be lifelong penance, but only in the hope that God would forgive at death (*de Pud* 2 and 4). Others, in Rome (or Carthage or both) were teaching differently (*de Pud* 1). It was too much for Tertullian that the 'bishop of bishops' (presumably in Rome) had declared remission of the sins of adultery and fornication for those whose penitence was complete (possibly, though we do not know this, as part of an on-going engagement with New Prophecy and other rigorists). In the mid-third century there were North African bishops who, like Tertullian, would not offer reconciliation to adulterers (Cyprian, *Ep* 51.21). It is beyond the scope of this paper to consider whether and to what extent Tertullian was innovatory in treating some sins as not remissable, though there is much debate on the matter.

53   Tertullian, *de Paen* 12.1, but contrast *de Pud* 6. 7 and 13. Tertullian, *de Paen* 7, had initially allowed a single post-baptismal repentance. It was a view which became widespread in the Church. Release from penalty (*poena*) was achieved through 'satisfaction' made, in compensatory penitence (*poenitentia*: see *de Paen* 5 and 6): see below, John Bossy, 'Satisfaction in Early Modern Europe, *c*.1400–1700', 106–18, 106. The idea of remission through compensation had as its paradigm the death of Christ. For Origen (*Homiliae in Lev.* 2; *de Oratione* 28; *Exhoratio ad martyrium* 30), acts of penitence and not just martyrdom acted as a second baptism for remission of sins. Day and night the penitent's couch was tear-drenched. Similarly, Clement of Alexandria likened a Christian-turned-outlaw's repentant tears to his second (self-) baptism, followed by prayer and fasting by others for and with him, until he was restored (see Clemens Alexandrinus, *Quis dives salvetur*, ed. Otto Stählin, revised edn Ludwig Früchtel, GCS (Berlin, 1970), 39–42, especially the last chapter).

54   Cf. Irenaeus, *AH* 3.4.3. Here Cerdon, predecessor of Marcion in heresy, was said to

sin, would bring no place in God's Church (*Man* 4.3.1–7). There could be post-baptismal (re)conversion as a 'once only',[55] last chance affair.[56] Lack of repentance spelt death,[57] he made clear, but there was hope. Hermas seized on the verb *renew* (*anakainizo*), which Hebrews had used (Heb. 6: 6), and on the time which was left.[58]

Again it must be stressed that matters of geography and kinds of theology come into play when discussing second-century concerns. Thus, at much the same time as Hermas was writing in the West, in the East in the third year of Trajan's reign (101 CE) and among Aramaic speakers, the visionary Jewish-Christian teacher Élchasai had also started to preach what was termed 'the Gospel of a new forgiveness of sins'.[59] Here was an advocate of prayer facing Jerusalem, of re-baptism for remission of (especially sexual) sins,[60] and unlike Hermas he was promoting early marriage rather than a celibate lifestyle. Hermas did not represent *the* early second-century view, but one of a number[61] and the second century saw teachers who would have none of Hermas's reconciling and who would not have countenanced the interpretations of Élchasai.

Indeed, some scholars have suggested that in general the wind of

have been in the Roman church for some time, frequently making public confession, once confessing after having been teaching in secret and finally being denounced for wrong doctrine.

55 Cf. Clement, *Strom* 2.13. Hermas gives no details of a process. *2 Clement* tells of acts of penitence —fasting, prayer and almsgiving (16.4 and cf. *Didache* 4.6; *Ep Barn* 19.10). *1 Clement* (90s of the first century) mentions confession (52), seeking pardon from the offended (51.2; 57.1), humility and receipt of correction (56) from the presbyters (57). Origen (*Contra Celsum* 3.51) writes of a disciplinary period prior to reintegration.

56 Though, as Carolyn Osiek notes in *The Shepherd of Hermas*, 115, this should not be treated too literally —*The Shepherd* allows that what is difficult, in terms of salvation, is not impossible.

57 See especially Hermas, *Sim* 9.19.1: those who are apostates, who betrayed 'the servants of God'. *The Shepherd* is less than clear on the matter of apostasy. Its seeming 'shifts' may be due to an extended period of composition.

58 Hermas, *Vis* 3.8.9: here during the building of the unfinished Tower (the Church) was a time when repentance and mercy and acceptance were possible for 'all who call upon His name'; Hermas, *Sim* 8.6.3; 9.14.1–3. Otherwise only in *Ep Barn* 6.11 in the Apostolic Fathers.

59 *Hippolytus Werke, Refutatio omnium haeresium*, ed. Paul Wendland, GCS 26.3 (Leipzig, 1916, repr. Hildesheim and New York, 1977), 9.13.3 [hereafter *Refut*]. The sources are few for Élchasai, notably Hippolytus and Epiphanius (e.g. *Refut* 9. 13–17; 10.29; Epiphanius, *Ancoratus und Panarion*, ed. Karl Holl, 3 vols, GCS 25, 31, 37 (Leipzig, 1915–33), *Pan* 19 and 30). The possibility of forgiveness even for apostasy was common to both writers: Hermas, *Sim* 9.26.5; Epiphanius, *Pan* 19.1.8–9. See J. Irmscher, 'The Book of Elchasai', in *New Testament Apocrypha*, 2: 745–50.

60 Hippolytus, *Refut* 9.15.1–3.

61 Cp. Tertullian, *de Paen* 7, but contrast Clement, *Strom* 2.23.

forgiveness was blowing in the opposite direction in the second century, towards greater rigour. Hence contemporary catacomb representations of the meticulous and saving Shepherd of the Gospel parable, the seeker after the one strayed sheep, may have been responses to the tendency towards *greater* rigorism and abandonment of the lost.[62] Certainly, Hermas was coming down on the side of an allowable repentance followed by reconciliation, albeit limited to once only,[63] but others preferred the uncompromising stance which 'some teachers' had represented. There is evidence of both points of view in second-century sources and now I shall turn briefly to some of it.

* * *

Matthew's teaching on the treatment of sinners (Matt. 18: 15–18) countenanced rejection as a last resort.[64] It lay sandwiched in the Matthaean text between the salvation of the hundredth, straying sheep, on the one hand (Matt. 18: 10–14), and, on the other, the statements about the Church's prayer and unlimited ('seventy times seven') forgiveness (Matt. 18: 19–22). Matthew's Gospel, originating probably in Antioch, had pointed in the direction of forgiving and receiving and his was the most-used Gospel in the second century. Ignatius the bishop and martyr stemmed from Antioch too, and in his letters, written in and to Asia Minor in the first decade of the second century,[65] forgiveness and reconciliation with your co-religionists was possible even if you had denied Jesus Christ by way of doctrinal error (such as docetism). That

---

[62] See Josef Schrijnen, 'Die Entwicklung der Bussdisziplin im Lichte der altchristlichen Kunst', in idem, *Collectanea Schrijnen: Verspreide Opstellen* (Nijmegen, 1939), 277–94. For Tertullian's determinedly different slant on the matter of the lost sheep, see *de Pud* 7.

[63] The stance of *The Shepherd* bore on the life-choices of the guiltless also. Thus the husband of an adulterous Christian wife had to divorce her (which matched both the Roman Augustan legislation and the sentiment of Matthew 19: 8–9), but not remarry in order to leave open the route to forgiveness and reconciliation. He was obliged to receive her back (which did *not* accord with the *Lex Iulia de adulteriis coercendis*), for it was necessary to receive the repentant, 'but not often': 'for the servants of God there is one repentance' (Hermas, *Man* 4.1.4–8).

[64] R. Hiers, 'Binding and Loosing: the Matthaean Authorizations', *Journal of Biblical Literature* 104 (1985), 233–50. Cf. the pre-150 CE *Epistula Apostolorum*, 47–8, which makes no reference to the part of 'the Church' in the process. See *Epistula Apostolorum*, in *New Testament Apocrypha* I: 276–7.

[65] Despite the latest attempts (e.g. Hübner and Lechner) to redate the *Middle Recension* of the Ignatian corpus, I hold, with most writers, to an early second-century date for the letters (to Ephesus, Magnesia, Tralles, Philadelphia, Rome, Smyrna and to Polycarp). See William R. Schoedel, *Ignatius of Antioch: a Commentary on the Letters of Ignatius of Antioch*, Hermeneia Commentary Series (Philadelphia, PA, 1985); Christine Trevett, *A Study of Ignatius of Antioch in Syria and Asia* (Lewiston, N.Y., 1992), 1–14.

was, provided of course that the guilty parties repented (*metanoein*)[66] of all that it entailed and made confession of (*homologein*)[67] the true doctrine. Ignatius thought it was unlikely that they would – but that was another matter.[68]

Ignatius's witness is interesting in several respects. 'The Lord forgives all who repent', he maintained,[69] provided that the repentance was such as to promote Church unity, which was closely interwoven with loyalty to emerging officialdom. What the Ignatian letters give us are clues about a developing second-century understanding of the Church and its officials (cf. *Trall* 1–3). Without this (and the ecclesiology of some sources is not easy to determine), it is hard to contextualize other clues about repentance and reconciliation.[70] Nevertheless, Ignatius gave no hint that a power of absolution lay with an episkopos, which, given his determined concentration of various kinds of rights in the hands of bishops, must be significant.[71]

Docetism was that same error being perpetrated in those Asian communities reflected in the New Testament Johannine letters.[72] Docetism's denial of the fleshly reality of Jesus Christ was so aberrant

[66] *Smyrnaeans* 4.1; 5.3 [hereafter *Smyrn*]; cf. *Philadelphians* 3.1–2 [hereafter *Phld*].

[67] *Smyrn* 5.2; 7.1.

[68] *Smyrn* 4.1; 5.3 cf. 7.1. In Hermas, those who introduced strange doctrine and corrupted Christians thereby might still repent and be reintegrated into the Tower of the Church (*Sim* 8.6.5–6). Ignatius was not optimistic that they would repent, but Jesus Christ had the power; cf. Eph. 7: 2: where a cure was unlikely, only the Lord as physician held the cure.

[69] Ignatius, *Phld* 8.1.

[70] Reference to the *synedrion* of the bishop in *Phld* 8.1 may be suggestive of those who formally 'received' the penitent. *1 Clement* 57.1 advised submission to the presbyters to receive correction, 'bending the knees of your hearts'. Pre-eucharistic confession and reconciliation with co-religionists is mentioned in *Didache* 14; see the discussion in Kurt Niederwimmer, *The Didache: a Commentary*, Hermeneia Commentary Series, transl. Linda M. Maloney and Harold W. Attridge (Minneapolis, MN, 1998), 193–9. The *Two Ways* material in *Didache* 4.14 speaks of confession of sins 'in the ecclesia' (an [editorial?] phrase not found in the parallel *Two Ways* material in *Ep. Barn* 19.12). Ecclesiastical confession figures in Justin, *Dial* 141. Ignatius was describing a church order which was in its infancy and not yet universal and an understanding of the church which was not shared by all ('orthodox') Christians in the region. It is inappropriate, in my opinion, to discuss passages such as *Trallians* 6–7 [hereafter *Trall*]; *Phld* 2–3; 8; *Smyrn* 9 in terms of a preceding act of 'excommunication'. Ferguson, 'Early Church Penance', 82, rightly sees a lack of finality in the drawing of 'lines of fellowship' in such passages about 'rebellion and division'.

[71] E.g. the oversight of Christian marriages, knowledge of a decision for celibacy, the care of widows, control of eucharistic and baptismal rites, as seen especially in his two letters to Smyrna. Cf. A. Brent, 'The Relations between Ignatius and the *Didascalia*', *The Second Century* 8 (1991), 129–56, 155: 'the absence of any power of absolution in the hands of the bishop unites Hermas with Ignatius against the Didascalist'.

[72] E.g. 1 John 4: 1; 2 John 10.

and abhorrent in Ignatius's eyes that he would not give its advocates the oxygen of publicity. He refused to write their 'unbelieving names'[73] to the frustration of scholars ever since. Yet repentance of the error and confession of the truth would be enough.[74] Like the author of 2 John 10, however, Ignatius was advocating that such people were not to be received in a church context, indeed were to be shunned and if possible not met with at all or even spoken about privately or publicly, until they did make confession of the true nature of Jesus Christ (cf. 1 John 4: 2–3)[75] and repented of their views about his Passion.[76] The churches were only to continue in prayer for the sinners' repentance.[77]

This social avoidance figures also in another first- or second-century writer with Syrian associations, namely the Didachist (15.3), who advocated Christian reproof of Christians but the shunning of one who had wronged another.[78] There was to be no spoken communication until repentance.

Ignatius was writing as though he was responding about a matter which he knew to be at issue. This was surely whether the errorists, people who had themselves refrained for reasons of doctrine from aspects of the Church's life,[79] might still have any contact with its members.[80] Ignatius was for forgiveness and reconciliation after repen-

[73] *Smyrn* 5.3. Jerry L. Sumney, 'Those Who "Ignorantly Deny Him": the Opponents of Ignatius of Antioch', *Journal of Early Christian Studies* 1 (1993), 345–65. Cf. the interpretation of Michael Goulder in his recent articles: 'Ignatius' "Docetists"', *Vigiliae Christianae* 53 (1999), 16–30; idem, 'A Poor Man's Christology', *New Testament Studies* 45/3 (1999), 332–48.

[74] Such 'confession' is publicly of faith, made, as in this case, after Christians' prayerful support. It may also (and probably did) involve acknowledgement of sins. As usual in this period we have no details.

[75] Ignatius described their present position in terms of denial (rather than confession) and blasphemy of Jesus Christ (*Smyrn* 5.1–2; 7.1).

[76] *Smyrn* 7.2; 4.1; cf. 1 John 4: 2–3. A 'bodiless' or 'phantasmal' person could not truly suffer, though might 'seemingly' do so (cf. *Smyrn* 2.1; cf. *Trall* 10.1). The Greek verb 'to seem/appear to be' lies behind the term 'docetism'.

[77] The imperatives were insistent where this error was concerned: 'shun', 'flee from', 're-frain from. . . heresy', 'abstain from evil growths. . .'; 'beware', 'Be deaf. . .'. Cf. similar language in the anti-docetic *3 Corinthians* (in the Asian *Acts of Paul*) 3.21 and 29: W. Schneemelcher, 'Acts of Paul', in *New Testament Apochrypha* II, 255–7.

[78] See Niederwimmer, *The Didache*, 203: 'The community itself exercises the right of discipline, and the most extreme means at its disposal is excommunication'. Cf. too Poschmann, *Poenitentia Secunda*, 95–6.

[79] E.g. 'prayer' and eucharist, through being at odds with ('not confessing') what others assumed about the *flesh* of the Lord (*Smyrn* 7.1). The matter was one of separate gatherings (and there were others beside these in the regions Ignatius was addressing), not one of grevious wrongdoing having brought exclusion from prayer and eucharist. Cf. Tertullian's pre-Montanist *Apol* 39.4.

[80] *Smyrn* 7.2 (I am following the readings of MS Gg): 'It is right therefore to refrain from

tance, even in a case of teachers who seemed to him to threaten the very promise of salvation. He drew the line against continued contact with the Church in the interim.

The verb *ekklinō*[81] suggests that he is not describing a formal act of excommunication.[82] Nevertheless it seems to me that Ignatius did regard these people as out of the Church already; being 'godless' they were beyond the pale.[83] There was no mention of any formal process, however,[84] and Ignatius's language was geared towards Christians avoiding action and staying free of pollution until the guilty saw the error of their ways.[85] Ignatius did not want errorists spoken to or spoken about. This is surely 'practically the equivalent of excommunication'.[86] Without contact it is hard to see that moves to regain the strayed would have been possible. The initiative would have had to come from them.

So while *The Shepherd* at the start of the second century had things to say on both great and lesser sins,[87] Ignatius, his contemporary to the

---

(*apechesthai*) such and not to speak about them even privately or in public (*koiné*)'. Cf. Eph. 7: 1: shun them (using *ekklinō*) as the surreptitiously biting wild beasts that they were.

[81] I.e. to *avoid* and not *ekkleiō* meaning to shut out.

[82] Cf. Hermas, *Sim* 1.5, where the city (the Church) might determine to exclude the compromising Christian who had abandoned its law but now sought to return. Also Hermas, *Vis* 3.9.6, where the thoughtless rich, wanting to do good and be part of the Church (the Tower), on its completion are shut out.

[83] *Atheoi* in *Trall* 10.1; cf. 3.2. For Ignatius Christ is 'our God'. The christology of these errorists is not made clear, but this may be a comment on it. See Trevett, *Ignatius*, 155–69.

[84] The 'insider' or 'outsider' status of the advocates of docetism is not easy to determine. I think that by the time of writing they were to be regarded as 'outside', but perhaps the lack of a formalized process had created opportunity for contact and uncertainty. Ignatius's advice may have been intended to clarify some matters.

[85] Paul had used the same verb in Rom. 16: 17, about avoiding contact with those who caused trouble and questioned the teaching given. 1 Cor. 5: 9–12 contained not dissimilar advice, namely, that believers should cease association with certain people presently *within* the Christian circle. They should not keep company or eat with them. The aim in that case was to drive them firmly from the local church (*exarate*: 1 Cor. 5: 13). Cf. too 2 Thess. 3: 14, where the same verb was used. This was a disciplinary move, a withdrawal of support and shaming of the individual into compliance. But that person was not an *enemy* (*echthros*). The process of exclusion in Anabaptist communities and Amish social avoidance ('shunning', in the German *Meidung*) comes to mind, based as it is on interpretation of just these New Testament passages. See John A. Hostetler, *Amish Society* (4th edn, Baltimore, PA and London, 1993), 85–7 and the literature there.

[86] These are Niederwimmer's words (*Didache*, 204) on *Didache* 15, and are applicable to Ignatius too, I think. The Greek of *Didache* 15.3b has its difficulties.

[87] It is the nearest thing we have in second-century Christian writing to a systematic consideration of these matters, even though it is far from being that precisely and in any case offers more than a doctrinaire theory of repentance.

East,[88] had something to say on 'heresy' (hairesis), which was the word he used to speak of the error of the teachers of docetism (Eph 6.2; Trall 6.1). Still, we should not assume that to have found one view on any matter is to have found the second-century Christian view of things or that what was determined in Rome or Smyrna matched belief and practice in Macedonian Philippi or Phrygian Hierapolis. I am much more cautious than O. D. Watkins who, in his well-known 1920 study of *The History of Penance*, maintained that only one post-baptismal penance was a rule of the Church by the time of Clement of Alexandria, that is, by the end of the second century and beyond.[89]

For when we look more generally for second-century clues about penitence and forgiveness, we find them to be occasional and scattered and showing that throughout the second century rigorism vied with a less inflexible stance. From Smyrna, in the Roman province of Asia and probably in the decade of the 130s, Bishop Polycarp wrote to the Church in Macedonian Philippi.[90] Christians there had previously written to him, pointedly inviting his comments on matters of 'righteousness' (Phil 3.1),[91] but we do not have their letter. His response suggests that the Philippian Church had felt itself polluted by some happenings in its midst. Well-versed in the Scriptures, the letter-writers of that Church – where Lydia, a 'god-fearer', had been Paul's first convert on the European mainland[92] – had been strongly dismissive of two people who had let it down.[93] The guilty parties were a presbyter called Valens and his unnamed wife (*Phil* 11).[94] The

---

[88] Ignatius was writing to the region where the Johannine teaching on confession and on 'mortal' sins may well have been known: 1 John 1: 9; 4: 15–17.

[89] See Watkins, *History of Penance,* 105–7. Clement was one of those on the side of *The Shepherd*, which he knew, reproducing much of its teaching on sin and repentance. His evidence does show that similar practices were to be found far East of Rome.

[90] Polycarp's *Phil* is probably a composite of two letters in its present form. The earlier of the two concerned the progress of Ignatius on his way to martyrdom. The portions on righteousness and Valens belong to the later document. The 'classic' study of this document was that by P. N. Harrison, *Polycarp's Two Epistles to the Philippians* (Cambridge, 1936). Contrast Paul Hartog, *Polycarp and the New Testament: the Occasion, Rhetoric, Theme and Unity of the Epistle to the Philippians and its Allusions to New Testament Literature,* Wissenschaftliche Untersuchungen zum Neuen Testament, 2. Reihe 134 (Tübingen, 2002).

[91] Cf. Polycarp, *Phil* 2.3; 3.3; 4.1; 5.2; 8.1; 9.1–2 and also 2.2. The kinds of behaviour he advocates and deplores as unrighteous probably contain clues to what had happened in Philippi.

[92] Despite a dearth of archaeological evidence for a Jewish community on Philippi, the book of Acts and other sources indicate Jewish presence there.

[93] Harry O. Maier, 'Purity and Danger in Polycarp's *Epistle to the Philippians*: the Sin of Valens in Social Perspective', *Journal of Early Christian Studies* 1 (1993), 229–47.

[94] 'The Valens affair' may have been the chief cause of the letter. In my forthcoming

language of dishonour, avarice and pollution by the pagan world was to the fore.

Polycarp's irenic response to them included a determined use mostly of the sentiments of the Sermon on the Mount and 1 Peter (*Phil* 2.2), echoing sayings about not judging so as not to be judged, forgiving so as to be forgiven, and so on. It was not given to him to quote as they had done, he wrote (*mihi non est concessum*, 12.1).[95] He appealed only to the sentiments of Psalm 4: 5 on anger and sinning and to New Testament Eph. 4: 26, 'Let not the sun go down on your wrath' (where the same Psalm quotation also occurs). Hence the Philippians were referred to indisputably Christian sentiments. This suggests to me that the letter he had received on the matter of these wrongdoers had been larded liberally with the language of judgement which seemed to Polycarp reminiscent of a different dispensation.

Polycarp addressed himself to the Philippian presbyters whose task, in his view, was pastorally to lead miscreants back through repentance. He advised moderation:[96] Valens and 'Mrs' Valens were in fact being treated as enemies. Thus, at least one faction in Philippi was not for promoting reconciliation but rather it had employed condemnatory tactics. Is it coincidental, or indicative of a certain ideology on their part, that Polycarp closed this section of his letter with a benediction echoing some of the language of the Epistle to the Hebrews?[97]

We are not told what steps this couple had sought to take towards being reconciled. In Polycarp, however, we have the man who was credited with refusing to 'recognize' Marcion and with labelling him 'first-born of Satan'.[98] It was in Smyrna, Polycarp's city (according to Hippolytus in his homily against Noëtus some decades later) that the said Noëtus was expelled from the Church for his Modalism. Thus Polycarp's advice to Philippi on one matter of boundary-maintenance was no necessary clue to the response in Smyrna on other and perhaps weightier ones.

---

study *Christian Women and the Time of the Apostolic Fathers*, I suggest that the couple had formerly been part of the church in Smyrna.

[95] Echoes of Psalms and Proverbs, favourite second-century sources, do appear in the letter.

[96] Polycarp, *Phil* 11.4: 'sobrii ergo estote et vos in hoc. . .'. The Latin version, which complements eight defective Greek manuscripts of this document, appears at this point in the Loeb edition of the text.

[97] Polycarp, *Phil* 12.2; cf. Heb. 6: 20; 7: 3, wishing the Philippians patience and freedom from wrath.

[98] Irenaeus, *AH* 3.3.4; Eusebius, *HE* 4.14.7.

Before I turn finally to martyrology and the New Prophecy I offer one further example of differences of opinion. When Bishop Dionysius of Corinth began his spate of letter-writing (c.170 CE) to areas as diverse as Crete and Rome, Pontus, Bithynia and Athens,[99] he wrote not just against heresy and on the interpretation of Scripture, but especially about the developing tendency towards asceticism and (to Pontus) of refusal to receive the penitent. He gave instructions, Eusebius reported, that the penitent should be received, whether their sin had been a matter of straying in conduct (apostasy) or what Eusebius termed heretical error (4.23.6). His advice was not always well received.

At the same time, Dionysius had been complaining that adulterated copies of his letters were already in circulation. Such adulteration may be evidence of strong conflicts of interest with regard to these matters or perhaps of dislike of this Corinthian's seeming liberality. Certainly we have evidence that his advice on matters of asceticism had its critics. Eusebius had some of the correspondence and he noted that Pinytos of Knossos had taken particular umbrage at the Corinthian's advice to him. Dionysius's letter had suggested that he (Pinytos) was 'burdening' his flock with requirements about chastity (*hagneia*). Eusebius cited the Cretan's polite and teeth-gritted response, in which he paid respect to Dionysius and hoped next time that Christians would get guidance a little less undemanding and 'milky'![100]

I surmise that there would have been others at this time responding equally negatively to the bishop's letters about receiving the penitent. That matter was being debated in churches and high-profile Christians like Dionysius, and confessors among them (as we shall see) were taking it upon themselves to express an opinion.

* * *

Tertullian, not even a Christian until the very end of the period which this study addresses, was never a man to mince his words. He was never one knowingly to understate. In ways which are not entirely clear from the second-century sources, the churches' right to mediate forgiveness and rituals associated with its seeking and finding had been established by Tertullian's time, in the early third century, certainly in North Africa, in Rome and probably in other places too. How consistently they were applied we do not know, nor how many swam against such a tide, as Tertullian did.

---

99 We know of these 'general epistles' only from Eusebius, *HE* 4.23.
100 Eusebius, *HE* 4.23.7–8.

In Carthage, for example, the right of intercession for wrongdoers was so firmly associated with confessors that Tertullian wrote scathingly about Christian prisoners no sooner being put in dark prisons than they were immediately being besieged by the adulterous, polluted and disfellowshipped, weeping, praying aloud and kissing the martyrs' bonds.[101] There were habitual sinners – women and men – in the dark, the now-Montanist Tertullian mused.[102] Recourse to confessors was easier than lengthy and humiliating rites of penance, easier perhaps than having to deal with a possibly unsympathetic and demanding bishop. But no, Tertullian averred, the martyr's merit availed for him/herself and no more. He would not accord to such the power of the keys, to grant absolution to the guilty.

Was he being typically New Prophet/Montanist in this? Had there indeed been an upsurge of refusal of forgiveness with the advent of the New Prophecy/Montanism in the second half of the second century? The evidence points to the answer yes, but such evidence is limited and flawed not least in that for some of it we have to rely on Tertullian himself, and he was scarcely 'typical' in any respect!

What was the New Prophecy? It was a revivalist movement at first not separate from catholic congregations. Its leading figures had been the prophetesses Priscilla and Maximilla and the eponymous Montanus, who had emerged into the public sphere in Asia Minor through the 160s.[103] The New Prophecy grew and spread quickly, characterized by belief in a fresh outpouring of the Spirit, enthusiastic gatherings, eschatological expectation and increased discipline. The early anti-Montanist sources did not rage about wrong doctrine but rather accused it of being innovatory with regard to discipline, introducing extra (and obligatory) fasts, abstemiousness, the forbidding of digamy and the like.[104]

A number of later anti-Montanist sources put into words what we might expect – viz. that the New Prophets did not forgive lightly.[105] In

---

[101] Tertullian, II *Ad Uxor* 4.

[102] Tertullian, *de Pud* 22; *pace* Tertullian, in North Africa in the 250s soon-to-be martyrs in prison and some clergy were reconciling the lapsed.

[103] Trevett, *Montanism*, 26–45.

[104] Trevett, *Montanism*, 105–28.

[105] See for example Pacian of Barcelona to the Novatianist Sym04pronianus (1–2) on their hostility to penance; Jerome [*Ep* 41 *Ad Marcellam*, ed. I. Hilberg, *Epistulae*, Corpus Christianorum Ecclesiasticorum Latinarum 54 (Vienna, 1910), 3] on their unforgiving discipline. These and other anti-Montanist sources and translations are most easily accessible in Ronald E. Heine, *The Montanist Oracles and Testimonia*, Patristic Monograph Series 14 (Macon, GA, 1989). Cf. also Tertullian, *de Monog* 2.1 and 4.

this and other respects they were seizing the moral high ground from the catholic side, refusing pardon to digamists and penitent adulterers.[106] One particularly late source tells of Montanists' refusal to receive digamists, refusal of penance for post-baptismal sin and their teaching about fire-breathing dragons, lions and the punishment of the unrighteous by being suspended by the flesh. These things are reminiscent of the Apocalypse of Peter[107] and in like vein Tertullian was familiar with the sentiments of Heb. 6.[108] According to Jerome so too were the New Prophets.[109] They tended, it would seem, towards its denial of a second chance.

Yet it was not that the New Prophets did not acknowledge in the Church the right to mediate forgiveness and reconciliation (though according to Tertullian it depended what you meant by 'church', of course, de Pud 21–2). They did acknowledge it, but they would not use it. They would bind and not loose. They would supply a deterrent to sin.[110] The Spirit (the Paraclete) had declared through the Prophets (according to Tertullian, who is our only source for this Saying) that 'The Church can pardon sin, but I will not do it, lest they also commit other offences'.[111]

Hippolytus, a contemporary of Tertullian but in Rome, was implacably hostile. This new thing was claiming to bring fresh revelation. The New Prophecy was clearly a challenge to the right of clergy to determine the cycle of disciplined life and forgiveness.[112] Indeed its stand seemed a far cry from the limited forgiveness, even for the worst sins which *The Shepherd* had profferred, or Ignatius' belief in awaiting

---

[106] Tertullian, *de Jej* 1 was uncompromising —it was the guts and genitals of the psychics (the Catholics) which lay behind complaints and accusations, because the Prophets taught that 'our fasts ought to be more numerous than our marriages'!

[107] Germanus, patriarch of Constantinople (715–30), *Ad Antimum* 5, PG 98, 41–44. Cf. *Apoc.Pet.* 7 and 11 (Ethiopic), 22 and 24 (Greek, Akhmim): see D. G. Müller, 'Apocalypse of Peter', 628–32.

[108] Tertullian attributed the anonymous Hebrews to Barnabas, *de Pud* 20.1–2.

[109] Probably so, since for example both were concerned with a city of promise (Jerusalem); but see Trevett, *Montanism*, 117.

[110] See too F. E. Vokes, 'Penitential Discipline in Montanism', in Elizabeth A. Livingstone, ed., *Papers Presented to the Sixth International Conference on Patristic Studies Held in Oxford, 1971*, Studia Patristica 14 = Texte und Untersuchungen zur Geschichte der altchristlichen Literatur 117 (1976), 62–76.

[111] Hippolytus, *de Pud* 21 and cf. the challenge to mainstream tradition in *de Pud* 12 on the 'washing' of penitence. The 'I' of this Saying is anonymous. On other New Prophecy sayings and 'I' see Trevett, *Montanism*, 77–86, 163–70. This and other New Prophecy oracles and testimonia are collected in Heine, *Montanist Oracles*, 93, in his translation.

[112] Hippolytus, *Refut* 8.19; 10.25–6.

repentance and confession, even of those who denied the very humanity of Jesus Christ. In particular, and given that the New Prophecy's spread coincided with outbreaks of hostility against Christians, what of the lapsed in those difficult times? 'Ancient penance was shaped by controversy'.[113] The account of the events in Gaul in the year 177 may preserve clues about the ways in which churches responded to an upsurge of New Prophecy rigorism. In Gaul, a particularly vicious outbreak of hostility coincided with what was also the time when confrontation with the New Prophecy had become acute elsewhere.[114] The Gallic Christians ventured a view on the matter, perhaps at the request of Asia Minor catholics, or even of followers of the New Prophecy.[115] The account of the martyrdoms was itself part of the responses made on this occasion and it was sent to the Churches of Asia and Phrygia, regions in which the Prophecy had taken hold.[116] Another document was prepared and sent to Eleutherus, bishop of Rome, by the hand of no less than Irenaeus of Lyon. Eleutherus may have been petitioned already by Asia Minor's New Prophets or by catholic leaders.[117] With whole regions in turmoil, for the New Prophecy was probably a reality in Rome as well as Asia Minor and elsewhere by this time, and from out of this struggle for support and equilibrium, we have the witness of the martyrs of Gaul concerning the reconciling of the lapsed.

These Gallic Christians were not unsympathetic to the New Prophecy's concerns. As Eusebius observed, prophecy and the outpouring of the Spirit (which mattered in the New Prophecy) were things which still mattered to some Christians (HE 5.3.4) and claims to prophesying existed elsewhere. Moreover there were Asiatics in Gaul and some ascetics,[118] who may have carried the particular New Prophecy understanding of the Church and its witness to Gaul from its homeland.[119]

---

113 Dallen, The Reconciling Community, 31.
114 It was spread 'among many', Eusebius reported.
115 Eusebius, HE 5.3.4; see Trevett, Montanism, 36. Essays by G. W. Bowersock, R. M. Grant, T. D. Barnes and others on the Asian/New Prophet links with the Gallic Christians plus other background material are in Jean Rougé and Robert Turcan, eds, Les Martyrs de Lyon, Colloque International du Centre National de la Recherche Scientifique (CNRS), Lyon, 20–23 septembre 1977 (Paris, 1978).
116 Eusebius, HE 5.1.2.
117 See also Eusebius, HE 5.4.1.
118 Eusebius, HE 5.3.2–3. For discussion of such knowledge see Trevett, Montanism, 53, 58–60, 64.
119 Similarly the Martydom of Polycarp was sent to the church in Philomelium in Phrygia (MPol. Inscr) at its request (20.1) and contains passages which some take to be interpolations

Gallic churches were in contact with the East. Hence they devised their own statement on the matter of the New Prophecy, appending letters from the imprisoned, though we do not know their content (*HE* 5.3.4). The late 170s was at a time when the discord about Montanus and the rest was at a peak. The suffering Christians of Gaul, said Eusebius, were ambassadors for the peace of the Churches.

What did they say? We do not know in detail, but the account of the martyrdoms tells us that the Gallic Christians refused the title 'martyr' (the original sense of 'witness' is still strong in this usage), which was rightly Christ's. They, by contrast, had not yet witnessed unto death (*HE* 5.4.3; 5.2.2–4). Determinedly, then, they insisted on being known as 'confessors' (*homologoi*).[120] 'Martyr' was evidently widely used in this more general sense of 'witness' (and was used by Tertullian, for example, in contexts where the Gauls' 'confessor' might have seemed more appropriate). It may be, however, that the New Prophets were appropriating the term 'martyr' a great deal, so that this was one element of the Gallic Christians' disassociation from certain tendencies of the New Prophecy.[121]

Moreover, the martyrology stated pointedly that in Gaul the confessors gladly forgave – 'they loosed all and bound none' (*eluon hapantas, edesmeuon de oudena*) who had lapsed in the strain of the persecu- tion.[122] They were shown to be right, the work suggested, in that subsequently the majority of those Christians too had become martyrs proper. I take this document to be a further pointer to the fact that the New Prophets, by contrast, did not readily proffer the hands of forgiveness.[123] If Tertullian had had his way, confessors/martyrs would not even have considered it possible that the power to do so lay with them.[124]

engaging in debate with Montanism. See Gerd Buschmann, 'Martyrium Polycarpi 4 und der Montanismus', *Vigiliae Christianae* 49 (1995), 105–45 and B. Dehandschutter, 'The *Martyrium Polycarpi*: a Century of Research', *ANRW* II.27.1 (Berlin, 1993), 485–522; Trevett, *Montanism*, 41, 123–4.

120 There are variant forms of this word in the manuscripts.

121 Eusebius, *HE* 5.2.2–4; cf. 5.18.6–7 (Apollonius) and 5.16.20 (Anonymous).

122 Eusebius, *HE* 5.2.5; cf. 5.1.45–6; 5.18.6.

123 The very-much-alive New Prophet 'martyr' called Alexander (Eusebius, *HE* 5.18.6 [Apollonius]) was alleged to have been a convicted criminal who had in time past not been 'received' by Christians. When Apollonius demanded challengingly whether now the prophetess forgave him of robbery or he as martyr absolved her from greed, we should probably regard this remark as biting comment on the New Prophecy's famed rigour, rather than evidence that forgiveness was common. The Catholic 'martyr' Aurelius Cyrenaeus was also very much alive when he signed a document *against* the New Prophecy referred to by Eusebius in *HE* 5.19.3.

124 The North African *Passio Perpetuae*, post 203 in date, which was at least redacted by

* * *

In the preceding overview we have moved from the only document (*The Shepherd*) which in the second century gives us more than a brief consideration of the subjects of repentance, forgiveness and reconciliation, to particular examples illustrating more and less liberal interpretations of response to post-baptismal sin. These further texts touched on questions of aberrant doctrine (Ignatius), abuses relating to church office (Polycarp and Valens), the receiving of the penitent (Dionysius) and the forgiveness of the lapsed (Gaul). No coherent development has emerged, for reasons I outlined at the beginning, but some consistency in that no single interpretation ruled where these matters were concerned.

In the second century the ground was prepared for the insights and responses of heavyweights of the third century, for Tertullian and Hippolytus and Cyprian, for the events of the Decian persecution and the new crisis of Novatianism. 'I have heard from some teachers', Hermas had begun, and rigorist teachers of that ilk and hearers such as Hermas, who subsequently offered a different view of post-baptismal sin and penance, were still realities at the end of the century. Without a treatise or a single second-century description of decision-making or rite, it is nevertheless possible to discern in these sources the horror of hell, the fear that mercy breeds hypocrisy, the prayerful work for reconciliation and the anguish of the betrayed and the betrayer.

University of Cardiff

Montanists, is important witness to belief in the power of confessors/martyrs to intercede for the suffering dead and to bestow peace on the living. It can not be discussed here.

INFORMAL PENANCE IN EARLY MEDIEVAL CHRISTENDOM

by RICHARD PRICE

THROUGHOUT the modern period Catholic and Orthodox Christians alike have taken it for granted that forgiveness for sins committed after baptism is obtained first and foremost through confession to a priest and absolution by a priest, the humility of confession plus the power of the sacrament being deemed the most effective remedy for human weakness. Other elements in overcoming sin, such as regular religious observance and the avoidance of the occasions of sin, were not forgotten, but were put in second place. The falling away from sacramental confession in the Catholic Church today is doubtless a complex phenomenon, but one reason for the decline is the widespread perception that this remedy does not work, that a penitential discipline that places so heavy a reliance on the power of priestly absolution, without adequate attention to the other aspects of repentance and forgiveness, is ineffectual. It also represents what is arguably an impoverished and clericalized Catholicism. The aim of this paper is to explore those elements of penitential practice in the early middle ages that belong to a tradition at once richer and more flexible.

A starting point as good as any is a chapter in the *Conferences* of John Cassian, written in the 420s. He begins, 'There are many fruits of repentance by which the expiation of sins is achieved.'[1] He proceeds to list them – a loving disposition, almsgiving, the shedding of tears, the avowal of one's fault, correction of one's behaviour, the intercession of holy persons, acts of 'mercy and faith', forgiving the offences of others, helping others on the way to salvation. He concludes,

> You see, then, how many opportunities for mercy the clemency of the Saviour has disclosed, so that no one who desires salvation should be broken by despair, when he sees so many life-giving remedies at his disposal.[2]

It is striking that this long list includes no mention of the system of

---

[1] John Cassian, *Conferences*, transl. B. Ramsey, Ancient Christian Writers 57 (New York, 1997), XX.8, 698–9.
[2] Ibid.

public penance, with its enrolment in the ranks of the penitents and formal reconciliation by a bishop.[3]

The official system suffered from severe limitations – it involved public humiliation, it covered only sins so grave as to warrant excommunication, penance could not be repeated and was therefore unsuitable for the young and safe only for the dying, and the clergy were themselves excluded.[4] Moreover, canonical penance had never been the principal channel for the forgiveness of sin: sensibly enough, it was constant teaching that sins against one's neighbour were to be healed through reconciliation with one's neighbour rather than recourse to the clergy.[5] The system of canonical penance was never as important as the traditional histories of the sacrament have tried to make out, distorted as they have been by having as their prime objective not the description of early Christian practice, but finding a respectable ancestry for the discipline of a later period.

In addition, by the time of Cassian the official system was falling into disuse; John Chrysostom (d. 407), for example, never makes reference to it, whether at Antioch or Constantinople.[6] In the West the system lasted longer, but it appears to have fallen largely into disuse by the sixth century; it survived as an exceptional penalty for people who had gravely offended the Church, rather than as a form of penance that

---

[3] The same is true of the list of means of gaining forgiveness in John Chrysostom, *De diabolo tentatore*, Homily 2, 6 (PG 49, 263–4), which specifies five modes: self-condemnation, forgiving one's neighbour, prayer, almsgiving, and 'humility'.

[4] Members of the clergy guilty of grave sin were degraded; as laymen they could do public penance, but not as clerics: see Cyrille Vogel, 'Pénitence et excommunication dans l'Église ancienne et durant le Haut Moyen Âge', *Concilium* 107 (1975), 11–22, repr. in idem, *En rémission des péchés: recherches sur les systèmes pénitentiels dans l'Eglise latine* (Aldershot, 1994), IV, esp. 15. To the references he gives may be added for the earlier period Basil, Canon 32 (see n. 15 below) and Augustine, *De correctione Donatistarum* 45 (*ep.* 185), PL 33, 812. In the Carolingian period the distinction was made that, to reduce exposure, degraded clergy did 'canonical' penance rather than 'public' penance: Mayke de Jong, 'Power and Humility in Carolingian Society: the Public Penance of Louis the Pious', *Early Medieval Europe* 1 (1992), 29–52, esp. 34 n. 18.

[5] This is fully demonstrated by Karl-Josef Klär, *Das kirchliche Bussinstitut von den Anfängen bis zum Konzil von Trient* (Frankfurt am Main and New York, 1991). Klär cites quantities of texts from the early centuries which show that Matt. 18, 15–20 on the efficacy of repentance in response to rebuke by the person wronged remained one of the favourite forms of the forgiveness of sin. John Chrysostom, the most read of the Greek Fathers in the medieval period, was particularly emphatic on this (*In Mt. Hom.* 60–61, in Klär, *Bussinstitut*, 129–30).

[6] Pietro Rentinck, *La Cura Pastorale in Antiochia nel IV secolo*, Analecta Gregoriana 178 (Rome, 1970), 281–309, esp. 289–90. As was shown in Karl Holl, *Enthusiasmus und Bussgewalt beim griechischen Mönchtum: eine Studie zu Symeon dem Neuen Theologen* (Leipzig, 1898), 273–301, public penance was never formally abolished. It was, however, very rarely imposed.

penitents themselves might choose.[7] This left the remedies listed by
John Cassian in control of the field even in the case of those sins which,
because of their gravity, had formerly been subject to the rigours of
canonical penance.

Conventional histories of penance have laid stress on the influence
of the Celtic and Anglo-Saxon penitentials, which laid down precise
periods of penance for particular sins (in a system known as *paenitentia
taxata* or tariffed penance) and were circulating on the continent from
as early as the late sixth century.[8] But it would be a mistake to see the
penitentials as filling a gap left by the virtual demise of public penance,
since the latter had never been applied to more than a small range of
sins,[9] and the notion that the prime remedy for sin was works of
penance was already well established. All the penitentials did was to
codify existing practice, and to reinforce traditional penitential exercises, such as fasting and abstinence from holy communion, by the
authority of written texts. Nor did they dominate the scene. A study by
Cyrille Vogel of hagiographical texts from Gaul of the sixth to ninth
centuries shows how the variety of remedies listed by Cassian
continued long in use.[10] There were plenty of spiritual fathers, and even
spiritual mothers, who recommended penances without reference to
the penitential manuals; there was even a widespread belief that sins
could be forgiven without acts of penance at all – on the basis of a
simple avowal of guilt, or of the power of the intercession of the saints.
No one system, whether canonical or tariffed penance, predominated.

The position in the Byzantine East was much the same. Robert
Barringer's Oxford doctoral thesis of 1979 on penance in Constantinople plays particular attention to hagiographical texts, and comes up
with results strikingly similar to those of Vogel's study of comparable
western material.[11] Barringer notes that in the period down to the

---

[7] Groupe de la Bussière, *Pratique de la Confession* (Paris, 1983), 59.

[8] There is a huge literature on the early medieval penitentials and the influence of
Celtic practice. Klär, *Das kirchliche Bussinstitut*, 139–60, offers a useful summary.

[9] The classic triad of mortal sins requiring canonical penance – idolatry, murder and
adultery – was well established in the Late Antique period, as can be illustrated from Pacian
of Barcelona (PL 13, 1083f.), Augustine (PL 10, 636), Pope Leo (PL 54, 1209) and John of
Ephesus (PO XVII, 241).

[10] Cyrille Vogel, 'La discipline pénitentielle en Gaule, des origines au IXe siècle: le
dossier hagiographique', *Revue des sciences réligieuses* 30 (1956), 1–26, 157–86, repr. in idem, *En
rémission des péchés*, VI.

[11] Robert Barringer, 'Ecclesiastical Penance in the Church of Constantinople: a Study of
the Hagiographical Evidence to 983 A.D.', unpublished D.Phil. thesis, University of Oxford,
1979.

Council of Chalcedon (451), public penance continued but was already supplemented by the originally monastic practice of private confession to a spiritual director. He continues:

> What the evidence lacks, however, is any indication that an accepted rite or routine for securing forgiveness of sin and reconciliation after serious moral lapses was universally known and practised during this period – let alone required – either in Constantinople or in the rest of the Greek East. There is certainly no indication in the *Vitae* that the ordinary Christian in the normal course of their lives would have come into contact with the institutions of ecclesiastical penance, whether of the older episcopal or the newer monastic variety.[12]

Public penance steadily receded into the background, and did not in practice survive the iconoclast controversy.[13] But private confession took longer still to establish itself as the standard procedure for seeking forgiveness; not till after the end of the iconoclast controversy in 843 does it appear to a significant extent in hagiography. As Barringer comments,

> The Lives still plainly show that confession was not considered obligatory or necessary by many ordinary people who were guilty of serious sin. Forgiveness could be secured from God by many different means (διόρθωσις [change of life], intercession of the saints, almsgiving, fasting, prayer, entry into the monastic life); recourse to ecclesiastical penance was only one of the many courses open to the sinner.[14]

Nor was there any sense that certain sins because of their gravity required recourse to a more formal mode of penance.

Penitentials circulated in the East as in the West, and had an older history. The tariffed penance which is conventionally attributed to the originality of Celtic monks derived in fact from eastern practice developed in the fourth century, notably in the penitential epistles of Basil of

---

12 Barringer, 'Ecclesiastical Penance', 57.

13 The discipline of public penance remained officially in force for centuries; the ritual is described in Symeon of Thessalonica, *De sacro templo* (PG 155, 357–60), written in *c.*1420, but such descriptions bore no relation to contemporary practice.

14 Barringer, 'Ecclesiastical Penance', 193. John Chrysostom thought it necessary to argue against the belief that annual communion was adequate for attaining the forgiveness of sins even without works of penance (*De beato Philogonio*, PG 48, 755).

Caesarea, which list specific offences with a set period of penance for each, and make no reference to any need for formal reconciliation at the end of the process.[15] This is clearly because forgiveness from God was believed to be assured by the completion of the appropriate penance, which made absolution by a priest unnecessary. It remains the case that from the ninth century it became increasingly common for penitents not simply to fix their own penance but to have recourse to direction from spiritual fathers, who would apportion a penance and give the penitent ongoing support through the help of blessings and prayers. Miguel Arranz has assembled and classified a large number of manuscript versions of these, from the whole Byzantine period.[16] He has observed that, although some of the texts envisage confession to a priest, the confessor is normally referred to simply as 'the receiver', that is, the spiritual father who took on his own shoulders responsibility for the sins and penance of his spiritual children.

Ever since the appearance of Karl Holl's *Enthusiasmus und Bussgewalt* in 1898,[17] it has been a much trumpeted fact that some of the Greek Fathers were singularly outspoken in attributing the power to remit sins to holy men and women, to non-ordained ascetics, rather than to priests. Particularly assertive on this theme was Symeon the New Theologian (d. 1022). Symeon boldly attributed the creation of spiritual fathers and monastic hegumens to the apostles themselves, and noted that with the passing of time their pastoral role had become all the more important.[18] Indeed, he claimed that power to bind and loose had been lost by the ordained clergy because of their spiritual corruption and was now possessed by monks alone.[19] He insisted that the power to remit sins belonged to all those who are truly humble and spiritual, 'not to those who have merely received election and ordination from human beings'.[20] As an example of a man empowered to bind and loose

---

[15] These canons are contained in Basil, *epp.* 188, 199, 217 (written in 374–5) in Saint Basile, *Lettres*, ed. Yves Courtonne, 3 vols (Paris, 1957–66), 2: 120–31, 154–64, 208–17.

[16] Miguel Arranz, 'Les prières pénitentielles de la tradition byzantine', *Orientalia Christiana Periodica* [hereafter *OCP*] 57 (1991), 87–143 and 58 (1992) 23–82; idem, 'Les formulaires de confession dans la tradition byzantine', *OCP* 58 (1992), 423–59 and 59 (1993), 63–89.

[17] Holl, *Enthusiasmus* (see n. 6).

[18] Hilarion Alfeyev, *St Symeon the New Theologian* (Oxford, 2000), 197, quoting the unpublished *Third Letter*.

[19] *Letter on Penance* 11, pr. in Holl, *Enthusiasmus*, 119–20.

[20] *Cat.* 28, 291–3, in Syméon le Nouveau Théologien, *Catéchèses*, ed. Basile Krivochéine, French transl. Joseph Paramelle, Sources chrétiennes 96, 104, 113 (Paris, 1963–65), 3: 150.

without having 'received ordination on the part of human beings', he cited his own spiritual father, Symeon the Devout.[21]

That the non-ordained were attributed with this power should not cause surprise in the context of the understanding of penance we have outlined, with its emphasis on the performance of penance by the penitent rather than the imparting of absolution by a confessor. Equally determinative was the emphasis in the Orthodox East, that went back to the Alexandrian theologians of the third century, on the confessor as doctor rather than judge: hearing confessions was linked with spiritual direction, and was therefore perceived to require charism rather than authority.[22]

As a result it was monks rather than members of the white, or secular, clergy who came to act as confessors; their status was enhanced by their sufferings in the iconoclast period, when monks were singled out for persecution by the emperors and for a new degree of veneration by an iconophile laity. The role of the bishops was therefore reduced to giving formal approval to particular monks to act as confessors; some monks even presumed permission without formally receiving it.[23] At the end of the Byzantine period, however, we find a greater stress on formal absolution, accompanied by the introduction of indicative formulae of absolution, where the confessor does not simply pray for the gift of forgiveness to the penitent but actually bestows it.[24]

Writing in the early fifteenth century Archbishop Symeon of Thessalonica argued that for bishops to delegate the power to bind and loose to non-ordained monks was inappropriate and unnecessary, though he did not deny that they could and sometimes chose to do so.[25]

Already in the ninth century we may note divergence between West and East. At a time when western councils were beginning to insist on confession to a priest, Byzantine piety continued to attach importance to holiness rather than ordination as a qualification for hearing confessions. Peter Brown has summed up a crucial confrontation at the Council of Constantinople of 869–70:

> Had the protospatharius Theodore been properly shriven by a priest? The delegate of the most holy see of Old Rome said: 'What

[21] *Letter on Penance* 16, in Holl, *Enthusiasmus*, 127.

[22] See Holl, *Enthusiasmus*, 226–39 on Clement of Alexandria and Origen, and Alfeyev, *St Symeon*, 197–201.

[23] Holl, *Enthusiasmus*, 324.

[24] Arranz, 'Les prières pénitentielles', *OCP* 58 (1992), esp. 64–82.

[25] Symeon of Thessalonica, *Responsa ad Gabrielem Pentapolitanum* 10–13, PG 155, 860–4.

was the name of your confessor?' 'I don't know. I only know that he was in the imperial chancellery. He became a monk. He did (*fecit!*) forty years on a pillar.' 'But was he a priest?' 'I don't know, he was a holy old man, and I put my trust in the man . . .'.[26]

The debate over the qualifications for a confessor reflects, of course, a developing consensus from the ninth century, in both East and West, that the forgiveness of sins required recourse to a confessor, in contrast to the looser discipline of the preceding period, when penitents often sought forgiveness through works of penance or mercy without any human mediator. As late as 813, the Council of Châlon-sur-Saône recognized as valid and efficacious confession to God alone.[27] But the Carolingian authorities soon came to demand confession to priest or bishop as a regular preparation for the reception of holy communion.[28] The resulting contrast between East and West remained, however, for some centuries more conspicuous in theory than in practice. A survey by Alexander Murray of saints' Lives and miracle collections from the ninth to the twelfth centuries has shown that in practice confession to a priest, except on one's deathbed, continued to be unusual, despite the exhortations of bishops and councils.[29]

Confession to God alone was, however, increasingly seen as inadequate: there was wide acceptance from this time onwards that, because of the social nature of sin, a purely inner act of contrition was less satisfactory than confession to a fellow human being. Where the Church authorities found it harder to convince the laity was over the principle that confession to a lay person was only adequate in the case of lesser

[26] Peter Brown, 'The Rise and Function of the Holy Man in Late Antiquity', *Journal of Roman Studies* 61 (1971), 80–101, repr. in idem, *Society and the Holy in Late Antiquity* (London, 1982), 103–52, 141. The significance of this episode was already appreciated by Johannes Morinus, *Commentarius historicus de disciplina in administratione sacramenti poenitentiae* (Paris, 1651; repr. Farnborough, 1970), 416.

[27] MGH, *Concilia* II.1 (Hannover and Leipzig, 1906), 280. Churchmen often tried to limit this principle to the case of minor sins: examples are Alcuin, *ep.* 112 (PL 100, 337–8), and Aelfric, *The Homilies of the Anglo-Saxon Church: The First Part, Containing the Sermones Catholici, or Homilies of Ælfric*, ed. Benjamin Thorpe (London, 1844), 124–5. It is significant that when Burchard of Worms mentioned confession to God alone in *c.*1000, he described belief in its efficacy as an error of the Greeks: Cyrille Vogel, *Le Pécheur et la pénitence au Moyen Âge* (Paris, 1969), 203.

[28] Rob Meens, 'The Frequency and Nature of Early Medieval Penance', in Peter Biller and A. J. Minnis, eds, *Handling Sin: Confession in the Middle Ages* (York, 1998), 35–55. For a survey of the history of the study of early medieval penance see Sarah Hamilton, *The Practice of Penance 900–1050* (Woodbridge, 2001), 1–13.

[29] Alexander Murray, 'Confession before 1215', *TRHS* ser. 6, 3 (1992), 51–81.

sins, while all serious sins required confession to a priest. Cases of necessity had to be respected, and it became universally accepted that even mortal sins could be forgiven through confession to a layman in situations where a priest was not available.[30] Scholastic theology acknowledged that such a confession was imperfect but still sacramental.[31] The practice is wittily parodied in the thirteenth-century mock epic *Reinaert de Vos* (Reynard the Fox), when Reinaert, on his way to trial, confesses his offences to his nephew Grimbert the badger, beginning with the curious words, 'Confiteor tibi, pater, mater'. Grimbert is disconcerted by the evident relish with which Reynard narrates his escapades, but lets him off with a brief admonition and the minimal penance of giving himself three blows on the back with a switch and then hopping over it.[32]

What happened in eastern Christendom outside Byzantium? In the new Churches of the South Slavic lands, from the ninth century, the hearing of confessions was not restricted to monks, as in contemporary Byzantium, but was widely entrusted to the white (or secular) clergy; and even though there is evidence of non-ordained monks being recognized as confessors, this was not usual, while in the new Church of Russia, from the end of the tenth century, there is, apparently, no evidence at all for non-ordained monks hearing confessions.[33] In these countries, then, the balance of power between ordained and non-ordained, between institution and charism, was different than in Byzantium. Meanwhile, in the contemporary Near East we find widespread evidence for the forgiveness of sins without individual confession, either to monk or priest. The early Armenian order of penance, of which the earliest known manuscript dates to the tenth century, prescribes a non-repeatable rite of public penance; later Armenian rituals contain a rite of private penance, and also a rite of general confession and absolution, for use at the beginning of the Sunday liturgy.[34] However, a late fifth-century sermon on penance by the

---

[30] The classic study is Amédée Teetaert, *La Confession aux laïques dans l'Église latine depuis le VIIIe jusqu'au XIVe siècle: étude de théologie positive* (Wetteren/Paris, 1926).

[31] Aquinas, *Summa Theologica, Supplementum* 8.2, *ad primum*.

[32] John Flinn, *Le Roman de Renart dans la littérature française et dans les littératures étrangères au Moyen Âge* (Toronto, 1963), 624–6. For an English version of this episode, see *The History of Reynard the Fox*, transl. William Caxton, ed. N. F. Blake (London, 1970), 25–8.

[33] S. Smirnov, *Drevnerusskij dukhovnik: Izsledovanie po istorii tserkovnago byta* [The Old Russian Confessor: A Study in the History of Church Life] (Moscow, 1913; repr. Farnborough, 1970), 15–17.

[34] Alphonse Raes, 'Les Rites de la Pénitence chez les Arméniens', *OCP* 13 (1947), 648–55.

Catholicos John Mandakuni makes no mention of any form of confession or ritual and recommends tears of repentance and almsgiving as the best way to obtain the forgiveness of sins, including mortal ones.[35] Meanwhile, in the medieval Syrian rites, we find an insistence that all sins are forgiven through a general absolution contained in the prayers of the eucharist.[36]

In all, the penitential systems of the early Middle Ages, whether in the West, the Orthodox East, or the ancient oriental Churches, show an extraordinary variety of forms, or lack of form. All the following received emphasis, with plenty of local variation: sorrow for sin, serious performance of penance (preceding absolution), almsgiving and other good works, some form of avowal, reconciliation with persons one had wronged, guidance and prayer from a spiritual father, the involvement of the whole Church through liturgical prayer and (occasionally) public penance, recourse to the intercession of the angels and saints. There was no sense of a need to define the relative importance of these various elements. Questions as to the qualifications and appointment of confessors could lead to tension, and there were periodic but ineffective attempts by church councils to insist on public penance in the case of gravely scandalous sin; but generally the laity enjoyed a wide variety of options as to how to seek forgiveness, although we have noted a shift by which from the ninth century in both East and West confession to a fellow human being, even if not a priest, was generally seen as preferable to confession to God alone.

To this may be contrasted the pattern of penance standard in the Catholic and Orthodox Churches in recent centuries – confession to a priest, absolution, and a token work of penance.[37] Penance in the early medieval period may seem chaotic in comparison, but it had the advantage of drawing attention to a variety of important aspects of penance that were subsequently obscured: the need for serious acts of penance if the penitent is to develop the self-discipline without which recidivism is predictable, the need for varying forms of reconciliation relating to various categories of sin (such as sins against religion and sins against

---

[35] Simon Weber, *Ausgewählte Schriften der armenischen Kirchenväter*, 2 vols (Munich, 1927), 2: 58–68.

[36] L. Ligier, 'Pénitence et Eucharistie en Orient', *OCP* 29 (1963), 5–78, esp. 18–24.

[37] Note the development in the West by *c.*1000 of a practice by which absolution followed immediately on confession and preceded penance: P. F. Palmer, *Sacraments and Forgiveness: History and Doctrinal Development of Penance, Extreme Unction and Indulgences* (London, 1960), 173–4. This fatally undermined the importance of acts of penance.

one's neighbour), and a sense of the involvement not just of ecclesiastical officialdom but of the whole communion of the Church, supremely through the intercession of holy men and women, both living and dead. The later system of private confession to a priest exploited scrupulosity as to whether one's sins had really been forgiven, and offered the reassurance of the sacramental power of the priest. But the resultant clericalization has left us with a system of penance that is inflexible, inexpressive of the involvement of the whole Church in sanctification and reconciliation, and ineffective in promoting true contrition and change of life. The early Middle Ages are not generally looked upon as one of the normative epochs in the history of Christianity, but in the matter of penance they were arguably exemplary.

Heythrop College, University of London

A TOKEN OF REPENTANCE AND RECONCILIATION: OSWIU AND THE MURDER OF KING OSWINE

by CHRISTOPHER M. SCARGILL

A S ANY parish priest will tell you, the first step in repentance and reconciliation is a recognition that you have done wrong. When, in 651, Oswine of Deira was betrayed into the hands of his enemy, Oswiu of Bernicia, and was put to death, Oswiu was left in little doubt about the sinfulness of such an action, for, if Bede is to be believed, the killing was met with universal disgust.[1] Oswiu might, I think, have been forgiven had he at first wondered why his action provoked such horror. After all, Oswine was not trying to make peace when he was killed. Even Bede, who condemns the murder, admits that Oswine was lying low, awaiting an opportune time to re-open hostilities.

Nor was Oswiu himself – as far as one can tell from the account in the *Historia Ecclesiastica* – responsible for Oswine's betrayal. This seems to have been a bit of private enterprise on the part of the Deiran nobleman Hunwald. Oswiu simply took advantage of the opportunity with which he was presented. Nor would it seem that Oswiu's contemporaries would have found political assassination *per se* a shocking act. Oswiu was clearly implicated in the murder of King Penda of the Middle Angles by his wife, Oswiu's daughter.[2] Any reader of Bede quickly comes to the conclusion that such assassinations were part of the common currency of relations between Early English kings.[3]

Yet Oswiu does seem to have responded to the wave of opprobrium which greeted the killing with a very clear and public display of repentance, founding a monastery at *In Getlingum*, the site of Oswine's murder, in expiation of his sin. Following the final defeat of Oswiu's great enemy Penda of Mercia at Winwaed in 655, Oswiu further dedicated one hundred and twenty hides of land, half in Deira and half in Bernicia, to provide for monks to pray for the peace of his nation.[4] As

---

[1] Bede, *Historia Ecclesiastica* III. 14, transl. and ed. Leo Sherley-Price, *A History of the English Church and People* (Harmondsworth, 1968) [hereafter Bede, *HE*].

[2] Bede, *HE* III. 24.

[3] Bede, *HE* II. 12, II. 9, IV. 32, for instance.

[4] Bede, *HE* III. 24.

we shall see, this endowment can also be understood as a sign of reconciliation between the Deiran and Bernician peoples, Oethelwald of
Deira having taken Penda's side in the events leading up to Winwaed.
Clues to this linkage can be found on the banks of the Tees, at the
northern limits of Deira.

In Getlingum is of course normally identified with Gilling in the
North Riding of Yorkshire, which in Domesday Book appears as a soke
containing the berewicks of Barton, Eppleby, Cliffe on Tees, Cartun
(probably Carlton, parish of Stanwick), Barforth, Ovington, Girlington,
Wycliffe, Thorpe (parish of Wycliffe), Mortham, Egglestone, Brignall,
Scargill, Barningham, West Layton, East Layton and two vills in
Stanwick itself. In 1571, 'a free chapel of St Tilde' – clearly an error for
Hilda – was recorded as lying at Thorpe near Wycliffe. This continued
to be used during the next century by the local Roman Catholic recusant community, but appears to have vanished by 1700. The Teesdale
local historian H. D. Pritchett, writing in 1935, says the 'chapel stood
close to the Tees on the left hand side of the road from Thorpe to
Whorlton, just before you cross the river'. He also notes that in the very
dry summer of 1906, the outlines of walls could be seen under the grass,
suggesting that the chapel must have originally formed part of a larger
complex of buildings.[5]

It should be noted that Thorpe on Tees has never been a separate
parish from Wycliffe and St Mary's Wycliffe itself contains some late
Anglo-Saxon sculpture. Nearby, between Greta Bridge and Wycliffe,
fragments of Anglo-Saxon stone sculpture have been found, which
have been dated to between 725 and 850.[6] Yet Symeon of Durham
claims that Wycliffe was one of three vills founded by Bishop Ecgred of
Lindisfarne, who was only consecrated in 830.[7]

While it is not impossible that Symeon of Durham is correct and we
are looking at evidence for a ninth-century monastic foundation
between Thorpe and Wycliffe, the evidence seems to point to a religious site predating Ecgred – a site lying within the soke of Gilling and
linked to a saint of the royal house of Deira. Since the site of the monastery at *In Getlingum* itself has never been located at Gilling, it is within
the bounds of possibility that this is in fact the main monastic site,

[5] H. D. Pritchett, *John de Wycliffe* (Darlington, 1935), 14–15.

[6] J. D. Cowen and E. Barty, 'An Anglo-Saxon Inscription Recovered', *Archaeologia Aeliana* ser. 4, 44 (1966), 60–7.

[7] 'Historia Dunelmensis Ecclesiae', in *Symeonis monachi opera omnia*, ed. T. Arnold, 2 vols (London, 1882–5), I: 196–214.

though of course that monastery was founded two decades before the death of Abbess Hilda. In that case, the chapel dedication would be a later development. More likely, however, is that this is an outlier of that monastery, which developed on one of the estates granted by Oswiu on the boundaries of Deira and Bernicia. Nearby, on the other side of the river Tees, lies Coniscliffe, where the church is dedicated to another Deiran royal saint, Edwin.

Intriguingly there may be further evidence of a royal monastic estate at nearby Ovington, still within the parish of Wycliffe. Both Bede, in his Life of St Cuthbert, and the anonymous Life of St Cuthbert tell of how the saint came to meet with St Aelfflaed and to dedicate a church on an estate belonging to her monastic house of Whitby.[8] There he had a vision of a holy man being carried by the angels to heaven, and when Aelfflaed asked the man's name, she was told that she herself would tell the saint as he was celebrating mass the following day. The abbess sent a messenger back to Whitby, who returned the following day, and the prophecy was fulfilled.

The anonymous Life omits the detail that this house was an estate of Whitby, but names it as Osingadun. This would (if one follows Colgrave) become Ovington in modern English.[9] There are several places in the north of England called Ovington or Ovingdon which could be the place in question, but Ovington in the parish of Wycliffe is in an area where there are known remains indicating early Anglo-Saxon religious activity. We know from the period when Wycliffe was a centre for recusancy in the sixteenth and seventeenth centuries that Whitby was in reasonably easy reach for the pre-Industrial Age traveller.

There also appears to be some uncertainty as to whether Cuthbert was operating within his own diocese as the author of the anonymous Life indicates, or whether he was outside his diocese, as Bede seems to imply.[10] A site such as Ovington, close to the Tees, could account for such confusion. On the other hand, it must be said that the place-name evidence seems to militate against this identification, the name appearing in Domesday as Ulfeton.[11] That said, the evidence of

8   Bedae, 'Vita Sancti Cuthberti', XXXIV.261 and 'Vita Sancti Cuthberti Anonymae', IV.127: in *Two Lives of St Cuthbert*, ed. Bertram Colgrave (Cambridge, 1940, repr. 1985).

9   *Two Lives of St Cuthbert*, 336.

10   *Two Lives of St Cuthbert*, 127 and 263; see also Colgrave's note, 336.

11   A. H. Smith, *The Place-Names of the North Riding of Yorkshire*, English Place-Names Society Series 5 (Cambridge, 1928), 299.

Domesday is three hundred years later than Bede, so the matter cannot be considered entirely closed.

Even without the Ovington–Osingadun identification, with its implication of a link to Whitby, it is still notable that while there are no religious sites in the Tees valley dedicated to St Oswald, an equivalent Bernician royal saint,[12] we have evidence of two religious sites in the Tees valley linked to the Deiran royal house and in one case linked to Gilling. Aelfflaed, Oswiu's own daughter dedicated to the religious life as part of his act of thanksgiving for the defeat of Penda, enters and eventually becomes abbess of the monastic community at Whitby, which, as both Alan Thacker and Clare Stancliffe have pointed out, quickly came to fulfil the function of a Deiran royal mausoleum and centre for the diffusion of the cult of Edwin.[13] Aelfflaed's predecessor in this role was of course her mother Eanfled, daughter of King Edwin, while the house was founded by Hilda, daughter of Edwin's brother Hereric (murdered probably at the instigation of Aethelfrith, father of Oswald and Oswiu).

A pattern seems to emerge, however sketchily, which links the gift of one hundred and twenty hides and the dedication of Aelfflaed not simply to Oswiu's desire for intercession to be made for the 'perpetual peace of his nation', nor even to thanksgiving for the defeat of Penda, but to the monastery of *In Getlingum* established by Trumhere, himself a kinsman of Oswine, at the petition of Queen Eanfled, as a token of Oswiu's repentance for the murder of the Deiran king and to a desire to honour the Deiran royal house. Thus those one hundred and twenty hides, so neatly divided, Bede tells us, sixty in Deira and sixty in Bernicia, become a sign of reconciliation, tying the two parts of the single Northumbrian nation together.

For, whether or not Oswiu repented of the sin of killing the saintly Oswine, he almost certainly repented of the act as a grave political error. Rather than bringing Deira firmly under his control, it seems to have pushed the Deirans into the arms of Penda. As was noted earlier, at the battle of Winwaed in 655 we find King Oswald's son Oethelwald

---

[12] Alison Binns, 'Pre-Reformation Dedications to St Oswald in England and Scotland', in Clare Stancliffe and Eric Cambridge, eds, *Oswald: Northumbrian King to European Saint* (Stamford, 1995), 241–71.

[13] See Clare Stancliffe, '"Oswald, most Holy and Victorious King of the Northumbrians"', in Stancliffe and Cambridge, eds, *Oswald*, 33–83, 73, and also A. Thacker, '*Membra disjecta*: the Division of the Body and the Diffusion of the Cult', in ibid., 97–127, 105–11.

on the Mercian side – though ultimately standing aloof from Penda's final defeat. While he would have had reasons of his own to mistrust Oswiu (as indeed he would have to mistrust Penda), Oethelwald appears elsewhere in Bede as a faithful Christian, a patron of St Cedd and of his community at Lastingham,[14] rather than as a maverick or a traitor. It is difficult to believe that at Winwaed he was acting on his own account without the support of his Deiran subjects. Oethelwald disappears from the pages of history after the battle and Oswiu seems to have incorporated Deira firmly into his own kingdom, probably under his son Alhfrith as sub-king, as, for a short time, he did with Mercia. If his rule over Deira was not however to prove as ephemeral as it did over Mercia, which revolted after a mere three years, then a great gesture of reconciliation was needed.

The granting of land for a monastery in expiation of Oswine's murder was a clear sign of Oswiu's repentance, but with Eanfled, the heiress of King Edwin, safely married to himself and with Oswine's kinsman Trumhere accepting the gift and becoming first abbot of the monastery, it must have seemed a gesture he could safely make. There was little chance of anyone trying to capitalize on his admission of guilt. Paradoxically, not only did the foundation of *In Getlingum* mark a recognition by both sides of Oswiu's sin, but at the same time it drew a line under the conflict between Deira and Bernicia, implicitly recognizing the success of that apparently sinful policy.

Oswiu then, at the price of a public display of penitence, united Deira and Bernicia into a single kingdom, a union which would endure despite all the tensions right up to the founding of the Viking kingdom of York, rising phoenix-like once more under the later Anglo-Saxon monarchy, only to be finally extinguished by the Norman kings. One might feel that it was a success cheaply bought. Even his gift of land for the monastery at *In Getlingum* seems to have cost him little. The clear implication of Bede's narrative is that the killing of Oswine and his companion Tondhere took place at the house of the nobleman Hunwald.

We hear no more of Hunwald. However, since Domesday sokes in the North have, in a number of cases, been shown to preserve earlier tenurial arrangements, one may reasonably conclude that the soke of Gilling probably represents Hunwald's own estates and it was parts of those estates which Oswiu took to endow the monastery and to make

---

14 Bede, *HE* III. 23.

up the sixty hides of Deiran land given for the monks to pray for the peace of the kingdom. Those two endowments would of course form only a fraction of the land which made up the soke of Gilling, so on a purely practical level Oswiu's gesture of repentance may well have involved giving away parts of an estate which did not belong to him in the first place and retaining the rest in his own hands so that he came out of the situation richer than before.

Moreover, a dispute recorded by Symeon of Durham between Aella of Northumbria (863–7) and the Church of St Cuthbert over those estates at Wycliffe, Iclife and Billingham which Symeon records Bishop Ecgred of Lindisfarne as having held, suggests that even two centuries later the Northumbrian kings felt they retained some sort of right over those lands in the soke of Gilling, though the Church might believe otherwise. As for Oswiu himself, one might well question the sincerity of his repentance when he was clearly implicated in the murder of Peada (by now king of the south Mercians) in 656 and the Mercians obviously feared that he would dispose of the young heir Wulfhere in a similar fashion.[15]

Yet had Oswiu genuinely escaped any retribution for the death of Oswine beyond his public, but apparently somewhat insincere, expression of repentance? On a purely pragmatic basis the answer must be yes. However, in a heroic culture, where reputation counted for so much, it could be said that Oswiu suffered the ultimate retribution. Despite N. J. Higham's suggestion that the replacement of Ceollach by Trumhere as bishop of the Mercians could be an attempt by Oswiu to put a reliable and politically astute candidate of his own in place to maintain, through ecclesiastical channels, the control over Mercia, which he had lost following Wulfhere's assertion of Mercian independence,[16] Wulfhere does not come over as a man so easily hoodwinked. Margaret Gelling's theory that the substitution of Ceollach by Trumhere as bishop of the Mercians is the replacement by King Wulfhere of Oswiu's nominee by a more independent-minded candidate seems to have considerable merit.[17]

If this is so, then it suggests that Trumhere was recognized as still retaining a certain antipathy towards Oswiu, despite having agreed to be abbot of *In Getlingum*. Whitby too may well have retained a tradition

---

[15] Bede, *HE* III. 24.

[16] N. J. Higham, *The Convert Kings: Power and Religious Affiliation in Early Anglo-Saxon England* (Manchester, 1997), 245–8.

[17] Margaret Gelling, *The West Midlands in the Early Middle Ages* (Leicester, 1992), 94–5.

of hostility towards the murderer of Oswine. Higham takes the view that Oswiu deliberately fostered the development of Whitby as a way of reorientating his kingdom and making it more southward looking and less centred on the old Bernician heartlands and on Lindisfarne. For Higham, the Synod of Whitby in fact marks the culmination of this policy and he suggests that Lindisfarne and Bamburgh may have been adversely affected by the fall of Oswald's son Oethelwald.[18]

However, as we saw earlier, Oethelwald actually wished to create a religious centre, an *eigenkirche*, at Lastingham and seems to have had little to do with Bernicia. Higham himself recognizes Hilda and the Whitby community as supporters of the Irish party at the Synod of Whitby. On the other hand, evidence of a cult of Oswine and a generally pro-Deiran (and by implication anti-Oswiu) tradition at Whitby and Gilling, continuing much later than the Synod of Whitby, is strong. The recovery of the body of King Edwin, showing a continuing interest in the old Deiran royal house, probably took place between 680 and 704, for instance.[19]

We noted earlier that Bede clearly regards the killing of Oswine as far more blameworthy than other such political assassinations. The sheer amount of text which he devotes to the incident testifies to that. Where would Bede have got his information? We know that one of his main sources for Deiran history was the community at Whitby, so does his grave view of the killing reflect the traditional view of the Whitby community, with its strong links to the Deiran royal house? Or is there an even closer link?

The Anglian inscribed stone found at Wycliffe bears an inscription which seems to read:

> Baeda [the settae]
> Aefter Berchtuini
> Becun aefter f[athorae
> Gebidaed der saule]

which translates as: Baeda [this set]/after Berchtuini/a beacon after [his father/pray for his soul].[20] Pritchett points out that a Bercthun or Berchtuini was first abbot of Beverley and a close associate of John of Beverley who ordained Bede to the diaconate.[21] We have of course no

---

[18] Higham, *Convert Kings*, 250–7.
[19] Thacker, '*Membra Disjecta*', 105.
[20] Cowan and Barty, 'Inscription Recovered', 63.
[21] Pritchett, *John de Wycliffe*, 5.

other evidence to link Bede to *In Getlingum* and there could well be other Baedas and other Berchtuinis. Moreover St Bercthun is usually thought to have died at Beverley.

At any rate, whether there is a genuine connection between Bede and *In Getlingum*, or whether Bede is drawing his material from a Whitby tradition at this point, a strong suggestion still remains that in the *Historia Ecclesiastica* he is drawing on a long-standing tradition which condemned Oswiu as the infamous murderer of the saintly Oswine, a tradition maintained in religious establishments closely linked to the old Deiran royal family. For Oswiu, who grew up in an Irish culture where bards were feared for their power to satirize a ruler and undermine his reputation and prestige, the presence of such a religious centre for ever preserving a record of his guilt may have seemed far worse retribution than the cost of having to found a monastery and create an endowment of one hundred and twenty hides of land.

Ipstones, Staffordshire

PENANCE IN THE AGE OF GREGORIAN REFORM

by SARAH HAMILTON

O N 28 January 1077 at the castle of Canossa in the northern Appenines King Henry IV was absolved from his excommunication by Pope Gregory VII.[1] Henry's reconciliation with the Church represented the successful conclusion to what had been a hazardous mission for both him and his small entourage, one which had involved a difficult journey through the alpine passes in winter.[2] It culminated in the king, having abandoned his royal garb for simple woollen clothing and with bare feet, standing for three days before the gates of the castle of Canossa, ceaselessly weeping and imploring divine mercy.[3]

The political significance of Henry's penance for his contemporaries is demonstrated by a substantial textual record.[4] Its importance for

---

[1] *Das Register Gregors VII*, ed. Erich Caspar, MGH Epistolae selectae (Berlin, 1920–3; repr. 1955), iv.12, 313 [hereafter *Reg.*].

[2] Lampert of Hersfeld, *Annales*, a. 1077, in *Lamperti monachi Hersfeldensis opera*, ed. O. Holder-Egger, MGH Scriptores rerum Germanicarum in usum scholarum separatim editi [hereafter SRG] 38 (Hanover and Leipzig, 1894), 286–7; Berthold of Reichenau, *Annales*, MGH Scriptores [hereafter SS], V: 264–326, 288. G. Meyer von Knonau, *Jahrbücher des deutschen Reiches unter Heinrich IV. und Heinrich V.*, 6 vols (Leipzig, 1890–1907), 2: 747; I. S. Robinson, *Henry IV of Germany, 1056–1106* (Cambridge, 1999), 160–1.

[3] *Reg.* iv.12, 313. See also Robinson, *Henry IV*, 161; H. E. J. Cowdrey, *Pope Gregory VII, 1073–85* (Oxford, 1998), 153–8.

[4] Texts include: *Reg.* iv.12, 312–14, iv.12a, 314–15, vii.14a, 484; *The Epistolae Vagantes of Pope Gregory VII*, ed. H. E. J. Cowdrey (Oxford, 1972), no. 19, 52; Lampert, *Annales*, 1077, 289–96; Berthold, *Annales*, 1077, 288–90; Donizo, *Vita Mathildis comitissae metrica*, ed. L. Bethmann, MGH SS, XII: 348–409, II.i, 381–2; Bernold of St Blasien, *Chronicon*, MGH SS, V: 400–67, 433; *Vita Heinrici IV imperatoris*, ed. W. Wattenbach and W. Eberhard, MGH SRG 58 (Hanover, 1899), 16–17; Peter Crassus, *Defensio Heinrici IV regis*, ed. L. de Heinemann, MGH Libelli de lite imperatorum et pontificum saeculi XI. et XII. conscripti, 3 vols (Hanover, 1891–97), 1: 432–53, ch. 6, 445–6; O. Holder-Egger, 'Fragment eines Manifestes aus der Zeit Heinrichs IV', *Neues Archiv der Gesellschaft für ältere deutsche Geschichtskunde* 31 (1906), 183–93, 189. See also the work defending royal penance, *De paenitentia regum et de investitura regali collectanea*, ed. H. Böhmer, MGH Libelli de lite, 3: 608–14; this text is preserved in a Bamberg codex which includes various polemics produced during the Investiture Contest, and was interpreted by its editor as a pro-royalist text, an argument developed further by Ute-Renate Blumenthal, 'Canossa and Royal Ideology in 1077: Two Unknown Manuscripts of *De penitentia regis Salomonis*', *Manuscripta* 22 (1978), 91–6. But Claudia Märtle argues, in 'Ein angeblicher Text zum Bussgang von Canossa: *De penitentia regum*', *Deutsches Archiv für Erforschung des Mittelalters* 38 (1982), 555–63, that the text is independent of Canossa. Nevertheless its inclusion in the Bamberg collection suggests Canossa may have given it a renewed relevance.

47

modern historians has been if anything greater. Bismarck said in 1872: 'We shall not go to Canossa, neither in body nor in spirit', whilst twentieth-century historians have seen it as contributing to the growth of papal power.[5] More recently historians have emphasized the parallels between the obviously staged formal royal penance at Canossa and the contemporary secular ritual of surrender and political reconciliation, *deditio*.[6]

To what extent his penance at Canossa was either a humiliating ritual or an empowering one for the king will continue to be debated, but this is not my concern here. Instead I want to draw out three other points. First, Henry did penance as an excommunicant, not as a voluntary penitent. Excommunication was a much-used weapon in the investiture contest; it had its own liturgical rituals of reconciliation and was also consciously regarded as distinct from penance in canon law.[7] Second, the reconciliation of excommunicants used the language of repentance and reconciliation which can, on occasion, make it hard to disentangle it from voluntary penance for sin. But, thirdly, what the example of Canossa undoubtedly demonstrates is the important role played by penitential language and penitential ritual in the age of Gregorian reform. Whilst historians have been endlessly concerned with political interpretations of this incident, little attempt has been

---

[5]   The historiography for Canossa is vast. Amongst other works see Harald Zimmermann, *Der Canossagang von 1077. Wirkungen und Wirklichkeit* (Wiesbaden, 1975); Walter Ullmann, *A Short History of the Papacy in the Middle Ages* (London, 1972), 157–9; Cowdrey, *Pope Gregory VII*, 153–67.

[6]   G. Althoff, 'Das Privileg der 'deditio': Formen gütlicher Konfliktbeendigung in der mittelalterlichen Adelsgesellschaft', in idem, *Spielregeln der Politik im Mittelalter: Kommunikation in Frieden und Fehde* (Darmstadt, 1997), 99–125; T. Reuter, 'Unruhestiftung, Fehde, Rebellion, Widerstand: Gewalt und Frieden in der Politiken der Salierzeit', in Stephan Weinfurter, ed., *Die Salier und das Reich*, 3 vols (Sigmaringen, 1991), 3: 297–325.

[7]   For the rituals associated with excommunication and the reconciliation of excommunicants, see *Le Pontifical romano-germanique du dixième siècle*, ed. Cyrille Vogel and Reinhard Elze, Studi e Testi 226, 227, 269 (Vatican City, 1963, 1972), 1: lxxxv–xci, 308–21 [hereafter *PRG*]; discussed by Roger E. Reynolds, 'Rites of Separation and Reconciliation in the Early Middle Ages', *Segni e riti nella chiesa altomedievale occidentale*, Spoleto 11–17 aprile 1985, Settimane di studio del Centro italiano di studi sull'Alto Medioevo 33 (Spoleto, 1987), 405–33. On the canonical distinction between penance and excommunication, see e.g. Burchard of Worms, *Decretum*, XI: De Excommunicatione and XIX, De Poenitentia, PL 140, 855–76, 949–1014; Bonizo of Sutri, *Liber de vita christiana*, ed. Ernst Perels (Berlin, 1930; repr. Hildesheim, 1998), ii.52, 60–2 (reconciliation of penitents), ix.4, 278–9 (reconciliation of excommunicants); Anselm of Lucca, *Collectio canonum*, XI (de poenitentia), XII (de excommunicatione): partial edition in *Anselmi episcopi Lucensis collectio canonum, una cum collectione minore*, ed. F. Thaner (Innsbruck, 1906–15); unfortunately most of book XI and all of book XII remain unpublished.

made to place Canossa in its contemporary penitential context. Canossa is therefore the starting point for this enquiry into penance in Italy in the second half of the eleventh century.

His submission at Canossa did not bring an end to Henry's troubles. At the Lent synod held in Rome in 1080 Henry IV was again excommunicated, and this time even deposed from the throne. The *Register's* record of this sentence recalled Canossa, when the pope 'seeing him humbled had received from him many promises about the amendment of his life (before he) restored him solely to communion'.[8] But, Gregory complained, this change had not been forthcoming and therefore Henry was 'cast out from the royal dignity for his pride, disobedience and falseness'.[9] The implication is that Henry's penance at Canossa had been false because it was not accompanied by a wholehearted change of life.

In highlighting the falseness of Henry's penance at Canossa, Gregory VII was drawing on a theme which had come to the fore in the previous eighteen months of his pontificate. At the November synod held in the Lateran in 1078, which seems to have been largely concerned with the reform of the Church, amongst other matters the assembled clergy considered 'what is false penance' and 'how true penance should be given'.[10] 'False penances' are those 'not imposed according to the

---

[8] *Reg.* vii.14a, 484: 'Quem ego videns humiliatum multis ab eo promissionibus acceptis de suae vitae emendatione solam ei communionem reddidi'; Gregory continues 'non tamen in regno, a quo eum in Romana synodo deposueram, instauravi nec fidelitatem omnium, qui sibi iuraverant vel erant iuraturi, a qua omnes absolvi in eadem synodo, ut sibi servaretur, precepi'; English transl. by H. E. J. Cowdrey, *The Register of Pope Gregory VII, 1073–85. An English Translation* (Oxford, 2002), 343. For the debate as to the truth of Gregory's claims, see A. Fliche, 'Grégoire VII, à Canossa, a-t-il réintégré Henri IV dans sa fonction royale?', *Studi Gregoriani* 1 (1947), 373–86; H.-X. Arquillière, 'La sens juridique de l'absolution de Canossa (1077)', in *Actes du Congrès de droit canonique: cinquantenaire de la Faculté de droit canonique: Paris, 22–26 Avril 1947* (Paris, 1950), 157–64; idem, 'Grégoire VII, à Canossa, a-t-il réintégré Henri IV dans sa fonction royale?', *Studi Gregoriani* 4 (1952), 1–26; K. F. Morrison, 'Canossa: a Revision', *Traditio* 18 (1962), 121–48.

[9] *Reg.* vii.14a, 486–7: 'Sicut enim Heinricus pro sua superbia inoboedientia et falsitate a regni dignitate iuste abicitur, ita Rodulfo pro sua humilitate oboedientia et veritate potestas et dignitas regni conceditur.' Transl. Cowdrey, *Register*, 344.

[10] *Reg.* vi.5b, 401: '[XIV] De falsis paenitentiis. [XV] Qualiter vera paenitentia detur'. On Gregory's actions in respect of penance, see Cowdrey, *Pope Gregory VII*, 510–13, 655; idem, 'The Spirituality of Pope Gregory VII', in *The Mystical Tradition and the Carthusians*, J. Hogg, ed., Analecta cartusiana 130 (Salzburg, 1995), 1–22, 14–17, repr. in *Popes and Church Reform in the Eleventh Century* (Aldershot, 2000), II; 'The Reform Papacy and the Origin of the Crusades', in *Le Concile de Clermont de 1095 et l'appel à la croisade: actes du Colloque universitaire international de Clermont-Ferrand, 23–25 juin 1995* (Rome, 1997), 65–83 and 'Pope Gregory VII and the Bearing of Arms', in B. J. Kedar, J. Riley-Smith and R. Heistand, eds, *Montjoie. Studies in Crusade History in Honour of Hans Eberhard Meyer* (Aldershot, 1997), 21–36.

authority of the holy fathers for the type of crimes', that is not according to church law, as recorded in the penitentials with their tariffs of the length of penance required for particular sins. According to the 1078 synod all those engaged in a profession which could not be performed without committing sin, such as a knight, trader or 'other office', or anyone 'who still bears hatred in his heart or who unjustly holds the goods of another . . . should recognize that (he) cannot complete true penance, through which (he) may avail to reach eternal life', unless he gives up his profession, or dismisses hatred from his heart, or restores the goods. The only true penance involved complete conversion away from sin. If he (or she) could not manage such an undertaking, then 'whatever good he shall be able to do we urge him that he should do so that Almighty God may illuminate his heart with penance'.[11]

A year later, in November 1079, Gregory wrote to the faithful of Brittany asking them to take action against the custom of false penance which he attributed in part to the negligence of priests. He warned that those who persist in serious crime – homicide, adultery, perjury – or who are 'engaged in a business that can scarcely be exercised without sin' cannot 'bring forth the fruit of true penance'.[12] True penance and

---

[11] *Reg.* vi.5b, 404: 'Falsas paenitentias dicimus, quae non secundum auctoritatem sanctorum patrum pro qualitate criminum imponuntur. Ideoque quicunque miles vel negotiator vel alicui officio deditus, quod sine peccato exerceri non possit, culpis gravioribus irretitus ad penitentiam venerit vel qui bona alterius iniuste detinet vel qui odium in corde gerit, recognoscat se veram penitentiam non posse peragere, per quam ad aeternam vitam valeat pervenire, nisi arma deponat ulteriusque non ferat nisi consilio religiosorum episcoporum pro defendenda iustitia vel negotium derelinquat vel officium deserat et odium ex corde dimittat, bona, quae iniuste abstulit, restituat; ne tamen desperet, interim, quicquid boni facere poterit, hortamur ut faciat, ut omnipotens Deus cor illius illustret ad paenitentiam.' Transl. Cowdrey, *Register*, 284. This decree is one of the few of Gregory VII's decretals to be taken up by the twelfth-century canonists: J. T. Gilchrist, 'Was There a Gregorian Reform Movement in the Eleventh Century?', *The Canadian Catholic Historical Association. Study Sessions* 37 (Ottawa, 1970), 1–10, repr. in idem, *Canon Law in the Age of Reform, 11th–12th Centuries* (Aldershot, 1993), no. VII; 'The Reception of Pope Gregory VII into the Canon Law (1073–1141)', *Zeitschrift der Savigny-Stiftung für Rechtsgeschichte: Kanonistiche Abteilung* 59 (1973), 35–82 and 66 (1980), 192–229, 223, repr. in idem, *Canon Law*, nos. VIII and IX.

[12] *Reg.* vii.10, 472: 'Qua in re hoc summopere vos cavere oportet aliosque monere debetis, quia, si quis in homicidium adulterium periurium vel aliquod huiusmodi lapsus in aliquo talium criminum, permanserit aut negotiationi, quae vix agi sine peccato potest, operam dederit aut arma militaria portaverit, excepto si pro tuenda iustitia sua vel domini vel amici seu etiam pauperum nec pro defendendis ecclesiis, nec tamen sine religiosorum virorum consilio sumpserit, qui aeternae salutis consilium dare sapienter noverunt, aut aliena bona iniuste possederit aut in odium proximi sui exarserit, vere penitentiae fructum facere nullatenus potest. Infructuosam enim paenitentiam dicimus, quae ita accipitur, ut in

remission of sins comes only from those who try to maintain the baptismal vows. Four months later, at the Lent synod held in 1080 at which Henry IV was excommunicated for a second time, Gregory returned to the topic warning against false penance which, like false baptism, does not work:

> Thus, just as false baptism does not wash away original sin, so false penitence after baptism does not blot out the wrong committed. [...] For this is true penance, that after committing some graver sin, such as homicide, premeditated and deliberately committed, or perjury committed on account of covetousness for office or money, or other things similar to these, each person should so turn himself to God that, having abandoned all his iniquities, he should thereafter continue in the fruits of doing good works.[13]

Outward penance in Gregory's eyes must be accompanied by inner conversion.

The emphasis on penance in Gregory VII's writings in the late 1070s has, inevitably, been connected by modern historians with his deteriorating relations with Henry IV. But Gregory's preoccupation with the importance of genuine contrition for true penance antedates the synod of 1078. On 16 February 1074 he advised his loyal supporter, Mathilda, countess of Tuscany, 'to put an end to the desire for sinning and, prostrate before (the Virgin Mary) shed tears *from a contrite and humble heart*.'[14] Gregory VII's call to penance should instead be seen as part of his wider reforming activities.

The pope's most recent biographer, H. E. J. Cowdrey, has suggested Gregory VII's views on penance were novel and ahead of their time, and that his emphasis on personal contrition and true conversion anticipated twelfth-century preoccupations.[15] Peter Abelard (1079–1142)

---

eadem culpa vel simili deteriori vel parum minori permaneatur'; transl. Cowdrey, *Register*, 334.

13 *Reg.* vii.14a (5), 481–2: 'Sicut enim falsum baptisma non lavat originale peccatum, ita post baptismum falsa paenitentia non delet nefas commissum. [. . .] Haec est enim vera penitentia, ut post commissum alicuius gravioris criminis, utpote meditati homicidii et sponte commissi seu periurii pro cupiditate honoris aut pecuniae facti vel aliorum his similium, ita se unusquisque ad Deum convertat, ut relictis omnibus iniquitatibus suis deinde in fructibus bonae operationis permaneat.'; transl. Cowdrey, *Register*, 341.

14 *Reg.* i.47, 73: 'Pone itaque finem in voluntate peccandi et prostrata coram illa *ex corde contrito et humiliato* (Ps. 50: 19) lacrimas effunde'; transl. Cowdrey, *Register*, 53.

15 Cowdrey, 'Spirituality of Gregory VII', 14: 'Gregory foreshadowed and prepared the way for twelfth-century developments both inside and outside the monastic order by his endeavours to base penance more largely upon personal contrition and penitence'.

famously identified the importance of intention in sin, and theologians distinguished *culpa*, guilt, from *poena*, punishment due for sin.[16] *Culpa* is the barrier to salvation but true contrition, inspired by grace, leads to forgiveness of *culpa*; therefore confession is important, but it does not eradicate the need to undergo *poena*; purgatorial suffering is needed for temporal penance.[17] Peter Abelard and his near-contemporary, Hugh of St Victor (1096–1141),[18] are the first authors to systematize the theology of penance. However, the emphasis on confession and inner contrition is already found in two works from around 1100: the tract on the need for frequent confession attributed to Lanfranc of Canterbury,[19] and the treatise *De vera et falsa poenitentia*, erroneously attributed to Augustine.[20] For Lanfranc it was possible to confess to God alone; what was important for reconciliation was avowal.[21]

There is therefore a plethora of material from the early twelfth century onwards testifying to a preoccupation with contrition. The traditional model for the history of medieval penance attaches great significance to this seeming switch from the early medieval emphasis on the external performance of penance, the penitential tariffs recorded in the penitentials, as necessary for reconciliation with the Almighty, to more emphasis being placed on the guilt and contrition felt by the

[16] *Peter Abelard's Ethics*, ed. and trans. D. E. Luscombe (Oxford, 1971), 42–8, 54–6. On twelfth-century theology of penance see P. Anciaux, *La Théologie du sacrement de la pénitence au XIIe siècle* (Louvain and Gembloux, 1949), 63–113; Karl Müller, 'Der Umschwung in der Lehre von der Busse während des 12. Jahrhunderts', in Adolf Harnack, ed., *Theologische Abhandlungen. Carl von Weizsäcker zu seinem siebzigsten Geburtstage, 11 December 1892* (Freiburg, 1892), 289–320; Mary C. Mansfield, *The Humiliation of Sinners: Public Penance in Thirteenth-Century France* (Ithaca, NY, 1995), 18–59.

[17] *Peter Abelard's Ethics*, 88, 101.

[18] Hugh of Saint Victor, *De sacramentis christianae fidei*, II.xiv, PL 176, 549–78.

[19] Lanfranc, *Libellus de celanda confessione*, PL 150, 625–32; although Margaret Gibson rejected Lanfranc's authorship of this work in her *Lanfranc of Bec* (Oxford, 1978), 244, I follow here the arguments of Alexander Murray, 'Confession before 1215', *TRHS* ser. 6, 3 (1993), 51–81, 53, and Mansfield, *Humiliation of Sinners*, 21–3.

[20] Pseudo-Augustine, *De vera et falsa poenitentia*, PL 40, 1113–30; this work has variously been attributed by modern historians to any time between the early eleventh and the early twelfth centuries: Müller, 'Umschwung', dated it to the late tenth–early eleventh century; Bernhard Poschmann, *Penance and the Anointing of the Sick*, trans. Francis Courtney (Freiburg, 1964), 158, to the eleventh century; Anciaux, *Théologie*, 15 at n. 2, to the second half of the eleventh century; but the modern consensus seems to be for the later dating: Ludwig Hödl, *Die Geschichte der scholastischen Literatur und der Theologie der Schlüsselgewalt*, Beiträge zur Geschichte der Philosophie und Theologie des Mittelalters. Texte und Untersuchungen 38.4 (Münster, 1960), 158–63.

[21] PL 150, 629.

individual.[22] Recent research has, however, identified certain problems with this model.[23]

These twelfth-century works are in large part a testimony to the increasing concern with the systematization of knowledge which is so typical of this period.[24] The Pseudo-Augustinian tract, *De vera et falsa poenitentia*, has been described as the first central medieval tract written on the theology of penance.[25] But we need to ask whether these new twelfth-century works testify to a change in penitential thought, or whether their existence represents instead a trick of the evidential light: are they perhaps a by-product of the new scholasticism, the so-called twelfth-century renaissance? Is it the genre, rather than its contents, which is new? Can we really accept the calls of Gregory VII and his fellow reformers to Christians to convert as representing new developments in penitential thought and practice?

In order to answer these questions, this paper will examine some of the works produced in reforming circles in central Italy in the second half of the eleventh century. It will focus principally on the evidence for penitential practice and thought revealed in rites for penance and in correspondence on this issue; the evidence of canon law will only be briefly considered in order to redress the preoccupation in the current historiography with canonical and theological works.[26] By concentrating on the Italian evidence, this paper will also try to redress another bias in the scholarship, this time towards the French evidence. This wholly understandable preoccupation with France came about through a desire to provide a context for the influential monastery of Cluny, for the First Crusade and for the origins of scholastic theology in the northern French schools.[27] Moreover, as modern scholarship has

---

[22] Müller, 'Umschwung'; Anciaux, *Théologie*, 65–76; Poschmann, *Penance*, 157–60; Cyrille Vogel, *Le Pécheur et la pénitence au Moyen Âge* (Paris, 1969), 27–36; Sarah Hamilton, *The Practice of Penance, 900–1050* (Woodbridge, 2001), 7.

[23] Hamilton, *Practice*, 13–15.

[24] For example Gratian's *Decretum*, the *Glossa Ordinaria* and Peter Lombard's *Sentences*. This trend had begun earlier with the production of systematic collections in the early eleventh century, such as Burchard of Worms's *Decretum*, *c*.1020; on eleventh-century systematization, see Anciaux, *Théologie*, 7–55.

[25] Anciaux, *Théologie*, 15.

[26] There is one important exception to this trend for a different period: Mary Mansfield's research on public penance in thirteenth-century northern France (see above, n. 16). She examined both liturgy and canon law and drew attention to the disjunction between the reality of penitential practice and the ideals of the new scholastic theology.

[27] On the French bias of current work on eleventh-century penance, see Marcus Bull, *Knightly Piety and the Lay Response to the First Crusade, the Limousin and Gascony, c.970–c.1130*

emphasized the importance of the Italian context for the papal reform movement, it also seems appropriate to study the papal reformers' writings about penance in their local context.[28] In what follows therefore I will begin by looking at the eleventh-century monastic antecedents for Gregory's penitential writings before turning to examine their more immediate context through the evidence of the eleventh-century Italian liturgy, letters and canon law.

* * *

Gregory VII's railings against the failure to perform penance properly were not new; they can be traced back to an earlier generation of eleventh-century reformers. Gregory's emphasis on the need for total conversion is a theme fundamental to all monasticism, and one avidly espoused by the exponents of monastic reform in the eleventh century. At the end of the eleventh century, the Burgundian abbey of SS Peter and Paul at Cluny was famously described by its long-serving abbot Hugh as 'the refuge of the penitent' (*asylum poenitentium*) when he was trying to persuade King Philip I of France to enter the monastery and die as a monk, thus avoiding the uncertain fate which awaited William Rufus and Henry IV, who had both died suddenly, by proving his true repentance through his monastic profession:

> Behold St Peter and St Paul, the princes of the Apostles, who are the judges of emperors and kings no less than of the whole world, are ready to receive you into their house. . . . We would devoutly intercede for you before the king of kings that as for his own sake he had called you from being a king to be a monk, so he would graciously restore you from being a monk to be a king, not, however, a king who ruled for a brief season in some narrow and poverty-stricken corner of the world, but a king who shared his own unending reign, in the boundlessly rich and happy realms of heaven.[29]

But Abbot Hugh's hard-sell was as nothing to the images evoked by the Camaldolese monk and member of the papal reform circles in the

(Oxford, 1993); H. E. J. Cowdrey, *The Cluniacs and the Gregorian Reform* (Oxford, 1970), 121–56; Mansfield, *Humiliation of Sinners*; the majority of the examples in Murray, 'Confession before 1215', are from northern France and Norman England.

[28] The argument for the importance of the Italian context for the eleventh-century papal reform movement is set out in John Howe, *Church Reform and Social Change in Eleventh-Century Italy. Dominic of Sora and His Patrons* (Philadelphia, 1997), *passim*, but especially xvi–xviii.

[29] Ep. viii, PL 149, 930–2; transl. Cowdrey, *Cluniacs*, 128.

1050s and 1060s, Peter Damian.[30] In a letter Peter wrote to an unknown
bishop sometime before 1045 he warned against taking gifts as a substitute for penance from evil men. He recounted in vivid terms a vision in
which a priest, who had been confessor to a Tuscan count called
Hildebrand, described how he, the priest, had contracted leprosy from a
cloak given him as alms by the count. The count had passed on the
disease of sin to his confessor, but the giving of alms had not alleviated
his burden of sin, for later the priest saw Hildebrand standing in a
'horrible river that was foul, pitch-black and filled with sulphur'. This
figure told the priest: 'I am that most unhappy count Hildebrand on
whom you used to impose a penance even though it proved to be
useless'.

Peter Damian told the story to warn the bishop that he should be on
his guard against gifts from evil men so that while avoiding sin himself
he also recoiled from association with the sin of another.[31] Confessors
must not be content with superficial penances, happy to be paid off
with alms; unless they ensured that those under their care were truly
repentant and willing to give up a way of life which was inherently
sinful, then such vicarious penance was a false penance, harming the
souls of both minister and penitent.

The prevalence and dangers of false penance and the call to true
penance were therefore part of the rhetoric of an earlier generation of
the eleventh-century reformers. What is deemed to be at issue is the
intention of the penitent, not just the efficacy of almsgiving. This is
made clear in one particular charter form popular in central Italy in the
first half of the eleventh century, which was used by the founders of the
small family of monasteries associated with the hermit and preacher St
Dominic of Sora (d. 1032). The donors recounted how they had
committed innumerable sins since they were born. Aware that those
who fail to atone for sins will be damned with the devil

> at the Last Judgement, having sought the counsel of religious men
> on how to atone for innumerable sins and avoid the eternal penal-
> ties from the anger of the eternal Judge, we learned that except for
> renouncing the world, nothing is better than the virtue of

---

[30] On Peter Damian's life and work see Jean Leclercq, *Saint Pierre Damien ermite et homme d'église* (Rome, 1960).

[31] *Die Briefe des Petrus Damiani*, ed. Kurt Reindel, MGH, Die Briefe des deutschen Kaiserzeit IV, 4 vols (Munich, 1983–93), Ep. 14, 1: 145–50.

almsgiving and to construct, from our own possessions and property, a monastery.[32]

Whilst it is difficult to make a connection between charter *formulae* and personal motives, this *formula* appears to record thoughts prevalent in Dominic's circle.[33] According to his *Vita*, Dominic himself also preached that almsgiving was second best to personal contrition and conversion. He reportedly exhorted citizens to strive for personal conversion, to fight sin with tears (the outward sign of contrition), with prayers and fasting as well as almsgiving.[34] But Peter, lord of Sora, failed to act fully on Dominic's advice to him. When he needed to atone for his killing of a cleric and other crimes, Dominic advised Peter not only to found a monastery, which he did, but also to put aside his arms, which Peter could not bear to do, eventually dying in battle.[35]

It is clear that the themes of true penance, that is personal conversion with genuine contrition, and false penance, that is insincere and vicarious penances, run through the writings of the eleventh-century reformers, from small local reformers like Dominic in the first third of the eleventh century, to the works of Peter Damian in the middle of the century, to Gregory VII in the third quarter and Hugh of Cluny at its end. But this rhetoric of true and false penance became in Gregory VII's writings part of his call to return the entire world to righteousness. In September 1080 Gregory wrote a general letter to the German faithful, clerical and lay, lamenting the Church's position in the face of the challenge from Henry IV and his supporters:

> Since *nothing on earth is without a cause* (Job 5: 6) – as the wise man's words bear witness –, the facts that up until now the holy church is stricken by a mass of floods and storms and that she suffers the raging of tyrannical persecution must be believed to occur for no reason save that our sins deserve these things; for indeed the judgements of God are most truly all just. . . . But if we shall apply the medication of penance to the disease of our faults and if by ourselves strictly correcting our excesses and negligences we shall

---

[32] The foundation charter of San Pietro Avellano (1026): *Historia abbatiae Cassinensis per saeculorum seriem distributa*, ed. Erasmo Gattula, 2 vols (Venice, 1733), I: 238; Howe, *Church Reform*, 108, 115.

[33] Howe also suggests it was a form prevalent in the region: *Church Reform*, 115–16. For a more positive interpretation of such formulae see Bull, *Knightly Piety*, 155–6.

[34] Howe, *Church Reform*, 60.

[35] Ibid., 107.

establish our manner of life according to the pattern of righteousness, then assuredly, with the help of power from above, both the
madness of our enemies will quickly perish and holy church will
receive her long-desired peace and security.[36]

For Gregory VII, like his namesake Gregory the Great, his and the
Church's tribulations could only be explained as a consequence of
mankind's sinfulness: the solution, therefore, was general penance.[37]
Gregory VII took his position as head of the Church seriously, and his
penitential expectations were a product of his overall concern with
salvation. But whilst this letter was produced for an immediate context
– it was a call to return to the papal side in the aftermath of the excommunication of King Henry IV in the spring of 1080 – it also reflects a
more general preoccupation with penance on the part of the pope.[38]
But where did Gregory get his ideas about penance from? One possible
source is the liturgy.

* * *

The meeting between priest and penitent is recorded in an idealized
form in the penitential liturgy. Such rites therefore provide a useful
perspective on the dry material of the canonical and theological works
upon which much earlier scholarship relied. It goes without saying that
the historian must tread warily when using liturgical evidence, shaped
as it is by a powerful textual tradition.[39] Liturgical manuscripts,
however, were not static compilations of texts, blindly copied and not
much used, and minor variations within recensions can sometimes
reflect the personal thoughts of the composer, or differences in local
practice. Used carefully liturgical rites can provide a useful source of

[36] *Reg.* viii.9, 527–8: 'Quoniam nichil in terra sine causa, sicut sapientis verba testantur,
quod dudum sancta aecclesia fluctuum procellarumque mole concutitur quodque tyrannice
persecutionis hactenus rabiem patitur, non nisi peccatis nostris exigentibus evenire
credendum est, nam iudicia quidem Dei verissime omnia iusta sunt . . . Quodsi culparum
morbis penitentiae medicamen adhibuerimus et excessus ac negligentias nostras ipsi districte
corrigendo ad iustitiae formam mores nostros instituerimus, profecto superna virtute
auxiliante et inimicorum rabies cito peribit et diu desideratam pacem atque securitatem
aecclesia sancta recipiet.' Transl. Cowdrey, *Register*, 374.

[37] On Gregory's conscious debt to Gregory the Great see G. B. Ladner, 'Gregory the
Great and Gregory VII', *Viator* 4 (1973), 1–26; Cowdrey, *Pope Gregory VII, passim*, but especially 695–7.

[38] On this letter see Cowdrey, *Pope Gregory VII*, 205–6.

[39] E. Bishop, *Liturgica historica: Papers on the Liturgy and Religious Life of the Western Church*
(Oxford, 1918), 298.

material for clerical teachings about penance,[40] and the evidence of the eleventh-century Italian rites for penance suggests that Gregory VII's message of true penance was already being preached in the liturgy.

The rite for receiving penitents recorded in an early eleventh-century copy of a Frankish penitential, written and kept at Monte Cassino (Monte Cassino, Cod. lat. 372), clearly states that no priest or pontiff can cure the wounds of sin, or remove sins from the soul unless signs of anxiety and tears are present in the penitent.[41] The minister is reminded that he too should humble himself with prayers, with sadness and tears, not only for his own faults but those of Christendom, because witnessing the minister's own sadness will make the penitent sad and afraid so that he is sorry with his whole heart; then the minister should take him by the right hand and the penitent should promise to amend his life and confess his sins.[42]

The penitent must display his contrition through external signs such as agitation and tears, avow his contrition and promise to amend his life. The importance of such a promise for effective penance is also made clear in the rite recorded in the collection of pastoral rites written by a scribe at Monte Cassino at the end of the eleventh century and probably intended for use outside the monastery (Rome, Biblioteca

---

[40] For this argument see Mansfield, *Humiliation of Sinners*, 159–247; Hamilton, *Practice*, 104–72.

[41] *Die Bussbücher und Bussdisciplin der Kirche: nach handschriftlichen Quellen dargestellt*, ed. H. J. Schmitz, 2 vols (Mainz, 1883 and Düsseldorf, 1898; repr. Graz, 1958) [hereafter *Bussbücher* I and *Bussbücher* II]. *Bussbücher* I, 397: 'Ita quoque nullus sacerdotum vel pontifex peccatorum vulnera curare potest aut animabus peccata auferre, nisi praestante sollicitudine et oratione lacrimarum'. This text is also found in Halitgar of Cambrai's ninth-century penitential: *Bussbücher* II, 291. For the manuscript's date: Francis Newton, *The Scriptorium and Library at Monte Cassino, 1058–1105*, Cambridge Studies in Palaeography and Codicology 7 (Cambridge, 1999), 273, n. 126. On this penitential see P. Fournier, 'Études sur les pénitentiels', *Revue d'histoire et de littérature religieuses* 7 (1902), 121–7; G. Motta, 'Collezioni canoniche dell'area cassinese nell'età dell'abate Desiderio', in Faustino Avagliano and Oronzo Pecere, eds, *L'età dell'abate Desiderio, III. I: Storia arte e cultura. Atti del IV Convegno di Studi sul Medioevo meridionale*, Montecassino–Cassino, 4–8 ottobre 1987, Miscellanea Cassinese 67 (Montecassino, 1992), 363–72, 365–6.

[42] *Bussbücher* I, 398: 'Sicut ergo superius diximus, humiliare se debent episcopi sive presbyteri et cum tristitiae gemitu lacrimisque orare non solum pro suis delictis, sed etiam pro Christianorum omnium, ut possit cum beato dicere Paulo: Quis infirmatur et ego non infirmor; quis scandalizatur et ego non uror? Videns autem ille, qui ad poenitentiam venit, sacerdotem tristem et lacrymantem pro suo facinore magis ipse timore Domini perfusus amplius tristatur et timet. Postea si vides eum ex toto corde conversum apprehende manum eius dexteram et promitte emendationem vitiorum suorum et duc eum amoto altare, ut confiteatur peccata sua.' The text of this *ordo* is derived from the Frankish tradition: cf. Halitgar of Cambrai, *Bussbücher* II, 291.

Vallicelliana, Cod. C. 32).[43] This rite includes a preliminary exchange which belongs to the ninth-century Frankish penitential tradition. Before interrogating the penitent about his sins and hearing his confession, the priest should ask him what he seeks, to which the penitent should answer he seeks to do penance for his sins.[44] The priest then asks, 'Are you converted to the all powerful God and redeemer of all souls with your whole heart?', to which the penitent must reply in the affirmative for the rite to continue.[45] But after interrogating and confessing the penitent, the priest should admonish him as follows. If he wishes to be saved, he ought to love the Lord with his whole heart and mind and avoid all serious sins – murder, adultery, theft, false testimony, incest – and instead castigate the body, love fasting, abandon rich clothing, care for the poor, visit the sick, bury the dead, avoid anger, sadness and false peace, choose charity, avoid perjury and other sins (which are listed), keep death before his eyes every day and pray with tears and sighs daily and prepare for judgement.[46] These admonishments are echoed in Gregory VII's own pleas to turn away from sin and convert wholeheartedly.

Whilst both these rites are heavily dependent on the ninth-century Frankish penitential tradition, it is too easy to dismiss the mechanics of penance as formulaic: the liturgies for these rites show a very real emphasis on the need for the penitent to display contrition and promise a heartfelt conversion. In a variant on the interrogation formulae common to the Frankish tradition recorded in a late eleventh-century pontifical from Arezzo, the priest should, before interrogating the penitent about his sins, ask each penitent about the orthodoxy of his belief: does he believe in God the Father, God the Son, God the Holy Spirit; does he believe in the Trinity; does he believe that he will arise on the day of judgement in the flesh which he is now, and be judged according to what he has done, both good and evil. These questions are a standard part of such rites from the ninth century onwards, but the final

---

[43] *Ein Rituale in beneventanischer Schrift: Roma, Biblioteca Vallicelliana, Cod. C 32. Ende des 11. Jahrhunderts*, ed. Ambros Odermatt, Spicilegium Friburgense 26 (Freiburg, 1980).

[44] Ibid., no. 111, 284: '*Postea interroget eum sacerdos et dicat*: Quid queritis, fratres, ut quid confugistis ad ecclesiam dei? *R. penitens*: Penitere, querimus de peccatis nostris'.

[45] Ibid.: '*Et sacerdos dicat*: Ex toto corde estis conversi ad deum omnipotentem et redemptorem omnium animarum? *R*. Ex toto'.

[46] Ibid., no. 128, 290–1. An alternative admonition which emphasises the parallels between penance and baptism and the need to turn away from sin follows: ibid., no. 129, 291–2.

question is more unusual: does he have faith that God can forgive all sins if he confesses and converts to him with *all* his heart?[47]

The evidence of the liturgies circulating within Italy in the second half of the eleventh century is that the penitential rite emphasized the need to confess all sins and to turn away from sin in the future after confession and penance. This is therefore the background to Gregory VII's own rhetoric of conversion and personal contrition. His was not a voice in the wilderness, anticipating the new twelfth-century theology, but rather he was a vocal exponent of current orthodoxy.

In his 1079 letter to the Bretons, Gregory VII made one exception to his argument that the truly penitent should give up any profession which might lead to further sin: in the event of a serious crime such as homicide, adultery or perjury, no man could 'bring forth the fruit of true penance' if he persists in such crimes, or unjustly possesses the goods of another or hates his neighbour, or is engaged in a business that can 'scarcely be exercised without sin', or

> bears military arms, unless it be to uphold his own justice or that of his lord or friend or also of the poor and also in defence of churches, nor, however, shall he take up arms without the counsel of religious men who know how to give with wisdom such counsel as makes for eternal salvation.[48]

This exception for those who bear arms in a good cause on the advice of religious men is usually interpreted as anticipating Urban II's call to the First Crusade in 1095, when Urban promised that whoever undertook this journey could substitute it for all penance.[49] In making this exception Gregory VII is seen as breaking with the past, when

---

[47] Vatican City, Biblioteca Apostolica Vaticana, MS Vat. lat. 4772, *Bussbücher* II, 405 (my emphasis). It is not found in the Romano-German pontifical: *PRG*, 2: cxxxvi.5, 235.

[48] *Reg.* vii.10, 472: 'Qua in re hoc summopere vos cavere oportet aliosque monere debetis, quia, si quis in homicidium adulterium periurium vel aliquod huiusmodi lapsus in aliquo talium criminum permanserit aut negotiationi, quae vix agi sine peccato potest, operam dederit aut arma militaria portaverit, excepto si pro tuenda iustitia sua vel domini vel amici seu etiam pauperum nec pro defendendis ecclesiis, nec tamen sine religiosorum virorum consilio sumpserit, qui aeternae salutis consilium dare sapienter noverunt, aut aliena bona iniuste possederit aut in odium proximi sui exarserit, vere penitentiae fructum facere nullatenus potest.' Transl. Cowdrey, *Register*, 334.

[49] R. Somerville, *The Councils of Urban II. 1. Decreta Claromontensia*, Annuarium historiae conciliorum. Supplementum 1 (Amsterdam, 1972), 74. For this interpretation, see Cowdrey, 'Pope Gregory VII and the Bearing of Arms', and also the earlier comments of Carl Erdmann, *The Origins of the Idea of Crusade*, trans. Marshall W. Baldwin and Walter Goffart (Princeton, NJ, 1977), 148–228, especially 171–2.

canon law had demanded that the penitent abstain from bearing arms, either for the length of the penance or for all time.[50] The breakdown of such a strict prohibition about the incompatibility of bearing arms and doing penance had already appeared in the early tenth century, when the bishops who met after the battle of Soissons in 923 enjoined a penance of three years' fasting on all the participants: they had to fast throughout Lent and Advent, and also every Friday, unless they were prevented by military service from observing the fast.[51] Despite such advanced practices, the liturgical rites appear more conservative, reflecting the attitude of *laissez faire*, or false penance, condemned by reformers like Peter Damian and Gregory VII.

One instruction on the penitent's future behaviour, Italian in origin, but recorded in the Romano-German pontifical composed in Mainz *c.*960,[52] tells the priest to establish the penitent's rank and profession and advise him accordingly: if he is a judge he should not accept bribes, if he is a money maker or trader he should not oppress anyone through trade or exchange.[53] The Romano-German pontifical was certainly known in Rome in the second half of the eleventh century.[54] But Gregory VII's demands were stricter: a trader should give up his profession if it could not be pursued without fraud; a century earlier the author of this *ordo* merely required that anyone in such a profession should ensure they practised it in future without recourse to sin. A moment's reflection, however, shows that Gregory VII's argument that the penitent knight can continue to bear arms if he does so with the

[50] Burchard, *Decretum*, xix. 66, PL 140, 999. On ninth-century interpretations of this law see K. J. Leyser, 'Early Medieval Canon Law and the Beginnings of Knighthood', in idem, *Communications and Power in Medieval Europe, I: The Carolingian and Ottonian Centuries*, ed. Timothy Reuter (London, 1994), 57–71.

[51] J. D. Mansi, *Sacrorum conciliorum nova et amplissima collectio* (Venice, 1759–98; repr. Graz, 1960), 18A: 345–6; Hamilton, *Practice*, 193.

[52] The possible Italian origin of this rite is suggested by the reference to 'castaldius', presumably meaning the Italian office of 'gastaldius'; cf. *PRG*, 2: cxxxvi.14, 240: 'Deinde interroga eum, quale ministerium faciat, si est comes, aut castaldius . . .'. On the history of the Romano-German pontifical see *Les Ordines romani du haut moyen âge*, ed. M. Andrieu, 5 vols (Louvain, 1931–61), 5: 72–9; C. Vogel, 'Précision sur la date et l'ordonnance primitive du pontifical romano-germanique', *Ephemerides Liturgicae* 74 (1960), 145–62; idem, 'Le Pontifical romano-germanique du Xe siècle: nature, date et importance du document', *Cahiers de civilisation médiévale* 6 (1963), 27–48; Hamilton, *Practice*, 104–35.

[53] *PRG*, 2: cxxxvi.14, 240.

[54] On the *PRG*'s *Nachleben* in Rome see *Le Pontifical romain au Moyen-Âge* I, ed. M. Andrieu, Studi e Testi 86 (Vatican City, 1938); Andrieu's argument has now been revised by Richard F. Gyug, 'The Pontificals of Monte Cassino', in Avagliano and Pecere, eds, *L'età dell'abate Desiderio III. I:* 413–39. This instruction is also repeated in Rome, Biblioteca Vallicelliana, Cod. C 32: *Rituale*, ed. Odermatt, no. 131, 292.

correct purpose is an extension of the logic of the Romano-German *ordo*; just as the judge can retain his position if he conducts it properly, so the knight can maintain his profession if he does so without sin. Instead of interpreting Gregory VII's arguments as a reaction against earlier penitential practice, it is at least possible that the liturgy served as a repository for his and other reformers' thought about what makes 'true penance'.

In order to call the faithful to true penance the reformers chose to condemn as false that penance which was not sincere: the penance of those who did not amend their sinful ways, those who, like Count Hildebrand, shrugged off their penitential responsibilities by giving leprous cloaks as alms to their confessors. There was a tendency amongst historians of the last century to interpret this reformist critique from a twelfth-century contritionist standpoint as a condemnation of the failure of the system of seemingly mechanical tariffs for sin, set out in the penitentials, through which penances of so many years' fasting were ordained for each sin.[55] Certainly some people were deterred from doing penance as the conditions imposed were too burdensome: both Peter, lord of Sora, and the French princes, reported by the Monte Cassino chronicler, Leo Marsicanus, were reluctant to perform penance as it would entail laying aside their arms and thus put them at a disadvantage.[56] But what was at stake in both cases was the temporary abandonment of their status as warriors, not the penance itself.

Penitential tariffs could be commuted either through payment of alms or in other ways. For example, Peter Damian records that the hermit Dominic Lorica, through flagellating himself whilst reciting three psalters, performed one hundred years' penance as follows: three thousand blows equals one year of penance, ten psalms equals one thousand blows, and

> since we know that the psalter contains one hundred and fifty psalms, five years of penance, if we count correctly, are contained in disciplining oneself through one psalter. Now if you multiply five by twenty . . . you arrive at a hundred. And so when one has chanted twenty psalters while taking the discipline one is sure that he has performed one hundred years of penance.[57]

[55] Vogel, *Pécheur*, 27–36.

[56] Howe, *Church Reform*, 107. *Chronica monasterii Casinensis*, iv.11, ed. Hartmut Hoffmann, MGH SS 34 (Hanover, 1980), 475.

[57] *Briefe des Petrus Damiani*, Ep. 44 (1055–7), 2: 22.

The arithmetic of commutation through flagellation was complicated: using two flails, one in each hand, Dominic completed one hundred years of penance in six days and in one Lent he completed one thousand years of penance.[58] Peter Damian, who elsewhere condemned the penitential canons as too soft, was a passionate exponent of the merits of flagellation for the commutation of penance. For him penance, in whatever manner it was performed, if undertaken with conviction, represented genuine contrition: 'when the faithful in reverent devotion recall their sins and punish themselves with strokes of the discipline they believe they are partaking in the passion of our Redeemer'.[59]

For Peter Damian, commutation of penance, even in its more conventional form, the payment of alms, did not represent an abdication of responsibility. In 1059 he was sent as a papal legate to Milan to reassert Rome's authority and arbitrate in the tensions between the established clergy and the Patarenes' objections to their endemic simony and nicolaitism.[60] At a public assembly of clergy and people outside the episcopal palace, Peter Damian investigated the clergy and discovered simony was the norm for ordination to any rank. He then extracted a promise of free ordination from the clergy to the bishop, who then prostrated himself and asked for penance for his failure to root out the crime. Peter Damian imposed a penance of one hundred years, prescribing that it could be redeemed by the annual payment of a fixed sum of money. Those clerics who had paid for their office unaware that it was a sin to do so were awarded a five-year penance, others who had paid more a seven-year penance, consisting of their fasting for two days a week on bread and water, and three days a week in Advent and Lent. However, they could commute one day's fasting per week by reciting a psalter, or by saying half a psalter accompanied by fifty prostrations, or by feeding a poor person, and after washing his feet, giving him a denarius. In addition, the archbishop promised to send all the clergy on pilgrimage, and only those deemed chaste, well educated and morally upright were allowed to return to clerical office. Commutation was not therefore, for Peter Damian, an easy option.

---

[58] Ibid.
[59] Ibid.
[60] *Briefe des Petrus Damiani*, Ep. 65, 2: 228–47. The dating is by no means certain: on the problems of dating this visit more accurately than *c.*1059–61, see ibid., 2: 230, n. 10. On the background to this visit, see H. E. J. Cowdrey, 'The Papacy, the Patarenes and the Church of Milan', *TRHS* ser. 5, 18 (1968), 25–48. For more detail on the penitential aspects: Hamilton, *Practice*, 186–8.

* * *

Peter Damian's own account of his legation to Milan also shows how crucial penance was to the reform process throughout the eleventh century. It was fundamental to the message of personal conversion preached by early eleventh-century monastic reformers such as Dominic of Sora and Romuald of Camaldoli. We have already examined Dominic's preaching, but penance was also central to Peter Damian's account of the life of the founder of his own house. Romuald himself entered the religious life in the late tenth century having been a passive observer of the fight in which his father killed his own brother in a dispute over property.[61] As a religious leader, Romuald specialized in telling important men to do penance and become monks: the Emperor Otto III went on penitential pilgrimage to Monte Gargano and promised to become a monk, whilst at Romuald's injunction Peter Orseolo, who had condoned the assassination of his predecessor as doge of Venice, gave up his position and entered the monastery of Cuxa in Catalonia.[62] In Peter Orseolo's case, the flight to Cuxa avoided him the publicity and the controversy which would have surrounded his open conversion in Venice.[63]

Penance was also key to the work of the first papal reformers who, from the mid-century, sought to reform the lives of the clergy and eradicate the sins of simony and clerical marriage from the Church: in 1049 the Lateran synod imposed a penance of forty days on all those who had knowingly been consecrated by a simonist.[64] Cases of individual penitents occupy a considerable proportion of the surviving correspondence from the reform popes of the 1050s and 1060s.[65]

[61] *Petri Damiani Vita Romualdi*, ed. Giovanni Tabacco, Fonti per la storia d'Italia 94 (Rome, 1957), ch. 1, 13–15.

[62] Ibid., ch. 5 (Peter of Orseolo), 21–5; ch. 25 (Otto III), 32–3; also ch. 11, 52–4 (Count Oliba of Cuxa confesses his sins to Romuald and is sent on pilgrimage to Monte Cassino). On Otto III's penance see Sarah Hamilton, 'Otto III's Penance: a Case Study of Unity and Diversity in the Eleventh-Century Church', in R. N. Swanson, ed., *Unity and Diversity in the Church*, SCH 32 (Oxford, 1996), 83–94.

[63] See also H. Tolra, *Saint Pierre Orséolo, doge de Venise puis bénédictin du monastère de Saint-Michel de Cuxa en Roussillon (Conflent). Sa vie et son temps (928–987)* (Paris, 1897).

[64] Mansi, *Conciliorum*, 19: 721; Ute-Renate Blumenthal, *The Investiture Controversy* (Philadelphia, 1988), 74.

[65] It should be noted that penance seems also to have played an important role in the work of the early eleventh-century popes, as demonstrated by the chance survival of several letters in English manuscripts. See the letters of Pope Gregory V (996–99) and Pope John [there is some debate as to whether they refer to John XVII (1003), XVIII (1003–9) or XIX (1024–33)] in *Councils and Synods with Other Documents Relating to the English Church I: AD 871–1204*, ed. Dorothy Whitelock, M. Brett and Christopher N. L. Brooke, 2 vols (Oxford,

Apparently chance survivals like Alexander II's letters show just how far penance constituted an important part of papal business.[66] Only severe cases were referred to Alexander II (1061–73), or at least only the records for these were thought worth preserving: he dealt with the sins of the clergy, including a priest who had fornicated with both a mother and her daughter, and who was told he should do penance for the rest of his days.[67] On other occasions, Alexander was more merciful. He expanded on the importance of contrition in a letter to one bishop: whilst the penance set out in the canons should always be observed, the bishop should remember the importance of the grace of mercy and of discretion, and take into account the contrition of heart, the degree of sadness expressed by the penitent, and the time he or she had spent waiting, and remember that the oil of mercy can be poured over the merits and fruits of penitence.[68]

Alexander practised what he preached in the penitential sentence he awarded to a certain Adam for setting fire to a church when drunk. He enjoined a five-year penance 'non iuxta modum culpae, sed moderamine benigne pietatis iniunximus'.[69] As in his other letters, the pope specified how Adam should undertake his penance: from this day (unfortunately the letter is undated) until the feast of St Martin (11

1981), 1: no. xliii.4–8, 234–7. See also one from Pope Leo IX (1049–54) to Archbishop Eadsige of Canterbury prescribing a seven-year penance for a priest, Andrew, who had committed homicide, but also absolving him and restoring him to priestly office: Robin Ann Aronstam, 'Pope Leo IX and England: an Unknown Letter', *Speculum* 49 (1974), 535–41.

66 These mostly survive in the *Collectio Britannica* (London, British Library, MS Additional 8873). Bull observed that the compiler of this manuscript seemingly had an interest in penance: *Knightly Piety*, 75. But on the compilation of what is really a canon law collection, probably drawn up in central Italy but copied in northern France between the end of the eleventh and the beginning of the twelfth century, see now Robert Somerville, *Pope Urban II, the Collectio Britannica and the Council of Melfi (1089)* (Oxford, 1996), 1–40. As Somerville noted elsewhere, the *Collectio Britannica* contains some eighty per cent of known papal letters 'from a crucial period in the history of the eleventh century': idem, 'Mercy and Justice in the Early Months of Urban II's Pontificate', in *Chiesa, diritto e ordinamento della 'Societas christiana' nei secoli XI e XII*, Atti della nona settimana internazionale di studio, Mendola, 28 agosto–2 settembre 1983 (Milan, 1986), 138–54, 148; repr. in idem, *Papacy, Councils and Canon Law in the Eleventh and Twelfth Centuries* (Aldershot, 1990), IV.

67 Ep. 141, PL 146, 1414.

68 *Epistolae pontificum romanorum ineditae*, ed. S. Loewenfeld (Leipzig, 1885; repr. Graz, 1959), no. 112, 55–6: 'Stephano Alvernensi episcopo. Que in canonibus determinata est, penitentia est omnino observanda. Sed misericordie gratia, que nulla lege concluditur, nullo temporis spatio cohercetur, non est pie penitentibus deneganda. Pastoralis itaque discretionis est, uniuscuiusque contrictionem cordis et doloris affectum magis quam temporis spatium attendere, et pro meritis operum fructuque penitentiae misericordiae oleum adhibere'.

69 Ibid., no. 107, 53.

November) he should fast for six days every week on bread and water, and from St Martin's day until Christmas three days' fasting in the week, from epiphany to Lent one day's fasting in the week, for the whole of Lent three days' fasting, from Pentecost until St Martin's one day, and so on for the whole five years. In the first year he 'should not enter a church nor take communion unless through necessity of death',[70] the implication being that Adam would be formally reconciled by the bishop and restored to communion on Maundy Thursday at the end of the year, but have to continue with his penance for a further four. In another case Alexander imposed the rigours of canonical public penance on a fratricide: he should give all his patrimony to the poor to pray for his brother's soul, and reserve only a usufruct for his own necessity; he should enter a monastery and fast for one year on bread and water, abstain from holy communion for three years, never bear arms again nor marry within a period of seven years.[71]

Gregory VII's own letters testify to his continuing concern with penance and the conservatism of his own penitential thinking. He condemned Rainerius, son of Count Uguccio, who had failed to pay the alms he had promised as penance for killing his brother, and further compromised the salvation of his soul by marrying; Gregory thus maintained the traditional canonical thinking that public penitents, guilty of scandalous crimes such as fratricide, should withdraw from the world and not marry, nor carry arms.[72] He also maintained another canonical tradition in his teaching on how clerics who kill should be treated. Clerics who kill should spend forty days in prison, then spend fourteen years doing penance when they must stand with the laity in church, for two of which they are forbidden communion.[73] But the hardship such severe penances entailed was brought to the attention of Pope Urban II (1088–99) by some penitents from the province of Rouen who petitioned against being sent into exile for, as they 'tearfully pointed out in our presence, wives, sons and even a widowed mother are known to stand greatly in need of their support' and 'lest perchance their wives, may it not happen, are overwhelmed by the ruin of fornication'. Urban

---

[70] Ibid.: 'Hoc anno ecclesiam ne ingrediaris, neque communices nisi pro necessitate mortis'.

[71] Ep. 100, PL 146, 1386.

[72] Reg. ii.48, 188.

[73] Epistolae vagantes, no. 68, 151–2. Attributed to Gregory VII in a canonical collection (Paris, Bibliothèque Nationale, MS lat. 8922, fol. 173r), and accepted by Cowdrey as having 'probably emanated from Rome during the pontificate of Gregory VII', ibid., 150.

II therefore wrote to their archbishop that these penitents should be allowed to return home after one year's penance in exile, to serve the remaining years at home but 'in such a way, nevertheless, that you add a small amount to their penances in place of exile'.[74]

At the same time as imposing strict canonical penances, Gregory VII, like both his predecessors and his successor, emphasized the importance of mercy towards those who showed the 'fruits of penitence'. In one case the pope suggested that a penitent cleric who had committed homicide, whilst he should not be restored to the priesthood, should be allowed to retain an ecclesiastical income lest the loss of this turn him again to sin.[75] The hints these papal letters give us is of a system of active penance – penance for harsh sins such as adultery, incest, murder – but it was not inhuman or rigid, emphasizing the importance of taking into account each penitent's state of mind, both their intent when they committed the sin and the degree of contrition now felt, and displayed.

* * *

Although many of these papal letters spell out in detail how penance should be undertaken, they do not indicate how it should be administered. A system of two-step penance is often implied, as in the case of the church arsonist: penance is awarded in one ceremony, but the penitent is not reconciled with the Church until the end of the first or second year.[76] Under the system of canonical public penance, as set out by the Carolingians, public penance was an episcopal prerogative; the penitent entered into formal penance on Ash Wednesday, and was formally reconciled on Maundy Thursday. But the penitential rites produced and used in Italy discussed earlier provide for a one-stop ceremony combining the awarding of penance and the reconciliation of the penitent at the same time.[77] On these grounds, and also because the revised version of the Romano-German pontifical made in southern Italy in the late eleventh century omitted a rite for public penance, it has been suggested that public penance was unknown in tenth- and eleventh-century Italy.[78]

[74] *Epistolae pontificum*, no. 132, 64; also in Somerville, *Pope Urban II*, 164. Somerville suggests this case might be linked to the interdict placed by Archbishop William of Rouen (1079–1110) on the entire duchy of Normandy in 1090 because of an attack by Duke Robert on the castle of Gisors. See also Cowdrey, 'Pope Gregory VII and the Bearing of Arms', 21.

[75] *Reg.* i.34, 55.

[76] *Epistolae pontificum*, no. 107, 53.

[77] Josef A. Jungmann, *Die lateinischen Bussriten in ihrer geschichtlichen Entwicklung* (Innsbruck, 1932), 190–6; Hamilton, *Practice*, 166–70.

[78] Whilst Andrieu, *Pontifical romain*, thought the twelfth-century Roman pontifical was

Certain of the reform canon law collections, however, testify to an attempt to promote the practice of public penance on the part of the reformers. Whilst some of the influential collections of the papal reform, like the *Collection in Seventy-Four Titles*, composed in Rome in the 1070s,[79] and the collection composed by Cardinal Deusdedit in the 1080s,[80] barely touch on the subject of penance, others, including the influential early eleventh-century south Italian *Collection in Five Books*,[81] Anselm of Lucca's *Collection*,[82] composed 1081–6, and Bonizo of Sutri's *Liber de vita christiana*,[83] composed 1089–95, devote entire books to the subject.

Anselm of Lucca repeated in his canon law collection the so-called Carolingian dichotomy first articulated *c*.800: manifest sins should be manifestly purged, public sins deserve public penance, hidden sins, secret penance.[84] What was at stake was the degree of *scandala* – offence against the public weal – so homicide could, theoretically, be a secret sin but it is hard to see how perjury, one of the sins identified by

composed in Rome, Gyug, 'The Pontificals of Monte Cassino', has suggested the origins of this influential text lie in the revision of the Romano-German pontifical made at Monte Cassino under Abbot Desiderius. There is no rite for public penance in the twelfth-century Roman pontifical. On the absence of evidence for this practice from tenth- and eleventh-century Italy see Hamilton, *Practice*, 170, 208.

[79] *Diuersorum patrum sententie siue Collectio in LXXIV titulos digesta*, ed. J. T. Gilchrist, Monumenta iuris canonici, series B: Corpus collectionum 1 (Vatican City, 1973); the absence of penitential material may explain the penitential tinge of the south Italian appendix to the *Collection in Seventy-Four Titles*, identified by Roger E. Reynolds in Florence, Biblioteca Medicea Laurenziana, MS 16.15: 'The South Italian *Collection in Five Books* and its Derivatives: a South Italian Appendix to the *Collection in Seventy-Four Titles*', *Mediaeval Studies* 63 (2001), 353–65.

[80] *Die Kanonessammlung des Kardinals Deusdedit*, ed. Victor Wolf von Glanvell (Paderborn, 1905; repr. Aalen, 1967).

[81] *Collectio Canonum in V libris* (Lib. i–iii), ed. M. Fornasari, CChr.CM 6 (Turnhout, 1970); unfortunately the penitential books iv and v remain unedited. See the description of Monte Cassino, Cod. Lat. CXXV (second quarter of the eleventh century) in *Bibliotheca Casinensis seu codicum manuscriptorum qui in tabulario Casinensi asservantur*, Monachorum ordines S. Benedicti abbatiae Montis Casini, eds, 5 vols (Montecassino, 1873–94), 3: 51–9.

[82] See above, n. 7. The manuscripts of Anselm's *Collection* fall into two main groups, A which includes the penitential book XI, and B which excludes book XI. I have consulted an Italian twelfth-century manuscript of recension A: Cambridge, Corpus Christi College, MS 269; see Lotte Kéry, *Canonical Collections of the Early Middle Ages (ca. 400–1140). A Bibliographical Guide to the Manuscripts and Literature* (Washington, DC, 1999), 218–19. On this collection see now K. G. Cushing, *Papacy and Law in the Gregorian Revolution: the Canonistic Work of Anselm of Lucca* (Oxford, 1998), although she does not consider book XI in any detail.

[83] *Liber de vita christiana*, ed. Perels (see n. 7), book IX, 277–304; on Bonizo's work, see Walter Berschin, *Bonizo von Sutri: Leben und Werk*, Beiträge zur Geschichte und Quellenkunde des Mittelalters 2 (Berlin and New York, 1972).

[84] Anselm, *Collectio*, XI.20.

Gregory VII as a serious sin, currently atoned for all too often by false penance, could be anything other than a public sin. Anselm of Lucca not only repeated the Carolingian dichotomy, but also included the standard provision, dating back to Late Antiquity, that in the case of public penitents 'no one should return to military service after doing penance'.[85] These provisions are both found in the early eleventh-century German collection, Burchard of Worms' *Decretum*, which was very influential on the work of the reformers.[86]

The references to public penance in Anselm's *Collection* are the first hint that reform-minded canonists of the 1080s seem to have been trying to lead a revival of public penance as part of their attempts to provide a blueprint for the Christian life. This emphasis is clearer in Bonizo's later *Liber*. According to him,

> we accept from the holy fathers the ancient tradition that on Maundy Thursday penitents ought to be specially reconciled because the tradition of the sacraments, those of baptism and the Lord's blood [i.e. the eucharist], was given by Lord Christ to the apostles on that day, and because this office, that is both reconciliation and the making of chrism, ought to be the bishop's alone.[87]

Bonizo distinguishes between those who have been excommunicated in soul only, in body only, and in both soul and body. The fate of those excommunicated by their own unpublicized sinfulness will be decided on judgement day. One need not save those excommunicated in both body and soul, that is those over whom anathema has been pronounced; but those who have been 'delivered *to Satan for destruction of the flesh that the spirit may be saved on the day of the Lord* (1 Cor. 5: 5)' will be reconciled by the bishop on Maundy Thursday according to church custom.[88]

Bonizo also set out the liturgy for this reconciliation of the

---

[85] Ibid., XI.29.

[86] Burchard, *Decretum*, xix.37 and 66, PL 140, 987, 999. On this work's rapid and wide diffusion in Italy, see O. Meyer, 'Überlieferung und Verbreitung des Dekrets des Bischofs Burchard von Worms', *Zeitschrift der Savigny-Stiftung für Rechtsgeschichte: Kanonistische Abteilung* 24 (1935), 141–83; Hamilton, *Practice*, 33 at n. 40.

[87] *Liber de vita christiana*, ii.52, 60: 'In cena Domini antiqua traditione a sanctis patribus accepimus reconciliari specialiter debere penitentes, ideo quia eo die sacramentorum, baptismi scilicet et sanguinis Domini, apostolis a domino Christo donata fuit traditio. Et quia hoc officium, scilicet reconciliatio et confectio crismatis, solis debetur episcopis'.

[88] Ibid., 61: 'Nunc vero de his, qui iuxta apostolum traditi sunt *sathane in interitum carnis, ut spiritus salvus sit in die Domini*, qualiter in cena Domini secundum aecclesiasticum morem ab episcopo debeant reconciliari, breviter enarremus'.

penitents.[89] The penitents should come before the bishop seated outside the doors of the church. The bishop should call the penitents, 'come my sons' (*venite filii*). Then the penitents at the command of the deacon should genuflect, then again rise at his command. The process of episcopal calling and penitential genuflection is repeated three times, until the penitents come to the middle of the pavement and prostrate themselves at the feet of the bishop. The deacon then petitions the bishop to show mercy. Then, after the psalms have been sung and the Lord's prayer said, the deacon asks the bishop to restore these penitents to the Church. After that, the bishop preaches a sermon to the penitents. The antiphon, *Venite*, is sung followed by psalms, and then the penitents are handed by the archdeacon to the bishop; the bishop places his hand on each of them and leads them into the church.

According to Bonizo, this was a Roman rite, which all easterners and Germans imitate the Church by following.[90] But it was not. This liturgy is not Roman. It is not even the service for the reconciliation of penitents on Maundy Thursday recorded in the Romano-German pontifical.[91] The liturgy which Bonizo records is that of the north-central family, found in Lotharingia and northern France from at least the early eleventh century, and still being used in northern France in the twelfth and thirteenth centuries.[92] I know of no other evidence that the north-central rite was used in Italy or, indeed, that it was used or known outside its core region in the Low Countries.

How did Bonizo come by such a rite? An ardent reformer – he viewed Urban II as a moderate –, he was originally from Lombardy. Banished from Sutri by imperial supporters, he took refuge with the countess Matilda and acted as bishop of Piacenza before being banished from there also in 1089.[93] His wholly Italian background does not therefore provide a clue to this Lotharingian trait, but one obvious route for such a liturgy to have come to Italy is with the Lotharingian train of Bishop Bruno of Toul when he was elected Pope Leo IX in

---

[89] Ibid., 61–2.

[90] Ibid., 62: 'Et hoc secundum Romanos, quos omnes orientales et Germanorum imitantes aecclesiae'.

[91] *PRG*, 2: xcix.224–51, 59–67; on this liturgy see Hamilton, *Practice*, 118–28.

[92] For eleventh-century records of this rite: Hamilton, *Practice*, 150–66; on its twelfth-, thirteenth- and fourteenth-century life, see Mansfield, *Humiliation of Sinners*, 188–247.

[93] Berschin, *Bonizo*; Paul Fournier and Gabriel Le Bras, *Histoire des Collections canoniques en Occident depuis les fausses décrétales jusqu'au Décret de Gratien*, 2 vols (Paris, 1931–32), 2: 139–50; Paul Fournier, 'Bonizo de Sutri, Urbain II et la comtesse Mathilde, d'après le *Liber de vita christiana* de Bonizo', *Bibliothèque de l'École des Chartes* 78 (1917), 117–34.

1049.[94] Whatever its origins, Bonizo was obviously unsure that the rite would be accepted; hence his insistence that this *was* a Roman custom which had influenced practice north of the Alps, and not vice-versa.[95] By deliberately including such a rite, Bonizo attempted to fill a *lacuna* in the Italian liturgy: neither the so-called twelfth-century Roman pontifical, composed in the 1070s, which omitted the rites for public penance found in its main source, the Romano-German pontifical, nor the other Italian liturgical books I have studied include any rites for public penance.

* * *

Bonizo recorded this liturgy for the reconciliation of penitents in the section of his collection devoted to episcopal power and duty, not in that on penance. Other eleventh-century canonists were content to cite decretals and other texts on the need to bring penitents to the bishop for reconciliation, including one by Hincmar, the ninth-century archbishop of Rheims.[96] It is therefore helpful to look at the Carolingian bishops' own interest in public penance in order to explain this renewed interest under the papal reformers.[97] The Carolingian reforming bishops had sought to revive the practice of public penance in the ninth century as part of their attempt to revive the Christian life

---

[94]   This evidence goes against the trend of modern scholarship which tends to dismiss the Lotharingian influence on the canon law of the papal reformers: Horst Fuhrmann, *Einfluß und Verbreitung der pseudoisidorischen Fälschungen: von ihrem Auftauchen bis in die neuere Zeit*, MGH Schriften 24, 3 vols (Stuttgart, 1972–4), 2: 340; I. S. Robinson, *Authority and Resistance in the Investiture Contest: the Polemical Literature of the Late Eleventh Century* (Manchester, 1978), 1–11; Ute-Renate Blumenthal, 'The Papacy and Canon Law in the Eleventh-Century Reform', *CathHR* 84 (1998), 201–18, 205.

[95]   He also records a variant on this rite, ascribed to 'certain westerners', for which I have not been able to discover any precedent; see *Liber de vita christiana*, ii.52, 62: 'Sciendum tamen est, quia non omnes, qui redduntur per manus episcopi ecclesiae, eo die sacre communionis merentur gratiam, set hii tantum, qui peracta penitentia celestis mensae redintegrantur convivio'.

[96]   Burchard, *Decretum*, xix.100, PL 140, 1003–4; the *Collection in Five Books*, iv.34; Anselm, *Collectio*, xi.8–10 and 19. See also *Collectio canonum Barberiniana*, ed. M. Fornasari, *Apollinaris: commentarius iuris canonici* 36 (1963), 127–41, 214–97, ch. lxiii, 259; the source for this canon is Hincmar of Rheims, *Epistola synodica*, PL 125, 776; the collection was composed in Italy between 1050 and 1073: Kéry, *Canonical Collections*, 283. Finally, cf. the early twelfth-century collection, *The Collectio canonum Casinensis duodecimi seculi (codex terscriptus). A Derivative of the South-Italian Collection in Five Books. An Implicit Edition with Introductory Study*, ed. Roger E. Reynolds, Studies and Texts 137 (Toronto, 2001), V; its source is Burchard, *Decretum*, xix.100.

[97]   On their influence in the tenth and early eleventh centuries, see H. Fuhrmann, 'Pseudoisidor in Rom vom Ende der Karolingerzeit bis zum Reformpapsttum', *Zeitschrift für Kirchengeschichte* 78 (1967), 15–66.

and 'purify' the realm.[98] According to the Council of Châlon held in 813, doing penance according to the 'ancient custom of the canons' had fallen out of use in many places, and the *ordo* was not followed, either for excommunication or reconciliation,

> so we implore the aid of the emperor that if anyone does sin publicly he should do public penance and according to the canons for his merit be excommunicated and reconciled.[99]

At the same time the west Frankish bishops condemned the penitentials as 'little books . . . of which the errors are certain, the authors uncertain.'[100] In 828, the Carolingian rulers Louis and Lothar called councils to be held the following year to bring an end to widespread famine and hardship, 'calling for *correctio* and *emendatio* as the only way to placate God's wrath'.[101] At one of these councils, that held in Paris in 829, the bishops went so far as to order the burning of penitentials as part of their effort to 'satisfy the offended deity'.[102]

Mayke de Jong has demonstrated how the revival of public penance accompanied the revival of public power under the Carolingian rulers: the Franks portrayed themselves in Old Testament terms as God's Chosen People, and therefore the 'correction' of the realms became the king's business, and 'the authoritative model of 'canonical' (penance) served as the main instrument for cleansing the realm of moral pollution'.[103] It is not surprising that in similar circumstances, though almost three centuries later, ardent papal reformers like Bonizo and Anselm of Lucca should have returned to this model of what constituted canonical penance. And as historians of the ninth century have shown, the

---

[98] Mayke de Jong, 'What Was Public about Public Penance? *Paenitentia publica* and Justice in the Carolingian World', in *La Giustizia nell'Alto Medioevo: secoli IX–XI*, Settimane di studio del Centro italiano di studi sull'Alto Medioevo 44 (Spoleto, 1997), 863–902; eadem, 'Power and Humility in Carolingian Society: the Public Penance of Louis the Pious', *Early Medieval Europe* 1 (1992), 29–52.

[99] C. 25: *Concilia aevi Karolini*, ed. Albertus Werminghoff, MGH Concilia II.1, 2 vols (Hanover, 1906), 1: 278: 'Paenitentiam agere iuxta antiquam canonum constitutionem in plerisque locis ab usu recessit, et neque excommunicandi neque reconciliandi antiqui moris ordo servatur. Ut a domno imperatore impetretur adiutorium, qualiter, si publice peccat, publica multetur paenitentia et secundum ordinem canonum pro merito suo et excommunicetur et reconcilietur'.

[100] C. 38: ibid., 1: 281.

[101] Janet L. Nelson, 'Kingship and Empire', in J. H. Burns, ed., *The Cambridge History of Medieval Political Thought c.350–c.1450* (Cambridge, 1988), 225–6.

[102] C. 32: *Concilia aevi Karolini*, 2: 633; this description is by de Jong, 'What Was Public about Public Penance? ', 901.

[103] Ibid.

critique of existing penitential systems was in large part rhetorical: criticism of the penitentials in 813 and 829 did not lead to their disappearance; rather, new penitentials were composed and circulated with the *imprimata* of official episcopal authority by Halitgar, the bishop of Cambrai, and Hrabanus Maurus, abbot of Fulda and archbishop of Mainz, no less.[104]

It is against the background of this Carolingian revival that Bonizo's work on penance, and that of other eleventh-century canonists, needs to be seen. For it seems to me that the attempt made in the 1070s and 1080s to revive penance in Italy was part of an attempt to revive ecclesiastical authority as a whole, as it had been in the ninth century. Just as the Frankish bishops in the ninth century constructed a rhetoric of 'bad' penance – referring to the circulation of unauthorized penitentials and slackness in the administration of penance – and 'good' penance – performed according to the canons as part of their reforms –, so Gregory VII's own rhetoric of true and false penance must be seen in the context of his wish to convert the whole world. In criticizing the penitential practice of his age and calling for a return to true penance, Gregory VII was not so much anticipating the new twelfth-century penitential theology of Abelard and the Victorines, but rather subscribing to an existing and influential reformist theme. For the rhetoric of true and false penance was a powerful one, and it would reappear, having undergone yet another metamorphosis, in the sixteenth century, with Martin Luther's criticisms of the late-medieval penitential system and his own emphasis on personal conscience.[105]

University of Exeter

---

[104] For the view that Carolingian reforms were effective see Rosamond Pierce, 'The "Frankish" Penitentials', in Derek Baker, ed., *The Materials, Sources and Methods of Ecclesiastical History*, SCH 11 (Oxford, 1975), 31–9; for the view that penitentials continued to circulate, see Allen J. Frantzen, 'The Significance of the Frankish Penitentials', *JEH* 30 (1979), 409–21; on the penitentials composed by Halitgar and Hrabanus Maurus and their manuscripts see Raymund Kottje, *Die Bussbücher Halitgars von Cambrai und des Hrabanus Maurus: ihre Überlieferung und ihre Quellen* (Berlin and New York, 1980).

[105] Thomas N. Tentler, *Sin and Confession on the Eve of the Reformation* (Princeton, NJ, 1977), 349–62. See in this volume the essays by David Bagchi, 'Luther and the Sacramentality of Penance', 119–77 and John Bossy, 'Satisfaction in Early Modern Europe, c.1400–1700', 106–18.

PENANCE AND RECONCILIATION IN THE CRUSADER STATES: MATTHEW PARIS, JACQUES DE VITRY AND THE EASTERN CHRISTIANS

by ANDREW JOTISCHKY

MEDIEVAL popes can scarcely have expected such spectacular results from a bull as Gregory IX achieved in 1237. His bull *Cum hora undecima* of 1235, a fundamental statement of the Church's missionary function, gave specific licence to the Dominican William of Montferrat to preach, dispense the sacraments, absolve and excommunicate in the lands of schismatics and heretics of the East.[1] Two years later, Philip, the Dominican provincial of the Holy Land, wrote to the pope announcing the conversion to Rome of the Syrian Orthodox (Jacobite) patriarch of Antioch, Ignatius II, the anticipated conversion of the Nestorian catholicos in Baghdad and possibly also the conversion of the Coptic patriarch. It was a staggering return from a mission only two years old, and represented a triumph for the Dominican Order as well as for the papacy.

In the West, the news attracted the interest of two monastic chroniclers: Alberic of Trois Fontaines and Matthew Paris in St Albans, both of whom reproduced the provincial's letter to the pope in full.[2] Matthew, who learned the news from a Dominican visitor to St Albans, also provided one of his customary digressions to explain the nature of the heresies from which the Syrian patriarch was converting. Properly speaking, the three errors that Matthew lists are religious – one might say cultural – customs rather than beliefs. They are: (i) the circumcision of children, (ii) the lack of auricular confession, and (iii) the practice of branding the sign of the cross on children's foreheads. It is the second of these, the absence of confession, on which I will concentrate here, though in fact all three are interrelated in the mind of the original

---

[1] *Acta Innocentii PP. IV (1243–1254)*, ed. T. Haluscynski and M. Wojnar, *Pontificia commissio ad redigendum codicem iuris canonici orientalis, Fontes*, ser. 3 [hereafter CICO] (Rome, 1966), 286–7 (the reissue by Innocent IV).

[2] Alberic of Trois Fontaines, *Chronicon*, ed. F. Schaffer-Boichorst, MGH (SS) XXIII, 941–2; Matthew Paris, *Chronica Majora*, ed. H. R. Luard, *RS* 57, 7 vols (London, 1872–83), 3: 396–9.

author of the passage: Matthew Paris had actually lifted the passage directly from a slightly earlier source, the *Historia Orientalis* of Jacques de Vitry.[3] Although he sometimes distorted or altered the documents he incorporated into his chronicle, on this occasion Matthew quotes his source with absolute accuracy. Matthew Paris is justly admired as a chronicler for the breadth of his interests, but in this case it is surely more than simply intellectual curiosity about Syrian Orthodox customs that induced him to lift a passage over a thousand words long from Jacques de Vitry. Like Jacques, Matthew was aware of the increasing role that confession and penance had come to play in lay spirituality in his own lifetime.[4] After examining the content of the passage more closely, I shall therefore suggest some ways in which the wider significance of this western commentary on eastern Christian practices might be understood.

Jacques de Vitry begins by explaining briefly the origin of the term 'Jacobites' to identify the Syrian Orthodox. He knows that they are to be found both in the east and in Africa, although he seems to confuse the Ethiopians, who were also Monophysites but had their own Church, with the Jacobites of Syria and the Copts of Egypt.[5] He understands in essence how the Monophysite theology of the nature of Christ differs from the Chalcedonian orthodoxy of the Greek and Latin Churches, but he is preoccupied chiefly with what he sees as deviant religious customs. Circumcision he attacks as a Jewish and Muslim custom, and quotes Paul's letter to the Galatians on the futility of the old law. The other deviant custom, the branding of the cross on children's bodies, is associated with John the Baptist's prophecy about Jesus baptizing in the Holy Spirit and in fire, and also serves to distinguish the Jacobites from the Muslims among whom they live.[6]

Jacques has more to say on the subject of confession. The Jacobites, he claims, do not confess to a priest, but to God alone. They burn incense and expect that their sins will rise to God's presence with the smoke from the brazier. In so doing, they ignore Scriptural texts that

---

[3] Jacques de Vitry, *Iacobi de Vitriaco . . . libri duo, quorum prior Orientalis, siue Hierosolymitanae: alter, Occidentalis historiae nomine inscribitur*, ed. F. Moschus (Douai, 1597), ch. 76, 144–8 [hereafter *Historia Orientalis*].

[4] For an introduction to the genre of confessional literature, see Leonard Boyle, 'The Fourth Lateran Council and Manuals of Popular Theology', in Thomas J. Heffernan, ed., *The Popular Literature of Medieval England* (Knoxville, TN, 1985), 30–43.

[5] *Historia Orientalis*, ch. 76, 144–5.

[6] Ibid., 145–6.

recommend confessing one's sins openly rather than in secret. Jacques then gives a brief defence of the practice of auricular confession, using the imagery of the priest trained to distinguish one sin from another as a doctor recognizes diseases,

> whose responsibility it is to judge between one sickness and another, and to impose penances by pondering on the circumstances of the sins committed, and to bind and release according to the keys entrusted to them, and to pray specially for those who have confessed.[7]

A little further on he remarks that 'the blushing with shame, and the embarrassment, and the humility one feels to the person to whom one confesses, is the most important part of penance'.[8] The presence of a priest in confession is thus essential for two reasons: first, so that sins confessed can be treated properly, as symptoms of a diseased soul, and second, because the act of confessing to another person, and the humility that this induces on the part of the sinner, is in itself part of the therapy. Without either of these elements, the Jacobites' confession is worthless.

Jacques's insistence on the importance of auricular confession is also a feature of his preaching. I will cite just one anecdote from his collected *exempla*. A man is guilty of such a great sin that he dares not confess it until he is close to death. The devil disguises himself as a priest and hears his confession. When the man dies, the devil demands his soul because the man has not made a true confession to a priest. The angel replies that it is the sinner's intention that counts, and that he is not held responsible for the devil's deceit. God then allows the man's soul to return to his body to make a true confession and do penance for it.[9]

Two points seem particularly important to Jacques: the right intent of the sinner and the need not only to confess to a priest, but also to do penance for sins. These points amplify the sentiments in his defence of auricular confession in the *Historia Orientalis*: the role of the priest as spiritual doctor and the importance of the act of confession itself as a stimulant to humility on the part of the penitent. Jacques's thinking

---

[7] Ibid., 145.
[8] Ibid.
[9] *The Exempla, or Illustrative Stories from the Sermones vulgares of Jacques de Vitry*, trans. Thomas F. Crane (New York, 1890; repr. 1971), no. CCCIII, 127.

about confession and penance comes directly from the Fourth Lateran Council's decree on confession, *Omnis utriusque sexus,* in which confession is enjoined on all Christians at least once a year. The decree, like Jacques in the *Historia Orientalis,* characterizes the priest as a spiritual doctor, and emphasizes the importance of understanding the context of sinful acts:

> Let [the priest] carefully inquire about the circumstances of both the sinner and the sin, so that he may prudently discern what sort of advice he ought to give and what remedy to apply, using various means to heal the sick person.[10]

Omnis utriusque sexus was the culmination of a century of theological development in the area of confession and penance.[11] The influence of Abelard, and his preoccupation with interior motive, is striking. Equally so is the expectation that sinners will be treated as individuals, and their sins understood in the context of the sinner's life and circumstances. Leonard Boyle, drawing a distinction between the role of the priest in discerning spiritual remedies for sinners as opposed to the mechanical use of penitential handbooks to assign punishments, called the decree the beginning of 'a revolution in spirituality'.[12] The underlying assumption of the decree was that priests would have sufficient education and training to fulfil such high expectations. This is one respect in which Jacques de Vitry and, following him, Matthew Paris seek to contrast western and eastern practices. The underlying feature of Jacques's critique of the Jacobites is their ignorance.

All three Jacobite customs that Jacques exposes are the result, he says, of a failure to understand the Scriptures. The peculiar custom of branding is 'crass ignorance, redolent of darkness'.[13] But ignorance in a different way is also a feature of his discussion of the theology that underpins these customs. In refuting Monophysite doctrine, Jacques implies that the Jacobites do not even understand their own theology. When he asked some Jacobites to confirm that their custom of making the sign of the cross with one finger alone represented their belief in

[10] *Decrees of the Ecumenical Councils,* ed. and trans. Norman Tanner, 2 vols (London and Washington, D.C., 1990), 1: 245.

[11] For background, see P. Anciaux, *La Théologie du sacrement de pénitence au XIIe siècle* (Louvain, 1949); J. C. Payen, 'La Pénitence dans le contexte culturel des XIIe et XIIIe siècles', *Revue des sciences philosophiques et théologiques* 61 (1977), 399–428.

[12] Boyle, 'Fourth Lateran Council', 37.

[13] *Historia Orientalis,* 145–6.

the single, divine nature of Christ, they denied that they held such beliefs, and claimed that it represented instead their belief in the unity of the Trinity.[14] Some Jacobites do seem to have understood the implications of Monophysitism, although they confused the single nature with the single will of Christ. The Dominican provincial's report of the reconciliation of Patriarch Ignatius II in 1237 deliberately contrasts Jacobite complacency and ignorance with Dominican industry and learning. Once the Catholic faith had been explained to him, the patriarch immediately abjured his errors.[15] The provincial goes on to explain that the Dominicans had established language schools in all the convents of his province, and already many of his friars could preach in Arabic.[16]

The theme of ignorance, on the part of both clergy and laity, runs throughout all of Jacques de Vitry's writing on the Jacobites. He first commented on Jacobite customs and doctrine, including their lack of auricular confession, in a letter written from the east in 1216–17 soon after he had taken up his new post as bishop of Acre.[17] He describes his attempts to reform them by preaching against circumcision and in favour of auricular confession in the Jacobite church in Acre. He found them, he says, only too willing to abandon their practices, 'now that they had heard the word of God, which they were unaccustomed to hearing'.[18] The implication, clearly, is that Jacobite clergy did not preach – or at least, they did not preach in ways that could be understood by the laity. In the *Historia Orientalis*, Jacques points out that the laity do not understand what their priests tell them, because they use Arabic, rather than the liturgical language, Syriac.[19] In contrast, efforts were being made in the West to bridge the gap between vernacular and sacerdotal languages. Provincial synods in England in 1217 and 1229 had enacted that the laity be taught the Creed in the vernacular before being admitted to confession – as Matthew Paris presumably knew when he inserted the passage from the *Historia Orientalis* into his *Chronica Majora*.[20]

Preaching and confession were clearly linked in the minds of those

---

[14] Ibid., 148.

[15] *Chronica Majora*, III, 397.

[16] Ibid., 398–9.

[17] *Lettres de Jacques de Vitry*, ed. R. B. C. Huygens (Leiden, 1960), no. II, 79–97.

[18] Ibid., 83.

[19] *Historia Orientalis*, 148.

[20] *Councils and Synods, with Other Documents Relating to the English Church. Vol 2. AD 1205–1313*, ed. F. M. Powicke and C. R. Cheney, 2 vols (Oxford, 1964), 1: 61, 172.

who were intimately associated with Innocent III's reforms in pastoral care. In 1217, during Jacques's first year in Acre, the Dominicans were recognized by Honorius III as both 'preachers in general' and 'confessors at large' throughout Christendom. Jacques's letters show how seriously he took his episcopal responsibilities of preaching and hearing confessions. Describing his daily life as a bishop, he says that he typically devotes the whole morning to hearing confessions.[21] When he visited Byblos, he preached and heard the confessions of the inhabitants.[22] He even resorted to a practice that he may have learnt from the friars, going into the Italian quarters in Acre to preach to the residents in the street, when they would not go to hear his sermons in the cathedral.[23] Taken together with the critique of confessional practices, Jacques de Vitry seems to be contrasting the pastoral vigour of the post-Lateran IV western clergy with the unreformed degeneracy of the Jacobites.

Such a stark contrast was wishful thinking on Jacques's part. The *Historia Orientalis* was, of course, written for a western audience, and one of the themes he wished to drive home was the pastoral responsibility of the clergy. The decree on confession in Lateran IV may seem in hindsight the logical outcome of a developing theology of penance, but the practice it prescribed was still unfamiliar to many Christians. As Innocent III himself observed, on the eve of the Council there was only one church in the town of Montpellier in which the sacrament of penance was administered.[24] Nor was *Omnis utriusque sexus* signalled in local councils. The synods of Avignon in 1209 and Montpellier in 1215 had nothing to say about confessional practices, and that of Paris in 1212 mentioned only confession by priests.[25] Jacques, who had been part of the inner circle of reform-minded clergy who had Innocent III's ear,[26] was promoting the benefits of auricular confession by contrasting its usage among the Latin clergy to the neglect of it by the schismatic Jacobites.

Jacques, moreover, has a clear agenda before him with regard to the Christian east. The *Historia Orientalis* is designed to expose the moral

---

[21] *Lettres*, no. II, 90.

[22] Ibid., 92–3.

[23] Ibid., 85–6.

[24] *Innocentii III Regesta, Pontificatus anno XV*, PL 216, 641.

[25] H. C. Lea, *A History of Auricular Confession and Indulgences in the Latin Church*, 3 vols (London, 1896), 1: 227.

[26] John W. Baldwin, *Masters, Princes and Merchants: the Social Views of Peter the Chanter and his Circle*, 2 vols (Princeton, 1970), 1: 36–9.

failings of the East and its indigenous inhabitants – both eastern and western. Jacques devotes a chapter to each of the eastern Christian peoples he had encountered in the Holy Land – Jacobites, Armenians, Georgians, Nestorians and the indigenous Arabic-speaking Greek Orthodox – and in each lists their errors of belief, custom and morals.[27] His ethnographic survey of indigenous peoples also included a critique of the westerners native to the Crusader States, whom he found incontinent and degenerate, the failure of the Italians to go to church being one example.[28]

Like most contemporaries, Jacques thought that the Holy Land, which was the responsibility of Christendom, has been lost through the sinfulness of its inhabitants. He used the biblical imagery of the 'serpent in the dust' to portray the degradation into which Jerusalem had fallen, and the 'sparrow on the housetop' to represent the deprivation experienced by its inhabitants.[29] How can this generation, he implies, expect to be entrusted by God with the care of the holy city when they have fallen so far from the ardour shown by the first crusaders? In this sentiment Jacques was following established tradition. The defeat of Christians in the east at the hands of Muslims had long been explained on moral grounds, and in the minds of western chroniclers both crusaders and the inhabitants of the Crusader States bore a share in the blame. As William of Newburgh put it, the Holy Land had initially welcomed the crusaders, but their descendants had been judged unworthy to possess it.[30] The solution, of course, was repentance. For if the holy city had been lost to the Muslims through sinfulness, it must follow that it could be regained by doing proper penance for those sins. Perhaps the most thoughtful critic of crusading, Ralph Niger, thought that crusaders should be required to confess their sins and to make an adequate penance before setting out for the east.[31] On the face of it, this seems reasonable enough – until one recalls that the crusade itself was regarded by popes ever since Urban II, and by canon law, as being in

[27] *Historia Orientalis*, chs 75–80, 137–57.
[28] Ibid., chs 73–4, 133–6.
[29] Brenda Bolton, ' "Serpent in the Dust: Sparrow on the Housetop": Attitudes to Jerusalem and the Holy Land in the Circle of Pope Innocent III', in R. N. Swanson, ed., *The Holy Land, Holy Lands and Christian History*, SCH 36 (Woodbridge, 2000), 154–80, 155–6.
[30] William of Newburgh, *Historia rerum anglicarum*, ed. R. Howlett in *Chronicles of the Reigns of Stephen, Henry II and Richard I*, 4 vols, RS (London, 1884–5), I: 254–5.
[31] Ralph Niger, *De re militari et triplici peregrinationis Ierosolimitane*, ed. L. Schmugge (Berlin, 1977), 92–3, 182–3, 218–19. See also Elizabeth Siberry, *Criticism of Crusading 1095–1274* (Oxford, 1985), 41–3, 45–6, 83–4.

itself a penance for sins confessed to a priest.[32] By the time of Lateran IV, the rhetoric of crusading acknowledged that, in order for any crusade to succeed, the internal reform of Christian society had to be a prerequisite.[33] Thus the decrees of Lateran IV, listing and explaining how such reform is to be achieved, can be seen to build up to the climax of the final decree, *Ad liberandam*, which details the practical arrangements for Innocent's proposed crusade.[34] Although only one of the decrees deals explicitly with confession and penance, in a sense the whole council was confessional, in so far as the reforms enacted can be seen as the necessary penances for healing the sick body of the Church.

Jacques de Vitry first came to prominence as a preacher of this crusade.[35] It is therefore in the broader context of crusading and reform, I would suggest, that we must read Jacques's critique of Jacobite confessional practices and his justification of the reforms enacted by Lateran IV. Confessing sins, as Jacques makes clear from his exposure of Jacobite practices, was not a casual affair. It was not something to be done in secret, nor could it be accomplished by mystical fumes of incense wafting heavenward. Confession was a practical matter in which individuals were enabled by the discernment of a spiritual doctor to confront the circumstances of their sinfulness, and thereby to treat the causes as well as the symptom of the disease. Moreover the act of confessing was painful and humiliating for the penitent, as any cure must be in order to be effective. The cure that Jacques had in mind was nothing less than the return of the Holy Land to its rightful ownership and, to accomplish this, not only western, but crusader society also, had to be purged.[36]

This point brings us back to Matthew Paris's appropriation of Jacques de Vitry's chapter on the Jacobites. In appending Jacques's defence of auricular as opposed to private confession to the letter of the Dominican provincial, Matthew is linking two different kinds of reconciliation – the sacrament of reconciliation, and the reconciliation of the Jacobite patriarch to Rome. Although, of course, he does not use

---

[32] H. E. Mayer, *The Crusades* (2nd edn, Oxford, 1988), 23–6.

[33] See for example the bull *Audita tremendi* (1187), *Historia de expeditione Friderici Imperatoris*, ed. A. Chroust, MGH Scriptores Rerum Germanicum V (Berlin, 1928), 6–10.

[34] Tanner, *Decrees of the Ecumenical Councils*, 1: 267–71.

[35] On Jacques's career, see Jessalynn Bird, 'Reform or Crusade? Anti-Usury and Crusade Preaching during the Pontificate of Innocent III', in John C. Moore, ed., *Pope Innocent III and his World* (Aldershot, 1999), 165–85, and in general Ilse Schöndorfer, *Orient und Okzident nach den Hauptwerken des Jakob von Vitry* (Frankfurt and New York, 1997).

[36] *Historia Orientalis*, ch. 1, 1–2.

the same terminology for both, I would suggest that Matthew is making this link quite consciously. We know that he was interested in and well informed on the affairs of the Holy Land: this letter is one of several from the east that he either inserted into the *Chronica Majora* or included in the *Liber Additamentorum*.[37] On this occasion, however, he is pasting together two separate pieces from other sources.

The key to the link lies in the Dominican provincial's perception of the Jacobite patriarch's attitude to his reconciliation and of the significance of that reconciliation. The Dominican clearly regards the affair as the submission of a heretic to the true faith:

> When we explained the Catholic faith to him, with the aid of divine grace, we came to him in solemn procession like that which descends from the Mount of Olives to Jerusalem on Palm Sunday, and he promised and swore obedience to the holy Church of Rome, forsaking all heresy. He submitted his confession of faith, written in Chaldean and Arabic characters, in perpetual witness, and received ours in return.[38]

Hermann Teule has recently suggested that what the Dominicans, and doubtless the papacy, chose to see as submission, was from the Jacobite point of view more likely to have been little more than an expression of diplomatic friendship in faith, and moreover that not all Jacobites took such a favourable view of the Franks.[39] Coupling Philip's letter with the chapter about Jacobite errors, however, leaves little room for seeing the episode as an exchange of theological views between equal parties. Moreover, the news that the submissions of the Nestorian and Coptic patriarchs were also anticipated adds to the overall implication that eastern Christians in general were abandoning heretical customs in favour of correct Roman ones. As Philip the Dominican noted, once all these had returned to Rome, 'only the Greeks would continue to persevere in their wickedness'.[40]

Matthew Paris's own hostility to Greek Orthodoxy is clear from

---

[37] E.g. *Chronica Majora*, II, 391; III, 161; IV, 288–91, 337–45, 488–9, 307–11; V, 221; VI, 203–5.

[38] *Chronica Majora*, III, 397.

[39] H. Teule, '"It is Not Right to Call Ourselves Orthodox and the Others Heretics": Ecumenical Attitudes in the Jacobite Church in the Time of the Crusades', in K. Ciggaar and H. Teule, eds, *East and West in the Crusader States: Context, Contacts, Confrontations*, 2 vols, Orientalia Lovaniensia Analecta 75 and 92 (Leuven 1996, 1999), 2: 13–27, 23–6.

[40] *Chronica Majora*, III, 398.

other episodes in the *Chronica Majora*, even to the extent of supporting the anti-Byzantine policy of the papacy, which he normally excoriated.[41] Matthew has been criticized as a 'bigoted, undiscerning scandal-monger',[42] and both Richard Vaughan and Antonia Gransden have pointed to his resistance to authority, both ecclesiastical and secular, as the unifying theme of the *Chronica Majora*.[43] I suggest, however, that the two passages pasted next to each other in his chronicle, the Dominican letter and the chapter on the Jacobites from Jacques de Vitry's *Historia Orientalis*, when taken together, demonstrate not only Matthew's interest in the East, but his understanding of where authority in the Church lay. The submission of the Jacobite patriarch to Rome is, he says, 'joyful news'. Touched by the Holy Spirit, the chief of the eastern heretics has abandoned superstition and error.[44] The long passage from the *Historia Orientalis* not only describes the nature of that error, but provides a firm justification of the correct, papal doctrine that the Jacobite patriarch has adopted in its place. In Matthew's view, as in Jacques de Vitry's, the sacrament of reconciliation is the path to the deeper reconciliation of Christian society within itself.

Lancaster University

---

[41]   Richard Vaughan, *Matthew Paris* (Cambridge, 1958), 142.

[42]   Helen Nicholson, *Templars, Hospitallers, and Teutonic Knights: Images of the Military Orders, 1128–1291* (Leicester, 1993), 46.

[43]   Vaughan, *Matthew Paris*, 142; Antonia Gransden, *Historical Writing in England. Vol. I, c.500–c.1307* (London, 1974), 356.

[44]   *Chronica Majora*, III, 396.

THEOLOGIES OF RECONCILIATION
IN THIRTEENTH-CENTURY ENGLAND

by WILLIAM H. CAMPBELL

One of [the Pharisees], a lawyer, asked [Jesus] a question, to test Him. 'Teacher, what is the great commandment in the Law?' And [Jesus] said to him, 'You shall love the Lord your God with all your heart, and with all your soul, and with all your mind. This is the first and greatest commandment. And a second is like it, You shall love your neighbour as yourself. On these two commandments depend all the Law and the Prophets.'[1]

RECONCILIATION of the relationships broken by sin, or the fall, is one of the central themes of Christianity, as this collection of studies duly highlights. The themes of reconciliation to God and reconciliation to neighbour run throughout both the New Testament, with special emphasis in Paul's letters to the Corinthians, and the Hebrew Scriptures, for in this passage from the Gospel of Matthew Jesus was quoting from Deuteronomy and Leviticus.[2] This text would have been well-known to Christian authors on the subject of reconciliation in Western Europe in the thirteenth century; and the passage, or at least its message, should have been familiar to most clergy and many of their people. As an item of catechesis, one of its virtues is that it is short, and thus easy to teach and to remember.

While the authority of these two commandments was not in question, churchmen did have to decide how to arrange them in their pastoral care. Long before the thirteenth century dawned, many pastors had discovered from accumulated experience that reconciling the individual to the community, both as the body of one's neighbours and as the microcosm of the Church, was necessary for establishing and maintaining a Christian society, which would have to precede the individual's reconciliation to God. This discovery may be understood socially, though this does not preclude theological explanations. Seeking to understand the fundamental fabric of society, the French sociologist

---

[1] Matt. 22: 35–40 (RSV).
[2] Deut. 6: 5; Lev. 19: 18.

Emile Durkheim realized that the 'Social Contract Theory' of the Enlightenment was insufficient, because contracts cannot function without a 'pre-contractual solidarity', an unspoken agreement to keep contracts.[3] In much of medieval society, the Church provided that pre-contractual solidarity without which the verbal and written contracts of the community could not have been held together:[4] witness, for example, the clauses in many mediaeval charters threatening violators of the agreement with excommunication and damnation.

It would be a reasonable position, and one with broad Biblical authority, to argue that a Christian community torn by internal strife could not be reconciled to God. However, we shall see below that theologians were rethinking this premise in the thirteenth century, changing the nature of pastoral care, and that the development and dissemination of different theologies of reconciliation was not uniform throughout England. This resulted in noteworthy differences from place to place, creating a geography of pastoral care which has not so far been adequately considered.

* * *

Reaching back to the early eleventh century, we find a benchmark of the earlier social and theological understanding of reconciliation in the *Corrector et Medicus*, a work on confession and penance written by Burchard, bishop of Worms, *c.*1008–12.[5] The opening directions express his theology of reconciliation:

> In the week before the beginning of Lent, let the priests of the people call together to themselves the populace, and reconcile the discordant by canonical authority, and settle all quarrels, and then, first, let them give penance to those who confess; so that, before the beginning of the fast arrives, all those who have confessed should have received penance, so that they may be able to say more freely: 'And forgive us our debts, as we also have forgiven our debtors.'[6]

---

[3] Randall Collins and Michael Makowsky, *The Discovery of Society* (6th edn, Boston, MA, 1998), 104.

[4] See the works of John Bossy, especially *Christianity in the West, 1400–1700* (Oxford, 1985), 35–56.

[5] The *Corrector et Medicus* is Book XIX of Burchard's *Decretum*.

[6] PL 140, 943–1014, 949: 'Hebdomada priori ante initium Quadragesimae, presbyteri plebium convocent ad se populum, et discordantes canonica auctoritate reconcilient, et omnia jurgia sedent, et tunc primum confitentibus poenitentiam dent; ita ut, antequam caput jejunii veniat, omnes confessi poenitentiam acceptam habeant, ut liberius dicere possint: Dimitte nobis debita nostra, sicut et nos dimittimus debitoribus nostris'. The trans-

At the end of this confession, the penitent and priest kneel and pray together to God for His forgiveness of the penitent's sins.[7] For Burchard, mutual forgiveness among the members of the Church is a prerequisite to the sacrament of penance, which then reconciles each believer to God. A priest enacting this theology in his parish would have given his parishioners an annual exhortation to forgiveness and settling of scores amongst the members of the parish community, followed by Lenten penances undertaken to restore individuals' relationships with God.

There remains the question: was Burchard's theology of reconciliation used in pastoral care in thirteenth-century England? I believe that it was. The *Corrector et Medicus* was a manual for confessors, a member of an important genre in the high middle ages. Burchard's manual and others based upon it would have influenced both parish priests and mendicant friars, directly and indirectly, in England and elsewhere. As Sarah Hamilton highlights, Burchard's *Decretum*, of which the *Corrector et Medicus* was a part, was an instant best-seller and was widely disseminated.[8] There were certainly copies in England by the thirteenth century, probably more than the extant records show.[9] Moreover, the world of ideas could change slowly at the level of the rural parish, and the mediaeval Church was an institution that held tradition in high regard. The fact that Burchard wrote around 1008–12 would not mean that his theology would be *passé* for thirteenth-century parish priests. Thus there is a strong possibility that Burchard's pastoral theology was used in pastoral care in thirteenth-century England, affecting people's relationships to God and to one another, especially within the parish community.

---

lations in this paper are mine, but selected passages are translated in 'The Corrector of Burchard of Worms', in *Medieval Handbooks of Penance: a Translation of the Principal Libri Poenitentiales and Selections from Related Documents*, ed. and trans. John T. McNeill and Helena M. Gamer (New York, NY, 1938, repr. 1980), 321–45.

[7] PL 140, 977–8: Tunc prosternat se poenitens in terram, et cum lacrymis dicat: Et in his, et in aliis vitiis, quibuscunque humana fragilitas contra Deum et creatorem suum, aut cogitando, aut loquendo, aut operando, aut delectando, aut concupiscendo peccare potest, in omnibus me peccasse, et reum in conspectu Dei super omnes homines esse cognosco, et confiteor. Humiliter etiam te sacerdos Dei exposco, ut intercedas pro me, et pro peccatis meis ad Dominum et creatorem nostrum, quatenus de his et omnibus sceleribus meis veniam et indulgentiam consequi merear. [Prayers follow.]

[8] See Sarah Hamilton, 'Penance in the Age of Gregorian Reform', 47–83.

[9] Zachary Nugent Brooke, *The English Church and the Papacy from the Conquest to the Reign of John* (Cambridge, 1931), 237–9. There is also textual evidence suggesting a copy at Salisbury: *Thomae de Chobham Summa confessorum*, ed. F. Broomfield (Louvain, 1968), *passim*.

Thirteenth-century England was particularly productive of hand-books for pastoral care, including works on the sacrament of penance. In 1217–19, Richard Poore, bishop of Salisbury, issued a set of statutes for his diocese, consisting mostly of pastoral instruction; in 1228, he was translated to Durham, and reissued them there.[10] Poore's

> practical good sense was much in demand in the settling of ecclesi-astical disputes ... he was clearly keen not simply to find a settle-ment as between two conflicting claims, but as far as possible to reconcile those claims by compromise, so that all parties could derive something from the outcome.[11]

This bishop's character of a wise and reconciliatory judge shows through in his statutes, particularly in statute 12, *De bono pacis*:

> Beloved sons, the great injunction to us is the necessity of peace being observed, since God Himself is the author and lover of peace, Who came to reconcile not only the heavenly ones to the earthly ones, but also to reconcile the earthly ones to one another. And since the peace of eternity will not come except through temporal peace and peace of the heart, we admonish you and strictly direct that *so far as it depends upon you, live peaceably with all* (Rom. 12: 18). You should admonish your parishioners that, by the bond of unity in faith and peace, there should be one body in Christ: diligently settling animosities, if they should arise in your parishes; conjoining friendships; recalling the discordant to concord; and, so far as you may, not permitting that *the sun should set upon the anger* (cf. Eph. 4: 26) of your parishioners.[12]

A textual parallel suggests that Poore's source, direct or indirect, was the passage quoted above from Burchard's *Corrector et Medicus*. Poore took Burchard's general directions to heart, but he changed the task of reconciling people to one another from an annual matter into a daily one. He also explained in his statutes that the sacraments of penance and the eucharist reconciled the individual to God, and had to be performed in that order; but he did not explicitly connect any sacra-ments with the principles of his statute *De bono pacis*. Poore promul-

---

10 *Councils and Synods, with Other Documents Relating to the English Church*, ed. F. M. Powicke and C. R. Cheney, 2 vols (Oxford, 1964) II: *A.D. 1205–1313*, 57–96 [hereafter C&S II]; C. R. Cheney, *English Synodalia of the Thirteenth Century* (London, 1941, repr. 1968), 51–89.
11 *English Episcopal Acta, 18: Salisbury, 1078–1217*, ed. Brian Kemp (Oxford, 1999), lix.
12 C&S II: 64.

gated his theology in two dioceses; other bishops copied his statute to do likewise.[13] Priests following his instructions should have provided their parishioners with more harmonious parish communities with fewer opportunities for internal strife to grow.

Another scholarly bishop who wrote for parish clergy was the diligent pastor Robert Grosseteste, bishop of Lincoln from 1235 to 1253. He was renowned both in and after his lifetime for his vast learning, and he taught the Franciscan friars at Oxford before his episcopate.[14] Because of his deep concern for the quality of pastoral care, Grosseteste wrote a treatise on confession, probably during his episcopate.[15] Before his exposition on sins and their correction, he explained his own theology of reconciliation, placing it in the framework of creation, fall and redemption.

Bishop Grosseteste wrote that Jesus, in His Resurrection, released from hell those who deserved release; but, continued the prelate, Jesus could not die again and harrow hell a second time for those who had not yet lived and died, and so the sacraments were instituted as the means of salvation – the means of reconciliation to God. But Grosseteste followed a different theological path from those of Burchard and Poore on what the sacraments offer. He wrote:

> There exist for us two Sacraments which reconcile to God and the Church, namely, Penance and the Sacrament of the Altar. It is fitting that first we should be led back to the Church by Penance, so that the Church should be able to reconcile us to God through the Sacrament of the Altar. . . . there are three essential parts to Penance: Confession with the mouth, Contrition of the heart, and Satisfaction of works, through which [the sinner] ought to be restored to the Church, so that he might be reconciled to God. . . . He gave His Son Himself to the Church so that she might offer Him as the Host, to the placation of the justice of God the Father for the sin of the penitent.[16]

Grosseteste's argument that the sacrament of penance should have

---

13 Cheney, *English Synodalia*, 62–7.

14 J. McEvoy, *Robert Grosseteste* (Oxford, 2000), 3–30 and *passim*; idem, *The Philosophy of Robert Grosseteste* (Oxford, 1982), 492–3.

15 McEvoy dates it from after 1239, but admits that 'Further precisions must, however, await new evidence': see *Philosophy*, 492–3. For text and notes, see the edition by S. Wenzel, 'Robert Grosseteste's Treatise on Confession, "Deus Est"', *Franciscan Studies* 30 (1970), 218–93.

16 Wenzel, 'Grosseteste's Treatise on Confession', 245. My translation.

harmony within the Church as its result, rather than its prerequisite (as Burchard and Poore would have it), can also be seen to have solid practical sense. Visible acts of Satisfaction, known as public penance, surely had a role in defusing tensions in society by the perception that the guilty were being punished. Satisfaction could, however, pay a more tangible debt to society in the cases of good works (such as feeding the poor) or indulgences. Indulgences were considered to be worthless without true Contrition of the heart; countless documents of indulgence explicitly state that benefit would only be had if the recipient were 'contrite and confessed'. Although the system of indulgences did have its abuses, Roy Haines has reminded us that proceeds from the sale of indulgences could go to help needy individuals, especially victims of accidents, and to maintain bridges, roads and hospitals.[17] Thus, the sacrament of penance, especially in Satisfaction, could result in very tangible manifestations of the penitent's 'paying back' of Christian society.

In addition, one of the seminal works from which medieval penitential manuals derived was Gregory the Great's *Pastoral Care*, according to which

> some active behavioural response was required for the proper reception of the Eucharist. . . . This behavioural realism anticipates much of modern notions of behavioural modification. For if you are serious about behavioural change, Gregory thought, you will work incrementally by small steps to modify actually revisable behaviour as evidence of your earnest desire for change. One cannot truly repent and then sit around and do nothing.[18]

Thus Grosseteste could marshal support from both practical experience and patristic authority to bolster his argument that the sacrament of penance should reconcile the sinner to the Church and precede the eucharist, which in turn reconciled to God. In addition to the dissemination of his manual, Grosseteste may have imparted this theology to the Franciscans he taught at Oxford and possibly included it in his sermons to the parish clergy of his diocese;[19] so it too was probably being used in pastoral care in England from about the 1230s into the

[17] R. M. Haines, 'The Indulgence as a Form of Social Insurance', in idem, *Ecclesia Anglicana: Studies in the English Church of the Later Middle Ages* (Toronto, 1989), 183–7.

[18] Thomas C. Oden, *Care of Souls in the Classic Tradition* (Philadelphia, 1984), 51–2.

[19] R. W. Southern, *Robert Grosseteste: the Growth of an English Mind in Medieval Europe* (Oxford, 1986, 2nd edn, 1992), 258–60.

fourteenth and fifteenth centuries, as it continued to be copied and read.[20] Under his theology, probably found more often in his diocese of Lincoln than in other parts of England, a priest might be more inclined to assign penances based on reconciling to community and neighbour, such as charitable works and almsgiving, than recitations of psalms and prayers, at least in comparison to confessors working primarily along the divine axis.

Bishop Peter Quinel of Exeter issued a set of statutes for his diocese in 1287 and included among them a treatise on the sacrament of penance. In the statutes, he wrote that priests hearing confession should not look at the face of the penitent, 'except to the point of being able to judge the contrition and blushing of [the penitent's] heart, which is the greatest part of penance' (*que est maxima pars penitentie*).[21]

Likewise, in the treatise on the sacrament of penance, Quinel wrote:

> Let [the priest] teach [the penitent] that he should have contrition of the heart ... chiefly on account of God (*precipue propter deum*) ... let the priest ... admonish him that he should have a true and naked confession... and that he should do this on account of God (*propter deum*) ... let the priest admonish him that his Satisfaction should correspond to all his sins, and that all of this should be on account of God (*hec totum sit propter deum*).[22]

In sequence and in significance, Quinel placed inward Contrition ahead of auricular Confession and the outworkings of Satisfaction. Moreover, Quinel carefully wrote of each of the three parts of the sacrament of penance that it should be done, not to reconcile one to neighbours nor to the Church, but rather *propter deum* (on account of God or with regard to God).[23] For Quinel, the sacrament of penance was not about reconciling the sinner to his neighbours at all.

Following the pattern of other bishops, one might expect Quinel to tie in the eucharist with some thoughts on reconciliation among parishioners. Concerning the eucharist, he wrote that it is to be adored, and that it is a *viaticum*, food for the spiritual journey; this is nothing new. But Quinel was silent about any aspect of reconciliation signified or achieved through the eucharist, or any reconciliation to Church or neighbour. Priests using Quinel's statutes and treatise as their only

---

20 Wenzel, 'Grosseteste's Treatise on Confession', 226–7.
21 C&S II: 992.
22 C&S II: 1074.
23 C&S II: 1061, prologue to Quinel's treatise.

pastoral handbook (excepting liturgical books) – possibly a common situation in his diocese, where every parish priest was required to have a copy of his treatise for use in confession[24] – would only be given a theology of reconciliation to God and, accordingly, instructions for its use.

* * *

Thus far I have considered writings by bishops for the benefit of parish clergy, but these were not the only providers of pastoral care in thirteenth-century England. The Dominican friars arrived in England in 1221, the Franciscans following three years later; in the 1240s the Carmelite and Austin (Augustinian) friars joined them. The friars shared an emphasis on preaching and hearing confessions for their pastoral care, though the different orders did have different theological and pastoral priorities. They formed a separate system of providing pastoral care, overlapping that of the parish churches. Their different priorities and practices brought them into conflict with parish priests countless times in thirteenth-century England; among their disagreements were issues surrounding repentance and reconciliation. In order to simplify the spectrum of views of the different orders of friars, the Dominicans alone will be considered here.

The Dominicans' standard textbook on the sacrament of penance during the thirteenth century was the *Summa de casibus poenitentiae* by Raymund of Peñafort, a Spanish Dominican canonist. This was the text used both for reading and for lecturing on the subject in Dominican convents, and, from the later 1230s, every brother should have been familiar with its contents and ideas.[25] At no point in this work did Raymund present the sacrament of penance as requiring or effecting reconciliation to Church or fellow-man; he is exclusively concerned with effecting reconciliation between the sinner and God. The absence of concern for reconciling interpersonal relationships is most marked in his discussions of scandalous and notorious sins, where one might expect some consideration of the need for communal healing. Other Dominicans were still more explicit about the purely man–God

[24] C&S II: 1077.
[25] Leonard Boyle, 'Notes on the Education of the *Fratres Communes* in the Dominican Order in the Thirteenth Century,' in *Xenia Medii Aevi Historiam Illustrantia oblata Thomae Kaeppeli O.P.* (Rome, 1978), 253–66, repr. in idem, *Pastoral Care, Clerical Education and Canon Law, 1200–1400* (London, 1981), VI; Raimundus de Pennaforte, *Summa de paenitentia*, ed. X. Ochoa and A. Diez (Rome, 1976).

relational aspect of the sacrament of penance: Thomas Aquinas, typifying the viewpoint, elevated Contrition (part of the inward relationship with God) far above Confession and Satisfaction.[26]

Aquinas's is the best-known Dominican exposition of the eucharist from the thirteenth century. In his discussion of the eucharist in the *Summa Theologiae*, Aquinas followed the metaphor of St Paul (1 Cor. 12: 12–27): the Church is 'the Body of Christ'; each person in the Church is one of the 'members' of the Body of Christ; in the eucharist, all 'participate' in the Body of Christ, thereby being reconciled to it and to Him. This model includes also that part of the communion of saints which is already in Heaven.[27] There is an implicit connexion between reconciliation to Christ, to neighbour, to the Church, and to the communion of saints in Thomas's eucharistic theology. Here Aquinas gave 'communion' its fullest meaning, deliberately conflating Christ and the Church into one unity – almost one entity.[28] While John Bossy argues that 'the sacramental theology of the scholastics, obsessed with philosophical considerations about the elements, did little to diffuse a social conception of communion', he also illustrates what he believes to have been widely-held eucharistic sacramental and sacrificial theology in essential agreement with Aquinas's position.[29]

In addition to his writing, Thomas was a teacher of long standing, and his ideas would have been imparted to his students and the other Dominicans whom they subsequently taught. This eucharistic theology of reconciliation was probably circulating among English Dominicans earlier than might be suggested by the time Aquinas finished writing the work, 1274. This theology would then have been taken to the laity via the Dominicans' preaching and hearing of confessions, focusing communality on the eucharist, rather than on penance, but considering both as reconciling the believer to God.

* * *

In this brief and preliminary examination, we have found indications of five different Christian theologies of reconciliation that were probably being used in pastoral care in thirteenth-century England; it is likely

---

[26] Thomas Aquinas, *Summa Theologiae, Tertia Pars*: 90.3.

[27] Ibid., 73.4.

[28] Ibid., 73.4; 79.5; 80.4, most clearly expressed, but also found throughout his discussions of the eucharist.

[29] J. Bossy, 'The Mass as a Social Institution, 1200–1700', *Past and Present* 100 (1983), 29–61, especially 50–5.

that there were other such theologies, and different shades and variations within each. This shows us how careful we must be in making broad assessments of theological trends and how they affected the laity, especially in this century of great dynamism in theology and pastoral care. By paying close attention to their geographical distribution, we may assess the manner, extent, and geography of the dissemination of these and other pastoral theologies.

Some of this must remain opaque, but we are not wholly in the dark; diocesan statutes were geographically limited in their theoretical enforcement, some bishops were more diligent than others in examining, disciplining and instructing parish clergy, and the theologies espoused by friars naturally would have been found where friars were to be found – in towns and their pastoral hinterland – more than in remote areas of the countryside where friars seldom ventured.

At this time, the parishes and the friars formed overlapping systems of providing pastoral care, sometimes differing in pastoral theologies and priorities. By considering these, we may arrive at a more complex insight into the quarrel between friars and parish priests: for all the good the friars surely did, perhaps they also undermined good work being done by parish priests, or even by friars of other orders, simply because of conflicting theologies of reconciliation. This is evident in the parish priests' perennial complaint, continuing into the fourteenth and fifteenth centuries, that the friars assigned penances that were too light,[30] which would induce more people to come to Confession (the remainder of their Satisfaction could be served in Purgatory), but would do less to induce communal reconciliation (which required settling of disagreements in the present life). This makes sense within Dominican theology as described here, but not from the point of view of the first three theologies considered in this paper, given to parish priests by their bishops.

At worst, churchmen following different theologies of reconciliation could have impeded one another. For instance, in a parish community in which some members confessed to friars, the parish priest would be deprived of opportunities to exhort those parishioners to reconciliation with their neighbours. Likewise, confusion and doubt could be

---

[30] C. H. Lawrence, *The Friars: The Impact of the Early Mendicant Movement on Western Society* (London, 1994), 152–65; M. Haren, 'Confession, Social Ethics and Social Discipline in the *Memoriale Presbiterorum*', in Peter Biller and A. J. Minnis, eds, *Handling Sin: Confession in the Middle Ages* (York, 1998), 109–22; J. R. H. Moorman, *Church Life in England in the Thirteenth Century* (Cambridge, 1945), 390–3.

sown: a parish priest who used and taught Grosseteste's theology might find that a Dominican preaching Aquinas's theology, roughly the reverse of Grosseteste's, would confuse his people. This situation might be found in Grosseteste's vast diocese of Lincoln, which had no fewer than thirty-one friaries by the end of the thirteenth century, seven of them Dominican. Thus friars could, with the best of intentions, divide communities and undermine parish priests' pastoral work.

Much historical literature has been biased towards the friars; parish clergy deserve equal sympathy. At best, however, the pastoral gifts offered by friars and parish clergy could have supported one another: it seems likely that many a parish priest used the sacrament of penance to reconcile his community and taught his flock to attend Mass in order to encounter God.[31] If an itinerant Franciscan were to preach Grosseteste's theology of reconciliation in his parish, it would reinforce the priest's pastoral work to the people. By studying the localities where different theologies and varieties of pastoral care were promoted and used, where they overlapped (such as around convents of friars), and how they developed through time, we may discover a more subtle and colourful vision of the spiritual landscape of England in the thirteenth century than has been known hitherto.

University of St Andrews

---

[31] Bossy, *Christianity in the West*, 35–56; Eamon Duffy, *The Stripping of the Altars* (New Haven, CT, 1992), 93–154.

CHURCH DISCIPLINE IN THE LATER MIDDLE AGES: THE PRIORS OF DURHAM AS ARCHDEACONS

by MARGARET HARVEY

IT is often forgotten that the medieval Church imposed public penance and reconciliation by law. The discipline was administered by the church courts, among which one of the most important, because it acted at local level, was that of the archdeacon. In the later Middle Ages and certainly by 1435, the priors of Durham were arch-deacons in all the churches appropriated to the monastery. The priors had established their rights in Durham County by the early fourteenth century and in Northumberland slightly later. Although the origins of this peculiar jurisdiction were long ago unravelled by Barlow, there is no full account of how it worked in practice. Yet it is not difficult from the Durham archives to elicit a coherent account, with examples, of the way penance and ecclesiastical justice were administered from day to day in the Durham area in this period.[1] The picture that emerges from these documents, though not in itself unusual, is nevertheless valuable and affords an extraordinary degree of detail which is missing from other places, where the evidence no longer exists. This study should complement the recent work by Larry Poos for Lincoln and Wisbech,[2] drawing attention to an institution which would reward further research. It is only possible here to outline what the court did and how and why it was used.

The prior's exercise of his archidiaconal jurisdiction conformed to the account given by William Lyndwood in his *Provinciale*, finished about 1430.[3] It involved regular visitation of local churches certainly triennially, but even yearly, paying particular attention to good order, lay and clergy instruction, discipline, care of the fabric and tithe-paying. The archdeacon could also enquire in general whether there was anything among clergy or laity in the parish which needed

---

[1] Details in Frank Barlow, *Durham Jurisdictional Peculiars* (London, 1950), esp. 47–50.

[2] *Lower Ecclesiastical Jurisdiction in Late-Medieval England: the Courts of the Dean and Chapter of Lincoln, 1336–1349 and the Deanery of Wisbech, 1458–1484*, ed. L. R. Poos, Records of Social and Economic History, NS 32 (Oxford, 2001), xiii–xiv gives the latest bibliography; the introduction gives an excellent account of the type of jurisdiction described in this paper.

[3] William Lyndwood, *Provinciale (seu constitutiones Anglie)* (Oxford, 1679, repr. Farnborough, 1968), Lib. 1, tit. 10.

correction, though Lyndwood points out that this would concern notorious matters, pertaining to church laws. Lyndwood says that a gathering of clergy at local level was known as a *capitulum*.[4]

The prior of Durham certainly summoned general gatherings of clergy from all the appropriated churches. They were known as *capitula generalia* or synods and seem the equivalent of the twice-yearly visitations of rural deaneries elsewhere.[5] The prior also had archidiaconal courts at one or two tiers below the bishop's consistory court by which he dealt among other matters with the results of visitations. Appeal from them ultimately went to the bishop.

The evidence for the prior of Durham as archdeacon is probably the best for any archdeaconry.[6] He usually worked through commissaries or officials, with good evidence for their functioning at least from the fourteenth century. Durham owns a precedent book which gives relevant documents for the archdeacon.[7] The documents date between 1370 and 1381, drawn from York archdiocese or the bishopric of Durham, with several referring to the prior as archdeacon. There are also two books from the archdeacon's court in Durham itself: the *Capitula Generalia* 1435–56 and the Court Book of the Prior's Official, 1487–98.[8] Several separate accounts of visitations survive also with references in the priory letter-books to the prior as archdeacon.[9]

The prior/archdeacon's centre of operations was Durham city. Twice yearly, at least by 1435, the clergy from the appropriated churches in Durham were summoned to a *capitulum generale* in that city, usually in St Oswald's Church, though from 1487 onwards some meetings were held in Witton Gilbert chapel, near Bearpark.[10] Later, these plenary meetings were called *capitulum generale cum sinodo*. They were usually in early October and mid-April.[11] Probably then the clergy paid their *synodalia*.[12] Clergy who did not attend the general chapter when summoned were fined, individual vicars in the later period 3s. 4d, parochial priests 2s and clerks 6d.[13] Those not present

4   Lyndwood, *Provinciale*, Lib. 1, tit. 2, under *capitula ruralia*.
5   See below. For other *capitula generalia* see *Lower Ecclesiastical Jurisdiction*, xxix.
6   Most recently, see *Lower Ecclesiastical Jurisdiction*.
7   Durham Cathedral Muniments [hereafter DCM], Misc. Ch. 421.
8   Both these books are in the DCM.
9   See below, nn. 69 and 72.
10 Court Book, e.g. fols 86r, 93r.
11 *Capitula*, fols 2r, 5v, 8r, 14v and *passim*; Court Book, fols 49v, 57v.
12 *Capitula*, fol. 113v, vicar of [Monk] Heselden, accused of usurping jurisdiction; the Officer also claimed money *pro sinodalibus*.
13 Court Book, fol. 29v for instance; in *Capitula* the sums vary: cf. fols 87v, 105v.

were noted as ill, absent, appearing by proctor or excused, for instance because the priest was celebrating a marriage.[14]

In the 1435–56 volume the list of those expected to attend a *capitulum generale* was given as: the vicars of Pittington, Dalton-[le-Dale], [Monk] Hesleden, Billingham, [Bishop] Middleham, Aycliffe, Heighington, [Kirk] Merrington and St Oswald's Durham, with chaplains from Jarrow, [South] Shields, Monkwearmouth, Hilton, Croxdale, Witton [Gilbert], Whitworth, St Margaret's Durham, Wolviston and Castle Eden.[15] Sometimes between 1435 and 1456 the vicar of Bedlington occurs, but not after 1439 and Wallsend is usually included.[16] Sometimes from about 1452 and always by about 1487 vicars and parish chaplains were listed, including the vicars and chaplains of Northumberland, with, in addition, the vicar of Muggleswick and Edmundbyers, with their parish chaplains. Furthermore the *clerici* (holy water clerks?) of Jarrow, Monkwearmouth, Hilton, Witton, Whitworth, St Margaret's Durham, Wolviston, Castle Eden and Holy Island were also expected. A group of 54 should have assembled in the 1490s. By that time Wallsend was omitted.

Scattered evidence exists for visitation by the prior's representative of the Durham churches with several full accounts and some evidence of a follow-up between the late fourteenth century and 1498.[17] The evidence for visitation of Northumberland is better than for Durham in the fourteenth century because the jurisdiction was being contested by the archdeacon of Northumberland and the priory exercised it assiduously and saved the evidence. In 1391, when the archdeacon of Northumberland took Durham to the Roman curia, the priory produced detailed evidence about exercising its visitation rights in its Northumberland churches from 1361.[18] There is documentation for visitation from 1361,[19] 1369,[20] 1371,[21] 1382,[22] 1391,[23] July 1392 with a

---

14 *Capitula*, fol. 12v, vicar of Dalton.
15 *Capitula*, fol. 1v; Barlow, *Durham Jurisdictional Peculiars*, 48.
16 *Capitula*, fols 48r, 56v, 59r.
17 DCM, Misc. Ch. 421, fols 13v–14v; DCM, 2.2. Archd. Dunelm. 4; DCM, Bursar's accounts, under expenses; *Capitula*, fols 11v, 12v, 98r, 97v, 99v–100r, Misc. Ch. 7069 for Merrington and Court Book, fol. 130r, *yconomi* indicted for not following up the injunctions; R. L. Storey, *Thomas Langley and the Bishopric of Durham, 1406–1437* (London, 1961), 174.
18 Now DCM, Misc. Ch. 5643.
19 DCM, 1.1. Archd. North. 11 and 14; DCM, Misc. Ch. 5643.
20 DCM, Misc. Ch. 5643 and for Norham only 1.1. Archd. North., 11.
21 DCM, Misc. Ch. 5643.
22 Ibid.; DCM, Loc. XII:17.
23 DCM, Loc. XII:17.

follow-up in December,[24] 1409,[25] 1417[26] and 1422.[27] There are dossiers of mandates to clergy, summons of laity with names, *comperta*, and injunctions.

The administration was Durham-based. Most officials for the Northumberland courts were supplied from Durham. In 1362 in Bywell Peter, as well as the notary John de Nissebit, master William Farnham and John Hyndely among the witnesses were part of the Durham staff of the prior.[28] Mandates by messenger from the prior, letters to Northumberland citing, suspending and excommunicating people, all went from there.[29] Local vicars probably acted as apparitors or summoners on the spot both for visitations and for *capitula*.[30]

The vicar or his deputy received a mandate telling him when to expect the visit, to assemble the clerics serving all the chapelries including the holy water clerk (*aquebavilus*), with their letters of orders and representatives of the parish and its chapelries, numbers according to the villages served, to recount the problems of their church and denounce those guilty by *publica fama* of grave sins or crimes. The clergy showed their orders and swore obedience to the prior as archdeacon, defects were denounced, missing villagers were suspended. A sermon preceded questioning the villagers. In 1392 in Bywell the visitors remedied some things on the spot, setting dates for repairs and obliging the villagers to elect overseers. In the December follow-up *sedens pro tribunali*, sexual offenders accused in July were given a penance if they confessed, or were not believed and given a penance in any case, or deferred. Those previously declared contumacious appeared and swore obedience.

Probably the local official of the prior as archdeacon held regular local *capitula* in the fourteenth century. In 1392 a *capitulum* was clearly distinguished from a visitation.[31] The same system as in Durham may have applied in Northumberland; the evidence is patchy, though

24 DCM, 1.1. Archd. North., 12, 13.

25 DCM, 2. 2. Archd. North., 1–3, 6.

26 Ibid., 7, 8.

27 Ibid., 9, 10, 11.

28 For Farnham see *Historiae dunelmensis scriptores tres: Gaufridus de Coldingham, Robertus de Graystanes, et Willielmus de Chambre*, ed. James Raine, Publications of the Surtees Society 9 (London, 1839), cli, clxxvii.

29 Bursar's Accounts 1362, 1383/4 for instance, under necessary expenses.

30 DCM, 2.2. Archd. North., 1–4, 9–11, with 5 showing a summons to a *capitulum* in 1392 distinguished from a visitation.

31 Ibid.

regular *capitula* are mentioned in the Priory Bursar's accounts: *de perquisitis capitulorum domini archidiaconi prioris*. In 1392 at Norham the Commissary ordered someone to come on 13 January 1393 with oath-helpers to Kyloe chapel.[32]

Probably the prior's court in Durham was the higher court, one step below the bishop's; even Northumbrians could be summoned to it. The parish chaplain of Holy Island in July 1392, negligent in summoning people, had to answer for his contempt by Michaelmas in Durham before the prior.[33] In 1451 two couples who failed to clear themselves before the vicar of Edlingham for alleged incontinence after correction had to come to Durham to receive public penance.[34]

The court books, like others elsewhere, are summaries of the cases on any court day, by no means containing full information. They include some cause papers, some witness statements, definitive sentences, and even a few visitation records. *Capitula Generalia* is the most systematic, a session-by-session record, in standard format, giving the place, usually an exact date and always the month, of a session, sometimes with the judge's name (often a monk). The cases are listed, usually with two names one above the other, joined by a bracket, information about one party being indicated by a line. This outline was probably prepared first, listing all the cases to be dealt with, the outcomes completed later, often in different ink. Frequently the status of the accused is given (*S: suspensus*, or *ex: excommunicatus*, or *extra: extra jurisdictionem*). Sometimes the parish and some occupations are also given. Summaries explain whether parties came in person or by proctor, the charge (*Imponitur*), whether the accused confessed, or fled. After a confession, sentence followed immediately, for moral lapses usually some public penance, a public flogging, or carrying a candle before the main procession into mass whilst wearing penitential garb, or a fine. In pleas about breach of faith (*lesio fidei*) the money value involved might be queried and evidence called for. If the charge was denied the accused produced oath-helpers (neighbours to swear to good character) or evidence. The Court Book is similar in content but chaotic, considerably less well written on pages of different sizes not always in order, suggesting papers bound together later. Inter-

---

[32] DCM, 1.1. Archd. North., 13. See also DCM, Misc. Ch. 5643; DCM, 1. 1. Archd. North., 12 (Bedlington): *nec alibi solent antiquitus clerus et parochiani ipsius ecclesie hac occasione trahi.*

[33] DCM, 1.1. Archd. North., 12.

[34] *Capitula,* fols. 93v, 111r; other examples *Capitula,* fols 82r, 83r, 106r; Court Book, fols 21r, 40v.

vening courts are always called *sessio*. This book distinguishes *pars actrix* from *pars rea*, which the earlier record often does not.

From 1435 the prior as archdeacon held a court about once every three weeks in Durham, usually in St Oswald's Church but sometimes elsewhere. In the later period the courts were held approximately weekly. Both books give various meeting-places, apart from St Oswald's.[35] These were often called *sessiones* presumably to distinguish them from fuller *capitula*. Thursday was the standard court day, but Fridays were sometimes used and cases could be completed on other days. The prior seldom presided. In 1494, sitting *pro tribunali*, he punished Sabbath violators,[36] but usually his official or a commissary, who was sometimes the chancellor, acted.

Capitula has a larger proportion of cases of sexual misdemeanour, though both books include such cases, including separations and claims of marriage. The Court Book, in line with findings elsewhere, has many more cases of *lesio fidei* (small debts).[37] *Capitula*, but not the Court Book, has several accusations of witchcraft and enchantment, occurring as defamation.[38] Both contain breaches of the Sabbath and feast-day observance and failure to attend one's parish church to receive communion at Easter. Some cases came *ex officio*, brought by court officials. This may be stated but the origin of many is obscure. Sometimes the priory Sacrist as rector of churches began proceedings,[39] but other times the Prior did so, not apparently *ex officio*.[40] He and priory obedientiaries used this court to collect dues, debts and tithes.[41]

Many of the cases, however, were brought by locals against other locals. The social level of litigants is often unclear. Sometimes the defendants pleaded poverty. On 11 April 1454 Agnes Hepburne, accused of fornication, alleged that she could not do public penance because she had no chemise (in which to do it) and no power to buy one. The judge ordered her to complete her penance in her tunic 'having one garment called le napron'.[42]

---

[35] *Capitula*, fols 89v, 96r, 104v; Court Book, fols 84r, 85r, 111r.

[36] Court Book, fol. 74v.

[37] R. H. Helmholz, 'Assumpsit and *Fidei Laesio*', *The Law Quarterly Review* 91 (1975), 406–32.

[38] See an example below, *Capitula*, fol. 105r.

[39] *Capitula*, fols 86v, 106r, 130v.

[40] *Capitula*, fols 83r, 86r; Court Book, fol. 43v.

[41] Court Book, prior or terrar, *lesio fidei*, fol. 22r; communar, fol. 26v; bursar, *lesio fidei*, fols 59v, 66r, 72v; almoner, fol. 65r, tithes.

[42] *Depositions and Other Ecclesiastical Proceedings from the Courts of Durham, extending from*

Notaries and clerks attached to the court litigated within it. The Berehalghs were a family of clerks resident in the Durham district of Elvet. In February 1454, John Berehalgh, in fact registrar of the court,[43] brought a case against Thomas Knott, presenting certain articles in English for Knott to answer. Knott refused to accept these, requiring that they be presented in due form of the law (in Latin?).[44] On the next court day, the judge handed Knott his articles in due form and assigned the parties the next court day for their case to be heard. They agreed to compromise, each selecting two substantial local men, being bound under forfeiture of £10 to come to an agreement by Palm Sunday.[45]

A further group of easily identifiable litigants were clerics and laity ministering in city churches. In 1436 the *procuratores* of the fabric of St Oswald's asked the court that the *villani* of Croxdale and Sunderland [Bridge], rural parts of the large parish, be obliged to pay to the fabric of St Oswald's. The representatives of the *villani* asserted that they were only obliged to pay half of what others paid and were given until the following Saturday to produce their proof *et interim ad deliberandum cum senioribus parochie*.[46] In February 1452 the procurator *incolarum et inhabitacionum de Elvett* asked that *dominus* John Runcorn should be compelled to minister in the divine offices in St Oswald's.[47] Runcorn had been since 1413 chantry chaplain of St Andrew and St James on Elvet Bridge in the city.[48] Already by 1422 he was pursuing a career as notary in Durham, including in the archidiaconal court.[49] The court ordered him to produce the *ordinacio* of his chantry at the next session.[50]

When parishioners did not wish to pay dues they might confront their fellow parishioners as church wardens (*yconomi*). In June 1451 the *yconomi* of the parish of Dalton le Dale brought a case against the

---

1311 to the Reign of Elizabeth, ed. James Raine, Publications of the Surtees Society 21 (London, 1845), 35, from *Capitula*.

[43] *Capitula*, fols 9v, 10v, 11r; R. B. Dobson, *Durham Priory, 1400–1450* (Cambridge, 1973), 141.

[44] *Capitula*, fols 123v, 124r.

[45] Ibid., fols. 150, 122, 152v.

[46] Ibid., fol. 7r.

[47] Ibid., fol. 110r.

[48] DCM, *Registrum* III, fol. 40v; *The Register of Thomas Langley, Bishop of Durham, 1406–1437*, ed. R. L. Storey, 6 vols, Publications of the Surtees Society 164, 166, 169, 170, 177, 182 (London, 1956–70), II: no. 287; Lichfield Joint Record Office, B/A/1/7, Register of John Burghill, Coventry and Lichfield, fol. 157r.

[49] *Register of Thomas Langley*, IV: nos 1027–8, V: no. 1496; *Capitula*, fol. 99r, acting as a witness/notary in the Prior's archidiaconal court. See also *Register of Thomas Langley*, II: nos 287, 296, 297; York, Borthwick Institute, Register 18, (Bowet), fols 276v, 277r, exchange of his benefice with previous holder of chantry.

[50] *Capitula*, fol. 110r.

parishioners about the repair of their cemetery, which was referred to the Consistory court.[51] The locals used the court very freely, for morality which offended local norms. It is often unclear who initiated accusations of fornication and adultery, but certainly not all arrived *ex officio*. In 1452 an accusation by Johanna Smythson against Agnes Thomson of St Margaret's parish was backed by Johanna Barker and Agnes Patry alleging that they had heard Agnes publicly defaming Johanna of '*sortilegia*' and saying that John Smyth, chaplain of St Margaret's in the city, was so enamoured of her that he had been imprisoned because of gifts he had given her.[52]

Enforcing morality in this way apparently did not lead to deep resentment. Visitations show locals willing to denounce each other for sexual offences but so do the secular court books. In May 1436 of Alice Wood (of St Margaret's) we read: *respituatur de penitencia sua ex bona gubernacione sua*.[53] John Preston of St Nicholas's parish, and *Alicia de Wod quam tenet* had been accused of fornication. Alice had failed to produce enough oath helpers to get her off.[54] The church court's definition *bone gubernacionis* probably also governed the secular court's judgement of a woman. The priory's unfree tenants were regularly presented by their neighbours and fined for *leyrwit* (fornication). Likewise the secular courts forbade the harbouring of women *non bone gubernacionis sui corporis*.[55] In 1493 Alice Johnson, servant of Thomas Watson, was called by Alice White, servant of John Richardson, a fornicator and a Scot.[56] Both qualifications were equally defamatory.

The abbey was watchful of its jurisdiction. Some accused even tried to escape by claiming that their offences, often sexual, had occurred under another jurisdiction.[57] The court preserved its rights against both the bishop's and the royal court (in Durham vested in the bishop). In 1454 in a testamentary case a writ of prohibition was presented. The judge accepted, protesting that he did not thereby intend to give up the

---

[51] Ibid., fol. 94v. See also Court Book, fol. 20r.
[52] *Capitula*, fol. 105r.
[53] Ibid., fol. 7r.
[54] Ibid., fols 2r, 3r.
[55] 'Harbouring fornicators': e.g., Court Book, fol. 55v, Michael Preston and his wife. 'Scots': e.g., DCM, Crossgate Court Book, fols 13v, 15r; 'women': ibid., fol. 56r; DCM, Loc. IV: 136, from Halmote court of Shincliffe, forbidding tenants to harbour Scots, 4 Henry IV (1402–3).
[56] Court Book, fol. 50v.
[57] *Capitula*, fol. 123r, February 1454, Cristina Johnson: *fatet crimen tamen allegat quod non deliquit infra jurisdictionem*. See also *Capitula*, fol. 110v.

case nor curtail the prior's jurisdiction.[58] In 1453 the court summoned the vicar of Hesleden because he had usurped jurisdiction by summoning John Forester to the bishop's court without sufficient mandate.[59] There were cases which were beyond the powers of the immediate judge. The Official's commissary or assessor in 1497, John Walker, facing a case of negligence in which a child was burnt to death, *senciens se non habuisse nec habere potestatem dispensandi cum eis* (the parents), sent the case on to Thomas Swalwell, the Official, who gave a long, tough penance to the grieving parents.[60] But the court was willing to send cases to the Consistory court. In 1498 the judge agreed to a request to refer a case *eo quod non habet consilium nec potest adquirere consilium.*[61]

The court was also anxious to get the parties to compromise, accept arbitration and otherwise agree. The case in 1493 between Alice Johnson and Alice White was remitted to their masters to return to the court next time if unresolved.[62] Litigants could also use the jurisdictional limits of the court in their own interest. In 1493 a group alleged that they had been cited to the Consistory and not to this court at all.[63] Some cases arrived which had already been dealt with in the bishop's court or by his various officials.[64] It was clearly quite difficult for the judges to ensure that the guilty did not fall between the jurisdictional stools.

The ecclesiastical and secular courts were closely linked in Durham.[65] The prior, for example, used the bishop's secular court to round up contumacious people who remained excommunicated for more than forty days.[66] In October 1435, Margaret Bryan of St Oswald's parish fled after accusation of fornication in the prior's court and was suspended (not allowed to enter church).[67] In May the next year she

[58] *Capitula,* fol. 136r; for the writ see R. N. Swanson, *Church and Society in Late Medieval England* (Oxford, 1989, repr. 1993), 183, 186–7.

[59] *Capitula,* fol. 112v; see also fols 122r, 106v.

[60] Court Book, fol. 119v.

[61] Ibid., fol. 128v; see also fol. 18v and *Capitula,* fol. 105v.

[62] Court Book, fol. 50v.

[63] Ibid., fol. 60v.

[64] E.g. Court Book, fol. 37v.

[65] Margaret Bonney, *Lordship and the Urban Community: Durham and its Overlords, 1250–1540* (Cambridge, 1990), 196.

[66] F. Donald Logan, *Excommunication and the Secular Arm in Medieval England: a Study in Legal Procedure from the Thirteenth to the Sixteenth Century,* Studies and Texts 15 (Toronto, 1968), 112–15.

[67] *Capitula,* fol. 2r.

confessed and was given a public penance which she then refused to perform.[68] In November 1436 the prior's official applied to the bishop who wrote to his chancellor to order his sheriff of Durham to have Margaret arrested for contempt and contumacy.[69] On 20 December she surrendered and was given public penance on two days and fined.[70]

Boundaries were blurred. A man could be prosecuted in the prior's church court for poaching in the prior's estate at Bearpark, thereby invading ecclesiastical property and liberty, punishable by major excommunication.[71] Numerous cases of debt and breaking of agreements came up in secular and church courts. In 1378 the bishop's secular chancellor prohibited the prior's archidiaconal official from attempting to recover by excommunication £15.5s.4d, based on a recognizance made by Thomas Diker to Richard de Fysshburn. The official was reminded that only recognizances of debt concerning marriage or testament were his.[72] But in the court books the prior's court shared debt recovery with the secular court under the guise of *lesio fidei*.[73] In March 1493 Thomas Bittleston, a Durham tanner and assiduous litigator, brought a case of *lesio fidei* in the prior's court against Richard Tadcaster demanding a debt of eight shillings with expenses already spent in the secular court for recovery of the money.[74] On 25 April Richard pleaded that he had already paid.[75] But Bittleston alleged the record of his successful plea in the secular court, that is, says the prior's court account, 'in the Old Borough of Durham before William Bichburn once seneschal, as appears by the rolls of the same court' for proof of which he was given a date. The choice of courts was often because the secular court would do when there was a written obligation whereas the church case involved breach of a spoken promise.

Lesio fidei could involve all sorts of promises to perform. In June 1493 Edward Glenton, probably a dyer, pleaded against Robert Jacson for 3s.4d for linen sold where Jacson alleged that he had already paid 20d.[76] John Richardson, from Elvet, alleged that he had seen Jacson's

---

68 Ibid., fols 7v, 8r.
69 DCM, *Registrum* III, fol. 203v.
70 *Capitula*, fols 8r, 10v.
71 Ibid., fol. 141v.
72 DCM, *Registrum* II, fol. 255r.
73 Court Book, fol. 87v.
74 Ibid., fol. 48v; for him as a tanner, see Bonney, *Lordship and the Urban Community*, 181.
75 Court Book, fol. 50r. See also DCM, Crossgate Court Book, fols 1r, 18r, 19v, 27v, 28r.
76 Court Book, fol. 52v.

wife buy two *lez boundez lini* from Glenton and paying 20d for one.[77] William Rogerson had been present in Glenton's house when Jacson's wife bought *lez boundez* and when she paid for one before she left. He had had part of the money for carriage of *le wadde* (woad) from Sunderland. Cuthbert Tailfer agreed; he helped the woman with four pennies from his own purse. In 1491 the widow of John Bell sued John Hall for *lesio fidei* in keeping from her eight ells of linen and eleven ells of hardin and asked for him to be excommunicated for breaking the last will of her husband.[78] He said she had not paid his wages for weaving the cloth.

Durham's court not only publicly punished public sin, but effectively did much more, so that the boundaries between it and the secular court were blurred. My study has shown that the secular and ecclesiastical jurisdictions overlapped, which in turn suggests that the concepts of punishment and penance were intertwined. Of course, in Durham the bishop had both secular and ecclesiastical jurisdiction, but some of the blurring certainly occurred as a result of the choice of the laity. By using the prior's court so readily, the laity practically extended its function from the enforcement of good morals to the collection of local debt and the sorting out of quarrels.

University of Durham

---

[77] Ibid., fol. 53r.
[78] Ibid., fols 24v, 26r.

PRACTICES OF SATISFACTION,
1215–1700

by JOHN BOSSY

THE title, and subject, of this piece is 'satisfaction', though its main locus in time is the sixteenth and seventeenth centuries. I chose the subject because it fitted in with our president's preoccupations, and because it interested me; it turns out, to my surprise, to jog our elbow about some contemporary matters, as I guess he wished.

We had better start with the word, where there are two distinctions to be considered. The obvious one is between making up for, paying for, making amends, making reparation; and contentment, gratified desire, giving satisfaction, what you can't get none of. I shall say that the first is the strong meaning, the second the weak one. The first is always other-directed, and entails an offence previously committed; the second is principally self-directed. 'To content' is a classical meaning of *satisfacere*, but it means to content someone else: to do something (*facere*), as against receiving something. A short history of the word in Latin and English records that the strong meaning emerged into late Latin as a description of church penance, and so passed into English in the fourteenth century. Its heyday was from then until the eighteenth. It referred to ecclesiastical penance (interrupted by the Reformation), the theology of the Redemption (encouraged by the Reformation), and in general public usage to the meeting of any kind of obligation, payment, atonement or compensation. From the eighteenth century it passed from public use, superseded by the weak meaning except in technical or professional fields. One professional usage, to which *The Oxford English Dictionary* gives a good deal of attention, is 'to satisfy the examiners': they think it is a case of 'content'; may it be a case of 'avert wrath'?[1]

There is another distinction, which is more subtle and may actually have more to tell us. It is a distinction within the strong meaning between what we may call a common and a learned version. In the

---

[1] *The Oxford English Dictionary*, 2 vols (Compact edn, Oxford, 1971), *s.v.* 'satisfaction', 'satisfy', etc. [hereafter *OED*]; *An Elementary Latin Dictionary*, ed. C. T. Lewis (Oxford, 1947), *s.v.* 'satisfacio', 'satisfactio'; A. Rey *et al.*, eds, *Dictionnaire historique de la langue française*, 2 vols (Paris, 1992), *s.v.* 'satisfaire', 'satisfaction'.

common sense, I think, satisfaction is the same as restitution, that is to say a recompense equal to the damage caused by the offence, a full and equal payment. That, for example, is the meaning in the doctrine of the Redemption expounded by Anselm in *Cur Deus homo*. But it is not the proper sense, which is from Roman Law and puts the stress on the *satis* (enough): '*Satisfactio est tantum facere quantum satis est irato ad vindictam*' (i.e., satisfaction is to *do enough* to prevent the angry party from taking vengeance). It is, for example, to make some kind of a payment on a debt in order to show willing and in the hope that the creditor will remit the rest or some of it, and not pursue you at law or otherwise. In the centuries I am dealing with, people were well up in Roman Law, and it showed in the matter of satisfaction.[2]

From words to facts. I shall talk about three sets of facts about the theory and practice of satisfaction, of which the first and most obvious is the sacramental theory and practice of the Roman Church. Satisfaction is or was one of the three performances in response to which the Church administered to its members the forgiveness of sins, the others being contrition and confession. Formally the case since the Council of Trent, this has actually been the case since the thirteenth century, perhaps the twelfth, partly because of the decree *Omnis utriusque sexus* of the Fourth Lateran Council of 1215, partly because of the doctrine of Peter Lombard and the thirteenth-century scholastics. Satisfaction is called penance, but is distinguished from previous forms of canonical or tariff penance by being voluntary on the penitent's part and arbitrary on the priest's. It is non-ritual; private, to the extent that it may not be such as to reveal to the curious what the penitent is satisfying for; not, in any possible sense, 'equal' to the offence committed; different from restitution, where that is relevant; and performed after absolution, not before it. It is directed toward God, not towards the neighbour; and the *poena* that it is supposed to avert appears in effect to be the pain of purgatory.[3]

The history of this sacramental satisfaction is not impressive. I

---

[2] Anselm, *Cur Deus Homo*, PL 158, 359–431, 393–3 and 403–4; P. Galtier, 'Satisfaction', in A. Vacant and E. Mangenot, eds, *Dictionnaire de théologie catholique* XIV (1939), 1129–1210, col. 1135.

[3] Henry Charles Lea, *A History of Auricular Confession and Indulgences in the Latin Church*, 3 vols (Philadelphia, PA, 1896), 2: 107, 169–231; Thomas N. Tentler, *Sin and Confession on the Eve of the Reformation* (Princeton, NJ, 1977), 318–40; the text of *Omnis utriusque sexus* in *Enchiridion definitionum et declarationum de rebus fidei et morum*, ed. Henricus Denzinger and Adolfus Schönmetzer (Freiburg, 1976), 264. B. Poschmann, *Penance and the Anointing of the Sick* (London, 1964), and Cyrille Vogel, *Le Pécheur et la pénitence au Moyen Âge* (Paris, 1969) supply a theological and historical perspective.

suspect that, if the Lateran Council had not required it, the thir-teenth-century masters would have abandoned it altogether. Their doctrine was, as I understand it, that sin, in so far as it concerned the sacrament, was an interior matter to be radically distinguished from the matters of exterior social readjustment to be dealt with by the *forum externum*. They suffered from the nightmare that the infliction of meaningful penances would keep people away from confession; Aquinas added a psychological elaboration of the theme with the thought that, if a priest required such a penance, the penitent would be so angry with him as to lose the pacific disposition with which, in prin-ciple, he had come to confess. Since the *poena* to be remitted was gener-ally understood to be not a worldly *poena* but a purgatorial one, it was widely held that a penitent who not only neglected, but absolutely refused to perform any satisfaction enjoined would nevertheless be absolved of his sins, and would simply have to do his satisfaction in purgatory. This was roughly the view of Jean Gerson (1363–1429) and of Antonino of Florence (1389–1459), and explicitly of the sixteenth-century Thomist Cajetan (1439–1534).[4]

So the practice of satisfaction settled down, so far as we can see, into a modest or token offering of prayers and almsdeeds, excluding fasting as perhaps too public: at the tough end, 'to say every day three Ave Marias, three Pater Nosters and one Creed, and to give three pence to three poor folks.'[5] It hangs around the sacrament between 1215 and 1517 like a relic, perhaps a ball and chain, from an earlier epoch.

As we come to the sixteenth century, in a Renaissance intellectual climate where the notion of retribution for sin was coming to be thought a barbarous anachronism, we find three solutions being offered. One was indulgences, which were in principle remissions of satisfactory *poena* required on earth or in purgatory. Since what they were remitting, in so far as they were remitting anything on earth, were the penalties of the old regime, indulgences had no direct effect on sacramental satisfaction; but they are relevant as an indication of the general failure of belief among the authorities in the idea of painful retribution for sin, though also of a vigorously persisting belief in it among the faithful.[6]

---

[4] Galtier, 'Satisfaction', 1200, 1205.

[5] John Bossy, *The English Catholic Community, 1570–1850* (London, 1975), 271; H. Aveling, *The Catholic Recusants of the West Riding of Yorkshire, 1558–1790*, Leeds Philosophical and Literary Society (Leeds, 1963), 251. This was the penance of a convert.

[6] Lea, *Auricular Confession*, vol. 3; Poschmann, *Penance*, 210ff. The widely held opinion

Another direction taken was to argue, against history and language, that the purpose of satisfaction was not vindicative (the appeasement of God's wrath), but what was called medicinal or reformative. We have heard that story before. There was a problem about the relation between this proposal and a minimal practice of satisfaction in the sacrament, but it was probably a better idea than indulgences. It could be supported by the text of *Omnis utriusque sexus*, had been pushed by Aquinas, and became something of a particular doctrine of the Dominicans; its warmest exponent in the sixteenth century was Cajetan, who tended to the view that *all* satisfaction was medicinal. The doctrine fitted conveniently with the fifteenth-century movement towards the systematic examination of conscience before confession and otherwise, a polishing, one might say, after the scraping of the soul, and a congruous adjunct to sacramental grace. It turned compensatory pain into a phase of the continuous process of self-monitoring which was the Counter-Reformation's complement to confession. By the middle of the twentieth century, to judge by the *Dictionnaire de théologie catholique*, it had become the standard defence of the satisfactory aspect of the sacrament.[7]

The simplest thing to do was to get rid of satisfaction altogether, and this of course is what the Reformers did. Or perhaps we should say that where the old Church had shifted the responsibility on to Purgatory, the Reformers shifted it on to Christ. Luther came to this position out of opposition to the practice of systematic examination of conscience and the implications about self-improvement carried by it and by the Dominican doctrine of medicinal satisfaction. He was an Augustinian, and under the guidance of Johann von Staupitz concluded that the proper frame of mind in which to approach the sacrament was an unspecific recognition of sinfulness and dependence on God's mercy in which the penitent should confess and receive absolution – 'a cure without equal for distressed consciences'.[8] And satisfaction? Well,

---

(as by Cajetan, in Lea, 3: 9) that indulgences only remit 'enjoined penance' seems to mean that they only apply to earthly penance; but for the complications see Tentler, *Sin and Confession*, 328f.

  [7] Lea, *Auricular Confession*, 2: 229; Galtier, 'Satisfaction', 1208; T. de Vio Cajetani, *De peccatis summula* (Paris, 1530), fols 260–2; H. Outram Evennett, *The Spirit of the Counter-Reformation* (Cambridge, 1968), 20–42.

  [8] *Luther's Works*, ed. Jaroslav Pelikan and H. T. Lehmann, 55 vols (Saint Louis, MO, and Philadelphia, PA, 1958–1986), 48: 64–70 (Luther to Staupitz, 30–v–1518); 36: 86 (*The Babylonian Captivity of the Church*, 1520). Luther ignored medicinal satisfaction in the Ninety-Five Theses, but these were defended by the Dominican indulgence-seller Johan Tetzel in his

JOHN BOSSY

Luther is known for his radical hostility to the notion: it was the theme
of his account of his tower-experience, the possibly fictional and
certainly undatable life-event which dramatized his getting out from
under the notion of divine justice by which an angry God required to
be placated for sin by works of satisfaction; it followed from his
doctrine, which some have found difficult to square with the above, of
the single satisfaction made by Christ on the cross, 'a full, perfect and
sufficient sacrifice, oblation and satisfaction for the sins of the whole
world'; it governed the demolition of purgatory and of masses satisfactory.[9]

I am not sure that the water here is entirely clear. The Ninety-Five
Theses, after all, seem to place against the theory and practice of indulgences a defence of redemptive pain. So Thesis 40, which argues that a
true contrition looks for and loves *poenas*; and Thesis 94, which
contrasts the spurious tranquillity given by preachers of peace on earth
and in heaven with the 'pains, deaths and hell' which should be the lot
of a true disciple of Christ. You might have thought that a decent
doctrine of satisfaction could have been constructed on these grounds,
but Luther did not take that road. Perhaps he was put off by the course
of the controversy sparked by the theses; perhaps by a 'tower-
experience'; perhaps by Melanchthon with his humanist contempt for
barbarous and antiquated mores. Anyway, what he came out with was a
radical rejection well expressed by William Tyndale: 'Whoever goeth
about to make satisfaction for his sins to Godward . . . the same is an
infidel, faithless and damned in his deed doing, and hath lost his part in
Christ's blood'.[10]

Naturally, the defenders of Catholicism were bound to stick up for
satisfactory pain. Thomas More did so against Tyndale, and so did the
Fathers of Trent, who said that *poena* was not necessarily remitted with

counter-theses, which claim that indulgences do not remit them: Ian D. Kingston Siggins,
Luther (Edinburgh, 1972), 60–1. Luther's doctrine of confession is expounded by Tentler, *Sin
and Confession*, 349–63.

[9] *Luther's Works*, 34: 336–7 (Preface to Latin Writings, 1545); P. S. Watson, *Let God be
God! An Interpretation of the Theology of Martin Luther* (Philadelphia, PA, 1970), 119–20; Prayer
Books of Edward VI, in *Liturgies of the Western Church*, ed. Bard Thompson (New York, 1962),
257, 280.

[10] *Luther's Works*, 35: 25–33 (Ninety-Five Theses); 48: 68 (Luther to Staupitz, 30-v-1518).
Sermons on Indulgences, 1516 and 1517, in Siggins, *Luther*, 55ff. and B. J. Kidd, *Documents
Illustrative of the Continental Reformation* (Oxford, 1911, repr. 1967), 29; *Luther's Works*, xlviii,
68. Thesis 40 seems to be taken from Augustine: Galtier, 'Satisfaction', 1145. Tyndale quoted
by Thomas More, *The Confutation of Tyndale's Answer*, in *The Complete Works of St Thomas
More*, ed. Louis L. Martz *et al.*, 15 vols (New Haven, CT, and London, 1963–97), 8.1: 90.

culpa; that it was necessary that sins should not be forgiven 'without any satisfaction'; that priests should 'enjoin convenient satisfactions according to the quality of the offence', and not 'trivial works for very serious sins'. Satisfaction was not just improving or medicinal, but also vindicative; but people could also satisfy by accepting patiently temporal plagues inflicted by God.

This strong view was followed by the theological faculty of Salamanca, which argued for 'proportional' satisfaction, but by nobody else. Jesuits sometimes did not bother with it at all; and rigorists like Borromeo and the Jansenists took an entirely different line. The tradition established after 1215, the presumption that the powers of the priest in enjoining satisfaction were arbitrary, and the general intellectual climate ensured that it gently faded away. Henry Charles Lea concluded that in the eighteenth century it became effectively obsolete.[11] The decline, I would suggest, goes along with the introduction of the confessional-box: not that that mysterious event was an obvious contributor to it, but that both were equally symptoms of a decay of the idea that sin was a social matter.[12]

For good or ill, that was probably not what the population thought. I think of the miller Menocchio, who took the view that, except that it was an opportunity to talk theology, the only point in going to confession was to find out what the penance was, and if you knew that already you could stay at home. I also think of the Florentine penitent of Archbishop Antoninus, who, having confessed a respectable sin and been given one *Pater* as a penance, complained that this was an insult. It was all very well for the learned on both sides to say that dealings with their neighbour were one thing, and dealings with God another, but the separation was rather contrary to instinct; it also jarred with the feeling, explained by a perceptive parish priest, that what *he* thought were offences against God, his parishioners thought were offences against *him* (the priest).[13] And they all lived in a social world where reparation, restitution, satisfaction, *amende honorable*, were constant preoccupations. These furnish the theme of my next two stories.

[11] Lea, *Auricular Confession*, 2: 186.

[12] More, *Confutation*, 66–90; *Enchiridion symbolorum*, 397–9, and the comment in Hubert Jedin, *Geschichte des Konzils von Trient*, 4 vols (Freiburg-im-Breisgau, 1970), 3: 327, 330; Galtier, 'Satisfaction', 1206; On the confessional-box, see my article, 'The Social History of Confession in the Age of the Reformation', *TRHS* ser. 5, 15 (1975), 29–33.

[13] Carlo Ginzburg, *The Cheese and the Worms: the Cosmos of a Sixteenth-Century Miller*, transl. John and Anne Tedeschi (London, 1980), 10; Galtier, 'Satisfaction', 1205; Gérard Bouchard, *Le Village immobile: Sennely-en-Sologne au XVIIIe siècle* (Paris, 1972), 339.

* * *

The first is about the duel, on which the Council of Trent also took a view. The duel was an invention of the early sixteenth century.[14] It arose from a dispute among noblemen, where a man who thought that his honour had been flouted challenged the offender to a single combat of a conventionalized kind, which would normally lead to the death of one or other party. Although invented in Italy, we are told that it did not flourish there because the institutions of peace-making were too strong.[15] Its heyday was in France between the reign of François I and that of Louis XIV: here it emerged out of the *combat judiciare*, a form of ordeal granted by and held in the presence of the king. It was encouraged by the wars of religion, but flourished especially after it. The crown, until Louis XIV, dithered between banning it under the death penalty and countenancing it underhand; so did the French Church, officially demanding its suppression, but allowing some latitude for it in practice, as in the case of François de Sales (1567–1622) and many casuists.[16]

The duel, as such, appears to be a form of satisfaction; we think that if somebody challenges somebody else to a duel, he is demanding satisfaction. This is true in a large sense: a duel is a vindicative action, assuming the *lex talionis*; it was, in particular, a form and means of restitution, a restitution of honour, which is why a lot of spiritual advisers were relatively sympathetic to it; it was satisfactory because at the end of it the surviving party, whichever he was, would be 'satisfied': the matter would be at an end. In that sense it was thought at the time, as by Jean Bodin (1520–96), and has been thought since, as by Lawrence Stone, to be a step forward in the civilizing process, by comparison with the simple feud.[17]

There are two reasons for taking a different view. In France at least, institutionally and in the sixteenth-century interpretation, it was not a form of feud but a form of ordeal, and the objection to it, as to ordeals in general, was that it was an attempt to force God's providence by a ritual obliging him to reveal the truth. This is clearly so up to a point;

14 François Billacois, *Le Duel dans la société française des XVIe–XVIIe siècles: essai de psychosociologie historique* (Paris, 1986); Lawrence Stone, *The Crisis of the Aristocracy, 1558–1641* (Oxford, 1965), 242–50.

15 Billacois, *Le Duel*, 70–81, 185.

16 Ibid., 137–89 and 163 for François de Sales.

17 Stone, *Crisis*, 243ff.; objections by Billacois, *Le Duel*, 397 and Stuart Carroll, 'The Peace in the Feud in Sixteenth- and Seventeenth-Century France', *Past and Present*, no. 178 (2003), 74–115.

but I do not think that anybody in the sixteenth century believed that a victor in a duel was necessarily the person in the right in the original argument, and after 1600 this line of argument was dropped in favour of more conventional legal and moral ones.[18]

The other reason is, on the face of it, purely verbal; it has a root in the distinction I drew at the beginning of the paper. If, in Early Modern France, you demand satisfaction from somebody, you are not challenging him to a duel; you are asking him to *do enough* in the way of a relative climb-down to make a duel or the pursuit of vengeance unnecessary. What is enough is a public verbal acknowledgement by the offending party that an offence has been committed, though it is unlikely to go so far as a straight apology; if a blow has been struck some kind of offer of a return blow may be made; the offender will say that he would accept the satisfaction if it were offered to him in a similar case. The pair are then said to be friends, but do not exchange a kiss of peace, so it is not clear that they are necessarily reconciled in the normal or theological sense.

The great practitioner of this kind of satisfaction among the French nobility was King Henri IV: my colleague Stuart Carroll has kindly passed on to me a collection of cases dealt with by him, which includes a very funny account of a dispute at his Council table between the duke of Epernon and M. de Rosny his treasurer, who had accused the duke of pocketing the tax receipts. Satisfaction of this kind is not something people demand, but something they have their arms twisted to consent to; and according to François Billacois it is often unsuccessful. Most people, it seems, would sooner fight; or, at least, will not be reconciled unless a bit of blood has been shed on both sides. An English observer contrasted French enthusiasm for instant challenges with the 'English gentleman, who with mature deliberation . . . judiciously determineth his manner of satisfaction according to the quality of the offence', like the priest according to the Council of Trent, and perhaps as inaccurately.[19]

My third story takes us, perhaps to your surprise, into the field of grand international politics, and to a strip in that field with which I have a certain personal relation, since it was, and indeed is, the particular province of a great historian to whom I have a debt outstanding,

---

[18] Billacois, *Le Duel*, 31ff., 175; cf. Robert Bartlett, *Trial by Fire and Water: the Medieval Judicial Ordeal* (Oxford, 1986), 103–26, 118 and 123.

[19] Ibid., 182–5 and 56, n. 62, quoting from Robert Dallington; Carroll, 'The Peace in the Feud', *passim*; Paris, Bibliothèque Mazarine, MS 2887, fols 10–15 for Rosny and Epernon.

which I now attempt to do something to pay. The field is the Thirty Years' War. I have a respectable German colleague who has said that he proposed to teach the history of seventeenth-century Germany without mentioning it, and that may be fairly typical of a cohort in German historiography which is interested in non-events like confessionalization and not in what actually happened. I try now, in a modest way, to put a little politics back.

On 26 June 1630 King Gustaf II Adolf of Sweden, our Gustavus Adolphus, arrived with an army at Peenemünde on the coast of Pomerania, scene of more explosive memories. He published a statement in justification of this armed incursion into the territory of the Empire in which he claimed that he had come to secure, among other things, 'satisfaction' from the Emperor Ferdinand II for various offences the emperor had committed against him.[20] It was a curious list, including a number of petty injuries like opening the king's diplomatic correspondence, and a larger offence, which it was nevertheless difficult to bring under the code of honour, of sending military aid to his enemy the king of Poland and so effecting a serious defeat of his own army by the banks of the Vistula.

During the remaining, dramatic, two years of his life, as his intervention in Germany proceeded to astonishing success and mortal dénouement, Gustavus continued to insist that *satisfactio* was one of the essential purposes of his campaign; the other was a new coinage, *assecuratio* (security). Satisfaction for the past; security for the future. Satisfaction was something that cropped up as a war aim in all the negotiations he undertook with the Lutheran princes of north Germany: they obliged themselves, after a great deal of arm-twisting, to fight on against the emperor and his allies until Gustavus had received 'an acceptable, sufficient, royal satisfaction'. Satisfaction continued to be a prominent object of Swedish policy, and an obligation upon German allies, after the battle of Lützen in 1632, which one might have thought, as by a duel in which the party challenging had been killed, to have rendered the claim defunct. The claim did indeed slumber during the following years, when a heavy defeat at Nördlingen and political successes on the imperial side put the Swedes' position in Germany in dire straits. But when things

---

[20] Michael Roberts, *Gustavus Adolphus: a History of Sweden, 1611–1632*, 2 vols (London, 1953–8), 2: index *s.v. satisfactio*; *The Thirty Years' War*, ed. Geoffrey Parker (London, 1984), 121–44, 156–61, 182ff., 186.

picked up again it was vigorously reawakened, and at the peace of Westphalia *satisfactio*, along with *assecuratio*, was royally achieved.

In the meantime, what was meant by satisfaction, and who and what were required to make it, had changed a good deal. Starting as a claim upon Ferdinand II and his supporters rather strictly defined (it excluded the Bavarians, protected by Gustavus's treaty with the French), it became by creep a claim upon the Protestant princes whose lands he had liberated in the course of his campaigns, as compensation for his efforts in liberating them; it ended as a claim upon the Empire as a whole, which the emperor himself succeeded in evading. In its substance the claim drifted from the unspecified requirement of 1630, to a claim for compensation in money, until it emerged as a claim for compensation in territory.

This transition meant a shift in the meaning of the terms *satisfactio* and *assecuratio*; the original instrument of security (occupation of Baltic coastline or ports) became the new satisfaction, while security came to mean a constitutional reconstruction of the Empire. Since what became envisaged as satisfaction was the whole Duchy of Pomerania, the new claim provoked the enmity of the Elector of Brandenburg, to whom the inheritance of the duchy belonged, and helped to cause the disintegration of the Swedish position between 1634 and 1636. But Gustavus had become convinced of the doctrine that *jure belli* conquered territory belonged to the conqueror, and applied it to the territories of friends as well as of enemies: at the minimum, he was entitled to territorial compensation if these territories were given up. At Westphalia Sweden got half of Pomerania as well as a whacking financial indemnity. I add, for the usage, that it also got from the Empire an undertaking to pay the massive arrears of wages of the Swedish army: what was called 'the contentment of the soldiery'.

The Swedish insistence on talking about satisfaction was a puzzle to the statesmen who dealt with Gustavus and his chancellor Oxenstierna: it seemed a special term like, in the internal history of Sweden, the term *reduktion*. How shall we explain it? I pursue three lines of thought.

(1) It came from the point of honour, and from the practice of satisfaction alternative to the duel. The chronology might well suggest this, and the idea gets support from some of the discussion of the subject on the Swedish side. One of the reasons for the drift from financial to territorial satisfaction was the belief that to accept financial compensation, or only financial compensation, was dishonourable. Gustavus himself said this to the German Protestants when they proposed it to

him after his triumph in 1631: he was not a mercenary, he said, to be paid off at the end of a campaign. And so, in the disastrous days of 1635, did a member of the Council of the Realm, Count Per Brahe. The question being discussed was on what conditions they might make peace with the then triumphant emperor: with some territory, if possible; if not possible, with some 'satisfaction' in money; if that was not on offer, to run for it. Brahe said that the second alternative was inconceivable: 'we could not accept compensation in money, and preserve our honour', so if no territory was on offer, they must fight on, win or lose.[21]

(2) It came from somewhere or other in penitential or judicial doctrine. It is a point against the argument from honour that what was demanded was an equivalent, not a token; and it *was* demanded, not pressed upon the Swedes. Of the two meanings of satisfaction described at the beginning of this paper, it is the first and looser meaning we are dealing with: what I thought we might call restitution. Restitution proper was certainly in the air around 1630: the imperial act of 1629 had required a massive resumption of ecclesiastical territories secularized since the Reformation. German Protestants used the term to describe one of their political objectives, a return to the status quo of 1618; it was later borrowed in England to describe the return of King Charles II to his kingdom. Gustavus could not ask for restitution because he was claiming what had never belonged to him. Hence, one might suppose, his resort to satisfaction. This line of thought seems over-abstract and less persuasive than the first.[22]

(3) It came from Hugo Grotius. Grotius and Gustavus never met, but had a lot to do with each other. After his escape from the Netherlands in the wake of the Arminian crisis (1621), Grotius looked for a political job and finally found it when he was recruited for the Swedish service in 1633: he was Swedish ambassador in Paris for ten years. Queen Christina, who preferred Descartes as her tame intellectual, recalled and dismissed him, and he died after a shipwreck in the Baltic in 1645. He was not a great political influence in Sweden, but he was certainly a considerable intellectual influence on Gustavus, by means of his *De jure belli et pacis*, published in 1625, read by Gustavus on its appearance, and

---

[21] Michael Roberts, ed., *Sweden as a Great Power, 1611–1697. Government, Society, Foreign Policy* (London, 1968), 149ff.; idem, 'The Political Objectives of Gustav Adolf in Germany, 1630–1632', in his *Essays in Swedish History* (London, 1967), 82–110, 99.

[22] Roberts, *Sweden as a Great Power*, 136, 139, 153; *OED, s.v.* 'restitution', no. 4.

said to have been taken with him on his campaigns; he certainly consulted it quite a lot.

What he found there was: that war was a natural and legitimate human activity; that it was caused by injury committed by one party upon another where there was no superior legal authority; and that, in a public war, or war between states, the party injured who effectively conquered territory belonging to somebody else acquired a title to it. What he did not find was anything about satisfaction, beyond a very general reference in the prolegomena to rights of restitution and reparation; Grotius did not get around to talking about peacemaking. He was the one person in Europe really qualified to sort out my subject, since he understood all the contexts I have talked about, and several more: Roman and other law, high politics, feud and the duel, Roman manuals for confessors. . . . He might have written a *Summa* on satisfaction, but did not.[23]

But he had said something about it, in a context which I have skipped over: the theological. Earlier in his career he had written a work on the theology of the Redemption, called *De satisfactione Christi,* a defence of the traditional doctrine against the view, influential at the radical end of the Reformation and nervously acknowledged by the orthodox, that it was an unchristian theory, incompatible with the doctrine of the forgiveness of sins. Grotius proceeded from a definition of satisfaction which was linguistically careful and historically accurate, but strictly designed to make his theological point:

> A satisfaction is a payment which may either be accepted or refused, and is the opposite of a payment strictly speaking [which is equal to the debt and cannot be refused].[24]

Hence, if we assume that vicarious satisfaction is in order, Christ's satisfaction for human sin may in principle be accepted or not accepted by God the Father; in accepting it he is exercising the forgiveness of sins:

> The term satisfaction signifies in law and common use the

---

23 Roberts, *Gustavus Adolphus,* 2: 423, 639–40, and *Essays,* 95; C. G. Roelofsen, 'Grotius and International Politics in the Seventeenth Century', in Hedley Bull, Benedict Kingsbury and Adam Roberts, eds, *Hugo Grotius and International Relations* (Oxford, 1992), 95–131 and Peter Haggenmacher, 'Grotius and Gentili. A Reassessment of Thomas E. Holland's Inaugural Lecture', ibid., 133–76, 146, n. 50 and 154, n. 77.

24 Hugo Grotius, *Defensio fidei catholicae de satisfactione Christi adversus Faustum Socinum senensem* (Leiden, 1617: Oxford, 1636 edn), 120. I have not seen the new edition and translation by E. Rabbie and H. Mulder (Assen, 1990).

tendering of an act or thing, from which liberation follows, not *ipso facto*, but by an act of the will [from the party offended]; this often happens, not only in matters of monetary debt, but also in the settlement of crimes, and it is called in the Latin languages *aliquem contentare*, to content somebody.[25]

This definition, I have to say, would not have helped Gustavus or Oxenstierna, who were looking for something different from the 'contentation' of their soldiery: a satisfaction 'full, perfect and sufficient', as we saw above. It cannot be the direct source of their usage. There are incidental remarks in *De satisfactione* which may be thought to look forward to the *De jure belli* and to Gustavus, like the defence of the legitimacy of rulers being judges in their own case, as in cases of *laesae majestatis* 'and in wars which are declared by one king against another on account of an injury inflicted upon him'.[26] I cannot but think that Grotius's doctrine of satisfaction had something to do with Gustavus's, but that is as far as I dare go.

At the end of this circuitous piece, I offer some concluding, not thoughts, but thoughts about thoughts. We may think about the history of a word, its roots, its branches of reparation and contentment, restitution and contentation, the flourishing of one and the withering of another. We may think about an item in the history of Christianity: a theological panic, perhaps unnecessary, about the idea of satisfaction for sin; more largely, a parting of the ways, a separation of thoughts and doings about God from thoughts and doings about other people, of religion and society properly speaking. We may think about the state of the world: about offence and retaliation, war on the pavements, war in the sky, war in the Gulf.

University of York

---

25 Ibid., 138.
26 Ibid., 54.

LUTHER AND THE
SACRAMENTALITY OF PENANCE

by DAVID BAGCHI

AT the beginning of his *De captivitate Babylonica ecclesiae prae-ludium* of early October 1520, Luther announced that there were not seven sacraments of the Church, but only three – baptism, penance, and the Lord's Supper.[1] By the end of the treatise, the three had been reduced to two.[2] His reasoning was starkly logical. A sacrament, to be a sacrament, must contain the promise of forgiveness of sins, and have attached to it a visible sign instituted by Jesus Christ. Because no such visible sign is associated with the rite, penance cannot be a sacrament. A reasonable inference to draw is that Luther must have come to reject the sacramentality of penance by the time he composed *De captivitate Babylonica*, in perhaps August 1520.

The matter is not, however, as straightforward as this. In his next major work, a detailed defence of those of his views which had been condemned in the bull *Exsurge Domine*, Luther repeatedly refers to penance as a sacrament, not in any perfunctory or casual manner, but in a way that is integral to his argument.[3] And in the most important theological work of his last years, the *Genesisvorlesung*, the power of the keys is very frequently bracketed with baptism and the eucharist as God's principal means of grace.[4] I propose to demonstrate that Luther's understanding of the sacramentality of penance was a good deal more complex than the argument of *De captivitate Babylonica* would suggest, and to offer an explanation for this. We shall see that this matter was not of purely personal significance for Luther, but that his ambivalence on the question of sacramentality led to a much wider ambivalence

---

[1] See *D. Martin Luthers Werke. Kritische Gesamtausgabe*, ed. J. C. F. Knaake *et al.*, 67 vols (Weimar, 1883–), 6: 501, ll. 33–38; English transl. in *Luther's Works*, ed. Jaroslav Pelikan and H. T. Lehmann, 55 vols (St Louis, MO, and Philadelphia, PA, 1955–86), 36: 18 [hereafter *WA* (*Weimarer Ausgabe*) and *LW* respectively].

[2] *WA* 6: 572.12–17, *LW* 36: 124.

[3] See his *Grund und Ursach aller Artikel so durch römische Bulle unrechtlich verdammt sind*, 1521 (*WA* 7: 308–57), transl. as *Defence and Explanation of All the Articles Condemned by the Pope* (*LW* 32: 7–99) *passim*, but esp. on Article 16.

[4] E.g. *WA* 43: 526.2–4, *LW* 5: 142; *WA* 43: 528.19–20, *LW* 5: 145.

concerning penitential practice within the Lutheran tradition as a whole.[5]

* * *

There is little sign in Luther's early writings that he was especially interested either in penance or in sacraments in general. On the contrary, scholars have remarked how little he refers to them. For example, in the half-a-million words he wrote in preparation for his first lecture series on the Psalms (1513–15), there are only 101 references to the sacraments, of which fewer than one-third concern penance.[6] This is surprising, considering that Luther was dealing with the Psalms of David, the most famous penitent of the Old Testament. But while Luther has less to say about the sacrament of penance than might have been expected, he has a very great deal to say about repentance, forgiveness, judgement, self-accusation, and humility as indispensable features of the Christian life. Indeed, all these elements coalesce in the course of his early lecture series to inform his new definition of faith.[7] Significantly, Luther describes the Christian in his lectures on Romans not only as '*simul iustus ac peccator*', but also as '*semper peccator, semper penitens, semper iustus*'.[8]

The idea of the Christian life as one of continuous repentance also lies behind Luther's critique of indulgences. The first two of the Ninety-Five Theses read:

> 1. When our Lord and Master Jesus Christ said '*Poenitentiam agite* etc.*', he meant that the whole life of believers should be one of repentance.
>
> 2. This command cannot be understood as referring to sacramental penance (that is, to confession and satisfaction administered by the priestly ministry).[9]

---

5   For a recent collection of essays which considers penitential theory and practice across all the major confessions of the Reformation era, see K. J. Lualdi and A. T. Thayer, eds, *Penitence in the Age of Reformations* (Aldershot, 2000). The select bibliography provides a useful guide to scholarship in this field.

6   See especially W. Jetter, *Die Taufe beim jungen Luther: Eine Untersuchung über das Werden der reformatorischen Sakraments- und Taufanschauung* (Tübingen, 1954), 115–35, 175–6; B. Lohse, *Martin Luther's Theology: its Historical and Systematic Development* (Edinburgh, 1999), 57; and Jonathan D. Trigg, *Baptism in the Theology of Martin Luther*, Studies in the History of Christian Thought 56 (Leiden, 1994), 133.

7   See esp. E. G. Rupp, *The Righteousness of God: Luther Studies* (London, 1953), 153, 195.

8   *WA* 56: 442.17, *LW* 25: 434.

9   *WA* 1: 233.10–13, *LW* 31: 25.

Although Luther goes on to stress the importance of priestly absolution (in Thesis 7), here we see for the first time the explicit subordination of sacramental penance to continuous repentance that perhaps best explains his reluctance to mention the sacrament in his Psalms lectures. During the course of the indulgences controversy, Luther found himself writing very frequently on issues concerning penance. Even after the controversy had moved on to other topics, Luther remained with the subject and indeed published a major treatment of it every six months for three years, always with reference to the pastoral problems which penitents encountered in confession.[10] The most important of these treatments were *Ein Sermon vom Sakrament der Buße* (1519) and *Von der Beicht, ob die der Bapst Macht habe zu gepieten* (1521, pr. 1522). Between these came *De captivitate Babylonica*, written in Latin rather than German and aimed at fellow-priests rather than lay people. His concern throughout these works was to demonstrate that penance should be seen not as an unwelcome imposition, the annual duty prescribed by Lateran IV,[11] but as liberation. For this reason, he stresses the voluntary nature of the sacrament. No-one can be forced to undergo it, but those who are oppressed by guilt will want to seek relief through it.[12] No-one should be required to recite all their sins individ-ually before the priest (which would in any case be impossible), but only those which are troubling the conscience.[13] And, if no priest is available, any Christian (including women and children) can give abso-lution, since the power of the keys, of binding and loosing, has been granted by Christ to the whole Church.[14] In particular, the third part of the sacrament in traditional theology, satisfaction, is to be dispensed

---

[10] These writings were: *Pro veritate inquirenda et timoratis conscientiis consolandis conclusiones*, summer 1518 (*WA* 1: 629–33); *Eine kurze Unterweisung, wie man beichten soll*, early 1519 (*WA* 2: 59–65); *Ein Sermon vom Sakrament der Buße*, mid-Oct. 1519 (*WA* 2: 714–23, *LW* 35: 9–22); *Confitendi ratio*, Apr. 1520 (*WA* 6: 157–69, *LW* 39: 27–47); the discussion of penance in *De captivitate Babylonica*, Oct. 1520 (*WA* 6: 543–9, *LW* 36: 81–91); *Ein Unterricht der Beichtkinder über die verbotenen Bücher*, Feb. 1521 [*WA* 7: 290–98; Eng. transl. by Bertram Lee Woolf, *Ref-ormation Writings of Martin Luther*, 2 vols (1956), 2: 89–98]; *Von der Beicht*, summer 1521 (*WA* 8: 138–85). Also important is the rather later work *Von den Schlüsseln*, 1530 (*WA* 30.II: 465–507, *LW* 40: 325–77).

[11] Constitution 21 ('Omnis utriusque sexus') in *Decrees of the Ecumenical Councils*, ed. and trans. Norman Tanner, 2 vols (London and Washington, D.C. 1990), I, 245,*245.

[12] *Von der Beicht*, *WA* 8: 157.24–7.

[13] *Sakrament der Buße*, *WA* 2: 721–2, *LW* 35: 20–21; *Confitendi ratio*, *WA* 6: 161–4, *LW* 39: 33–8; *Kurze Unterweisung*, *WA* 2: 60.11–20; *Von der Beicht*, *WA* 8: 158–62.

[14] *Sakrament der Buße*, *WA* 2: 716.25–35, *LW* 35: 12; *WA* 2: 719.16–19, *LW* 35: 16; *Von der Beicht*, *WA* 8: 155–6 and 182.23–8.

with entirely, for God's absolution is absolute, and no human being can, or is required to, make restitution to God for their sins.[15]

The ideal reader of Luther's pastoral writings was a devout Christian with a fragile conscience, constantly aware of their failings before God and in need of hearing Christ's promise of forgiveness. In other words, Luther had in mind a person not unlike himself, or at any rate not too dissimilar to the penitents who came to see him at the city church and castle-church at Wittenberg, or to the friars whose father-confessor he was. The so-called 'Wittenberg Movement' of 1521–2 was a rude awakening for him, for it showed that not everyone was like this. The success of the radicals in converting even educated people like Karlstadt to extreme positions on infant baptism and Christ's presence in the eucharist demonstrated to him the need for basic instruction in the faith and in the true meaning of the sacraments. When he came to draw up a service book for the Wittenberg congregations in 1523, he therefore stipulated that everyone intending to receive communion would have to satisfy the priest beforehand of their understanding of the eucharist, and of their moral uprightness as the fruit of that under-standing.[16] Although this examination was not intended as confession, it came to take place after vespers on the Saturday before communion on Sunday, and it ended with the priest assuring the intending commu-nicants that their sins were forgiven.[17] It is not surprising that clergy and lay people alike came to regard this examination (*Exploration*) as confession, and Luther himself contributed to the confusion by speaking of it in these terms.[18]

At the same time, something strange was happening to the sacra-mentality of confession in the nascent Lutheran Church. In the *Unterricht der Visitatoren an Pfarrherrn in Kurfürsten zu Sachsen* (1528), penance is again reckoned a sacrament: the wording was Melanchthon's, but Luther, who provided the preface, did not correct it.[19] The same point is made in the Augsburg Confession of 1530, and in the Apology of the Augsburg Confession, also very largely products

---

[15] *Sakrament der Buße, WA* 2: 719.38–720.3, *LW* 35: 21.

[16] *Formula missae et communionis*, 1523, esp. *WA* 12:215.21–3, *LW* 53: 32–3.

[17] Ernst Bezzel, *Frei zum Eingeständnis: Geschichte und Praxis der evangelischen Einzelbeicht*, Calwer Theologische Monographien, Reihe C: Praktische Theologie und Missions-wissenschaft 10 (Stuttgart, 1982), 14.

[18] Ibid., 15.

[19] *WA* 26: 217.29–31, *LW* 40: 295.

of Melanchthon's pen.[20] And in local ecclesiastical ordinances, the existence of three sacraments, including penance, was affirmed.[21]

In the period of Lutheran Orthodoxy, the dogmaticians therefore had to come to terms with a double legacy. On the one hand were the official confessions of the Lutheran Church, which explicitly stated that penance was a sacrament. On the other was Luther's own testimony, which explicitly stated the opposite, but which included a significant body of writings, including some of his most mature statements, which seemed to give the power of the keys a quasi-sacramental status. Opinion was divided, but most of the dogmaticians conceded that penance was a *res sacra* and close to a sacrament, but not a sacrament as such. Their main sticking points were, first, the lack of dominical authorization for the practice, and also the historical fact that the earliest Church knew only two sacraments.[22]

* * *

The Lutheran understanding of penance is therefore a complex one, and it is difficult to avoid the conclusion that a good deal of its complexity stems from Luther himself. Two questions in particular may be raised: why did Luther abandon his belief in the sacramentality of penance in the first place, and why in later life did he once again bracket it so frequently with the dominical sacraments?

An overriding concern for Luther in all his treatments of penance was the avoidance of compulsion. Despite imposing the *Exploration* on all would-be communicants, he continued nonetheless to characterize auricular confession as helpful when voluntary, unhelpful when compulsory. For instance, in his 1528 *Vom Abendmahl Christi Bekenntnis* he wrote:

> Thus [auricular confession] is a precious, useful thing for souls, as long as no-one is driven to it by laws and commands, but left free to make use of it, each according to his own need, when and where he wishes (just as we are free to obtain counsel and comfort, guidance and instruction whenever and wherever necessity or desire moves us); and as long as no-one is forced to list or describe all his sins, but only those which are more burdensome to him or which

---

[20] Bezzel, *Eingeständnis*, 28–30.
[21] E.g. the influential Nuremberg *Kirchenordnung* of 1533, and, as late as 1553, that of Hohenlohe. See *Die evangelischen Kirchenordnungen des XVI. Jahrhunderts*, ed. Emil Sehling, 15 vols (Leipzig & Tübingen, 1902–), 11: 186, 14: 57, 60.
[22] Bezzel, *Eingeständnis*, 53.

he happens to mention, as I have discussed in my *Little Book on Prayer*.[23]

A second vital concern was to shift the centre of gravity of the rite. In his 1519 *Sermon vom Sakrament der Buße* Luther divides the sacrament into three parts. One expects him to use the traditional division into contrition, confession, and satisfaction; but instead he lists absolution, grace, and faith.[24] The centre of gravity of the sacrament has shifted to absolution, because both contrition on the one hand, and satisfaction, on the other, emphasize human agency instead of divine forgiveness. This is, I think, why Luther opposed detailed interrogation; not because it represented the 'burden of late-medieval religion' (as Steven Ozment has argued),[25] nor because of the opportunities for titillation it offered prurient priests (as many reformers feared),[26] but because it focused on the penitent's ability to remember and the priest's skill at setting the appropriate tariff. The focus should have been, as Luther had learned from Staupitz, the cross of Christ.[27]

A third concern was that penitence should be thought of as a way of life more than a sacrament. Erasmus's Greek Testament had shown Luther that Jesus had said in Matt. 3: 2 not *Poenitentiam agite* ('Do penance') but *Metanoeite* ('Change your mind'). Therefore the mark of the true Christian is not annual penance but continual penitence:

> Sin is not destroyed, as the sophists dream, by our acts of contrition, preparation, and satisfaction. . . . We are not in a state of perfection, but of becoming and transition, in a state of daily movement from virtue to virtue, from purgation to purgation. Having been sanctified, we are still being sanctified.[28]

The fourth and most important factor is what we might call the 'gravitational pull' of the dominical sacraments. In *De captivitate Babylonica*, Luther assigns a massively enlarged role to baptism.[29] Penance is no longer the flotsam that can save the Christian sailor who

23 *WA* 26: 507.20–7, *LW* 37: 368. The reference is to his *Betbüchlein* of 1522.
24 *WA* 2: 715.21–30, *LW* 35: 11.
25 Steven E. Ozment, *The Reformation in the Cities: the Appeal of Protestantism to Sixteenth-Century Germany and Switzerland* (New Haven/London, 1975, repr. 1980), 22–32.
26 Jacob Strauss, amongst others, made this accusation and graver ones about the Catholic clergy. See Ozment, *Reformation in the Cities*, 51–4.
27 See the letter to Staupitz of 30 May 1518 (*WA* 1: 525.21–3, *LW* 40: 66).
28 *Genesisvorlesung*, on Gen. 49: 11–12 (Sept.?, 1545), *WA* 44: 775.1–2, 8–11, *LW* 8: 267.
29 'In these pages [*sc.* the baptismal section of *De captivitate Babylonica*], rather, we see nothing less than a *rediscovery* of baptism by Luther': Trigg, *Baptism*, 145, emphasis original.

has made a shipwreck of his faith by post-baptismal sin, because baptism is an unsinkable ship. Penance is no longer anything in itself, but simply a means of returning to baptismal grace.[30] Penance was also intimately linked with the eucharist, as a necessary preparation for communion, and Luther seems to elide one into the other. In his *Sermo de digna praeparatione cordis pro suscipiendo sacramento eucharistiae* of 1518, Luther, with his gift for the counter-intuitive, states that the only worthy preparation for receiving communion is to be aware that one never can be worthy.[31] Since the point of penance for most people was to prepare them for Easter communion, one could argue that Luther had at a stroke destroyed the purpose of the exercise. Luther goes some way to admitting this. In the *Confitendi ratio* (1520), he writes:

> I advise, as Jean Gerson also advised several times: that one should sometimes go to the altar or sacrament with a scruple of conscience, that is, without confessing. . . . Do you want to know why such advice is given? It is so that one learns to trust in God's mercy more than in one's own confession or effort.[32]

So with one part of its function (restoration to a state of grace) taken over by an enlarged conception of baptism, and another (preparation for communion) taken over by a new understanding of worthy reception, the sacrament of penance for Luther is pulled apart by the gravity of the two larger bodies.

I think that these factors explain why Luther came to deny the sacramentality of penance. But we need also to ask why the power of the keys came to assume quasi-sacramental status in the Genesis lectures. The first point to note is that Luther never lost sight of the importance of confession, even when least convinced of its sacramental status. It was, he believed, 'necessary', and 'a cure without equal for distressed consciences', because in it one hears God's own word of consolation through the voice of another.[33] But secondly, three stages in the 'rehabilitation' of the keys can be detected. In the first stage (from *c.*1520 to *c.*1530) penance is demoted, and in its place the gospel is ranked along-

---

[30] Penance is nothing more – or less – than 'the way back to baptism' ('via et reditus ad baptismum': *De captivitate Babylonica*, *WA* 6: 572.17, *LW* 36: 124).

[31] *WA* 1: 330.25–31.

[32] *LW* 39: 40, *WA* 6: 166.1–7. Luther mitigates the scandalous potential of this advice by assuming that the sinner has committed only the light (monastic?) sins of drinking, talking, or sleeping too much, or missing the canonical hours.

[33] *De captivitate Babylonica*, *LW* 36: 212.

side the remaining sacraments. This is clear from the statement of belief that forms the third part of Luther's *Vom Abendmahl Christi*:

> Nor should one make sacraments out of matrimony and the priestly office. These are holy orders in their own right. And penance is nothing else than the application of the power of baptism. Thus two sacraments remain, baptism and the Lord's supper, along with the gospel, in which the Holy Spirit richly offers, bestows, and accomplishes the forgiveness of sins.[34]

The second stage (from *c*.1530 to *c*.1542), sees Luther concentrate much more on the idea of the keys, with its biblical grounding in Matt. 16: 19, and by extension Matt. 18: 18 and John 20: 22–3. In his 1530 treatise *Von den Schlüsseln* he gives due emphasis to the key which binds as well as the key which looses. He writes:

> Both of these keys are absolutely essential to Christianity, and God can be fully thanked for them. For no human being [*sc.* unlike the key which looses] can console a truly frightened sinful conscience. . . . The strong, iron key which binds is for pious Christians a mighty shield, wall and stronghold against evil-doers. But it is also an effective, useful and holy medicine for evil-doers, though terrifying and frightening to the flesh.[35]

It is clear from his exposition that Luther is equating the key that binds to the Law (with its double effect of protecting the true Church from the wicked reprobate while convincing the wicked elect of their sin), and the key that looses to the Gospel. And so the conditions are in place for him to equate the power of the keys to the ministry of the Word as Law and Gospel.

In the final stage, at the time of the Genesis lectures, Luther is therefore again able to rank the power of the keys with the dominical sacraments: 'For this, too, we learn from experience – we who are in the same profession and to whom *baptism, the power of the keys, and the sacrament of the altar* have been given'.[36] Luther is not consistent in this equation, but he makes it sufficiently often to demonstrate that the power of the keys and the ministry of the Word are strongly associated in his thought.

---

[34] *WA* 26: 508.25–9, *LW* 37: 370.
[35] *WA* 30.II: 503.34–504.11, *LW* 40: 373.
[36] On Gen. 27: 28–29 (*WA* 43: 528.18–20, *LW* 5: 145). My emphasis.

It is tempting to conclude that Luther had come full-circle, from a conventional view of penance in the 1510s, to denying its sacramentality in the 1520s, to bracketing the power of the keys with the dominical sacraments in the 1540s. But such a view is not satisfactory, because Luther clearly did not end where he began. Indeed, it could be argued that the complexities of Luther's – and Lutheran – penitential theology are attempts to come to terms with the tensions implicit in Luther's initial paradigm shift on penance. What he learned from Staupitz enabled him to see penance as liberating rather than oppressive, but what he learned from Erasmus's Greek Testament prevented him from seeing Matt. 3: 2 as divine authority for penance.[37] When Luther came to write *De captivitate Babylonica* two years later, he simply made this tension explicit: on the one hand, private confession is 'a cure without equal for distressed consciences'; on the other, it lacks direct divine authority.

Luther's later thought on the subject can be interpreted as a search for an appropriate biblical basis for a practice which was eminently justifiable on pastoral grounds. Some possibilities put forward by conservative opponents, such as Luke 17: 14 ('Go and show yourselves to the priests'), were unjustifiable.[38] Others, such as Matt. 9: 8 ('They glorified God, who had given such authority [*sc.* to forgive sins] to men') become very important to Luther for a time.[39] Only the 'binding and loosing' passages retained an abiding significance for him. First used polemically as a means of denying papal jurisdiction over Purgatory, these passages assume an increasing importance as the biblical basis for confession, and finally (as we have seen) are used as the basis of the ministry of the word itself. In this sense, confession for Luther comes to partake more of the character of 'word' than of 'sacrament'.

University of Hull

---

[37] Behind the influence on Luther of Staupitz's radical view of repentance lay that of Johann Tauler. On this, see most recently Volker Leppin, ' "Omnem vitam fidelium penitentiam esse voluit" – Zur Aufnahme mystischer Traditionen in Luthers erster Ablaßthese', *Archiv für Reformationsgeschichte* 93 (2002), 7–25.

[38] Letter to Spalatin, 17 Sept. 1521: *D. Martin Luthers Werke. Kritische Gesamtausgabe: Briefwechsel*, ed. Otto Clemens (Weimar, 1930–), 2: 391–2, *LW* 48: 312–14.

[39] E.g. *Sermon vom Sakrament der Buße, LW* 35:21; *Von der Schlüsseln, LW* 40: 366.

JUDGEMENT AND REPENTANCE
IN TUDOR MANCHESTER:
THE CELESTIAL JOURNEY OF ELLIS HALL

by PETER MARSHALL

AMONG the diversions for Londoners in the early summer of 1562 was the sight of a man confined in the pillory at Cheapside, bizarrely dressed in grey animal skins, and accompanied with the caption: 'For seducinge the people by publyshynge ffallce Revelations'. Ellis Hall had come to London from his home in Manchester with the intention of presenting to the Queen a 'greate booke' containing secret revelations written in verse. He went to the palace at Greenwich, but was denied his interview with Elizabeth. Instead, Hall was interrogated by the bishop of London, Edmund Grindal, on 12 June, and castigated in a sermon by the bishop of Durham, James Pilkington, two days later. On 18 June he was questioned by five members of the Privy Council, and on 26 June, after his spell in the pillory, he was sent on Grindal's orders to Bridewell, where he died three years later.[1]

From the records of the two interrogations an extraordinary autobiographical story emerges.[2] Hall was no youthful zealot, but a man of sixty, born in 1502. As a child he claimed to have 'dyffred moche from all my fathers Children . . . geven to solitarynes abstinence and prayer'. But he turned his back on childhood piety, married at 27 and made a fortune as a draper, earning £500 'in the tyme of Kinge Edwarde the sixte when the great fale of money was'. One night in 1552, however, while poring over a set of accounts, he was interrupted by a voice,

---

[1] *The Diary of Henry Machyn: citizen and merchant-taylor of London, from A.D. 1550 to A.D. 1563*, ed. John Gough Nichols, Camden Society ser. 1, 42 (London, 1848), 284; John Strype, *Annals of the Reformation and Establishment of Religion, and other various occurrences in the Church of England, during Queen Elizabeth's happy reign: together with an appendix of original papers of state, records, and letters*, 4 vols in 7 tomes (Oxford, 1824) I.1: 433–5; I.2: 196; London, BL, Lansdowne MS 24, no. 81; London Guildhall MS 33011/1, fol. 222r.

[2] Public Record Office, SP 12/23/39; Oxford, Bodleian Library, MS Tanner 50, fols 16r–17r. The latter was edited by W. P. M. Kennedy, 'A Declaration before the Ecclesiastical Commission, 1562', *EHR* 37 (1922), 256–7, though it seems more likely to have been an *ad hoc* grouping of available councillors: cf. *Acts of the Privy Council of England*, 44 vols (London, 1890–1958), 7: 105.

calling out three times, 'Elye thow Carpenters sonn . . . rise watche & praye for the daye drawethe nighe'. This was followed by a vision of 'a man clothed in white havinge fyve woundes bleadinge'. Believing this to be 'but a dream or phantasye', Hall continued in his 'covetous & worldly affayres', and in consequence was shortly afterwards struck down by a painful illness. As he lay tormented in his bed, the figure in white returned, telling Hall that he was 'electe & chosen of god to declare & pronounce unto his people his word', that he was to write of a revelation that 'shalbe putt in to thy hed by the holye ghoste . . . & shew hit to the magistrates & rulers'. After this Hall was 'taken owt of my bed as it were in a tuft of fethers' and blown up into heaven where he beheld Christ seated in majesty, compassed about with angels, one of whom held a book in his hand. Then Hall was carried down into hell 'where I saw all the tormentes therof & also a place prepared for me, yf I wolde not amend my corrupte lyfe, & also a place prepared for me yn heaven if I wolde follow godes holy will'. Hall calculated that he was absent from his chamber two nights and a day, from 9 to 11 April 1552, 'in which tyme I was not sene of anye mann in the yearth lyvinge'. He was commanded to watch and pray for seven years, and then to write for a further three and a half, during the last year of which he would suffer persecution. Accordingly, at the end of Mary's reign he began to work on his book, but found no inspiration till he had distributed his goods to kinsmen and the poor, given up meat, fish and wine, and 'apparrelled myself thus as ye se'. He had also, he claimed, 'wrote everie worde of this booke on his knees'.

Between his second interrogation on 18 June, and his committal to Bridewell on the 26, Hall barely qualifies as a nine-day wonder. But he has retained a marginal claim on the attention of historians of the English Reformation since John Strype took notice of the case in the early eighteenth century. More recently, there have been passing mentions in surveys of early modern prophecy by Keith Thomas, Richard Bauckham, and Alexandra Walsham, and in assessments of the early Elizabethan ecclesiastical scene by Norman Jones and Christopher Haigh.[3] The two latter scholars agree that Hall was evidently an unreconcilable Catholic opponent of religious reform. Jones comments that

[3] Keith Thomas, *Religion and the Decline of Magic* (London/New York, 1971), 157; Richard Bauckham, *Tudor Apocalypse* (Appleford, 1978), 187–8; Alexandra Walsham, *Providence in Early Modern England* (Oxford, 1999), 204; Norman Jones, *The Birth of the Elizabethan Age: England in the 1560s* (Oxford, 1993), 41–2; Christopher Haigh, *Reformation and Resistance in Tudor Lancashire* (Cambridge, 1975), 144–5.

'his revelation must have called the nation to repent its sins, probably including the Reformation', and Haigh, with tongue perhaps partially in cheek, observes that 'although Hall was clearly a madman, it is interesting that his mind was apparently unhinged under Protestant governments only'.

There are, it must be admitted, compelling reasons for approaching the case from this perspective. Having interrogated Hall, Bishop Grindal considered him to be 'of the popishe Iugement in Religion which verie manifestlye appeared by divers of his speaches'. Perhaps we should expect no less of an emigré from Lancashire, that notoriously intractable North-West Frontier of the Tudor Reformations. Though Hall's Manchester housed a Protestant presence, and was the target of preaching by John Bradford in Edward's reign, Mancunians were regularly in trouble with the Elizabethan authorities for a variety of assertively conservative behaviours.[4] Moreover, and most suggestively, the alleged experience at the heart of Hall's claim to prophetic authority seems to belong securely in a recognizably Catholic and medieval genre.

The other-worldly journey, in which a privileged visionary is able to travel, either in dream-state or bodily through the territories of the next life, and to return from them carrying cautionary messages for the living, is a much-studied phenomenon of late-medieval popular religious culture.[5] In addition to their sheer entertainment value, such visions served to underscore conventional morality by advertising the fate awaiting the lecherous, the gluttonous and the proud. They confirmed, in a particularly flamboyant way, the truth of the Church's teaching about purgatory, limbo, heaven, and hell, and they encouraged various forms of preparation for death, and intercession for the dead. They constituted, it has been aptly remarked, 'a folklore which had the imprimatur of the Church on it'.[6]

[4] Haigh, *Reformation and Resistance,* 168–9, 209, 219–20; R. Hollingworth, *Mancuniensis; or, An history of the towne of Manchester, and what is most memorable concerning it* (Manchester, 1839), 75–6.

[5] Howard Rollin Patch, *The Other World according to Descriptions in Medieval Literature* (Cambridge, MA, 1950, repr. New York, 1970); J. Le Goff, 'The Learned and Popular Dimensions of Journeys in the Otherworld in the Middle Ages', in Steven Laurence Kaplan, ed., *Understanding Popular Culture: Europe from the Middle Ages to the Nineteenth Century* (Berlin and New York, 1984), 19–37; A. Morgan, *Dante and the Medieval Other World* (Cambridge, 1990); Aron Gurevich, *Medieval Popular Culture: Problems of Belief and Perception,* transl. János M. Bak and Paul A. Hollingsworth (Cambridge, 1988), ch. 4: 'The *Divine Comedy* before Dante', 104–52; Gwenfair M. Walters, 'Visitacyons, Preuytes, and Deceytys: The Vision in Late Medieval English Popular Piety', unpublished Ph.D. thesis, University of Cambridge, 1992.

[6] Walters, 'The Vision in Late Medieval English Popular Piety', 21.

These traditions had by no means run their course by the generation into which Hall was born. Several well-established visionary accounts (*The Vision of the Monk of Evesham, The Pilgrimage of the Soul, The Gast of Guy*) were put into print in the last years of the fifteenth century, and some new ones continued to be written down.[7] In 1465, a Somerset gentleman, Edward Leversedge of Frome, lying sick with the 'plage of pestylence', felt his spirit to be 'raveschyd and departyd from my body'. His disembodied soul was then led by his 'good angell' through a valley filled with hostile demons, and up a high hill whence a ladder of crystalline stone led to a place of overpowering light. On the way he was admonished by the Virgin Mary about the perils of fashionable apparel and unchaste living.[8] A similar 'vision in a trance' was experienced in 1492 by a man called John Newton, like Leversedge 'vesited with the plage of pestelence'. An unspecified 'leder' guided Newton through a wilderness where souls were being tormented in numerous horrific ways. This, he was informed, was not hell, but purgatory, though he also saw there a place beyond a wall of crystal whence joyful souls passed up to heaven. Newton believed 'that he was walkyng bodely upon the erth' for the space of three days, a little longer than Hall's physical removal from his chamber of 'two nights & one day'. Interestingly, Newton was, like Hall, a draper, and hailed from Congleton, just across the Cheshire border from Hall's Manchester.[9]

Such accounts surely constitute the genus of which Ellis Hall's is a late evolved species, a medieval dinosaur alive and well in the Lost World of Elizabethan Lancashire. But there are a number of departures from the conventional patterning which should give us pause for thought. In the first place, Hall's tour through the otherworld took in heaven and hell, but made no mention of purgatory, focal point of the experiences of Leversedge, Newton and most other late-medieval visionaries. Indeed, this omission seems to have struck Bishop Grindal as odd. Hall was pressed for his views on a number of doctrinal matters '& especially of purgatorie, for it is like that if he sawe heaven & helle he shulde have seene purgatorie also if there be anye'. Grindal's mocking tone echoed the Protestant polemic which regularly

---

[7] Peter Marshall, *Beliefs and the Dead in Reformation England* (Oxford, 2002), 8.

[8] E. M. Thompson, 'The Vision of Edmund Leversedge', *Notes and Queries for Somerset and Devon* 9 (1904–5), 19–35.

[9] Oxford, Bodleian Library, MS Lat. Misc. c. 66, fols 21r–23v. See D. Marsh, 'Humphrey Newton of Newton and Pownall (1466–1536)', unpublished Ph.D. thesis, University of Keele, 1995, 311–17.

lambasted papists for their absurd and specious precision about the geography and topography of the next life – a theme much in evidence in a lively dialogue entitled *The Huntyng of Purgatorye to Death*, which John Veron, a prebendary of Grindal's cathedral of St Paul's, had published only the previous year.[10]

The vivid descriptions of purgatory in late-medieval visions often served a didactic purpose, inculcating the right understanding of the sacrament of penance and the importance of prayer for the dead. But doctrinal specifics of this kind are absent from the statements made by Hall. 'Beinge demaundett what his iugement is of the masse and of Transubstantiation', Hall refused to answer, saying he was commanded not to speak of those matters until he had delivered his book to the Queen.[11] Late-medieval visionaries usually journeyed through the otherworld with the assistance of a spiritual guide, an angel, saint or other departed soul, but Hall was swept up into heaven and carried down into hell without any such companion. Hall's account also seems out of tune with the dominant late-medieval English visionary tradition in its overtly apocalyptic refrain, the charge he received to preach 'repentaunce & amendment of lyfe' to people and magistrates alike because 'the daye drawethe nighe'.

There may be no great mystery here. The distinctive features and omissions of Hall's revelation are the product of his personal pathology, and of the fact that, unlike many medieval accounts, it comes to us relatively unmediated, without passing through the filter of scribal or clerical culture. But there is another possibility, and one which invites us to think again about the ways traditionally-minded parishioners may have responded to the reforming initiatives of the crown in the mid-sixteenth century. I wish to argue that Hall's revelations are difficult to fit unproblematically into a tradition of late-medieval visionary literature for the reason that they are closely patterned on the themes and phraeseology of vernacular Scripture.[12] The proposition seems at first glance perversely counter-intuitive. Hall confessed to Bishop Grindal 'that he hath nott muche redde in the byble', and to the

---

[10] MS Lat. Misc. c. 66, fols 155r–176r. For further examples, see my ' "The Map of God's Word": Geographies of the Afterlife in Tudor and Early Stuart England', in Bruce Gordon and Peter Marshall, eds, *The Place of the Dead: Death and Remembrance in Late Medieval and Early Modern Europe* (Cambridge, 2000), 110–30.

[11] SP 12/23/39.

[12] *Pace* the view of Alexandra Walsham in her entry on Hall for the new *DNB* that he 'showed little knowledge of the Bible', though I am immensely grateful to Dr Walsham for allowing me to see this in advance of publication.

authorities his 'ffallce Revelacions' and 'Counterfet practyce' represented the worst sort of unscriptural accretions to Christianity. But Hall's diffidence about his scriptural knowledge may have been the proper humility of the acolyte, rather than the grudging concession of the *illiteratus*. He went on to claim 'that he is hable havinge penne yncke & paper to write, & to cite and allege authorities forthe of the scripture', and there are grounds for taking him at his word.[13]

My point of entry here is the injunction Hall received right at the outset of his supernatural experiences: 'watche and pray'.[14] This, of course, is the charge which in the synoptic gospels Christ gives to the weary disciples in the garden of Gethsemane on the eve of his passion. He returns to repeat it three times, just as Hall heard a voice 'which spake these words unto me thre tymes havinge a lyttle dystance betwene them'. Immediately preceding the passion narratives in Matthew, Mark and Luke is the set of verses which modern biblical scholars term the 'eschatological discourse' or the 'synoptic apocalypse', an exposition of a final judgement with eternal life for the righteous and endless punishment for the ungodly.[15] Here too Mark has Jesus urging his disciples to 'watche and praye for ye knowe not when the tyme is'. Other passages in Hall's confessions suggest a close reflection on these signs of the impending end. Christ's warning that his disciples will be persecuted (Matt. 24: 9) is given to Hall *ad hominem* in the vision of 1552: 'thowe shalte be trobled & falle into persecjution'. Hall's anxiety that 'yf I shuld preach wryte or teach the thinge which I could not prove, neyther weare agreable to the scryptures, I shulde not be beleved' is conceivably connected with the synoptic apocalypse's warnings about the appearance of false prophets and messiahs. But his vision of Christ 'syttinge in his royall seate compassed abowte w[i]t[h] aungels' surely evokes the promise of 'the sonne of man commynge in the cloudes of heaven, with power and greate glorye' in Matt. 24: 30–31, sending forth his angels to 'gather together his chosen from the hyghest partes of heaven'. Indeed Hall had been assured that 'thow arte elect & chosen of god'. The revelation to Hall that 'the daye drawethe nighe' or

---

[13] The most frequently-printed version in the period before 1552 was the 'Great Bible', a 1541 edition of which (STC 2075) has been used for explicating Hall's statements, employing modern chapter and verse divisions.

[14] Tanner MS 50, fol. 16r has the alternative 'faste and pray' – conceivably a mistranscription, though this linkage too has scriptural resonances: Matt. 17: 21; Mark 9: 29; Luke 2: 37; Acts 10: 30; 13: 3; 14: 23; I Cor. 7: 5.

[15] Bruce M. Metzger and Michael D. Coogan, eds, *The Oxford Companion to the Bible* (New York and Oxford, 1993), 193; *The Jerusalem Bible: New Testament* (London, 1967), 69.

'draweth nere' is evocative of Christ's words in Matthew (26: 45) that 'the houre is at hande', and in Luke that 'the tyme draweth neare' and that when the Son of Man comes in glory 'loke up, and lyfte up your heades; for your redempcion draweth nye' (21: 8, 27–28). Hall may have been drawing on a wider range of biblical allusions, for there are echoes too in the epistle of James (5: 8) – 'the commyng of the Lord draweth nye' – as well as in the prophetic warning of Ezekiel that 'the tyme commeth, the daye draweth nye' (7: 12). Christ's injunction that Hall should 'aryse & mak thine accompte' is redolent of St Paul's monition (Rom. 14: 10–12) that every person will have to stand before the judgement seat of Christ and 'geve accomptes of hymselfe to God'. The vision of an angel 'havinge a book in his hand' and another asking 'whether the tyme weare com' calls to mind the angel in Revelation (5: 2), proclaiming 'Who is worthy to open the boke, and to lose the seales thereof?'

Ellis Hall may have been well into middle age before he had the opportunity to immerse himself in the Scripture in English. We do not know whether he owned a Bible, or whether he was one of those who went into his parish church to peruse the copy the Henrician and Edwardian injunctions had compelled parishes to acquire.[16] We cannot even be certain that his scriptural awareness was not absorbed in a primarily oral/aural context, though he was clearly literate. The full inwardness of his response to the Word of God in Scripture will always elude us, but it seems beyond question that it triggered an overpowering sense of personal vocation. Hall heard his name being called in the Scriptures, and perhaps in a rather literal way. Before the councillors he termed himself 'Elye otherwyse called Ellys Hawle', while to Grindal he confessed that 'his name emong[es] the comon people is (as he sayethe) Elizeus Halle, but he writethe him selfe Ely the Carpenters sonne'.

Hall's evident concern with these various redactions of his given name is interesting, and surely significant: recent work by historians such as Scott Smith-Bannister and Stephen Wilson has made clear the importance that early modern people attached to personal names and the messages and meanings they were believed to carry.[17] Ellis, the

---

16 Haigh, *Reformation and Resistance*, 114 argues that 'it is very unlikely that vernacular Bibles reached the county in any number'. The one surviving set of churchwardens' accounts (Prescot) gives no sign of a purchase until after the 1547 royal visitation (ibid., 115).

17 Scott Smith-Bannister, *Names and Naming Patterns in England 1538–1700* (Oxford, 1997); Stephen Wilson, *The Means of Naming: a Social and Cultural History of Personal Naming in Western Europe* (London, 1998).

name by which Hall seems to have been known in Lancashire, is an anglicization of Elias, the Greek transliteration of Elijah, while Eliseus is the latinate rendering of Elisha – both Elias and Eliseus were the forms used in early English translations of the Scripture.[18] Between them, Ely–Elias–Eliseus–Elijah wove a spiritual identity for Hall criss-crossing the Old and New Testaments. Hall's career as a prophet and visionary began with an unseen voice calling out to him three times in the night. An obvious biblical propotype suggests itself here: God's three-fold calling of Samuel, ward of the priest Eli, against whose house God threatens judgement for the iniquity of Eli's sons.[19] The word 'Eli' appears more poignantly in the New Testament, in the anguished Hebrew of the crucified Christ: 'Eli, Eli, lama sabachthani?' ('My God, my God, why hast thou forsaken me?': Matt. 27: 46). The bystanders misunderstand, and remark 'this man calleth for Helias . . . let us se whether Helyas will come and delyver him'. But it may be that Hall too felt in some sense this was a call meant for him. 'Elye thow Carpenters sonn' is the appellation with which Christ greets him in the vision. Perhaps, as historians have assumed, Hall was indeed the son of a carpenter, but the phrase surely has more intimate and compelling associations. 'Is not this the carpenters sonne?', the crowd in Nazareth disparagingly ask when Jesus returns to teach there, a prophet without honour in his own country (Matt. 13: 55).

But ultimately it was in the guise of the prophet Elijah that Hall understood the pattern of what he was being called to undertake. In almost the last words of the Hebrew Old Testament, Hall would have encountered God's promise in the mouth of Malachi (4: 5): 'Behold, I will sende you Elias the prophet before the commynge of the daye of the great and fearful Lorde'. The New Testament abounds with references to the appearance of Elijah as the herald of the last days (Matt. 16: 14; 17: 10–12; Mark 6: 15; 8: 28; 9: 11–13; Luke 9: 8, 19; John 1: 21, 25). Moreover, at the Transfiguration, the disciples were accorded a vision of Elijah/Elias, Peter foolishly offering to erect him a tabernacle (Matt. 17: 2–5; Mark 9: 3–7; Luke 9: 29–34). Hall's vision of the glorified Christ is surely heavily indebted to the Transfiguration narratives, in its

---

[18] E. G. Withycombe, *The Oxford Dictionary of English Christian Names* (3rd edn, Oxford, 1977); Patrick Hanks and Flavia Hodges, *A Dictionary of First Names* (Oxford, 1990). 'Elys Hall' was junior constable of Manchester in 1557: *A Volume of Court Leet Records of the Manor of Manchester in the Sixteenth Century*, ed. John Harland, Chetham Society os 63 (Manchester, 1864), 170.

[19] I Kgs 3: 1–18 = I Sam. in AV.

references to the appearance of a dazzling light, to 'a man clothed in white', and to a 'veale or courteyne drawn betwene me & the light', corresponding in the Gospels to a cloud that overshadowed the disciples. We can only speculate as to whether Elijah's charge to convert King Ahab has any connection with Hall's mission as 'a mesenger sente from godde to the Quene & to all princes', or whether he used the name Eliseus to indicate that he, like the prophet Elisha, was Elijah's chosen successor. But the Manchester draper's close identification of himself with the Old Testament prophet and harbinger of the Second Coming must be considered settled by the manner of his bodily ascent to the judgement seat of Christ: 'Elia went up thorow the whyrlewynde into heaven';[20] so too did Ellis Hall, 'taken owt of my bed as it were in a tufte of feathers with a worlewynde up into heaven'.[21]

There is then, I would argue, a close and complex pattern of scriptural 'self-fashioning' underlying the delusions of grandeur that impelled an obscure Lancashire draper to pursue his fifteen minutes of fame on the national stage. But what in the end does this tell us? Was Bishop Grindal prejudicial and premature in declaring Hall to be 'of the popishe Iugement in Religion', and have historians like Christopher Haigh been too eager to see him as an extreme but yet somehow representative type, 'an anguished Catholic' taking a stand against the Reformation? Due to the non-survival of the 'greate booke' of Hall's revelations it is simply impossible to say for certain. In his two appearances before the authorities, the acknowledged themes are fasting and prayer, 'dewtye towardes god', 'vertuous lyvinge', 'baptisme repentaunce & amendment of lyfe', the forsaking of 'all thinges pleasante to the flesshe'. Stripped of their apocalyptic wrapping, these are the common denominators of early modern Christian morality. Hall's implicit advocation of a works-based soteriology, along with his allusion to the Five Wounds of Christ, seems to place him in a distinctly traditionalist milieu, but on points of disputed doctrine, as on the question of his conformity to the established Church, he maintained a studied silence.

Was Hall a Catholic, a 'papist' even? The ambiguities of the case serve as a warning to Reformation historians that they should exercise

---

20 IV Kgs 2: 11 = II Kgs in AV.
21 Tanner MS 50, fol. 16v. Strype, *Annals*, I.2: 196, suggested that the gown of skins worn in the pillory was 'perhaps in mockery to him, calling himself Elias, and going in camel's hair, in imitation of that prophet.' For later examples of *soi-disant* prophets claiming to be Elijah, see Bauckham, *Tudor Apocalypse*, 187; Walsham, *Providence*, 204.

caution before seeking to ascribe pristine confessional labels to their subjects, particularly in the case of those like Hall whose lives spanned the reigns of all five Tudor monarchs, and whose adult experience was thus of a bewildering succession of advances, reversals and false-starts in ecclesiastical policy. In many ways this hardly seems necessary advice. In recent years the work of David Cressy, Norman Jones, Alexandra Walsham, Tessa Watt and others has encouraged us to identify distinct traces of pre-Reformation religious culture in the private and public discourses of post-Reformation England, to see the lived cultural impact of the English Reformation as one of gradual accomodation rather than of rapid conversion or rabid resistance.[22] But the celestial journey of Ellis Hall invites us to look at these processes of religious inculturation through the other end of the telescope. It reveals not a slow and ameliorating acceptance of enforced change, but rather the capacity of a long-established cultural form – the revelation of an otherwordly journey – to appropriate, absorb and adapt elements of the 'new learning'. It also suggests how an acute interest in vernacular Scripture might be neither the mark nor the making of a predictably evangelical Protestant. In Ellis Hall we appear to have an example of that classic Reformation type: a mid-Tudor layman galvanized into thinking afresh about retribution, repentance and reconciliation, both personal and collective, through his encounter with the Word of God in Scripture. Yet in this, and perhaps other cases, the conjunction did not lead in the directions that contemporary reformers would have wished, or that modern historians have come to expect.

University of Warwick

---

[22] David Cressy, *Bonfires and Bells: National Memory and the Protestant Calendar in Elizabethan and Stuart England* (London, 1989); Norman L. Jones, *The English Reformation: Religion and Cultural Adaptation* (Oxford, 2002); Walsham, *Providence*; Tessa Watt, *Cheap Print and Popular Piety 1550–1640* (Cambridge, 1991; 2nd edn, 1993).

DID CALVINISTS HAVE A GUILT COMPLEX?
REFORMED RELIGION, CONSCIENCE
AND REGULATION IN
EARLY MODERN EUROPE

by GRAEME MURDOCK

THIS essay assesses ideas and evidence about the response of Calvinists to sin during the Early Modern period. It takes as a starting-point the analysis provided by Max Weber about the development of Reformed salvation theology in later Calvinism. Weber suggested that Calvinists came to connect the eternal fate of their souls with their behaviour on earth, and attempted to exert systematic controls over their own conduct. Calvinists, Weber argued, developed a mind-set of methodical self-analysis and exhibited constant vigilance, concern and guilt about ongoing sin. Some early modern Calvinists certainly did demonstrate this highly refined personal anxiety about their wrong-doing, and worried about what their lack of enthusiasm and commitment to true religion and moral conduct might mean. However, most Reformed ministers across the Continent seem to have been rather more concerned that members of their congregations did not feel guilty enough about their sins, and alongside encouraging self-discipline through sermons and catechizing, turned to elders and, where possible, to state authorities, to enforce high standards of morality on often recalcitrant parishioners.

I will first briefly describe Calvin's ideas about salvation and Weber's analysis of the impact of later predestination theology. Evidence which supports the view that Calvinism produced characters who internalized these theological insights, and who responded by attempting to impose strict self-discipline on their thoughts and behaviour will then be assessed. However, it will be argued that, across most of the Calvinist world, moral discipline was not only a private matter for individual reflection but also an institutionalized, community project, which was more concerned with external forms of behaviour than with internal systems of belief, and which was not driven by any great attention to ideas about predestination. I will consider the value of consistory records in revealing the behaviour and intentions of early modern Calvinists, and suggest that the demands made on individuals to repent

of their sins were increasingly bolstered by a return to detailed regulation of external conduct. This reaction followed the perceived failure of
reform to effect significant moral change in Calvinist congregations,
and was undertaken where possible in alliance with secular authorities.
I will highlight this process by looking at the attitudes of Reformed
clergy in Geneva and France to the challenge posed to the moral health
of their communities by abuses in clothing and appearance.

Calvin's theology asserted that God is an all-mighty, all-knowing
power, whose sovereignty extends over the span of human life and over
the history of the universe. God has determined, through his sovereign
will, the fate of the souls of all his created children, and has chosen
those whom he has desired to save from a fallen humanity. Those
divine decrees cannot be altered by any individual's will or action, nor
are God's decisions bound by prior knowledge of the lives which individuals were to lead, nor can individuals discern God's judgement on
their souls while they are alive. As Calvin made clear in the *Institutes of
the Christian Religion,* God's eternal decrees of predestination are
'founded on his free mercy, without any respect to human worth'.
During their lives, Christians were charged to believe in their creator
God, to trust in his justice, and to look to their saviour Jesus Christ for
the hope of salvation. Faith in Christ would turn their hearts from sin,
and lead them to aspire after piety and live according to God's
commands.[1]

Calvin's explanation of salvation and predestination was challenged
by any number of theologians within the Reformed tradition from
Jerome Bolsec to Jacobus Arminius, and also by confessional opponents.
Such challenges led to an increasingly dogmatic expression of
Reformed orthodoxy, which was defended, clarified, elaborated and
rationalised in the heat of polemic debate from the tracts of Theodore
Beza to the resolutions of the synod of Dordrecht.[2] Calvin had advised
against searching 'hidden recesses of the divine wisdom' about the
predestined fate of individual souls, and suggested that this ought not to

---

[1] John Calvin, *Institutes of the Christian Religion* (Geneva, 1559), 3/24/7, transl. Henry
Beveridge, 3 vols (Edinburgh, 1845), 2: 540. For biographies of Calvin see William J.
Bouwsma, *John Calvin. A Sixteenth-Century Portrait* (Oxford, 1988), and François Wendel,
Calvin: the Origins and Development of his Religious Thought (London, 1963).

[2] Philip C. Holtrop, *The Bolsec Controversy on Predestination, from 1551 to 1555: the Statements of Jerome Bolsec, and the Responses of John Calvin, Theodore Beza, and other Reformed Theologians,* 2 vols (Lewiston, NY, 1993); John S. Bray, *Theodore Beza's Doctrine of Predestination*
(Nieuwkoop, 1975); Joel R. Beeke, *Assurance of Faith: Calvin, English Puritanism and the Dutch
Second Reformation* (New York, 1991).

be a matter which ministers focused on in sermons and teaching. He argued:

> But what proof have you of your election? When once this thought has taken possession of any individual, it keeps him perpetually miserable, subjects him to dire torment, or throws him into a state of complete stupor.[3]

However, some Reformed theologians, for example William Perkins, plunged headlong into the abyss marked out by Calvin, and took up the question of how men and women might know whether they were saved or not as a pastoral issue in tracts on practical divinity. Perkins suggested that any sense of assurance on the part of believers about their future salvation did not in fact have to wait until death, and that there were signs of election among those predestined to be saved under a covenant of grace which bore fruit in believers' lives.[4]

This increase in the attention given to ideas about predestination, which took place only in some parts of the Reformed world, led to a variety of intellectual and social responses. One extreme reaction pointed towards antinomianism, with some reckoning that whatever they did, God was going to save them. More commonly, preaching on the signs of election tended to encourage the reconnection of moral behaviour with the scheme of salvation. This emphasis stimulated perfectionism and the perception that a visible boundary between those God was going to save and those he was going to damn was apparent in people's everyday conduct and commitment to spiritual exercises. This tradition was notably present in the deformed Calvinist Church in England, which lacked the institutional framework for the regulation of community discipline which for other Calvinists was an essential mark of a true Church.[5] Patterns of self-regulation and group-regulation filled this vacuum, marked most strongly among those self-obsessed enough to compose daily accounts of their lives.[6]

---

[3] Calvin, *Institutes*, 3/24/4, 2: 585.

[4] I. Breward, 'The Significance of William Perkins', *Journal of Religious History* 4 (1966–7), 113–28; Richard A. Muller, *Christ and the Decree. Christology and Predestination in Reformed Theology from Calvin to Perkins* (Durham, NC, 1986).

[5] Scottish Confession of Faith (1560) and Belgic Confession of Faith (1561) in *Reformed Confessions of the 16th Century*, ed. Arthur C. Cochrane (London, 1966), 176–7, 210.

[6] Patrick Collinson, *The Puritan Character. Polemics and Polarities in Early Seventeenth-Century English Culture* (Los Angeles, CA, 1989); idem, *The Elizabethan Puritan Movement* (Oxford, 1990); Peter Lake, *Moderate Puritans and the Elizabethan Church* (Cambridge, 1982); idem, 'Calvinism and the English Church 1570–1635', *Past and Present* 114 (1987), 32–76;

While authors of spiritual autobiographies can hardly be taken as typical of early modern Calvinists in England or elsewhere, Richard Rogers serves as a useful example of this religious culture. Rogers, educated at Christ's College, Cambridge, was suspended from the ministry at Wethersfield in Essex for his presbyterianism by Archbishop John Whitgift in 1583, and was called before High Commission in 1598. Rogers wrote some treatises on Christian living, and kept a journal full of accounts of successes and failures in a mostly private and internal war between his mind, heart and body. Rogers' anxiety and uncertainty about his own character emerges almost daily, as on 18 August 1587, when he recorded that

> we may observe by exper[ience] that even the most zealous doe somewhat in time decline and waxe remisse in careinge for the matters of God. . . . For mine owne part, I see cause to feare this in my self, and I hope I will look more diligently to my selfe than I have done and weane my selfe from some lawfull profites and pleasures, much more to mak[e] more consc[ience] of such as be unlawful, yea even of thoughts which are with delight in thinges that ought not to be.[7]

However, on 30 August, the next entry in Rogers' journal records that, despite this stated commitment to continue in a 'godly manner', on riding to London with his wife, 'wandringe by litle and litle in needlesse speach, somewhat of my former fervency was abated'. Rogers noted how easy it was to backslide and, but for a fast held on his return home, 'I thinck I should have further fallen some wayes'.[8] Again on 12 September that year Rogers wrote that

> this after noone I felt a strongue desire to injoy more liberty in thinkinge uppon some vaine thinges which I had lately weaned my selfe from . . . and if I had not either written this immediately, or by some other means mett with it, I had allmost been gone from this course and become planely minded and idle as before.[9]

By 29 November, Rogers' battle to watch over his heart had still made

---

Philip Benedict, *The Faith and Fortunes of France's Huguenots, 1600–85* (Aldershot, 2001), 208–28.

[7] 'The Diary of Richard Rogers', in *Two Elizabethan Puritan Diaries by Richard Rogers and Samuel Ward*, ed. Marshall Mason Knappen (Chicago, 1933), 57.

[8] Ibid., 58.

[9] Ibid., 59–60.

little progress; 'I saw that the love of worldly th[ings] cleaveth so neer to my hart that I must purge it out strongulier than yet it hath been'. Rogers' diary thus provides an account of his ongoing struggle to live by his constant motivation to serve God, and not be swayed by temporary emotion and desires.[10]

Richard Rogers' search for certainty about salvation and guilty reckoning of ongoing sin and moments of tepid religiosity was later reflected in the words of the 1646 Westminster *Confession of Faith*, which described the long struggle which faced true believers before they could gain assurance of grace.[11] The generations of Calvinists in England from the 1580s to the 1640s were, according to Max Weber in *The Protestant Ethic and the Spirit of Capitalism*, those who began to create a conviction about their salvation not, as did Catholics, through a gradual accumulation of individual good works to one's credit, but rather through systematic self-control which was thought to be a fruit of election. As Weber put it, 'the God of Calvinism demanded of his believers not single good works, but a life of good works combined into a unified system'.[12]

Weber therefore argued that Calvinism demanded a 'rational asceticism', in which all aspects of life were subjected to examination as to whether they were in accordance with God's will. According to Weber, ideas of calling or vocation in this context had the effect of sacralizing worldly activity. Callings had to be lived out with self-discipline, sobriety, decency and anti-eroticism. Weber also suggested that Calvinists were called not to struggle against the rational acquisition of wealth but were to restrict their consumption of goods to non-luxurious purposes. For Weber, these Calvinist beliefs structured patterns of behaviour which eventually helped to form the formalistic, hard, correct character of the Western capitalist bourgeoisie, and provided the source of their sober economic virtue and utilitarian worldliness. Weber concluded that Calvinism more than any other system of religious belief held an elective affinity with the spirit of capitalism, which he described as the desire to seek profit rationally and systematically.[13]

---

[10] Ibid., 65.

[11] *The Westminster Confession of Faith* (1646), ch. 18: '. . . a true believer may wait long and conflict with many difficulties' before receiving assurance that they are in a state of grace.

[12] Max Weber, *The Protestant Ethic and the Spirit of Capitalism*, transl. T. Parsons (s.i., 1930; repr. London, 1996), 115. See also E. Troeltsch, 'Calvin and Calvinism', *The Hibbert Journal* 8 (1909–10), 102–21.

[13] Weber, *Protestant Ethic*, 98–128, 155–85; Michael H. Lessnoff, *The Spirit of Capitalism*

Some of England's Puritans perhaps most closely match the model of early modern Calvinist belief and behaviour identified by Weber. However, the Church in England lacked the key institution of Reformed moral discipline, the congregational consistory. In much of the rest of the Reformed world, the work of these disciplinary bodies offers a very different perspective on the responses of ordinary people to Reformed teaching about sin and salvation. The goal of consistorial discipline was to provide clear guidance about normative behaviour within a Christian community, and to challenge offenders against those norms to offer heart-felt repentance of their wrong-doing. Ministers were charged to respond to the sins of members of their congregations in their sermons, catechism classes, and prayers, and to work with elders to cajole, warn, investigate and confront offenders. At first, wrong-doers were commonly only required to offer a sincere apology for their misconduct to an elder or the minister in private. If this apology seemed unsatisfactory or the sinful behaviour continued, then the oxygen of publicity was applied to engender appropriate guilt, embarrassment and repentance. If being compelled to repent before the whole consistory still failed to stimulate a change in lifestyle, offenders were then temporarily excluded from participation in Communion.

Re-admission to the Christian community normally required offenders to appear in church in front of all their neighbours and describe what they had done wrong and how sorry they were about it. A few weeks of this public humiliation for the most serious offences, which was sometimes also marked by wearing a hood, or sack-cloth, or by carrying a torch or going bare-legged while having their offences denounced by ministers, was seen to be the best means to help the most recalcitrant to express true repentance and have their offences forgiven by God and his Church. Ministers and elders only very infrequently gave up altogether on members of their congregations, and rarely imposed the ultimate sanction of permanent excommunication on reprobate offenders as beyond hope of redemption.[14]

A range of historians have undertaken analysis of surviving consis-

and the Protestant Ethic. An Enquiry into the Weber Thesis (Cambridge, 1994); David Little, 'Max Weber Revisited. The "Protestant Ethic" and the Puritan Experience of Order', *HThR* 59 (1966), 415–28; Gordon Marshall, *In Search of the Spirit of Capitalism: an Essay on Max Weber's Protestant Ethic* (Aldershot, 1982; repr. 1993); Malcolm H. MacKinnon, 'The Longevity of the Thesis: a Critique of the Critics', in Hartmut Lehmann and Guenther Roth, eds, *Weber's Protestant Ethic: Origins, Evidence, Contexts* (Cambridge, 1993), 211–43; Gianfranco Poggi, *Calvinism and the Capitalist Spirit: Max Weber's Protestant Ethic* (London, 1983).
[14] Raymond A. Mentzer, ed., *Sin and the Calvinists: Morals Control and the Consistory in the*

tory records across the Continent to attempt to reconstruct how Reformed beliefs alongside the activities of the Church's disciplinary bodies affected behaviour in Calvinist communities. The results of this work certainly confirm the extent of the commitment of clergy and elders to the project of moral discipline. Some local records have permitted historians to identify differences in the impact of Reformed discipline on men and women, on the social elite and ordinary people, and on people in towns and in the countryside. They have also noted the range and proportion of those brought under discipline by their local elders for a variety of religious and moral offences such as sexual misconduct, swearing, violence, arguing with their neighbours, drinking to excess and gambling.[15]

However, statistical analysis of these formal records of consistorial action only reveals part of the story of Calvinist discipline, and fails to take account of the many informal warnings given by elders or of unrecorded disciplinary action undertaken by consistories.[16] Consistory records also only infrequently offer sufficient detail about any individual's life and offences to construct any sort of account of how and why their behaviour may have changed over time. For example, what should be made of Jean Maupille, who was repeatedly brought before his local consistory at Coutras in south-western France in the 1580s for dancing? Maupille apologised for his offence, then re-offended, offered a formal apology before the congregation, then immediately re-offended, was given a final warning about his behaviour, and then disappears from the consistory records altogether. Had Maupille become a reformed character, full of sincere regret for his sin of dancing, and for challenging

Reformed Tradition (Kirksville, MO, 1994); Robert White, 'Oil and Vinegar: Calvin on Church Discipline', *Scottish Journal of Theology* 38 (1985), 25–40.

15 K. M. Brown, 'In Search of the Godly Magistrate in Reformation Scotland', *JEH* 40 (1989), 553–81; B. Vogler and J. Estèbe, 'La Genèse d'une société protestante: étude comparée de quelques registres consistoriaux Languedociens et Palatins vers 1600', *Annales* 31 (1976), 362–88; Geoffrey Parker, 'The 'Kirk by Law Established' and the Origins of 'the Taming of Scotland': St Andrews, 1559–1600', in Leah Leneman, ed., *Perspectives in Scottish Social History: Essays in Honour of Rosalind Mitchison* (Aberdeen, 1988), 1–33; Michael F. Graham, 'Equality before the Kirk? Church Discipline and the Elite in Reformation-Era Scotland', *Archiv für Reformationsgeschichte* 84 (1993), 289–309; Heinz Schilling, *Civic Calvinism in Northwestern Germany and the Netherlands. Sixteenth to Nineteenth Centuries*, Sixteenth Century Essays and Studies 17 (Kirksville, MO, 1991).

16 Judith Pollmann, 'Off the Record: Problems in the Quantification of Calvinist Church Discipline', *Sixteenth Century Journal* 23 (2002), 428–38; Heinz Schilling, ' "History of Crime" or "History of Sin"? – Some Reflections on the Social History of Early Modern Church Discipline', in E. I. Kouri and Tom Scott, eds, *Politics and Society in Reformation Europe: Essays for Sir Geoffrey Elton on his Sixty-Fifth Birthday* (Basingstoke, 1987), 289–306.

the consistory's power? Or, had the Church's persistence merely won an empty victory of resentful acquiescence, or had Maupille merely learned to evade his elders' attention and continued to dance in secret?[17] Given the problems for elders to assess the quality of repentance offered before them in consistory meetings, the room for historians to offer any judgement on such cases is limited, and when the records fall silent, it becomes almost impossible to assess the motivation behind the behaviour of early modern Calvinists.

Charting the impact of congregational discipline on an individual basis seems very difficult, and contemporary assessments on the overall impact of the work of consistories on Reformed communities also varied wildly. Some visitors to Geneva, where the consistory only operated with the council's full support from the mid-1550s, offered very rosy opinions on the city as 'the maist perfyt schoole of Chryst'.[18] Towards the end of his life, Calvin himself argued that the two most important elements of reform in the city had been the consistory and the catechism. However, despite the best efforts of Geneva's elders to encourage and enforce moral discipline, and decades of preaching and catechizing, Calvin remained distinctly unimpressed by the behaviour of Genevans, and in one sermon described the impiety of the city as like 'seeing down a chasm into the very mouth of hell'.[19]

One issue which seemed to Calvin to present endless problems and opportunities for sin was clothing. After first highlighting Calvin's views on apparel and appearance, the reaction of the Reformed clergy to the apparent failure of Genevans to abandon sinful behaviour in how

[17] This document is edited by Alfred Soman, 'Le Registre consistorial de Coutras, 1582–1584', *Bulletin de la Société de l'Histoire du Protestantisme Français* 126 (1980), 209–12.
[18] John Knox's letter to Anne Locke of December 1556, in *The Works of John Knox*, ed. David Laing, 6 vols (Edinburgh, 1846–64), 4 (1855): 240–1; J. H. Hexter, 'Utopia and Geneva', in Theodore K. Raab and Jerrold E. Siegel, eds, *Action and Conviction in Early Modern Europe. Essays in Memory of E. H. Harbison* (Princeton, NJ, 1969), 77–89; Nicolas Bouvier, 'Geneva', in idem, Gordon A. Craig and Lionel Gossman, eds, *Geneva, Zurich, Basel: History, Culture and National Identity* (Princeton, NJ, 1994), 17–40; Francis Higman, 'The Origins of the Image of Geneva', in John B. Roney and Martin I. Klauber, eds, *The Identity of Geneva. The Christian Commonwealth, 1564–1864* (Westport, CT, 1998), 21–38.
[19] Robert M. Kingdon, 'The Control of Morals in Calvin's Geneva', in Lawrence P. Buck and Jonathan W. Zophy, eds, *The Social History of the Reformation* (Columbus, OH, 1972), 3–16; idem, 'Calvin and the Establishment of Consistory Discipline in Geneva: the Institutions and the Men who Directed it', *Nederlands Archief voor Kerkgeschiedenis* 70 (1990), 158–72; E. William Monter, 'Women in Calvinist Geneva (1550–1800)', *Signs* 6 (1980), 189–209; idem, 'The Consistory of Geneva, 1559–1569', *Bibliothèque d'Humanisme et Renaissance* 38 (1976), 476–84; Jeffrey R. Watt, 'Women and the Consistory in Calvin's Geneva', *Sixteenth Century Journal* 24 (1993), 429–39.

they dressed will be considered. Calvinists, or indeed Churches, did not of course hold any monopoly of interest in individuals' appearance and dress. In early modern societies clothing was a crucial means of establishing, and reflecting, social rank, gender identity, ethnic difference and occupational group. State laws had been commonly established across the Continent which set out the various colours, fabrics and decorations which different social ranks were allowed to use in items of clothing.[20]

However, Reformed Churches took a particular concern to check the immorality of abuses in clothing and appearance for a number of reasons. Clothes and sin had been intimately connected from the beginning of society, as clothing was an immediate consequence of Adam's rebellion against God. Clothes were the result of sin, made necessary by human corruption, but also the cause of sin, if God's gift of clothing was abused (Gen. 3: 7–21). Sumptuous apparel was seen as a particular problem, a sign of pride, vanity, selfishness and self-indulgence. Inappropriate and immodest display of the body risked encouraging sexual appetites in others, and revealed a shamelessness and indecency in the wearer. Economic and social injustices were also laid at the door of excesses in the luxurious consumption of clothing which replaced appropriate charitable concern for the poor. Immorality was also seen to occur when people ignored or challenged how clothing marked out differences in the social hierarchy.

Calvin had plenty to say about clothing in tracts, sermons and commentaries. He particularly instructed ministers to give a good example to their communities in their everyday dress, and Theodore Beza thought it important to comment in his biography of Calvin that the reformer's clothes were 'neither careful nor mean, but such as became his singular modesty'.[21] Calvin also required ministers to abandon wearing traditional liturgical vestments during church services to avoid giving the impression to the congregation that the clergy had any special powers, especially important during Communion services. However, rather than wear everyday clothing in church, clergy in Geneva and across the Reformed world instead came to wear

---

[20] For a view of sumptuary laws as a secular project against conspicuous consumption see Alan Hunt, *Governance of the Consuming Passions: a History of Sumptuary Law* (Basingstoke, 1996); idem, 'Moralizing Luxury: the Discourses of the Governance of Consumption', *Journal of Historical Sociology* 8 (1995), 352–74.

[21] Theodore Beza, *Life of John Calvin* (Geneva, 1564) in *Tracts Relating to the Reformation*, ed. Henry Beveridge, 3 vols (Edinburgh, 1844–51), 1 (1844): xcvii.

loose-fitting, full-sleeved, black gowns. This reflected Calvin's view that the clergy ought to appear as a professionally-trained, disciplined, preaching elite.[22]

Calvin also set out broad ethical principles for the consumption of goods. He insisted that Christians must learn 'to avoid squandering their resources in unnecessary expenditure', arguing that God 'has commanded frugality and temperance to us and prohibited luxuriating wantonly in abundance'. In a short tract of 1546 or 1547, 'On Luxury', he also reflected on Classical and Biblical sources which advised a frugal and moderate attitude to clothing and appearance.[23] Calvin advised neither excessive luxury nor excessive austerity in attitudes towards clothing. He demanded that everyone ought to be 'exhorted to forgo superfluous pomp and vain foolishness', suggesting that 'those who exert great effort in caring for the body are not much concerned about the cultivation of the soul'. He required that attitudes towards dress should lie closer to a humble simplicity than to luxury, suggesting that if 'you have cultivated your appearance with great care, you should be ashamed to be outdone by many animals, and ashamed that there is nothing in your clothing to show frugality'.[24] Calvin also argued that while 'a filthy and torn garment dishonoureth a man, a handsome and clean garment doth greatly beautify him', but on the other hand wrote that 'it's no sweet smell always to have a sweet smell'.[25]

Calvin's comments identified true beauty with modest decorum in clothes and with cleanliness. These positive injunctions directed Calvinists away from paying undue attention to their appearance, and towards conforming to customary standards of dress according to their social status. Calvin also provided a series of negative statements about the perils of certain forms of dress and appearance. He suggested, for example, that a 'few things need to be said about the honest use of a mirror', and that 'we are worse than children [who are] delighted with

---

22 Graeme Murdock, 'Dressed to Repress? Protestant Clergy Dress and the Regulation of Morality in Early Modern Europe', *Fashion Theory. The Journal of Dress, Body and Culture* 2 (2000), 179–99; Paul Romane-Musculus, 'Histoire de la robe pastorale et du rabat', *Bulletin de la Société de l'Histoire du Protestantisme Français* 115 (1969), 307–38.

23 John Calvin, 'De Luxu' (1546/7), in Ford Lewis Battles, 'Against Luxury and Licence in Geneva. A Forgotten Fragment of Calvin', *Interpretation* 19 (1965), 182–202, 192–5; see also the translation by Mary Beaty and Benjamin W. Farley, *Calvin's Ecclesiastical Advice* (Edinburgh, 1991). Calvin's sources included reflections on Cato's opposition to the repeal of the Oppian Law, which had introduced restrictions on women's dress in response to Hannibal's attack on Italy.

24 Ibid., 193 and transl., 83–7.

25 Ibid., 192, 195.

cheap necklaces; we go in for expensive absurdities'. Wearing sumptuous clothing also harmed the poor, and Calvin warned that 'your whole body has become infected [with the blood of the poor] because it is decked out in such clothing'.[26] Calvin was also concerned about clothing which disguised the wearer's appearance:

> How many persons are there who – if one should deprive them of clothing or of hair – would not think their very limbs torn off, so that now they no longer seem the same to themselves? This is the slave dealer's art; to hide defects under some sort of finery.[27]

Clothing could also lead to sexual immorality, through the 'seduction of another's modesty with wanton dress and obscene gestures and foul speech'.[28] Calvin followed texts in the New Testament which particularly advised modesty for women in dress, and objected to the claim that women were only trying to please their husbands by dressing in finery.[29] Calvin also paid significant attention to how men dressed. He quoted Seneca with approval that 'elegant dress is not a manly adornment'. He wrote against long hair for men, and was concerned that items which used to be carried around only by women are 'now a man's baggage, nay a soldier's pack'. Those who gave too much concern to their appearance were rendered 'effeminate and dissolute', and again 'not effeminate but castrated', and not only 'weakened by soft living but emasculated'.[30] Clothing's Catholic past was also of concern to Calvin. He thought that the attention previously given to clothing had misdirected spirituality from the Gospel and the sacraments onto the material world of images and their clothing and appearance. Calvin spoke out against the pomp of traditional funeral attire, and attacked how priests and monks had sought sanctity from vestments, tonsures, hoods and tunics.[31]

---

[26] Ibid., 193–5.

[27] Ibid., 193–4.

[28] Ibid., 201, using the *Institutes* 2/8/41–4.

[29] 1 Tim. 2: 9–10 and 1 Peter 3: 3–4; cf. Marie-Lucile de Gallatin, 'Les Ordonnances somptuaires à Genève au xvie siècle', *Mémoires et documents publiés par la Société d'Histoire et d'Archéologie de Genève* 36 (1938), 193–275, 198–9.

[30] Calvin, 'De Luxu', 192–3, 195. See also Deut. 22: 5.

[31] John Calvin, *Advertissement tresutile du grand proffit qui reviendroit à la Chrestienté s'il se faisoit inventaire de tous les corps sainctz, et reliques, qui sont tant en Italie, qu'en France, Allemaigne, Hespaigne, et autre Royaumes et Pays* (Geneva, 1543), ed. Francis M. Higman in *Jean Calvin. Three French Treatises* (London, 1970), 49–97, 49; Calvin, 'De Luxu', 194.

Calvin expressed concern about the potential consequences for Geneva if offences related to clothing went uncorrected. This was based on the dire warnings of judgement given in Isaiah 3 in response to excesses in the appearance of the women of Judah. Calvin warned that God would soon intervene to correct Geneva's faults in apparel, if people proved unwilling to act themselves.[32] Calvin offered advice about the need for moral clothing in Geneva, and gave guidance on the principles for reform. He was, however, certain that issuing specific and detailed laws would not be of any use:

> . . . we cannot pass a certain law to say that this is prohibited, that is permitted: to see treatment in minute detail of each thing. One might well in general extract an unerring principle: but if one wanted to decipher all this fine baggage of the apparel of women, what would that be?[33]

Calvin had also argued in the *Institutes* that individual consciences should not be entangled by the need to observe detailed rules in matters which were indifferent to salvation. Although it was of no consequence in the sight of God 'whether they are clothed in red or in black', Christians were not 'to roll and wallow in luxury' or to use their liberty over things indifferent as a cloak for their lust. This was especially dangerous for the wealthy, since 'there is scarcely any one whose means allow him to live sumptuously, who . . . does not plume himself amazingly on his splendour'.[34] However, Calvin concluded that without an understanding of true Christian liberty

> . . . our consciences will have no rest, there will be no end of superstition. In the present day many think us absurd in raising a question as to the free eating of flesh, the free use of dress and holidays, and similar frivolous trifles, as they think them; but they are of more importance than is commonly supposed. For when once the conscience is entangled in the net, it enters a long and inextricable labyrinth, from which it is afterwards most difficult to escape. When a man begins to doubt whether it is lawful for him to use linen sheets, shirts, napkins, and handkerchiefs, he will not long be secure as to hemp, and will at last have doubts as to tow [sackcloth].[35]

---

32 De Gallatin, 'Ordonnances somptuaires', 198.
33 Ibid., 200.
34 Calvin, *Institutes* (1559), 3/19/9, 2: 436–8.
35 Ibid., 3/19/7, 2: 434.

However, some regulations against specific items of dress, in particular slashed clothes, were introduced in Geneva during the 1550s. The council, apparently without prompting from the Company of Pastors, introduced some further regulations in 1558. Although Calvin had warned against trying to compose and enforce regulations on clothing, Nicolas des Gallars was then delegated by the consistory to consult with the council about how to provide some remedy against luxurious consumption in Geneva.[36] The resulting city regulations of 1560 were later translated into English by the exile Robert Field. As Field explained, preaching in Geneva ought to have sufficed to inspire Christian behaviour, but experience had shown that many continued to offend through excessive drinking and by wearing sumptuous clothing. Proclamations were thus needed to get the people of the city to turn from their love of excess which could provoke divine wrath. The 1560 ordinances therefore compelled Genevans to dress honestly, simply, and according to their rank, under threat of fines. The immodesty of slashed garments, the use of foreign clothing, and excesses of costly decoration, golden jewellery, and extravagant hairstyles and head-dresses were particularly highlighted, and no-one was to wear more than two rings, except on their wedding day.[37]

Despite Calvin's view that regulations which tried to provide a detailed differentiation between moral and immoral clothing would prove pointless and even counter-productive, Geneva's regulations on clothing were soon extended and became more and more detailed, especially once Calvin was safely dead. Already by 1562 some clarification had proved necessary on exactly what sort of head-dresses and bracelets were permitted for women in the city. These laws also explained that it had only been intended in 1560 to outlaw silver and gold chains worn around shirt collars out of pride, but not to ban silver belts which were merely worn to be useful.[38] Twelve days after Calvin's

[36] On Geneva see E. William Monter, *Calvin's Geneva* (2nd edn, Huntington, NY, 1975); Gillian Lewis, 'Calvinism in Geneva in the Time of Calvin and Beza, 1541–1608', in Menna Prestwich, ed., *International Calvinism, 1541–1715* (Oxford, 1985), 39–70; William G. Naphy, *Calvin and the Consolidation of the Genevan Reformation* (Manchester, 1994); Mark Valeri, 'Religion, Discipline, and the Economy in Calvin's Geneva', *Sixteenth Century Journal* 28 (1997), 123–42.

[37] *The Lawes and Statutes of Geneva, as well concerning ecclesiastical discipline, as civil regiment, with certeine proclamations, duly executed, whereby God's religion is most purelie maintained; and their common wealth quietly governed: translated out of Frenche into Englishe by Robert Fills* [Field] (London, 1562), fols 74v–75v.

[38] De Gallatin, 'Ordonnances somptuaires', 219–20: '. . . que quant aux chaines d'or ou

death in 1564, new ordinances were agreed by the Company of Pastors and the council on clothing, with yet further clarifications of the previous laws. These new ordinances demanded that Genevans dress modestly as honest Christians, and stated that after already issuing ordinances,

> joined with the ordinary warnings from God's word, we would have hoped that each person would order themselves voluntarily to all sobriety and honest moderation, according to their rank and vocation. However, the total opposite has happened, to our great regret, and more new and superfluous styles of clothing and other excesses have reached us from foreign countries, instead of correcting the faults which are already here, and it is not possible that more great vices and wrongs should occur, without provoking God's anger . . . it thus seemed good and necessary to us to specify the following things. . . .[39]

The 1564 ordinances then set about the detailed regulation of all sorts of outlawed forms of dress. The use of gold and silver in embroidery, trimmings and fringes, wearing of gold or silver chains, bracelets, gold belts, cut silk clothes, use of silk sheaths for swords, and low collars and revealing neck-lines for women, were all banned. While silver hooks for cloaks were permitted, any enrichment of shoes made out of a different material from those of the shoes themselves was outlawed, as were gold or silver buckles, head-dresses made of gold or silver, and women were not allowed to twist or curl their hair. The regulations also specified particular restrictions for different groups, which reflected the way codes on dress were related to establishing social status. For example, the families of artisans were not allowed to wear any garments made of silk or other expensive cloths. Female servants and chamber-maids were not allowed to wear any silk head-dresses. Finally, 'so that the present ordinances are better observed', penalties were also imposed on any dressmakers or clothiers responsible for making any items of prohibited dress for Genevans.[40]

Despite issuing such detailed regulations, only a very small number

---

d'argent on entend celles qui se portent au col ou au bras par orgueil ou autrement en fasson de brodure et non pas des ceintures d'argent ny autres qui servent à l'usage'.

[39] Ibid., 223–4.

[40] Ibid., 224–5: '. . . que les présentes ordonnances soyent mieux observées, défendons sous mesme peine à tous cousturiers, ou autres ouvriers de faire habillemens, ou ouvrages contrevenans à icelles pour les citoyens, bourgeois, habitans, ou sujets de ceste cité'.

of prosecutions were subsequently brought under these laws.[41] Without commenting on this limited enforcement of the ordinances, the consistory went back to the council in 1569 to request a further revision of the regulations to prevent people from making expensive decorations for their shoes. Ordinances were issued in 1570 which repeated the previous ban on embellishing clothes with silver, gold and silk, and outlawed wearing chains, bracelets, gold belts and costly jewellery. New items also now joined the list of banned clothes, such as velvet bonnets, all superfluous collars and ruffs, and silk or padded shoes. Artisans' wives could not wear head-dresses of a value of more than five florins, and any tailors or other clothiers who contravened these regulations were threatened with the loss of their livelihood.[42]

Between 1570 and 1572 there were no cases brought against any Genevan under these ordinances on clothing, and then only occasional cases emerged mostly relating to women wearing velvet, silk or other expensive materials and jewellery. Still, in 1573 the consistory wrote to the council about their concern over women's hairstyles. In June 1574 the pastors, led by Theodore Beza, Lambert Daneau and Simon Goulart, claimed that the clothing ordinances were not being well observed, especially by foreigners, that golden bracelets were still commonly worn, that servants were wearing clothes fit for their masters, and that women were wearing too many rings.[43] The council responded to these complaints by having the most recent ordinances printed in an effort to increase awareness of the rules. They also asked the ministers to provide the names of any known to have contravened the regulations. The ministers replied sourly that the councillors knew very well how poorly their ordinances were being obeyed.[44] In 1575 the council re-issued the clothing ordinances, which included a relaxation of the law on rings allowing people to wear up to four rings instead of only two. They issued the ordinances again in 1579, and distributed between two and three hundred copies of the regulations in the city. The pastors remained very concerned about the lack of rigour in

---

[41] Ibid., 210, 220, 228.
[42] Ibid., 230–2. The Italian refugee community at Geneva, which specialized in the trade of silk and velvet, had grown substantially in the 1560s: cf. E. William Monter, 'The Italians in Geneva, 1550–1600: a New Look', in Luc Monnier, ed., *Genève et l'Italie* (Geneva, 1969), 53–77.
[43] Ibid., 235.
[44] Ibid.

enforcement, and continued to press for firm action against gold bracelets, belts and silk clothes.[45]

In 1580 minister Lambert Daneau, who had fled France for Geneva in 1572, translated and published two classical tracts on clothing, and completed his own *Traite de l'estat honneste des Chrestiens en leur accoustrement*.[46] This treatise built on scriptural texts and Genevan ordinances, with Daneau defending the need for specific laws on appropriate clothing. He acknowledged the strength of the argument that questions of clothing should be left to the conscience of each individual rather than be dealt with as a matter for formal regulation. However, he suggested that public discipline was particularly needed in this aspect of life. While Daneau conceded that Christians were free to use all the things which God had provided in the world, he argued that the right use of those resources demanded prudence, moderation and sobriety. So, although Christians could live according to their consciences, according to Daneau 'all liberty is slippery and dangerous'. Therefore, magistrates were to ban excesses in clothing, and Christians were obliged to observe these laws. While the consciences of Christians remained free, for Daneau this freedom had to be adjusted to rules on clothing as it was important not only for Christians to guard against 'evil, but also all appearance of evil'.[47]

New clothing regulations appeared again in Geneva in 1581, which repeated familiar concerns about excessive display, luxury, cost and novelty in clothes, and prohibited a long list of specific items of dress. The council complained that previous ordinances had not been observed as they required, and demanded that social distinctions be observed in clothing. The 1581 ordinances were even more detailed than previous laws, including rules against men having long hair, prohibitions against women styling and curling their hair, against the luxury of jewellery and expensive cloths, and against clothes which displayed too much of the body. No women were to wear velvet bonnets, except for those married to men from the social elite of the

---

[45] Ibid., 236, 239, 241–2.

[46] Lambert Daneau, *Deux Traitez de Florent Tertullian, docteur tres-ancien, et voisin du temps des apostres, environ CLXX ans apres l'incarnation de Iesus Christ: l'un des parures et ornemens: l'autre des habits et accoustremens des femmes Chrestiennes. Plus un traité de sainct Cyprian evesque de Carthage, touchant la discipline et les habits des filles* (Geneva, 1580); idem, *Traite de l'estat honneste des Chrestiens en leur accoustrement* (Geneva, 1580). Christoph Strohm, 'Zur Eigenart der frühen calvinistischen Ethik: Beobachtungen am Beispiel des Calvin-Schülers Lambert Daneau', *Archiv für Reformationsgeschichte* 90 (1999), 230–54.

[47] Daneau, *Traite de l'estat honneste des Chrestiens*, 10, 30–1, 97, 99.

city. Tailors and clothiers were again warned against producing any new styles of clothes. The fine for a first offence against these regulations were set at five florins, at ten florins for the second offence, and twenty-five florins on the third occasion with the confiscation of any banned items. The council also offered a final catch-all article:

> ... that, in general, each person should dress honestly and simply according to their estate and quality, and that all, from the least to the greatest should give a good example of Christian modesty to each other.[48]

The frequent repetition of laws on clothing and appearance in Geneva, the litany of complaints from Geneva's clergy about the impact of the ordinances, the council's own admission of inadequate enforcement of the laws, and the small number of prosecutions under the regulations, all add up to a picture of the limitations of regulatory action by an early modern government. Many Genevans certainly failed always to abide by all the strict standards of simple and modest dress specified in the city's ordinances. However, this does not mean that decades of clerical and political effort did not achieve any results, nor that the regulations on dress relied only on enforcement from above. When moral standards of dress were flagrantly violated, some citizens protested. Nicolas Vimont was so struck by the appearance of a woman in expensive clothes in August 1585, with a grand ruff and styled hair, that he called out in the street against the offence she caused to God. However, Vimont ended up in trouble for his outburst, since the woman turned out to be the wife of a nobleman from Grenoble, and as a visitor to Geneva was not obliged to comply with the city's regulations.[49]

The clergy certainly also kept up their pressure on the council over the regulations on dress, complaining again in December 1587 about excessive ruffs and flared skirts.[50] The ministers then proposed to send elders to homes where they knew people owned excessively luxurious items of clothing, and to call offenders to appear before the consistory. While this meant ceding authority to the consistory, the council accepted this proposal perhaps with relief.[51] During the 1590s, cases

---

[48] De Gallatin, 'Ordonnances somptuaires', 244–8: '... et en général que chacun ait à s'accoustrer honnestement et simplement selon son estate et qualité, et que tous, tant petis que grands monstrent bon exemple de modestie Chrestienne les uns aux autres'.

[49] Ibid., 253.

[50] Ibid., 254.

[51] Ibid., 255.

were more frequently brought against individuals who offended against the clothing regulations. For example, in February 1593 Simon Berthier was asked by minister Charles Perrot in the name of the consistory not to wear his large velvet mittens, but instead to wear simple gloves if his hands were cold. The consistory remained vigilant against any perceived relaxation in their exacting standards, maintaining that excesses in jewellery and the luxurious embellishment of clothing brought ruin to the individual, endangered the community, and were offensive to God.[52]

Unlike in Geneva, the Reformed Church in France could not work in partnership with the secular authorities in the regulation of morality and clothing. State laws were introduced in France during the latter decades of the sixteenth century which specified approved dimensions of skirts, outlawed padded shoes, and regulated the decoration of clothes and use of gold, silver and silk. However, meetings of the Reformed national synod considered what further instructions should be issued to the faithful on how to dress, which particularly highlighted the connection between clothing and sexual morality.[53] The Church's *Discipline* ratified in 1572 set out that ministers were to exhort people to modesty, to refrain themselves from all excesses in their apparel, and to ensure that their families offered a good example to their local community on how to dress.[54] Regional assemblies in the Huguenot heartland of Guyenne and Languedoc also considered the issue of women's clothing and hairstyles. The assemblies responded to complaints from local ministers and elders about women who braided or curled their hair, or raised their hair with wire. Assemblies also warned against women wearing open collars and flared skirts.[55] The national synod held at La Rochelle in 1581 decided that people should be excluded from participating in the sacraments if they wore clothes with 'certain marked features of impudicity, dissolution or too ostentatious or

---

[52] Ibid., 262.

[53] *Tous les Synodes nationaux des églises reformées de France: auxquels on a joint des mandemens roiaux, et plusieurs lettres politiques, sur ces matières synodales, intitulées doctrine, culte, morale, discipline, cas de conscience*, ed. Jean Aymon, 2 vols (The Hague, 1710), I: 70, 129, 184.

[54] 'La Discipline Ecclesiastique des Eglises Reformées de France selon qu'elle a este arrestée aux Synodes nationaux par les deputes des provinces et ratifiée par toutes les Eglises, reveue et confermee par le dernier Synode tenu a La Rochelle le 12e Avril 1571 et a Nismes le 7e May 1572 regnant Charles 9 par la grace de Dieu Roy de France', ed. Glen S. Sunshine in 'French Protestantism on the Eve of St-Bartholomew: the Ecclesiastical Discipline of the French Reformed Churches, 1571–1572', *French History* 4 (1990), 340–77, 352–77: see 357, 375.

[55] Janine Garrisson-Estebe, *Protestants du Midi, 1559–1598* (Toulouse, 1980), 307.

indecent novelty, such as make-up, pleating, tufts of feathers, stitchings, ... exposed bosoms, ... and other similar things'.[56] The injunctions issued by the French Reformed national synod, and by regional synods, and the messages conveyed in published tracts on clothing were backed up by local disciplinary action taken by consistories, particularly in large towns. At Nîmes, issues relating to dress increased in importance in the business of the local consistory during the 1580s and 1590s.[57] In 1581 the region's synod had complained about the indecency of women's clothing which revealed too much of their bosoms. The Nîmes Church also received a letter from the Church in Orange with a fraternal warning about the bad example which was being set in the matter of dress and appearance by the women of Nîmes. The pastor and elders responded by giving new attention to these issues, feeling that they had fallen behind the standard set in other leading Calvinist towns such as Montauban and Castres. In 1589 the Nîmes consistory warned local apothecaries about the sale of rouge and other make-up. In 1592 the ministers and elders of the town of around 10,000 people went from house to house to demand that women dressed more modestly. Those in Nîmes who could afford the expense of wearing decoration in their hair, or who used wire to raise their hair were regularly warned by the elders, as were those who wore clothes with low necklines which displayed too much of the body, or who used hoops to flare their skirts. Even male students in the town were occasionally brought before the elders and told to get a haircut.[58]

Max Weber proposed that during the early modern period a system of belief emerged which valorized systematic self-control over all aspects of life, and in particular restricted the consumption of goods to rational and non-luxurious uses. As Weber described them, Calvinists were bred with a complete suspicion of culture without religious value, and that

[56] *Tous les Synodes nationaux des églises reformées de France*, 1: 152–3.

[57] Ann H. Guggenheim, 'The Calvinist Notables of Nîmes during the Era of the Religious Wars', *Sixteenth Century Journal* 3 (1972), 80–96; Raymond A. Mentzer, 'Le Consistoire et la pacification du monde rural', *Bulletin de la Société de l'Histoire du Protestantisme Français* 135 (1989), 373–89.

[58] Raymond A. Mentzer, Jr, '*Disciplina nervus ecclesiae*: the Calvinist Reform of Morals at Nîmes', *Sixteenth Century Journal* 18 (1987), 89–115; Philippe Chareyre, ' "The Great Difficulties One Must Bear to Follow Jesus Christ": Morality at Sixteenth-Century Nîmes', in Mentzer, ed., *Sin and the Calvinists*, 63–96, 86–7.

the conceptions of idle talk, of superfluities, and of vain ostenta-
tion, all designations of an irrational attitude without objective
purpose, thus not ascetic, and especially not serving the glory of
God, but of man, were always at hand to serve in deciding in
favour of sober utility as against any artistic tendencies.[59]

This was especially true, Weber argued, in the case of the decoration of
the person, and in clothing, with 'the strict exclusion of the erotic and
of nudity from the realm of toleration'.[60] For Weber, the attitudes and
forms of behaviour which Calvinists exhibited reflected their attempts
to sustain some conviction about their status as elected for salvation.
Indeed Puritans in England, who paid most attention to such an understanding of predestination, were commonly identified by their
commitment to external signs of election including their conduct on
the Sabbath, use of language, sexual morality, and patterns of dress and
appearance. Although understanding of the clothing adopted by Puritans requires further research, issues of appropriate dress were certainly
a constant theme of piety tracts and works of practical divinity in
England. Hungarian Reformed students who visited England during
the early seventeenth century, and who returned to their homeland
dubbed as Puritans, were also noted to give particular attention to
maintaining pious, simple dress.[61]

However, in most Calvinist Churches predestination played a more
limited role in public teaching, and congregational institutions shaped
responses to sin and made decisions about when to exclude offenders
from the sacraments of the Church. This provided individual believers
with a more ordered escape from personal guilt about sin by admitting
wrong-doing before local elders and being formally accepted as part of
a disciplined, Christian community. During the second half of the
sixteenth century, the notable development in this process of Calvinist
discipline was a marked turn to formal and specific regulation of
offences through synodal injunctions and civil laws. Calvinist regulatory enthusiasm, however, did not become a mere reflection of a
general elite zeal to control aspects of ordinary people's lives, and relied
for its effectiveness on some degree of popular support and acceptance.
The Reformed turn to regulation on clothing, and growth in detailed

[59] Weber, *The Protestant Ethic*, 9.
[60] Ibid., 169.
[61] Graeme Murdock, *Calvinism on the Frontier, 1600–1660. International Calvinism and the Reformed Church in Hungary and Transylvania* (Oxford and New York, 2000), 178.

rules concerning patterns of dress in Geneva, France, and elsewhere, rather aimed to bolster the established framework of community spiritual discipline when the liberty allowed to Christian consciences seemed to prove 'slippery and dangerous'. A more rigid nexus of boundaries was to be provided by regulations on external behaviour, implemented by the Church's institutions and, where possible, also through co-operation with civil bodies. This aimed to prod believers more firmly with fines as well as demands for apologies and other spiritual punishments towards recognizing their sins, repenting of them, and living as true Christians.

Calvin had warned that introducing detailed rules on clothing among other issues risked turning moral discipline into a legalistic process which would ensnare consciences. However, when rightly-ordered ideas about God did not lead many ordinary people willingly and voluntarily to initiate for themselves an equally rightly-ordered pattern of daily life, the temptation for clergy to compose rules and regulations as the means by which to encourage progress towards these goals proved irresistible. This moral discipline was at the heart of Calvinism in practice, so perhaps rather than assess the psychological impact of guilt and ideas about salvation on individuals within early modern Calvinist societies, it might be more rational to look to the impact on communities of life under moral regulations and to the development and effectiveness of Calvinist and civil disciplinary institutions as a potential source for the long-term cultural and social changes in Europe noted by Weber, such as the formalism, and hard, correct character ascribed to the Western bourgeoisie.

University of Birmingham

RECANTATION AND RETRIBUTION:
'REMEMBERING FRANCIS SPIRA', 1548–1638

by M. A. OVERELL

B Y 1600 many, perhaps most, English people knew the story of Francesco Spiera, whom they usually called 'Francis Spira'.[1] Spiera, an Italian lawyer, recanted his Protestant beliefs in 1548, then he despaired and died, convinced of his own damnation. For Protestants during the mid sixteenth-century persecutions, the moral of the tale was urgent and could not have been clearer: recant and you will meet with God's retribution – in agony, like Spiera.

Spiera's story was part of the 'anti-Nicodemite' propaganda campaign aimed at faint hearts who would not stand up and be counted. Contemporaries called them 'Nicodemites' after Nicodemus in the Gospels, who came to Christ by night.[2] This theme was begun by Protestants in the 1540s and 1550s, but was later taken up by Catholics, when they too faced persecution.[3] One particular quotation from Scripture was hammered home relentlessly: 'The one who disowns me . . . I will disown'. Recantation was that sin against the Holy Ghost for which there was no forgiveness.[4] In this European polemic, Spiera acquired a totemic significance.

But stories are adaptable. Over the three centuries of its popularity, this one sustained dramatic shifts in interpretation. Ten years ago Michael MacDonald published a study of its reception in the version most widely read in England, *The Fearfull Estate of Francis Spira*, a compilation by Nathaniel Bacon, published in 1638, some ninety years after

---

[1] In this study the Italian name, 'Spiera', will be used except in English titles and quotations which adopt 'Spira'. There is variation in the sources.

[2] John 3: 1; 7: 50; 19: 39. There is a complex relationship between anti-Nicodemite propaganda and two different contemporary literatures: the martyrologies and resistance theory; see Brad S. Gregory, *Salvation at Stake: Christian Martyrdom in Early Modern Europe* (Cambridge, MA, 1999), 154–7; Carlos M. N. Eire, 'Prelude to Sedition: Calvin's Attack on Nicodemism and Religious Compromise', *Archiv für Reformationsgeschichte* 76 (1985), 120–45.

[3] Alexandra Walsham, *Church Papists: Catholicism, Conformity and Confessional Polemic in Early Modern England* (Woodbridge, 1993); M. A. Overell, 'Vergerio's Anti-Nicodemite Propaganda and England: 1547–1558', *JEH* 51 (2000), 296–318; A. Dillon, *The Construction of Martyrdom in the English Catholic Community, 1535–1602* (Aldershot, 2002), 286–90.

[4] Cf. Matt. 10: 33; 12: 32; Mark 3: 29; Luke 12: 10.

the original recantation.[5] MacDonald highlighted two themes in the English understanding of Spiera: first, he was 'God's Warning to Apostates'. Second, he symbolized religious despair. MacDonald devoted most attention to his second theme, citing especially seventeenth- and eighteenth-century writers who quoted Spiera to comprehend the despair and fear that they themselves experienced on their tortuous road to final conversion. He concluded that telling this story was one of the ways people constructed or 'fashioned' their own religious identity.

John Stachniewski, too, worked from mostly seventeenth-century evidence and concluded: 'It was Spiera's exemplification of the reprobate experience rather than anything special to apostates that gripped the Puritan imagination'.[6] More recently, Alexandra Walsham has set the Spiera stories among those judgement tales which form part of her illuminating study of the dark workings of Providence in Early Modern England.[7] It should be evident from all the above that Spiera – chameleon like – came to symbolize different things at different times: recantation, despair, reprobation, judgement. Recantation, originally the dominant theme, faded as fear of retribution began a crescendo.

The main focus of this study is the second half of the sixteenth century, a time when Spiera's sad end was becoming known in England, but before Nathaniel Bacon's *Fearfull Estate* imprinted it on the English Protestant psyche. My purpose here is to examine how and why this one supremely adaptable medium came to convey different messages. Spiera stories will be set within what Peter Burke called the 'polymorphism' of cultural diffusion, with influences flowing 'upward', 'downward', 'interacting' and 'cross fertilising', and changing on the way.[8] Borrowing themes from the medieval *ars moriendi*, these tales were written up by anti-Nicodemite polemicists, disseminated by preachers, and then re-emerged in English culture. Subjected to reconfiguration,

---

5 Michael MacDonald, ' "The Fearful Estate of Francis Spira": Narrative, Identity and Emotion in Early Modern England,' *JBS* 31 (1992), 32–61; *STC*, 12365, 1177.5–1179; D. G. Wing, *A Short Title Catalogue of Books Printed in England, Scotland, Ireland, Wales and British America and of English Books printed in other countries, 1641–1700*, 3 vols (2nd edn, New York, 1972–88), B 357–366 [hereafter *STC* Wing].

6 John Stachniewski, *The Persecutory Imagination: English Puritanism and the Literature of Religious Despair* (Oxford, 1991), 38.

7 Alexandra Walsham, *Providence in Early Modern England* (Oxford, 1999), 86, 326–7.

8 Peter Burke, 'Learned Culture and Popular Culture in Renaissance Italy', in idem, ed., *Varieties of Cultural History* (Cambridge, 1997), 124–35; idem, *Popular Culture in Early Modern Europe* (London, 1978), 281.

they by-passed, let down and livened up orthodox theology no end.[9]
Spiera's retribution became more important than his recantation.
The authors of the first accounts of Spiera's misery were: Pier Paolo
Vergerio, a Catholic bishop who fled from Italy to become a Protestant
shortly after witnessing Spiera's state; Matteo Gribaldi, Protestant
Professor of Civil Law at Padua; Sigismund Gelous 'from Transylvania';
Henry Scrymgeour, a Scottish Protestant from St Andrews. The radical
humanist Caelio Secundo Curione edited an important collection of
Spiera narratives which included accounts from all of the above.[10] The
writers were anti-Nicodemite polemicists, not historians, and they
produced an uneasy blend of fact and fiction. Popular tropes crept in,
lifted from the late-medieval texts and woodcuts of the *ars moriendi*,
transcending theological divisions. Spiera experiences deathbed despair,
a fly in the sick room is Beelzebub; devils come to stick pins in his
pillow.[11] But parts of the Protestants' story are corroborated facts. The
lawyer Francesco Spiera certainly lived in Cittadella, north of Venice,
was brought before the Venetian Inquisition in 1548 and admitted
some mildly Protestant activities, such as owning a Bible, translating
the Lord's Prayer and having doubts about purgatory. At his trial he
recanted, was fined and ordered to make a public recantation. He did
so, then fell into a despairing illness. He was taken to Padua for medical
help.

⁹ For similar discrepancies between orthodoxy and popular beliefs, see R. W. Scribner,
'Incombustible Luther: the Image of the Reformer in Early Modern Germany', in idem,
Popular Culture and Popular Movements in Reformation Germany (London and Ronceverte, WV,
1987), 323–53; Leigh Eric Schmidt, *Holy Fairs: Scottish Communions and American Revivals in the
Early Modern Period* (Princeton, 1989), 213.
¹⁰ Matteo Gribaldi, *Historia de quodam [F. Spira] quem hostes Evangelii in Italia coegerunt
abiicere cognitam veritatem* (Padua, 1549); the place of publication is probably false. Next from
the continental presses was Caelio Secundo Curione, *Francisci Spierae qui quod susceptam semel
Evangelicae veritatis professionem abnegasset . . .* (Basel, 1550), which includes the pieces by
Gribaldi, Vergerio, Gelous and Scrymgeour. The best known account was *La Historia di M. F.
Spiera, il quale per havere in varii modi negata la conosciuta verità dell'Evangelio, cascò in una misera
desperatione*, ed. P. P. Vergerio (Basel, 1551). For detail on the Italian background, see M. A.
Overell, 'The Exploitation of Francesco Spiera', *Sixteenth Century Journal* 26 (1995), 619–30.
¹¹ Cf. the image 'The temptation to despair' from the *Ars Moriendi*, reproduced in
Eamon Duffy, *The Stripping of the Altars: Traditional Religion in England, 1400–1580* (New
Haven, 1992), fig. 117. Several early reformers developed the medieval tradition that desper-
ation was 'the sin that is death' (1 John 5: 16). See, for instance, John Frith, *A Disputacion of
Purgatorye* (?1531), *STC* 11386.5, Book 2, sig. f8r. Sister Mary Catherine O'Connor, *The Art of
Dying Well: the Development of the Ars Moriendi* (New York, 1942; repr. 1966); M. A. Overell,
'The Reformation of Death in Italy and England, *circa* 1550', *Renaissance and Reformation* 23
(1999), 5–21, 6–7; Peter Marshall, *Beliefs and the Dead in Reformation England* (Oxford, 2002),
4–5, 241, 316.

There the audience gathered in his sick room included the writers of the main Protestant accounts: Vergerio, Gribaldi, Scrymgeour and Gelous. They suggested that Spiera was something of a predestinarian who believed that the elect went to heaven, but of course *he* was not going there.[12] All these Protestant narratives stressed the anti-Nicodemite interpretation: his recantation, leading to despair and his own certainty of imminent retribution. But Spiera's family said his despair had nothing to do with recantation but set in because he had been a money-grabbing lawyer – a trait which some Protestant accounts also mention.[13] Both sides had axes to grind.

* * *

Matteo Gribaldi's version reached England in 1550, less than a year after its first appearance on the Continent, and was given a red carpet entry to elite culture. It was published by the King's Printer in Wales, John Oswen, and the translator Edward Aglionby was a kinsman of Catherine Parr. The full title had a clear recantation–retribution spin: *A Notable and Marveilous Epistle [. . .] concerning the terrible Judgement of God upon him that for Fear of Men denieth Christ*.[14] This was strong stuff. As Peter Marshall pointed out, the reformers never aimed 'to restore society to a condition of feeling at ease with itself'.[15] The preface from John Calvin added further horror – suicide. Certainly the chroniclers said Spiera refused food and unashamedly they themselves had put suicidal ideas into the poor man's head: 'I demand of you . . . would ye kill yourself'.[16] But Calvin was sure he had done it.[17]

Then a theologian tried to make sense of it all. The Italian Protestant

---

[12] Gribaldi's *Historia de quodam (F. Spera)*, published in England as *A Notable and Marveilous Epistle . . .*, trans. E. A. [Edward Aglionby] (Worcester: J. Oswen, 1550), *STC* 12365, sig. C ii.

[13] For instance Sigismund Gelous in Curione's collection, *Francisci Spierae*, 98.

[14] *A Notable and Marveilous Epistle*, *STC* 12365; John N. King, 'The Book Trade under Edward VI and Mary I', in Lotte Hellinga and J. B. Trapp, eds, *The Cambridge History of the Book in Britain, 3: 1400–1557* (Cambridge, 1999), 167–70; London, British Library, MS Lansdowne, 2, 28, Edward Aglionby to Cecil, 3 December 1549; Susan E. James, *Kateryn Parr: the Making of a Queen* (Aldershot and Brookfield, VT, 1999), 148; see below n. 34. For Italian Protestant books in England, see M. A. Overell, 'Edwardian Court Humanism and *Il Beneficio di Cristo*, 1547–1553', in Jonathan Woolfson, ed., *Reassessing Tudor Humanism* (Basingstoke, 2002), 151–73.

[15] Peter Marshall, 'Fear, Purgatory and Polemic in Early Modern England', in William G. Naphy and Penny Roberts, eds, *Fear in Early Modern Society* (Manchester and New York, 1997), 150–66, 161.

[16] *A Notable and Marveilous Epistle*, sigs Aviii and Ciii.

[17] Ibid., sig. Aiiii.

exile Peter Martyr Vermigli (1499–1562) lectured on the Epistle to the Romans in Oxford in 1550.[18] He used Spiera to illustrate the hoary problem about whether God wills sin and damnation, acknowledging that Spiera 'persuaded himself that he had sinned against the Holy Ghost'.[19] Vermigli, ever systematic, looked at the alternative explanations. Either God used Spiera to frighten others, 'Howbeit this neither customably happeneth', or alternatively, 'Peradventure God did not put this into the head of Spira but the Devil, whose bond slave he was'.[20] There was no clear conclusion. Spiera, God and the Devil were left vying for responsibility.

Preaching in 1552, Hugh Latimer was very sceptical. It was the last time for several decades that an Englishman dared to question the recantation–retribution sequence. But then Protestants were not persecuted and Spiera had not acquired the terrible relevance soon to be imposed upon him. Latimer expected his noble audience to know the story: 'I know now that Judas had sinned against the Holy Ghost, also Nero, Pharoah and one Franciscus Spira'.[21] He agreed that Spira recanted, but the retribution part was rubbished:

> Ask remission of sin in the name of Christ and then I ascertain you that you sin not against the Holy Ghost. For *'gratia exsuperat supra peccatum'*; the mercy of God far exceedeth our sins.[22]

This was tantamount to a bucket of cold water on the whole drama. According to Latimer (and in contradiction to three Gospels), the sin against the Holy Ghost could be forgiven.[23]

The Marian persecution put a stop to such leisured critique. John Bradford, Lady Jane Grey and Myles Coverdale used Spiera's story to stop Nicodemism and strengthen resolve.[24] Bradford urged Lord

---

18 *Original Letters Relative to the English Reformation*, ed. H. Robinson, PS, 2 vols (Cambridge, 1846–7), 2: 401, John ab Ulmis to Henry Bullinger, 25 March 1550.

19 These lectures were published later: Pietro Vermigli, *In Epistolam S. Pauli Apostoli ad Romanos* (Basel, 1558) and then translated into English, *Most Learned and Fruitfull Commentaries of D. Peter Martir Vermilius Florentine, Professor of Diuinitie in the Schole of Tigure, vpon the Epistle of S. Paul to the Romanes : wherin are Diligently [and] Most Profitably Entreated All Such Matters and Chiefe Common Places of Religion Touched in the Same Epistle [. . .] Lately tra[n]slated out of Latine into Englishe, by H. B.* [Sir Henry Billingsley, d. 1606] (London, 1568), *STC* 24672, 301.

20 Ibid.

21 H. Latimer, *Sermons*, ed. George Elwes Corrie, PS, 2 vols (Cambridge, 1844–5), 1: 425.

22 Ibid.

23 Latimer's reference suggests quite widespread knowledge of the story by 1552.

24 For English Protestant anti-Nicodemism, see Thomas Freeman, 'Dissenters from a

Francis Russell, in sheriff's custody in 1553: 'Remember Lot's wife which looked back; remember Francis Spira'.[25] In 1554, when Bradford was in prison, his 'Exhortation to the Brethren' included a prayer intended to steel himself and others:

> Oh let us not so run down headlong into perdition, stumbling on those sins from which there is no recovery.... as it chanced to Lot's wife, Judas Iscariot, Francis Spira and to many others.[26]

Bradford was tough talking at a desperate moment, arguing that recantation had 'no recovery'. Myles Coverdale in his own 'Sermon on the carrying of Christes Cross' used exactly the same words about Spiera as Bradford.[27]

Taught by John Aylmer and moving within court humanist circles, Lady Jane Grey had encountered the Italian story. Before her death she tried to dissuade her father's chaplain, Thomas Harding, against recanting 'like a white hewred milk soppe':[28]

> Remember the horrible history of Julian of old, and the lamentable case of Spira of late, whose case (me thynke) should be yet so green in your remembrance, that being a thing of our time, you should fear the like inconvenience seeing you are fallen into the like offence.[29]

As they 'remembered Spiera', John Foxe (1516–87) recorded their message. In the *Actes and Monuments* he reprinted Lady Jane's reference

---

Dissenting Church', in Peter Marshall and Alec Ryrie, eds, *The Beginnings of English Protestantism* (Cambridge, 2000), 129–57, 130, esp. n. 3, 135, 152; on anti-Nicodemism and women, idem, ' "The Good Ministrye of Godlye and Vertuouse Women": the Elizabethan Martyrologists and the Female Supporters of the Marian Martyrs', *JBS* 31 (2000), 8–33, 12–16. For English Nicodemism, see Andrew Pettegree, 'Nicodemism and the English Reformation', in idem, *Marian Protestantism: Six Studies,* St Andrews Studies in Reformation History (Aldershot, 1996), 86–117 and Overell, 'Vergerio's Anti–Nicodemite Propaganda', 298–9, 317–18.

[25] John Bradford, *Writings*, ed. Aubrey Townsend, PS, 2 vols (Cambridge, 1848–53), 2: 80.

[26] Ibid., 1: 433.

[27] Myles Coverdale (1488–1568), *Writings and Translations* and *Remains*, ed. George Pearson, PS, 2 vols (Cambridge, 1844–46), 2: 276.

[28] Lady Jane Dudley, *An Epistle of the Ladye Jane to a Learned Man of late falne from the Truth of Gods Word* (n.p., J. Day?, 1554?), STC 7279, sig. A iiii; another version, *Here in this Booke ye have a godly Epistle made by a Faithful Christian* [Successor of A. Scoloker? 1554?], STC 7279.5. See also STC 25251–2. For Lady Jane Grey's *Epistle* and John Day, see L. P. Fairfield, 'The Mysterious Press of "Michael Wood" ', *Library* ser. 5, 27 (1972), 220–32, 226–7. For an important advance in research on John Day's secret printing, see Elizabeth Evenden, 'The "Michael Wood" Mystery: William Cecil and the Lincolnshire Printing of John Day', *Sixteenth Century Journal*, forthcoming.

[29] *Epistle of the Ladye Jane*, sig. Bii.

in full and the first one of Bradford's.[30] Spiera fitted Foxe's agenda. First, as Tom Freeman has pointed out, *Actes and Monuments* included 'a virtually endless parade of divine judgements'.[31] Second, recantations of Englishmen like James Bainham and Edward Crome presented him with problems, but Spiera's was useful in that, like all other standard examples of apostates – Lot's wife, Judas Iscariot and Julian the Apostate – he was both foreign and dead. Thus the nasty business of naming and shaming Englishmen could be kept to a minimum.[32]

So *Actes and Monuments* was almost certainly Spiera's passport into English popular culture. Other versions of the story in English appeared in John Daus's translation of Sleidan's *Chronicle* in 1560 and in Vermigli's influential *Commonplaces* of 1583.[33] Aglionby's translation had further reprints in 1570 and in 1582,[34] and a 'Ballad of Master Ffrauncis' of 1587, now lost, also told the tale.[35]

By the 1580s, as memories of persecution receded, there were some obvious jitters about Spiera's retribution. Edwin Sandys hedged his bets, saying apostates '*hardly ever* or never doth rise again'. His list of examples was brought up to date: 'Judas, Julian, Arius, Franciscus Spira, Staphylus, Baldwin (Baudouin)', still all foreign, of course.[36] Writing in

---

[30] Lady Jane Grey's *Epistle* appears in John Foxe, *Actes and Monuments of these Latter and Perillous Dayes, touching Matters of the Church* (1563), 922, and in every edition thereafter. Bradford's 'Exhortation' is not printed in any edition of Foxe's *Actes and Monuments* but does appear in *Certain Most Godly Fruitful and Comfortable Letters of Such True Saints and Holy Martyrs of God . . .* , ed. Henry Bull (London, 1564), STC 5886, 445. This work has been attributed to Myles Coverdale. I am grateful to Dr Thomas Freeman for his generous help on these points. In the 1576 edition of Foxe's *Actes and Monuments* (2 vols), the Spiera reference appears at 1: 1351, but is misnumbered 1341; see also *The Acts and Monuments of John Foxe*, ed. Stephen Reed Cattley and George Townsend, 8 vols (London, 1838), 6: 421, 7: 219.

[31] Thomas Freeman, 'The Importance of Dying Earnestly: the Metamorphosis of the Account of James Bainham in "Foxe's Book of Martyrs"', in R. N. Swanson, ed., *The Church Retrospective*, SCH 33 (Woodbridge, 1997), 267–88, 281.

[32] Ibid.; Susan Wabuda, 'Equivocation and Recantation during the English Reformation: the "Subtle Shadows" of Dr Edward Crome', *JEH* 44 (1993), 224–42.

[33] Johannes Sleidan, *A Famouse Cronicle of oure Time, called Sleidanes Commentaries concerning the State of Religion and Commonwealth during the Raigne of the Emperour Charles the Fift* (John Day, 1560), STC 19848, vol. 21, fols cccxxii–cccxxviii; the original had appeared in 1555. *The Common Places of [. . .] Peter Martyr with a Large Addition of manie theologicall and necessarie Discourses. Translated and partlie gathered by Anthonie Marten* (London, 1583) STC 24669, part 3, 23–4.

[34] *A Notable and Marveilous Epistle*, STC 12366; W. T. Lowndes, *The Bibliographer's Manual of English Literature*, ed. Henry G. Bohn, 4 vols (London, 1871), 2: 945.

[35] E. Arber, *A Transcript of the Registers of the Company of Stationers of London, 1554–1640*, 5 vols (London, 1875–94), 2: 472.

[36] Eighteenth Sermon preached at St Paul's Cross, probably between 1570 and 1576; *The Sermons of Edwin Sandys*, ed. John Ayre, PS (Cambridge, 1841), 362.

the early 1580s, Thomas Rogers swung right back to forgiveness. He argued that the very idea that Christ could not wash away grave sins was an error, 'which was Cain's, Francis Spiera's and other desperate persons'.[37] In 1581, Nathaniel Woodes's play about Spiera, *The Conflict of Conscience*, came in two issues in the same year with different endings. In the second, happy ending Spiera is converted – not at all what the anti-Nicodemites had had in mind.[38] This inclination to turn the whole story on its head was most clearly revealed in the writing of William Perkins, ever suspicious of fables. He took everyone to task for cocksure conclusions 'which inconsiderately tax him [Spiera] for a castaway'. Perkins thought of English examples 'which match Francis Spiera, whether we regard the matter of his temptation or the deepness of his desperation, who yet through the mercy of God have received comfort'.[39]

Despite his claims about Englishmen sharing the 'matter of his temptation', real inquisition at the hands of a real Catholic power had ended in the year Perkins was born. The intervening decades of Protestant government presented a problem. To tell Spiera's or any other anti-recantation story was to encourage refusal to conform, fan the flames of radical resistance and cast Elizabeth I's and then James I's governments in the role of persecuting powers. Educated hesitation was understandable.

Nonetheless, around the turn of the century, Spiera had an enduring resurrection in the judgement books. Thomas Beard in his *Theatre of Gods Judgements* (1597) let the Italian off lightly, putting him in the *least* bad category of apostates, 'who through infirmitie and fear have fallen away'. The genre was a European phenomenon and the story kept crossing frontiers. Beard based his account on Sleidan's *Chronicle*. Spiera appears among the 'desperate persons' in the English translation of Simon Goulart's *Admirable and Memorable Histories containing the Wonders*

---

[37] Thomas Rogers, *The Catholic Doctrine of the Church of England: an Exposition of the Thirty-Nine Articles*, ed. J. J. S. Perowne, PS (Cambridge, 1854), Article 2, 46–59. The first nineteen articles were first published in 1585.

[38] Nathaniel Woodes (fl. 1580), *The Conflict of Conscience: 1581*, ed. Herbert Davies and Frank Percy Wilson (Oxford, 1952): cp. ll. 2410–13 in first and second issues. William A. Jackson, 'Woodes's Conflict of Conscience', *Times Literary Supplement*, 7 September 1933, 592; Celesta Wine, 'Nathaniel Wood's *Conflict of Conscience*', *Publications of the Modern Language Association of America* 50 (1935), 661–78; Leslie Mahin Oliver, 'John Foxe and *The Conflict of Conscience*', *Review of English Studies* 25 (1949), 1–9.

[39] *The Workes of that Famous and Worthy Minister of Christ in the University of Cambridge, M. VV. Perkins (1558–1602)*, 3 vols (London, 1626–31), 3: 407, cited by MacDonald, ' "Fearfull Estate" ', *JBS* 31 (1992), 48; Walsham, *Providence*, 104.

of Our Time (1607). In his turn, Goulart relied heavily on the earlier account of the Scottish lawyer Henry Scrymgeour.[40]

Nathaniel Bacon's famous compilation of Spiera stories secured their place in English literature. His manuscript, circulating as early as 1628, was destined to become a best seller reissued about fifty times and reworked still more.[41] Bacon's use of several Italian sources was viewed as proof that Spiera was fact, a cut above chap-book fictions. Robert Bolton's highly regarded *Instructions for a Right Comforting [of] Afflicted Consciences* (1631) analysed Spiera's state and had liberal quotations from Bacon crammed into the margin, with the comment 'I have the original Relations of the story and find this excellent translation to answer exactly to them'.[42] He was wrong. The Italian originals were not reliable and Bacon's *A Relation of the Fearfull Estate of Francis Spira*, finally published in 1638, was not a translation but a free blend of originals, laced with Bacon's own interpolations, but it saved Spiera for posterity.[43]

Recently, Alexandra Walsham showed how the story of a young apothecary, William Rogers, published in 1636, had 'arresting similarities' to Spiera's: a religious young man forsook the Church, became a drunkard, rejected his minister's warnings, despaired and died expecting hell.[44] Retribution had eclipsed formal recantation and the Italian tale had become a template for any final fall.[45]

Anti-Nicodemite polemic was written in a hurry, its shelf life dictated by the continuance or resumption of persecution. There was

---

[40] Thomas Beard, *The Theatre of Gods Judgements: or, A Collection of Histories out of Sacred, Ecclesiasticall, and Prophane Authours, concerning the Admirable Judgements of God upon the Transgressours of His Commandements. Translated out of French, and augmented by more than three hundred examples* (London, 1597) *STC* 1659, 63; Simon Goulart, *Admirable and Memorable Histories containing the wonders of our Time collected into French*, transl. Edward Grimeston (London, 1607), *STC* 12135, 187–96.

[41] Brian Opie, 'Nathaniel Bacon and Francis Spira: the Presbyterian and the Apostate', *Turnbull Library Record* 18 (1985), 33–50; Nehemiah Wallington copied out the text in 1635: Paul S. Seaver, *Wallington's World: a Puritan Artisan in Seventeenth-Century London* (Stanford, CA, 1985), 202; *STC* 1177.5–1179 and *STC* Wing B 359–366.

[42] Robert Bolton, *Instructions for a Right Comforting [of] Afflicted Consciences* (London, 1631), *STC* 3238, 18.

[43] David Renaker, 'John Bunyan's Misattribution to Francis Spira of a Remark by Nathaniel Bacon', *Notes and Queries* NS 25 (1978), 25.

[44] Robert Abbot, *The Young-Man's Warning-Peece; or a Sermon preached at the Buriall of William Rogers, Apothecary* (London, 1636; 1639), *STC* 60.3–60.7, 10, 14; Walsham, *Providence*, 326–7.

[45] *STC* Wing B359–366. For instance, *The Second Spira: being a Fearful Example of an Atheist*, ed. Richard Sault (London, 1693).

no time to consider its deeper implications. Three phases of urgent anti-recantation propaganda have been examined here. First, writers in Italy blended a few facts about Spiera into a fiction based on medieval models and intended to make Italian Protestants resist or, failing that, flee. Second, during the Marian persecution in England, John Bradford and Lady Jane Grey cited Spiera's recantation to make their fellow Protestants hold firm. Last – and often overlooked – this particular anti-recantation message reappeared in John Foxe's great martyrology. He recorded the Marian martyrs as they remembered Spiera. His positive English exemplars meditated on a negative exemplar whose recantation could be readily admitted because he was a dead Italian. But once Elizabethan Protestantism had taken root, focusing on Spiera's sin could produce an 'own goal'. Condemning his feeble conformity might well create more nonconformists.

Minority groups facing persecution continued to fix on Spiera's recantation, but people not at odds with official religion made far more of the story's end – retribution, expected and deserved. For Thomas Beard and others, judgement was good copy: it attracted readers and might even make sinners into saints. Walsham has shown how many 'respectable' Protestant writers and preachers disseminated clearly unorthodox stories: 'They allowed people to believe . . . that flagrant offenders came to bad ends and descended automatically to hell.'[46]

This study has traced how one such popular tale ran out of control. A few recognized the theological chasms it opened. Vermigli could not tell if God or the devil was to blame, Latimer, Rogers and Perkins were troubled by the absence of forgiveness and Perkins knew that such certainty about God's judgements was absolutely forbidden to men. They were a small chorus. Spiera's very foreignness made it easy to consign him to retribution and to claim that, even if this was hard doctrine, it was nonetheless reliable Italian history. *That* it had never been. Medieval popular conventions of despair and judgement had passed through the unreliable filter of anti-Nicodemite polemic and emerged as a tale of despair and retribution.

The Open University

---

46 Walsham, *Providence*, 330; cp. Margaret Spufford, *Small Books and Pleasant Histories: Popular Fiction and its Readership in Seventeenth-Century England* (London, 1981), 207.

'THE PARTIAL CUSTOMS OF THESE FROZEN PARTS': RELIGIOUS RIOT AND RECONCILIATION IN THE NORTH OF ENGLAND*

by ANDREW CAMBERS

JOHN Bossy's recent book, *Peace in the Post-Reformation*, should, I think, finally lay to rest Thomas Hardy's notion that 'War makes rattling good history; but peace is poor reading.'[1] In it he suggests that the 'moral tradition' was a feature of traditional religion, transformed by the religious and social changes taking place between about 1500 and 1700, and eroded by a current of civility. Furthermore, Bossy argues that in England even the godly sought the moral tradition and attempted to make peace with their neighbours. In this article, I will trace peace-making between the godly and their Catholic neighbours in the North of England in the early seventeenth century. In doing so, I will suggest some alternatives to Bossy's argument: that the language of civility was exploited by the godly to make peace on their terms; that it was changing in this period; and that it appropriated rather than ran directly against the moral tradition.

To sustain my hypothesis that the godly and their Catholic neighbours had competing conceptions of civility, I will consider in detail the riot against the Hoby family, committed in their home at Hackness, North Yorkshire on the 26 and 27 August 1600. The case presents a large body of material, from court records and correspondence, that allows a reconsideration of the godly and the moral tradition. I want to introduce the parties involved in this ritual, riotous assault, before describing the course of events and the subsequent legal battle, and finishing with a discussion of the changing nature of civility, retribution and reconciliation in the North of England in this period.[2] Although the assault was far from unique and the records of the Star

---

* The quotation in the title is taken from the letter of Thomas Hoby to Robert Cecil, 5 September 1600. See, *HMC: Salisbury MSS* (1883–1923), X: 303. For discussions of this material and help clarifying my ideas, I would like to thank Mark Jenner, Bill Sheils and Michelle Wolfe.

[1] John Bossy, *Peace in the Post-Reformation* (Cambridge, 1998); Thomas Hardy, *The Dynasts: a Drama of the Napoleonic Wars*, 3 vols (London, 1903–8), 2: v.

[2] The source material for the dispute is at Public Record Office [hereafter P.R.O.] STAC 5/H50/4, 5/H16/2, 5/H22/21 and 5/H42/12. The correspondence can be found in

Chamber are somewhat formulaic, I think we are privileged to hear the proponents of two conflicting religious cultures working out two very different meanings of civility. I hope that the discussion will advance the current state of scholarship on civility, which has been focused on issues of continuity and change rather than accommodation and appropriation.[3]

In theory, there was no-one better placed to appreciate the nature of civility than Thomas Posthumous Hoby. His father, who had died shortly before his birth, had translated Castiglione's *Book of the Courtier*,[4] providing instruction for the behaviour of morally upstanding gentlemen. His mother, however, tempered these noble instincts with a boisterously litigious spirit. For her, peace-making was all very well in theory, but not at the expense of a relationship with God. Finally publishing her childhood translation of Martin Bucer in 1605, she advised her readers that

> To seeke the attonement of men is to be commended, and it hath a sure promise of God: *Blessed be the peace-makers*. But I feare me, lest in greedily following the same, it happen to me which chanceth to them that part fraies, while they seeke others safetie, they beare the blowes themselves. And I, while I study to make enemies friends, perhaps shall have small thanks of them. Which if it happen, the example of him shal comfort me, which said: If I should please men, I should not be the servant of Christ.[5]

Thomas Posthumous Hoby was a rather unscholarly son of these most scholarly parents. He was, however, zealous in his pursuit of godly reform, particularly after his marriage to Margaret Dakins in 1596, and his move up to the wilderness of Hackness, near Scarborough, in the North Riding of Yorkshire. Margaret had been twice widowed by the

---

HMC: Salisbury MSS (1883–1923), X: 302–4, 325, 391–2, XI: 11–12, 456, 546, XII: 22–3, 32, 105, XXII: 81.

3 Anna Bryson, *From Courtesy to Civility: Changing Codes of Conduct in Early Modern England* (Oxford, 1998), suggests change; John Gillingham, 'From *Civilitas* to Civility: Codes of Manners in Medieval and Early Modern England', *TRHS* ser. 6, 12 (2002), 267–89, advocates continuity. Also important is Peter Burke, Brian Harrison and Paul Slack, eds, *Civil Histories: Essays Presented to Sir Keith Thomas* (Oxford, 2000).

4 Baldassare Castiglione, *The Courtyer of Count Baldessar Castilio divided into foure bookes. Very necessary and profitable for yonge Gentilmen and Gentilwomen abiding in Court, Palaice, or Place, done into Englyshe by Thomas Hoby* (London, 1561).

5 Lady Elizabeth Russell, *A Way of Reconciliation of a Good and Learned Man: Touching the Trueth, Nature, and Substance of the Body and Blood of Christ in the Sacrament* (London, 1605), sig. A1v.

age of twenty-four, marrying first Walter Devereux and then Thomas Sidney. On Sidney's death in 1595, and after the death of her father which made her the sole inheritor of a wealthy estate, Margaret was one of the most eligible and firmly Protestant women in the land. Thomas Hoby stretched out the tentacles of his influential family, which included the Cecils and the Bacons, to draw in his prey and they lived together, happy but childless, at Hackness Hall. They transformed their house into a miniature godly commonwealth, educating the children of families such as the Askes and Sydenhams, before sending them on their way to such pillars of the godly establishment as Emmanuel College, Cambridge. They employed a young chaplain, Richard Rhodes, whose puritanism would get him into trouble even in staunchly puritan Beverley in the 1630s.[6]

The Hobys were held up to Protestants as the ideal model for implanting reform in the North. They were the dedicatees of Nicholas Byfield's *The Rule of Faith* (1626), in which they were described as 'paternes of piety . . . patrons of pious and godly men, and of their labours', and praised for being 'more excellent than your neighbours'.[7] They were fervent Protestants but no lovers of peace; difficult, controversial and unpopular with their unreformed Yorkshire neighbours. There had been trouble as soon as Thomas Hoby arrived, in particular a dispute about land and religion with Henry Cholmley, a member of the Whitby recusant gentry family. Thomas Hoby, whose interest was to prize from the Cholmleys the Liberty of Whitby Strand, bore the brunt of a public shaming by Cholmley at the Topcliffe sessions at Easter, 1597. So much is well-known, and Lady Margaret Hoby has gone down in history as the first female English diarist, for the record she kept of her godly life between 1599 and 1605.[8] The diary gives many insights into the daily life of the godly, the ritual observance of prayers and sermons, and the intensity of religious reading matter. It also gives some information into the animosity that her husband's public, godly zeal created in this largely unreformed area.

---

[6] For Richard Rhodes, see Ronald Albert Marchant, *The Puritans and the Church Courts in the Diocese of York, 1560–1642* (London, 1960), 271–2.

[7] Nicholas Byfield, *The Rule of Faith: or an Exposition of the Apostles Creed* (London, 1626), sig. A2v–A3r.

[8] *The Private Life of an Elizabethan Lady: the Diary of Lady Margaret Hoby, 1599–1605*, ed. Joanna Moody (Stroud, 1998).

* * *

Lady Hoby's diary gives only the briefest outline of the assault on her family by their Catholic neighbours. For 26 August 1600, she recorded that she 'made some provision for som strangers that Came'. For the 27, a little more: 'I spake with Mr Ewrie, who was so drunke that I sone made an end of that I had no reason to stay for: and, after, praied, brake my fast, praied and then dined . . .'. The following day, she 'talked with Mr Hoby about the abuse offered by Mr Ewere and his Companie'.[9] The motives for the assault and the sequence of events become clearer upon examination of the complaints, correspondence and court records surrounding the case.

On 26 August 1600, rousing the county, about eighty men and boys arrived at Hackness Hall to mock their neighbour and to prevent him sitting on a subsidy commission on the following day. In advance of the party's arrival, William Eure sent his footboy to the Hobys' house to explain that they had been hunting and needed to stay that night. Thomas Hoby replied that, though he would usually have obliged, he could not put them up because his wife was ill. The footboy, however, told Hoby that since his master was on the move, he could not pass this message on, and so, at about five o'clock in the afternoon, the hunting party came to Hackness Hall, armed with 'rapyers, swords and daggers' and 'with bluddy entents and murderous mynds'.[10] They were not simply a mob but a group of local Catholic gentry. They included Sir William Eure and his nephew William Eure, Richard Cholmley, William Dawny, William Hylliarde the Younger, Stephen Hutchinson and George Smyth.

The Eures were the major players in enacting local justice, and they were heavy-weights in the borders. Sir William's father, Ralph Lord Eure, was the vice-president of the Council in the North, and though the family were to be tainted by their closeness to the Earl of Essex, they remained powerful. The Cholmleys were an important local gentry family too, some of whom were also to be implicated in the Essex rebellion. The remainder of the party included aggrieved locals such as George Smyth, who was upset at Hoby's use of the stocks 'to punish poor folkes', and at his plans for renovating the parish church. Smyth

---

[9] Ibid., 108.
[10] P.R.O. STAC 5/H50/4, evidence of Peter Campelman and John Thornborough, Bishop of Limerick.

also had a menacing reputation: he had been in trouble for attacking the godly preacher of Thirsk, putting him in 'feare of his lyffe'.[11]

This party entered the house and went into Hoby's dining room. They brought out cards and played until supper time, amusing themselves

> discoursing of horses and dogs, sports whereunto Sir Thomas never applied himself, partly with lascivious talk where every sentence was begun or ended with an oath, and partly in inordinate drinking unto healths, abuses never practised by Sir Thomas.[12]

Well-fed, they stayed up playing cards and dice and later disturbed the Hoby family in their prayers. Hoby complained that when he

> and his family had begun to sing a psalm, the company above made an extraordinary noise with their feet, and some of them stood upon the stairs at a window opening in the hall, and laughed all the time of prayers.[13]

One of the servants, Robert Nettleton, said the party stamped their feet and made 'strange and wyld noyses' that drowned out the psalm and that young William Eure and two others 'did remayne with their backes towards those that were at prayers, callyng and laughing moste unreverently and most prophanely untyll prayers wer ended'.[14] Another servant, William Jorden, believed it a 'black sanctus'[15] and Thomas Hoby deplored these 'atheistical contempts'.[16]

The next morning, the company were provided with breakfast, but Hoby 'willed his servants to fyll noe more wyne, but to brynge the keye of the wyne seller into his bedchamber'.[17] Hoby told the party that they were welcome to stay if they behaved themselves, but if they continued their rowdiness, they would have to leave. Young William Eure, who was denied a conference with Lady Hoby, told Robert Nettleton:

> By god thy master send me such scurvy messages as I care not for them. I came to see my ladye and not for his meate and drinke.

---

11 Ibid., evidence of John Reynes and Robert Nettleton.
12 *Salisbury*, X: 304, Thomas Hoby to the Privy Council, 5 September 1600.
13 Ibid., X: 304.
14 P.R.O. STAC 5/H50/4, evidence of Robert Nettleton.
15 Ibid., evidence of William Jorden.
16 *Salisbury*, X: 325, Thomas Hoby to Robert Cecil, 26 September 1600.
17 P.R.O. STAC 5/H50/4, evidence of Robert Nettleton.

Bidd him send word what that lyeth him in, and I will pay him for it and sett up hornes at his gate and begone.[18]

Hoby added that Eure had said, 'Tell thy master he hath sent me scurvy messages, and the next time I meet him I will tell him so, if he be upon the bench, and will pull him by the beard'.[19]

Eventually, William was allowed to see Lady Hoby in her bedchamber, despite her illness (which rather unusually is not recorded in her diary), on condition that the party then left. Lady Hoby's serving woman claimed that Lady Hoby was distressed at Eure's behaviour: that he walked up and down her bedchamber, calling Thomas Hoby 'scurvy urchin', 'spindleshanked ape' and 'sundry other names not seemly'. She claimed that his speeches were more fit for a drunkard than a gentleman, being 'outrageous and uncyvyl'.[20] William Eure claimed that Lady Hoby agreed that the party had been ill-treated, 'with some show of dislike of her husband's strange fashions', and asked them to leave. He also suggested that Thomas Hoby listened to the conversation from behind the adjoining study door 'as I may now conjecture, to take advantage if I should use any unseemly speeches'.[21] Whatever the truth of it, the party then left, breaking some windows on their way out, young William Eure boasting that he would 'play the young Devereux' (that is, take the place of Hoby in the bedroom) and George Smyth tearing up the Hoby's driveway with his horse.[22]

* * *

This was, as Robert Cecil admitted, 'a very fowle riot', though he urged Hoby that, 'when I consider the nature of railings especially in that kind, I never found any that took less scandal than they cold after have wished they might have avoyded'.[23] Undeterred, Hoby resolved to take the matter to Star Chamber, and the details of the process afford some insight into the working out of peace. Shortly after the events, Hoby wrote to Cecil to complain about the matter, which he suggested arose from his 'want of partiality' as a commissioner. He demanded the rioters come to York to answer his complaint, boasting: 'I shall easily

18 Ibid., evidence of Robert Nettleton.
19 *Salisbury*, X: 304, Thomas Hoby to the Privy Council, 5 September 1600.
20 P.R.O. STAC 5/H50/4, evidence of Everill Aske.
21 *Salisbury*, XI: 11–12.
22 Ibid., X: 304, Robert Cecil to Thomas Hoby, 1 November 1600.
23 Ibid., XXII: 81.

derive this outrage against me conceived from envy and malice for want of partiality in me in the executing of my place and calling.'[24]

Not least because Lord Eure presided over the Council in the North, Hoby found proving his case a little more difficult than he had thought. At York he was accused of wronging the gentlemen, before a pacification was arrived at, whereby Hoby signed a paper of peace and the gentlemen said they had meant no offence to Lady Hoby. The pacification pleased Cecil, who wrote back to Hoby on 1 November 1600, saying: 'I am very gladd that the matter is reconciled, not doubting but you have very good satisfaction for so great an injury.'[25] Hoby, however, felt threatened by Lord Eure's subsequent 'long discourse of duelles . . . that one caryed not swords in vaine but to defend there reputacions as occasion required' and became determined on a court settlement.[26] Lord Eure, whose relatives were involved in the riot, and on whom Hoby ultimately blamed it, remained convinced he would win, writing to Cecil shortly before the trial in the Star Chamber in early 1602:

> I shall be pressed in defence of my honour to present the true state of the cause to the open view of the world, which hitherto I have forbone to do in regard of yourself [Cecil] and some other of his friends.[27]

The judgment went against the Eures. Lady Hoby, with some satisfaction, recorded the reconciliation of 29 May 1602:

> This day came the lord Ewry his men to Hacknes to pay 100li: which was appointed them and others to pay, by the Lordes of the privie Counsill in the starr Chamber, for their riott Comitted and unsivill behauiour att Hackenes: and so it fell out that, as it was done in the sight of our tenantes, so many of the tenants were bye when the mony was brought: which I note, as seeing the Iustice and mercie of god to his servants in manifestinge to the world, who little regards them, that he will bringe downe their enemes unto them.[28]

Thus far the story has appeared to be a simple narrative of the Eures's retribution on the Hobys for their godliness and legalism, avenged by

24 Ibid., X: 303.
25 Ibid., XXII: 81.
26 P.R.O. STAC 5/H50/4, evidence of John Thornborough.
27 *Salisbury*, XII: 22, Ralph Lord Eure to Robert Cecil, 16 January 1602.
28 *Diary of Lady Margaret Hoby*, 180–1.

Hoby in the courts and reconciled in the public payment at Hackness. However, this is the narrative that Hoby was trying to present and in fact misses out some of the details, such as the allegation that he was set on Star Chamber and its monetary rewards from the start, that show Hoby less sinned against than sinning.

* * *

This case also offers material to discuss the way in which civility was changing, as a word and code of behaviour, particularly in relation to the process of reconciliation. Norbert Elias argued in *The Civilizing Process* that civility was of growing importance in the early modern period, its importance clear from the output and content of conduct literature.[29] Whilst in the past civility was pretty similar to chivalry and the crusading spirit, as time went on it became associated with secularism and a strengthened social control. Among the problems of Elias's approach is the focus on conduct literature at the expense of other sources. Examining the language in the Hoby case, which is complicated by differences of opinion between the northern gentry and the central court in the South about the nature of civility, I think we can see civility, in the early seventeenth century, as a term open to interpretation, and up for grabs. This would suggest a later and more nuanced development of the precise meaning of civility, and its regional and temporal variations. The particular modern resonance of the word further complicates any analysis of the meanings of civility in the early modern period. For instance, violence is seen today as the antithesis of civilization, whereas in the seventeenth century only certain forms and uses of violence were described as 'uncivil'.

In describing the riot, Thomas Hoby and his supporters used the concept of civility to justify a certain lifestyle and to complain about its violation. Their theory of civility, particularly in the depositions of the servants, was perhaps a little too consistent: it is certainly possible that Hoby coached them to further his cause. Nevertheless, their 'civility' was the peaceful, lawful and above all Protestant way of life. Hoby appropriated a narrative of the popish past cleansed by the new civil society. Incivility went with threats, madness, violence, drinking and recusancy. Henry Cholmley, in one of the lists of questions addressed to the defendants, was accused of 'verie uncyvill and disgraceful speaches'

---

[29] Norbert Elias, *The Civilizing Process: Sociogenetic and Psychogenetic Investigations*, Eric Dunning, Johan Goudsblom and Stephen Mennell, eds, transl. Edmund Jephcott (revised edn, Oxford and Cambridge, MA, 2000).

at the Topcliffe sessions in 1597.[30] Linking these 'speech acts' to a perceived threat against Thomas Hoby, violence became associated with incivility. Furthermore, in the case itself, Everill Aske recorded Lady Hoby's saying that young William Eure's behaviour was 'outrageous and uncyvyl', more fit for someone overcome by 'drynke or dystracted in his wytte then for a gentleman of honourable birth and brynging up to offer in a ladys bedchamber'.[31] Lady Hoby recorded in her diary that the fine for the Eures was both for their riot and their 'unsivill behavour'.[32] Aske said that Eure was 'railing very maliciously'. Robert Nettleton, another servant, said that the defendants showed 'unkindness' and 'discurtesie' in their gaming at the Hobys' house. He stressed that the defendants violated 'the lawes of hospytalitye', coming without warning and not being content with the household's 'cyvyll and lawfull' entertainment.

The party's excessive drinking, and the offering of 'extraordinary healths' ran contrary to their code of civility.[33] Furthermore, the nicknames by which Hoby was called were brought up in court, not for their illegality but for their uncivil usage. Hoby was commonly called a 'busy little Jack' and 'Sir Pastiferous hubby', equating his grasping, litigious nature with alleged violence towards his wife.[34] William Eure's description of Hoby as 'spindleshanks' in front of Lady Hoby, and 'scurvy urchin' in front of his servant, were taken as evidence of Eure's inversion of the proper order.[35] The public use of the private 'nickname' was an aspect of incivility, heightened by the associations these names had with the bodily grotesque.[36]

Hoby's collecting of these misdemeanours under the label of incivility linked misbehaviour, such as drink and dice, with the more serious problems of violence and recusancy. However, the depositions show that the defendants had a different conception of civility. They associated civility with hospitality, honour and tradition. It was civil to

---

[30] P.R.O. STAC 5/H22/21, interrogatories.
[31] P.R.O. STAC 5/H50/4, evidence of Everill Aske.
[32] *Diary of Lady Margaret Hoby*, 180–1.
[33] P.R.O. STAC 5/H50/4, evidence of Robert Nettleton.
[34] Ibid., evidence of Michael Wharton. For the accusation that Hoby beat his wife, see P.R.O. STAC 5/H22/21, interrogatories *ex parte* Eure, no. 44.
[35] Ibid., evidence of Everill Aske and Robert Nettleton.
[36] See Anton Blok, *Honour and Violence* (Oxford, 2001), 168–70. The best analysis of nicknames is Norbert Schindler, 'The World of Nicknames: on the Logic of Popular Nomenclature', in idem, *Rebellion, Community and Custom in Early Modern Germany*, trans. Pamela E. Selwyn (Cambridge, 2002), 48–92.

allow hunting and to put up guests properly. They objected to the way that when they arrived at the house, there was no one there to greet them. They were forced to seek stables in the town and on their return were kept waiting for a further fifteen minutes.

They came, they said, in 'kindness' and they behaved 'in peaceablie manner',[37] but were made 'coldly welcome' by Hoby.[38] Hoby's complaint about their games and the implications of his hiding the key to the cellar were, claimed Sir William Eure, 'not answerable to our Northern entertainments'.[39] The Eures claimed Hoby was 'uncivil against the table', thus linking a very different set of rules to the code of civility, suggesting that sobriety was uncivil since it violated the laws of hospitality. This they connected to the privacy of Thomas Hoby's domestic religious practice. They argued that it was uncivil not to be informed that prayers were to about to begin and not to be invited to join in.[40] Their own sets of questions both challenged the timing and manner of the Hoby prayers and asked 'whether ys yt ordenarye to entreate strangers . . . to accompanye them in prayer'.[41] They included honour and peace in their version of civility. Lord Eure said that this code of conduct involved not revealing everything publicly: this he only threatened to do 'in defence of my honour'.[42] Eure's speech of duels and the use of swords was designed to instruct Hoby in proper and civil behaviour in the honour culture of the North of England.

This discussion of the place of civility in the post-Reformation, when people were learning to live with religious changes, has highlighted its importance on either side of the confessional divide as a prominent yet contested category. Clearly it was not everything: it was the physical damage of the riot that secured prosecution. And yet, civility would appear to have been close to the heart of the matter: at the time of crisis in the (contested) community, its key values appear to stare at us through the often cloudy historical record. Civility had much to do with peace for both sides, but after that their conceptions differed widely. To the Hobys it was a case of Protestantism and sobriety, to the Eures one of hospitality, honour and tradition.

---

37 P.R.O. STAC 5/H42/12, evidence of William Eure.
38 *Salisbury*, XI: 11–12.
39 Ibid., XI: 11–12. For honour in this incident, see Felicity Heal, 'Reputation and Honour in Court and Country: Lady Elizabeth Russell and Sir Thomas Hoby', *TRHS* ser. 6, 6 (1996), 161–78.
40 P.R.O. STAC 5/H50/4, evidence of William Jorden.
41 P.R.O. STAC 5/H22/21.
42 *Salisbury*, XII: 22–3.

However, resorting to the courts at best brought reconciliation, which appears to have meant something like 'cease-fire', rather than peace. In this case, the resolution was superficial. Lord Eure did his penance in the form of an embassy with the Essex puritan, Richard Crakanthorpe. Stephen Hutchinson went on to become the MP for Scarborough in 1626. Dismissing the offer of traditional peace at York, Hoby achieved a lucrative reconciliation. However, he remained in a lifelong feud with the Cholmleys, arising from personal animosity, contradictory magisterial and religious viewpoints, and a continued struggle over property. Hoby had never really wanted peace. He was, as Hugh Cholmley later recalled, a 'perverse troublesome neighbour' who 'delighted to spend his mony and time in sutes'.[43] And true to form, he was regularly in the Star Chamber, for instance in 1615, accusing Sir John Hotham of bearing him a 'scornfull and insolent manner'.[44] Again he pressed for settlement with an aggressive notion of civility, one that appropriated the notion of peace and reconciliation but had none of its meaning.

Keble College, Oxford

---

[43] *The Memoirs and Memorials of Sir Hugh Cholmley of Whitby, 1600–1657*, ed. Jack Binns, Yorkshire Archaeological Society Record Series 153 (Woodbridge, 2000), 76 and 72.
[44] P.R.O. STAC 8/175/4, Bill of Complaint.

CONFESSION AND ABSOLUTION
IN CAROLINE CAMBRIDGE:
THE 1637 CRISIS IN CONTEXT

by ERIC JOSEF CARLSON

IN June 1637, Anthony Sparrow and Sylvester Adams, two Cambridge scholars, preached in Great St. Mary's Church on the subject of confessing sins. Their sermons caused such a scandal that a deeply divided vice-chancellor's court had to act. These sermons have not gone unnoticed by historians, but they have not been contextualized in a way that makes complete sense both of the sermons and of their reception.[1] Sparrow's sermon, published shortly after it was delivered, is the better-known of the two, but not the more radical. Although no complete text of Adams's sermon survives, there are manuscript sources that make it possible to reconstruct the gist of it and to prove that it made novel claims concerning the necessity of confession for salvation. Moreover, in defending Adams his supporters challenged the sources of doctrinal authority in the English Church in unprecedented ways.[2]

Adams's text was John 20: 23, 'Whosoever sins ye remit, they are remitted unto them; and whosoever ye retain, they are retained.' John Cosin, the head of Adams's college, Peterhouse, and too supportive of Adams to distort what he said for polemical effect, summarized the sermon in a lengthy report to Dr Steward, Dean of Chichester and Clerk of the Closet, written on 12 March 1638: 'The Scope of his whole Sermon was to declare, th[a]t Confession of Sins to a Priest was implicitly required by this Text as an act necessary ... p[re]vious to Absolution, so as w[i]thout it there was no such Absolution', and without absolution, no salvation.[3] An anonymous hostile source reported that Adams said:

[1] See, for example, Peter McCullough, 'Making Dead Men Speak: Laudianism, Print, and the Works of Lancelot Andrewes, 1626–1642,' *HistJ* 41 (1998), 401–24, 417–18, and Anthony Milton, *Catholic and Reformed: the Roman and Protestant Churches in English Protestant Thought, 1600–1640* (Cambridge, 1995), 72–5.

[2] William Prynne reported reading Adams's sermon in Archbishop Laud's papers, but its fate is unknown: *Canterburies Doome: or, the first part of a compleat history of the commitment, charge, tryall, condemnation, execution of William Laud* (London, 1646), 192–3; Anthony Sparrow, *A Sermon Concerning Confession of Sinnes, And The Power of Absolution* (London, 1637).

[3] London, Public Record Office, State Papers [hereafter SP] 16/385, fol. 137r.

Because neither the Apostles nor we either were or are otherwise acquainted with the secrets of mens hearts, without confession there could not, there cannot be remission, & without remission noe salvation. And againe if Christ ordayned a tribunall seate of judgement where synnes should be remitted or retained at the discretion of the Preist (as it appeareth most Evidently by my text he did) then without all doubt it was his Intention that the faithfull should necessarily confesse all theire synnes before the preist (so farre forth I meane as they remember) for the purchasing of his pardon & remission.[4]

The concurrence of two sources from men of very different views makes it highly probable that Adams indeed argued that confession of sins to a priest was necessary for salvation.

Some of the college heads understandably found this to be a 'scandalous & popish sermon'[5] and the Vice-Chancellor, Thomas Comber of Trinity College – a genuine non-partisan among the increasingly polarized heads – summoned Adams to appear before his court.[6] It took some effort to get both Adams and a text of his sermon (which he originally claimed to have lost),[7] but the copy he eventually produced on 9 October was no self-serving exercise in selective memory. According to a contemporary report, Adams wrote that it was primarily to God that we confessed and only secondarily to the priest as his delegate: 'For the power of remission is primitive and originall in God, derivative and dependant in the Priest; in God imperiall, in the Priest Ministeriall; in God absolute, in the Priest, Delegate; in God Soveraigne, in the Priest instrumentall'. But he went on to say that the priest's power was

Judiciary too . . . no less then a temporall Judge hath a Judiciary power, though he be subject to Soveraignty. The Priest then is a Judge, and therefore must have cognizance of the cause, before he gives his Sentence. He is our Spirituall Physician and therefore

---

[4] London, British Library, MS Harley 7019, p. 57.

[5] SP 16/385, fol. 137r.

[6] On college heads, see David Michael Hoyle, ' "Near Popery yet no Popery": Theological Debate in Cambridge 1590–1644', unpublished Ph.D. thesis, University of Cambridge, 1991, 182–8. The vice-chancellor's court, made up of the heads of the colleges, and presided over by the vice-chancellor (himself one of the college heads), was responsible for disciplining Cambridge scholars and fellows.

[7] Cambridge University Library [hereafter CUL], Vice-Chancellor's Court Book [hereafter: VC CB] I.57, fols 64r, 74v.

must know the diseases of our Souls before he administers his Physick.

Adams distinguished between a worthwhile thing done by papists and a 'point of Popery', arguing that confession was the former since 'it was instituted by our Saviour, practised by the Apostles, Holy Fathers, and all succeeding Ages'. If private confession to God were enough, he argued (citing Augustine), then God gave the keys to the Church in vain; it must have been Christ's intention that sins be confessed 'in speciall' before the priest 'for a necessary means to bring us to Salvation. Without confession there could not, there cannot be remission, and so without remission there can be no salvation'. While he accepted that God *may* dispense with this requirement, he considered it dangerous to presume it; therefore, confession was not absolutely necessary but was necessary 'in a sorte', i.e. for all practical purposes.[8]

Adams failed to satisfy many of the college heads, including the new (and very hostile) Vice-Chancellor Brownrigg, with his attempts to distance himself from Rome. Someone made a motion that 'a forme of submission & Recantation' should be prepared, 'for the vindication of the Religion professed in o[u]r Church' against this assault from 'popish & false doctrine'. Cosin objected that a recantation should not be drawn up unless a majority of the heads concluded that what Adams had spoken was 'directly contrary & repugnant to the publick authorized doctrine of the Church'.[9] Brownrigg, however, determined to proceed with the recantation itself.

On 18 December, Adams was presented with the recantation. He was to acknowledge that he had said

> that a speciall confession unto a Priest (actually where time or opportunity presents itselfe or otherwise in explicite intention & resolution) of all o[u]r sins comitted after Baptisme, soe farre forth as we doe remember is necessary . . . [and] there can be noe Salvation without the aforesaid confession

and admit that his views were

> erronious & dangerous, having noe warrant from the word of God & Crossing the doctrine of o[u]r church as may appeare by her Liturgy in the second exhortation at the Com[m]union, & in the

---

[8] CUL, MS Mm.2.23, pp. 209–10.
[9] SP 16/385, fol. 138r.

visitation of the Sick & in the second part of the Homily of repentance.[10]

Brownrigg placed particular weight on the homily, noting its crucial phrase: 'It is against true Christian libertie that any man should be bound to the numbring of his Synnes, as it hath bene used heretofore in the tymes of Ignorance & blindnesse'.[11] When Adams refused to submit, the heads had to decide whether to compel him.[12]

Three of the first six heads who spoke – Samuel Ward of Sidney Sussex, Thomas Bainbrigg of Christ's, and Thomas Batchcroft of Caius – condemned Adams's doctrine. Ward called it 'most scandalous, & false & popish' and Batchcroft believed that Adams had 'contradicted the doctrine of the Church of England as it had now bin held & preachd a great while, & likewise B[isho]p Jewell & all the Protestant divines'. Both Thomas Comber (the former vice-chancellor) and Samuel Collins of King's voted against imposing the recantation because they wanted more time to reflect, while the independent-minded Henry Smyth of Magdalene 'pleaded much for the use of Confession, & for the necessitie of it'.[13]

When Cosin spoke he admitted that 'he wished many things in Mr Adams & in his sermon amended', but he could not accept that he had contradicted the Church's doctrine:

> That the Church of England in the 39 Articles where it condemned all the opinions & points of poperie . . . did not yet condemne the opinion th[a]t some men had of the Necessitie of speciall Confession & that the Book of Com[m]on Pray[e]r seemed rather to give a man libertie to be of th[a]t opinion, then to condemne him for it.[14]

He considered it wise of the Church to have left the matter unsettled and 'dangerous' for the heads 'to doe otherwise, or at least to determine it und[e]r the name of the publick autorized doctrine of the Church of England'.[15] As Anthony Milton has pointed out, 'Taken to its logical extreme, Cosin's argument would have denied that any point of popery could be rejected if the Thirty-Nine Articles did not explicitly

10 MS Harley 7019, p. 58. See also VC CB I.57, fol. 104Br; SP 16/385, fol. 138r.
11 Ibid.
12 SP 16/385, fol. 138r; see also VC CB I.57, fol. 91r.
13 SP 16/385, fol. 138r–v.
14 Ibid., fol. 138v.
15 Ibid.

renounce it'.[16] Cosin might simply have been giving his opponents a dose of their own poison. On 10 February 1629, the Commons had ordered both universities to send in all 'Recantations, Censures, and Submissions . . . for Popery or Arminianism'. They were to use the Thirty-Nine Articles as the measure of orthodoxy, and report the names of any who 'have written or published any points of doctrine contrary to the Articles'.[17] Cosin turned their chosen test against them.

After Cosin spoke, Benjamin Laney of Pembroke rejected the Vice-Chancellor's view that 'speciall Confession' was explicitly contrary to church doctrine. Then Richard Love of Corpus, surely without intending to do so, placed a lethal weapon in the hands of Adams's supporters by raising the subject of the *Homilies*. Love argued that they were part of the 'publick established and autorized doctrine of o[u]r church' and plainly condemned 'speciall and auricular Confession . . . as having no warrant from the word of God, nor testimonie from the auncient Fathers, & being contrary to [Christ]ian libertie'; Adams had caused a grave scandal to the University and 'true reformed Religion' by trying to introduce popery and the recantation was 'very moderate & just' under the circumstances. Edward Martin of Queens', an enthusiastic Laudian, launched himself into the debate and completely recast it by rejecting the notion that the *Homilies* were in fact part of 'determinate & established doctrine'. The vice-chancellor's court had no statutory power to censure Adams or require a recantation unless he had spoken against the Articles of Religion.[18]

Richard Sterne of Jesus then asserted that the 'Church of England spake very much for Confession both publick & private' and nowhere condemned it. He understood the *Homilies* only 'to condemne popish auricular Confession as they had abused it in times of blindnes & ignorance', not confession itself.[19] Thomas Eden of Trinity Hall joined him in supporting Adams, but Richard Holdsworth of Emmanuel approved of the recantation, accepting the *Homilies* as a source of 'established doctrine' and that Adams had 'taught contrary doctrine thereunto'.[20]

Eight heads had spoken against the recantation. Vice-Chancellor Brownrigg had not yet voted, though he clearly sided with the five who

[16] Milton, *Catholic and Reformed*, 74.
[17] Hoyle, 'Near Popery', 180–1.
[18] SP 16/385, fols 138v–139r.
[19] Ibid., fol. 139r. Sterne was later remembered for giving 'greate offence' in a sermon on absolution, 'w[hi]ch he made to a Judiciary formall act of remission': MS Harley 7019, p. 63.
[20] SP 16/385, fol. 139r.

had already voted to impose it. Neither side had the nine votes necessary for a decisive end. Brownrigg saw the only way open to him and seized it: he would not cast his vote in order to give the matter more time. Sterne, Martin and Eden objected that this was unfair to Adams since 'the major p[ar]t of the Court' sided with him, but unnamed 'others' decided that 'it were well to deliberate a while longer' and that was that as 1637 drew to a close.[21]

On 2 March 1638, Brownrigg 'suddenly' called a new meeting of the heads, knowing that four of those who had voted against the recantation in December (Comber, Eden, Martin, and Smyth) would be unavailable. Two previous absentees attended this session: William Beale of St. John's, siding with Adams, and Thomas Paske of Clare with Brownrigg. With seven heads present in favour of the recantation, five opposed, and four absent, it was presented once again,[22] and they voted. Although none changed his vote, the argument on both sides had shifted to one over the definition of authority – the 'worde[s] of the Liturgie & Homily of o[u]r Church' versus the exclusive, narrowly construed authority of the Thirty-Nine Articles. For example, Samuel Collins, who earlier had sought more time, now noted that the 'Book of Articles, w[hi]ch condemned many points of poperie, condemned not' Adams's views, and neither would he. Paske, weighing in for the first time, stated that he 'thought it wold be better w[i]th us if it [i.e., confession] were more in use then it is', but he could find no warrant for 'the Necessitie of it' and he believed the *Homilies* – 'the autorized doctrine of o[u]r Church' – were clear on that; Adams's sermon was, therefore, 'Scandalous, & repugnant to' official doctrine.[23]

It was a hollow victory for Brownrigg. As Ward wrote to James Ussher soon after,

> The major pars præsentium did concurr in a form præscribed by the Vice-Chancellor, protesting against his doctrine, as contrary to the Doctrine of the Church of England, but we could not make the number of 9. And though complaynt, be made to higher powers, yett the party escapeth for any thing I hear.[24]

---

21 Ibid., fol. 139v.
22 Cosin, who was outraged by Brownrigg's political shenanigans, surely would have complained if the text of the recantation had been altered since the December meeting: SP 16/385, fol. 140r; see also VC CB I.57, fol. 104Br.
23 SP 16/385, fol. 140r.
24 Oxford, Bodleian Library, MS Cherry 23, p. 181. I am grateful to Greg Cowley for transcribing this letter.

Ward could do little more than sigh that 'such are the tymes now, th[a]t, both Homilies & Liturgy are sleighted'.[25] Brownrigg's sentence was written on the recantation. The seven heads who supported it signed their names, while the five opponents penned dissents.[26] But the sentence could not be carried out for all that Brownrigg might have wanted to pretend otherwise. Instead, as Cosin records, 'when this was done, all was done . . . & Mr Adams had his liberties to goe into the country, where now he is'.[27]

*   *   *

What is the significance of this case? First, it is apparently the earliest instance in which the authority of the *Book of Common Prayer* and the *Homilies* was formally challenged. The way that the argument emerged during the debate suggests that it was novel. The anti-Calvinist George Hakewill, for one, had been content to argue not long before that, because the *Book of Common Prayer* and the *Homilies* were authorized in the Articles of Religion, 'whatsoever is doctrinally delivered in any of these, may safely bee called, The doctrine of the Church of England'.[28] Adams himself seemed prepared to base his defense on the *Homilies*, rather than rejecting the book's authority as doctrine, since he stated

> that he did most willingly & hartily Subscribe to the doctrine & Religion established in the church of England, wherin he wold constantly persist and that he wolde admit the words of the Homily where it said It is against [Chris]tian libertie th[a]t any man shold be bound in confession to the numbring of his Sins, as it hath bin used heretofore in the time of blindness & ignorance.[29]

It was one of Adams's *opponents* who brought up the *Homilies*, never expecting it to serve the other side. Cosin and his allies were not lying in wait for a chance to spring a trap, and it is perhaps just blind luck that Edward Martin had not yet spoken when Love brought up the *Homilies*, since Martin was a rabid Laudian and the ideal person to see the explosive potential of denying that they had any status as doctrinal statements.

At this point, the case ceased to be entirely about the necessity of

---

25 Ibid., p. 183.
26 MS Harley 7019, pp. 58–9; VC CB I.57, fol. 104Bv.
27 SP 16/385, fol. 141r. Adams was vicar of Rudgwick, Sussex.
28 George Hakewill, *An Answere to a Treatise Written by D'. Carier* (London, 1616), 138.
29 SP 16/385, fol. 137r.

confession and became a row over the locus of the Church's 'established and authorized doctrine'. The Thirty-Nine Articles, as Cosin rightly stated, do not explicitly condemn mandatory confession to a priest. But it never occurred to those constructing the Elizabethan settlement that they should. Official intentions were clearly set forth in the liturgy, and explained in the 'Homily of Repentance': confession was an option in the English Church, encouraged for comfort and to be sought as needed; it was not to be confused with forgiveness, which came from God and could be obtained without any human intermediary.

This approach to confession was both embraced and defended by divines all along the ecclesiological spectrum right into the 1630s, although the broad consensus in support of optional private confession has been obscured by historians focusing only on episcopal visitation articles from the 1620s and 1630s. It is certainly true that, starting with John Overall, many bishops associated with an anti-Calvinist and ceremonialist approach used visitations to promote private confession by asking if the minister read the exhortation to confession before administering the Lord's Supper, but they always did so specifically invoking the authority of the *Book of Common Prayer*. For example, Richard Neile's 1624 articles for Durham asked: 'Doth [your minister] admonish [the parishioners] to cleare their consciences (if they be in any way grieved) by confession and absolution, according to the booke of common prayer'.[30] These bishops embraced the liturgy's authority and anyone who accused them of ceremonial innovations would be met with the response that they did nothing but quote from the prayer book. Rejecting its authority in 1637 opened up a gaping chasm between these bishops and the Cambridge heads defending Adams. Moreover, although only bishops now labelled Laudian or Arminian (and not all of them) made this a visitation issue, there was a much broader consensus not only that confession as an *option* was a good thing, but also that it was 'much neglected' (to use Adams's words) and should be talked up.[31]

Many writers emphasized the optional character of confession as a distinctive feature of the English Church. In his rebuttal to the convert

---

[30] Nicholas Tyacke, *Anti-Calvinists: the Rise of English Arminianism c.1590–1640* (Oxford, 1987), 116, 206–7. For the articles, see *Visitation Articles and Injunctions of the Early Stuart Church*, ed. Kenneth Fincham, Church of England Record Society 1 & 5, 2 vols (Woodbridge, 1994–8), I: 86–9, 164, 169–73; II: 28, 136–7, 145, 150.

[31] For the substantial evidence for this, see Eric Josef Carlson, 'Confession and Absolution in the English Church from the Reformation to the 1630s' (in progress).

Benjamin Carier's critique of the English Church, George Hakewill wrote in 1616 that 'people are indeed freed from the necessity of that which we call auricular [confession], though not from the *possibility*, as you falsely pretend'.[32] In 1625, the Calvinist bishop, James Ussher, in response to an Irish Jesuit's attack, also wrote favorably about confession noting

> that no kinde of Confession, either publick or private, is disallowed by us, that is any way requisite for the due execution of the ancient power of the Keyes which Christ bestowed upon his Church: the thing which wee reject, is that new pick-lock of Sacramental Confession, obtruded upon mens consciences, as a matter necessarie to salvation.[33]

The Caroline bishop, Griffith Williams, in a court sermon printed in 1636, urged the necessity of *repentance*, but that was generally joined with confession directly to God. Confession to priests could sometimes be good 'because they know best how to yeeld us comfort', but Williams added immediately that 'this doth no waies prove, or patronize the necessity of that unjustly imposed auricular confession'. He was content to emphasize over and over that God was the source of mercy, and that confession of sins to God was all that was necessary for forgiveness.[34]

So where did Adams get his ideas? According to Samuel Ward, in a letter to Ussher shortly after the case fizzled out, 'Adams would have B[isho]pp Andrewes in his sermon of absolution to patronage him, w[hi]ch I cannot conceyve he doth'.[35] Ward was right on both points. There are several phrases in Adams's sermon that appear to have been lifted directly from the court sermon on absolution preached by Lancelot Andrewes in 1600 and published in 1629 in *XCVI Sermons*, very likely a conscious effort by Adams to create the illusion of his orthodoxy.[36] But if his language mimicked that of Andrewes's sermon, his argument did not.

Andrewes was certainly a great enthusiast for private confession, who lamented its neglect and used his office as penitentiary canon at St

---

32 Hakewill, *Answere to Carier*, 266.
33 James Ussher, *An Answer to a Challenge Made by a Jesuit in Ireland* (London, 1625), 81–2.
34 Griffith Williams, *The Best Religion* (London, 1636), 191.
35 MS Cherry 23, p. 183.
36 Lancelot Andrewes, 'A Sermon Preached at Whitehall', in *The Works of Lancelot Andrewes*, ed. J. P. Wilson and J. Bliss, 11 vols (Oxford, 1841–54), 5: 88–94, 102–3.

Paul's to promote it,[37] but he never advocated the *necessity* of private confession. In his sermon, he focused on the role and power of the minister in absolution. It was fairly common at the time, as it continued to be into the 1630s, for many divines to argue that it was adequate to confess to any 'discreet and faithfull Christian'[38] who could bring comfort to the penitent. As Arthur Hildersham put it,

> As we finde in the diseases of the body, men run not alwayes to the Physitian, but receive that counsell and medicine sometimes from a neighbour, that hath had the same infirmitie, that doth him more good, then he could have received from the most learned Doctour: So in the wounds and distemper of the soule, that helpe may some-times bee found from a private Christian that hath had experience of the same tentation, that cannot bee had from many a learned and godly Minister.[39]

Hildersham and most of the other writers who took this line still felt that the minister was the best qualified to help but accorded him no definitive advantage over a godly lay person, and typically emphasized the very limited nature of the minister's power. Andrew Willet, for example, stated that a minister's duty was only to *declare* and not to *decide* forgiveness, which only Christ did; ministers were ambassadors and not judges.[40] Joseph Bentham wrote,

> Ministers have power to forgive onely ministerially, by declaring whose sins are forgiven, whose not. As the priests under the law cleansed the lepers, pronouncing the cleane to be cleane, not making him to be so; so Ministers of the Gospell have received power to remit where God remits but no where else.[41]

But Andrewes felt that the words with which Jesus commissioned the apostles needed to be read differently:

> For the Apostles' part is delivered in the active, *Remiseritis*, and His own part in the passive, *Remittuntur*. . . . He fully meaneth . . . to

---

[37] McCullough, 'Making Dead Men Speak', 417–18.

[38] Nehemiah Rogers, 'The Indulgent Father', in *The true conuert: or, An exposition vpon the XV. chapter of St. Lukes Gospell* (London, 1632), 261.

[39] Arthur Hildersham, *CLII Lectures Upon Psalme LI* (1635), 152, 165–8.

[40] Andrew Willet, *Synopsis Papismi* (5th edn, London, 1634), 288.

[41] Joseph Bentham, *The Saints Societie* (London, 1636), 38.

ratify in heaven that is done on earth, to the sure and steadfast comfort of them that shall partake it.[42]

God was the 'original' of the power to forgive sins, only in God was that power absolute, and God also retained the power to forgive sins Himself, but ministers had real judicial power, and were not merely mouthpieces for God. However, Andrewes never departed in the slightest way from the clear voice of the liturgy: private confession was optional. The issue for him was how, if the option were sought, it could be most effective for the troubled person.

If not in Andrewes, then perhaps in Richard Montagu there is some precedent for Adams's words. There was, after all, a direct personal connection since Adams had been tutor to Montagu's son. In *A New Gagg*, Montagu, like Andrewes, said there were two ways in which sins were forgiven: an original power (God) and a delegated power (the priest). Among human beings, only priests had this power. Confession to priests was 'of excellent use and practice, being discreetly handled' and the English Church made it available to all who wished it and encouraged it for some, though it was always understood to be 'of conveniency, not of absolute necessity'; confession was 'never necessary necessarily'.[43] Thus, not even Montagu can provide an historical precedent for Adams.

In spite of his connection with Montagu, and while he was protected by the Cambridge 'Arminian bloc',[44] Adams was not being accused of Arminianism. In fact, he made some of the Durham House crowd uneasy and John Cosin, his most stalwart defender, pointedly did not endorse the necessity of confession but tried feebly to craft a compromise in which Adams's views would receive only the back-handed endorsement of being private opinions on things indifferent.[45] It was actually popery – or at least 'near popery' – with which Adams stood charged.[46] Vice-Chancellor Brownrigg's citation of the *Homilies* made this clear: in making confession to a priest necessary for salvation, Adams recalled the 'tymes of Ignorance & blindnesse' when people had 'against true Christian libertie . . . [been] bound to the numbring of

---

[42] Andrewes, 'A Sermon Preached at Whitehall', 103.

[43] Richard Montagu, *A gagg for the new Gospell? No: a new gagg for an old goose* (London, 1624), 78, 83; see also *Appello Cæsarem* (London, 1625), 310, 314–15.

[44] McCullough, 'Making Dead Men Speak', 417.

[45] SP 16/385, fol. 140v.

[46] On this distinction and its importance in Cambridge, see Hoyle, ' "Near Popery" ', *passim*.

[their] Synnes'. It had always been the core of the Protestant critique that it was impossible to confess every sin ever committed and that to require people to do this was to transform what was supposed to be a great comfort into a cause for anxiety and a terrible burden. This was what they derogatorily called 'eare-confession', to distinguish it from the practice of the ancient Church as set forth in the Bible.[47]

Early in the process against him, when Adams was given the opportunity to show how his views differed from those of Rome, he tried first to associate himself with the ancient practice of the Church, but it is hard to believe that anyone with even a nodding acquaintance with early Church history would have bought that argument. The more pressing problem was for him to define 'necessity' in a way that would be acceptable and not popish. First, he argued that in making confession necessary he did *not* mean that it was necessary to name all sins and that he condemned the canons of the Council of Trent on this subject. This was a shrewd polemical strategy, since it was a point that brought together Calvinist and Laudian divines. For example, Ussher made it the core of his argument cited above: the English Church, like the Fathers of the ancient Church, exhorted people to confess to their ghostly fathers; it rejected only the necessity of confession required in

> the Canons of the late Conventicle of Trent, where those good Fathers put their curse upon everie one, that either shall deny, that Sacramentall confession was ordayned by divine right, and is by the same right necessary to salvation: or shall affirme, that in the Sacrament of Penance, it is not by the ordinance of God necessarie for the obtayning of the remission of sinnes, to confesse all and every one of those mortall sinnes, the memory whereof by due and diligent premeditation may bee had. . . .[48]

When the Laudian pamphleteer Christopher Dow tried to clarify the orthodoxy of his views on auricular confession, he wrote that

> if any shall call it, auricular, because it is done in private, and in the eare of the Priest, I know not why hee should therefore bee condemned of Popery. But if [he] by Auricular Confession, meane that Sacramentall Confession, which the Councell of Trent hath defined to bee of absolute necessity by Divine ordinance, and that which exacts that (many times impossible) particular enumeration

---

[47] Willet, *Synopsis Papismi*, 734.
[48] Ussher, *Answer to a Challenge*, 82.

of every sinne. This wee justly reject, as neither required by God, nor so practiced by the ancient Church.[49]

Thus, Adams affirmed that it was neither necessary nor possible to confess every sin ever committed and was 'Sufficient to confesse [only] those knowne Sinnes' of which penitents were conscious, establishing some common ground and sounding reasonable while putting distance between himself and the 'tymes of Ignorance & blindnesse'.[50] Adams seemed to be staking out precisely the line taken in the 'Homily of Repentance'.

But the larger problem was the sovereignty of God – always a central concern for Calvinists – and the possibility of salvation if one confessed one's sins to God alone. This clearly had been the teaching of the English Church since the Reformation and it was embraced without exception by divines of every stripe. Adams might say

> that he made no such absolute necessitie of private Confession for all Sorts of men, & for every p[ar]ticular & primary offence, as th[a]t w[i]thout it there cannot possibly be any remission or p[ar]don hoped for from Gods hands, this being one, though not the only means to Salvation,

but it was hard to square that with other statements that he seems to have made in his sermon and which he never denied making.[51] While he might try to associate himself with Montagu's view that confession was 'never necessary necessarily', what he had to ignore was that Montagu had written immediately before that confession was 'of conveniency, not of absolute necessity'. Adams never said that he espoused only the 'conveniency' of confession.

There are, then, two things that appear to explain the furore over Adams's sermon. The first is the content of his argument, which exceeded even the claims of the most controversial Laudians. The second is the way in which authorized doctrine was recast in order to defend Adams. What is remarkable is that, however uncomfortably, so many of the Cambridge heads felt it necessary to do so. Unless someone

---

[49] Christopher Dow, *Innovations Unjustly charged upon the Present Church and State* (London, 1637), 55–6.
[50] SP 16/385, fol. 137v.
[51] Ibid. Although Cosin was not uncritical of Adams, he did want to cast him (and, by extension, his own support of Adams) in the best light. Since Cosin makes no mention of him denying the necessity of private confession when doing so would exonerate him, it seems unlikely that he did.

preached obvious heresy, it was preferable to find a way to protect what we now call free speech, since any restrictions could potentially be turned against them on another day. In the process, the Laudian heads made it easier for their enemies to associate them with 'near popery' and they may ultimately have done great damage to their cause while trying to protect a platform from which to promote it.

Gustavus Adolphus College

'THERE VERY CHILDREN WERE SOE FULL OF HATRED': ROYALIST CLERICAL FAMILIES AND THE POLITICS OF EVERYDAY CONFLICT IN CIVIL WAR AND INTERREGNUM ENGLAND

by MICHELLE WOLFE

IN Ugborough, Devonshire, in the mid-1640s, the young son of Emmanuel Sharp, the former Royalist rector of Bathealston, Somerset, joined a group of children at a bonfire.[1] As people gathered to hear news of another battle won by Parliament, a local tailor spotted one child and denounced him as a 'priest's bastard'. Mrs Sharp flew to the defence of her son's legitimacy and her own marital honour. Heavily pregnant, Mrs Sharp miscarried as a result of the commotion. The involuntary abortion was allegedly acclaimed by local Puritans, who purportedly celebrated '[t]hat ye calf was dead, & if ye cow had died also they would have made a Bonfire ... [up] to Heaven'.[2]

Reported fifty or sixty years after the fact by Sharp's grandchild, this account may be more family and parish legend than reliable fact.[3] Yet even as rhetoric, it captures the character of the interpersonal politics that surrounded the ejection and sequestration of Royalist ministers in Civil War and Interregnum England. The verbal assault on the Sharp child and the celebration of Mrs Sharp's miscarriage as a providential expression of God's Parliamentarian sympathies highlight the identification of a minister's family with his ecclesio-political allegiances. Meanwhile, Mrs Sharp's vociferous defence of clerical parentage at the

---

[1] Thanks are due to Margaret Spufford for pointing me to the Manby family, and to W. J. Sheils and Carla Pestana for their incisive comments.

[2] Oxford, Bodleian Library [hereafter Bodl.], MS J. Walker c.3, fols 304–305; A. G. Matthews, *Walker Revised: Being a Revision of John Walker's Sufferings of the Clergy during the Grand Rebellion, 1642–1660* (Oxford, 1948), 336.

[3] The Walker MSS comprise a diverse set of sources, from official papers to reports of parish hearsay regarding the ejections of past parsons. I am using here official papers and the signed accounts from clerical wives, children and grandchildren. See Anne Laurence, ' "This Sad and Deplorable Condition": an Attempt Towards Recovering an Account of the Sufferings of Northern Clergy Families in the 1640s and 1650s', in Diana Wood, ed., *Life and Thought in the Northern Church c.1100–c.1700: Essays in Honour of Claire Cross*, SCH.S 12 (Woodbridge, 1999), 465–88, 465–9, for the problems of family 'mythology'.

bonfire demonstrates how the context of war and ejection turned everyday events into acts of political conflict. It made women and children combatants in a domestic and neighbourly theatre of war.

Previous scholarship on women in the English Civil Wars has either emphasized their suffering on the sidelines or their opportunistic transgression of conventional gender roles in religion, culture and society. Important essays by Barbara Donegan, on atrocities, and Ann Laurence, on northern Royalist clerical families, have clearly demonstrated the collateral economic and bodily injury inflicted by the Civil Wars on women and children.[4] However, the ecclesio-political meanings of that suffering, and women's and children's active responses to it require further examination. Additionally, starting with the work of Keith Thomas and Phyllis Mack, an ongoing historiographical debate has continued to probe the degree to which social and confessional upheaval of the wars and Interregnum created new or unconventional roles for women in worship, work and political expression.[5] However, the debate over women's liberation and transgression has often obscured the potential power of women's conventional activities during a time of conflict.[6] It has frequently deflected our attention from the conservative investment many women felt in the authority and status they already possessed as mistresses of patriarchal households, and turned us away from their political passion to defend and preserve the position of their husbands and households within the patriarchal hierarchy of English society.

Here I will step outside the two historiographical frameworks of gender passivity or gender role transgression and subversion. In Royalist clerical families, the conventional positions, work and representations of subordinate household members had political and confessional meaning and impact. In peacetime, the parish visibility, influence and charitable responsibilities of the entire clerical household could and

---

[4] Barbara Donegan, 'Atrocity, War Crime, and Treason in the English Civil War', *AHR* 99 (1994), 1137–66; idem, 'Did Ministers Matter? War and Religion in England, 1642–1649', *JBS* 33 (1994), 119–56; Laurence, ' "Sad and Deplorable" ', 465–88.

[5] Keith Thomas, 'Women in the Civil War Sects', in Trevor Aston, ed., *Crisis in Europe 1550–1650: Essays from Past and Present* (London, 1965); Phyllis Mack, *Visionary Women: Ecstatic Prophecy in Seventeenth-Century England* (Berkeley, 1992); Patricia Crawford, *Women and Religion in England, 1500–1720* (London, 1993), 119–84 and idem, 'Historians, Women and the Civil War Sects, 1640–1660', *Parergon* 6 (1988), 19–32.

[6] See Ann Hughes, 'Gender and Politics in the Leveller Literature', in Susan D. Amussen and Mark A. Kishlansky, eds, *Political Culture and Cultural Politics in Early Modern England: Essays Presented to David Underdown* (Manchester, 1995), 162–88.

often did enable clerical wives and sometimes children to locally exercise unofficial but nonetheless significant forms of influence.[7] This influence arose from what, in the Early Modern context, Sara Mendelson and Patricia Crawford have termed 'public housekeeping': the conventionally feminine labours of nurturing and domestic care performed by the wives, daughters and dependants of men in public positions, for a larger clientele or community outside their own private household.[8] Such 'public housekeeping' was always performed in the name of the patriarchal household head. Thus, in peacetime, 'public housekeeping' comprised elite women's political collaboration in maintaining patriarchal household honour and in conserving the larger social *status quo*.

For Royalist clerical wives and dependants during the Civil Wars and Interregnum, family property, domestic survival and neighbourly relations became zones of political and religious conflict, as they became objects of confessional retribution. Thus, housekeeping and play became practices of political and confessional resistance. These acts of resistance, however, were themselves conservative, rather than subversive. Like peacetime 'public housekeeping', they were performed in defence of the patriarchal identity and status of the clerical household head.[9]

These practices of Royalist political housekeeping reflected a two-way dynamic of professional and ecclesio-political identification. Targeting them as objects of political and confessional hostility, Parliamentarian officials, soldiers and parishioners associated clerical wives, sons and daughters with the profession and ecclesiastical politics of their husband or father. Thus dependant family members of ceremonialist clergy were locally treated as convenient personal symbols of polluted Protestantism and the encroachment of stealth popery. Resisting sequestration and Presbyterian intrusion, the wives and children of ejected ministers identified themselves with the ecclesio-political posi-

---

[7] Jacqueline Eales, 'Gender Construction in Early Modern England and the Conduct Books of William Whately (1583–1639)', in R. N. Swanson, ed., *Gender and the Christian Religion*, SCH 34 (Woodbridge, 1998), 163–74; Jeremy Gregory, 'Gender and the Clerical Profession in England, 1660–1850', in ibid., 235–71.

[8] Sara Mendelson and Patricia Crawford, *Women in Early Modern England, 1550–1720* (Oxford, 1998), 341.

[9] Susan Dwyer Amussen, *An Ordered Society: Gender and Class in Early Modern England* (New York, 1993); Elizabeth Foyster, *Manhood in Early Modern England: Honour, Sex and Marriage* (London, 1999); Laura Gowing, *Domestic Dangers: Women, Words and Sex in Early Modern London* (Oxford, 1996).

tion of their husband and father. For some this meant fully embracing the identity of the Royalist clergy and the confessional politics of King, Episcopacy and Common Prayer.

In the rest of this paper I will briefly describe the process and procedures of clerical ejections in the 1640s and early 1650s. Then, using both the contemporary records of the committee for scandalous ministers and (with some caution) the later accounts given by widows, children and grandchildren of Royalist clergy, I will examine how ejection gave rise to politicized acts of resistance by clerical wives and children, as they engaged in sustained conflict with sequestrators, intruders and parishioners.

* * *

During the first English Civil War, a Parliamentary ordinance passed in January 1644 authorized the Earl of Manchester to establish committees in the seven associated counties of Cambridge, Essex, Hertford, Huntingdon, Lincoln, Norfolk and Suffolk, to identify clergy suspected of pastoral insufficiencies, ceremonialist sympathies or opposition to Parliament. The ordinance authorized the Earl of Manchester to remove such 'scandalous' ministers from their posts, sequester their benefices and personal estates, and replace them with ministers – popularly termed 'intruders' – approved by the Westminster Assembly. It also gave him discretionary power to grant as maintenance a fifth of the income from any such sequestered living to the petitioning wife or children of the ejected clergyman. As the ejections commenced, Parliament's existing Committee for Plundered Ministers assumed responsibility for complaints and appeals from both ejected families and stymied sequestrators. Petitions and paperwork swelled as further areas fell under Parliamentarian control and greater numbers of Royalist ministers were ejected. A subsequent ordinance, passed in 1654 by the first Protectorate Parliament, established a committee for scandalous ministers in each county of the Commonwealth, with uniform procedures for ejection and the maintenance of the evicted wives and children.[10]

Clerical ejection and sequestration combined a programme of religious

---

[10] J. W. F. Hill, 'The Royalist Clergy of Lincolnshire', *Lincolnshire Architectural and Archæological Society Reports and Papers* 2 (1938), 36–40; *The Suffolk Committees for Scandalous Ministers, 1644–1646*, ed. Clive Holmes, Suffolk Records Society 13 (Ipswich, 1970), 9–14; *Acts and Ordinances of the Interregnum, 1642–1660*, ed. C. S. Firth and R. S. Rait, 3 vols (Holmes Beach, FL, 1969) [hereafter *A&O*], I: 371–2; II: 968–90.

reform with a policy of military pacification. Ejection allegedly cleansed parish churches of ineffectual preaching and prayer-book ceremony. Ejection also silenced articulate opponents of Parliament, whose subversive pronouncements from the pulpit could sway the sympathies of their parish. The meagre and irregular 'fifth' of sequestered clerical income granted to wives and children served as an economic method of suppressing Royalist resistance. Petitions for fifths were granted on condition that the clerical wife and her husband swear to 'yiel[d] all due obedience to the . . . sequestracon [sic]' and offer no opposition to the sequestrators or intruder.[11]

The economic element of clerical ejection and sequestration was essential, in its conception and its effect. And it was this element that most effectively implicated clerical wives and children. Evicting the clergyman from his house and life-interest freehold, it subjected the entire clerical family to ecclesio-political punishment. The sins of Laudian fathers were visited upon school-age sons. The impact of ejection on families was explicitly integrated into County Committee proceedings, which appended to each inquiry the number of offspring and marital status of the scandalous minister under investigation.[12] It was acknowledged in the ordinances that authorized the institution of the wife's fifth, and continually enacted in the petitioning process that resulted.[13]

* * *

Early Modern England's system of political and social governance was constituted around the patriarchal household.[14] Among the landed elite in particular, and to a lesser degree among the merchant and mandarin classes of lawyers and clerics, the seventeenth-century family was a base of political power and social authority. The markers of household honour were essential to that authority, and household dependants as well as household heads bore those markers in their day-to-day carriage and conduct.[15] Thus, clerical dispossession visited both political and material retribution upon the family, as it stripped the clerical household of its status, authority and economic livelihood.

[11] *Minute Book of the Committee for Plundered Ministers* [hereafter CPM] 1644–1647, British Library, Additional Manuscripts [hereafter BL, MS Addit.] 15669–15670, *passim*.
[12] Cambridge University Library [hereafter CUL], MS William M. Palmer B. 58, *passim*; Holmes, *Suffolk Committee*, 28–91.
[13] *A&O*, I: 371, II: 986; BL, MS Addit. 15669, *passim*; BL, MS Addit. 15670, *passim*.
[14] Amussen, *Ordered Society*, 34–66.
[15] Gowing, *Domestic Dangers*, 105–19.

Sequestration unmanned the minister himself by depriving him of the basic masculine ability to provide for his family.[16] Reducing those clerical wives of landed or professional birth to 'see out for Bread' by the mean labours of subsistence such as begging or commercial spinning, sewing and brewing, was a pointed humiliation that further diminished the honour of the entire household.[17] As mistresses of the parsonage, clerical wives were often predominant dispensers of parish charity. As a social and domestic labour, dispensing regular charity was one form of 'public housekeeping' that endowed these women with status and moral authority. Receiving charity, on the contrary, was an activity that degraded status and credit. Ejection subjected the clerical wife to a dramatic reversal in status. It transformed a socially esteemed 'instrumen[t] under God in the Relief of the Poor', such as Mrs Anne Goodwin, wife of the vicar of Cransfield, Suffolk, into the socially demeaned recipient of 'meere charity'.[18]

Whereas seventeenth-century clerical children had been previously pressured by parents to represent the parsonage by serving as visible models of conduct to their schoolfellows and playmates, they were now real targets of hostility and scorn.[19] They were taunted, like the Sharp child. The children of John Manby, rector of Cottenham, Cambridgeshire, were ostracized and attacked. 'There very children were soe full of hatred', Manby's daughter recalled, that they would often run from her and her sister whenever they attempted to join in games.[20] Attention from local children was even worse. Pretending to befriend her, Frances Manby's schoolmates led her out of the schoolyard, where 'a boy, sone to an adversary' thrust the tines of a fork into her forehead.[21] In a society where household honour was a communal attribute shared by every family member, these attacks reinforced the loss of status of Royalist clerical families. They reiterated their position as outcasts and as symbols of a so-called 'scandalous' Church regime.

The most powerful material fact of sequestration was the eviction of

---

[16] A. J. Shepard, 'Meanings of Manhood in Early Modern England, with Special Reference to Cambridge, *c.*1560–1640', unpublished Ph.D. thesis, University of Cambridge, 1998, Ch. 3.

[17] Bodl., MS J. Walker c.2, fol. 458r; c.3, fol. 214r; c.4, fol. 87r; c.8, fols 83–84.

[18] Bodl., MS J. Walker c.1, fol. 397r; Matthews, *Walker Revised*, 336.

[19] See [William Bedell, Jr.], *A true relation of the life and death of the Right Rev. Father in God William Bedell, Lord Bishop of Kilmore in Ireland*, ed. Thomas Wharton Jones, Camden Society Publications, NS 4 (London, 1872), 18 and 20, from the manuscript *c.*1670 or 1682.

[20] CUL, MS William M. Palmer B. 58, fol. 3r.

[21] Ibid., fols 3r–4r.

the clerical family from the parsonage house. When husbands were imprisoned or in hiding, the wives and children of Royalist clergy endured the harsh process of eviction and sequestration alone. Representatives of the absent clergyman, they became the *de facto* objects of Parliamentarian retribution. Evicted from the rectory of Broughton, Northamptonshire, while her husband was in hiding, Mrs Martha Bentham was supposedly 'not suffer[ed]' by sequestrators 'to take one peck of corn out of her Barne . . . nor one peny but what was in their [pockets]'.[22] As Parliamentarian agents evicted his family from the parsonage of Otterton, Devonshire, the eight-year-old son of the Rector Richard Venn, was allegedly 'struck . . . with a violent blow' as the irritated sequestrator 'was turning ym out of doors'.[23]

The domestic objects of everyday family life became tools of material retribution, as sequestrators and intruding ministers detained or destroyed the families' basic moveables and household goods. Jane Darnelly, wife of the ejected rector of Teversham, Cambridgeshire, was not unusual in appealing to the central Committee for Plundered Ministers for recovery of the 'household stuffe . . . of the said Mris [*sic*] Darnelly by him [i.e. the intruder William Sharp] destroyed'.[24] Ordinary household moveables were not officially under sequestration, a principle that was often ignored. John Reeve, the son of the ejected rector of Allerton, Norfolk, recalled with bitterness that parishioners and troopers 'brought carts & carried away my father's Librirary [*sic*] & all the Household goods'.[25] The punitive centrepiece of clerical ejection, eviction from the parsonage house, punished the entire clerical household. Subjecting clerical wives and children to material, physical and social humiliation, it assaulted both the honour and the economic integrity of the entire clerical family.

* * *

Punishment of the family through dispossession and dishonour reflected a policy and a mental attitude that associated the clerical family with the confessional and political stance of the clerical household head. This made clerical wives and children passive objects of ecclesio-political retribution, but it also made them potential political

22 Bodl., MS J. Walker c.2, fol. 97a recto.
23 Bodl., MS J. Walker c.2, fol. 415r.
24 CPM minutes, Teversham: 18 April 1646 and 4 September 1646, BL, Addit. 15670, fols 143 and 207.
25 Bodl., MS J. Walker c.1, fol. 78r; see also Bodl., MS J. Walker c.3, fol. 214r.

actors. The anthropologist James Scott has suggested a dual model of political opposition: public opposition, which comprises formal or open action in a public or official arena, and 'infrapolitical resistance' which comprises everyday forms of resistance in the unofficial arenas of labour, domestic life and local relations.[26] Ejection prompted clerical wives, and to a lesser degree clerical children, to resist the retribution of sequestration by official and unofficial means.

The process of petitioning for her fifth did not enfold the clerical wife into the fluidly enfranchised 'political nation' of seventeenth-century England. But it did endow the clerical wife with an official political status. The process recognized her as a subject of political sequestration and engaged her as a potential opponent of the regime by requiring her to swear her obedience.[27] The orders and acts of these Parliamentarian committees against clerical wives suggests the potential political influence they held in their parishes, and the potential problems it posed for the government. Mrs Rachel Procter, wife of the ejected rector of Stradishall, Suffolk, was instructed by the Committee for Compounding that her fifth was conditional on her residing outside the parish and avoiding contact with parishioners.[28] Mrs Hester Manby, wife of the ejected Rector John Manby, organized a highly successful tithe strike in the parish of Cottenham. In response, the Committee for Plundered Ministers issued orders for the arrest of Mrs Manby as a 'malignant' – an official opponent of Parliament.[29]

As official petitioners, clerical wives were constrained by a rhetoric of deference; even the troublesome Mrs Procter declared her humility when petitioning the Committee for Plundered Ministers.[30] Yet within the tight rhetorical formulas of maintenance petitions, some clerical wives found an official opportunity to express confessional disapproval. Martha Bentham, wife of the ejected rector of Broughton, called into question the pastoral superiority of some Westminster replacements when appealing to the Northamptonshire County Committee. She

[26] James Scott, *Domination and the Arts of Resistance: Hidden Transcripts* (New Haven, CT and London, 1990), 1–16; 183–201; my thanks to Jennifer Anderson for the reference.

[27] Children could also petition and did: BL, MS Addit. 15670, fol. 235. See also Geoffrey L. Hudson, 'Negotiating for Blood Money: War Widows and the Courts in Seventeenth-Century England', in Jenny Kermode and Garthine Walker, eds, *Women, Crime and the Courts in Early Modern England* (Chapel Hill, NC, and London, 1994), 146–69.

[28] Bodl., MS Bodley 324, fol. 2r.

[29] BL, MS Addit. 15671, fols 188v and 200v.

[30] BL, MS Addit. 15669, fol. 236v.

archly noted that the intruder Mr. Bazely had 'preached not one sermon . . . nor tooke care for any'.[31]

Scott also argues that people often seize on infrapolitical strategies when the dominant regime mixes political repression, or in this case political punishment, with material exploitation. Under those conditions, infrapolitical resistance does double duty as both a strategy of material subsistence and expression of political, and in this case confessional, dissent.[32] Thus, in the process of securing food or finances or charitable support for their family, clerical wives could express resistance to their family's sequestration and the regime that imposed it. When the intruder Richard Herring of Drewsteignton, Devonshire, refused to pay the ordered fifth to Jane Short, wife of the ejected rector, his tithe corn was 'violently taken away by her' and effectively held for cash ransom.[33] Mrs Peckham, wife of the ejected rector of Fostead Parva in Sussex, was found guilty of resisting sequestration by the Committee for Plundered Ministers. She 'contemmed the said sequestration by keeping possession of the house till she was from there expelled'. She further articulated her contempt by subjecting the parsonage to 'much willful spoyle'.[34]

For some clerical wives, attempting to preserve their husband's library was an attempt to save a valuable piece of family property and a politicized and confessionally charged effort to defend their family's honour as a *clerical* family. Judith Whitford, wife of the rector of Ashford, Northamptonshire, helped hide her husband's books.[35] And Royalist legend recounted that Mrs Willington, widow of the ejected vicar of Ospringe, Kent, braved Parliamentarian pistols as she attempted to block their way to her deceased husband's study.[36] Both materially valuable and professionally meaningful, clerical libraries represented at once a family repository of monetary investment (for some clerical families, the library was probably financially on a par with plate) and a tangible symbol of the minister's special status and profession.[37] In accounts of sequestration, both widows and children referred repeatedly and specifically to the trauma of watching sequestrators

[31] Bodl., MS J. Walker c.4, fol. 315r.
[32] Scott, *Domination*, 183–201.
[33] Bodl., MS J. Walker c.4, fol. 163r.
[34] BL, MS Addit. 15669, fol. 78v.
[35] Bodl., MS J. Walker c.4, fol. 33r.
[36] Bodl., MS J. Walker c.2, fol. 458r.
[37] On the gendered and family meanings of the clerical library see my paper, ' "Sacred Imployments": Gendering Spiritual Space and Labour in the Clerical Household', presented

seize their husbands' or fathers' books.[38] The sting with which wives and children recalled that loss revealed the degree to which the family possessed a shared investment in the patriarch's clerical honour and clerical identity.

In a significantly lesser fashion, both adult and younger children of Royalist clergy were also politicized in their household roles, generally by assisting their father or mother. Older children such as Thomas Couckson, son of the ejected parson of Marston, Bedfordshire, assisted his father in going door-to-door to organize a tithe strike against the intruder.[39] Typically, young children might perform small household chores while also being themselves an object of substantial household labour and care. When petitioning, begging and negotiating with sequestrators, clerical wives sometimes invoked the needs and number of their young children when protesting against eviction or financial deprivation. However, sometimes the children themselves participated in these engagements, as their parents put their youth and vulnerability to use. The wife of Joseph Barnes, ejected rector of East Isly, reportedly 'sent her little daughter' to entreat the intruding minister to pay his arrears of fifths, 'hopeing her innocens might move him'.[40]

Although their status as household dependants excluded them from most forms of public politics, clerical wives and children were subordinate members of what we might term a 'public household' with a privileged political status and a unique spiritual standing. 'Public housekeeping' and 'infrapolitical resistance' represented two sides of the political life of women, children and dependants within such households. Both were modes of practical and nurturing labour and action conventional to women and household subordinates. Both employed these conventional forms to either produce and exercise neighbourly influence from an uncontested position of household power, or engage in resistance and opposition from a contested position of household weakness. Both were ultimately conservative expressions of support for the patriarchal household, by subordinate members of that household.

at the Religion and Society in Early Modern England Conference, St. Mary's College, Surrey, UK, 22 April 2001.

[38] See CUL, MS William M. Palmer B. 58, fol. 1v; Bodl., MS J. Walker c.1, fols 264r, 78r and 57r; c.2, fols 211r and 458r; c.3, fol. 263r.

[39] BL, MS Addit. 15671, fol. 189r; see John Morrill, 'The Church in England, 1642–1649', in idem, ed., *Reactions to the English Civil War 1642–1649* (London, 1982), 89–114.

[40] Bodl., MS J. Walker c.3, fol. 329r.

Clerical wives and children were well aware that they derived their political resources and religious status from the clergyman who headed their family. When Royalist clerical wives and children sabotaged parsonage barns, organized tithe strikes and incited parish discontent, they did so in defence of their husband or father and his professional position, expressing support for the Episcopal cause from which he drew his status and authority. Thus, the ecclesio-political identity expressed by Royalist clerical wives and children was a dependant identity, in which identification with the Royalist/Episcopal cause and identification with the Royalist husband or father was one and the same. As Mrs Sharpe, late of Bathealston, defiantly claimed of her minister husband during another neighbourly exchange: 'he was a Cavalier, he is a Cavalier & will live & dy a Cavalier'.[41]

Ohio State University

---

[41] Bodl., MS J. Walker c.3, fols 304r–305r.

'IN LOVE AND CHARITY
WITH YOUR NEIGHBOURS . . .':
ECCLESIASTICAL COURTS AND JUSTICES
OF THE PEACE IN ENGLAND
IN THE EIGHTEENTH CENTURY

by W. M. JACOB

THE aim of this paper is to account for the busyness of the ecclesiastical courts in England during the first half of the eighteenth century, and to suggest why, apart from matters of strictly ecclesiastical business, and defamation, matrimonial and probate causes, their business declined during the second half of the century.

The ecclesiastical courts in the first part of the century were a popular part of the lowest level of judicial activity in England. That the churchwardens of St Mary's Beverley paid the ringers 2s. 6d in 1721 for ringing when 'the Spiritual Court Men came' suggests the arrival of the consistory court to conduct business in a town was an occasion of note.[1] Archdeacons' and consistory courts show evidence of considerable activity in almost every diocese in which research has been undertaken about eighteenth-century church life.[2] The diocese of Ely seems to be the exception, where the evidence for much activity in the courts peters out in 1704.

Until the revived interest in religion in the eighteenth century of the past thirty years or so, Ely's case was taken to be the norm.[3] In fact, improving the procedures of the ecclesiastical courts was a recurring item of business for convocations from 1689 until 1717.[4] Recent research about crime and criminal law in the eighteenth century, however, has recognized the importance of the church courts in

---

[1] East Riding of Yorkshire County Record Office, PE1/1111; St Mary's Beverley Churchwardens' Accounts, 1721-2.

[2] For a summary of recent research and an account of the church courts in the eighteenth century, see W. M. Jacob, *Lay People and Religion in the Early Eighteenth Century* (Cambridge, 1996), 135-54.

[3] See M. Cross, 'The Church and Local Society in the Diocese of Ely *c*.1630-*c*.1730', unpublished Ph.D. thesis, University of Cambridge, 1991, 288-302.

[4] See Tony Claydon, *William III and the Godly Revolution* (Cambridge, 1996), 168, and G. V. Bennett, 'The Convocation of 1710: an Anglican Attempt at Counter-Revolution', in G. J. Cuming and Derek Baker, eds, *Councils and Assemblies*, SCH 7 (Cambridge, 1971), 311-19.

regulating the lives of people in local communities, with the approval and consent of a wide range of parishioners.[5] The activity of the church courts in the eighteenth century illustrates Alan Hunt's view that moral regulation is often initiated 'from below' and that the primary initiators and agents are frequently not holders of institutional power. Further, it suggests that his point that women played an important role as agents of moral regulation in the nineteenth century is also true in the previous century.[6]

The success of all courts rested upon a willingness by neighbours to mind each others' business. Courts, even criminal courts, depended, until the advent of a national pattern of policing, on the willingness of people as individuals or officers of their communities to bring complaints or actions in the courts. To survive, courts had to be seen to be effective and to offer the service that people required. Without sufficient business to provide an income from fees for the officials of a court, there would be no officials, no people with expertise in that branch of the law, and the court itself would wither away. The church courts seem to have provided for an orderliness in society for which most people, at least of the middling and the better-off of the poorer sort, craved, in the face of miscellaneous communal disorderliness.

* * *

On the face of it, ecclesiastical courts, based in cathedrals, those of the 'old foundation', like Lincoln, or even the rebuilt St Paul's, and usually situated on the south side, at the west end of the south aisle, surrounded as they were by the formal pomp of prayers and processions preceded by a mace, seem unlikely expressions of a popular enthusiasm for justice. Their business was religion and morality – church attendance, behaviour in church, payment of dues to the incumbent and for the upkeep of the parish church, the repair and maintenance of church buildings and parsonages, the supervision of the clergy, the moral, including sexual, conduct of parishioners, marriage and its breakdown, defamation, and the supervision of deceased persons' estates. The only real constraint on the business of the courts was that cases required a moral interpretation.[7]

---

[5] See J. A. Sharpe, *Crime in Early Modern England 1550–1750* (London, 1984), 81–93.

[6] Alan Hunt, *Governing Morals: a Social History of Moral Regulation* (Cambridge, 1999), 1–2.

[7] The best recent introduction to church courts and their procedures is Anne Tarver, *Church Court Records: an Introduction for Family and Local Historians* (Chichester, 1995).

The courts – whether consistory courts acting on behalf of bishops, archdeacon's courts acting on behalf of archdeacons in their archdeaconries, and peculiar courts exercising the jurisdiction of the archdeaconry or the consistory court in the territory of the peculiar, depending on whether the peculiar was exempt from the archdeacon's or the bishop's visitation, or both – had an 'office' jurisdiction concerning disciplinary matters, and also heard 'instance' cases arising when one party in a dispute brought the case before the court. Even office jurisdiction was exercised on the basis of consent, for cases usually arose from visitations, conducted triennially in most dioceses (except Norwich and Winchester where by ancient custom visitations were septennial or only once in an episcopate, respectively), and bishops and archdeacons were largely dependent on churchwardens and clergy reporting offences. Episcopal visitations were of value not so much as policing exercises, but as reminding churchwardens and clergy, by means of the visitation articles inquiring into the state of a parish, of what might be amiss. After a visitation a court's business might significantly increase. Even in 1784, after Bishop Bagot's primary visitation of the diocese of Norwich, there was a marked increase in the number of office cases in the consistory court in the first half of 1785, continuing for the next three years.[8]

During the first half of the eighteenth century there was considerable business in office cases in the ecclesiastical courts and sometimes there seem to have been specific campaigns. During the 1730s in the diocese of Carlisle there was a sharp increase in the numbers of presentments for fornication, 361 men and 542 women being presented between 1731 and 1740, compared with 199 men and 329 women between 1704 and 1715.[9] In Norfolk, Devon and Lancashire the church courts continued busy with office cases during the first half of the eighteenth century.[10] The great majority of the cases coming before the courts, apart from technical offences on the part of schoolmasters, physicians, and

[8] Norfolk Record Office [hereafter NRO], NDR ACT 102 and 103, Consistory Court Act Books, 1778–86 and 1786–98.

[9] Mary Kinnear, 'The Correction Court in the Diocese of Carlisle 1704–1756', *Church History* 59 (1990), 191–206.

[10] See NRO, NDR ACT 92–99; Arthur Warne, 'Church and Society in Eighteenth-Century Devon', unpublished Ph.D. thesis, University of Leeds, 1963, 116–39; idem, *Church and Society in Eighteenth-Century Devon* (Newton Abbot and New York, 1969), 74–86 (the published version is less detailed than the thesis); Jan Maria Albers, 'Seeds of Contention: Society, Politics and the Church of England in Lancashire 1689–1790', unpublished Ph.D. thesis, Yale University, 1988, 222.

midwives failing to exhibit their licences, and churchwardens failing to exhibit terriers at episcopal visitations, were of bastardy and fornication. The presentation of such offences has sometimes been regarded as illustrative of social and moral control exercised over a parish by the 'parish gentry', from whose ranks churchwardens were recruited, and who paid the poor rates, which supported unmarried mothers and their children. However, the case may be more complex than that. The presentments of churchwardens may have represented a moral consensus in parish communities; there is considerable evidence, for the first half of the century at least, that offenders appeared willingly before the courts, and accepted the sentence of the courts.

This view is supported by the large number of instances cases, brought into the courts on the complaint of an individual, for defamation. In noting booming business in the church courts in Wiltshire, Ely and York in the first half of the previous century, Martin Ingram pointed out that such cases reflected the small-scale tensions and rivalries characteristic of local communities which were relieved if not resolved by legal action.[11] The church courts provided people, particularly women and especially wives of artisans and tradesmen, with an opportunity to defend themselves against gossip, loss of reputation and general undermining, as against innuendo or suggestions of sexual impropriety. The church courts provided a forum where communal tensions could be defused and anger allowed to cool. Often cases were not pursued to a final verdict, but were merely ventilated, and settled out of court, presumably with an apology from the defendant. Defamation was a mainstay of the business of the church courts in the eighteenth century. In the five terms in 1720–21, 116 of the 141 new causes entering the York Chancery Court were for defamation.[12] In the London consistory court between 1735 and 1745, there were 237 cases of defamation representing sixty per cent of the cases coming before the court, almost all 'instance' cases, brought by one of the parties.[13] Defamation cases continued to be an important part of the church courts business until the mid-nineteenth century.[14]

---

11   Martin Ingram, *Church Courts, Sex and Marriage in England 1570–1640* (Cambridge, 1987), 292ff.

12   J. A. Sharpe, *Defamation and Sexual Slander in Early Modern England: the Church Courts at York,* Borthwick Papers 58 (York, 1980), 9.

13   Tim Meldrum, 'A Women's Court in London: the Bishop of London's Consistory Court', *The London Journal* 19 (1994), 1–20, 2.

14   See S. M. Waddams, *Sexual Slander in Nineteenth-Century England: Defamation in the Ecclesiastical Courts 1815–1855* (Toronto, 2000).

Other cases indicative of social tensions came before the church courts. The parish church, as usually the only building of local public assembly, was often the site and focus of community disputes, especially relating to status in the community. This probably accounts for the significant numbers of cases about allocation of seats in churches that came before consistory courts, and the rows that might erupt in churches and churchyards.[15] As late as 1801 James Parker Curties, a farmer of Wormegay in Norfolk, was cited before the court for 'quarrelling, Chiding and brawling within the parish church', which complaint was found proved and he was sentenced and admonished and ordered to pay costs, as also were three other parishioners.[16]

The church courts met a need in a small-scale society, where even the great metropolis of London was really only a series of small parishes, where anonymity seems to have been difficult to achieve and where reputation and social status were important. For at least the first half of the eighteenth century, by contrast with other judicial systems, as we will see, they offered an accessible process for settling local disputes and communal tensions, particularly over matters of reputation and social standing, which were a source of potential tension in communal life.

The basis of the canon law administered by the church courts was the establishment of the 'peace of God' in the Church. It provided procedures for the reconciliation of human beings to one another and to God, and to ensure that the nation itself did not fall under divine judgement and wrath. The aim of the courts was to ensure that people lived 'in love and charity with their neighbours', and were able to participate in the life of their communities and the sacraments of the Church, not to convict and award punishments. The sentences of the courts were admonitions and penances, aimed at securing repentance and amendment of life, to secure the forgiveness of God and the person or persons who had been sinned against and offended. They were formally pronounced. In the London consistory court, the vicar general began his sentence '. . . having called upon God and set Him alone before our Eyes, and having taken council thereupon, [I] do pronounce, decree and declare . . .'. He then noted that the offence was 'contrary to good manners and the bond of Charity'.[17] Public penance, while a

---

[15] See Meldrum, 'A Women's Court', 3.

[16] NRO, NDR ACT 104.

[17] London Metropolitan Archives [hereafter LMA], DL/C166 Allegations, Libels and Sentence Book 1734–36.

shaming and punishing ordeal, was an act of repentance and reconciliation with God and the community. This is made clear in the form of penance the penitent was required to read. The form varied between dioceses, but included the same essentials. In Norwich the penitent was required to stand

> Penitently in the Middle Alley, before the Minister's Seat or Pulpit, cloathed in a White Sheet holding a White Rod or Wand in [his or her] hand, having a Paper pinn'd upon [his or her] Breast, describing [his or her] Fault or Sin; and then and there in such Sort to continue during the whole Time of Divine Service and Sermon, and at the End of the same before the Congregation is dismissed, and the Blessing given, shall upon [his or her] Knees make . . . humble Confession, repeating every Word after the Minister with an audible Voice.[18]

Public penances continued to be undertaken until the early nineteenth century. The performance of a public penance could provide an opportunity for appropriate instruction by the incumbent. On 25 November 1705 Henry Prescott, Deputy Registrar of the Chester Consistory Court, noted that Richard Bebbington performed a penance 'in a great Congregation today at St Michaels [Chester] solemnly when Mr Leftwich had prorenatu a Sermon on Marriage is honourable, &c . . .'.[19] For an offence that had not caused public outrage a private penance before the incumbent and churchwardens might be ordered. A woman who admitted to fornication before the Oxford consistory court was required to do penance 'without sheet' in her normal clothes, before the rector in the vestry at Nuneham Courtney in 1761.[20] Excommunication, which had punishing civil implications, was only used as a last resort.

The physical arrangement of surviving courts, for example in Chester Cathedral, and at St Nicholas Chapel in King's Lynn, illustrates the reconciling aim of the courts. The proceedings of the court were conducted round a table, which reduced the opportunity for adversarial conflict. There was also a degree of formality in church courts which

18 NRO, NDR ANF/10/3.
19 *The Diary of Henry Prescott, LL.B., Deputy Registrar of Chester Diocese, Vol. 1, 28 March 1704–24 March 1711*, ed. John Addy, The Record Society of Lancashire and Cheshire 127 (Gloucester, 1987), 79.
20 *The Deserted Village: the Diary of an Oxfordshire Rector, James Newton of Nuneham Courtenay 1736–1786*, ed. Gavin Hannah (Stroud, 1992), 131 and 135, n. 8.

may have been reassuring. Proceedings were held in the context of the prayers of the Church. Henry Prescott (1649–1719), registrar of the diocese of St Asaph, noted in 1712 that: 'The 2 proctors and I in our Gowns go to prayers, after which the Court is held.'[21] There was a written record of the proceedings. There were officers of the court present in addition to the chancellor or vicar general or a surrogate as judge, namely the registrar or his deputy, and the proctors or notaries, who acted as the advocates. All of them had some training in canon law. A case described in detail by Henry Prescott, that of the negotiation of alimony following a legal separation of a couple 'between bed and board' which lasted a whole day, involved complex and frequent consultations between proctors and their clients and lengthy negotiations over financial details about the maintenance for the wife and children. This case illustrates the detailed care taken over achieving a satisfactory result for an abandoned wife and her involvement in the negotiations.[22] Often, especially in archdeacons' courts, people appeared in person, without a notary.

The courts were accessible. They sat frequently: in Lichfield and Norwich the consistory courts sat several days a month. The courts were peripatetic, to compensate for the vast geographical size of most diocese and many archdeaconries. In Carlisle diocese, the court was held usually for one morning in October, November and December in each of the four deaneries, in Carlisle, Wigton, Penrith and Appleby, which must have made the court more accessible in such a remote and mountainous diocese.[23] Prescott's diary illustrates the progress of the Chester consistory court around Cheshire and Lancashire. In the archdeaconry of Derby, a late seventeenth-century initiative led to the archdeacon's court meeting twice a year in All Saints' Derby and at Chesterfield, as well as in Lichfield Cathedral, thus making the court more accessible to the inhabitants of the archdeaconry.[24] On circuit the court might meet in an inn rather than a church. In October 1751 the Norwich consistory court Act Book noted the court met at the 'Black Lyon, Little Walsingham, the proctors first Consenting to the Judge's

---

21 *The Diary of Henry Prescott, LL.B., Deputy Registrar of Chester Diocese, Vol. 2, 25 March 1711–24 May 1719*, ed. John Addy and Peter McNiven, The Record Society of Lancashire and Cheshire 132 (Stroud, 1994), 350. The three volumes of Prescott's diary provide excellent evidence of the activities of an official of the church courts.

22 *Diary of Henry Prescott*, I: 253, 257.

23 Kinnear, 'Correction Courts', 199.

24 Richard Clark, 'Anglicanism, Recusancy and Dissent in Derbyshire 1603–1703', unpublished D.Phil. thesis, University of Oxford, 1979, 225.

Time and Place as if in open Court' to hear a case against the Minister, churchwardens and parishioners and inhabitants of Little Walsingham.[25] The Norwich archdeaconry court met, amongst other places, at the Bull at Litcham, and at the Wrestlers at Great Yarmouth.[26]

Cases were usually dealt with expeditiously. Unusually a case in Norwich consistory court in the 1750s continued for two and a half years before appeal to the Court of Arches.[27] Many cases disappear from court records, and appear not to reach a resolution or conclusion. This, however, may be a symptom of the courts' reconciling role, rather than of their inefficiency. Disappearance of cases from the records may mean that they were resolved between the parties, and there was no need to continue through the court, the communal tension having been relaxed, honour having been done, and a name cleared.[28]

* * *

Decline in the moral jurisdiction of the church courts was not uniform. In 1738 the incumbent of Watlington in Oxfordshire thus complained to Bishop Secker:

> One great complaint I must make and I am afraid is a pretty general one, is the little regard had in the Spiritual Courts to presentments for bastardy &c. Or the easy Commutation for penance. . . . This I think has been some encouragement to Vice and I am Sure a great Occasion of Contempt and disdain of the Spiritual Courts and authority.[29]

His other comments suggest that he may have been of a complaining disposition. In the 1740s there were significant numbers of cases before the Norfolk ecclesiastical courts, and significant numbers of offenders came into the courts to confess their offence and voluntarily undertake a penance.[30] In the 1763 visitation of the diocese of Norwich, comprising Norfolk and Suffolk, 144 cases of bastardy were presented.[31] Only in the 1770s do presentations for fornication disap-

---

[25] NRO, NDR ACT 100.

[26] NRO, NDR Norwich Archdeaconry General Visitation Books, Book 9.

[27] NRO, NDR ACT 96.

[28] Cf. similar methodological considerations in this volume in the article by Graeme Murdock, 'Did Early Modern Calvinists Have a Guilt Complex?', 138–58 and n. 16.

[29] *Articles of Enquiry Addressed to the Clergy of the Diocese of Oxford at the Primary Visitation of Dr Thomas Secker, 1738*, ed. H. A. Lloyd Jukes, Oxfordshire Record Society Series 38 (Oxford, 1957), 165.

[30] NRO, NDR Norfolk Archdeaconry ANF/10/2.

[31] NRO, NDR VIS/20.

pear from Lancashire consistory courts.[32] By 1790 in Norfolk public penance was sufficiently unusual for the rector of Morton to consult the rector of Weston Longueville, James Woodforde, about one of his parishioners doing a penance 'for calling Mrs Michael Andrews a Whore'.[33] The sense that defamation constituted a breach of charity within the community between neighbours and undermined social harmony, which James Sharpe has noted as a characteristic of early modern England,[34] was a feature of English life until at least the mid-nineteenth century. He also noted that people seemed less interested in pecuniary damages than in a healing of a breach, possibly including a public retraction, in the form of a public penance. The church courts provided a means of resolving these tensions, but recent research about justices of the peace in the eighteenth century has indicated that they too exercised a mediating role in their localities.[35]

Evidence for the judicial activities of justices outside quarter sessions during the eighteenth century is limited, for formal records of their justicing work were not kept. For most of the eighteenth century, justices' administrative role in governing counties was more significant, especially to central government, than justicing, and only the minutes of their meetings in quarter sessions, kept by the clerk of the peace, have survived. Proceedings of adjourned 'petty sessions' comprising meetings of two or three justices, held between quarter sessions to deal with urgent administrative matters, such as granting licences and releasing debtors from prison and the administration of the Poor Law, were not recorded. In the case of minor offences, most justices acted alone. Four personal notebooks kept by justices, recording their justicing activities, are known to survive, from Middlesex, Surrey, Wiltshire and County Durham.[36] An analysis of them shows that by far

---

[32] Albers, 'Seeds of Contention', 248.

[33] James Woodforde (1740–1803), *Diary of a Country Parson*, ed. John Beresford, 5 vols (London, 1924–31), IV (1793–96): 155.

[34] J. A. Sharpe, ' "Such Disagreements betwyx Neighbours": Litigation and Human Relations in Early Modern England', in John Bossy, ed., *Disputes and Settlements: Law and Human Relations in the West* (Cambridge, 1983), 167–87, 178–9.

[35] Robert B. Shoemaker, *Prosecution and Punishment: Petty Crime and the Law in London and Rural Middlesex c.1660–1725* (Cambridge, 1991), 23–7 and 82–93.

[36] *The Justicing Notebook of William Hunt, 1744–1749*, ed. Elizabeth Crittall, Wiltshire Record Society 37 (Devizes, 1982); *The Deposition Book of Richard Wyatt, JP, 1767–1776*, ed. Elizabeth Silverthorne, Surrey Record Society 30 (Guildford, 1978); *Justice in Eighteenth Century Hackney: the Justicing Notebook of Henry Norris and the Hackney Petty Sessions Book*, ed. Ruth Paley, London Record Society 28 (London, 1991); *The Justicing Notebook (1750–64) of Edmund Tew, Rector of Boldon*, ed. Gwenda Morgan and Peter Rushton, Surtees Society 205 (Woodbridge, 2000).

the largest group of offences with which they dealt were offences against the peace, involving private disputes in which plaintiffs sought settlement of conflicts, not the punishment of offenders. One justice, William Hunt, in the area around West Lavington in Wiltshire in the 1750s, recorded an agreement between parties in three-quarters of such cases. Binding over, or seeking a recognizance from an offender, provided an opportunity to extract an apology and a promise not to offend in the same way again, on forfeiture of a sum to the Crown.[37]

Individuals often wanted restitution in the case of a theft of wood or fruit or vegetables or grain by a neighbour, or an apology arising from profane swearing or defamation in a dispute between neighbours rather than a lengthy prosecution and punishment. Justices seem to have encouraged informal settlements after complaints. About half the hearings William Hunt noted in Wiltshire were informal. Most complainants knew one another. Most complaints of assaults and of disputes came from members of the labouring poor, more complaints seem to have been brought by servants than masters. The labouring poor were not afraid to come before a justice even to complain against their masters. Poaching was not a particularly significant issue. Only about two per cent of cases in notebooks concern poaching, and justices seem to have treated it leniently.[38] As in the church courts, women seem to have been frequent users of the mediation process.[39]

From the limited evidence available for justices' activities, a picture emerges of the lowest levels of the eighteenth-century English criminal law system as providing a forum for the settlement of conflicts and for negotiating compromises between individuals, as well as for providing opportunities for forgiveness and the maintenance of love and charity between neighbours, rather than it being an instrument to punish offenders and to protect public safety in the interests of the parish or county gentry. Perhaps significantly, there was less tendency by justices from Hackney, then a rural suburb of London, or on a busy Surrey turnpike or on the Thames, to come to record informal settlements in their notebooks, than the two justices from traditional communities.[40]

The Revd Edmund Tew's justicing notebook is particularly interesting because he was a clergyman acting as a justice in the 1750s, just

---

[37] Dietrich Oberwittler, 'Crime and Authority in Eighteenth-Century England: Law Enforcement on the Local Level', *Historical Social Research* 15 (1990), 3–34, 11.
[38] Oberwittler, 'Crime and Authority', 15.
[39] Shoemaker, *Prosecution and Punishment*, 207.
[40] Oberwittler, 'Crime and Authority', 19.

before a major increase in numbers of clerical justices of the peace. He was a member of the commission for the peace in a county where there were already a significant number of clerical justices, perhaps because the bishop of Durham was *ex officio* lord lieutenant of the county palatine. Tew's notebook shows him acting to re-establish peace in his neighbourhood, negotiating and mediating settlements to disputes and censoring anti-social behaviour. Most of his activity as a justice seems to have involved resolving individual problems and ensuring good community order rather than prosecuting offenders. The bulk of Tew's justice business consisted of complaints by victims of the behaviour of neighbours, employers and family members. In June 1757, for example, he noted twenty-three cases including six of issues arising from the master–servant relationship, six concerning assaults, five relating to poor law administration, one of theft, three of defamation, and one of bastardy. His role seems to have been as much that of a problem-solver as that of a judge. The purpose of going to law before a magistrate seems to have been less to secure a conviction than to settle personal disputes between neighbours, by restoring their relationship of 'love and charity' and ensuring the maintenance of the customary social behaviour upon which communal life depended.

Tew's notebook provides a link between the world of the church courts and the developing role of justices of the peace in the later eighteenth century. In the second half of the eighteenth century increasing administrative responsibilities were given to justices by successive ministries,[41] but many county gentry who might have been expected to be available to act as justices spent little time on their estates, and complainants often had to travel long distances to see a justice.[42] The rector of Watlington in Norfolk complained in 1784 that: 'We have more than twenty miles to go for ye Punishment of Offenders' and lamented the cost of the journey to the poor rate. He suggested clergy should be permitted to act as magistrates in their own parishes.[43]

In the second half of the eighteenth century, increasing numbers of justices were appointed to county commissions for the peace from among lesser county gentry and people striving to establish gentry status, as well as from among the more prosperous clergy. There was a

---

[41] See Norma Landau, *The Justices of the Peace 1679–1760* (Berkeley, CA, and London, 1984), 125–40.

[42] For the absenteeism of the county gentry, see James M. Rosenheim, *The Emergence of a Ruling Order: English Landed Society 1650–1750* (London and New York, 1998), 102–23.

[43] NRO, NDR VIS 29.

steady increase in the numbers of clerical magistrates, who seem to have become the work-horses of the local judicial and administrative system. In the early eighteenth century there were barely fifty clerical justices, but by 1761 there were over a thousand.[44] In Wiltshire there were five clerical justices in 1728, nine in 1760, and sixteen in 1786.[45] In Norfolk there were only two clerical justices in 1761, which was well below the national average,[46] but in 1787, of twenty new justices who 'qualified' to sit, seven were clergy, whilst in 1788 nine out of twelve new justices were clergy, in 1789 eleven out of fifteen, in 1790 nine out of eighteen.[47] By 1785 clerical justices comprised twenty-eight per cent of the active magistrates in Essex, and in the 1780s they included five of the seven most active justices in the county.[48] In Leicestershire in the 1790s clergy outnumbered gentry among magistrates attending quarter sessions meetings whereas a hundred years before there had been no clergy.[49] There was some regional variation in the presence of clergy among the justices on commissions for the peace. In Sussex there were no clerical justices because the lord lieutenant, the duke of Richmond, objected to clergy as justices.[50]

In the last quarter or so of the eighteenth century, with a higher proportion of resident justices in most parts of England, justices were more accessible than earlier in the century to people seeking mediation in their disputes and the admonition of troublesome neighbours. When considering the mediatorial role of justices in maintaining peace in their area of a county, it is important to remember that lay magistrates could be expected to be as conscious of the duty to live in love and charity with their neighbours, and to foster neighbourly love and charity, as were clergy. Almost all justices of the peace would have been familiar with the words of the Bible and the Book of Common Prayer, with their emphasis on communal peace and order. As from the 1760s clergy were more frequently recruited to serve on county commissions

[44] Paul Langford, *Public Life and the Propertied Englishman 1689–1798* (Oxford, 1991), 411.

[45] Donald A. Spaeth, *The Church in an Age of Danger: Parsons and Parishioners 1660–1740* (Cambridge, 2000), 49.

[46] Eric J. Evans, *The Contentious Tithe: the Tithe Problem and English Agriculture, 1750–1850* (London, 1976), 11.

[47] W. M. Jacob, 'Clergy and Society in Norfolk 1707–1806', unpublished Ph.D. thesis, University of Exeter, 1982, 429.

[48] Peter King, *Crime, Justice and Discretion in England, 1740–1820* (Oxford, 2000), 117–18.

[49] Christopher Chalklin, 'County Building in Leicestershire 1680–1830', *Georgian Group Journal* 9 (1999), 69–85.

[50] Peter Virgin, *The Church in an Age of Negligence: Ecclesiastical Structure and Problems of Church Reform 1700–1840* (Cambridge, 1989), 118.

for the peace, and became active magistrates, they were taking up a role not inconsistent with their clerical office, as has often been claimed.[51] The clergy who were appointed to the magistracy were the sort of people who had served as surrogates in the ecclesiastical courts, labouring in both systems to maintain 'love and charity' between neighbours.

Examining the limited evidence for the local activities of justices of the peace helps to put into context the attitudes of lay people towards the ecclesiastical courts. In both systems of justice people sought means of reconciliation, while both systems encouraged repentance and forgiveness by the offended parties. However, the increasing accessibility of justices, and the increasing numbers of clergy among them, may have been a contributory factor in the decline of the ecclesiastical courts for cases other than defamation and strictly ecclesiastical matters. This may be a more plausible explanation for the decline of the church courts, apart from their strictly ecclesiastical business in the second half of the eighteenth century, than other hypotheses that have been advanced for the decline. Such reasons include the decision of Lord Hardwicke in 1736, in the case of *Middleton v Croft*, that the post-Reformation canons were binding on laity only in so far as they had been specifically confirmed by statute, and changes in the pastoral practice of clergy, who ceased to use the ecclesiastical courts to support their pastoral ministry, and changes in attitudes to moral offences and the sanctions of the ecclesiastical courts. It may simply be that justices acting alone and in petty sessions, especially if they were clergy, began to usurp the communal functions of the ecclesiastical courts.[52]

London

---

[51] For example by E. J. Evans, 'Some Reasons for the Growth of English Anti-Clericalism *c*.1750–*c*.1830', *Past & Present* 66 (1975), 84–109.
[52] For the various hypotheses advanced for the decline of the church courts, see Jacob, *Lay People and Religion*, 151–4.

PUBLIC ORDERS INTO MORAL COMMUNITIES: EIGHTEENTH-CENTURY FAST AND THANKSGIVING DAY SERMONS IN THE DUTCH REPUBLIC AND NEW ENGLAND

by PETER VAN ROODEN

IN the eighteenth century, both in the Dutch Republic and in the colonies of New England, collective repentance and social reconciliation with God were institutionalized in great common rituals. In both polities, Fast and Thanksgiving Days were proclaimed by civil authority, and these occasions brought people together into churches to hear ministers interpret their common situation. These rituals were the main way in which the New England colonies and the Dutch Republic expressed their unity as political communities. It was this aspect of these sermons that made them of interest to nineteenth-century American and Dutch historians. In the nineteenth-century Kingdom of the Netherlands, N. C. Kist, the first holder of the newly instituted chair of Church History at Leiden University, finished his career with his two-volume *Neêrlands Bededagen en Biddagsbrieven*, offering both an interpretation and an antiquarian overview of all the Fast Days proclaimed in the Netherlands.[1] In the United States, William de Loss Love published his exquisite *The Fast and Thanksgiving Days of New England* in 1895, similarly offering both an antiquarian list of all Fast and Thanksgiving Days and an analysis.[2] Kist was deeply involved with the nation-building project of the early nineteenth-century Kingdom of the Netherlands. De Loss Love, the first chaplain of the Connecticut Society of the Sons of the American Revolution, was as inspired by modern nationalism as Kist was. Both scholars interpreted the Fast-day ritual as an indication of the high moral purpose and commitment to the nation of their ancestors.

The relation between modern nationalism and Fast and Thanksgiving Day sermons is more complicated than Kist and de Loss Love supposed, but it is the right question to ask of these sources. Let me first

---

[1] N. C. Kist, *Neêrland's Bededagen en Biddagsbrieven*, 2 vols (Leiden, 1848–9).
[2] William de Loss Love Jr., *The Fast and Thanksgiving Days of New England* (Boston, MA, 1895).

make some clarifications. I will use the concept 'nationalism' in a sense inspired by the work of Benedict Anderson and Ernst Gellner.[3] I am not interested in nationalism in the sense of love of country, place of origin, or a particular dynasty. Nationalism, as I will use the term in this essay, is part political programme, part social imaginary. It is the political notion that the nation-state, the organization of socially free, legally equal, and culturally related citizens, is the only legitimate form of political authority. The social imaginary focuses upon this notion of a community of free and equal men, who constitute themselves by being morally committed to each other and their community. A loyalty to France or to the French king arguably goes back to the Middle Ages. However, the notion that all French should feel such a loyalty to each other and to their nation, that this feeling constitutes their primary social identity and is the core of their moral selves, and that the main job of the French state is to ensure that this all actually comes to pass, is something quite new, with staggering consequences for social life in general and religion in particular. When this notion of politics as the creation of a moral community is heavily determined by religious language, I will use the concept 'religious nationalism'.[4]

I use Fast and Thanksgiving Day sermons mainly because they offer a methodologically justifiable way to study the development of the religious imaginary of the social world during the Early Modern period. About three hundred Fast and Thanksgiving Day sermons were printed in America before 1790, something between five and ten per cent of all sermons published there.[5] In the Dutch Republic, curiously, far fewer sermons were published, but Fast and Thanksgiving Day sermons made up a much larger proportion, so that there too we have something like two hundred published sermons.[6]

The organization of the Dutch days of prayer duplicated the

---

[3] Ernest Gellner, *Nations and Nationalism* (Oxford, 1983); Benedict Anderson, *Imagined Communities: Reflections on the Origin and Spread of Nationalism* (revised edn, London, 1991).

[4] Peter van der Veer, *Religious Nationalism: Hindus and Muslims in India* (Berkeley, CA, 1994).

[5] I used the *Early American Imprints, 1639–1800* [microform], ed. Clifford K. Shipton, American Antiquarian Society (New York, 1962–74). A description of these 22,000 microfiches is to be found in: John H. Jenkins, *Early American Imprints: a Collection of Works Printed in America between 1669 and 1800* (Austin, TX, 1977).

[6] I have read all printed Dutch Fast-day sermons preserved in the Royal Library of The Hague, and the University Libraries of Amsterdam and Leiden. These three libraries possess most of the Dutch printed sermons, if the period 1750–1800, for which a bibliography of sermons exists, is any indication: Jelle Bosma, *Woorden van een gezond verstand: de invloed van de Verlichting op de in het Nederlands uitgegeven preken van 1750 tot 1800* (Kampen, 1997).

particularistic and decentralized political structure of the Dutch Republic. Public days of prayer were proclaimed by a political authority, usually the States-General. The official proclamation, explaining why it was necessary to implore God's blessing or mercy, and setting a date for the public day of prayer, was sent to the Provincial States, which passed it on to local authorities. These, finally, handed the proclamation over to the ministers of the public Church, who were legally obliged to find a fitting text of Scripture and to base their sermon on the proclamation.[7] The ritual was in use from the very beginning of the Dutch Revolt (1572–1609) until the end of the eighteenth century. From 1713 onwards, national days of prayer became a regular annual event. They were no longer proclaimed on special occasions, but took on the character of State of the Union messages. The proclamations were printed and consisted of an evaluation of the political, social and moral welfare of the Republic.

Already in the seventeenth century, Protestant dissenters had joined the ritual. Gradually, they were officially invited by the local authorities to do so as well. The burgomasters of Utrecht, for instance, started to invite the Lutheran minister in 1676.[8] Those of Haarlem decided in 1742 to send the proclamation to the Arminian, Lutheran and five Mennonite Churches of their city.[9] In the archive of the Sephardic Jews of Amsterdam, all official proclamations from 1741 to 1794, sent them by their burgomasters, have been lovingly preserved.[10] In the last quarter of the eighteenth century, the village of Graft, north of Amsterdam, even invited its Catholic priest to take part in the ritual.[11]

The official proclamations of public days of prayer show a marked development in the way the Republic was represented.[12] Traditionally, descriptions of the Republic as a social body distinguished three elements: its political order, its religious establishment, and its inhabitants. At the occasion of the coronation of Stadholder William III as

---

[7] *Kerkelijk Placaatboek*, 5 vols ('s-Gravenhage, 1722–1807), III: 26.

[8] Muncipal Archive of Utrecht: Stadsarchief, Vroedschapsresoluties, 6 November 1676.

[9] Municipal Archive of Haarlem: Stadsarchief, Burgemeestersresoluties, 9 February 1742.

[10] Municipal Archive of Amsterdam: Archief van de Portugees-Israelitische Gemeente, no. 66.

[11] G. J. Schutte, *Een Hollandse dorpssamenleving in de late achttiende eeuw: de banne Graft 1770–1810* (Franeker, 1989), 116. On the other hand, even in 1771 some Catholics of Zevenbergen, south of the great rivers, were fined because they refused to close their doors and windows on the day of prayer: National Archive, Oud-Synodaal Archief, Acta Particuliere Synode van Zuid-Holland 1771, a. 10.

[12] All proclamations are published in Kist, *Neêrland's Bededagen*.

king of England in 1688, for instance, the proclamation expressed the wish that this event would tend towards 'the conservation of the true reformed religion, our liberty, and the welfare of the nation (*vaderland*)'.[13] It is quite clear that this last word refers to the subjects of the Republic. These three elements are not conceptually integrated. There is no single word which denotes their connection or unity.

It is only from the 1750s onwards that the word 'nation' (*vaderland*) in the proclamations by the States General evolves into an overarching concept which denotes all aspects of the Dutch Republic as a political community.[14] This conceptual shift is immediately coupled with a new sense of history and moral well-being. The moral state of the Republic, in the sense of both its public morality and the private morals of its citizens, is linked to its political power and continuing existence within a world history of struggling states. This link between private morality and public power is made in two different ways. Following a classic republican topos, a virtuous citizenry is said to support the power of the state. Sins, on the other hand, call down God's wrath. In the proclamations, there is no tension at all between these natural and supernatural mechanisms: they have both been instituted by God. In the seventeenth century, too, every defeat of Dutch arms and every natural disaster had been depicted as the wages of sin, but these sins had never been made concrete or personalized. Living in sin is the human condition, the ongoing consequence of Adam's fall, not an occasion for, reason of or invitation to moral improvement or social transformation. Sin leads to repentance, not to reform. Pre-1760 Fast-day sermons were meant to deplore sin, not to improve the moral fibre of the Dutch. The social imaginary in these years circles around the notions of order and origin, not those of community and history.

The emergence of the nation as a moral community in the official proclamations developed quite quickly. In 1754 the nation was, for the first time, said to have a moral claim on its inhabitants. They are now obliged to further its welfare.[15] In 1759, the stakes were raised and the inhabitants were called upon to love their nation.[16] This expansion of the moral claim of political authority on its subjects found its mirror-

---

13 Kist, *Neêrland's Bededagen*, II: 259–60.
14 Peter van Rooden, 'Godsdienst en nationalisme in de vroeg-moderne tijd. Het voorbeeld van de Republiek', in N. C. F. van Sas, ed., *Vaderland: een geschiedenis van de vijftiende eeuw tot 1940* (Amsterdam, 1999), 201–36.
15 Kist, *Neêrland's Bededagen*, II: 366–7.
16 Ibid., II: 382.

image in an enormous extension of the duties of the government. In 1756 God was asked to bless its endeavours

> tending towards the preservation of our peace, the stimulation of our commerce, the furthering of virtue, the continuation of useful arts and sciences, and the restoration of the welfare and happiness of the commonwealth.[17]

In general, the proclamations of these years identify love of the nation with religious duties. Already in the 1750s, the proclamations consciously depicted the public rituals of Fast and Thanksgiving Days as means to further patriotism. In 1764, the proclamation called upon 'true lovers of the nation and right-minded Christians'.[18] In 1765, love of the nation was said to inspire a desire for religion, as the welfare of the nation depends upon virtue, and virtue upon religion.[19]

The awkward question concerning what kind of religion produced civic virtue was never explicitly tackled. Traditionally, the proclamations had ended with a prayer to God to further the interests of the Reformed Church of the Republic. In 1765 the citizens of the Republic were, for the first time, exhorted to pray for

> the welfare of all Protestant churches in the whole world, and especially for those of these United Provinces, to the end that the labours of their ministers may bear more and more fruit, affirming Christian belief and spreading piety and justice, love and concord.[20]

This conception of the links between the nation, virtue and religion governs all proclamations for public days of prayer during the second half of the eighteenth century. *Vaderland* has become the word for the political community of which every inhabitant of the Republic is a member. This community has a moral claim upon its members. Its citizens realize their moral selves by performing good acts not just because these are duties, but because they further the welfare of the nation. The Dutch Republic is consistently depicted as a moral community. The most important virtues of its members are patriotism and piety, the latter being understood as a universal, not confessionally determined source of civic virtue.

---

[17] Ibid., II: 373. My translation.
[18] Ibid., II: 394.
[19] Ibid., II: 402.
[20] Ibid., II: 403.

Such a conception of the nation as a community of moral selves lent itself to radical political uses. When God's blessings ceased, and the nation suffered reverses, the government could be held responsible for the lack of moral virtue. This is what happened after the catastrophic defeat of the Republic at the hand of the English in 1780–1, when the Dutch had come out on the side of the American revolutionaries. The following years saw a slowly developing radical and democratic revolution, meant to restore the civic virtue and political power of the Dutch Republic. It was crushed by Prussian troops in 1787.[21]

The new social imaginary, despite its religious components, was not produced by ecclesiastical forces. In stark contrast to the proclamations of public days of prayer by the States-General, the use of the concept 'nation' by ministers of the public Church in their Fast-day sermons was quite rare until deep into the eighteenth century.[22] This is all the more remarkable, as they usually reflected the text of the official proclamations quite accurately.

Bernard Smytegelt of Middelburg was considered the best Dutch preacher of the eighteenth century, and the first Dutch minister of whom a really large number of sermons have been preserved, including ten Fast-day sermons. He hardly ever used the word 'nation', preferring 'Country and Church' (*Land en Kerk*). In 1729 he said:

> Today is a day of prayer. Sit a little while longer. In this country one day of covenant follows another. Last Sunday it was the 845th day of communion of this church. That was a covenant for the soul, that we would be redeemed by the blood of Christ, and today, three days later, there is another day of covenant, for the external world, for Country and Church.[23]

Smytegelt depicted the relation between religion and political community in a slightly more complicated way than most of his fellow ministers. He did not construct an opposition between personal piety and

---

[21] Wayne Ph. te Brake, 'Provincial Histories and National Revolution in the Dutch Republic', in Margaret C. Jacob and Wijnand W. Mijnhardt, eds, *The Dutch Republic in the Eighteenth Century: Decline, Enlightenment and Revolution* (Ithaca, N.Y., and London, 1992), 60–90; F. Grijzenhout *et al.*, eds, *Voor Vaderland en Vrijheid. De revolutie van de patriotten* (Amsterdam, 1987); N. C. F. van Sas, 'De Nederlandse revolutie van de achttiende eeuw', *BMGN* 100 (1985), 636–46; idem, 'The Patriot Revolution: New Perspectives', in Jacob and Mijnhardt, eds, *The Dutch Republic in the Eighteenth Century*, 91–122.

[22] Van Rooden, 'Godsdienst en nationalisme', 215–17.

[23] Bernardus Smytegelt, *Keurstoffen of verzameling van vyftig uitmuntende predicatien* (Middelburg en Den Haag, 1765), 429.

social order, or between Church and nation. Instead, he distinguished between outer and inner forms of religion, between the politically and ecclesiastically ordered society of the Republic and interior piety. His Fast-day sermons invariably end with an overview of the duties of magistrates, ministers, elders, heads of households and employers, in short, the duties of all those who bear authority, followed by a second series, which contrasts the sins, obligations and situations of pious and nominal Christians. Smytegelt located religion in two different places: on the one hand in the social and ecclesiastical order of the political body, and on the other in the hearts of the truly pious. In the course of the eighteenth century, making such a distinction would become more and more common in Dutch Reformed Fast- day sermons. In the seventeenth century, only the public order had been represented in these sermons, yet this new emphasis on the importance of personal piety never led to attempts to intellectually integrate the two notions: public religious order and personal piety were distinguished, but were never connected. Religion in the form of a public order can be produced socially and politically, by those who bear social and political authority, but personal piety cannot be produced by social actions. People knew about social order, while knowing about personal piety too. Public discourse did not integrate civil or political and religious duties.

* * *

The Dutch Protestant dissenters, too, religiously imagined the Republic by making a distinction between public order and personal piety. The prominent Arminian theologian Simon Episcopius held a sermon on the public day of prayer of 1627, just some weeks after he had returned from his exile following the Synod of Dordrecht. His is actually the oldest preserved Dutch Fast-day sermon.[24] Episcopius found the reason for God's blessing of the Republic in its religious-political order, which made true religion possible. True religion, in his eyes, rests upon sincere personal conviction, which is not forced and which bears fruit in a moral life. The Republic's upholding of the principle of freedom of conscience made such a non-hypocritical piety possible. Although Episcopius in this way established a link between public order and personal piety, he did not depict the Republic, or even the pious, as a moral community. The public order of the Republic makes individual

---

[24] Simon Episcopius, *XVII Predicatien (. . .) by verscheide gelegentheden, en inzonderheit op Feestdagen* (Amsterdam, 1693), 245–65.

piety possible, but the virtue of the pious remains an individual affair. Episcopius did not consider the Republic to be a moral agent, creating pious selves. The Dutch Arminians would not deviate from this conception until after 1750.[25]

The Dutch Mennonites had always been characterized by their intense stress on the importance of the moral purity of their own communities, an alienation from general society perfectly expressed by their rejection of infant baptism and celebration of martyrdom. In their thirty or so preserved Fast-day sermons, late seventeenth- and early eighteenth-century Mennonite preachers still upheld this awareness of being a different community, visibly standing apart.

Like the Arminians, the Mennonites praised the tolerant policies of the Dutch Republic, yet they never integrated their justification for taking part in the civil ritual of the public Fast-day with their interpretation of public weal or disaster. In their eyes, the Republic was no moral agent, and it was not the public order of the Republic, but the acts of the Mennonites which caused public disaster: war, cattle sickness, the ship worm destroying the wooden piles of the Dutch dykes – these were all God's punishment for the sins of the Mennonites.

The obvious road to integrate justification and interpretation (we pray for the Dutch Republic because it protects us and we are the moral core of the Dutch community) was never taken, because it would involve a rejection of the Mennonite notions of martyrdom and pacifism. All Mennonite sermons held on the days of prayer during the great wars with France around 1700 display a decided reluctance to identify fully with the war effort of the Republic. The rhetorical ploy that the moral acts of the Mennonites cause the sufferings of the Republic, functions as an appeal to the Mennonites to take their belief seriously. It does not lead to a rhetorical incorporation of the Mennonites into the nation.

In short, all Protestant groups in the Netherlands continued to uphold a difference between public order and inner piety in their Fast-day sermons for some two decades after the civil authorities had collapsed both into the notion of the moral community of the nation. But, in the last quarter of the eighteenth century, this distinction dissolved. The sermons of Jacobus Hinlopen, a prominent orthodox Reformed minister at Utrecht, offer excellent examples.[26] Hinlopen still

25 Van Rooden, 'Godsdienst en nationalisme', 218.
26 Jacobus Hinlopen, *Leerredenen* (Utrecht, 1781).

ended his sermons with an overview of the duties of magistrates, ministers and parents, but he did not follow these exhortations with an
address to the pious. It is not that he does not know them. He constructs
the relation between authority and interiority in a new way. In
Hinlopen's sermons, magistrates, ministers and parents are no longer
responsible for the religious order of external, visible and public social
life; instead, their main task is to influence individuals morally. As the
government attempts to moralize its subjects, piety is every citizen's
duty. 'May I hope that you, as good patriots, will [. . .] request me to
pray the Lord for redemption and peace in your name?'[27]

The foreword of the edition of Hinlopen's Fast-day sermons,
published in 1781, was addressed to 'every pious lover of his nation
(*vaderland*), in whose veins still flows a drop of Dutch blood'. Religious
and political community coincide. Both religion and the nation rest
upon individual moral selves, not upon public orders. In the late 1770s,
this new conception of the nation as a moral community was shared by
all Dutch Protestant ministers, both Reformed and Dissenters. It is the
nation which enables its citizens to create their moral and religious
selves, because the proper field of moral action is the nation. Once one
imagines the nation in this way, it is no longer possible to consider the
public Church the only legitimate embodiment of religion. In the foreword to his book, Hinlopen addressed the Dutch Dissenters, expressing
the hope that his work would make clear that the Reformed, too, cared
about personal morality. Implicitly, he conceded the right of other
Dutch groups to judge the contribution of the public Church to the
moral State of the nation.

In the case of the dissenters, who had always emphasized personal
piety, a similar process can be observed. More and more they described
piety as something which their members shared with all other virtuous
citizens of the Republic. In the last quarter of the eighteenth century,
dissenting ministers addressed their audience as members of the nation,
no longer as individuals or as a special group. You had to be moral
because you were Dutch, not because you were a Mennonite.[28]

[27] Ibid., 128.

[28] S. Ysbrandi, *Vaderlandsche Dank- en Biddagsrede over Jozua vii 12b* (Amsterdam, 1782); F.
A. van der Kemp, *Het gedrag van Israel en Rehabeam, ten spiegel van Volk en Vorst. Leerrede over I
Kor xii: 3b–20a* (Leiden, 1782); D. Hovens, *Onze tegenwoordige toestand vergeleken by dien onzer
voorouders, (. . .) op den bedestond, den 2den, en op den gedenkdag van Leydens ontzet, den 3den october
1782* (Leiden, 1782); J. A. S. Hoekstra, *Leerredenen en bedestonden* (Utrecht, 1787).

Religious nationalism seems to me to be a perfectly good term to describe this new conception of the proper place of religion. Everybody knew that the nation was neither God nor Church. Yet the moral community of the nation had become the social context in which true religion and morality had to be realized. This emergence of modern nationalism in Fast-day sermons in the Dutch Republic took place before the political upheavals at the end of the eighteenth century. Already in the 1770s, a religious and cultural nationalism was firmly embedded in Dutch Fast-day sermons. The Patriot Revolution of 1782–7 and the policies of the Batavian Republic installed by the French revolutionary armies in 1795 would be deeply influenced by this religious nationalism.[29]

* * *

This, it seems to me, is the great difference between America and the Dutch Republic. The development of the New England Fast and Thanksgiving Day sermons mirrors the Dutch development. In New England, too, the overall move is one from a public order to a vision of a national community of moral selves. In New England too, the crucial decade is the 1770s. But whereas this transformation of the religious imagination of the social and political order in the Netherlands took place before the political upheavals of the 1780s and 1790s, in America these were part and parcel of the Revolution.

Even in 1775 though, at the height of the Revolution, there still were many sermons which expressed unease with a modern religious nationalism.[30] Typically, they would explain the need and legitimacy of political and military resistance against British tyranny, and press upon their hearers the need to defend true religion. Yet, at the end of the sermon, the preacher would change gear, and point out the importance of the immortal souls of his hearers, and how they, as citizens of eternity, would cease to be interested in earthly things in a few years:

> Nay, this globe itself, the mighty theatre of contention, must ere long crumble into atoms, and leave not a wreck behind of all the trophies of ambition.[31]

---

[29] Simon Schama, *Patriots and Liberators: Revolution in the Netherlands, 1780–1813* (London, 1977).

[30] Henry Cumings, *A sermon, preached in Billerica, on the 23d of November, 1775: Being the day appointed by civil authority, for a public thanksgiving throughout the province of Massachusetts-Bay*, Early American Imprints. First series, no. 14723: 28.

[31] Thomas Coombe, *A sermon, preached before the congregations of Christ Church and St.*

Thomas Coombe, the very enlightened and revolutionary minister whose words these are, ended his sermon with the prediction that 'the kingdoms of this new-world, with their honor thick upon them, shall sink into the general abyss of empires'. Before the emergence of the USA, its demise could already be imagined. The new religious nationalism would find it much harder to accommodate this fact, and Coombe's opinion has not been repeated as a prediction by many American ministers.

In the United States too, religious nationalism made political authority responsible for the pious and virtuous conduct of the citizens of the nation. Like the Utrecht minister Hinlopen, Joseph Duché, preaching before the Continental Congress in 1775, used the traditional distinction between the duties of the people, the ministers and the magistrates. Yet the nature of these duties had changed: all now had to create moral selves.

> From [the Ministers] let the Magistrates take the alarm – Let them boldly rebuke vice – Let them punish immorality and profaneness without respect to rank or fortune – Let them become Ministers of the Gospel as well as Ministers of Justice – Let them inculcate the knowledge and practice of true religion and virtue, as far as their influence and authority extends.[32]

The duty of individuals correspondingly became to create a moral self, oriented towards the nation. John Witherspoon, at a national Fast-day in 1776, began his sermon with the political commitment and national ardor of his listeners, which he took for granted.[33] He then argued that they ought to be even more concerned with their soul's salvation: 'is your state on earth for a few fleeting years of so much moment? And is it of less moment, what shall be your state through endless ages?'[34] This looks like a throwback to the older patchwork of the thanksgiving

Peter's, Philadelphia, on Thursday, July 20, 1775: Being the day recommended by the Honorable Continental Congress for a general fast throughout the twelve United Colonies of North-America, Early American Imprints. First series, no. 42801: 26.

32 Jacob Duché, *The American vine: a sermon, preached in Christ-Church, Philadelphia, before the Honourable Continental Congress, July 20th, 1775. Being the day recommended by them for a general fast throughout the united English colonies of America*, Early American Imprints. First series, no. 14012: 29.

33 John Witherspoon, *The Dominion of Providence over the Passions of Men: A Sermon Preached at Princeton, on the 17th of May, 1776. Being the General Fast Appointed by the Congress through the United Colonies: To which is added, an address to the natives of Scotland residing in America*, Early American Imprints. First series, no. 15224.

34 Ibid., 30.

sermons, like that of Coombe. Yet Witherspoon depicts real piety as preconditioned by political and social factors:

> The knowledge of God and his truths have from the beginning of the world been chiefly, if not entirely confined to those parts of the earth, where some degree of liberty and political justice were to be seen.[35]

On the other hand, true piety and morality make a nation strong.

> What follows from this? That he is the best friend to American liberty, who is most sincere and active in promoting true and undefiled religion, and who sets himself with the greatest firmness to bear down prophanity and immorality of every kind. [. . .] Do not suppose, my brethren, that I mean to recommend a furious and angry zeal for the circumstantials of religion, or the contentions of one sect with another about their peculiar distinctions. I do not wish you to oppose any body's religion, but everybody's wicked-ness. Perhaps there are few surer marks of the reality of religion, than when a man feels himself more joined in spirit to a truly holy person of a different denomination, than to an irregular liver of his own.[36]

Witherspoon ended by identifying a set of social, political and religious duties:

> . . . remember that your duty to God, to your country, to your families, and to yourself is the same. [. . .] It is in the man of piety and inward principle that we may expect to find the uncorrupted patriot, the useful citizen, and the invincible soldier. God grant that in America true religion and civil liberty may be inseparable, and that the unjust attempts to destroy the one, may in the issue tend to support the establishment of both.[37]

After the end of the war with Great Britain, in the 1780s, these senti-ments were generally shared: 'Let us, my brethren, become real and sincere Christians. Vital Christianity will secure and hold us steady in a course of right conduct to promote our own and the public welfare'.[38]

---

35 Ibid., 51.
36 Ibid.
37 Ibid.
38 David Osgood, *Reflections on the Goodness of God in Supporting the People of the United States through the Late War, and Giving Them so Advantageous and Honourable a Peace: A Sermon*

In the 1790s, the new religious nationalism led to an explosion in the number of printed Fast and Thanksgiving Day sermons. The New England clergy felt themselves obliged and justified to intervene in all kinds of political questions, because they supposed politics aimed at creating moral individuals, which coincided with their own duty. This intense politicization of the New England clergy ended with the destruction of the Federalist party at the hands of Jefferson, but would live on in the great reform societies.[39]

I want to stress the originality and abrupt appearance of this American religious nationalism, which collapsed political, ecclesiastical and personal duties into the morals of the membership of a national community. New England Congregationalism had always been about owning the Covenant, about the personal appropriation of faith. Yet this piety had always been intellectually and discursively separated from the social order. In 1741, Ernst Bucknam, minister at Medway, preaching a traditional Fast-day sermon, routinely declared that a fast was necessary, because there were too many sins to mention, although he managed to order them under four headings.[40] People neglected the regular church services. This was the worst sin of all:

> We have all the private helps that can rationally be desired for our advancement in knowledge and holiness, and furtherance in the way to happiness, besides the publick administrations of God's house from time to time, as duly and regularly performed as in any place perhaps in the whole World: and yet how are they profaned, neglected and abused by many amongst us? What numbers are there that absent themselves from the publick worship of God's house, that stay away from Sabbath to Sabbath?[41]

People neglected to have their children baptized, to join the covenant, and to take part in the Lord's Supper. Morning and evening prayers in families were neglected, as were private prayers.

The other great sins were swearing and oath taking, profanation of the Sabbath, and disobedience to parents, which Buckham takes in

---

Preached on the Day of Annual and National Thanksgiving December 11, 1783, Early American Imprints. First series, no. 18670: 33.

[39] Jonathan D. Sassi, A Republic of Righteousness: The Public Christianity of the Post-Revolutionary New England Clergy (Oxford, 2000).

[40] Nathan Bucknam, The Just Expectations of God, from a People, when his Judgments are upon Them for Their Sins: Shewn, in Two Sermons, on Deut. XIII. 11. Preach'd at Medway, on a day of publick fasting and prayer, April 23, 1741, Early American Imprints. First series, no. 4682.

[41] Ibid.

general as 'a great want of that respect and reverence that is due from Inferiors to Superiors according to the Gospel of Jesus Christ.' This interpretation is echoed in scores of sermons until the 1770s. All these sins are public. They are infractions upon a public order. Bucknam points out that we know from scripture and history that these sins lead to collective judgements and social punishments. That is why he calls his hearers to repentance:

> Oh let everyone of us search and try our hearts and ways, and return again to the Lord [. . .] Let us reform the neglect of duties, publick, private and secret: [. . .] Let us reform our deadness and formality in duty: let us not satisfy ourselves with the form of Godliness without the life and power of it.[42]

Everyone is called to examine himself, confess his sins before God, and engage in introspection. This introspection and the hoped-for transformation of the self takes place to avert God's judgement, yet remains a deeply private act, without social effects or preconditions.

> Let everyone look to himself, and reform one, and hope and pray that it may be so through the Land. If ever there be a general Reformation brought about, it must begin in individuals, for generals are made up of particulars and the Sins of each help to draw down God's Judgements upon the Land; and if we amend, if others don't do in general, the People among whom we dwell may fare the better for us; a few righteous in a place may preserve it.[43]

This is a view of society which is quite similar to that of Smytegelt. Society is hierarchically ordered, and a very important aspect of the Christian life is that people fulfill the duties of their stations in life. Religion, in its social manifestation, is made up of a complex of 'public, private and secret duties'. The neglect of these religious and social duties leads to collective punishment. Piety stands apart from these social and religious duties and is an individual affair. It is not socially created. It is not a social duty. It has no social consequences. It may avert God's judgement, but it does not make society a better place. Socially, religion is public order, entailing duties. Over against this public order stand invisible, intensely individual pious selves, which are not known to each other.

42 Ibid., 68–9.
43 Ibid., 76.

* * *

The most thorough study of the New England sermon has been under-taken by Harry Stout.[44] In reaction against various attempts to docu-ment a decline or transformation of New England Puritanism, he argued for an essentially unchanging style of New England preaching, which until the Revolution engaged in both social moralism and the furtherance of piety. He divides these tasks between the regular Sunday sermons, concerned with personal salvation through faith in Christ, and the 'occasional' weekday sermons (of which, besides Fast and Thanksgiving Day sermons, election and militia sermons were the most important), where the ministers would tell the community what to do to retain God's blessing. A close re-reading of the hundreds of printed Fast and Thanksgiving Day sermons leads one to the same conclusion. Within these occasional sermons too, morality, in the sense of doing your social and religious duties,[45] and piety, a private inner state, are strictly distinguished and not integrated.[46]

Early in the eighteenth century, a number of Fast-day sermons worried about the neglect of religion by children, and exhorted parents to take care that their children would take their duties seriously. The means they offered were not educational in the modern sense of the word. Parents have to pray for their children, even before they are born, have them baptized, take them to church or hold Fast days.[47] Real piety is not the fruit of education, but of grace:

[44] Harry S. Stout, *The New England Soul: Preaching and Religious Culture in Colonial New England* (Oxford, 1986).

[45] Samuel Chandler, *Ezekiel's parable of the boiling pot.: Considered in a Discourse Preached at Glocester, on the Provincial Anniversary Fast, Thursday, March 20. 1755*, Early American Imprints. First series, no. 40743: 22–3; Aaron Burr, *A discourse Delivered at New-Ark, in New-Jersey. January 1, 1755*, Early American Imprints. First series, no. 7373: 32–5; N. Appleton, *The Right Method of Addressing the Divine Majesty in Prayer; so as to support and strengthen our faith in dark and troublesome times: Set forth in two discourses on April 5, 1770. Being the day of general fasting and prayer through the province: and in the time of the session of the General Court at Cambridge*, Early American Imprints. First series, no. 11554: 30ff.

[46] Perry Miller, the dean of Puritan studies, noticed the change I am trying to describe as well: see his article 'From the Covenant to the Revival', in Nelson R. Burr, ed., *Religion in American Life 1: The Shaping of American Religion* (Princeton, 1961), 322–68, arguing that until the revolution, ministers had supposed that men would persistently sin, and so would have to be recurrently summoned to communal repentance. With the revolution, political action had succeeded, and they inferred that Americans were virtuous and could look to the future. The evangelical scholar Mark Noll describes the same changes in his article, 'The American Revolution and Protestant Evangelicalism', *Journal of Interdisciplinary History* 23 (1993), 615–38, without the benefits of the concepts 'moral community' or 'nationalism'.

[47] Joseph Belcher, *Two Sermons Preached in Dedham, N.E.: The first on a day set apart for prayer with fasting, to implore spiritual blessings on the rising generation. The other (some time after) in*

Alas! There are many that mistake Morality for grace! Because they are not so bad as some others are, they think they are good. All their godliness is the mere effect of a good Education. Had they been born amongst Papists, they would have been Papists.[48]

Although the general development in New England and the Dutch Republic is the same – from public order to moral community – there are also important differences. The most important difference, perhaps, is methodological. There were more Dutch than New Englanders in the eighteenth century, and the Dutch were richer too. Even in the international world the eighteenth-century Dutch Republic – a shadow of its seventeenth-century predecessor – was still much more important and powerful than the New England colonies. At the beginning of the twenty-first century, this is no longer the case.

There are, probably, three important recent books about the religious history of the eighteenth-century Dutch Republic, and a score of articles. The number of important American studies of New England simply is of a different order of magnitude: scores of books, hundreds of articles. A focus on Fast-day sermons and the comparison with the Dutch Republic enables one to cut through many of the American discussions, and to place them in context.

In the first place, pietism as such, taken in a wide sense, as a stress on the importance of the personal appropriation of religious doctrines, was not enough to bring about the transformation of the social imaginary. In the Dutch Republic pietism was an important current within the public Church, gaining strength in the eighteenth century. Yet it always easily accommodated a location of Christianity in a public, hierarchical order. In New England, conversion stood next to social order from the very beginning of the colony, without piety and public order being integrated.

Secondly, millennialism, of which American scholars have made so much, also seems to be less important.[49] Undoubtedly, there were strong millenerialist elements in certain American revolutionary

<hr />

private, to a considerable number of young persons in the aforesaid town, Early American imprints. First series, no. 1443.

[48] Increase Mather, *The Duty of Parents to Pray for their Children: opened & applyed in a sermon, preached May 19. 1703*, Early American imprints. First series, no. 1132; 1133: 39.

[49] Sacvan Bercovitch, *The American Jeremiad* (Madison, 1978); Nathan O. Hatch, *The Sacred Cause of Liberty: Republican Thought and the Millennium in Revolutionary New England* (New Haven, 1977); Ruth Bloch, *Visionary Republic: Millennial Themes in American Thought, 1756–1800* (Cambridge 1985).

sermons, maintaining that the new American Republic would herald in the end of time. In the Dutch Republic such sentiments were very rare, but we do find in the Dutch days of prayer sermons from the 1770s onwards a new and thorough awareness of world history, the time through which the national community moves. Hierarchies and public orders have an origin and ought to stay the same. Moral communities move through time, have a history and change.[50] Such an historical awareness, quite apart from millenarialist speculation, is also an important part of late eighteenth-century American Fast-day sermons, often expressed in terms of an amazing demographic awareness of the millions of Americans yet unborn:[51]

> If twenty-five Years will double the Number of Inhabitants in the Colonies [. . .] than one hundred Years will give sixteen for one, without Importation of Foreigners [. . .] one Century and a half will people the British Empire in America, with upwards of Sixty Million Souls.[52]

In the third place, in the Netherlands, enlightened sociability and literature deeply influenced the imagination of the nation as a moral community. During the eighteenth century the Dutch Republic experienced an inexorable decline. The decades-long wars with France around 1700 had been the last the Republic had been able to fight as a great power. In the eighteenth century, it could no longer afford to engage in such world-historical acts. This perceived decline led to a moralizing, proto-nationalistic programme of renewal, developed by enlightened writers in new Dutch-language journals from the 1730s onwards.[53] The cause of Dutch decline was seen in a loss of civic virtue, and the remedy in a return to simple, ancestral life-styles. The journals

---

50 Peter van Rooden, 'Dutch Protestantism and its Pasts', in R. N. Swanson, ed., *The Church Retrospective*, SCH 33 (Woodbridge, 1997), 254–63.

51 See, for example, Timothy Hilliard, *The Duty of a People under the Oppression of Man, to seek Deliverance from God*. The substance of two sermons, delivered at Barnstable, July 14th, 1774. A day set apart for humiliation and prayer on account of the present dark and melancholy aspect of our public affairs, Early American Imprints. First series, no. 13329; and Thomas Coombe, *A Sermon, Preached before the Congregations of Christ Church and St. Peter's, Philadelphia, on Thursday, July 20, 1775*, Early American Imprints. First series, no. 42801: 20.

52 John Mellen, *A Sermon Preached at the West Parish in Lancaster, October 9. 1760: On the general thanksgiving for the reduction of Montreal and total conquest of Canada: Containing a brief account of the war, from the year 1755; and a review of the first settlement and several expeditions against (with some of the reasons for holding) Canada*, Early American Imprints. First series, no. 8669: 36–7.

53 J. Hartog, *De Spectatoriale Geschriften van 1741–1800. Bijdrage tot de kennis van het huiselijk,*

attempted to spread a kind of morality which would try to benefit not only one's concrete neighbour, but the imagined society as a whole. They deplored the influence of French culture, attempting to replace it with traditional and simple Dutch virtue and manners. In the 1750s, this enlightened language of moral reform as a means of regaining national strength was taken up in the States-General's proclamations of days of prayer; and in the 1770s they were, as we have seen, present in Fast-day sermons as well. There is no similar development in New England. The eighteenth-century American colonies certainly suffered their share of horrors, but over all they did very well, with their traditional war with France and its Indian allies culminating in total victory when Canada was conquered in 1760. New Englanders too, just like the Dutch, used the French as the main 'Other', but they did not describe them as insiduous sappers of national morals and individual selves, but much more brutally and directly as religious tyrants, bent upon enslaving Protestants both civilly and religiously. This was a much cruder and much more political anti-Catholicism than is to be found anywhere in the eighteenth-century Dutch Republic.[54] Although this anti-Catholicism explicitly opposed tyranny and freedom, liberty and enslavement, it did not function in the same way as the enlightened programme for national renewal in the Netherlands. The tyrannical French threatened above all the religious and political order of New England, not the individual selves of the New Englanders, and the eighteenth-century French threat thus did not lead to a programme of individual reform.

Fourthly, political structures account for the most important difference between New England and the Dutch Republic. In the 1770s, the Dutch Republic was an existing political entity, and, although it was highly decentralized and absurdly particularistic, its new imagination of itself as a moral community grew out of the concerns of its ruling group about its international status and was spread by the national organization of the days of prayer. Internal political upheavals followed the application of this new discourse. The Patriot revolution of the

---

maatschappelijk en kerkelijk leven onder ons volk in de tweede helft der 18e eeuw (Utrecht, 1872); P. J. Buijnsters, *De Nederlandse literatuur van de achttiende eeuw* (Utrecht, 1984).

54 Cotton Mather, *The Wonderful Works of God Commemorated: Praises bespoke for the God in Heaven in a thanksgiving sermon; delivered on Decemb. 19. 1689. Containing just reflections upon the excellent things done by the great God, more generally in creation and redemption, and in the government of the world; but more particularly in the remarkable revolutions of providence which are every where the matter of present observation. With a postscript giving an account of some very stupendous accidents, which have lately happened in France*, Early American imprints. First series, no. 540.

1780s was triggered by military defeat, but can be called a revolution because it rested upon a political application of the new religious nationalism. Its main ideologue, Johan Derk van der Capellen, started his revolutionary career as a publicist with the translation of a Walloon Fast-day sermon, which already contained the whole Patriot political diagnosis.[55] The colonies in America, on the other hand, were only growing towards a common self-awareness during the eighteenth century, with war with France playing the most important role in this development. The political crisis within the British Empire led to the sudden emergence of modern nationalism in the United States, which was religiously expressed. Yet this nationalism had not been religiously prepared.

* * *

All this implies a rather thorough rejection of the argument Alan Heimert made in 1966 in his monumental *Religion and the American Mind: From the Great Awakening to the Revolution*.[56] Heimert argued that the Great Awakening, the wave of religious revivals which supposedly swept the American colonnies in the 1740s, prepared the way for the American Revolution. When his book was published, it received withering reviews. Still, a strange combination of evangelical and postmodernist scholars, united in their rejection of a liberal interpretation of the American Revolution, has managed during the last twenty years to elevate Heimert's thesis into the leading model for understanding the social role of religion in eighteenth-century America.[57] Heimert argued that Calvinism, and especially Edwardsian New Light Calvinism, had provided Americans with a radical political ideology, had fostered democracy, and had contributed towards American nationalism. Since then his thesis, never easy to understand in the first place, has mutated in so many ways, that it has become very hard to refute. Jon Butler, in a blistering article, has argued, quite convincingly in my eyes, that the whole concept of a Great Awakening in the eighteenth century is an interpretive fiction: there simply was no single religious movement sweeping all the American colonies in the 1740s

---

55 Isaac du Puy, *Leerrede over Ps V:13 op den algemeenen dank- vast- en bededag den 14 February 1781, uit het Fransch vertaald door Johan Derk Baron van der Capellen* (Zwolle, 1781).

56 Alan Heimert, *Religion and the American Mind: from the Great Awakening to the Revolution* (Cambridge, MA, 1966).

57 Philip Goff, 'Revivals and Revolution: Historiographic Turns since Alan Heimert's *Religion and the American Mind*', *Church History* 67 (1998), 695–721.

and transforming them, while the religious movements there were did not have 'proto-nationalist' consequences.[58] Actually, according to Butler, the confessional state, linking religion to social hierarchy, was doing very well in the American colonies up to the Revolution.[59]

The use of a single literary genre over a longer period is an excellent way to explore such questions. An analysis of the Fast and Thanksgiving Day sermons does not support Heimert in any way. A new imaginary of the social place of religion only emerged with the Revolution. Yet neither would I completely agree with those opponents of Heimert, who interpret the Revolution as an instance of secularization: scholars like Edmund Morgan, arguing that a secularized, moralized form of Puritan virtue animated the Revolutionary generation; or Bailyn, stating that religion served to spread Whig ideology by employing moral arguments; or Hatch, concluding that ministers during the Revolution combined Whig ideology with a millenarianism that resulted from the French and Indian wars, so raising the political stakes with powerful religious images.[60] I do not find these interpretations very helpful. Religious nationalism, the notion that the political world ought to be made up of moral communities of religiously informed individuals, was really something new, and although this notion was not religiously produced, it did not lead to secularization. Instead, we have to think of this new location of religion as an opening up of new opportunities, a radical new way to make religion socially relevant, a new vision of how to create Christian societies and Christian selves. In a famous quotation, W. R. Ward has stated that

> The generation overshadowed by the French Revolution was the most important generation in the modern history not only of English religion, but of most of the Christian world. For the Revolution altered forever the terms on which religious establish-

---

[58] Jon Butler, 'Enthusiasm Described and Decried: the Great Awakening as Interpretative Fiction', *The Journal of American History* 69 (1982), 305–25. He emphasizes, for instance, that even the Calvinist revivalists of the 1740s continued to draw sharp distinctions between the rights of ministers and the duties of the laity (314). He also makes clear that not the revivals, but the eighteenth-century colonial wars raised intercolonial unity.

[59] Jon Butler, 'Coercion, Miracle, Reason: Rethinking the American Religious Experience in the Revolutionary Age', in Ronald Hoffman and Peter J. Albert, eds, *Religion in a Revolutionary Age* (Charlottesville, VA, 1994), 1–29.

[60] Hatch, *The Sacred Cause of Liberty*; Bloch, *Visionary Republic*; Edmund. S. Morgan, 'The Puritan Ethic and the American Revolution', *William and Mary Quarterly* 24 (1967), 3–43; Bernard Bailyn, *The Ideological Origins of the American Revolution* (Cambridge, MA, 1967).

ments, the chief device on which the nations of the West had relied for christianising the people, must work.[61]

Yet it was not simply that religious establishments after 1800 worked on different terms: their whole purpose had changed. Before the emergence of religious nationalism, creating a Christian society always involved strenghtening a public order. Having an establishment was the goal, because having an establishment was the only way to socially produce Christianity. With the emergence of religious nationalism, establishments became means to produce Christian selves, the form the social production of Christianity would henceforth take. Before the revolutions, sin invited repentance; after the revolutions, it led to reform.

To finish, I would like to offer some observations about the status or nature of this, presumably new, religious nationalism. Theologically, the best expression of the new religious nationalism is to be found in Schleiermacher, specifically in his *Reden über die Religion*: piety lies at the root of all social and cultural manifestations of religion.[62] This notion proved to be an extremely powerful research agenda, determining the historical scholarship of the nineteenth-century German theological faculties, the intellectual powerhouses of modern Christianity. Their conception of religion as deriving its social force and cultural power from individual piety has deeply stamped modern views of the religious past, determining not only historical and theological scholarship, but cultural and social anthropology as well.

But the new conception of the relation between inner selves and social action, between piety and power, is not a particular view, a peculiar theology, or a theory about the nature of religion. Up until now I have carefully avoided the word 'discourse', but in this conclusion, I am afraid, I have to use the concept or a word which tries to express the same thing. Fast-day sermons, both in the Netherlands and in America, explicate a certain way of conceptualizing the social world, which makes possible certain kinds of political and social action, while suppressing others.

This is also the main reason why I refuse to interpret the new location of religion in inner selves as secularization. It certainly was something new, but it also opened up a whole new array of possible ways of

61 W. R. Ward, *Religion and Society in England, 1790–1850* (London, 1972), 1.
62 Peter van Rooden, 'Friedrich Schleiermachers *Reden über die Religion* en de historische bestudering van godsdienst', *Theoretische Geschiedenis* 23 (1996), 419–38.

acting.[63] Everything we think of as the vital aspects of modern Christianity (or of any modern religion, actually), like missions, the involvement of the laity, social movements, a market for a religious print culture, only makes sense within the new discourses and practices of religious nationalism. To put it starkly, before the end of the eighteenth century, general sin was an occassion for collective rituals of repentance. Since then, particular sins have been a motive or justification for projects by the state or for the actions of social movements. The discursive change in the conceptual relation between power and piety transformed penance into reform.

University of Amsterdam

[63] Peter van Rooden, 'Secularization and the Trajectory of Religion in the West', in Henri Krop, Arie Molendijk and Hent de Vries, eds, *Post-Theism: Reframing the Judeo-Christian Tradition* (Leuven, 2000), 169–88.

IMPRISONMENT AND RELEASE IN THE WRITINGS OF THE WESLEYS

by TIM MACQUIBAN

THIS essay focuses on repentance, with respect to one particular aspect of the work and witness of the Methodists as exemplified in the writings of their founders, John and Charles Wesley (1703–91 and 1707–88 respectively). A predominant motif of their preaching and hymn-writing came from the experience of working with condemned prisoners in Oxford and London gaols, an experience which became paradigmatic for the evangelical conversionist stance of the movement. The metaphors of imprisonment and freedom were realities arising from the physical conditions of the few, pressed upon a general population perceived to be languishing in spiritual stupor and captivity as the *kairos* of Gospel revelation called all those under sentence of death to repentance: 'This is the time, no more delay; This is the Lord's appointed day'.[1]

After sketching the historical background to imprisonment in the eighteenth century and looking at the Wesleyan context, the involvement of the Wesleys in prison work will be examined, leading to a detailed analysis of the hymns and sermon material. Linking the cultural context of such writings with an analysis of the way in which they illustrate praxis can help the religious historian fathom the motives of those engaged in social action.

* * *

Dostoevsky once commented that the soul of society 'can be measured by its prisons'.[2] In today's British society with its rising prison population and growing tensions, this is a sad indictment of the current state of law and order which seeks to imprison ever greater numbers despite the alternative options available to magistrates and judges. Snyder characterizes this choice as a 'spirit of punishment' which pervades the penal system, in which the Churches collude through the imposition of

---

[1] *Hymns and Psalms*, prepared by representatives of the British Methodist Conference (Peterborough, 1983), 460.

[2] T. Richard Snyder, *The Protestant Ethic and the Spirit of Punishment* (Grand Rapids, MI, 2001), 2.

a Protestant notion of grace. The Protestant theology of grace places greater stress on total depravity and the individual's need to appropriate the redeeming work of Christ compared with a more positive view informed by a gracious God whose justice restores rather than condemns.[3] Lee Griffith comments, in his critique of the place of prisons in society, that 'cages, chains, pits, dungeons, jails and prisons are biblically identified with the power and spirit of death'.[4] Whatever his rationale, the continuing presence of clergy and lay people from churches in prisons bears witness to the engagement of Christianity with issues of the care of humanity imprisoned by society for a variety of reasons.

Prisons in the eighteenth century were primarily places of containment, ensuring the safe custody of suspects arrested, those condemned to die or waiting for transportation, or those to be coerced into repaying debts. Very few expected to be incarcerated for a long fixed term. These were places of 'unrelieved misery, sexual promiscuity, disease, squalor and extortion',[5] guaranteed to reduce the will to live and an ability to recover. To some Christians, the social and moral conditions of prisons caused concern. John Howard was prominent in his call for reforms to the system.[6] The place of the chaplain was limited and often neglected: 'His business was not to seek to reform the living . . . but . . . to administer to those appointed to die "the consolation of religion".'[7] Nevertheless the example of Matthew Henry, a non-conformist preacher (1662–1714), and the ordinaries who served in prisons should not be overlooked.

From 1688 to 1820 the number of hanging offences rose from fifty to about two hundred. Those so convicted and executed were mainly the victims of a social system in which the pressures of poverty and incidence of crime were clearly linked.[8] There was a scant use of imprisonment for criminal offences. The gallows was the indispensable tool for maintaining the authority of the criminal law: 'It, not religion, became the chief ideological weapon which, in the name of equality, could facilitate and justify the hegemony of an elite.'[9]

[3] Ibid., 11–15.
[4] Lee Griffith, *The Fall of the Prison* (Grand Rapids, MI, 1993), 188.
[5] Sean McConville, *A History of English Prison Administration, 1750–1877* (London, 1981), 49.
[6] McConville, *English Prison Administration*, 49–54.
[7] Ibid., 74, with reference to Kingsmill in 1854.
[8] John Rule, *Albion's People: English Society 1714–1815* (Harlow, 1992), 227.
[9] Ibid., 240, 245.

As Hay has demonstrated, the Tyburn tree was at the heart of this ideology, to protect the property of a privileged elite.[10] Such public punishment was pure theatre, 'didactic theatre . . . to provide lessons and warnings for other would-be transgressors of the Law'.[11] Large crowds gathered to witness the scenes of impending death, to inflict further pain on the condemned or sometimes to rescue their self-declared heroes in defiance of the authorities and ruling classes who had condemned them.[12] Here was a supreme theatrical moment for religion to intervene and demonstrate its power, a chance for criminals to repent, to blame others and to seek forgiveness; here was a chance for evangelists to shine, using this moment of drama to intensify the opportunities for life-saving conversion not merely for those condemned to hang, but also for all convicted sinners who gathered to gape and tremble at human weakness in the face of death.[13]

One example will suffice here. John Lancaster, born in Whitechapel in 1726, attended the Foundery charity school and was apprenticed to a velvet weaver from whom he stole some pieces at the Bartholemew Fair and fled abroad. When he returned years later, his habit had not been broken. He was discovered selling the cloth he stole to a Jewish fence in Houndsditch. He was convicted and sentenced to be hanged. In the Newgate Gaol (later to be the scene of the prison visiting of the Quaker Elizabeth Fry) where he was held prior to execution, Sarah Peters, a Methodist, visited him and supervised his conversion.

The procession to the gallows at Tyburn, according to John Wesley's account, was more like a revival meeting than a hanging match. The condemned sang a Wesley hymn, *Lamb of God whose bleeding love*, before John Lancaster and his companions died. Wesley deduced signs of divine intervention from the fact that Lancaster's face was neither bloated nor otherwise disfigured. The body, taken off by surgeons for dissection, was rescued by eight sailors and returned to his mother who gave it a decent burial, sure evidence that the conversion was efficacious. Like the dying thief on the Cross, in the words of the Wesley hymn: 'O remember Calvary, And let us go in peace'. No butchery therefore at the hands of surgeons if at all possible![14]

---

10 Douglas Hay, *Albion's Fatal Tree: Crime and Society in Eighteenth-Century England* (London, 1975), 13.
11 Clive Emsley, *Crime and Society in England 1750–1900* (2nd edn, London, 1996), 259.
12 Ibid.
13 Ibid., 260.
14 Hay, *Albion's Tree*, 87.

The account is a powerful piece of religious propaganda supporting the evangelistic opportunity available through prison and beyond, offering the desire for peaceful translation of the soul from this life to the next. But the Wesley brothers' regular missions to Newgate and other prisons from 1738 onwards often provoked opposition from the authorities and the crowds.[15] Were the Wesleys through their involvement in prisons challenging one of the 'chief ideological instruments' of the ruling class?[16] Or was their involvement an instance of the social control sought by evangelicals in reclaiming the ground stolen by secular authorities?

The origins of the Methodist involvement in prison work and in the evangelistic ministry to the condemned lie in the decade earlier, when John and Charles were in Oxford. Such practical engagement in this work had a significant effect on their sermons and writings, becoming a leitmotif in the *ordo salutis* (order of salvation) they framed as a distinct Arminian contribution to the Evangelical Revival of the eighteenth century. The fact that even today *And can it be* remains the best known and sung hymn of the Wesleyan movement is indication of the way in which this Aldersgate experience – the personal moment which followed the conversion of Charles and John Wesley at Aldersgate in London in May 1738 – became encapsulated in the imagery of imprisonment and freedom which their practical ministerial work had taught them.

* * *

Prison visiting, concern for prisoners and the experience of being in prison was central to the Wesley family. When, in 1705, Samuel, rector of Epworth in Lincolnshire, was cast into Lincoln Castle gaol for debt, he took the opportunity to write to the Society for the Promotion of Christian Knowledge to obtain books to distribute among the prisoners as well as lead services for them, reflecting that 'I am getting acquainted with my brother jail-birds as fast as I can.'[17] His eldest son Samuel wrote to his mother Susanna to comfort her in the family difficulty.[18] This Samuel, then a scholar at Westminster School, later wrote a poem, *The Prisons opened,* in honour of James Oglethorpe and fellow members

15 McConville, *English Prison Administration*, 74.
16 Emsley, *Crime*, 10.
17 Maldwyn Edwards, *Family Circle: a Study of the Epworth Household in Relation to John and Charles Wesley* (London, 1949; repr. 1961), 19.
18 Edwards, *Family Circle*, 103.

of a 'Committee . . . appointed to inquire into the state of the Jails of this kingdom'[19] in 1728. Oglethorpe was a great friend of debtors and felons whose conditions he highlighted. Samuel Wesley voiced these in his poem:

> Piecemeal alive they rot, long doom'd to bear
> The pestilential foul imprison'd Air:
>
> As if the Pris'ners were condemned to dwell
> With Pains with Darkness and with Fiends of Hell.[20]

Out of Oglethorpe's concern came the great project to create the colony of Georgia, suggested to his mind by the situation of those 'whom he had rescued from the fangs of the jailer and the horrors of imprisonment'.[21] His colony became a haven of hope for over a thousand whom he enabled to find asylum abroad. Samuel Wesley senior supported his endeavours and tried to find recruits for the work of evangelism. Ironically, it was his own two sons, supported through their years at Oxford by their elder brother Samuel, who were sent by the Society for the Propagation of the Gospel after Samuel's death in 1735, perhaps with the encouragement of Dr Burton, President of Corpus Christi College, Oxford, and a Trustee of the Colony.[22]

It was at Oxford that John and Charles first became involved in the sort of prison visiting that their own father had engaged in whilst at University. Encouraged by William Morgan in August 1730, they began to visit first the Castle Gaol (for felons) and then the Bocardo (for debtors), preaching and praying and caring for the prisoners.[23] These activities soon earned them opprobrium and the nickname of 'The Holy Club', a title which Samuel senior urged them not to disdain nor give up the work.[24] For Charles Wesley, such visits were central to the social concerns embodied in the evangelistic works of mercy they engaged in. From their pens flowed a distinctive theology, in the hymns and sermons shaped by this pastoral context.[25] Charles, as ever under

---

[19] [Samuel Wesley the Younger], *The Prisons Open'd: a Poem occasion'd by the late glorious proceedings of the Committee appointed to enquire into the State of the Goals [sic] of this Kingdom* (London, 1729), title page.

[20] Ibid., 8.

[21] *The Journal of the Revd Charles Wesley*, ed. Thomas Jackson, 2 vols (London, 1849), 1: x.

[22] Ibid., viii–xxvii.

[23] Richard Heitzenrater, *Wesley and the People Called Methodists* (Nashville, TN, 1995), 40.

[24] Edwards, *Family Circle*, 35.

[25] This idea was expressed in an unpublished paper by Peter Forsaith, 'Christmas Dinners for Wretched Sinners: the Wesleys' Ministry in Oxford Castle', delivered at the

the shadow of his elder and more prominent brother, was no mean theologian in his own right; he was, according to Newport, 'of not insignificant ability in his attempt to explain the plight of the human condition'.[26] A number of sermons which have survived were preached by him and his brother John at the Castle, particularly the first post-Pentecost sermon on the text 1 John 3: 14 in August 1738.[27] Newport regards these as indicative of a change of heart in the light of an optimism which conversion brought, compared with his earlier soteriological pessimism.[28]

In that same year, Charles moved away from Oxford, that until then was the sole theatre of his good works and evangelism, to the larger cities of Bristol and London, and then beyond, fired by the Aldersgate spirit. For several intense periods, both in 1738 and in the years following, he concentrated on the prison at Newgate in London where he ministered to condemned prisoners in July and September 1738, February 1739 and January/February 1741, according to his journal accounts. The encounters in the cells and the death scenes at Tyburn are evidence of the importance of this aspect of his ministry in these early years after conversion.[29] It was there that the 'spirit of faith' came upon him again as he preached to the malefactors and offered them salvation.[30] Charles described the night before the execution, as they sang *Behold the Saviour of Mankind* in July 1738, as 'one of the most triumphant hours I have ever known'.[31] The next day he described the condemned at the hanging scene as 'all cheerful, full of comfort, peace, and triumph; assuredly persuaded Christ had died for them, and wanted to receive them into paradise'.[32]

* * *

The motif of the dying thief is a powerful trigger for much of the concern for such condemned prisoners and the offer and promise of salvation for all people, irrespective of their human condition, to whom

---

Research Seminar, Wesley and Methodist Studies Centre, Westminster Institute, Oxford, in October 2002.

[26] *The Sermons of Charles Wesley: a Critical Edition*, ed. Kenneth G. C. Newport (Oxford, 2001), 48.

[27] Ibid., 132.

[28] Ibid., 57.

[29] Ibid., 117–23, 130–45, 303–6.

[30] Ibid., 117.

[31] Ibid., 120.

[32] Ibid.

the promise of eternal life is held out as a hope in trouble. Taking up themes prevalent in his Journals of 1738–9, a hymn written by Charles and published in 1749 uses the biblical metaphor of the dying thief (Luke 23: 42) as a motif for the redemptive gospel the Wesleys sought to proclaim to all. In it, the condemned malefactor asks:

> Hast thou not wrought the sure belief
> I feel this moment in Thy blood?
> And am not I the dying thief?
> And art not Thou my Lord, my God?
>
> Forgive, and make us fit to die,
> Alas! We are not fit to live.[33]

Charles uses the experience and example of the dying thief as indicative of the reconciling death of Christ on the Cross, sealed in his blood shed for all, available to all whatever their condition.

Watson reminds us of the way in which Wesley uses strongly physical metaphors for the spiritual state. Amongst these, *melting* and *breaking* the *stony hearts* of the unredeemed individual are central, picking up on biblical allusions of transformation of lives (cf. Ez. 11; 21; 22). So for Wesley the dying thief, like the condemned prisoner, becomes a metaphor for the human condition dependent on the mercy of God for life or death. Christ's redeeming work on the Cross demonstrates that offer of grace. The inevitability of death needs to be faced in the hope of the promise of eternal life which relieves us from the threat of eternal death.[34]

While the 'cords of sin and death' bind the unbeliever, the 'chains of sin and death' can be loosed by the offer of eternal life to those who believe in the atoning death of Christ upon the Cross. Charles Wesley's birthday hymn of 1741 is a throw-back to his conversion experience of 1738, when he was confirmed through the power of the Spirit as a newly liberated soul, aware of the New Birth or New Creation. Wesley became a person who is no longer bound by sin and death, but a 'prisoner of hope':

> The tyranny of sin is past;
> And though the carnal mind remains,
> My guiltless soul on thee is cast,

---

[33] J. Ernest Rattenbury, *The Evangelical Doctrines of Charles Wesley's Hymns* (London, 1941), 238–49.

[34] J. R. Watson, *The English Hymn: a Critical and Historical Study* (Oxford, 1997), 261–2.

> I neither hug, nor bite my chains;
> Prisoner of hope; to thee I turn,
> And bless the day that I was born.[35]

Wesley uses the figure of imprisonment under the law of sin and death as a legal metaphor for the human condition, given his awareness of the reality of its social impact on the lives of his contemporaries. The pardon of sin and deliverance from the forces of evil draws on the powerful images of freedom from the dark and from the dungeon of the prison, out into the light of a new dawn with no chains, no 'iron yoke', the 'fetters broken', as a 'Freeman of the Lord [. . .] to life restor'd'.[36]

Of all the hymns included in the 1780 *Collection of Hymns for the Use of the People called Methodists* [hereafter CH], the most significant and universal in application in modern hymnals is *And can it be*, in which Charles Wesley likens his pre-Aldersgate condition to the 'imprisoned spirit' waiting for deliverance from the dungeon in which he lies 'fast bound in sin and nature's night'. The awareness of God's infinite mercy, 'immense and free', brings him a sense of new freedom and the reconciliation with God which he sought.[37] But the imagery is scattered throughout the collection, drawing on the rich veins of biblical allusions of deliverance from Isaiah, Luke, ch. 4 and Paul's Letter to the Romans. The Gospel of Jesus Christ sets prisoners free 'from the pit' (CH 144, v. 7: cf. Ps. 40: 2) which brings 'sweet release' (CH 215, v. 3). All can find grace, even 'the foulest offender' (CH 5, v. 1), or the 'outcasts of men . . . harlots and publicans and thieves', since Christ 'came the lost to seek and save' (CH 29, v. 5), emphasizing the inclusivity of the social message of the gospel. As the second Adam, Christ has come to

> . . . set the plaintive prisoners free.
> Bring forth out of this hellish pit
> This dungeon of despairing grief.[38]

The condition of such captive souls is hellish; they are 'guilty spirits oppressed', 'groaning souls' waiting to be released (CH 28, vv. 1 and 3), as instanced in the following hymn:

---

35 Rattenbury, *Charles Wesley's Hymns*, 253.
36 Ibid., 240–2.
37 Watson, *English Hymn*, 222.
38 CH 125, vv. 4–5.

O let the pris'ners mournful cries
As incense in thy sight appear.
Their humble wailings pierce the skies
If haply they may find thee near.

The captive exiles make their moans
From sin impatient to be free;
Call home, call home, thy banished ones!
Lead captive their captivity![39]

Out of the dungeon of despair, grief, and oppression, like Daniel in the den (CH 156, v. 2), tied down by the 'tyrant's chain' of sin and death, the believer is, as the Israelites, 'out of the house of bondage brought, and freed from th' Egyptian yoke', when 'the open door of hope' is offered (CH 284, vv. 2 and 4). Paradoxically, the believer, released from one condition of imprisonment, becomes for Christ 'the sinner's friend' (CH 138, v. 1), 'the prisoner of thy love' (CH 102, v. 3) which brings 'life and liberty' (CH 135, v. 2) to all 'happy sinners' (CH 336, v. 1). Because Christ for the Wesleys has been found in the experience of meeting those who were prisoners and strangers, the outcasts of society shunned by conventional Christians of their day, they hold up the work of evangelism amongst the poor and oppressed for their followers:

The prisoner release
The stranger relieve
Supply all their wants
And spend and be spent in assisting his saints.[40]

Towards the end of his life, a collection of hymns *For Malefactors* was published in the Jackson edition of Charles Wesley's Journal, which was particularly indicative of the continuing importance of this ministry to the prisoners in shaping the spiritual development of the 'people called Methodists'. The collection consisted of six hymns, two of these for those in prison, and four for condemned malefactors. The tone of such hymns was to encourage those who ministered to such 'stupid slaves of sin' who were regarded 'with pity and pain' by fellow sufferers. The power of Christ's death on the Cross to forgive, remove

---

[39] CH 28, vv. 1, 3.
[40] CH 482, v. 3.

sin and death and rescue these 'lost sheep' was invoked, and for those who repented, the promise of entry into his eternal kingdom made.

* * *

In his recent edition of the Charles Wesley's sermons, Kenneth Newport has given us the detailed textual tools needed to make a more thorough analysis of the development of Charles's theological thought.[41] Newport has developed a greater awareness of how different was his pre- and post-Aldersgate preaching, and how significant was the context in which both Charles and John found the exercise of their ministry. The social concern which characterized the Oxford years remained. But the 'conversion' experience of 1738 reshaped and revitalized the sermons of Charles in the light of the 'New Birth' he and John came to know.

The regular visitation of the Castle prison to engage with the condemned prisoners was, as we have seen, a particular concern in the 1730s. This experience had a significant impact on Charles's endeavour 'to explain the human condition' and to offer the 'optimism of grace' which he had come to experience for himself.[42] The edited sermons provide further evidence of how this change contributed to dispel the earlier gloom and soteriological pessimism.

Contrast two sermons drawing on images of imprisonment. The first comes from the pre-1738 period, taking a text from Phil. 3: 14–15. The darkness of Charles Wesley's own dungeon and the gloom of his attempts to strive towards perfection are evident, as he seeks release both for those to whom he ministers and himself.[43] The second example is his first surviving post-Pentecost sermon, delivered at Oxford Castle on 29 August 1738, 'preached to the poor prisoners' on a theme from the First Letter of John (1 John 3: 14). The familiar contrasting pairs of darkness/light and captivity/freedom are clearly drawn from the context of prison ministry and given soteriological significance in the context of the preacher's own conversion experience. Those in captivity are proclaimed by the modern-day follower of Isaiah's prophecy (Is. 61: 1 and Luke 4) to be 'prisoners of hope', allowing the spirit of God to take them out of darkness into light, out of bondage into glorious liberty. He exhorts in conclusion:

41 See n. 21.
42 *Sermons of Charles Wesley*, 48, 57.
43 Ibid., 57.

Believe that he is able to do this!
Believe it according to thy faith.[44]

A similar sermon preached on 4 April 1742 at a time of intense activity as a prison minister in London, on the text 'Awake thou that sleepest' (Eph. 5: 14), depicts the human condition as one of bondage: 'fast bound in misery and iron, he dreams he is happy and at liberty'.[45] Such a delusion is exposed by the preacher who declares that all are under sentence of death, that is, the 'spiritual death' which awaits the coming of the second Adam (i.e. Christ), whose 'quickening spirit' raises from death, that of sin, 'pleasure, riches or honours'.

Charles goes on to develop in the same sermon the image of Peter in the prison cell, 'lying in the dark dungeon between the soldiers' (Acts 12: 6), as a metaphor for those 'fast asleep in the devil's arm, on the brink of the pit, in the jaws of everlasting destruction' to whom the angel of deliverance is to come to bring 'light (to) shine into thy prison!' and set the prisoner free.[46] The preacher himself takes on the role of the angelic messenger, aided by the power of the Spirit of God to bring such deliverance. No longer is he enslaved by sin and death, because he has found the experience of release which he wants to share with others in his evangelistic ministry.

Brother John's sermons are more extensive and wide-ranging in scope. He too has his post-Aldersgate preaching shaped by the reflection on the spiritual experience in the light of the prison ministry he continues to exercise. His sermon *Salvation by Faith,* preached at St Mary's in Oxford on 11 June 1738, takes the text from Rom. 8: 1 and proclaims that there is no condemnation for those who believe in Jesus Christ: they are saved from guilt and fear, the 'fear of punishment . . . of the wrath of God'.[47]

In *The Spirit of Bondage and of Adoption*, developing the text in verse 15 of the same chapter of Romans, Wesley describes the three states of man: one is natural, as man is burdened by original sin; one is legal, as man is subject to the Law and is fearful; one is evangelical, as man discovers his salvific hope in Christ. The images of darkness and captivity are crucial to the contrast between the latter condition and the

---

[44] Ibid., 144. The quotation is printed in verse, perhaps because it came from a hymn.
[45] Ibid., 213.
[46] Ibid.
[47] *The Works of John Wesley: the Bicentennial Edition*, ed. Albert C. Outler *et al.*, 26 vols (Nashville, TN, 1975–), 1: 122–4.

former. By his own, man is unable to break free: 'The more he strives, labours to be free, the more does he feel his chains, the grievous chains, wherewith Satan binds him . . . his servant he is'.[48]

But the 'Spirit of Adoption' replaces the 'Spirit of Bondage' and overcomes the 'sin and misery' of the human condition without God.[49] This comes about as human beings find themselves forgiven. Then the 'chains fall off' and there is no condemnation.[50] In other sermons, such as *Origin, Nature, Properties and Use of the Law, General Deliverance*, similar images of chains loosed and bondage ended are used.

Unlike Charles, John seems to have enjoyed a more optimistic outlook on the ability of human beings to respond to the offer of a transforming grace. We know from surviving notes that John preached at regular weekly intervals at the Castle Gaol, often using notes abridged from the sermons of others for over thirty minutes.[51] In his sermon *In Earth as in Heaven*, preached in Oxford Castle in April 1734, he expresses a high doctrine of human potential for goodness and truth. This outlook enables him to preach with confidence, despite the wretchedness of the conditions of the condemned and their expectations of God's love for them. In *A Single Intention*, preaching on a text from Matt. 6: 10, John contrasts the terrors of the deep and its darkness with the light of God's abundant providence, thus exhorting his congregation: 'Be ye likewise new creatures! Let God be your aim and God only! Let your one end be to please and to love God!'[52]

* * *

The importance of the prison ministry in shaping the early theological development of the Wesleys' preaching can be judged by the inclusion within tracts published in 1746 of *A Word to a Condemned Malefactor* (1745) and in subsequent editions of this work. The tract represented the various practical expressions of the Wesleys' ministry and mission, displaying a breadth of concern for mind, body and soul of all people.[53]

This tract continued to represent the interest of the bold succession of Methodists who engaged in prison visiting, like Sarah Peters and Silas Told to the Newgate in London, John Valton and others.[54] Clearly this

---

[48] Ibid., 1: 258.
[49] Ibid., 1: 253–8.
[50] Ibid., 1: 386 ('Sermon on the Mount' sermon).
[51] Ibid., 4: 525.
[52] Ibid., 4: 371–7.
[53] Heitzenrater, *People Called Methodists*, 156–7.
[54] Leslie F. Church, *More About the Early Methodist People* (London, 1949), 201; *The Works*

commitment to work with the marginalized had an abiding influence within Methodism and the Evangelical Revival. John Fletcher, at one time thought to be a candidate for the apostolic succession in the Methodist movement, published in 1773 a tract entitled *The Penitent Thief,* commending ministry among those condemned with a stirring narrative of the visitation to John Wilkes in Stafford prison prior to his execution.[55] John Fletcher wrote to the nineteen-year-old condemned of theft from a poor widow, asking him to confess his sins, or suffer 'an eternity of torments'. He held before him the example of the Dying Thief and encouraged him to listen to the two women who were sent to minister to him. Echoing the one held up as exemplar, he did indeed come to repentance on the day of execution. His last recorded words were: 'Lord, from this place receive me into thy heavenly kingdom'.[56]

Those who today visit or write to prisoners on death rows stand in succession to Methodists, Quakers and others who in the eighteenth century made this work central to their social outreach, as an expression of the evangelical response to the perceived needs of people in captivity to sin waiting to be released by the Christian Gospel. Was this Wesleyan approach to prisoners markedly different from the response of Calvinist clergymen in the Church of England and Nonconformity? More comparative work deserves to be done in investigating this issue. A related question appears to be the link to the development of anti-slavery writing, drawing on similar imagery. John Wesley, in his dying days, commended the work of Wilberforce (1759–1833) in the growing movement in opposition to slavery. Having been the earliest religious leader to join the protest against slavery, he wrote his last letter to Wilberforce on 24 February 1791 in support of his work in Parliament.[57] The shift of emphasis for concern for oppression at home to that found abroad is perhaps symptomatic of Britain's emerging role as a world colonial power.

Sarum College, Salisbury

of John Wesley, ed. Thomas Jackson, 14 vols (London, 1831; repr. Grand Rapids, MI, 1958–9), 11: 179–82.

55 [John Fletcher], *The Penitent Thief: or, a Narrative of two women fearing God, who visited in prison, a highway-man, executed at Stafford, April the 3rd, 1773, with a letter to a condemned malefactor* (London, 1773), 35–6.

56 Ibid.

57 See D. M. Lewis, *s.v.,* in Timothy Larsen, ed., *Biographical Dictionary of Evangelicals* (Leicester, 2003), 721–5.

RELATIONSHIPS HUMAN AND DIVINE:
RETRIBUTION AND REPENTANCE
IN CHILDREN'S LIVES, 1740–1870

by MARY CLARE MARTIN

THE place of repentance and retribution in children's lives between 1740 and 1870 has not been viewed positively. E. P. Thompson famously claimed that 'the child' in Methodist Sunday schools and in pious homes, from about 1780, was subjected to 'the worst kind of emotional bullying to confess his sins and come to a sense of salvation'. In the 1840s children in the mines allegedly reported that they had been taught at Sunday school that hell was a place full of fire and brimstone.[1] Nor have such assertions been made only about working-class children. Lawrence Stone, James Walvin, Walter Houghton and others claimed that the young of the middle and upper classes were intimidated by stories such as Mrs Sherwood's *The Fairchild Family*, and other Evangelical tracts threatening hell and retribution and urging immediate repentance.[2] In 1995, Hugh Cunningham still followed Stone's chronology in suggesting that the early nineteenth century was a period of 'reaction' in religious terms for children.[3]

Christopher Tolley and Doreen Rosman have provided a relatively sympathetic treatment of the religious upbringing of the children of members of the Clapham Sect and other leading 'Evangelical' families between 1780–1830.[4] John Tosh, writing in 1999, echoed their arguments, but also referred to 'the sobering fear that if death came before conversion, damnation would follow'.[5] Moreover, in 2001, Callum Brown argued that: 'Children in the first sixty years of the nineteenth

---

[1] E. P. Thompson, *The Making of the English Working Class* (London, 1963), 414–15.

[2] Lawrence Stone, *The Family, Sex and Marriage in England, 1500–1800* (London, 1977), 669–71; James Walvin, *A Child's World: a Social History of English Childhood, 1800–1914* (Harmondsworth, 1982), 30–9; Walter E. Houghton, *The Victorian Frame of Mind, 1830–1870* (New Haven, CT, 1957), 63.

[3] Hugh Cunningham, *Children and Childhood in Western Society since 1500* (Harlow, 1995), 55–6.

[4] Christopher Tolley, *Domestic Biography: the Legacy of Evangelicalism in Four Nineteenth-Century Families* (Oxford, 1997), 1–55; Doreen M. Rosman, *Evangelicals and Culture* (London, 1984), 110.

[5] John Tosh, *A Man's Place: Masculinity and the Middle-Class Home in Victorian England* (New Haven, CT, and London, 1999), 41–2.

century were subjected to shock treatment in the evangelical press by being bombarded with the issue of death' and that such accounts included didactic challenges to come to repentance.[6] Although this refers to Evangelical literature in general, rather than specifically to the treatment of children, it nevertheless suggests that fear was an aspect of most children's lives.

This essay will explore the psychological and social significance of the concepts of repentance and retribution in the period 1740–1870, in relation to the recorded experiences of children, as well as in didactic literature. It will present a more nuanced and complex picture of the place of these phenomena in children's lives and their family relationships than formerly, and thus address a key and neglected aspect of the history of childhood.[7] Even where retribution and repentance were an aspect of children's upbringing, their presentation could be more attractive than has been realized. The tendency to associate a religious upbringing with 'Evangelicalism', which has been a characteristic of the history of childhood, underplays the extent of denominational difference and affiliation which will be explored in this essay, also in relation to chronology.

'Evangelicalism' as it developed within the Church of England, and, arguably, much of Nonconformity, 'lays special stress on conversion and salvation by faith in the atoning death of Christ'.[8] The early eighteenth century witnessed a religious revival in Europe and America. In England, Wesleyan Methodism stressed the doctrines of justification by faith, sanctification and perfection. Calvinist theology survived, notably in the preaching of Howell Harris, George Whitfield, and the Countess of Huntingdon's Connexion. Both strands, although popular with many artisans, and certain sections of the labouring poor, such as Cornish tin-miners, were frequently regarded with suspicion by social elites, and their proponents attacked by plebeian mobs.[9] From the

6 Callum Brown, *The Death of Christian Britain: Understanding Secularisation, 1800–2000* (London and New York, 2001), 65.

7 Colin Heywood, *A History of Childhood: Children and Childhood in the West from Medieval to Modern Times* (Cambridge, 2001), 102, noted the lack of knowledge about children's response.

8 F. L. Cross, ed., *The Oxford Dictionary of the Christian Church* (Oxford, 1997), 580.

9 Michael Watts, *The Dissenters: Volume I, From the Reformation to the French Revolution* (Oxford, 1978), 394–470; David Bebbington, *Evangelicalism in Modern Britain: a History from the 1730s to the 1980s* (London, 1989, repr. Cambridge, 1995), 27–74; D. Bruce Hindmarsh, *John Newton and the English Evangelical Tradition between the Conversions of Wesley and Wilberforce* (Cambridge, 1996), 1–11, 49–82, 119–68; Paul Edwin Sangster, *Pity My Simplicity: the Evangelical Revival and the Religious Education of Children, 1738–1800* (London, 1963), 18–23.

1790s, when a group of mainly upper-middle-class Evangelical MPs were particularly active in philanthropic causes, Evangelicalism became more acceptable to Anglicans, as well as Dissenters (but not 'rational Dissenters' and Unitarians).[10] Whereas it could be difficult to distinguish between Evangelicals and High Churchmen before 1833, the boundaries between 'church parties' allegedly hardened after that date.[11] According to Houghton and Newsome, however, both Evangelicals and Tractarians shared a common goal in 'the pursuit of holiness'.[12]

The specific locus of this study is the two Essex villages of Walthamstow and Leyton, six miles north-east of the City of London, which provided a 'pretty retiring place' as either second, weekend or first home to a wealthy mercantile elite. This social group provided employment for a number of artisans, trades and crafts people and domestic servants, while agricultural workers (which, until the 1830s, included 'husbandmen') supplied the London food market. There were many schools and places of worship, representing a wide range of religious denominations. Due to its presumed healthy location near London, the area was a popular site for residential institutions, whether for elites or poor children. Besides workhouses, founded from the 1720s, these included a Methodist orphanage (1763-8), the Forest (Proprietary) school for sons of the local elite, founded in 1834, and an interdenominational school for missionaries' daughters, founded in 1838.[13]

A case-study of this kind can be valuable in exploring the nature of childhood experience, drawing on new research. Although the area was geographically limited, at least fifty sets of family records were consulted. These families were not only connected with Walthamstow and Leyton, but with the metropolis and elsewhere, particularly Essex and Norfolk. While most of those studied were from the local elite, rather than the poor, this still addresses a gap in the historiography. I have taken the age at which childhood ends as twenty-one, until when

---

[10] Boyd Hilton, *The Age of Atonement: the Influence of Evangelicalism on Social and Economic Thought, 1795-1865* (Oxford, 1988), 7-35; Michael Watts, *The Dissenters: Volume II, The Experience of Evangelical Nonconformity* (Oxford, 1995), 1-3 and *passim*; Linda Wilson, *Constrained by Zeal: Female Spirituality among Nonconformists, 1825-75* (Cumbria, 2000), 43-64.

[11] Arthur Burns, 'W. J. Conybeare: "Church Parties"', in Stephen Taylor, ed., *From Cranmer to Davidson: a Church of England Miscellany*, Church of England Record Society 7 (Woodbridge, 1999), 213-385; Peter Benedict Nockles, *The Oxford Movement in Context: Anglican High Churchmanship, 1760-1857* (Cambridge, 1994), 1-43, esp. 16-21, 32-5.

[12] Houghton, *Victorian Frame of Mind*, 237-9; David Newsome, *The Parting of Friends: a Study of the Wilberforces and Henry Manning* (London, 1966), 5-15.

[13] Mary Clare Martin, 'Children and Religion in Walthamstow and Leyton, 1740-1870', unpublished Ph.D. thesis, University of London, 2000, 44-131.

many elite children could not inherit. Also, the teenage years have been regarded as those of greatest religious turmoil.[14] As has frequently been noted, sources relating to the history of childhood pose problems of memory.[15] Pat Jalland argued that the sources for discussing Victorian family experiences of death constitute a continuum of reliability, from published tract to private diary.[16] Besides biographies, which often contain reprinted family correspondence, I have used other contemporary evidence: letters between adults and children, children's diaries and school records. Relevant didactic literature includes sermons by William Wilson, vicar of Walthamstow 1822–48, addresses by school headmasters and published accounts of dying children. The wide range of sources used offsets the frequent use of spiritual autobiographies, which frequently contain conversion narratives, as a source to discuss spirituality, which also underlines the emphasis on Evangelicalism.[17] Nevertheless, whatever the problems of autobiographical sources as a record of childhood experience, identification of the 'stories' which they tell about retribution and repentance are important in gauging attitudes to childhood.

* * *

Retribution and repentance are not merely abstract theological concepts, but implicate deep human emotions of guilt, humiliation, suffering, and catharsis. Retribution can be defined as punishment, human or divine, for evil done, repentance as the feeling and expression of sorrow for one's actions.[18] Retribution can be considered from two perspectives: divine retribution, including fear of hell and of God, and immediate, human retribution from parents, family and other authority figures.

The most conventional historiography of 'Evangelical' childhoods claimed that children were terrified with threats of death and hell.[19] Similarly, Hilton, Brown and Knight identify the period 1800–50 as

---

14 Robert Currie, Alan Gilbert and Lee Horsley, *Churches and Churchgoers: Patterns of Religious Growth in the British Isles since 1700* (Oxford, 1977), 90–1; Thomas Laqueur, *Religion and Respectability: Sunday Schools and Working Class Culture, 1780–1850* (New Haven, 1976), 166–7.

15 Harry Hendrick, 'The Child as Social Actor in History', in Pia Christensen and Alison James, eds, *Research with Children: Perspectives and Practices* (London and New York, 2000), 36–59.

16 Pat Jalland, *Death in the Victorian Family* (Oxford, 1996), 22–6, 124, 129, 134–8, 168.

17 Watts, *Dissenters*, I: 407–23; II: 49–81; Wilson, *Constrained by Zeal*, 17–36.

18 *Concise Oxford English Dictionary* (Oxford, 1990), *s.v.*, has been consulted here.

19 See, for example, Sangster, *Pity*, 124, 139, 140, 142, 148–9, 153–4; Stone, *Family*, 251–3; Houghton, *Victorian Frame of Mind*, 63–4; Walvin, *Child's World*, 29.

one in which great emphasis was placed on hell. Whereas Knight's and Brown's evidence was derived mainly from printed Evangelical tract literature, Hilton drew on government documents and the 'public' statements of well-known figures.[20] However, Michael Wheeler, who used literature, theology and personal memoirs, claimed that 'the contributors to *Essays and Reviews* had known that there was a gap between doctrine preached by the Church of England and the actual beliefs of educated people'.[21] Pat Jalland argued that from 1700, and especially the 1830s, liberal Christians had been increasingly unhappy about the existence of hell, and concluded from family records that heaven was given more emphasis from this date.[22] While Watts found fear of hell to be a constant feature of spiritual autobiographies of late eighteenth- and early nineteenth-century Nonconformists, especially Methodists, Wilson found it to be almost absent from her study of Nonconformist female obituaries between 1825 and 1875.[23] This essay will explore whether the difference in type of source accounts for such varying conclusions.

In Walthamstow and Leyton, between 1740 and 1870, fear of hell, or evidence of teaching about it, was recorded by children of different religious denominations, but none retrospectively felt it was damaging. The fears of Mary Bosanquet (1739–1815) were apparently nurtured within a conventionally Anglican elite eighteenth-century family, though of Huguenot antecedents. She recalled that from the age of four or five, 'I began to have much concern for my eternal welfare and frequently enquired of those about me whether such and such things were sins.'[24] When told not to take the Bible too seriously, 'I began to believe there was no hell at all, or at least not half so terrible as I had been taught to think.'[25] In the 1760s, Bosanquet taught the orphans in the community she ran in Leytonstone for destitute children and adults about hell, because 'We wished to save ... their souls from eternal destruction.'[26] One such eleven-year-old child, Betty Lawrence, expressed fears of hell during

[20] Hilton, *Atonement*, 271–9, 281–2, 301, 335–6; Frances Knight, *The Nineteenth-Century Church and English Society* (Cambridge, 1995), 48, 54; Brown, *Death*, 65.

[21] Michael Wheeler, *Heaven, Hell and the Victorians* (Cambridge, 1994), 16.

[22] Jalland, *Death*, 21, 60–1.

[23] Watts, *Dissenters*, II: 49–81; Wilson, *Constrained by Zeal*, 63.

[24] *The Life of Mrs Mary Fletcher, Consort and Relict of the Rev. John Fletcher, Vicar of Madeley, Salop. Compiled from her Journals, and Other Authentic Documents*, ed. Henry Moore (5th edn, London, 1824), 1.

[25] Ibid., 2–3.

[26] Ibid., 38.

her conversion experience, but these were quickly overcome.[27] Retrospectively, the Methodist William Pocock (1813–99), son of a surveyor, whose conversion was stimulated by the cholera outbreak of 1833, did not consider it problematic that fear of hell, rather than the attraction of heaven, brought him to conversion.[28] Burne-Jones, the friend of William Morris (1834–1896), argued that though the Last Judgement 'did fill our childhood with terrors, it was an incitement to our imaginations, and there's no telling what good there is in that.'[29] Daisy Maynard (1861–1938), from a gentry background, retrospectively claimed of the 1860s that: 'the Heaven and Hell of that day were too vague and shadowy to influence conduct. I neither feared the punishments, nor coveted the rewards of an after-life.'[30] Gipsy Smith (b.1860) recalled his mother's fear of hell on her death-bed about 1870, when he was a boy.[31]

Rather than being threatened with hell, children in many families were advised to be prepared for death. In 1825 the Anglican Mrs Sarah Cotton reminded her twelve-year-old son after his grandparents' death that 'sleeping is in awful opposition to the very different dispositions of mind found in the faithful servants who alone will be received as blessed.'[32] In most cases, the advice given was in a cheerful sense – to be ready to meet Jesus, rather than in terms of retribution.[33] Anglican young people expressed awareness of the need to prepare for death in the same vein: the dying Teddy Cotton, aged twenty, in 1842; Elizabeth Fry, aged sixteen, in 1842; Arty Buxton, aged seventeen, in 1867.[34]

There was, however, a difference between personal memory and public rhetoric. In the 1830s, William Wilson, the Evangelical vicar of Walthamstow, instructed children, to think, during sermons, 'And I may die, and go to heaven above – or to hell beneath! I will lose no

27 Ibid., 44–5.
28 Extracts from the Reminiscences of William Willmer Pocock (1814–99), Vol. I, manuscript privately held by Stephen B. Arch, ARIBA 88 [hereafter WWP Reminiscences].
29 Burne-Jones Talking: his Conversations 1895–1898 Preserved by his Studio Assistant Thomas Rooke, ed. Mary Lago (London, 1981), 95 (26 February 1896).
30 Frances, countess of Warwick, Life's Ebb and Flow (London, 1929), 25.
31 Gipsy (Rodney) Smith, His Life and Work: by Himself (London, 1903), 13–14.
32 Oxford, Bodleian Library, Papers of William Charles Cotton, MS Acland d. 182, fol. 1: Mrs Sarah Cotton to William Charles Cotton, 29 January 1825.
33 Memoir of the Life of Elizabeth Fry with Extracts from her Journal and Letters, Edited by Two of her Daughters, 2 vols (London, 1847–8), 2: 445; Herbert Alfred Birks, The Life and Correspondence of Thomas Valpy French: first Bishop of Lahore, 2 vols (London, 1895), 1: 308.
34 Oxford, Bodleian Library, MS Acland d. 189, fol. 102: Teddy Cotton to William Charles Cotton, 3 February 1842; A. F. J. Brown, ed., Essex People, 1750–1900: from their Diaries, Memoirs and Letters, Essex Record Office Publications 59 (Chelmsford, 1972), 151, 24 June 1842; Memorials of Fowell Arthur Buxton (for private circulation, London, 1886), 4–5.

time. I will hear what God will say to me.'[35] Printed works emphasized the need to prepare for death. *The Missionary Souvenir*, a volume collected to raise money for the Mission School, stated in 1850 of Jane, the missionary's daughter, that: 'it was well she was ready, or how terrible it would have been'.[36] The memoirs of the Baptist William Knibb and Congregationalist Emily Judson Lillie also stressed the suitable frame of mind of these dying young people.[37]

Divine retribution is also connected with concepts of God. According to Paul Sangster, between 1738 and 1800, God the Father represented Law, Judgement, Hell and Damnation.[38] Hilton's view was that the dominant image between 1780 and 1850 was of Christ on the Cross, propitiating an inexorable, if not a wrathful, God.[39] Noel Annan commented on the early nineteenth-century belief that it was God's duty to judge.[40]

Few references to God as Judge have been found in this study, and these were rarely frightening. Mary Bosanquet believed in the 1750s that: 'Jesus will be the Judge, and I cannot be afraid of Jesus.'[41] The most frightening example came from the High Church Mary Young in the 1820s. She reminded her children through the story of Ananias and Sapphira (also cited by Rosman), who fell down dead for telling a lie, of the 'sad hatred God bears to liars' and the 'severe punishment he has inflicted upon them'.[42]

The word 'fear' was most frequently used to mean 'awe and reverence' rather than 'terror'. Thus, in 1800, the nineteen-year-old Presbyterian/Unitarian Rebecca Solly listed 'a fear of offending that is humble and not mean' as one of her religious duties.[43] Between 1820–64,

35 London, Waltham Forest Archives, W96/Wilson, *The Instructor, conducted by the Parochial Ministers of Walthamstow*, I. 2 (February 1836), 19; IV. 3 (March 1839), 49.

36 Elizabeth, 'The Missionary's Daughter', in Thomas William Aveling, ed., *The Missionary Souvenir* (London, 1850), 96.

37 James Hoby, *Memoir of William Knibb, Son of the Rev. W. Knibb, Missionary, who died at the Refuge near Falmouth, Jamaica* (2nd edn, Bristol, 1840); *The Missionary's Daughter: a Brief Memoir of Emily Judson Lillie* (London, 1865), 13–14.

38 Sangster, *Pity*, 134–7.

39 Hilton, *Atonement*, 4–5, 8, 177–80, 185, 188–9, 270–1, 278, 281–2.

40 Noel Annan, *Leslie Stephen: the Godless Victorian* (2nd edn, London and New York, 1984), 148.

41 *Life of Mrs Mary Fletcher*, 4–5.

42 London, Museum of London [hereafter MOL], Young Manuscripts Collection, Education Scheme, 1825–31, 48.85/6: Letter 'To My Children', 1825; Rosman, *Evangelicals and Culture*, 101.

43 Oxford, Bodleian Library, John Johnson Collection, Journal of Rebecca Solly Shaen, MS e. 7, fol. 122.

Anglican, Quaker-Anglican and Baptist parents told their children to 'fear God' and gave advice such as 'the fear of the Lord is the beginning of wisdom'.[44] The Forest Proprietary School opening address in 1834 began: 'Let us humbly cherish the hope that our labours may be begun and ended in the fear of God.'[45] In my study of Walthamstow and Leyton, I found that images of God as Loving Father and Almighty Creator were more prevalent and powerful than those of an avenging God.[46] Similarly, whereas Rowell claimed that Evangelical journals and tracts popularized an intimidating doctrine of 'petty providentialism',[47] most references from these two villages, whether from personal memoirs or published works, suggest a view of Providence as benign, though recognizing that it could have painful effects.[48]

* * *

The contexts in which repentance occurred will be considered in three categories: as an aspect of the experience of conversion, on death-beds, and within personal, particularly family relationships. Throughout, there will be a comparison of the Pauline-like experience of an immediate inrush of apparently divinely-inspired grace with the cultivation of a 'self-critical spirit' or the 'inner life of Christian discipline' as described by Walter Houghton.[49]

Bebbington and Newsome, for example, describe well-known parents pressurizing their children to come to conversion (and therefore repentance).[50] By contrast, Annan argued that the young Stephens 'were never troubled by their parents looking for an "illumination" '.[51] The sources in this study describe conversion as inner-directed rather than as a result of parental pressure, with perhaps the exception of the families of the Baptist William Knibb (in the 1840s) and Free Church

---

[44] Citing Psalm 111: 10. Oxford, Bodleian Library, MS Acland d. 179, fols 4–5, 9–10, William Cotton to William Charles Cotton, 12 September and 2 October 1826. Hoby, *Memoir of William Knibb*, 57; Chelmsford, Essex Record Office, Buxton Letters, T/G 88, 156–7: Catherine Buxton to Louis Buxton.

[45] London, Forest School Archive, Box 1820–40, *Prayers and Address delivered at the Opening of Forest Proprietary Grammar School, October 1st, MDCCCXXXIV*, 22.

[46] Martin, 'Children and Religion', 145–53.

[47] Geoffrey Rowell, *Hell and the Victorians: a Study of the Nineteenth-Century Theological Controversies concerning Eternal Punishment and the Future Life* (Oxford, 1974), 1–2.

[48] Martin, 'Children and Religion', 166–8.

[49] Houghton, *Victorian Frame of Mind*, 237–9.

[50] Bebbington, *Evangelicalism*, 7; David Newsome, *The Parting of Friends: a Study of the Wilberforces and Henry Manning* (London, 1966), 9.

[51] Annan, *Stephen*, 16.

Gipsy Smith, which suggests that such pressure was more likely to be exerted in such non-Anglican denominations. Thus, William Knibb wrote to his teenage daughters in the 1840s: 'Go to him then as poor guilty sinners, and he will accept and bless you.'[52] Before his conversion, Gipsy Smith's father would say 'Lord save my Rodney.'[53]

Pressure was also exerted in institutions, particularly for girls. The aim of the weekly family-meeting in Mary Bosanquet's Methodist community was to bring sinners to repentance. Thus, after such a meeting, in about 1764, eleven-year-old Betty Lawrence implored God to forgive her sins, saw a vision of Jesus, and received assurance of forgiveness.[54] After revivals in the School for Missionaries' daughters in the 1840s, it was claimed in the *Evangelical Magazine* that 'several had given their hearts to the Lord'. Here, however, no reference has been found to the drama of repentance and forgiveness.[55]

Most personal accounts described repentance during or before conversion as the culmination of an inner-directed process. The Methodist William Pocock described his experience aged twenty as stimulated by the cholera outbreak of 1833. After hearing a sermon by the Revd Charles Atherton, 'I believed that God had pardoned my soul.'[56] Others experienced painful feelings of inadequacy before conversion. The eleven-year-old Quaker Ann Barclay's journal from the 1840s, cited in her obituary, recorded a 'scrupulous and painful recording of faults with the mind centred on self' and a 'self-righteousness and scrupulosity that produced an outward improvement but no peace of mind'.[57] Similarly, William Mallinson, aged twenty, who worked for a timber-merchant, recalled his feelings of personal failing before conversion.[58]

An integral aspect of the Evangelical 'good death', as described by Pat Jalland and others, was an act of repentance made by the dying person, who would receive assurance of forgiveness and perhaps a glimpse of heaven. Jalland has argued that published accounts tended to

---

[52] John Howard Hinton Sr, *Memoir of William Knibb* (London, 1847), 389, 454–5, 480.
[53] Smith, *Life*, 65.
[54] *Life of Mrs Mary Fletcher*, 44–5.
[55] *Evangelical Magazine and Missionary Chronicle*, NS 18 (April 1940), 19.
[56] WWP Reminiscences, 88.
[57] *The Annual Monitor for 1914, or Obituaries of the Members of the Society of Friends in Great Britain and Ireland for the Year 1914*, NS 102 (1914), 42.
[58] Sir William Mallinson, Bart, *A Sketch of My Life* (London, 1936), 36–8 (based on diary entries).

be more formulaic than family memoirs or private diaries.[59] Knight, however, suggested that the widely available literature on the early nineteenth-century death-bed provided a form of words which people might produce *in extremis*.[60]

The only accounts which follow the scenario of the 'good death' were published versions of the deaths of Nonconformist missionaries' children. They include a lengthy description of the death of twelve-year-old William Knibb, who allegedly desired to be saved through the blood of Jesus.[61] The story of 'Jane' in *The Missionary Souvenir* (1850) stressed her anxiety to have her sins forgiven, and messages to relatives, particularly urging her siblings to prepare themselves for death.[62] Instead, the published memoir of Emily Judson Lillie in 1860 only emphasized her suitable state of mind, and readiness for death.[63] Similarly, accounts from family memoirs, letters and diaries stressed children's sweet nature, and piety, rather than any death-bed testimony or repentance.[64]

Finally, I will consider the place of repentance in family life and personal relationships, exclusive of the conversion experience. The first aspect is the role played by adult family members in mediating children's relationship with God. This included giving advice. In 1844, Elizabeth Fry senior stressed 'God's saving grace to all who repent' to her grand-daughter.[65] In the 1840s, the Baptist missionary William Knibb urged his daughters, 'Go to Him then, as poor guilty sinners, and he will accept and bless you'.[66] Bishop Valpy French wrote a prayer stating: 'May his precious blood cleanse me from all my sin' for his children in the 1860s.[67] Adults could also act as role models. Thus, Gipsy Smith was impressed by his parents' state of repentance in the 1860s and 1870s.[68]

Parents also acted as confessors for their children. This could have

---

[59] Jalland, *Death*, 22–6, 124, 129, 134–8, 168.

[60] Knight, *Nineteenth-Century Church*, 50–1.

[61] Hoby, *Memoir of William Knibb*, 46–7.

[62] *Missionary Souvenir*, 96.

[63] *Memoir of Emily Judson Lillie*, 13–14.

[64] Martin, 'Children and Religion', 198–200.

[65] ' "Reminiscences in Old Age": Elizabeth Fry's Memories, as Recorded by her Grand-Daughter', *Journal of the Friends Historical Society* 45. 1 (Spring 1953), 22.

[66] Hinton, *Knibb*, 389; Mrs M. E. Smith, *William Knibb, Missionary in Jamaica, A Memoir* (London, 1896), 103.

[67] Birks, *Thomas Valpy French*, 1: 135.

[68] Smith, *Life*, 13–14, 48–9.

mixed results. When Mary Bosanquet voluntarily confessed her continuing adherence to Methodism to her parents in the 1750s, aged sixteen,
she was, as she feared, prevented from seeing her Methodist friends.[69]
Lying could have severe consequences. Mary Young warned her children in the 1820s that they should confess immediately if they told lies,
otherwise 'no one will ever believe you again'.[70] Incidents of parental
retribution for lying often remained in people's memories for a lifetime
and were represented as crucial to the formation of conscience. Henry
Solly (1813–1902) described his terrible feelings, in his memory of the
'one great sin and punishment of my childhood', when his mother, who
'till then had never looked at me but with affection' sent him to his
room for the rest of the day, for stealing 'some delicacy' and lying about
it. When he repeated the offence, and stole some plumcake, he
confessed immediately, and was so remorseful that he received little
rebuke.[71] Gipsy Smith recalled being beaten by his father after he and
his sister had eaten some plum-puddings intended for his family:
'Never since that day have I had the least appetite for plum-pudding.'[72]

Solly's autobiography demonstrated the overlap between repentance, and the development of a 'self-critical spirit'. Solly later recalled
listing his faults (aged seven) after hearing a story about a similar
incident. He then threw the list into the fire and could only remember
'I said "Devil" too much.'[73] When the twenty-year-old William Cotton
'confessed' his indolence during the holidays to his mother, in 1833,
Sarah responded: 'in no earthly confessor can you ever meet with a
more sincere desire to benefit you than in your mother', though 'I did
much regret seeing you put off the work you had to do.'[74]

The language of repentance was used humorously in her children's
correspondence. Thus, in 1836, in an exchange of letters about why
they had not written, the Anglican Sarah Cotton (aged twenty-one)
wrote to her brother, an Oxford undergraduate,

> It was very good of you to give me absolution before you had heard
> my confessions, and also we are always admonished that repen-

[69] *Life of Mrs Mary Fletcher*, 11.
[70] MOL, Education Scheme, 48.85/6, 1825.
[71] Henry Solly, '*These Eighty Years*', or, *the Story of an Unfinished Life*, 2 vols (London, 1893),
1: 44–6.
[72] Smith, *Life*, 67–8.
[73] Solly, '*Eighty Years*', 1: 19.
[74] Oxford, Bodleian Library, MS Acland d. 183, fol. 60, Mrs Sarah Cotton to William
Charles Cotton, 7 May 1833.

tance is best [l?]earned by its friends. I hasten to give you a full proof of mine in as long and as . . .[75]

Repentance, regarding behaviour to others, could be recorded privately. According to the obituary of the Quaker Jane Barclay, her diary in 1833 included 'confessions of hastier temper and still hastier tongue', when having to cope with a large household and six motherless siblings, aged seventeen.[76]

While, as has been indicated, many young people used diaries for the purposes of self-scrutiny or to record their conversion experiences, these were not always self-critical. From 1800, the Presbyterian/Unitarian Rebecca Solly recorded an annual accounting of faults and virtues, usually summing up on a positive note.[77] The journals of the Anglican Elizabeth Fry in the 1840s, and her cousin Ellen Buxton in the 1860s were more concerned with everyday events, but occasionally interspersed with comments about religion. Elizabeth in particular would take herself to task for wasting her time.[78] Ellen's contained no self-criticism, although she was clearly conscientious.[79]

* * *

This micro-study challenges the claim of Brown, in particular, but also of earlier historians of childhood and the family, that fear of retribution and pressure to repent were frequent and disturbing features of children's lives between 1740 and 1870, particularly in the early nineteenth century. Little evidence survives of children being taught about hell, and these few did not record it as harmful. Very few recorded being pressured by their parents into conversion, and these were of Free Church or Baptist parents, and in an eighteenth-century Methodist community. The only records found of children repenting on their death-beds were in published tract accounts of two missionaries' children, between 1840 and 1870.

Instead, the records present a more nuanced picture of the place of retribution and repentance in children's lives. 'Fear' was most commonly used in the sense of awe and reverence rather than terror. The more

75 Oxford, Bodleian Library, MS Acland d. 186, fol. 32r, 1833, Sarah Cotton to William Charles Cotton.
76 London, Library of the Society of Friends, Temp. MSS, 400/4, 41; *Annual Monitor* NS 58 (1900), 22–3.
77 Oxford, Bodleian Library, MS Johnson e. 7, fols 69–74, 89–91, 124.
78 *Essex People*, 154–5.
79 *Ellen Buxton's Journal, 1860–61*, arranged by her grand-daughter, Ellen R. C. Creighton (London, 1967).

common death-bed pattern, expressed in a tract in 1860, and in family memoirs, stressed the piety and sweet nature of the dying child, rather than repentance. The language of confession and repentance was woven into the web of family interaction and journal-writing, sometimes humorously, and was an integral part of personal relationships.

Superficially, it might appear that an 'Evangelical' mentality, rather than chronology, accounts for the differential treatment and response of children over time: both eighteenth-century Methodists and mid to late nineteenth-century members of Free Churches put pressure on children to repent and be converted. Yet denominational boundaries are hard to draw. In the 1820s, the High Church Mary Young also urged her children to confess immediately if they told lies, and a Presbyterian/ Unitarian such as Rebecca Solly described God as a judge in the 1800s. Both encouraged the cultivation of a 'self-critical spirit', Young in her role as mother, Solly in her journal as a young, unmarried woman.

Clearly, there are issues about the reliability and validity of the sources. The strength of this study lies in the range of personal memoirs used, which include letters between different family members and diaries, besides retrospective autobiographies. My conclusions highlight the problems of making generalizations about piety based on didactic literature, as do Brown, Hilton and Knight. Yet neither does the evidence follow the pattern suggested by Jalland, with a continuum of reliability between private diary and published tract. Although 'awful warnings' were mainly recorded in print, there appears to be no direct relationship between the type of source and the message it conveyed. Published death-bed accounts could resemble journals or family letters and be rambling rather than formulaic.[80]

This study also raises issues about locality and regionality. Since many of the published texts were widely circulated, it would be inappropriate to attribute the attitudes they contained to a specific geographical area. Although many of the families cited here belonged to a specific mercantile elite, most moved or worked outside Walthamstow and Leyton, and therefore their experiences should be considered to have general significance, with regard to that social group at least. This essay therefore addresses a notable absence in the history of the family and of childhood.

University of Greenwich

---

80 *Life of Mrs Mary Fletcher*, 48–53; Hoby, *Memoir of William Knibb*, 44–8.

COMMUNITY AND DISCIPLINE
IN ULSTER PRESBYTERIANISM, c.1770–1840*

by ANDREW HOLMES

ULSTER Presbyterians in the eighteenth and nineteenth centuries formally dealt out retribution, repentance and reconciliation through church discipline administered by Kirk sessions and presbyteries. These institutional structures had given Presbyterians an organizational framework that enhanced their geographical concentration in the north-east of Ireland.[1] Hitherto, historians of Presbyterianism in Ireland have taken the view, often based on evidence from the period before 1740, that discipline was effective, broad in its coverage, and hard yet fair in its judgements, claims made all the more remarkable as the north-east had the highest illegitimacy rates in Ireland during the period under consideration.[2] It has been argued that though the system largely survived the eighteenth century, it collapsed at the turn of the nineteenth because of a loss of morale among Presbyterians after the failure of the 1798 rebellion in which many thousands of them had taken part.[3]

Studies of discipline in the Church of Scotland have suggested that both the public prominence and actual prosecution of discipline were virtually at an end by the 1780s. Several reasons for this decline have been offered, including the spread of Enlightenment and humanitarian ideas, the rise of religious dissent, greater population mobility, urban

* I am grateful to the AHRB for the award of a postgraduate studentship under which the research for this paper was carried out. I would like to thank Dr David Hayton for comments upon an earlier draft of this paper and Dr Paul Gray for permission to use his as yet unavailable thesis.
    [1] Raymond Gillespie, 'The Presbyterian Revolution in Ulster, 1660–1690', in W. J. Sheils and Diana Wood, eds, *The Churches, Ireland and the Irish*, SCH 25 (Oxford, 1989), 159–70.
    [2] J. M. Barkley, 'A History of the Ruling Eldership in Irish Presbyterianism', unpublished MA thesis, 2 vols, The Queen's University, Belfast [hereafter, QUB], 1952; idem, *The Eldership in Irish Presbyterianism* (n.p., 1963); W. P. Gray, 'A Social History of Illegitimacy in Ireland from the Late Eighteenth to the Early Twentieth Century', unpublished Ph.D. thesis, QUB, 2000, ch. 4.
    [3] Peter Brooke, *Ulster Presbyterianism: the Historical Perspective, 1610–1970* (2nd edn, Belfast, 1994), 157–8, n. 151.

and rural transformation, and the rise of evangelical individualism.[4] A recent commentator has pushed back the decline of discipline into the decades after 1840 and suggested that its purpose had changed from 'policing society' to regulating the membership of a congregation who voluntarily submitted themselves to censure.[5] The Scottish experience is not directly comparable to Ulster Presbyterianism, since the Church of Scotland was established and its structures of discipline 'straddled ecclesiastical and civil law with at best a hazy division between the two'.[6] The non-established status of Presbyterianism in Ulster arguably increased the efficiency of church discipline as sin and crime were not conflated, allowing church courts to establish clear boundaries between civil and religious offences.[7] More importantly, it was easier to regulate a population that willingly submitted itself to discipline. The 1809 pastoral address of the Synod of Ulster, the largest Presbyterian grouping, pointed out to their people, 'Ye have submitted yourselves to our pastoral inspection. We have taken the oversight of you in the Lord; and vowed before God to watch over your souls.'[8]

The aim of this paper is to assess the experience and persistence of discipline within Ulster Presbyterianism by examining the above themes within the context of communities. Though sectarian division is the obvious way of characterizing communities in Ireland, and consequently an important context for assessing the function of discipline in the formation of group identity, this essay will focus upon the meaning and purpose of discipline within Presbyterianism. In that context, the term community can be understood in at least two ways in this study.

First, there were various institutional groupings within Ulster Presbyterianism which had distinctive theological views and consequently formed one type of community. The largest group was the General Synod of Ulster, founded in 1690. Though subscription to the *Westminster Confession of Faith* was enjoined within the Synod,

---

[4] Leah Leneman and Rosalind Mitchison, *Sexuality and Social Control: Scotland 1660–1780* (Oxford, 1989).

[5] C. G. Brown, *Religion and Society in Scotland since 1707* (Edinburgh, 1997), 73.

[6] Ibid., 69.

[7] For an elucidation of this distinction see Heinz Schilling, ' "History of Crime" or "History of Sin"? – Some Reflections on the Social History of Early Modern Church Discipline', in E. I. Kouri and Tom Scott, eds, *Politics and Society in Reformation Europe: Essays for Geoffrey Elton on his Sixty-Fifth Birthday* (Basingstoke, 1987), 289–310.

[8] *A Pastoral Address from the Ministers of the Synod of Ulster, Assembled at their Annual Meeting, to the People under their Care* (n.p., 1809), 1.

non-subscribing views known as New Light gradually came to the fore. In 1726, the non-subscribing Presbytery of Antrim was expelled from the Synod, although New Light remained a powerful influence within the parent body for the rest of the century. The New Light tendency was fitfully opposed in the Synod by an Old Light party and assailed from without by the Seceders who had arrived in Ulster from Scotland in the 1740s. During the first decades of the nineteenth century, the Old Light party, revived by evangelicalism, gained ascendancy in the General Synod and forced out virtually all the remaining non-subscribers, many of whom were now Arians, into an association of their own known as the Remonstrant Synod. This action paved the way for the union of the Synod of Ulster with the Seceders in 1840 to form the present-day Presbyterian Church in Ireland.

The second aspect of community refers to the actual expression of these theological differences in the local congregations belonging to each group. By submitting themselves to the oversight of the Kirk session, they supposedly upheld the theological and moral values represented by each. The importance of local communities was reinforced by the location and size of settlements in Ulster. Though Belfast grew rapidly during the nineteenth century, Ulster retained much of its rural character and even by 1851 only one-eighth of the population lived in settlements of over 2,000 persons.[9] As will be shown, the existence of tightly-knit rural communities would have a marked effect upon how discipline was experienced by the laity in certain areas.

The broad themes adumbrated at the outset of this paper will be examined within this dual context. By outlining the interaction between the types of Presbyterian community concerned, the intensity of discipline brought to bear on such communities, and the activity of the laity, the experience of discipline within Ulster Presbyterianism may be better understood.

* * *

Theoretically, church discipline was calculated to deal with the conscience in order to convince offenders both of their sin and the need to live a holy life in the sight of God and man. Discipline, therefore, was more than punitive in intent and had a strong communal function by

---

[9] W. H. Crawford, 'Economy and Society in Eighteenth-Century Ulster', unpublished Ph.D. thesis, QUB, 1982, ch. 6.

publicly upholding proper behaviour and acting as a deterrent.[10] Though Ulster Presbyterians agreed in general with these principles, they asserted them in different ways according to the characteristics of the branch of Presbyterianism to which they belonged. One nineteenth-century commentator argued that the non-subscribers of the previous century 'quietly ignored' offences such as neglect of family worship or irregular marriage, leaving the Old Light party and the Seceders to uphold strict moral and religious standards through discipline.[11] This view is supported by evidence from Kirk session and presbytery records. Ballycarry, a non-subscribing congregation, tried 59 cases between 1740 and 1780; 56 were for sexual offences alone. Only two of the 59 cases were tried after 1750 and from 1765 the session book records only financial deliberations.[12] The records of both non-subscribing congregations in eighteenth-century Belfast report no cases of discipline at all and neither did the Presbytery of Bangor after its re-formation in 1774.[13] The most prominent Remonstrant, Revd Henry Montgomery, argued that discipline was an unnecessary imposition on an individual's conscience and ought to be set aside if it excluded penitent sinners from the Lord's table.[14] It is little wonder that this should have been the case, as the views of non-subscribers were profoundly shaped by Enlightenment humanitarianism that saw public discipline as uncivilized. It should also be pointed out that the number of adherents to the various non-subscribing bodies in 1834 amounted to less than 30,000 and that membership was largely confined to the upper echelons of society.[15] The non-subscribing community was in some ways easier to discipline because it was small, and it may be that anti-social behaviour was not actually prevalent amongst their adher-

10 *The Confession of Faith; the Larger and Shorter Catechisms, with the Scripture Proofs at Large* (London, 1646; repr. Inverness, 1976), 121.
11 W. T. Latimer, *A History of the Irish Presbyterians* (2nd edn, Belfast, 1902), 340.
12 Belfast, Public Record Office of Northern Ireland [hereafter PRONI] Ballycarry session book, 1740–80, CR/3/31/2.
13 S. Shannon Millin, *History of the Second Congregation of Protestant Dissenters in Belfast 1708–1896* (Belfast, 1900); A. G. Gordon, *Historical Memorials of the First Presbyterian Church of Belfast* (Belfast, 1887); Belfast, Presbyterian Historical Society [hereafter PHS], Minutes of Bangor Presbytery, 1774–90.
14 R. G. Crawford, 'A Critical Examination of Nineteenth-Century Non-Subscribing Presbyterian Theology in Ireland', unpublished Ph.D. thesis, 2 vols, QUB, 1964, 2: 309–10.
15 George Matthew, *An Account of the Regium Donum, Issued to the Presbyterian Church in Ireland* (Dublin, 1836), 27. For the same problem in a different context, cf. Irina Paert, 'Penance and the Priestless Old Believers in Modern Russia, 1771–1850s', 278–90 below.

ents. On the other hand, the risk of alienating important benefactors must have been a deterrent to the disciplining of wealthier members, a fact not lost on evangelical commentators in the nineteenth century.[16] The Seceders, on the other hand, were proud of their strict discipline and often lambasted their Synod of Ulster neighbours for apparent indifference and lack of scrupulosity.[17] They firmly held to confessional Presbyterianism and the importance of upholding discipline to ensure purity of Church communion.[18] The Seceding Kirk session of Cahans congregation, County Monaghan, tried 69 cases between 1752 and 1758, 23 for fornication, 20 for irregular marriage, 3 for adultery, and 23 other offences. Between 1767 and 1836 there were a further 188 cases recorded: 50 for fornication; 22 for 'antenuptial fornication' (i.e. sexual intercourse between a couple who subsequently married); 14 for adultery; 61 irregular marriages; and 41 others.[19] The same pattern could be repeated many times, but this example illustrates not only the number of cases but also the variety of offences considered. Though some were repelled by the rigour of discipline, many seem to have been attracted by the self-disciplined lifestyle it promoted, an important reason for the remarkable growth of Seceding congregations in the eighteenth century.[20] Those who submitted to this level of discipline consciously set themselves apart from the perceived moderatism of the Synod of Ulster. Seceder session books often quoted the following verses from Num. 33: 1–2, indicating what was at stake when an individual or family joined that community: 'These are the journeys of the children of Israel. . . . And Moses wrote their goings out according to their journeys, and these are their journeys'.[21]

The continued importance of discipline in some Old Light congregations offers a corrective to the caricature of the Synod of Ulster painted by Seceder polemicists. Carnmoney session, for example, tried no less than 171 sexual offences between 1767 and 1805.[22] Nevertheless,

---

16 William Oliver, *Pastoral Provision: or, the Income of the Irish Presbyterian Clergy Shown to be Insufficient* (Belfast, 1856), 70.
17 Thomas Clark, *New Light Set in a Clear Light* ([Dublin], 1755), 50–67; *Christian Freeman* [hereafter *CF*] 2 (1834), 198–202.
18 David Stewart, *The Seceders in Ireland: with Annals of their Congregations* (Belfast, 1950), 406–9.
19 PRONI, Cahans session book, 1752–8, 1767–1836, CR/3/25B/1 & 2.
20 Stewart, *Seceders*, 65.
21 For example, PHS, Minutes of the Down Presbytery (Seceder), title page.
22 Gray, 'Illegitimacy', 115. Other examples may be found in Barkley, 'Ruling Eldership', vol. 2.

nineteenth-century evangelicals in the Synod of Ulster agreed that despite the efforts of a few godly ministers discipline had degenerated from the Presbyterian ideal. Revd Samuel Dill declared in 1802 that discipline was 'looked upon as nothing short of ecclesiastical tyranny', and urged his fellow ministers to ensure standards were raised once more.[23] Evangelicals directly attributed this malaise to the influence of New Light Presbyterianism in the previous century. Recognizing the importance of community pressure in the enforcement of discipline, they argued that the prevalent mood of eighteenth-century non-subscribing theology had dulled public opinion to flagrant religious and moral failings.[24] As a result, evangelicals sought to improve discipline within their own congregations, though it was only with the publication of the Synod's *Code* in 1825, produced by a theologically mixed committee, that the proper procedures were codified.[25]

Under the growing influence of evangelicalism in the 1830s, the Synod of Ulster ordered the reorganization of presbyteries and the regular examination of Kirk session records at presbytery visitations.[26] Evangelicals believed that discipline had to be enforced, not only to eliminate moral and religious failings, but also to promote religious revival. According to the Presbytery of Magherafelt, along with preaching and prayer, 'the strict exercise of church discipline is also a Scriptural means of attaining this most desirable consummation, in as much as the Holy Ghost will not take up his abode in a polluted temple'.[27] It is no surprise to find that Synod of Ulster Kirk sessions were swept along by the zeal of evangelicalism in the nineteenth century with many, particularly recently-established charges, both prosecuting more cases and resorting to more public rebukes than before.[28] Similar developments occurred within the Secession Synod and it is little wonder that the themes of discipline and revival paved the way for the union of 1840.

---

[23] Samuel Dill, *A Sermon on the Duty of Ministers and their Connexion with Christ; Preached at the Meeting of the Particular Synod in Londonderry, May 18th, 1802* (Londonderry, [1802]), 21–2.

[24] *Annual Address of the General Synod of Ulster to the Churches under their Care* (Belfast, 1833), 10; *Orthodox Presbyterian* [hereafter *OP*] 6 (1835), 240–3.

[25] *The Constitution and Discipline of the Presbyterian Church. . . . Published by Authority of the General Synod of Ulster* (Belfast, 1825) [hereafter *Code*].

[26] *Records of the General Synod of Ulster* (Belfast, 1831), 32–4 and (Belfast, 1837), 28.

[27] *OP* 6 (1834), 69.

[28] PRONI, Ballymoney session book (Synod of Ulster), 1827–66, CR/3/1/B/4; Barkley, 'Ruling Eldership', 2: 297; PRONI, Portstewart session book (Synod of Ulster), 1826–77, MIC/1P/83/1.

From this brief overview, it is clear that how church discipline was experienced depended upon the wider Presbyterian community to which a minister and his congregation belonged. It is also clear that variations in the level of discipline experienced could occur for a number of other reasons, particularly the zeal or otherwise of ministers and Kirk sessions. With the virtual abandonment of visitation presbyteries in the Synod of Ulster in the eighteenth century, presumably due to the influence of New Light ideas, there was no incentive for either ministers or elders to prosecute cases or indeed keep proper session records. This situation in part accounts for the poor survival of Ulster session books for the period before 1800 when compared with the richness of Scottish sources.[29] Even after presbytery visitations were reintroduced in the Synod of Ulster, some ministers still attempted to get away with the bare minimum by either ignoring discipline completely or prosecuting only high profile cases such as adultery.[30] On the other hand, in the late eighteenth century, a zealous minister usually ensured that discipline was properly enforced.[31] In terms of procedure, variations in sentencing could be determined by various factors including the type of offence, its notoriety, how recently it had occurred, or the nature of the evidence.[32] Specific circumstances such as a spate of irregular marriages or the political turmoil following 1798 could also call forth special measures.[33] It is worth noting that being a woman may not have been a significant determining factor in the type of discipline experienced. The evidence from presbytery records suggests a greater preponderance of males tried for sexual offences than in Scotland where women were apparently 'criminalized' by male-dominated Kirk sessions.[34]

At a congregational level, offences came under the cognizance of Kirk sessions through rumours, complaints, reference, or appeal.[35] The oversight of ministers and elders would uncover some offences, but it was the active involvement of the laity that brought cases to light. In a different context, that of late sixteenth- and early seventeenth-century

29 For a list of the surviving pre-1800 records see Barkley, *Eldership in Irish Presbyterianism*, 22.
30 *Annual Address of the General Synod of Ulster to the Churches*, 10–11.
31 For example, J. R. Dill, *The Dill Worthies* (Centenary edn, Draperstown and Ballymena, 1992), 48–73.
32 *Code*, 19, 78–83.
33 *Records of the General Synod of Ulster*, 3 vols (Belfast, 1897–8), 3: 212.
34 Gray, 'Illegitimacy', 105–6; Leneman and Mitchison, *Sexuality and Social Control*, 50–2.
35 *Code*, 64.

Holland, Charles Parker has suggested that Reformed church discipline was largely 'a collaboration between the consistory, church members and townsfolk'. This process, he argues, was facilitated by the daily interaction of the local community and church members whose 'gossip, innuendo, rumour and speculation . . . enabled the consistory to identify deviance in ordinary members'.[36] Though the source of information is not always specified, Ulster session books, by reference to neighbourhood rumours or 'reports' by which cases were brought to their attention, indicate a similar process at work.[37] Informing was, however, a double-edged activity for the laity, for if the report were discovered false, the individual who had spread it would be liable to censure for either gossip or slander.[38]

For discipline to work effectively depended upon the interaction of the community and the willingness of individuals not only to uphold the values being enforced but also to inform on their neighbours. Indeed, given the size of communities in Ulster, good neighbourliness must have been important. Kirk sessions were often used by church members to deal with personal grievances, solve interpersonal conflict, or quash false rumours concerning alleged bad behaviour.[39] Yet the contingent nature of discipline should not be overemphasized. In many instances, discipline was enforced simply to control a widespread breach of morality. The prevalence of sexual offences recorded in Carnmoney session books can be partly explained by the fact that premarital sex was common in the locality, being customarily used by couples to force unwilling parents to give them their inheritance.[40] Similarly, Ballybay session recorded that a spate of irregular marriages tried in May 1820 had been owing to the activities of a degraded clergyman and resolved that all couples so married would be publicly rebuked for fornication.[41] Discipline was not always imposed from the top down, but in efforts to contextualize experiences, this aspect must not be dismissed.

---

[36] Charles Parker, 'The Moral Agency and Moral Autonomy of Church Folk in the Dutch Reformed Church of Delft, 1580–1620', *JEH* 48 (1997), 44–70: 47, 51.

[37] Barkley, 'Ruling Eldership', 2: 231–2, 236, 256, 271.

[38] *Code*, 69.

[39] Barkley, 'Ruling Eldership', vol. 2. For the importance of good neighbourliness in another context see D. B. Rutman, 'Assessing the Little Communities of Early America', *William and Mary Quarterly* 3rd ser., 43 (1986), 163–78.

[40] *Ordnance Survey Memoirs of Ireland, vol. 2: Parishes of County Antrim 1, 1838–9*, ed. Angélique Day and Patrick McWilliams (Belfast, 1990), 86.

[41] PHS, Ballybay session book, 23 May 1820.

Despite the lack of legal sanction to compel offenders to appear, it is remarkable how few people did not submit to discipline. Out of the 1,275 cases recorded in the surviving nine Kirk session books in the 1640–1740 period – there were a total of 181 Presbyterian congregations by 1740 –, only two per cent of individuals tried showed verbal dissent from the sentence passed or deserted the Church.[42] The visitation returns of Synod of Ulster and Seceder presbyteries in the later eighteenth and nineteenth centuries confirm this pattern.[43] Why did people appear before Kirk sessions, often submitting themselves to the ignominy of a rebuke before friends and relatives at public worship? Many did so from sincere religious convictions and a desire to still their guilty consciences by reconciling themselves with both God and man. In addition, if an individual had failed morally, it was difficult within close-knit rural communities to escape the inevitable gossip. This was especially true if the offender was a woman who had become pregnant because of an illicit liaison. Being the subject of a scandal or scandalous rumour damaged an individual's place within a community upholding high standards of conduct and it was only through the rituals of confession, rebuke and restoration, often in public, that a person could be reintegrated into the religious and social community.[44] Furthermore, by remaining unrepentant, individuals excluded themselves and their children from the sacraments. Given the importance many attached to baptism, failure to submit and have the child baptized was thought to have had serious consequences for its eternal well-being.[45] It is significant that, according to the *Code*, a private rebuke should be given for those offences that were not public knowledge, indicating the desire of church authorities to protect not merely the reputation of the individual but also the public testimony of the Church.[46]

Community pressure could also work in the other direction, making the system a divisive rather than a unifying feature. This is particularly noticeable with the revival of discipline within the Synod of Ulster in

[42] R. M. Browne, 'Kirk and Community: Ulster Presbyterian Society, 1640–1740', unpublished M.Phil. thesis, QUB, 1998, 94–8.

[43] PHS, Down Presbytery (Seceder) 1785–1800, 1818–39; Minutes of Ballymena Presbytery (Synod of Ulster), 1808–19; Minutes of Route Presbytery (Synod of Ulster, typescript), 1811–34.

[44] Charles D. Cashdollar, *A Spiritual Home: Life in British and American Reformed Congregations, 1830–1915* (University Park, PA, 2000), 146–8.

[45] James Denham, *Public Baptism Vindicated by an Appeal to Scriptural Authority, and the Nature and Uses of the Ordinance; with an Answer to Prevailing Objections* (Derry, 1844), 24–30.

[46] *Code*, 65–6, 78–83.

the early nineteenth century. Visitation presbyteries, the imposition of stricter procedures, and the creation of a 'godly' public opinion through tracts, sermons, religious societies and so on, profoundly altered the moral and religious character of nineteenth-century religion. It is little wonder that presbyteries began to report more instances of fugitives from discipline than seems to have been the case in the previous century.[47] Some ministers reported that the laity would only submit to moderate discipline; others that owing to efforts to impose stricter standards, members of their congregations had joined other less closely regulated churches.[48]

The imposition of previously less prominent standards of moral and religious conduct partly explains the reported increase in the defiance of discipline. This impression may also be influenced by the better survival of evidence from the early nineteenth century owing to the increased scrupulosity of session clerks and the examination of congregational records by presbyteries. Nevertheless, there was a decline in the absolute number of cases recorded over the nineteenth century, and in some areas, this trend had begun in the 1820s.[49] Urbanization, the disruption of cohesive rural communities, the rise of individualism, and the desire for privacy, all fed into the relative decline of the public importance and prosecution of discipline in the Victorian era.[50] The experience of discipline depended upon a variety of factors and those factors, in various combinations, determined the persistence of discipline in a particular congregation.

At the same time, public opinion against certain moral failings was strengthened in the 1830s and 1840s. Though sexual offences continued to dominate the business of church courts, the number of cases of drunkenness tried increased as the temperance movement propelled the issue into public consciousness by creating a godly public opinion against what was an endemic social problem.[51] One of the reasons why this and other movements for social and moral reform made such remarkable progress in Ulster was because it articulated the

---

47   PHS, Down Presbytery (Seceder), 28 August 1827, 11 August 1829, 17 August 1830: 8, 98 and 142 respectively.
48   PHS, Route Presbytery (Synod of Ulster), 10 May 1831, 295; A. P. Goudy, *Zion's Good; or, the Position and Duty of the Irish Presbyterian Church, at the Present Time* (Derry, 1848), 14.
49   Gray, 'Illegitimacy', 105–6.
50   Cashdollar, *Spiritual Home*, 148–50; Brown, *Religion and Society*, 72–3.
51   *CF* 1 (1833), 116; Stewart, *Seceders*, 216–20; Elizabeth Malcolm, *Ireland Sober, Ireland Free: Drink and Temperance in Nineteenth-Century Ireland* (Dublin, 1986).

views of large sections of the working and middle classes who were striving for respectability through sobriety, chastity and hard work.[52] In doing so, they created precisely the public opinion that would enable discipline in these areas to continue to function. It may be legitimately suggested that the *quantitative* decline in the number of cases tried over the nineteenth century was an outcome of the success of discipline in inculcating the moral and religious standards of both the church and the dominant social groups.[53] The persistence of high levels of illegitimacy does not necessarily invalidate this point, as submitting to discipline in Ulster had normally been voluntary and it is by no means clear that all who were labelled 'Presbyterian' were committed to the Church. Similar levels of bastardy were also to be found in Catholic areas of the north-east, suggesting the importance of industrialization to any explanation of this phenomenon.[54]

In the long term, social and economic change made it almost impossible to uphold discipline amongst a population that increasingly prized individual privacy. Particularly in urban areas from the 1820s onwards, evangelicals realized that inculcating correct behaviour would be better achieved through town missions, Sunday Schools, tract distribution and visitation work.[55] Even in the countryside, discipline was increasingly placed within the context of pastoral visitation and not appearance before the Kirk session. The Presbytery of Raphoe's visitation questions, published in 1837, included the following to be addressed to the elders: 'When visiting his congregation, does he [the minister] admonish those whom he knows to be addicted to gross sins; such as drunkenness, rioting, fornication, Sabbath-breaking or profane swearing?'[56] More generally within transatlantic Protestantism, this concern gradually drifted into a therapeutic understanding of pastoral care and discipline in the second half of the nineteenth century that conceived of sin in social rather than religious terms.[57]

---

[52] For general comments see David Hempton and Myrtle Hill, *Evangelical Protestantism in Ulster Society 1740–1890* (London, 1992), 113–21.

[53] Cashdollar argues that this was the case amongst Reformed communities in Britain and America during the nineteenth century: *Spiritual Home*, 139, 148.

[54] This is not to suggest that religious differences were unimportant in determining levels of illegitimacy. See the comments of Gray, 'Illegitimacy', 159–63, 314–15.

[55] Hempton and Hill, *Evangelical Protestantism*, 105–28.

[56] *OP* 8 (1837), 167.

[57] Cashdollar, *Spiritual Home*, 138–50.

* * *

It is clear that community, in both senses of the term used here, was an essential factor in determining how discipline was experienced by lay Presbyterians. It is also obvious that in order to explain continuity and change within church discipline over time, the symbiotic relationship between church courts and the laity must be carefully considered in order to determine the form of discipline experienced. The creation of a godly public opinion in the nineteenth century, through various movements for social and religious reform, allowed high standards of personal conduct to be upheld without the overt threat of formal church discipline. If needed, censure was always in reserve as the ultimate sanction against inappropriate behaviour.[58] Although the nature and application of discipline changed over the two centuries, it did not disappear; rather, the form and content of church practice were adapted to meet the needs of a new age.

The Queen's University, Belfast

---

[58] Ibid.

PENANCE AND THE PRIESTLESS
OLD BELIEVERS IN MODERN RUSSIA, 1771–c.1850

by IRINA PAERT

THE epidemic of bubonic plague that spread in Russia between 1770 and 1772, claiming about 100,000 lives, was perceived as a divine punishment by many ordinary Russians.[1] In 1771, Moscow witnessed popular riots, which were partly caused by the unwillingness of ecclesiastical authorities to allow Muscovites to venerate the icon of the Mother of God placed above the St Barbara Gates in the Kremlin and which was believed to have miraculous powers against epidemic.[2] In order to stop the spread of the infection, the Moscow authorities established sanitary cordons around the city. In such an atmosphere of social crisis the Old Believers, a conservative current of Russian religious dissent, articulated popular fears and proposed a solution to these. The Old Believer merchants had received permission from the government to set up quarantine hospitals and cemeteries on the borders of the city. This led to the emergence of two Old Believer centres in Moscow in the suburb of Lefortovo: Rogozhskoe, that belonged to the priestly Old Believers, and Preobrazhenskoe, belonging to a branch of the priestless Old Believers, the Theodosians (fedoseevtsy).

One of the leaders of the Theodosian Old Believers, the peasant Ilia Ivanov who died in the epidemic, preached that the plague was a retribution for Russia's apostasy from the true Orthodox faith, and a sign of the approaching Judgement. To be saved one had to repent and be baptized by three immersions. Driven by the passionate preaching of Ivanov and other Theodosian leaders, hundreds of panic-stricken Muscovites were baptized in the Khapilov pond in the Lefortovo district of Moscow and renounced their former faith as heresy.[3] These newly baptized were required to promise a life of chastity, as the

---

[1] John T. Alexander, *Bubonic Plague in Early Modern Russia: Public Health and Urban Disaster* (Oxford, 2003).

[2] G. Freeze, 'Institutionalizing Piety: the Church and Popular Religion, 1750–1850', in Jane Burbank and David L. Ransel, eds, *Imperial Russia: New Histories for the Empire* (Bloomington, IN, 1998), 228.

[3] We can judge the scale of conversions from the growing number of Old Believers in Moscow: if in the 1760s there were only several dozen, in the 1790s there were about 1,000

Theodosians believed that marriage and procreation were those things 'passing away' on the verge of the Second Coming. But since human nature was not capable of sustaining the promise of celibacy, and given that eschatological fears receded with the end of the epidemic, the Old Believer congregation had to impose penances on those who breached their vows of chastity.

Penance was one of the two sacraments practised by the priestless Old Believers, who – unlike the Protestant reformers – did not abandon this sacrament as a ritual *poenitentia* and as a source of spiritual direction. On the contrary, Old Believer penance retained many features of medieval Orthodox penitential practice, but at the same time underwent certain changes. This paper will focus on the meaning, function and transformation of penance in the priestless communities. Although the priestless Old Believers abandoned a large portion of the Orthodox ritual inseparable from ordained priesthood, they retained some understanding and certain practices of penance that had more affinity with the medieval than with the contemporary Orthodox Church. The paper will touch upon the relationship between penance and communal politics in proto-industrial Moscow between the 1770s and 1850s, that is, in the period during which the conservative Old Believers encountered the mainstream culture of urban Russia. The focus will be on Preobrazhenskoe in Moscow, which during this period emerged as the leading centre for the priestless Old Believers in the face of the declining Vyg-Leksa community in the Russian North.

* * *

Old Believers were those members of the Russian Orthodox Church who refused to accept the liturgical reforms introduced in 1656–8 by Patriarch Nikon (1605–81), arguing that his reforms led to the distortion of the Orthodox faith.[4] The Old Believer movement was driven by fervent millenarian expectations that led many believers to mass self-immolations.[5] As millenarian fervour receded in the 1690s, Old

---

living in Preobrazhenskoe and several thousands of men and women associating themselves with Old Belief in the Lefortovo district of Moscow.

    4 On the early history of religious dissent see P. Pascal, *Avvakum et les débuts du raskol. La crise religieuse au XVIIe siècle en Russie* (Paris, 1938); R. O. Crummey, *The Old Believers and the World of the Antichrist: the Vyg Community and the Russian State, 1694–1855* (Madison, WI, 1970). For a revisionist interpretation of the Schism as having little to do with the Nikonian reform see Georg Bernhard Michels, *At War with the Church: Religious Dissent in Seventeenth-Century Russia* (Stanford, 1999).

    5 D. I. Sapozhnikov, *Samoszhiganie v russkom raskole* (Moscow, 1891).

Believers became divided into two major groups, the priestly and the priestless. The priestly Old Believers held that, despite the reform, grace was still present in the sacraments of the Church, thus making it possible for Old Believers to hire ordained Orthodox priests who would celebrate according to the pre-Nikonian rite. On the contrary, the priestless Old Believers, who in the 1690s were in turn divided into two currents, the Theodosians and the Pomorians (*pomortsy*), maintained that there was no grace in the Nikonian succession, because the reform had led to the interruption of the holy Orthodox tradition and to the advent of the Antichrist, who was understood as a spirit rather than as a person. In the absence of a trustworthy priesthood, only two sacraments were available to Christians in the 'last days', those of baptism and penance, both of which could be performed by a lay person.[6] Given that the sacrament of Holy Matrimony was no longer available to Christians, chastity was perceived as the normal post-baptismal state for all members of the priestless congregations.

Old Believers retained a kind of medieval approach to penance, seeing it as a therapy healing human nature distorted by sin. It was often interpreted as a second baptism, as the terms 'renewal' (*ponovlenie*) and 'cleansing' (*chistka*) implied. Penance had also an aspect of spiritual instruction: it was intended to correct spiritual faults and put one's soul to right. This function found expression in the Old Believer term for penance, *isprava* (correction). Old Believer spiritual leaders who administered penance were called *nastavniki* (mentors). Instruction was understood in familial terms, as a father admonishing his children, and designated by the Greek word, *paidevmata*. The pedagogical character of penance was conveyed through the structure of penitential rites, which included sermons and an admonition read by the priest to the penitent, besides special prayers that verbalized the feeling of contrition of illiterate penitents.[7] In the patriarchal peasant society penance thus served the function of a 'pedagogical rod', to use the expression of a nineteenth-century Russian historian, Kliuchevskii.[8] The seventeenth-century priest Avvakum, who later became the leader of the Old

---

[6] Old Believers drew examples from the ancient Church and the monastic practice of non-ordained men and women to minister Baptism and Penance. See A. and S. Denisov, *Pomorskie otvety* (Moscow, 1909). For the interpretation of the priestless Old Believers' history and beliefs see again Crummey, *Old Believers and the World of Antichrist*.

[7] A. I. Almazov, 'Tainaia ispoved' v Pravoslavnoi Vostochnoi Tserkvi', *Zapiski Imperatorskogo Novorossiiskogo universiteta* 65 (1895), 25.

[8] V. O. Kliuchevskii, 'Dva vospitaniia', in idem, *Sochineniia*, 9 vols (Moscow, 1990), 9: 12–16.

Believers, used to chain those parishioners who were late for the beginning of the church service and who failed to repent.[9]

Both the priestly and the priestless Old Believers appropriated the traditional practice of penance, using medieval collections of church canon law, found in manuscripts or in early printed penitential manuals.[10] They retained the Old Russian 'tariff' system and the use of public penance. In accordance with medieval tradition, the Old Believer practice of confession was specific and guided: confession continued to be administered with the aid of questionnaires rather than allowing a penitent to unburden his or her soul freely. The questionnaires differentiated between groups of penitents: men, women, married, unmarried, widowed, children, nuns, monks, merchants and their servants, reflecting a society in which the self was inseparable from one's social status. However, questions specific for each particular group were complementary to a standard confession, focusing on the sins against the faith, the Ten Commandments, and sexual sins.

Since religious dissent broke away from the institutionalized Church, disciplinarian penitential practices were not easily promoted. Many of the dissenters believed that a penitent had to confess his or her sins directly to God, either in front of an icon or addressing the earth.[11] Old Believers also practised the so-called 'Hermits' repentance' (*Skitskoe pokaianie*) that consisted of prayers designed to prepare a person who could not attend church, such as a hermit or the sick, for Holy Communion, distributed by a local bishop.[12] Although the leaders of Old Believer congregations accepted self-confession in times of crisis and persecution, they objected to this practice in times of relative stability, when communal discipline was of key importance.[13]

[9] S. Smirnov, *Drevnerusskii dukhovnik: Izsledovanie po istorii tserkovnago byta* [The Old Russian Confessor: A Study in the History of Church Life] (Moscow, 1913; repr. Farnborough, 1970), 215.

[10] A large number of Old Believer penitential manuals (*epitimiiniki*) can be found in the manuscript departments of the state libraries in Russia, such as Russian State Library, the Library of the Academy of Science, the Urals University Library [hereafter UrGU].

[11] The ritual of 'confession to the earth' is mentioned in Church records against the Strigol'niki heresy, *c.*1350–1450s. Smirnov commented on the origin of this ritual (which unfortunately he did not describe in detail) and characterized it as 'dual-faith', consisting of a syncretism of the pagan and Christian beliefs of the Russian folk. See Smirnov, *Drevnerusskii dukhovnik*, 255–83.

[12] Almazov, 'Tainaia ispoved', 115.

[13] Biblioteka akademii nauk [The Library of the Academy of Science: hereafter BAN], MS Chuvanova 6, fol. 340. N. Pokrovskii, 'Spory o ispovedi i prichastii u staroverov-chasovennykh vostoka Sibiri v XVIII v', in *Kul'tura slavian i Rus'* (Moscow, 1998), 526.

* * *

The leaders of the priestless communities tired to ensure that each member had a spiritual father (*dukhovnyi otets*) or *nastavnik*, who was responsible for administering confession and imposing penance (*epitim'ia*). Hence the traditional title for a confessor was that of 'penitential father' (*pokaial'nyi otets*).

The relationship between spiritual fathers and their 'children' was a combination of personal, economic and spiritual bonds. The *nastavniki* tried to reform the everyday behaviour of the lay members,[14] and their moral authority made an impact on the life of both rich and poor members. For example, fear of excommunication and heavy penance haunted many Muscovite merchants such as the leading textile industrialists, the Guchkovs, Morozovs and Prokhorovs, since almsgiving was often chosen as a penance for the failure to attain high moral standards. When conflicts between a spiritual father and a spiritual child arose, the community served as arbiter.[15]

To have a moral authority over his parishioners, a spiritual father had to demonstrate high moral standards himself. The *nastavniki* themselves were expected to confess annually to their own spiritual fathers. The rules of the 1694 Novgorod council, for example, prohibited spiritual leaders from hiring young female servants or cooks in order to prevent public disapproval and gossip.[16] However, police records of the 1840s suggest that, despite these rules, some *nastavniki* had secret mistresses: it was only in the case of giving birth to a child – which served as proof of illicit sexual relations – that a guilty father was excommunicated.[17] Police records attest that a *nastavnik*, Trofim Andreev, for example, was excommunicated from the community for eighty days for fathering an illegitimate child.[18] In a similar vein, according to official observers, priestly Old Believers tolerated the moral misconduct of their priests. Given the shortage of priests,

---

[14] *Dnevnye dozornye zapisi o raskol'nikakh*, 2 vols (Moscow, 1885), 1 (part 1–2): 171–2.

[15] Almazov, 'Tainaia ispoved', 47.

[16] Rossiiskaia gosudarstvennaia biblioteka [Russian State Library: hereafter RGB], MS Egorova 1330, fols 255–6.

[17] Rossiiskaia natsional'naia biblioteka [Russian National Library: hereafter RNB], MS Titova 2293, fols 150–66. After 1847 a police officer lived permanently on the territory of the Preobrazhenskoe community. The police reports, based on personal observations and rumours, were sent to the Governor-General of Moscow with the aim to provide evidence of Old Believer criminal activities and moral misconduct. This evidence was eventually used for the suppression of Preobrazhenskoe in 1853.

[18] Ibid., fols 150v–171v.

parishioners tended to excuse the excessive drinking and sexual liaisons of an ordained person who agreed to serve in Old Believer churches.[19] *Nastavniki* could not engage in economic activities apart from spiritual service. The Council of 1791 in Preobrazhenskoe condemned spiritual fathers who engaged in commerce. An accused spiritual father tried to justify himself saying that it was his assistants who traded, and that the trade was his only means of support, but the council did not accept his plea and dismissed him as unworthy.[20] According to the police records, none of the Preobrazhenskoe *nastavniki* in the 1840s had merchant status which would allow them to trade and have factories. Among seven *nastavniki* registered by the police officials, all but one came from a rural background and had the lowest urban status, while one, Zinovii Osipov, was a peasant.[21]

Women in the priestless communities could administer both baptism and penance when an experienced male *nastavnik* was not available.[22] In the nineteenth century some provincial Theodosian communities elected women as their *nastavniki* despite criticism from their Moscow brethren.[23] However, with the growth of moderate tendencies in the community in the nineteenth century, Old Believers tended to put restrictions on female leadership. The spiritual leaders of Preobrazhenskoe criticized lay women who 'impudently' practised the confession of members of their own sex.[24] A spiritual leader of Preobrazhenskoe, Sergii Gnusin, discouraged the female community in Sudislavl' from baptizing and confessing by referring to the authority of the Orthodox Church which did not allow women to minister sacraments.[25]

Old Believers suggested that, to minister penance, a person had to be skilled, experienced, mature and, preferably, male.[26] Administering penance was a skill which was usually transferred from one spiritual father to another. Thus, women were excluded from the 'profession' by their lack of spiritual training, self-control and reasoning powers.[27]

---

[19] P. Mel'nikov (Andrei Pecherskii), *Polnoe sobranie sochinenii*, 7 vols (Moscow, 1909), 7: 232–3.

[20] Livanov, *Raskol'niki i ostrozhniki*, 3 vols (St Petersburg, 1872), 2: 37.

[21] Ibid., 182–3.

[22] Natsional'nyi arkhiv Respubliki Karelii [National Archive of the Republic of Karelia: hereafter NARK], fol. 9, op. 1, d. 304/2950, l. 1.

[23] RGB, MS Egorova 1044, fol. 325.

[24] RGB, MS Egorova 1052, fol. 162.

[25] Ibid.

[26] RGB, MS Egorova 1869, fol. 223.

[27] RGB, MS Egorova 2066, fol. 24v.

Since women had to be excluded from the position of spiritual instructors, confession gave male spiritual leaders control over sexuality and over the reproductive capacity of female members of the community.

* * *

Penance had several functions in the priestless community: it regulated the relations with the outside world and ensured the morality and loyalty of its members. The priestless Old Believers used penance to guard the boundaries of the community. For example, communication with non-believers – either in partaking of the sacraments or in sharing meals – was penalized by penances that could last between a few weeks to several years, depending on the gravity of the transgression.

In deciding the degree of the severity of penance, confessors took into account whether a particular transgression was avoidable or not, sincerely repented or not. Outsiders were perceived as excommunicated members, so that any communication with them led to eternal damnation. When the relationship concerned members of one family who shared one household and had no choice other than sharing meals, the priestless advised the faithful members to keep their dishes separate from those of the 'unfaithful'. Thus, when the members of one family belonged to different religious groups, everyone had one's own spoon or cup or plate. This peculiar custom of keeping one's individual spoon and a set of dishes (the so-called *chashnichestvo*) may be interpreted as a kind of survival of the ancient practice of banishing penitents from communion.

Public penance had a disciplinary function: members who did not live in accordance with the rules of the community were excommunicated. As chastity was the ultimate goal of the priestless Old Believers, the leaders of the communities regulated sexual conduct of their members by means of penances. However, different branches of the priestless differed in their approach to marriage. While the Pomorians approved separation of married converts, who were called *starozheny*, the Theodosians recognized the validity of these marriages, but expected a husband and wife to live as brother and sister. By contrast, they disqualified marriages of those members who were baptized in the community either as infants or as adults (the so-called *novozheny*), treating their unions as fornication. Penance for sexual relations of *starozheny* in the Theodosian community was less severe than that of *novozheny*. Given that the birth of a child was the only visible evidence for the transgression of the rules of chastity, the Theodosian leaders suggested in 1694 that *starozheny* had to be excommunicated from the congregation of the faithful: for forty days for the birth of their first child, one year for the second and six years for the third child.[28] *Novozheny*, in contrast, were banned from sacraments and prayer for an indefinite period of time unless they promised to separate and live in chastity. Their infants could not be baptized and husband and wife could not receive the sacrament of penance.

In the 1750s, under pressure from married members of different communities, several leaders of the priestless Old Believers developed a new approach to marriage, deeming it to be a sacrament that did not require the presence of an ordained member of the clergy. In parallel to the sacrament of penance, marriage was perceived as a mystery that was taking place between the couple and God.[29] It was the consent of the couple and their marital vows given to God, to which the entire congregation was witness, that provided the validity of marriage as a sacrament.[30] The followers of the new teaching married in chapels, or, alternatively, in private houses in the presence of a congregation or of the respective families.

In response to these new developments, the conservative Theodosians in Preobrazhenskoe re-emphasized strict rules against *novozheny* marriages. The newly married were excommunicated for life. The leaders of the Theodosians differentiated between those who acknowledged their sinful behaviour, and those who appealed to pro-marriage arguments. The community leadership made some concessions to the former: their infants could be baptized in cases of grave illness. In contrast, those who failed to repent were considered to be heretics, and had no access to the sacraments. The parents who assisted their children in matchmaking and wedding arrangements were excommunicated for three years, during which period they had to make one hundred prostrations every day. The penance for parents included strict fasting rules: these members were not allowed to eat

---

[28] Ural'skii Gosuniversitet [The Urals State University: hereafter UrGU], MS XVII 119p, fol. 32v.

[29] Old Believers also dwelt on the idea that vows of the bride and the bridegroom constitute the essence of marriage as a sacrament, basing this thought on the seventeenth-century canon law collection (*Kormchaia Kniga*) by Petr Mohila, that was written under the influence of Tridentine canon law. See A. S. Pavlov, *50ia glava Kormchei knigi* (Moscow, 1887), 51–6.

[30] For more on the debate on marriage, see I. K. Paert, 'Gender and Salvation: Representations of Difference in Old Believer Writings from the Late Seventeenth Century to the 1820s', in Linda Edmondson, ed., *Gender in Russian History and Culture* (Basingstoke, 2001), 29–51; also my book, *Old Believers, Religious Dissent and Gender in Russia* (Manchester, 2003).

dairy products and meat on any other day except Saturdays and Sundays for the rest of their life.[31]

However, at the same time, the Moscow Theodosians relaxed the rules regulating procreation of *starozheny* in the Theodosian community in the early 1800s. While in official statements the leaders insisted on the policy of excommunicating couples who 'frequently gave birth', in practice they developed a differentiated approach to the majority of married members in their community.[32] While some spiritual conservative leaders abided by the rules of 1694, insisting on excommunicating *starozheny* for repeated procreation, other leaders of the community argued that no excommunication was necessary at all, as Christ taught that one should forgive sinners until seventy times seven (cf. Matt. 18: 23).[33] Relaxation of penances for procreation of *starozheny* was essential for the community's survival, especially when strict laws against religious proselytizing were introduced between 1816 and the 1850s.

Yet, despite this double-standard approach to married members in the priestless communities, penance functioned as a control of communal morality and gender *status quo*. In Preobrazhenskoe in nineteenth-century Moscow, a woman found in a drunken state had to wear a rough dress and make a few hundred prostrations in church during services.[34] Having served a period of excommunication, penitents had to reconcile themselves with the congregation by performing a rite of forgiveness that consisted of reciting some introductory prayers (*nachal*) and making prostrations in front of each member of the congregation.[35] Thus the ritual of reconciliation between the transgressor and his or her community was substituted for the absolution of sins that symbolized the reconciliation between the penitent and God.

Penance regulated the behaviour of the urban Old Believers who were too eager to adopt the new, Westernized culture. Old Believers opposed not only the liturgical reforms introduced by Nikon, but also more generally the Westernization of Russian culture that was taking place in the eighteenth and nineteenth centuries. The Theodosian leaders criticized their wealthy parishioners for adopting the life-styles

---

31 UrGU, MS XVII 119p, fols 16v–17.
32 UrGU, MS XVII 119 p, fol. 5.
33 RGB, MS Egorova 1044, l. 120, I. Nil'skii, *Semeinaia zhisn' v russkom rakole* (St Petersburg, 1869), 292.
34 *Dnevnye dozornye zapisi*, 2 (part 3–7): 47–8.
35 UrGU, MS XVII 119p, l. 17.

of an ungodly society. For example, a council of Theodosian fathers in 1847 discussing the transgressions of Moscow merchants and their spouses criticized them for smoking, gambling, betting on horses, drinking coffee, breaking fasts and attending clubs. They also rebuked their wives for attending theatre, dancing, riding, smoking cigars, and for wearing corsets, male hats, dresses 'with Satanic tail' and décolleté.[36] Impious parents were criticized for improperly bringing-up their children by reading fairy-tales instead of prayers and teaching children music and dancing.[37] For most of these transgressions penance entailed excommunication that would stop if the sinners changed their behaviour.

Public penance was imposed for violations of public morality and outward expressions of disloyalty to the communal rules. Sins committed and confessed in secret, in contrast, were subject to private penances, which consisted of a number of bows and prostrations, and fasting during the period of repentance, which could last from several days to several years. To safeguard the privacy of their spiritual children, some *nastavniki* introduced changes to the traditional penitential practice. The leader of the Moscow Pomorians who approved of marriage, Gavriil Skachkov, for example, argued that a woman who secretly committed adultery and repented her sin should not be separated from the congregation of the faithful, so that her husband should not find out.[38] Here the privacy of a woman rather than the interests of communal morality were preserved.

Outside observers were often shocked by the severity of traditional Orthodox penances.[39] However, all penances were subject to commutation. The Byzantine and Old Russian canons for calculating the volume of public or private penance always provided some guidance that allowed a reduction of the length of the penitent's excommunication taking into account his/her piety and good disposition, charity, observation of fasts and (young) age. The Russian penitential practice was not acquainted with the system of indulgences and penitential pilgrimages, but Old Believers followed a medieval custom of 'distributing' penance

---

[36] *Dnevnye dozornye zapisi*, I: 171. For a similar situation in a different context, see in this volume the essay by Graeme Murdock, 'Did Early Modern Calvinists Have a Guilt Complex?', 138–58, 156.

[37] RGB, MS Egorova 1354, fols 148–49.

[38] N. Popov, *Materialy dlia istorii bespopovshchinskogo soglasiia* (Moscow, 1870), 57.

[39] Smirnov mentions evidence of foreign travellers to Muscovy in the sixteenth and seventeenth centuries. See Smirnov, *Drevnerusskii dukhovnik*, 169.

among the members of the penitent's family and household.[40] For example, the members of one family could divide the number of prostrations and prayers prescribed to a transgressor. This form of commutation was preserved as a custom rather than as a canonical regulation. Despite the lack of written evidence, it was widely practised by members of Old Believer communities even unto the present.[41] Thus, carrying a penance was not an individual act, but a collective responsibility.

Old Believer manuals emphasized that sincere repentance, a good disposition of the heart and charity were the crucial factors that allowed a spiritual father to reduce a given penance. The spiritual leaders usually encouraged almsgiving in penitents: Moscow merchants, who, due to the nature of their business activities, found it difficult to keep up the strict rules of the community, donated generously to the poor living in the dormitories of Preobrazhenskoe.

The importance of penitence was conveyed through spiritual instruction, popular literature and visual art. Eschatological literature such as the *Life of St Theodora* and the *Vision of St Gregory*, including an apocryphal *Tour of the Mother of God in Hell*, communicated the possibility of punishment after death for different categories of sins.[42] Spiritual verses, popular among all Old Believer currents, also put much emphasis on judgement and punishment of sinners.[43] Popular culture has retained such a non-legalistic view of penance, as a contemporary anecdote may serve to illustrate. During one of the expeditions to the Old Believer communities in the Urals in 1998-9, we were told the tale of a thief who wept so much about his crimes that he needed a towel to wipe tears off his face. After the thief's death, demons put their hands on his soul attempting to take it to Hell, but the angels placed the thief's tears on the scales: the tears outweighed all his sins.[44] While penitential practice and admonition were methods imposed from above, spiritual verses and popular eschatological literature had a

---

[40] On the medieval Russian instances of 'distribution' of penance see Smirnov, *Drevnerusskii dukhovnik*, 188-9.

[41] Evidence from oral history interviews, taken in 1998-9 in the Russian Urals.

[42] See, for example, *Tsvetnik* (Moscow: Preobrazhenskoe, *c.*1909).

[43] See, for example, G. Fedotov, *Stikhi dukhovnye* (Moscow, 1991), 105-17.

[44] This is an oral version of the repentant thief from the Byzantine 'beneficial tales', known in Russia among Old Believers from medieval collections such as the *Prolog*. On the original story in Greek, see John Wortley, 'Death, Judgment, Heaven and Hell in Byzantine "Beneficial Tales" ', *Dumbarton Oaks Papers* 55 (2001), 53-69, 63. Many thanks to Barbara Crostini for drawing my attention to this source.

broader impact: they enabled the whole community and the individual families to keep control of morals and provide spiritual instruction of younger members.

* * *

The reforms in the Orthodox Church in the seventeenth and eighteenth centuries led to the transformation of penance, that became uniform, standardized and administered by ordained priests. In the nineteenth century the Orthodox Church experienced a gradual decline of public penance.[45] Thus penance lost its disciplinary function, while confession became closely linked with Holy Communion. The Old Believer tradition provides an insight into the traditional medieval understanding and practice of penance. In particular, in the priestless Old Believer congregations penance was dissociated from the institution of ordained priesthood: both lay men and women could take on the role of confessor and the congregation of the faithful was a witness to the penitent's reconciliation with God. Penance also served as an important instrument of moral discipline, guarding the boundaries of the community and ensuring the commitment of its members.

Old Believers retained the elements of medieval penance understood as spiritual instruction and reformation: it was legalistic, guided and specific, focusing primarily on behaviour and actions rather than on thoughts and the inner disposition of the penitents. Above all, penance remained a communal rather than an individual sacrament: certain penances could be distributed between the members of one family and parents carried out responsibility for their children's sins. Penance should not be interpreted as a disciplinarian method imposed by the community leadership: ordinary men and women contributed to penitential practice by articulating traditional visions of punishment after death through verses and story-telling. Eschatological narratives conveyed the centrality of repentance for salvation. Spiritual verses and popular apocrypha emphasized the torments of those who failed to repent of their sins before death.

Yet, at the same time, in the context of the modernizing of Russian society, Old Believer penitential practices underwent a transformation that was not dissimilar to that of the mainstream Orthodox Church. Facing the greater assimilation of conservative members into the

45   G. Freeze, 'The Wages of Sin: the Decline of Public Penance in Imperial Russia', in S. K. Batalden, ed., *Seeking God: the Recovery of Religious Identity in Orthodox Russia, Ukraine, and Georgia* (Dekalb, IL, 1993), 53–82.

dominant culture of urban society, the leaders of the conservative priestless communities had to relax their approach to penance, commuting public *epitim'ia* with private penances and encouraging charity as an alternative to excommunication. Despite their outward conservatism and legalism, in many ways, Old Believer penitential practices were flexible and irregular. At the end of the day, to quote the *Hermits' Repentance* (*Skitskoe pokaianie*), it was God who had 'the last word to forgive sins, have mercy and redeem' (*ty bo edin vlast' imashi ostavliati pregresheniia u tvoe bo est' ezhe milovati i spasati nas*).[46]

University of Wales, Bangor

---

[46] Almazov, 'Tainaia ispoved' v Pravoslavnoi Vostochnoi Tserkvi', 24–5.

JUDGING THE NATION:
EARLY NINETEENTH-CENTURY
BRITISH EVANGELICALS AND DIVINE RETRIBUTION

by JOHN WOLFFE

Long had the 'still small voice' been spoke in vain,
But God now thunders in an awful strain!
Commercial woes brought down our nation's pride,
Our harvest fail'd, and yet we God defy'd:
But now the 'voice' cries loud to all the Land,
The 'Rod' is felt, Oh! may we see the *Hand*.
'Tis God who speaks – 'Tis He who 'points the blow,
'Tis God who's laid the pride of Britain low![1]

IN these lines, written in November 1817, a lady member of a
Newcastle-upon-Tyne Nonconformist congregation unambiguously
attributed the death of Princess Charlotte to specific divine intervention. This conviction reflected that of her minister, James Pringle, in
a recent sermon preached on an Old Testament text widely expounded
at that time, the chastening rod (or voice) of God in Micah 6: 9.[2] Such a
perception of adverse national events as divine retribution for sin,
comparable to prophetic interpretations of the history of Old Testament Israel, was a noticeable strand in early nineteenth-century British
evangelical discourse.

Preaching of this kind during specific periods of armed conflict has
already received some attention from historians.[3] The intention in the

---

[1] Lines by 'Charintee' appended to James Pringle, *The Lord's Voice in the Rod: a sermon,
preached on the nineteenth of November, 1817, the day of interment of the much-lamented Princess
Charlotte of Wales* (Newcastle-upon-Tyne, 1817), 63–4.

[2] The text goes on to denounce commercial dishonesty, violence and deceit, and to
threaten famine, war and desolation. Other sermons on Micah 6: 9 published at the time of
Princess Charlotte's death include John East, *The Voice of God to the Nation* (Evesham, 1817),
Thomas Scott, *The Voice of God to Britain* (London, 1817) and Martin Richard Whish, *The
Lord's Voice to the British Zion* (Bristol, 1817).

[3] Olive Anderson, 'The reactions of Church and Dissent towards the Crimean War',
JEH 16 (1965), 209–20, 214–19; Deryck Lovegrove, 'English Evangelical Dissent and the
European Conflict 1789–1815', in W. J. Sheils, ed., *The Church and War*, SCH 20 (1983),
263–76, 271–4; Brian Stanley, 'Christian Responses to the Indian Mutiny', in ibid., 277–89,
279–83.

present paper is to build upon and complement this existing research by looking at the peacetime articulation by evangelicals of ideas of divine retribution. Material will be drawn particularly from published sermons and other writings on the deaths of Princess Charlotte in 1817 and of Prince Albert in 1861, on the cholera epidemics of 1832 and 1849, and on the Irish famine of 1847. It will thereby become possible to form some impressions of the overall nature and significance of such beliefs in Britain in the first two thirds of the nineteenth century, especially in relation to the development of national consciousness.

It needs something of a leap of the imagination to enter into the public mood at the time of the events under consideration, although experience of the responses to AIDS and the aftermath of Princess Diana's death and of 11 September 2001 suggests some limited contemporary parallels. Princess Charlotte's death, at the age of twenty-one shortly after giving birth to a stillborn child, in November 1817, was a poignant human tragedy, which also gave rise to well-founded concerns for the succession, and confirmed a sense of post-war national lack of self-confidence. When Prince Albert died prematurely in 1861, for a time the stability of the monarchy again appeared very uncertain. In the meantime visitations of cholera stirred widespread anxiety, not only because of the numerous fatalities, but also because of the apparently random incidence and rapid onset of the disease.[4] There was also a coincidence with political turbulence, with the Reform Bill crisis in 1832, and in 1849 with the aftermath of revolution on the continent. In such psychological environments supernatural explanations had enhanced plausibility and appeal. The mood was heightened by particular recognized days of collective national observance: fast days with reference to cholera, famine and war; funeral days in relation to the deaths of prominent individuals.

Evangelicals did not have a monopoly on the language of divine chastisement and retribution,[5] but their strong belief in the active interventionist providence of God, especially when undergirded by a Calvinist theology, particularly predisposed them to such an outlook. Further support came from a tradition of biblical exegesis in which God's dealings with Old Testament Israel were perceived as normative for the subsequent history of Churches and nations. For preachers and

4 For background on cholera see R. J. Morris, *Cholera 1832: the Social Response to an Epidemic* (London, 1976).

5 For a prominent non-evangelical example see E. B. Pusey, *Chastisements Neglected, Forerunners of Greater* (London, 1847).

writers with such convictions it seemed axiomatic that events such as the sudden premature death of the heiress presumptive to the throne, or the onset of an epidemic that killed thousands of previously healthy people, were directly inflicted by the Almighty. Consideration of perceived 'secondary causes', such as the medical management of the Princess's labour, or living conditions in cholera-infested towns, was quickly dismissed as irrelevant.[6] Moreover, once responsibility for such events was directly and unambiguously attributed to God, the imputation of a retributive and chastising divine intent followed naturally. The only logical alternatives – a deity responsible for evil as well as good, or a capricious one inflicting disaster at random – were theologically unthinkable.

Individuals would be subject to divine judgement and punishment after death, but according to the leading Hackney Independent minister John Pye Smith:

> Nations, as nations, that is in their corporate and connected capacity, have existence only in this life and therefore, so far as it is requisite, in the eyes of divine justice and wisdom, to punish national sins, as *national*, and separate from the future amenableness of the individuals who have perpetrated them, they *must* be punished in the present state.[7]

Preaching on Princess Charlotte's death, Smith maintained that the teaching of Scripture was that the premature deaths of 'good and valuable and promising characters' in prominent and powerful positions was one means by which the Almighty expressed his displeasure. Furthermore, he believed that there were British historical parallels, notably the premature death of Henry, Prince of Wales in 1612. Such judgements should be viewed as a mercy to those who died because they were taken away from subsequent manifestations of divine wrath.[8] According to William MacDonald, preaching at the Countess of Huntingdon Chapel in Brighton, the Princess's death (like the King's long illness) arose from her being a representative member of a sinful nation whom God had afflicted, and should not be seen as a punish-

---

[6] Scott, *Voice of God*, 3, 7–8; J. A. Begg, *The True Cause of the Prevalence of Pestilence, and other judgments of God; with the divinely appointed means of deliverance and safety* (London and Paisley, 1832), 6.

[7] John Pye Smith, *The Sorrows of Britain, Her Sad Forebodings, and Her Only Refuge* (London, 1817), 14.

[8] Ibid., 14, 21–2.

ment for particular sins of her own.[9] Thomas Scott, the biblical commentator and rector of Aston Sandford, dwelt on his sense of spiritual and moral identification between rulers and their people, which implied that the former were the channels for divine judgement upon the latter.[10]

A similar emphasis on corporate national responsibility was apparent in responses to cholera and famine. An anonymous Tyneside pamphleteer argued that the particular prevalence of cholera among drunkards and sabbath-breakers pointed to God's judgement on these individual sins,[11] but recognition that the relatively virtuous were also dying in large numbers stirred most preachers to more collective explanations. For example, James Taylor, a lecturer at St John's Church, Newcastle-on-Tyne, held that pestilence is a 'scourge particularly in the hands of the Almighty, to punish ungodly, unthankful, and wicked nations'. He cited the biblical examples of the last plague of Egypt (Exodus 12) and the deaths of twenty-four thousand Israelites following idolatrous worship of Baal (Numbers 25).[12] Similarly, William Trollope, curate of Ringwood, preaching about the famine on texts drawn from Amos 4, held that there was an invariable connection between national sin and national calamity, while stressing that individual afflictions should not be regarded in the same light.[13]

Identifications of the specific sins that prompted divine retribution were various. William Wilberforce had suggested in 1807 that lengthy war and the recent deaths of Pitt and Fox were a providential penalty for the continuance of the slave trade, and in 1823 in his appeal for slave emancipation he again counselled against presumption 'on the forbearance of the Almighty'.[14] The issue was indeed picked up by some writers and preachers. In 1832 the young James Begg, later to be a leading force in the Free Church of Scotland, described slavery as the

---

9 William MacDonald, *Jehovah's Voice to Britain* (London, 1818), 9–10.

10 Scott, *Voice of God*, 15–19.

11 Anon., *An Affectionate Address to the Inhabitants of Newcastle and Gateshead on the Present Alarming Visitation of Divine Province, in the Fatal Ravages of the Spasmodic Cholera* (Newcastle-upon-Tyne, 1832). Morris, *Cholera 1832*, 137–9, notes that there is an objective medical link between alcoholism and susceptibility to cholera.

12 James Taylor, *The Cholera: or God's Voice in the Pestilence* (London, 1832), 8.

13 William Trollope, *Three Sermons Having Reference to the Prevailing Famine* (Cambridge, 1847), 3.

14 William Wilberforce, *A Letter on the Abolition of the Slave Trade: addressed to the freeholders and other inhabitants of Yorkshire* (London, 1807), 4–6; idem, *An Appeal to the Religion, Justice and Humanity of the Inhabitants of the British Empire, in Behalf of the Negro Slaves in the West Indies* (London, 1823), 74–5.

'deadly drug in that cup of bitterness of which as a nation we must drink.' He was further concerned by 'open and unblushing idolatry' in India, which, he pointed out, was where cholera had originated.[15] John East, preaching at Campden Parish Church in 1817, saw failure to evangelize the enslaved Africans or the commercially exploited Indians as a significant sin of omission.[16] For Thomas Chalmers, in his sermon at the Tron Church in Glasgow on the day of Princess Charlotte's funeral, it was rather failure in home mission that had given rise to the judgement of God. He therefore proceeded to turn his sermon into an appeal for church extension.[17]

Countenancing of 'Popery' was, however, the most frequently identified spiritual defect in national policy.[18] In 1817 Pye Smith maintained that Britain had sinned in allowing the restoration of both the Pope and Roman Catholic monarchs to their dominions, without proper safeguards for religious liberty.[19] In his sermon Pringle focused rather on the advance of Roman Catholic proselytism and political aspirations at home.[20] In 1832 Joseph Irons, Independent minister of Grove Chapel, Camberwell, denounced Catholic Emancipation, passed in 1829, as an appalling national sin and declared his conviction that the 'day of divine visitation is at hand'.[21] In 1847 the Irish Famine was interpreted as a judgement on Roman Catholicism, not only by the leading anti-Catholic agitator, Hugh McNeile, preaching in Liverpool, but also by William Trollope in small-town Hampshire.[22] McNeile saw the encouragement of 'Romanism' as 'in a peculiar sense a *national* sin' because he held that it compromised 'the high principles of civil and ecclesiastical liberty'.[23] Trollope asserted the 'undeniable evidence of history' that national prosperity was directly related to the extent to which 'Popish error and corruption' had been discouraged.[24] In 1849,

---

[15] Begg, *True Cause of Pestilence*, 14, 16.

[16] East, *Voice of God*, 13–14.

[17] Thomas Chalmers, *A Sermon Delivered in the Tron Church, Glasgow, on the Day of the Funeral of HRH the Princess Charlotte of Wales* (Glasgow, 1817), 20, 26–7.

[18] On the wider context of Protestant agitation see John Wolffe, *The Protestant Crusade in Great Britain, 1829–1860* (Oxford, 1991).

[19] Pye Smith, *Sorrows of Britain*, 17.

[20] Pringle, *Lord's Voice*, 59–61.

[21] Joseph Irons, *Jehovah's Controversy with England: the substance of a sermon preached at Grove Chapel, Camberwell* (London, 1832), iii–iv, 13.

[22] Hugh McNeile, *The Famine a Rod of God* (London and Liverpool, 1847), 23; Trollope, *Three Sermons*, 36–7.

[23] McNeile, *Famine*, 23.

[24] Trollope, *Three Sermons*, 36–7.

McNeile stated his anti-Roman reading of events even more forcefully in a published letter to Sir George Grey, the Home Secretary. He explicitly attributed the cholera epidemic of 1832 to divine judgement on Catholic Emancipation, the Famine to the Maynooth Act of 1845, and the current 'visitation of Cholera' to further national encouragement of 'idolatry'.[25]

Preachers however were usually careful to avoid dwelling on specific single offences in this way. Even McNeile, in a footnote to his 1847 sermon, was at pains to deny the charge that he attributed the Irish Famine exclusively to God's judgement on Roman Catholicism.[26] Others tended to see the grounds of divine judgement in general issues such as widespread pride and arrogance, dissipation, disregard of religion, and lukewarmness among professing Christians.[27] In 1817 James Taylor listed a variety of offences including Sabbath-breaking, blasphemy, commercial fraud, and discontent among the lower orders.[28] An anonymous address in 1832 to the inhabitants of Fakenham in Norfolk also cited failures in Sabbath observance, together with drunkenness, adultery, and the inattention of parents to the religious instruction of their children.[29] The most comprehensive catalogue of sins appeared in a pamphlet by the leading Anglican evangelical Edward Bickersteth, written in response to the 1849 cholera epidemic. In block capitals he listed 'fearful' matters such as worldliness, and neglect of God and spiritual interest. The poor were oppressed, but they themselves were prone to lawless insubordination. The empire had been used for gain, not for the glory of God. The Church had sinned by the apostasy of some to Rome, the unfaithfulness of others, and its widespread divisions. Warming further to his theme, Bickersteth continued:

> By pride and vain glory, by ambition and rapacity, by open or secret profligacy and prostitution, by frauds in trade, by the traffic of opium in China, by oppressive exaction of labours in factories, mining, and of women and the lower orders generally, by slander

25 Hugh McNeile, *National Sin – What Is It?* (London and Liverpool, 1849), 34–5.
26 McNeile, *Famine*, 21–2.
27 For example Thomas Lewis, *Murmurs Silenced, or the Righteousness of the Divine Judgments Vindicated* (London, 1817), 24–5.
28 Taylor, *Cholera*, 12–14.
29 *An Appeal to the Inhabitants of Fakenham, in Reference to the Recent Visitation of Cholera*, by a Fellow Townsman (Fakenham, 1832), 10–16.

and quarrelling, by swearing, cursing, and perjuries, we have as a nation grievously sinned against God.[30]

Nevertheless, despite the strong emphasis on sin and retribution in these sermons and writings, God was perceived as fundamentally merciful. There was acknowledgement of ways in which the Almighty had favoured as well as judged the nation.[31] One preacher on the 1832 cholera epidemic noted that the ravages of the disease in Britain had been less severe than in other countries, which he regarded as a sign of relative divine mercy and restraint.[32] Above all, the judgements inflicted were viewed not as mere retributive punishment, but as fatherly chastisements and calls to repentance, through which God intended to draw people and nation back to himself, and thereby spare them further outpourings of his wrath.[33]

Hearers and readers were therefore exhorted to a personal response. Even when perceived sins at a level of national policy were identified, preachers usually stopped short of advocating specific legislative action to eliminate them. Their attention rather was directed primarily to their own congregations and localities. In 1817 William MacDonald maintained that there needed to be both a general and individual reformation of manners. While calling on the royal family to recognize the true source of their authority and responsibility under God and on Parliament to pass measures to control vice and secure the observance of the Sabbath, he then moved on to exhort ministers of religion to speak out as watchmen, magistrates to suppress immorality, and all families and households to consecrate themselves for God.[34] Pye Smith told his congregation that the fate of their country rested with them as 'sincere and practical Christians', and urged them to spend the day of Princess Charlotte's funeral in prayer, confessing sin, and interceding for divine mercy.[35] James Taylor struck a similar note in 1832, asserting the only true patriotism lay in confessing one's own sins and mourning for those of the people. The danger of cholera should be seen as an

---

[30] Edward Bickersteth, *Parochial and Congregational Fasting, on Occasion of the Cholera in 1849* (London, 1849), 4.

[31] MacDonald, *Jehovah's Voice*, 20; Bickersteth, *Parochial and Congregational Fasting*, 3.

[32] Charles Cator, *The Cholera Morbus, a Visitation of Divine Providence* (2nd edn, London, 1832), 25–6.

[33] See for example Lewis, *Murmurs Silenced*, 5–20; Irons, *Jehovah's Controversy*, iv; Trollope, *Three Sermons*, 13, 50.

[34] MacDonald, *Jehovah's Voice*, 23–6.

[35] Pye Smith, *Sorrows of Britain*, 27–30.

opportunity to lead children, relatives and servants to more immediate faith in Christ.[36] In his 1849 pamphlet Bickersteth proceeded to give instructions on the observance of the Fast: there should be seclusion, self-examination, confession of sin, resolution of amendment and intercession for others. He believed that without such signs of general repentance heavier judgements would follow.[37]

Public assertions about divine judgement could be controversial, even within evangelical circles. In 1831 two Anglican clergymen, Nicholas Armstrong and William Dalton, provoked uproar at a public meeting called to raise funds for the relief of prevalent famine and distress in Ireland, when they attributed these disasters to the judgement of God on 'Romish' apostasy. Roman Catholics were present at the meeting, and took understandable offence at the apparent gratuitous insult to their religion. Moreover other evangelicals, while sympathetic to Armstrong's and Dalton's theology, still felt that such a forceful and tactless expression of it on such an occasion was unjustified.[38] Still, when Armstrong's conduct was attacked in *The Times*, the evangelical *Record* newspaper, which had previously criticised him, rallied vigorously to his defence.[39]

As Olive Anderson and Brian Stanley have shown, the notion that national disasters were retribution for sin remained very widespread in the 1850s. In the face of the misconduct of the Crimean War, however, many preachers were quite prepared to attack human incompetence as well as to reverence divine judgement.[40] The Indian Mutiny though was generally seen in retributive terms, partly because of its cataclysmic nature, but also because specific related sins of maintaining Hindu idolatry and failing to propagate Christianity could readily be identified.[41]

In December 1861 Prince Albert's death led to more varied reactions. One preacher saw it as ongoing retribution for lukewarmness in missionary endeavour, while another spoke rather of intemperance,

---

36 Taylor, *Cholera*, 23–33.
37 Bickersteth, *Parochial and Congregational Fasting*, 7–10.
38 *The Record*, 30 May, 2 June 1831.
39 Ibid., 9 June 1831; Wolffe, *Protestant Crusade*, 57–8.
40 Anderson, 'Crimean War', 215–19. In 1853 there was a recurrence of cholera and Lord Palmerston, then Home Secretary, stirred considerable debate and strong Evangelical censure when he rejected demands for a Fast Day, on the grounds that this would be a distraction from endeavours to remove the material causes of cholera: see Robert Buchanan, *The Waste Places of Great Cities* (Glasgow, 1853).
41 Stanley, 'Indian Mutiny', 279–81.

irreligion and sensuality.[42] Bishop Samuel Wilberforce recalled his evangelical roots by also regarding it as a divine judgement. This view, however, excited controversy.[43] Notable evangelical criticism came from John Cumming, minister of the Church of Scotland church at Crown Court in London, and a popular writer and speaker on prophecy and judgement. On this occasion, however, Cumming asserted that 'It is neither for prelate nor presbyter to mount the judgement-seat and pronounce judicial sentences.' He held that the Prince's death was a 'paternal' rather than 'penal' outworking of providence, insofar as it would help to dissolve the hostile feelings that risked leading to war with the United States. Furthermore he noted that, four decades on, loyal subjects of Queen Victoria no longer regarded Princess Charlotte's death as a calamity.[44]

Cumming's sermon on Prince Albert's death may well be character-ized as marking something of a watershed between a widespread evan-gelical view of national disasters as divine chastisement, and a more open-ended understanding of the workings of providence, in which seemingly negative events were viewed rather as part of mysterious divine purposes that were currently perplexing but fundamentally benevolent. Such a transition is consistent with Boyd Hilton's view of the ending of the 'Age of Atonement' around 1860, concurrently with the arrival of limited liability in business and the decline of a purely retributive penal policy.[45] Moreover, the full rigour of a traditional view of eternal punishment of sin in the afterlife began to be diluted, even among some evangelicals.[46] A further factor may have been the simple absence, in the decades after 1861, of disasters of the kind that had stirred consciousness of divine judgement in the preceding half century. There were no royal deaths of comparable psychological impact to those of Charlotte and Albert until the Duke of Clarence succumbed to influenza in 1892; cholera was now understood and under control; there were no major subsistence crises, and no sustained military conflict until 1899.

In their heyday, however, evangelical ideas of divine retribution and

[42] J. W. Brooks, *The Rod of the Almighty* (Nottingham, 1861), 13; E. H. Carr, *The Nation Admonished* (London, 1862), 15.

[43] E. P. Hood, *Words from the Pall of the Prince* (London, 1862), 23.

[44] John Cumming, *From Life to Life* (London, 1861), 18–20.

[45] Boyd Hilton, *The Age of Atonement: the Influence of Evangelicalism on Social and Economic Thought, 1785–1865* (Oxford, 1991), 255–70.

[46] D. W. Bebbington, *Evangelicalism in Modern Britain: a History from the 1730s to the 1980s* (London, 1989), 145.

chastisement of the nation are likely to have been widely diffused. Hymns are a likely channel of such popularization, for example in lines published in 1833 that seem well to reflect the insecurities of the early 1830s:

> From pestilence or foreign foes
> Or worse and deadlier wars at home,
> Let us not know what heavy woes
> On sin and godless pride may come.[47]

A hymn written for the Stockport Sunday School annual sermon on October 1847 somewhat smugly evoked the wasting of Ireland by famine, but rejoiced that Britain had been spared:

> Lord, who dost in mercy chasten
> Nations that Thy law despise
> Yet to save them, swiftly hasten
> When thou hears't their contrite sighs . . .[48]

The sense of collective responsibility for the perceived sins of the nation engendered by such lines and by the sermons and other publications surveyed in this paper should be seen as a significant factor in the development of British national consciousness. They stimulated a sense of participation in the nation as 'imagined community'[49] with patriotism and piety fuelling each other rather than appearing to be in conflict. It was a form of religious discourse that transcended denominational divisions, and enabled Nonconformists to assert their patriotism even as they affirmed their dissent from the Established Church. While perceived divine retribution could be highly divisive when it was felt to arise from national countenancing of particular groups – Roman Catholics above all – it could also be a spur to repentance and to social reconciliation.

The Open University

47 *A Collection of Hymns for General Use Submitted to the Consideration of the Members of the United Church of England and Ireland* (London, 1833), No. CXXIX.
48 *Hymns Composed for the Use of the Children of the Stockport Sunday School* (Manchester, 1848), 31.
49 Cf. Benedict Anderson, *Imagined Communities: Reflections on the Origin and Spread of Nationalism* (revised edn, London, 1991), 7.

GLADIATORS OF EXPIATION:
THE CULT OF THE MARTYRS IN THE CATHOLIC
REVIVAL OF THE NINETEENTH CENTURY

by VINCENT VIAENE

IN the spring of 1802, the Roman catacombs of Priscilla were the scene of excavations in search of Christian antiquities and martyrs' bodies. Excavations of this kind had been going on in Rome since the late sixteenth century, though they had been temporarily interrupted during the occupation by French revolutionary troops in the last years of the eighteenth century. On 25 May, the *fossores*, or diggers, who worked under the authority of a religious dignitary, the Custodian of the Relics, hit on an elaborate tomb. The profuse symbols on the slab were (erroneously) believed to indicate martyrdom: arrows, an anchor and a lash for the instruments of torture, a luxuriant palm for the martyr's eventual triumph and reward in heaven. From the garbled inscription 'LUMENA PAX TECUM FI', the name of *Filumena*, or Philomena, could be deduced.[1]

In accordance with the rules laid down by the Congregation of Indulgences and Relics, the tomb was solemnly opened in the presence of the Custodian. Next to the fragmentary mortal remains of a young woman, it contained a broken vessel, the so-called *ampolla di sangue*, believed to hold the blood of the martyr, and considered at the time as conclusive proof of martyrdom. In this instance, moreover, as was later reported, when the brown-reddish substance was carefully scraped off from the sides of the vessel and transferred to a crystal bowl, it would suddenly have lit up as if composed of jewels, 'in all the colours of the rainbow'.[2]

---

[1] In reality, the garbled nature of the inscription was proof of re-use, implying that the remains the tomb contained were not those of a martyr, nor even those of Philomena (cf. H. Leclercq, 'Filumena', *Dictionnaire d'Archéologie chrétienne* V. 2 (Paris, 1923), 1600–06). Although the false identification was ascertained in the first decade of the twentieth century, Philomena was not removed from the saints' calendar until 1961. Cf. D. Balboni, 'Filomena', *Bibliotheca Sanctorum* 5 (Rome, 1964), 796–800. On the rise of the cult of Philomena, see S. La Salvia, 'L'invenzione di un culto: S. Filomena da taumaturga a guerriera della fede', in S. Boesch Gajano and L. Sebastiani, eds, *Culto dei santi, istituzioni e classi sociali in età preindustriale* (Rome and L'Aquila, 1984), 873–956.

[2] F. di Lucia, *Relazione istorica della traslazione del sacro corpo di S. Filomena vergine e martire da Roma a Mugnano del Cardinale*, 2 vols (5th edn, Naples, 1833), 1: 80–1. Don Francesco di

It proved only the first in a long series of miracles. The (semi)-lique-faction of Philomena's blood continued in her new home, the village church of Mugnano near Naples, where her relics (enclosed, after the Italian custom, in a life-like statue) were transferred for veneration by the faithful, after they had been acquired by a renowned local preacher, Don Francesco di Lucia. In a series of visions to Suor Maria Luisa, a devout Neapolitan Dominican tertiary, Philomena revealed the romantic story of her life – she had been the virgin daughter of a Greek king coveted by the emperor Diocletian – and the excruciating details of her martyrdom.[3] There seems to be little doubt that the acts of the martyrs served as a source of inspiration to both Don Francesco and Suor Maria Luisa.[4] Coming in 1833, the revelations to Maria Luisa were a result, rather than a cause, of the saint's success. It is not irrelevant to note that Maria Luisa's visions were written down by the chaplain of the Neapolitan court, and that she went on to found her own congrega-tion, the Oblates 'dal titolo dell'Addolorata e di S. Filomena'.

Next to the liquefaction, there was also an almost embarrassing panoply of other supernatural phenomena. St Philomena could make her statue 'sweat' a kind of manna, open its eyes and even change its pose or shake off its clothes – the original pose and attire being consid-ered too awkward and shabby.[5] Above all, her intercession obtained countless healings for all kind of afflictions. Everything was carefully recorded by Don Francesco in *acta* which would have made even the more imaginative medieval hagiographers blush. But perhaps this belief in the extraordinary powers of a godmother-saint to baffle, favour and also punish her 'clients' should not astonish us too much in the context of the European deep South.

Lucia, the great advocate of devotion to Philomena in Italy, compared the liquified blood to the gem-stones of the Heavenly Jerusalem, and explained how it symbolized the virtues of the martyr; it was just that God glorified the martyr in her (or his) blood, because martyrdom had been a victory over 'the passion of the blood'. Liquefaction was of course not uncommon in Southern Italy. On the famous model of San Gennaro, the patron saint of Naples, see V. Paliotti, *San Gennaro: Storia di un culto, di un mito, dell'anima di un popolo* (Milano, 1983).

  3 The respective roles of Don Francesco and Suor Maria Luisa in 'uncovering' Philomena's life remain somewhat unclear and would warrant further research.

  4 On the reality of female martyrdom in ancient Rome, see Stuart G. Hall, 'Women among the Early Martyrs', in Diana Wood, ed., *Martyrs and Martyrologies*, SCH 30 (Oxford, 1993), 1–22; C. Jones, 'Women, Death and the Law during the Christian Persecutions', in ibid., 23–34.

  5 Don Francesco commented that it was only proper that the martyr concerned herself with the splendour of her body and her outward appearance, because it were the bodies of the martyrs which were 'the occasion and the most rich wellspring of merits, triumphs and luminous crowns': di Lucia, *Relazione*, 1: 163ff.

If the kingdom of Naples was still largely an old world, however, it was one shaken by revolution. Through the 'santi scherzi' of Philomena, through her miracles beyond number and belief, God honoured the simple and shamed the 'superbi Filosofi' who had corrupted society into silence.[6] The new virgin martyr was an eminent model of chastity, moreover, in an offensive aimed at reinvigorating popular morality after years of French occupation and civil war. Don Francesco himself founded quite an original congregation of virgin women. Though they had a highly distinctive dress, each of them continued to live in the midst of her family as a discrete keeper of the morality of her relatives, and thus of social order, by preventing her sisters from having premarital sex and her brothers, uncles and father from keeping concubines – not to mention avoiding vendettas and keeping her dowry in the family.[7] According to pope Leo XII, this was the true miracle of St Philomena.

That Philomena was a saint for the modern age was underscored after 1835, when she went on to make a lightning career on a continental scale as 'la thaumaturge du XIXe siècle', defying an age of scepticism and religious indifference. Reborn religious orders such as the Jesuits, the Redemptorists or the Dominicans, *femmes d'oeuvres* such as Pauline Jaricot, founder of the *Association pour la Propagation de la Foi*, and activist parish priests like the curé d'Ars were particularly instrumental in spreading her cult. This new generation of religious men and women was a leading protagonist of the Catholic revival sweeping over much of Europe in the middle decades of the nineteenth century, an encompassing movement typically associated with (among other things) countryside missions, 'lay apostolate', the development of a network of confessional schools and charitable *oeuvres* promoted by a new type of (mostly female) congregations, the rise of Marian devotion or the affirmation of papal authority. Against the backdrop of this wave of religious enthusiasm, the book by Francesco di Lucia was translated in several other languages and went through numerous popular editions.[8] Soon, Philomena was credited with healings in France and Belgium. Parcels of her relics were brought across the Alps (something

---

[6] Di Lucia, *Relazione*, 1: 72–4, 144; 2: 3ff.

[7] See di Lucia's most interesting 'Apologia della Verginità', appended to vol. 1 of his *Relazione*, esp. 97ff.

[8] The most important translation/adaptation was by the French Jesuit J. F. Barrelle, *Vie et Miracles de Sainte Philomène, vierge et martyre, surnommée la thaumaturge du XIXe siècle* (Brussels, 1835).

no doubt facilitated by the miraculous growth of her body about this time). Popular confraternities were founded in her honour, liberally provided with indulgences for the faithful and the souls in purgatory by pope Gregory XVI. By the mid-1840s, *Philomène* had become one of the most popular girls' names in certain regions of France, and Mugnano a place of pilgrimage for devout *oltramontani*.[9]

The astonishing cult of St Philomena was only one of the more curious sides of a general renewal of interest in the early Christian martyrs among nineteenth-century Catholics. The phenomenon has long been underestimated as just another ultramontane devotion.[10] In reality, the essential elasticity of martyr saints as models of the religious life greatly facilitated the integration of crucial new developments – such as the growing role of lay elites, of congregations with simple vows and of women – in the traditional structures of the Church.[11] Within the context of this particular volume, however, I would like to focus on the role of early Christian martyrdom as an ideological linchpin of nineteenth-century Catholicism.

The revival's fascination with the martyrs was scarcely less important for the Catholic definition of self in the modern age than its better-known attraction towards the Middle Ages. Both forms of historical dramatization were complementary. The Middle Ages provided the imagery for Catholic reform and Catholic utopia; it was the language of the future. The epic of the martyrs was a more adequate mirror for the predicament of the present. In no other instance had Christianity better demonstrated its capacity of dealing with pain. It therefore suited 'an age matured by suffering', which had learned the lesson of transience the hard way.[12] Since, historically, martyrs had been

---

9   See, next to La Salvia, 'Invenzione', above all Philippe Boutry, 'Les Saints des Catacombes. Itinéraires français d'une piété ultramontaine (1800–1881)', in *Mélanges de l'Ecole Française de Rome, Moyen Age–Temps Modernes* 91 (1979), 875–930, 895–6. The spreading of the devotion in Belgium is illustrated by Anon., *Leven van de Heilige Philomena* (Gent, 1845).

10   Philippe Boutry was the first to offer a reassessment, in the article mentioned in the previous note.

11   The Roman martyrs had fulfilled a similar function in the Counter-Reformation: the important article by Simon Ditchfield, 'An Early Christian School of Sanctity in Tridentine Rome', in idem, ed., *Christianity and Community in the West. Essays for John Bossy* (Aldershot, 2001), 183–205. A more general framework is provided by Giulia Barone, Marina Caffiero and Francesco Scorza Barcellona, eds, *Modelli di santità e modelli di comportamento*, Sacro/Santo 10 (Turin, 1994).

12   See F. R. de Chateaubriand (1768–1848), *Les Martyrs ou le Triomphe de la religion chrétienne*, ed. Maurice Regard, *Oeuvres romanesques et voyages*, Bibliothèque de la Pléiade

considered as privileged channels of divine grace, cults like that of Philomena bore witness to the thirst for reconciliation after the social body had been lacerated by decades of revolution, war and displacement. At the same time, however, the new memory of the martyrs reverberated with an obsessive fear of divine retribution, and was a rallying cry for Catholics to avert God's wrath by expiating the sins of modernity.

The origins of Philomena's career as a saint coincided with the publication in 1809 of François-René de Chateaubriand's *Les Martyrs*, one of the most influential novels of the Catholic revival. In essence, the plot of *Les Martyrs* consists of a grand religious love story, a classic romantic tear-jerker. The Christian youth Eudore falls in love with the pagan girl Cymodocée, the last descendant of Homer. Although Cymodocée converts, profane passions threaten to undermine their commitment to the 'superior passion' of Christianity. In the end, after various temptations, both embrace martyrdom, dying in each other's arms in the Colosseum.

The numerous admiring references to *Les Martyrs* in Catholic travelogues to Rome underscore its importance. Chateaubriand's novel was a crucial stepping stone towards the construction of a specifically revivalist pilgrimage, in reply to the eclectic and secularized tourism summed up by Murray's or the Baedeker. The martyrs occupied a central place in the romantic religious experience of the modern pilgrim. The approach to Rome through the desolation of the *campagna* was transformed into an initiatic itinerary along sites associated with their memory. In the Eternal City, the highlights were no longer the Forum or baroque churches, but the Colosseum, the Mamertine prison (the alleged scene of St Peter's captivity, and of a large part of *Les Martyrs*), the early Christian basilicas and, above all of course, the catacombs.[13]

Subterranean Rome had not received so much attention since its rediscovery during the Counter-Reformation, when the catacombs had been a gold-mine of relics and the stakes of a major controversy with

209–10 (Paris, 1969), 2: 62–3. The text has also been made available electronically by the Bibliothèque Nationale, Paris: http://gallica.bnf.fr/scripto. There is an English transl. by O. W. Wight, *The Martyrs* (New York, 1976). Another key work is P. Gerbet, *Esquisse de Rome chrétienne*, 3 vols (Louvain, 1844), 1: iv.

13 See in general V. Viaene, *Belgium and the Holy See from Gregory XVI to Pius IX (1831–1859). Catholic Revival, Society and Politics in 19th-Century Europe* (Leuven, Brussels and Rome, 2001), 236–79.

protestantism.[14] Ultramontane devotion interacted with the start of early Christian archaeology in reinvigorating excavations and bringing about the discovery of many new sites. The research of the Frenchman Raoul-Rochette on the art of the catacombs (*Tableau des catacombes*, 1837) was followed by the more comprehensive work of the Jesuit Giuseppe Marchi (*Monumenti delle arti cristiane primitive nella metropoli del cristianesimo*, 1844) and especially of his pupil Giovanni Battista de Rossi (*Roma sotterranea cristiana*, 1864–77).[15] Until the ground-breaking studies of de Rossi, Christian archaeology remained closely tied up with the apologetical legacy of the Counter-Reformation, out of which it was born. Catholics did not limit themselves to the sound argument that the catacombs were an authentic testimony of the early Church. More than ever, they claimed these as their own, as a convenient arsenal of archaeological artefacts vindicating the antiquity of Catholic dogma, discipline, ritual and art. Certain recesses hewn into the rock could thus be seen as the ancestors of the confessional, for instance, or the arrangement of carved seats in subterranean churches interpreted as evidence of a clerical hierarchy culminating in the papacy – an interpretation symbolically consecrated when Gregory XVI blessed the bystanders from such a presumed papal throne during his first visit to the catacombs.[16]

The transformation of the catacombs into sites of religious tourism was new, however. Considered as unusual and dangerous places to visit until the mid-1830s, they rapidly became a must-see for the Catholic traveller over the following decade. 'The Christian Pompeii' was a major focus of the classic revivalist travelogues. Monsignor Philippe Gerbet – the former intimus of Félicité de Lamennais, the champion of Catholic intransigence – devoted some of his best pages to it in *Esquisse de Rome chrétienne* (1844–51): it was the perfect emblem of the dual character of Rome as memento of the *nihil* of the earthly City and as *umbra* of the City of God.[17] The notorious ultramontane polemicist,

---

14 G. Labrot, *Roma caput mundi. L'immagine barocca della città santa 1534–1677* (Naples, 1997), *passim*; Ditchfield, 'An Early Christian School of Sanctity'.

15 On the apologetical and archaeological literature about the catacombs since the Counter-Reformation, see W. H. C. Frend, *The Archaeology of Ancient Christianity: a History* (London, 1996); Simon Ditchfield, 'Text before Trowel: Antonio Bosio's *Roma Sotterranea* Revisited', in R. N. Swanson, ed., *The Church Retrospective*, SCH 33 (Woodbridge, 1997), 343–60; G. B. de Rossi's introduction to the first volume of *Roma sotterranea*, 1–82, remains useful as well.

16 Gerbet, *Esquisse*, vol. 2 (Paris, 1851) is the best example, based for the most part on Marchi (the anecdote on Gregory XVI is on p. 209).

17 Gerbet, *Esquisse*, 1: 50–60; 'Christian Pompeii', ibid., 183.

Father Gaume, reserved a whole volume for the catacombs in his more facile and popular *Les Trois Rome* (1847).[18] By the mid-1840s, the memory of the martyrs had so well succeeded in imposing itself that it was the leitmotif in the fourteen-day itinerary outlined by the first modern Catholic travel guide to Rome, Dalmières's *Itinéraire du voyageur catholique à Rome* (1846).[19] The vogue for Christian antiquity reached a high point in the 1850s with a new round of martyrs' novels, of which Cardinal Wiseman's *Fabiola or the Church of the Catacombs* (1854) and Newman's *Callista: a Sketch of the Third Century* (1856) were the most important. *Fabiola*, in particular, went through numerous editions and was translated into many languages, popularizing much of the apologetical scholarship mentioned above.

The revivalist pilgrimage along the sites of the martyrs was a romantic encounter, meant to speak to the heart. Between the rough-hewn, immemorial walls of the Mamertine prison, in the presence of St Peter and Eudorc, the Catholic traveller could find relief from empty baroque façades.[20] Visiting the Colosseum (preferably by moonlight) or following 'the trail of blood' around the City, he could relive the horror and the heroism of martyrdom.[21] Wandering through the ruins of the *campagna romana*, he could let himself be overtaken by 'sweet melancholy', suspended between an overwhelming sense of mortality and Christian hope.[22] In the catacombs, it was not always easy to make abstraction of 'packs' of tourists, and also to overcome an instinctive fear.[23] Yet this 'secret terror' was no doubt essential to the religious shock-effect of subterranean Rome, to a ripple of 'sensations de foi'. Exploring the austere 'labyrinth of death' by torchlight, the pilgrim could feel lost amidst 'the desert of time'. Progressing along mortal

18   Mgr Gaume, *Les Trois Rome. Journal d'un voyage en Italie*, 4 vols (Paris, 1847–8). I used the second edition of 1857.
19   Other travelogues referred to in this essay are: [C. de Lagranville], *Souvenirs de voyage, ou lettres d'une voyageuse malade*, 2 vols (Paris and Lille, 1836); E. de Beauffort, *Souvenirs d'Italie, par un Catholique* (Paris, 1838); and the unpublished 'Journal d'un voyage en Italie, 1847' by Victor Dechamps (Redemptorist archives, KADOC, Leuven). On the authors, see Viaene, *Belgium and the Holy See, passim*.
20   Dechamps, 'Journal'; Lagranville, *Souvenirs*, 1: 254–5.
21   Gaume, *Trois Rome*, 1: 369–88; 4: 88; Lagranville, *Souvenirs*, 2: 43–4.
22   Gerbet, *Esquisse*, 1: 7ff. ; Gaume, *Trois Rome*, 4: 165; Lagranville, *Souvenirs*, 2: 189–91. The association between melancholy and the *campagna* was first made by Chateaubriand in his *Lettre à M. de Fontanes* (1804).
23   Dalmières, Curé du Pont Saint-Esprit, *Itinéraire du voyageur catholique à Rome, en passant par Gênes, Pise, Florence, Assise et Lorette, suivi d'un pélerinage au tombeau de saint Janvier, à Naples* (Avignon, 1846), 177, 167; D. Raoul-Rochette, *Tableau des Catacombes de Rome* (Brussels, 1837), 85.

remains, he could observe what Gerbet called 'ce combat entre une mort et une mort' – all the stages of decomposition of the skeleton, until the bones were reduced to an outline of dust effaced by a mere breath. Before this 'end of the history of man in this world', he could ponder the significance of the 'sacred love' which was the wellspring of martyrdom.[24]

But beyond the thrills of Christian melancholy and vicarious sacrifice, the epic of the early Church was the central thread which made the patchwork of Rome's monuments into a seamless garment of Christian remembrance. It transformed the revivalist pilgrimage into a coherent tale of retribution, repentance and reconciliation, signed by the hand of divine Providence – a parable for the Catholic experience in the modern age. Les Martyrs was again seminal in this respect. Eudore and Cymodocée, the Christian soldier and the pagan virgin, are the victims chosen by God to expiate the sins of paganism and the short-comings of the early Church, thus ensuring the triumph of the Cross. The self-sacrifice is accepted at the end of the novel, in the arena of the Colosseum, when Eudore gives Cymodocée a ring drenched in his martyr's blood, exclaiming: 'c'est ici l'autel, l'église, le lit nuptial'.[25] Rome is redeemed and Christian civilization is born.

Half a century later, Cardinal Wiseman would harp upon the same string in his Fabiola, where the sacrifice of the martyrs Agnes and Syra operates the grace of the conversion of the occidental heathen Fabiola and the oriental heathen Orontius. In between, the idea that the voluntary sacrifice of the martyrs was the pivot of the history of Rome and, by extension, of the history of Western civilization became a commonplace of the travelogues codifying the modern pilgrimage. The nodal point of the City as a stage of Providence was the triangle formed by the Arch of Titus (at the far end of the Forum), the Colosseum and the Arch of Constantine. The Arch of Titus, erected by that Emperor to commemorate the suppression of the great Jewish revolt of AD 71, was an unwitting vindication of Daniel's prophecy about the destruction of the Temple. It bore witness to God's punishment of 'deicide' Judaism, as the ruins of the Colosseum signalled His punishment of pagan Rome, the second great rival of Christianity.[26] Transformed by the

[24] Gerbet, Esquisse, 1: 112–14, 184ff. and Chateaubriand, Martyrs, 440; similar emotions in Lagranville, Souvenirs, 1: 321–2; Dechamps, 'Journal'; Dalmières, Itinéraire, 176.
[25] Chateaubriand, Martyrs, 494; see also ibid., 105ff., 139ff., 444, 467.
[26] The most extensive version of this topos is in Gaume, Trois Rome, 1: 364–8; other examples in Chateaubriand, Lettre à Fontanes, in Oeuvres romanesques et voyages, 2: 1483 (but

popes into a monument in honour of the martyrs, Gerbet wrote that, in old age, the Colosseum had become a penitent.[27] The Arch of Constantine (built after the famous victory over Maxentius in 312) symbolized the triumph of Christianity, considered as a direct fruit of the martyrs' sacrifice.[28] Constantine's legions were but the rear-guard of the martyrs, 'gladiators' of faith who had been besieging pagan Rome for centuries from their underground metropolis.[29] They had been nothing less than 'co-redeemers of the world', their blood 'a continued effusion of the blood of Christ'.[30] Offering propitiation for the ceaseless 'profanation of the blood' by paganism – in sacrifice to idols and in sexual excess – the 'stream of [their] blood' purified 'the corruption that had penetrated the social order into its most intimate recesses'.[31] By the same token, it was the seed of faith; when the martyrs offered up their hearts as 'altars of sacrifice', they destined Rome to become 'the heart of Christendom'.[32]

The revival's vision of the world historical significance of early Christian martyrdom was a histrionic metaphor for its own providential role in a society believed to be wrecked by revolution and hollowed out by 'modern paganism'. The ills undermining the Roman Empire were readily recognizable to the nineteenth-century Catholic. The villain of *Les Martyrs*, the sophist Hierocles, was a transparent image of the eighteenth-century *philosophe* and his successors.[33] Philomena and other martyrs – the sensational story of their lives no less than their intercession – would be a powerful antedote against the 'poison' of 'bad books', popularizing the scepticism and the libertinism of the Enlightenment.[34] The debauchery of the ancient Romans mirrored modern 'sensualism', contrasting sharply with the virginity ascribed to almost all martyrs. According to Dom Prosper Guéranger, one of the first

without the anti-semitic odour, rather the contrary, see *Martyrs*, 172); Dechamps, 'Journal'; Wiseman, *Fabiola*, 42.

27 Gerbet, *Esquisse*, 2: 366–7.
28 See the last two pages of *Les Martyrs*, 498–9.
29 Gerbet, *Esquisse*, 1: 21, 115.
30 Gaume, *Trois Rome*, 4: 470; Beauffort, *Souvenirs*, 184. See already Chateaubriand, *Martyrs*, 489; J. de Maistre, *Les Soirées de Saint-Pétersbourg* (Antwerp, 1821), 2: 332ff. The idea goes back to Origen.
31 Beauffort, *Souvenirs*, 185; Lagranville, *Souvenirs*, 1: 68–9.
32 Chateaubriand, *Martyrs*, 443; Gerbet, *Esquisse*, 260.
33 Chateaubriand, *Martyrs*, 167.
34 Barrelle, *Vie et Miracles*, 46–7; the martyr St Alenia, whose relics were brought to Liège by the Redemptorists in 1843, was also to be invoked against bad books, see [V. Dechamps], *Translation de Sainte Alénie martyre* (Liège, 1843), 32.

advocates of the 'new saints' of the catacombs, the cult of the virgin-martyrs was a rampart against 'the frenzied instinct of pleasure' culminating in the free sex of the socialist *phalanstères*.[35] In ancient Rome, the political counterpart of the 'idolatry of the world' had been the divinization of the Emperor. According to the Belgian Redemptorist Victor Dechamps, future Archbishop of Mechelen, the 'pagan theocracy' of the Roman Empire prefigured the modern doctrine of the omnipotence of the State, ineluctable terminus of liberalism and socialism alike. As guardians of the sanctuary of conscience, the martyrs had died for civilization, and offered a stirring model for the political battles of the Church in the nineteenth century.[36]

The political subtext of early Christian martyrdom was in fact no small part of its attraction to the militant Catholicism of the revival. Whether invoked against the encroachments of the modern State or against socialism, the saints of the catacombs were eminently anti-revolutionary. In this respect, it is worth noting that the memory of the early Christian martyrs tended to coincide with and to reinforce the memory of the (religious) victims made by the French Revolution;[37] the (imaginary) millions of the former (11 million according to Gaume, of which 2.5 million in Rome alone)[38] compensated, incidentally, for the less staggering numbers of the latter. In a sense, the modern Catholic 'myth' of the martyrs was a long gloss on Joseph de Maistre's idea that the martyr-king Louis XVI had lifted France from the abyss of revolution....[39]

The trauma of the guillotine helps explain the extraordinary insistence of nineteenth-century Catholics, especially in France, on the salvific power of 'le sang des martyrs'. Blood, of course, had been considered the supreme seal of Christian martyrdom, 'the testimony of passion' (in the words of Gaudentius), since Antiquity. The historical fact that the early Christians collected and venerated the blood shed by their martyrs was the main argument for the thesis that the vessels outside many tombs in the catacombs served precisely this purpose.

[35] P. Gueranger, *Histoire de Sainte Cécile vierge Romaine et martyre* (Paris, 1853), iv–vii.

[36] Dechamps, 'Journal'; see also Wiseman, *Fabiola*, 145; *Le Livre de Sainte Theudosie, recueil complet des documents publiés sur cette sainte, cérémonies et processions qui ont eu lieu pour la translation de ses reliques de Rome à Amiens*, ed. P. Gerbet (Amiens, 1853), 138.

[37] Chateaubriand, *Martyrs*, 52; Dechamps, 'Journal'; *Livre de Sainte Theudosie*, 145.

[38] Gaume, *Trois Rome*, 4: 506. In his article 'Ampoules (de sang)', in *Dictionnaire d'Archéologie chrétienne* I. 2 (Paris, 1907), 1747–78, 1765, H. Leclercq suggested a maximum of 15,000 for Rome.

[39] De Maistre, *Considérations sur la France* (London, 1797).

The controversy surrounding the *ampolla di sangue* as the decisive mark of a martyr's tomb naturally reinforced the focus on their blood.[40] The multiple resonances of the blood theme lay bare the osmosis of religious and socio-political motifs in the revivalist cult of the martyrs. It is interesting to note that Francesco di Lucia, who still stood with one leg in the world of the Ancien Régime, makes much less of the blood theme than his more modern co-religionists from the north-west European heartland of the Catholic revival.[41]

The language of blood is first and foremost the language of propitiatory sacrifice in the Judeo-Christian tradition. The cult of the martyrs carries us right to the heart of the peculiar victimizing ethos of the Catholic revival. As Auguste Comte (1798–1857) and John Stuart Mill (1806–73) were laying the foundations of sociology as a science, Catholics reconsidered penance in the light of the all-encompassing social change they had witnessed in their lifetime. The old belief that one could atone for the sins of others was transformed into the notion that the individual could do penance for the transgressions of society as a whole. Joseph de Maistre outlined this bedrock of ultramontane spirituality, the twin axiom of 'the reversibility of merit' and 'the substitution of expiatory suffering', in his *Soirées de Saint-Petersbourg* (1820).[42] Like the martyrs of their dreams, revivalist Catholics were bent on expiating the social sins of a godless society. Their mission was to sanctify modernity in spite of itself, warding off the 'new barbarians' of social revolution, a nineteenth-century version of the providential 'lesson of ruins'.[43]

Blood is the language of fidelity. It establishes a bond; it suggests a debt to be paid. As Gerbet concluded his evocation of the catacombs, if the tangible confrontation with the martyrs could not break through 'le respect humain' and shake religious indifference, nothing else would.[44] Masters in the Christian school of suffering, they steeled the

---

40 For an overview of this controversy (which seems never to have been formally closed), see the introduction by A. Ferrua in his edition of G. B. de Rossi (1822–1894), *Sulla questione del vaso di sangue: memoria inedita con introduzione storica e appendici di documenti inediti*, Studi di Antichità Cristiana 18 (Vatican City, 1944), vii–xcix; and the essay by Leclercq on 'Ampoules (de sang)'.

41 For di Lucia, the martyrs' blood is a 'small theatre' of the martyrs' virtues, inviting the faithful to follow their example: *Relazione*, 1: 74, 144. Likewise, his virgin followers were not expiating the sins of society in their prayers and penitential exercises, but rather their own sins: 'Apologia', *passim*.

42 See above, n. 30.

43 Viaene, *Belgium and the Holy See*, 185ff., 89.

44 Gerbet, *Esquisse*, 1: 184.

nineteenth-century Catholic for a life of abnegation and self-sacrifice, whether in sexual continence, in mystical 'reparation' to the Sacred Heart or in good works.[45] Blood speaks of fertility. Self-sacrifice did not come without the promise of a rich (spiritual) harvest. Revivalist piety was never short on consolation, as it was never short on trepidation. The martyrdom of innocent victims was an inexhaustible well of grace. The romantic authors who revived their memory waxed lyrical in metaphors of fecundity. Chateaubriand compared the Colosseum to the marriage bed, as we have seen; Gerbet sang about the 'funerary Eden' of the catacombs; Wiseman extolled the 'stream [of] Christian blood [which] watered the paradise of the New Law'.[46] It is significant in this context that the more popular among the 'new saints' extracted from the catacombs were generally women. Philomena's first miracle in Mugnano was to bring rain; in other instances too, women martyrs were no less invoked against bad harvests than against the 'bad books' spread by proud men.[47]

The language of blood, finally, is the language of kinship, of heredity and, in modern times, of nationhood. The Roman martyrs were the ancestors of the Catholic 'family of God', the founding fathers (and mothers) of the 'sacred nation'.[48] They had always been there, reconciling God with their spiritual progeny. In the cult of martyrs' relics, the Church elevated the natural and irrepressible 'instinct of origins' into a universal bond of love.[49] This was a conscious reply of Catholic traditionalism to the 'pantheistic' cult of the nation and its 'great men' advanced by liberalism. The crowds thronging to venerate martyrs' relics underscored the inanity of all civil religion.[50] The imagined blood tie with the martyrs tapped into traditionalist discourse in another sense as well. On earth as in heaven, revivalist Catholicism envisaged society as an extended family, consisting of concentric circles of organic units, natural communities. The people and its natural patrician or

---

[45] Chateaubriand, *Martyrs*, 446; Gerbet, *Esquisse*, 1: 186–7; Barrelle, *Vie et Miracles*, 253ff.; *Neuvaine en l'honneur de Sainte Philomène* (Lille, 1840), 25–6.

[46] Chateaubriand, *Martyrs*, 494; *Livre de Sainte Theudosie*, 146 (a poem by Gerbet); Wiseman, *Fabiola*, 111.

[47] Barrelle, *Vie et Miracles*, 56; *Livre de Sainte Theudosie*, 131; other examples in Boutry, 'Saints des Catacombes', 902–3.

[48] Gerbet, *Esquisse*, 1: 74.

[49] Ibid., 2: 188–90.

[50] *Livre de Sainte Theudosie*, 178 (oration by Mgr Pie), 202ff. (article from Veuillot's *Univers*); and, more moderate, Gerbet, *Esquisse*, 2: 226.

aristocratic leaders were to join hands against the bourgeois upstarts who had disrupted this order. Without making too much of this, it is hard not to notice the echo of this ambivalent populism in the romantic production on the martyrs. Much emphasis was put on the equality of the catacombs, or on the 'plebeian' character of early Christian art;[51] yet many of the more famous martyrs were noble in more than one sense – from the embattled aristocrats Eudore and Cymodocée through the princess Philomena to the tight-knit group of 'recusant' patricians in Wiseman's *Fabiola*.[52]

Mesmerized by the 'noble blood' of the martyrs, Catholic pilgrims to Rome sent and took their relics home in increasing numbers. Individual travellers often returned 'loaded with relics like a donkey', in the words of one of them.[53] More spectacular, however, was the solemn translation of 'sacred bodies' like that of Philomena, often enclosed in life-like wax statues dressed after the fashion of the Roman Empire. Between 1814 and 1847, 2,500 of them were asked, and sent, for veneration to the four corners of the globe.[54]

One of the most important translations of martyrs from Rome was that of St Theodosia to Amiens in 1853. Not much more was known about this woman, whose remains were found in the catacombs of St Hermes in 1842, than about Philomena. Her tombstone simply mentioned that she was a pious and loving wife, and that she hailed from the region of Amiens. This information was enough to ensure her translation, and her elevation into a revivalist model. The stagemasters of the event were, next to the local cleric canon Dumont, Gerbet and Bishop Salinis, one of the closest associates of the radically ultramontane Louis Veuillot. The act was part and parcel of the romanization forced through by Salinis in his diocese. But beyond that, it was meant to have a national and even a European dimension – and so it did. An estimated 150,000 faithful attended, together with the Veuillot brothers and twenty-eight bishops, archbishops and cardinals, representing the *fine fleur* of the ultramontane clergy from France, Belgium and the British Isles.

The ceremony subsumed many of the themes developed above; because of the context of reaction in these early years of the Second

---

51 Gerbet, *Esquisse*, 1: 134–5, 149ff.; Raoul-Rochette, *Tableau*, 24.
52 For the recusant echo, see notably Wiseman, *Fabiola*, 67.
53 Beauffort, *Souvenirs*, 271.
54 Boutry, 'Saints des Catacombes'; idem, 'La Restauration de Rome', unpublished Ph.D. thesis, University of Paris–IV, 1994, 2: 153–97.

Empire, the political stakes of the devotion to the martyrs became more explicit than usual. The central part of the translation was an imposing procession; triumphal arches made for the occasion, costly draperies, saintly 'tableaux vivants' and the illumination of the city added to its lustre. There was an ascending order in the procession, from the parish priests and the common people through the religious congregations and the higher clergy to the princes of the Church at the end (the thorny question of the place of the notables was circumvented by having them join the procession hors catégorie, after it started). Towering above them all were huge statues of the saints of the diocese, with their relics. The stately, hierarchical rhythm of this choreography was punctuated yet softened by the hundreds of colourful banners (one for every parish, congregation or charity); the alternation of Gregorian chant and musical chapels must have had much the same effect.[55]

The relics of Theodosia were the culminating point of the procession both physically and symbolically. Their presence in the city was very welcome at a time when Amiens faced a harsh winter and the possibility of famine, a contingency which explains to a great extent the enthusiasm of the crowd.[56] The relics and Theodosia's tombstone were touched with thousands of scapulars and medals.[57] The need for protection and mediation was the perennial anthropological basis upon which the 'new saints' built their home. Popular devotion was encapsulated within a revivalist world-view. The trajectory of the procession enacted the providential theory outlined in Catholic travelogues: starting from a chapel which had been decorated as a catacomb for the occasion, the shrine proceeded under triumphal arches in ancient Roman and gothic styles to the Cathedral, one of the greatest monuments of medieval Christendom. 'The cathedral is the heir to the catacombs', in Gerbet's words.[58] Just as the sacrifice of the martyrs ushered in medieval utopia, the sacrificial zeal of the revival would build 'a new future with the debris of the past'.[59] The translation of Theodosia was a solemn public act of 'reparation' clearing the way for this silver age. The French Revolution had dispersed the relics of the saints as it had dissolved the social body. The return of the 'corps saints' gave the signal

55 *Livre de Sainte Theudosie*, 39–78.
56 Ibid., 120–1, 130–1.
57 Ibid., 34, 83.
58 Ibid., 111.
59 Ibid., 15–16.

for a recomposition of the 'social kingdom of Christ', prefigured in the procession.[60] With its numerous representatives of the clergy and of all Catholic schools and charitable institutions of the diocese, the procession was a show of strength at a time when Napoleon III was hailed as a new Charlemagne. The neo-gothic reliquary of Theodosia showed the Virgin Mary crushing a dragon with seven heads, representing Protestantism, Jansenism, rationalism, secret societies, socialism, anarchy and atheism.[61] The scenography of the procession highlighted the role of women and of charity in achieving this anti-revolutionary type of social reconciliation. Women transmitted the faith at a time when men had forsaken it;[62] religious women were also the leading actors in 'the martyrdom of charity'.[63] The instrumentalization of the language of victimhood reached an excruciatingly low point in Bishop Salinis's crass comparison of the money of the benefactor with the blood of the martyr.[64]

Functioning like a display of the Revival, the procession at once paraded the very social order it hoped to achieve. Bundling 'all classes of society' in a common effort, it was 'a vivid image of ancient times'. Assembling past (through the saints) and present generations of 'the great Christian family' around the primeval mother of the Roman catacombs, it represented the chain of tradition which would hold back revolution. The chain was unbroken because it was anchored in papal authority. Theodosia was a 'kiss of love' from Pius IX; the devotion to the martyrs sealed the quintessential union between the Catholic revival and the papacy.[65]

* * *

In holding up Theodosia for veneration, the enthusiasts of the martyrs were not only stretching the limits of exploitation, but also those of credulity. Her banal tombstone mentioned all kinds of things, save her martyrdom. The fuss made about her by radical ultramontanes triggered an internal Catholic debate about the *ampolla di sangue*, which marked the coming of age of Christian archaeology and ended with a

---

[60] Ibid., 130.
[61] Ibid., 184–5.
[62] Ibid., 172ff. (oration by Mgr Pie).
[63] Ibid., 52–3; see also 49. The oration by Cardinal Wiseman, 166ff., developed the same theme.
[64] Ibid., 84.
[65] Ibid., 42, 122, 78, 93–6, 118–19, 139, 180.

Roman embargo on further translations from the catacombs.[66] If the number of relics was no longer growing, the cult of the martyrs was unbroken; in a sense, the brake of a mature archaeological criticism made such devotion stronger, less vulnerable to outside attack. It would not end until the world descended from the revival imploded. The removal of the relics of the 'new saints' of the nineteenth century during the 1960s signalled a turning point. Dust returned to dust. At best, the remains of those early Christians now rest among the old paper of diocesan archives, sealed away in the green boxes that are the tombs of history[67] – mute testimony to the religious passions of another age.

F. W. O. Vlaanderen
Catholic University of Leuven

---

[66] The critics – an international band of courageous, mostly liberal-Catholic scholars – demonstrated that the vessels (whatever they may have contained) were no *certain* sign of a martyr's tomb. The Roman retreat, effective from the second half of the 1850s onwards, became official in 1881. Cf. Ferrua, *Sulla questione del vaso di sangue*, xli ff.

[67] This, at least, is where the author found the 'relics' brought to the Archdiocese of Mechelen in the nineteenth century.

VÖLKNER AND MOKOMOKO:
'SYMBOLS OF RECONCILIATION' IN
AOTEAROA, NEW ZEALAND*

by ALLAN K. DAVIDSON

O N 2 March 1865, the Revd Carl Sylvius Völkner, a Church Missionary Society (CMS) missionary, was hanged from a willow tree close to his own church and mission station at Opotiki in the Bay of Plenty, New Zealand. John Hobbs, who had arrived as a Methodist missionary in New Zealand in 1823, reported on 'the very barbarous Murder of one of the best Missionaries in New Zealand' and noted that Völkner's death marked 'a New Era in the history of this country'.[1] Völkner was the first European missionary of any denonomination to be killed in New Zealand since missionary work began in 1814.[2]

The events surrounding Völkner's death and the reasons for his hanging are complex and their interpretation shaped by varying perspectives. Some have seen Völkner's death as murder or martyrdom, while others, accusing him of acting as a spy or government informant have described his death as an execution. William Colenso, a former CMS missionary, wrote in 1871

> that although the Government received a very large amount of written information concerning the death of Mr Volkner (I having read more than twenty letters and statements, written and signed by a great number of persons, European and Maori, many of whom were resident on the spot), scarcely two of them agree, save in his having been killed: indeed, some of them strangely contradicted each other.[3]

---

* Note on style: most Maori words in this essay, following the current New Zealand convention, are reproduced in ordinary type. In quotations, Völkner's name appears without an umlaut as per the original source.

[1] John Hobbs to the Secretaries of the Wesleyan Missionary Society, Auckland, 7 April 1865: Auckland, St John's College Library, MS MET 003/4/33.

[2] Two Maori missionaries, Kereopa and Te Manihera, were killed on 12 March 1847. Ken Booth, ed., *For All the Saints: a Resource for the Commemorations of the Calendar* (Hastings, 1996), 85–9.

[3] William Colenso, *Fiat Justitia: being a Few Thoughts Respecting the Maori Prisoner Kereopa, now in the Napier Gaol, Awaiting his Trial for Murder . . .* (repr. Christchurch, 1999), 11.

Carl Völkner was born in Germany in 1819 and had come to New Zealand in 1849 under the auspices of the North German Missionary Society. He was accepted as a CMS lay catechist in 1852 and married Emma Lanfear in 1854, the sister of another CMS missionary. Völkner became a naturalized New Zealander in 1857. Bishop William Williams ordained him a deacon in 1860 and a priest in 1861. He was stationed at Opotiki in August 1861, where he gained a reputation as a hard-working, pious missionary among Whakatohea people, building with their help a school and a church.[4]

The influence and respect which missionaries gained among Maori were seriously eroded in the 1860s as a result of the increasing settler pressure both on Maori land and their rangatiratanga or sovereignty. The outbreak of war in Taranaki in 1860 and in the Waikato and eastern parts of the North Island from 1863 contributed to the breakdown of trust between many Maori and Pakeha (Europeans) in general, and between Maori and missionaries in particular. Maori, who were defending their own land and rights, were defined as rebels, leading the French Catholic bishop, J. B. Pompallier, to remark about Wiremu Tamihana in 1864 to the Governor, Sir George Grey, that 'a great many natives like that chief fought not from the vice of rebellion, but from sentiments of race, of nationality, and, in their mind, justice'.[5]

While some notable Anglican missionaries and Church leaders such as Archdeacon Octavius Hadfield, Bishop Selwyn and Sir William Martin tried to defend Maori and their rights, gaining from their Pakeha detractors the derogatory sobriquet 'philo-Maori',[6] increasingly throughout the conflict Maori disowned the missionary Christianity which they had accepted during the last thirty years. Selwyn's role as a chaplain to the British military forces, despite his altruistic motives, as he somewhat mournfully noted in 1865 after the death of Völkner, 'has destroyed my influence with many. . . . This has thrown me back in native estimation, more, I fear, than my remaining years of life will enable me to recover.'[7]

The emergence in the context of conflict of Pai Marire, which

---

[4] Evelyn Stokes, 'Carl Sylvius Völkner', *Dictionary of New Zealand Biography* [hereafter *DNZB*], 5 vols (Wellington and Auckland, 1990–2000), 1: 566–7.

[5] Cited in Evelyn Stokes, *Wiremu Tamihana Rangatira* (Wellington, 2002), 389.

[6] See Earle Howe, *Caught in the Crossfire: a Revisionist Approach to Philo-Maori in New Zealand History, 1850–1870* (Auckland, 2000).

[7] H. W. Tucker, *Memoir of the Life and Episcopate of George Augustus Selwyn*, 2 vols (London, 1879), 2: 206–7.

combined political, military and religious motivation and objectives, provided many Maori with an alternative to missionary Christianity. Bishop William Williams, who had been a missionary in New Zealand since 1826, reported to the CMS that a Maori messenger from Opotiki, after Völkner's death,

> Addressing me [. . .] said, 'We received our Christianity from you formerly, and now we give it you back again, having found some better way, by which we may be able to keep possession of our country'.[8]

Pai Marire originated in Taranaki in 1862 under the leadership of Te Ua Haumene. Following a vision, he believed that he was God's chosen prophet and commanded 'to cast off the yoke of the Pakeha and promised the restoration of the birthright of Israel (the Maori people) in the land of Canaan (New Zealand).'[9] Pai Marire, which meant 'good and peaceful', was seen by Te Ua as purifying Christianity. The Hauhau, the Pai Marire followers, were caught up in the Waikato War. Their use of the preserved heads of soldiers in their distinctive rituals and their dancing and chanting around the Niu pole or mast contributed to the growing Pakeha hysterical reaction. Two emissaries, Patara Raukatauri and Kereopa Te Rau, were sent by Te Ua in December 1864 to Turanga on the East Coast. Their arrival and presence at Opotiki in February 1865 were a significant catalyst in the events which resulted in Völkner's death and Te Ua's peaceable intentions were betrayed. William Williams, struggling to come to terms with Völkner's death, dismissed Pai Marire as a 'fanatical delusion . . . clearly a device of Satan'.[10] Pai Marire, however, like all new religious movements, had its own internal logic and rationality which made sense to its followers and gave them hope of deliverance from Pakeha oppression.[11]

Whakatohea, the people among whom Völkner ministered, were caught up in the inter-tribal tensions provoked by war. While many, according to Völkner, in mid-1863 initially opted for neutrality, they were increasingly drawn in 1864 into the war on the side of the followers of the King movement against the Crown and their tradi-

8   *Church Missionary Record* X.9 (September 1865), 262.
9   Lyndsay Head, 'Te Ua Haumene', *DNZB* 1: 512.
10   *Church Missionary Record* X.9 (September 1865), 261.
11   Bronwyn Elsmore, *Like Them That Dream: the Maori and the Old Testament* (Auckland, 2002), 123–31; *Mana from Heaven: a Century of Maori Prophets in New Zealand* (Auckland, 1999), 168–84.

tional enemies the Arawa confederation.[12] Paul Clark points to the decline in economic prosperity for the Whakatohea people in the 1860s and the impact of typhoid and measles and death in late 1864 and early 1865 which contributed to the context of social dislocation and instability in which Völkner was killed.[13] The violent murder in late 1864 of the Whakatohea chief, Te Aporotanga, by a rival tribe, and the 'vice-regal inaction' were also seen as a cause of complaint against the government Völkner represented.[14]

Questions had also been simmering away for some time about Völkner's role in the removal of the Catholic priest, Joseph Garavel, from Opotiki. Völkner had reported to the governor that a letter from Wiremu Tamihina was distributed by Garavel requesting Whakatohea to support the Kingites against the Crown.[15] Garavel was seemingly unaware of the letter's contents, but according to Völkner it had 'unsettled the natives at Opotiki and up the coast more than any they have had.'[16] Garavel in turn 'accused Volkner of being an informer of the Government.' It is possible that Garavel's conduct contributed to his removal to Australia on 1 August 1864. The rumour that Garavel had been hanged confirmed for some Whakatohea their doubts about Völkner.[17]

Völkner put himself in an ambiguous relationship with Whakatohea by both acting as their minister and providing information about their political disposition. Seven letters by Völkner to Sir George Grey between 13 January and 26 February 1864 clearly indicate that he was acting as what he conceived of as a loyal informant, but in the context of war could be seen by opponents as spying. Völkner also made five visits to Auckland between April 1864 and March 1865 when it is likely he passed on further information. While Völkner believed it was his 'duty' to provide information on 'the movement of the natives', he recognized 'that it would interfere with my future usefulness in the

12 Paul Clark, 'Hauhau': the Pai Marire Search for Maori Identity (Auckland, 1975), 32–3. See also James Belich, The New Zealand Wars and the Victorian Interpretation of Racial Conflict (Auckland, 1986), 128, 167, 194.
13 Clark, 'Hauhau', 33.
14 Ibid., 36.
15 Dom Felice Vaggioli, History of New Zealand and its Inhabitants, transl. John Crockett (Dunedin, 2000), 242–3.
16 C. S. Völkner to Sir George Grey, Opotiki, 13 January 1864, in Earle Howe, Bring Me Justice (Auckland, 1991), 44.
17 E. R. Simmons, In Cruce Salus. A History of the Diocese of Auckland 1848–1980 (Auckland, 1982), 73.

cause in which I am engaged' if this 'were publicly known'. He requested the governor to receive future letters 'as private communications to yourself'.[18] The role of missionaries as government informants was not unusual,[19] but given the growing volatility of the political and social context in Opotiki Völkner made himself very vulnerable. In one letter Völkner included a drawing of the Maori fortification at Rangiaowhia a month before it was attacked.[20]

Völkner's return in Samuel Levy's schooner to Opotiki on 1 March 1865, where Te Ua's emissaries were stirring up anti-missionary and anti-European sentiments, can be seen, given the warnings that his life was in danger, as either an indication of his devotion to duty, or his lack of appreciation of the unstable situation. He was accompanied by T.S. Grace, another CMS missionary, who distanced himself from the war and military chaplaincy and was seen as a champion of Maori self-government. Grace and Völkner, along with other Pakeha, were taken prisoners on landing. The Levy brothers, who were traders in Opotiki, as Jews were given a special status by the Hauhau and released. While Grace's life was in serious danger it is significant that Völkner and not Grace was killed.

No first-hand written accounts of Völkner's death survive. The various letters and documents referred to by Colenso depend on information supplied by eyewitnesses. Exactly who was responsible for hanging Völkner is disputed. What is not in dispute, however, is that after he was hanged Völkner was beheaded and both his head and body subject to various indignities.[21] Völkner was tried posthumously on the 5 March by Patara, one of Te Ua's emissaries. Grace, who was present at the trial, reported that three charges were brought against Völkner to

---

[18] C. S. Völkner to Sir George Grey, Opotiki, 16 February 1864, in Howe, *Bring Me Justice*, 48.

[19] John Whiteley, a Methodist missionary who was killed by Maori in 1869, and John Morgan, a CMS missionary, both corresponded with C. W. Richmond while he was Colonial Treasurer and Minister of Native Affairs giving information about Maori activities. See *The Richmond-Atkinson Papers*, ed. G. H. Scholefield, 2 vols (Wellington, 1960), 1: 292–4, 372–3, 389–90, 455–7.

[20] Völkner's letters, including the drawing, are reproduced in Howe, *Bring Me Justice*, 35, 43–9.

[21] Different accounts talk about such things as Völkner's headless body being put in a cesspit and attacked by dogs before it was buried outside his church. His eyes were taken out and swallowed by Kereopa, his head placed on the pulpit inside his church and later preserved in accordance with Pai Marire custom. While these reported actions confirmed Pakeha views of Hauhau fanaticism they need to be seen against the background of Maori traditional treatment of enemies and within the context of the rejection of missionary Christianity and Pakeha authority.

justify his death. The first related to Völkner 'going to Auckland as a spy for the Government'. The second charge, which Grace records 'broke down', possibly reflects the Völkner/Garavel, Protestant/ Catholic tensions, as it was to do with a cross having been found in Völkner's house. The third charge was that Völkner had 'returned to Opotiki after having been told to remain away'. Patara, who was not present when Völkner was killed, according to Grace 'tried to make it appear that he should have stayed away because he knew we were at war, but he did not say that he justified the murder; I think he regretted it'.[22]

A letter to the government dated 6 March 1865 in the name of four Maori tribes, including Whakatohea, indicated that Völkner had 'been crucified according to the laws of the New Canaan, in the same manner as it has been ordained by the Parliament of England, that the guilty man be crucified', that is by hanging. New Canaan represented the institution of the Pai Marire kingdom as an alternative to the British Crown. General charges were raised, the first against 'the deception practised upon our Island by the Church',[23] and two against the conduct of the war at Rangiriri and Rangiaowhia where Maori women were killed. The call to Maori to give up their guns led to the response, 'You catch Maories; I also kill the Pakehas. You crucify the Maories, and I also crucify the Pakehas'. The freeing of Grace was made conditional on the release of Maori prisoners.[24]

Grace was able to escape after sixteen days with the help of Samuel Levy and H.M.S. *Eclipse*. Levy's account of what happened at Opotiki resulted in the newspapers seeing him as a hero.[25] In contrast, Grace was seen as ungrateful, for his initial public thanks included everyone who helped with his rescue except Levy. While Grace attempted to correct this with a subsequent letter, his own account of what happened at Opotiki contained very critical remarks on Levy's behaviour during his capture.[26] The *New Zealand Herald* led a pro-settler, anti philo-Maori campaign. They pointed to Levy's account and told their readers to

---

[22] 'Mr Grace's Imprisonment at Opotiki', *Appendices to the Journals of the House of Representatives* (1865), A–5, 24 [hereafter *AJHR*].

[23] The Committee of Ngatiawa, Whakatohea, Urewera, Taranaki to the Government, Auckland, Opotiki, Place of Canaan, 6 March 1865: *AJHR* (1865), E–5, 9.

[24] Ibid., 10.

[25] *New Zealand Herald*, 20 and 23 March 1865 [hereafter *NZH*].

[26] *Daily Southern Cross*, 22 and 23 March 1865; 'Mr Grace's Imprisonment at Opotiki', *AJHR* (1865), A–5, 24–31.

place it in the hands of every child capable of reading and understanding, and ... tell them that these men who hold these accursed
doctrines, who perform these horrible rites, who drink the warm
blood and eat the flesh of murdered Europeans, are the men who
have been held up at Exeter Hall as better Christians than the colo-
nists themselves.[27]

While Völkner, the loyal missionary, was idealised as 'a really Christian
and pious man', and Levy, the Jewish trader, was described as having
'given his property to save the lives of others', Grace, the friend of the
Maori, was denounced as having 'for years past ... taken an active share
in bringing about the state of disaffection and disloyalty which has
ended in the present rebellion.'[28] In contrast, Grace pointed to 'the
insidious encroachment of colonization which throws missionary effort
into a wrong light, and makes us objects of suspicion'.[29]

On 2 September 1865, the governor issued a 'Proclamation of Peace'
in which he declared that he was 'sending an expedition ... to arrest the
murderers of Mr Volkner' and James Fulloon, the government agent
who had been killed at Whakatane in July 1865 along with three other
Pakeha. Justice would be satisfied if the murderers were given up, but
'if not, the Governor' declared that he would 'seize a part of the lands of
the tribes who conceal these murderers'.[30] The New Zealand Settlement Act of 1863 provided for the confiscation of land from Maori
who were declared to be in rebellion. Martial Law was proclaimed in
the Districts of Opotiki and Whakatane on 4 September 1865.[31] Four
days later five hundred soldiers were landed at Opotiki and Völkner's
church was garrisoned as a fort. Fifty-one Maori were killed during the
first month of engagements and accusations were made against the
soldiers of rape and pillage.[32]

There was an element of both punishment and retribution in the
government action with the confiscation by an Order in Council on 17
January 1866 of 448,000 acres of Whakatohea, Ngati Awa and Tuhoe
land in the Bay of Plenty. Over half of this land was later returned to its

---

[27] *NZH*, 22 March 1865.
[28] *NZH*, 23 March 1865.
[29] T. S. Grace to Henry Venn, Auckland, 31 March 1865: CMS Papers, Australian Joint
Copying Project Microfilm 223.
[30] 'Proclamation of Peace', *AJHR* (1866), A–9, 3.
[31] Ibid.
[32] Ibid., 'Return of Maoris killed or wounded at Opotiki'; A. C. Lyall, *Whakatohea of
Opotiki* (Auckland, 1979), 161–3.

traditional owners but 211,060 acres were confiscated and Whakatohea lost some twenty-nine percent of their very fertile productive land.[33] In 1920 a Commission reported that 'the penalty paid by Whakatohea, great as was their offence, was heavier than their deserts'. The Royal Commission to Inquire into Confiscations of Native Lands reported in 1927, however, that while 'In the case of the Whakatohea Tribe it [the confiscation] was excessive, we think, but only to a small extent', and they recommended that £300 be paid annually for education scholarships.[34] There was, however, no war when the troops entered the area and the 'rebellion' which gave rise to confiscation can be seen as a defensive reaction.[35]

* * *

Among those who gave themselves up to the militia at Opotiki was Mokomoko, a Whakatohea chief, who was arrested for his alleged role in the death of Völkner. 'He claimed that he went away after the decision was made to kill Völkner and was not present at the death'.[36] The courts-martial held in November 1865 had found twenty-eight Maori, including Mokomoko, guilty of the death of Völkner and Fulloon and sentenced them to death. But these proceedings were declared 'legal nullities'.[37] Mokomoko was then tried in the Supreme Court in Auckland with four others for Völkner's murder. Grace was the first witness and testified that he 'saw Mokomoko in the procession of natives who led Mr Volkner out'.[38] In his written description of his imprisonment Grace made no mention of Mokomoko by name but refers in general terms to 'a number of armed men (perhaps twenty)' who came and 'called to Mr Volkner as we supposed to go to the meeting'.[39]

The second witness, Joseph Jeans, a Portuguese, stated that he saw Völkner's murder and that 'Mokomoko carried the rope'. According to 'Waipea' or Wepiha Apanui, Mokomoko 'had the command' of the 'armed party' which he led following behind Völkner when he was taken out to be hanged. Völkner was accompanied by Heremita and

33 Lyall, *Whakatohea*, 173.
34 'Royal Commission to Inquire into Confiscation of Native Lands . . .', *AJHR* (1928), G–7, 21, 22.
35 Waitangi Tribunal, *The Ngati Awa Raupatu Report* (Wellington 1999), 63–8.
36 Tairongo Amoamo, 'Mokomoko', *DNZB* 1: 292.
37 Waitangi Tribunal, *Ngati Awa Report*, 71.
38 *NZH*, 28 March 1866.
39 'Mr Grace's imprisonment', *AJHR* (1865), A–5, 25.

Hakaraia, two of the other accused, and Wepiha also testified that Mokomoko carried the rope. Wiremu Te Paki 'corroborated the preceding witnesses in their account of the tragical occurrence, and said that the murder was committed in obedience to orders of Kereopa'. Te Paki does not name Mokomoko as being involved, but mentions Te Ika and Wihura, who were not charged, as responsible for cutting off Völkner's head. Te Paki, under cross-examination, indicated that Wepiha, who was a primary witness against the accused, had accompanied Kereopa to Opotiki as his second-in-command and had taken part in some of the events on 2 March.[40] It was later pointed out that 'for years past there' had 'been disputes between them [Wepiha and Mokomoko] as to land', calling into question Wepiha's motives in testifying against Mokomoko.[41]

The defence lawyer in summing up 'contended that the evidence adduced was insufficient for a conviction. . . . As for Mokomoko, it was in evidence that he was standing by a stream at some distance from the scene of the murder'. Sir George Arney, the Chief Justice, in his summation indicated the contradictory nature of the evidence in relation to Mokomoko, that

> He was deposed to have walked behind Mr Volkner carrying a rope, the very implement by which the unfortunate gentleman was killed. . . . other circumstances deposed . . . that Mokomoko had left the scene of action immediately before the body was hoisted up.[42]

After deliberating for just over three hours the jury found Mokomoko, Heremetia and Hakaraia guilty, Penetito guilty with a recommendation of mercy, and Paora not guilty.[43]

Mokomoko, Heremetia and Hakaraia were sentenced to death and were executed at Mount Eden Gaol in Auckland on 17 May 1866 along with Horomona and Mikaere Kirimanga who were found guilty of Fulloon's murder. T. S. Grace was among those who visited the condemned men the day before they were hanged. Mokomoko was baptized by an Anglican priest the night before he died. From the scaffold Mokomoko exclaimed, '*Hei konei ra, pakeha ma; tenei ahau e mate hara kore! kahore i tika taku matenga!*', which means, 'Farewell you pakeha! I die without a crime; it is not right that I should die'. After their death

40 *NZH*, 28 March 1866.
41 *Daily Southern Cross*, 18 May 1866.
42 *NZH*, 30 March 1866.
43 Ibid.

and an inquest, those executed were buried within the gaol, despite Mokomoko's anxiety 'that his body should be given up to his relatives'.[44] Grace was very critical of the trial with its all European jury, claiming that 'the counsel for the defence was far worse than no counsel'. He concluded that 'there is every reason to believe [Mokomoko] was innocent'.[45]

Kereopa Te Rau was captured in September 1871 and stood trial for Völkner's murder on 21 December. While it is likely that Kereopa provoked Völkner's death, 'he did not take part in the actual hanging'. He was, however, found guilty, largely on the basis of Samuel Levy's testimony 'that he had seen Kereopa among those who escorted Völkner to the willow tree' where he was hanged.[46] William Colenso's appeal for clemency was not heeded and on 5 January 1872 Kereopa Te Rau was hanged at Napier.[47]

* * *

Völkner acquired for some the status of a martyr, although he never received the recognition accorded to his contemporary, John Coleridge Patteson, who was killed at Nukapu in Solomon Islands in September 1871.[48] In Opotiki, Völkner's church was reconsecrated and named St Stephen the Martyr. In 1910 the building was extended to take in Völkner's grave at the east end and a parish publication in 1936 looked forward to the time when 'we shall be able to erect a suitable shrine for our Martyr'.[49] When the Anglican Church drew up its first New Zealand Calendar in 1972 Völkner was listed for 2 March as 'priest-martyr'.

Significant changes have taken place in Maori–Pakeha relations since the 1970s. The Maori renaissance, seen in their language and culture, was also given political expression. The growing significance given to the Treaty of Waitangi, the founding document between Maori and the British Crown in 1840, led the Anglican Church in the 1980s to move towards revising its constitution and structures to give effect to bicultural partnership between Maori and Pakeha. Questions

[44] *Daily Southern Cross*, 18 May 1866.
[45] T. S. Grace to Henry Venn, Auckland, 15 June 1866, CMS Papers, Australian Joint Copying Project Microfilm 223.
[46] Steven Oliver, 'Kereopa Te Rau', *DNZB* 1: 503.
[47] Colenso, *Fiat Justitia*, 25–7.
[48] David Hilliard, 'The Making of an Anglican Martyr: Bishop John Coleridge Patteson of Melanesia', in Diana Wood, ed., *Martyrs and Martyrologies* (Oxford, 1993), 333–45.
[49] Anon., *St Stephen the Martyr. Opotiki. N.Z.* (Opotiki, 1936).

were raised by Maori in 1988 about Völkner's status in the New
Zealand Calendar, given the ambiguity over his role in Opotiki and
unresolved Whakatohea grievances about Mokomoko and land confiscation. Völkner's name was listed in *A New Zealand Prayer Book – He
Karakia Mihinare o Aotearoa*, published in 1989, as 'Priest, Opotiki',
without the description 'martyr', with the note that 'General Synod,
1988 began the process of deleting the commemoration'.[50]

The retribution visited upon Mokomoko and Whakatohea for
Völkner's death had serious consequences for Mokomoko's descendants. The Mokomoko family carried the stigma of his conviction, they
were blamed for the confiscation of tribal land and suffered along with
their tribe from the loss of their economic base.[51] On 19 October 1989,
Mokomoko's remains, along with those of others executed at Mount
Eden Gaol, were exhumed and his bones reinterred in his own land at
Waiaua two days later. It was now recognized that it was culturally
inappropriate for bodies to be buried within the precincts of a gaol.[52]

In view of Mokomoko's reburial and the 'process of reconciliation'
underway, Whakahuihui Veroce, the bishop of Aotearoa, requested the
Anglican General Synod in 1990 to halt the process of the deletion of
Völkner's name from the calendar. He indicated that 'To say that the
hurt is gone, is not true. But the bones of our ancestors have come
home and are laid to rest – we are now in a state of forgiveness'. The
Synod recognized this as an action 'born out of aroha [love], forgiveness
and a desire for reconciliation'.[53] The Anglican Church committed
itself 'to gather new evidence supporting the innocence of . . .
Mokomoko'.[54] Earle Howe, a staff member of the Anglican Bicultural
Education Unit, published in 1991 an account of the history
surrounding Völkner's death and concluded that 'the deaths of both
Mokomoko and Volkner are memorials to us'.[55] The General Synod in
1992 agreed that the entry in the Church Calendar for 2 March should
read, 'Carl Sylvius Volkner, Priest, and Mokomoko, Rangatira [chief],
Opotiki, 1865, symbols for reconciliation'.[56]

On 25 July 1992 at Waiaua, the Minister of Justice presented

---

[50] *A New Zealand Prayer Book – He Karakia Mihinare o Aotearoa* (Auckland, 1989), 16.
[51] Ewan Johnston, *Wai 203 and Wai 339 Research Report*, A Report Commissioned by the
Waitangi Tribunal, June 2002, 7, appendix 2.
[52] *NZH*, 11 November 1989.
[53] Booth, *For All the Saints*, 75–6.
[54] *NZH*, 13 March 1991.
[55] Howe, *Bring Me Justice*, 42.
[56] *Proceedings of the Fiftieth General Synod – Te Hinota Whanui* (Auckland, 1992), 107.

Mokomoko's family with the document conveying a government pardon. It was taken by one of Mokomoko's elderly descendants and held up to the hill where he was buried with the words, 'At long last the long black cloud has been lifted off you, your family and the whole of Whakatohea'.[57] The pardon was placed in St Stephen's Church, Opotiki, 'as a symbol of reconciliation between Maori and Pakeha in this area'.[58]

While the pardon which both Mokomoko's descendants and the Church had worked for was a step towards reconciliation, the Whakatohea claim to the Waitangi Tribunal remained unsettled. The Tribunal was set up to deal with historical grievances arising from breaches of Maori rights under the Treaty of Waitangi. A deed of settlement was signed by Whakatohea representatives and the government on 1 October 1996 for a forty million dollar compensation package for actions taken against Whakatohea following Völkner's death. The deed, however, lapsed as there was not sufficient support from the beneficiaries to accept the settlement.[59] The New Zealand government, through the Waitangi Tribunal, is facing the implications of the colonial actions against Maori, seeking to recover the history of these events, to apologise for past wrongs, to provide compensation and to promote reconciliation.[60]

The events surrounding 2 March 1865 in Opotiki point to the complexities and ambiguities of history and the way in which the death of two men had reverberations which have continued to impact on people down to the present. Völkner's relationship with the government and the people to whom he ministered raises questions about the missionaries' duty and loyalty. His death also raises questions about the nature of martyrdom. The retribution visited upon Mokomoko and his people and the exercise of British justice has left what Heretaunga Pat Baker in his historical novel about the Opotiki incident called 'a legacy

---

57 Maramena Roderick, ' "Farewell, you Pakeha! I die without a crime" ', *Mana* 1 (January/February 1993), 87.
58 'Brief History of Hiona St Stephens Church', http://www.waiapu.anglican.org.nz/ bop/Opotiki/welcome.htm, accessed 17 June 2003.
59 'Whakatohea Deed Terminated', Rural Bulletin 1998, Ministry of Agriculture and Fisheries. See: http://www.maf.govt.nz/mafnet/publications/archive/rural-bulletin/1998/ index.htm, accessed 17 June 2003.
60 Alan Ward, *An Unsettled History: Treaty Claims in New Zealand Today* (Wellington, 1999). Ngati Awa, a neighbouring tribal group of Whakatohea, who also were affected by the deaths of Völkner and Fulloon and subsequent land confiscation, have 'accepted a treaty settlement from the Government, including an apology and about $42 million in cash and land', as reported in *NZH*, 3 February 2003.

of sorrow'.[61] Bishop Vercoe, speaking in St Stephen's Church in Opotiki on the anniversary of Völkner's death in 1991, 'reminded those present that "if we cannot redress the past we can address the future"'.[62] The conjunction of Völkner's and Mokomoko's names in the Anglican Calendar on 2 March each year as 'symbols of reconciliation' indicates a process begun rather than a goal achieved. One of the collects for the day remembers 'Carl, hanged and dishonoured . . . Mokomoko, unjustly condemned, and the oppression devastating the land' and ends with the invocation, 'Now may Maori and Pakeha live together in aroha'. Repentance and reconciliation are not end points but new starting points as people formerly divided begin to 'address the future' together.[63]

University of Auckland

---

61 Heretaunga Pat Baker, *The Strongest God* (Whatamongo Bay, 1990), 233.
62 *AD News*, May 1991.
63 Booth, *For All the Saints*, 77.

GOD AND THE GALLOWS:
CHRISTIANITY AND CAPITAL PUNISHMENT IN
THE NINETEENTH AND TWENTIETH CENTURIES*

by HUGH MCLEOD

AT the end of the eighteenth century the 'bloody code' was still in full force in England and Wales. There were some two hundred offences which carried the death penalty, ranging from murder to stealing goods worth five shillings from a shop. In the 1780s several hundred men, women and children were sentenced to death each year, and though rather over half were reprieved, there were still about two hundred executions. In London, condemned prisoners were confined in Newgate prison in the City, and until 1783 they were transported two miles to be hanged at Tyburn on the western outskirts of the metropolis. There were usually large crowds lining the streets, and particularly notorious criminals might expect up to thirty thousand spectators at their death. A clergyman would travel in the cart with the prisoners, his main purpose being to ensure that they died repentant, and, it was hoped, with better prospects in the next world than in the present one.

Repentance was most often the theme of the last words which the condemned were allowed as they stood on the scaffold, though occasionally they would seize this last opportunity of protesting their innocence, or declaring their contempt for God, the state, humanity in general, or whoever they blamed for their fate. The religious significance of the gallows had already been emphasized by the Assize Sermon attended by the judge on the Sunday before the opening of the court, and by the sermon to the condemned preached in the prison chapel on the Sunday preceding their execution.

Assize Sermons took as their favourite text Rom. 13: 4: 'for he [the ruler] is the minister of God to thee for good. But if thou do that which is evil, be afraid; for he beareth not the sword in vain . . .'. Since the magistrate was authorized by God to punish the wrong-doer, his calling

* I would like to thank all those who have made helpful comments or have supplied me with copies of their own, or other relevant publications, and in particular Martin Bergman, Jeff Cox, Mary Clare Martin, David Pugsley, Martin Ryan, Michael Snape, David Taylor, Peter van Rooden, Vincent Viaene and Ulrich Volp.

was a high one: he was entitled to judge with severity, since respect for and fear of the law were the chief means by which the majority of sinful human beings were kept out of temptation, and society saved from disintegration. The sermons at Newgate frequently used the fear of hell as a means of terrifying into repentance those prisoners who remained defiant. From 1783, hangings took place in front of the prison gates, but otherwise nothing changed.[1]

England and Wales were unusual in the number of capital offences, and also in the fact that the same method of execution was used in the overwhelming majority of cases. In other parts of Europe there was often a more complicated system of graduated punishments, with the method of execution being adapted to the nature of the offence and the extent to which it was seen as undermining the political or moral order. But otherwise the situation described above was typical of Europe and the newly established United States at the end of the eighteenth century. Death sentences could be imposed for a variety of crimes besides murder, including non-lethal violence, theft and forgery, and sometimes sexual or religious offences. Executions were frequent, public, highly ritualized, and had a strong religious dimension. The latter was especially emphasized in Roman Catholic countries where, for instance, there were confraternities whose task it was to accompany the condemned to the scaffold wearing distinctive robes.[2]

However, most aspects of these 'bloody codes' were beginning to come under attack in the latter years of the eighteenth century. Many people objected to the use of the death penalty for any but the most serious offences, to the cruel methods of killing that were commonly used, and to the fact that these punishments were inflicted in public places before a huge audience. A smaller number of more radical voices were already proposing that the death penalty should be abolished even in cases of murder. In 1786 this was done in Tuscany, though the experiment was short-lived.

---

[1] V. A. C. Gatrell, *The Hanging Tree: Execution and the English People, 1770–1868* (Oxford, 1994); Randall McGowen, ' "He Beareth not the Sword in Vain": Religion and the Criminal Law in Eighteenth-Century England,' *Eighteenth-Century Studies* 21 (1987–8), 192–211.

[2] Jürgen Martschukat, *Inszeniertes Töten: eine Geschichte der Todesstrafe vom 17. bis zum 19. Jahrhundert* (Cologne, 2000); John McManners, *Death and the Enlightenment: Changing Attitudes to Death among Christians and Unbelievers in Eighteenth-Century France* (Oxford, 1981), 379–408; Pieter Spierenburg, *The Spectacle of Suffering: Executions and the Evolution of Repression from a Preindustrial Metropolis to the European Experience* (Cambridge, 1984); Louis P. Masur, *Rites of Execution: Capital Punishment and the Transformation of American Culture, 1776–1865* (New York, 1989), 55–76.

Two centuries later, the situation was completely different. By 1995, the death penalty for all 'normal' crimes had been abolished in the great majority of European countries, the only exceptions being Belgium and some of the formerly Communist states in eastern Europe. Even Belgium was *de facto* abolitionist, the last execution having been in 1950. Some European states had retained the death penalty for treason, but had not executed any alleged traitor for forty or more years. Capital punishment had also been abolished in Canada and in twelve of the United States. On the other hand, thirty-eight of the United States retained the death penalty and in several of them executions were frequent.[3]

The purpose of this essay is to analyse the relationship between Christianity and the theory and practice of capital punishment in the traditionally Catholic or Protestant countries of Europe (excluding the Orthodox East) and North America from the late eighteenth century to the present day. Various campaigns to abolish the death penalty gradually brought about this change. Who has supported these campaigns, in what circumstances they have succeeded, and what part Christianity and the Christian Churches have played in contributing to their success or failure are some of the questions I shall focus on, drawing detailed examples mainly from the United Kingdom and the United States.

* * *

Two histories have influenced my formulation of these questions: Richard J. Evans's impressive study, *Rituals of Retribution: Capital Punishment in Germany 1600–1987*, which is in my view the best book yet published on the history of executions, and Harry Potter's *Hanging in Judgment: Religion and the Death Penalty in England.*[4] After more than a century of campaigns, the death penalty was abolished in the Federal Republic of Germany in 1949 and in the German Democratic Republic in 1987. Having discussed various explanations for the declining acceptability of capital punishment, Evans concludes that state killings were mainly legitimated by religious arguments and by the support of the Churches, and that their decline should be seen primarily as a consequence of secularization. Potter, a former Anglican prison chap-

---

3 Hugo Adam Bedau, 'The United States', in Peter Hodgkinson and Andrew Rutherford, eds, *Capital Punishment: Global Issues and Prospects* (Winchester, 1996), 45–76; Peter Hodgkinson, 'The United Kingdom and the European Union', in ibid., 193–213; Stanislaw Frankowski, 'Post Communist Europe', in ibid., 215–41.

4 Richard J. Evans, *Rituals of Retribution: Capital Punishment in Germany, 1600–1987* (London, 1997); Harry Potter, *Hanging in Judgment: Religion and the Death Penalty in England* (New York, 1993).

lain, and, like Evans, a committed abolitionist, agrees with Evans in according established religion, in this case the Church of England, a key role in support for the death penalty. Indeed he argues that abolition would have come about much sooner, but for the support for hanging given by the Anglican bishops. On the other hand, while Evans seems to regard religion as such as being favourable to the death penalty, Potter notes the opposition of many Nonconformists and various Anglican prison chaplains. He also discusses the conversion of the Anglican bishops to the abolitionist cause in the 1950s and gives them a significant role in its eventual triumph in the 1960s.

In reading these two books I found myself impressed by the quality of their research, yet to some degree sceptical of their arguments. Evans establishes that, in Germany, during the Wilhelmine and Weimar periods, the political parties that were closest to the Churches tended to support the death penalty, while those parties that were most active in seeking abolition tended to be more distanced from, or even hostile to, the Churches. He also cites examples of support for capital punishment by individual clergymen, including prison chaplains. On the other hand, there are some gaps in his argument.

One of Evans's basic assumptions is that the Enlightenment was non-religious or even anti-religious, and that, if the critique of the death penalty can be shown to be rooted in the Enlightenment, that is sufficient to establish its 'secular' credentials. However, this proposition needs to be demonstrated rather than assumed. The religious character of the Enlightenment was much more varied than this one-sidedly secular depiction would suggest. In particular, it varied considerably from country to country, the anti-religious Enlightenment being a mainly French phenomenon.[5] The same is of course true of nineteenth-century Liberalism, which was frequently anti-clerical, and sometimes secularist, but which in many countries had a strong Protestant dimension, and in some a significant Catholic aspect. In Germany, the link between the Churches and support for the death penalty seems to have been a result of their increasing conservatism from the 1850s onwards. In 1848, nine out of fourteen Protestant and Catholic clergymen in the Frankfurt Parliament and thirty-one out of thirty-eight in the Prussian National Assembly voted for abolition.[6]

---

[5] Roy Porter and Mikulás Teich, eds, *The Enlightenment in National Context* (Cambridge, 1981), 6, 73, 112.

[6] Bernhard Düsing, *Die Geschichte der Abschaffung der Todesstrafe in der Bundesrepublik Deutschland* (Schwenningen am Neckar, 1952), 52, 67.

Whereas in these two areas Evans is in danger of overstating his case, his biggest claim of all appears to be without any foundation in evidence. Citing Albert Camus, who argued that the death penalty could only be justified if one believed that there was the possibility of restitution in another life, Evans goes on to claim that 'it was the growing belief that death was final'[7] that led to rejection of the death penalty in the eighteenth and nineteenth centuries. Yet he gives no examples of anyone other than Albert Camus himself and one speaker at the Frankfurt Parliament who rejected the death penalty for this reason,[8] and indeed no evidence that belief in the finality of death was increasing in that period.

While this may have been so, the situation was certainly much more complex than any picture of a one-way secularization process would suggest. On the one hand, Keith Thomas has found plenty of evidence for the denial of immortality both at elite and at popular levels in sixteenth- and seventeenth-century England.[9] On the other, John McManners and Thomas Kselman have shown that many of those who rejected the Catholic Church in eighteenth- and nineteenth-century France continued to believe in an after-life, including Rousseau, Robespierre and Victor Hugo, to name only the most famous examples.[10] Furthermore, the very extensive practice of state killings by atheist governments in the twentieth century, including present-day China,[11] must lead one to doubt whether there is a general connection between belief in the finality of death and reluctance to apply the death penalty. The question seems to me rather: which are the specific historical conditions that have led to connections between secularism or religious scepticism and opposition to capital punishment?

In the case of Potter, I would question the influence which he ascribes to Anglican bishops. Given the predominance of Presbyterians in Scotland and of Dissenters of various kinds in Wales, and the existence of large Dissenting and Catholic minorities in England; given also the facts that the allegiance of many Anglicans to their Church has been

---

7 Evans, *Rituals of Retribution*, 901.
8 Ibid., 271.
9 Keith Thomas, *Religion and the Decline of Magic: Studies in Popular Beliefs in Sixteenth-and Seventeenth-Century England* (Harmondsworth, 1973), 198–205.
10 McManners, *Death and the Enlightenment*, 172–90; Thomas A. Kselman, *Death and the Afterlife in Modern France* (Princeton, NJ, 1993), 125–62.
11 Ger Peter van den Berg, 'Russia and the Other CIS States', in Hodgkinson and Rutherford, *Capital Punishment*, 77–103; Michael Palmer, 'The People's Republic of China', in ibid., 105–41.

little more than nominal, and that even very devout Anglicans have often been reluctant to take a political lead from their bishops, there seem good *a priori* grounds for doubting that the role of the episcopate was as great as Potter suggests.

* * *

In this section I shall offer an overview of the debate on the death penalty from the 1780s to the 1990s. Then I shall look at where, when and why abolitionist movements have succeeded. Finally, I shall attempt a summing up of the part played by religion in the story, and shall assess the validity of the arguments presented by Evans and Potter.

The modern debate over the death penalty in western, traditionally Catholic or Protestant societies began in the later eighteenth century and continues to the present day. It is usually said to have begun with Cesare Beccaria, whose *On Crimes and Punishments* was published in Italian in 1764, and soon translated into many other languages.[12] While not completely opposed to the death penalty, Beccaria objected to its present application primarily for utilitarian reasons: executions served no useful purpose, since other penalties could act as an equally effective deterrent. However, he also objected on more fundamental grounds by suggesting that capital punishment was counter-productive, since by its 'barbarity' it set a bad example.

While Beccaria had a considerable influence both on the intelligentsia and on those in government, at least three other currents of thinking contributed to dissatisfaction with the contemporary practice of capital punishment and sometimes led to demands for outright abolition. First, there was a humanitarian and religious current, associated with such figures as the English Quaker prison reformer John Howard, who believed that the principal objective of punishment should be reform rather than retribution.[13] Second, there was a political current, which was especially powerful in the new revolutionary states of France and America, where the death penalty was seen as a relic of the Ancien Régime. Third, there was a new culture of what Gatrell has termed 'squeamishness' in the upper and middle classes, which was repelled by brutal punishments inflicted in public, as well as by all the

---

[12] For instance, a German translation appeared in 1766 and an English translation in 1767. Petra Overrath, *Tod und Gnade: die Todesstrafe in Bayern im 19. Jahrhundert* (Cologne, 2001), 251–5, stresses that other writers had already prepared the ground for Beccaria.

[13] Richard R. Follett, *Evangelicalism, Penal Theory, and the Politics of Criminal Law Reform in England, 1808–30* (Basingstoke, 2001), 86–9, 141–2, and *passim*.

associated ritual, but which might be prepared to accept more humane, if equally deadly, punishments administered in private.[14]

As capital punishment began to be hotly debated from the later eighteenth century onwards, a repertoire of arguments emerged on either side that has changed very little over two centuries. There have been seven principal arguments for retaining the death penalty, each of which has faced an abolitionist counter-argument. I shall refer to examples of their use in the United Kingdom in evidence to the Capital Punishment Commission in 1864–5 and in the Parliamentary debates of 1948 and 1956. But the same arguments were used elsewhere in Europe, and continue to be used in the United States right up to the present day.

For most of these two hundred years the main argument for the death penalty has been that it acts as a deterrent.[15] Abolitionists have therefore tried to refute this claim by analysis of criminal statistics.[16] In fact, this is the only part of the debate that has now been settled to most people's satisfaction, as more and more studies have demonstrated that stopping executions does not lead to an increase in the number of murders.[17] A second argument is the need for proportionate retribution – 'life for life'.[18] Abolitionists have branded this demand as a thirst for revenge.[19] Third, it is said that the sacredness of human life is best defended by imposing extreme penalties on those who violate the principle.[20] However, the chief argument against the death penalty has always been that state killings undermine the sanctity of life.[21] Fourth, capital punishment has been justified by reference to certain biblical texts, notably Gen. 9: 6: 'Whoso sheddeth man's blood, by man shall his blood be shed'.[22] On the other hand, it is argued that the whole spirit of

---

14   Gatrell, *Hanging Tree*, 240, 267–72, 297, and *passim*.
15   'Report of the Capital Punishment Commission', *Parliamentary Papers*, 1866, XXI, Q. 2 [Lord Cranworth, judge]; *Parliamentary Debates (Lords)*, 5th series, 155 (1947–8), 407–9 [Lord Simon, former Home Secretary].
16   *Report from the Select Committee on Capital Punishment* (London, 1930), a major part of which was given to analysing statistics from abolitionist countries.
17   William C. Bailey and Ruth D. Peterson, 'Murder, Capital Punishment and Deterrence', in Hugo Adam Bedau, ed., *The Death Penalty in America: Current Controversies* (New York, 1997), 135–62.
18   *Parliamentary Debates (Lords)*, 5th series, 155, 481 [bishop of Truro].
19   *Parliamentary Debates (Lords)*, 5th series, 156 (1947–8), 124 [bishop of Chichester].
20   *Parliamentary Debates (Lords)*, 5th series, 155, 427–8 [bishop of Winchester].
21   *Parliamentary Debates (Lords)*, 5th series, 156, 124 [bishop of Chichester].
22   *Report of the Capital Punishment Commission*, Q 1175 [Revd John Davis, Ordinary of Newgate].

the New Testament is incompatible with it.[23] Fifth, executions are justified by reference to general human depravity and the incorrigibility of particular criminals,[24] while abolitionists claim that even the worst criminal is capable of reformation.[25] In spite of their often bleak view of human nature, proponents of the death penalty have sometimes had great faith in the ability of the gallows not only to concentrate the mind wonderfully, but even to produce a sudden and, from an eternal point of view, beneficial change of heart.[26] Opponents, however, argue that true repentance takes longer.[27] Finally, supporters of the death penalty warn that murderers who are not executed may kill again,[28] while opponents refer to the fallibility of human justice and the risk of sending the innocent to the scaffold.[29]

Public debate may largely have been conducted in terms of such rational arguments, yet more purely emotive rhetoric or language of a totally subjective nature kept breaking through. Opponents of the death penalty claimed that it was 'evil', 'horrible and beastly', 'uncivilised' and 'a barbarous relic of paganism'.[30] Clarence Darrow, the famous American defender of the 1920s, dismissed all high-minded justifications for capital punishment, claiming that its supporters simply enjoyed killing people.[31] The English Lord Chief Justice Goddard was alleged to derive an erotic thrill from sentencing people to death.[32] Meanwhile, supporters accused their opponents of caring more about the criminal than the victim, of being sentimentalists and (if male) of lacking virility.[33]

The death penalty arouses both fascination and horror at a very deep level, and ultimately beliefs about it depend more on emotional responses than on abstract reasoning. Death cells and executions play a

[23] Ibid., Q 3261 [Revd Lord Sydney Godolphin Osborne, rector of Durweston].

[24] *Parliamentary Debates (Lords)*, 5th series, 155, 493 [Lord Chief Justice Goddard].

[25] Ibid., 537 [Lord Rochester, former Liberal MP].

[26] *Parliamentary Debates (Lords)*, 5th series, 198 (1955–6), 698 [Lord Elton]; Potter, *Hanging in Judgment*, 195–7.

[27] *Report of the Capital Punishment Commission*, Q 1043 [Sir Fitzroy Kelly, former Attorney-General].

[28] Ibid., QQ 1154–8 [Revd John Davis].

[29] Ibid., Q 2498 [John Parry, barrister].

[30] *Parliamentary Debates (Lords)*, 5th series, 198 (1955–6), 594, 620, 712, 725 [Lords Rea, Wise, Darwen, Raglan].

[31] Philip English Mackey, ed., *Voices against Death: American Opposition to Capital Punishment, 1787–1975* (New York, 1976), 168.

[32] Marlene Martin, 'The fight for Derek Bentley: A full pardon – 46 years late,' www.nodeathpenalty.org/newaboog/bentley.html, consulted 2 April 2003.

[33] *Parliamentary Debates (Lords)*, 5th series, 198, 613–14, 656, 718 [Lords Glasgow, Teviot, Ailwyn]; Gatrell, *Hanging Tree*, 591–3.

part in novels and poems by Wordsworth, Dickens, George Eliot, Hardy, Housman, Graham Greene, Stefan George, Stendhal, Hugo, Zola, Camus, Pasternak, Dostoyevsky, and many others. Dostoyevsky, having himself been under sentence of death, was understandably obsessed by the subject. As a literary theme, executions probably rank second only to adultery. In the popular slang of eighteenth-century London, it is said that the number of words referring to hangings was exceeded only by the number of those referring to money.[34]

Most people have probably had ambivalent responses to actual executions, as opposed to capital punishment in the abstract – horror at what is being done by the state and at the macabre rituals associated with the killing, mingled with equal horror at the crime for which the victim is being punished, and some satisfaction that this cruel act is being avenged.[35] It was the recognition of this ambivalence that gave strength to the film *Dead Man Walking*, which some critics perversely accused of sitting on the fence, because in spite of its abolitionist message, it pulled no punches in depicting the crime or the anguish of the victims' families.

Such ambivalence also helps to explain the bewildering changes of front, in both directions, which have marked the history of capital punishment. The most spectacular defection from the abolitionist camp was that of Robespierre, who in 1791 delivered an eloquent denunciation of the death penalty to the National Assembly. There have also been many examples of democratic parties, including the German Social Democrats in the 1920s, and the British Labour Party and Indian Congress Party in the 1940s, which demanded abolition when in opposition but found the time unripe when they achieved power. In the early 1950s German Communists were *simultaneously* opposing the death penalty in the West, while declaring the time for its abolition unripe in the East.[36] On the other side, those who actually

---

[34] Peter Linebaugh, 'The Tyburn Riot Against the Surgeons', in Douglas Hay *et al.*, eds, *Albion's Fatal Tree: Crime and Society in Eighteenth-Century England* (Harmondsworth, 1977), 65–117, 66, n. 1.

[35] For discussion of the responses of those who witnessed executions, as reflected both in eye-witness accounts and literary treatments, see William B. Thesing, ed., *Executions and the British Experience from the 17th to the 20th Century: a Collection of Essays* (Jefferson, NC, 1990); Daniel Gerould, *Guillotine: its Legend and Lore* (New York, 1992); Gatrell, *Hanging Tree*, 242–58 and *passim*.

[36] David P. Jordan, *The Revolutionary Career of Maximilien Robespierre* (New York, 1985), 54; Victor Bailey, 'The Shadow of the Gallows: the Death Penalty and the British Labour Government 1945–51', *Law and History Review* 18 (2000), 305–49; Evans, *Rituals of Retribu-*

carried out executions or were professionally obliged to be present at them often became converts to abolitionism. This sometimes led to strange situations.[37] For instance, one of the leading American abolitionists of the 1920s and '30s, Lewis Lawes, was Warden of Sing Sing Prison, and thus responsible for numerous electrocutions.[38]

* * *

Successive phases in the struggles over the retention, restriction, or abolition of the death penalty are to be understood mainly in terms of the symbolic meanings which this form of punishment has carried at various times, and these meanings have been in constant flux.[39] Between 1786 and 1995, the abolitionist movement in Europe and North America has gone through six phases: a first in the 1780s; a second in the first half of the nineteenth century; a third in the later nineteenth and early twentieth centuries; a fourth immediately after World War II; a fifth in the 1960s and a sixth in the 1990s. The identities of the main protagonists have changed and so have the symbolic meanings attached to the death penalty.

The first abolitions in Tuscany in 1786 and in the Austrian Empire in 1787 took place under the Ancien Régime. They were enacted by decree of the Grand Duke Leopold and his brother the Emperor Joseph II, devout Catholics, disciples of Beccaria and, in the case of Joseph, an exponent of enlightened absolutism. As well as being influenced by utilitarian and humanitarian objections to the death penalty, they were – at least in Leopold's case – concerned with the possibility of reforming the criminal, and in view of the severe labour to which convicts were subjected, they were probably also influenced by the recognition that the death penalty was a waste of manpower. However, capital punishment in their states was progressively restored from 1790 onwards, as part of the reaction to the French Revolution.[40]

---

tion, 506; for India, information from David Taylor, formerly pro-director of the School of Oriental and African Studies, London, and a leading authority on twentieth-century Indian politics; Düsing, *Abschaffung,* 301, 309–10.

[37] In the Lords debate of 1948, Lord Douglas of Kirtleside who, as Military Governor in Germany, had been responsible for numerous executions, declared his conversion to abolitionism. For examples of prison chaplains who rejected capital punishment because of their experience of executions, see Potter, *Hanging in Judgment,* 133; James J. Megivern, *The Death Penalty: an Historical and Theological Survey* (Mahwah, NJ, 1997), 271–5, 357–9.

[38] Mackey, *Voices against Death,* 191.

[39] I am entirely in agreement here with Evans, who stresses this point in his overview of the German history: Evans, *Rituals of Retribution,* 873.

[40] Michael Schewardnadse, *Die Todesstrafe in Europa: eine rechtsvergleichende Darstellung*

The American and French Revolutions mark the beginnings of a second phase in this history. At first, it seemed that revolutionary France might get rid of the gallows, but in fact the debates of 1791 led only to the introduction of a more humane and egalitarian method of execution, the guillotine.[41] It was in the new republic in North America that a widespread abolitionist movement with popular support first developed. Its main proponents were political democrats and religious dissenters, who sometimes were the same people. For the former, the death penalty was a symbol of the old political order. For the latter, it was part of an archaic theology. In Massachusetts, where Congregationalism remained established up to 1833, the clergy of that Church were among the staunchest defenders of the death penalty. In some other states, where Church and State were formally separated, there continued to be an informal establishment, in that the clergy of certain denominations, often the Presbyterians or Episcopalians, were closely linked with the political and economic elite, and they too supported the status quo.[42]

The first American abolitionist is generally held to be Benjamin Rush, a Philadelphia doctor.[43] He was both a Unitarian and a fervent republican, and his critique of the death penalty, published in 1787, mixed political and theological points with ideas drawn from Enlightenment writers, such as Beccaria. Similarly eclectic was the leading penal reformer in New York, the Quaker Thomas Eddy, who drew on Beccaria and Montesquieu, on Rush, and on John Howard. But so far as many of his readers were concerned the most persuasive points in his critique were political. In a book of 1801 he claimed that it was not possible

> that a people enamoured of freedom and a republic, should long acquiesce in a system of laws, many of them the product of barbarous usages, corrupt society and monarchical principles, and imperfectly adapted to a new country, simple manners, and a popular form of government.[44]

mit einer rechtsgeschichtlichen Einleitung (Munich, 1914), 16–17; Evans, *Rituals of Retribution*, 132–3.

[41] Gordon Wright, *Between the Guillotine and Liberty: Two Centuries of the Crime Problem in France* (New York, 1983), 30–4.

[42] Masur, *Rites of Execution*, 54–76; Philip English Mackey, *Hanging in the Balance: the Anti-Capital Punishment Movement in New York State, 1776–1861* (New York, 1982), 214–17.

[43] Masur, *Rites of Execution*, 61–70.

[44] Mackey, *Hanging in the Balance*, 64.

Since the strongest advocates of abolition were often Unitarians, Universalists and Quakers, while many of the strongest advocates of the gallows were Calvinists, the death penalty was also at the heart of the debate between two rival theologies. Orthodox Calvinists emphasized divine justice; their critics insisted on divine mercy. Calvinists believed that certain texts in the Hebrew Bible provided an incontrovertible divine mandate for the gallows; their critics either disputed the exegesis of these texts or claimed that the New Testament superseded the Old. Quakers and Unitarians believed that criminals could be reformed, while Calvinists were much more sceptical. Louis Masur, a leading American historian of capital punishment, sees the conflict as focusing above all on two understandings of human nature: 'Most anti-gallows activists viewed man as moral, reasonable, educable, and savable'.[45] Their objective was a society of free 'self-governing' individuals. They also believed that social conditions contributed to crime, so that as well as reforming erring individuals, they had to reform society:

> Supporters of capital punishment, by comparison thought of man as a sinful depraved, and corrupt animal who had to be restrained by divine and civil laws. . . . for pro-gallows writers only strict disciplined order would permit any freedom at all.[46]

The American debate reached a peak in the 1830s and '40s, when numerous abolitionist organizations were founded, including one specifically for women, and public debates were staged. As always, abolition came as part of a package: in nineteenth-century America, it also included anti-slavery and temperance.[47] The main centres of the campaign were in New York, Philadelphia and Boston. But while abolitionist bills were narrowly defeated in the legislatures of New York and Massachusetts, the cause first triumphed in 1846 in the remote western state of Michigan. Wisconsin, Rhode Island and Maine soon followed. After these initial victories, however, the abolitionist movement lost momentum, partly because of the overriding claims of the anti-slavery cause, and it did not revive until the end of the nineteenth century.[48]

By that time, in Europe, abolition of the death penalty was back on

---

[45] Masur, *Rites of Execution*, 153–4.
[46] Ibid.
[47] Ibid., 118–24.
[48] David Brion Davis, 'The Movement to Abolish Capital Punishment in America, 1787–1861', *American Historical Review* 63 (1957), 23–46, 41–6.

the political agenda. In France there were several parliamentary debates on this issue in the early 1830s, and the United Kingdom Parliament debated an abolitionist motion for the first time in 1840. An analysis of the French debates highlights the centrality of religious arguments. Both Catholics, such as Charles Lucas, the leading French abolitionist, and deists, such as Victor Hugo, contended that life was a gift of God which men had no right to take away.[49] But for most of Europe the turning-point was 1848, when all time-honoured practices were thrown in the melting-pot. The Frankfurt Parliament voted to abolish capital punishment, though this resolution had no practical effect. Several German states did however stop all executions. Tuscany followed in the 1850s, and in the 1860s and '70s the majority of Swiss cantons, together with Portugal and the Netherlands, did the same.

There was also widespread opposition to the death penalty even in those countries (the majority) where it remained. The Belgian Senate rejected an abolitionist motion in 1867, but in practice executions had stopped in 1863, and were only resumed during or in the immediate aftermath of the two world wars.[50] In the United Kingdom five of the twelve members of the Capital Punishment Commission, which reported in 1866, declared their opposition to capital punishment.[51]

Opposition came mainly from political Liberals and Radicals and from religious Dissenters. For the former, the gallows was a symbol of arbitrary rule. 'Let us not bring the death penalty from the times of the police state into the times of the state ruling by law', pleaded one speaker in the Frankfurt Parliament. According to another, the retention of the death penalty would 'perpetuate submissiveness and serfdom for all time, since it really turns the condemned man into the bodily property of state and society'. Similarly, a pastor, who had turned against the death penalty after accompanying a condemned man to the scaffold, put their debate in context as follows:

> Gentlemen, many an upright man standing here would have counted as a political offender according to the laws and the erro-

---

[49] Paul Savey-Casard, 'Les arguments d'ordre religieux dans les controverses sur la peine capitale en France au XIXe siècle,' in *Pena de Morte: Colóquio internacional comemorativo do centenário da aboliçao da pena de morte em Portugal*, Universidade de Coimbra, 1967, 3 vols (Coimbra, 1970), 2: 219–27.

[50] Evans, *Rituals of Retribution*, 275, 282, 329; Stefan Suter, *Guillotine oder Zuchthaus: die Abschaffung der Todesstrafe in der Schweiz* (Basel, 1997), 17–44; Schewardnadse, *Todesstrafe*, 19–43; P. Cornil, 'La Peine de mort en Belgique', in *Pena de Morte*, 1: 143–51.

[51] *Report of Capital Punishment Commission*, 47–58; see also in this volume Michael Snape, 'British Army Chaplains and Capital Courts-Martial in the First World War', 357–68.

neous views prevailing forty years, and if he had been caught, punished with death [*Many voices*: Four months ago!]'[52]

The role of religious Dissenters was most prominent in England. The Quaker William Allen was one of the two founders of the Capital Punishment Society, set up in 1808 to call for the reduction of the number of capital offences from two hundred to only the one of murder. Quakers also took a leading part in the movement of petitions to Parliament for the restriction of the death penalty in 1818 and 1819, and their Yearly Meeting which considered the death penalty in 1818 looked forward to total abolition. The various abolitionist organizations formed during the nineteenth century all depended on Quaker support, and the Quaker MP John Bright was one of the most persistent opponents of the death penalty in Parliament. Witnesses to the Capital Punishment Commission repeatedly claimed that Nonconformists were widely opposed to the death penalty, and that in areas where Dissent was strong it was difficult to gain convictions in capital cases because of conscientious objections to the death penalty by jurymen.[53]

* * *

The abolitionist movement had a third wave of successes or near-successes in the early twentieth century. Ten more American states abolished the death penalty for murder between 1897 and 1917.[54] Sweden did the same in 1921, after a long period when executions had been rare. In France there was a moratorium between 1906 and 1908, but the Chamber of Deputies finally defeated the proposed abolition.[55]

In Britain the main growth of support for abolition came after World War I. A National Council for Abolition was established in 1925 with the Quaker Roy Calvert as its secretary and guiding force, and with support from a coalition which included both a variety of religious bodies and the National Secular Society. In 1930 a Select Committee of the House of Commons, chaired by Revd James Barr, a

---

52 Evans, *Rituals of Retribution*, 271–3, for all three quotes.

53 Potter, *Hanging in Judgment*, 39; Elizabeth Isichei, *Victorian Quakers* (London, 1970), 206, 250–1; *Capital Punishment Commission*, QQ 2498, 2680. Capital punishment was a popular subject at Nonconformist debating societies in the mid-Victorian years. At their first debate, in 1875, the Young Men's Improvement Society at Clifton Road Congregational Church, Brighton, voted for abolition. See N. Caplan, 'Young Men in the Church,' *Transactions of the Congregational Historical Society* 21 (1972), 102–5, 102.

54 Mackey, *Voices against Death*, xxxii–iii.

55 Julie Le Quang Sang, *La Loi et le bourreau. La peine de mort en débats (1870–1985)* (Paris, 2001), 39–113.

Labour MP who was also a Presbyterian minister, recommended that the death penalty be suspended for five years, though Macdonald's minority Labour government failed to implement this recommendation.[56] By now the strongest advocates of abolition were Socialists, for whom the death penalty was a symbol of class rule. The German Social Democrats included abolition in their Erfurt programme of 1891, and this was reaffirmed unanimously at their congress in 1912. While repeating many of the old liberal and humanitarian objections to the death penalty, they also condemned the legal system as an instrument of class justice, and they argued that the way to reduce crime was not through cruel punishments, but by getting rid of the 'poverty and destitution', the 'poor upbringing, schnapps and lack of education' which were the causes of crime.[57] Though the German Social Democrats were noted for their strongly secular orientation, the British Labour Party, which was under much greater religious influence,[58] was equally opposed to the death penalty. In 1930, all the Labour members of the Select Committee voted to suspend capital punishment, and in 1934 the party conference voted unanimously for abolition.[59] In some countries, notably Britain and Sweden, religious Dissenters also continued to have an important role in abolitionist campaigns.[60]

Also significant, especially in the United States, were theological developments within the larger Protestant Churches, expressed in two main trends. One was the Social Gospel movement, which had a big influence on Baptists, Congregationalists, Methodists, and other mainstream Protestants in the United States and Canada, and which influenced Protestant thinking in Britain too. According to Social Gospellers, of whom the most famous was the New York Baptist, Walter Rauschenbusch, the gospel was not only about the salvation of individuals, but also about the Christianization of society. This required a critique of all existing institutions, and also a recognition of the effects

---

[56] James B. Christoph, *Capital Punishment and British Politics: the British Movement to Abolish the Death Penalty, 1945–57* (London, 1962), 30–5.

[57] Evans, *Rituals of Retribution*, 456–7. In 1908 when the French Chamber of Deputies rejected an abolitionist motion by 330 votes to 201, the Socialists were all in the minority: Le Quang Sang, *Loi et bourreau*, 111.

[58] See Hugh McLeod, 'Religion in the British and German Labour Movements: a Comparison', *Bulletin of the Society for the Study of Labour History* 50 (1986), 25–36.

[59] Bailey, 'Shadow of the Gallows', 313–18; Potter, *Hanging in Judgment*, 140–1.

[60] For Sweden see Martin Bergman, *Dödsstraffet, kyrkan och staten i Sverige från 1700-Tal till 1900-Tal* (Lund, 1996), English summary, 203.

on individual behaviour of a harmful environment. These ideas found their main political expression in support for the Progressive Party, which had a brief but powerful impact in the years immediately before World War I.[61]

Meanwhile, in the Church of England and the American Episcopalian Church, incarnationist theology was having similar practical consequences. This provided the underpinning not only for much of the Anglican Christian Socialism of this era, but also for the thinking of such prominent abolitionists of the inter-war years as Revd Glanville Murray, a former chaplain of Holloway Prison, and Mrs Sarah Donaldson, vice-chairman of the National Council for the Abolition of the Death Penalty. They based their case against capital punishment on the claim that the Incarnation meant that all human life was sacred.[62]

However, in the 1920s, '30s and '40s, the abolitionist movement suffered a series of major setbacks. The establishment of totalitarian regimes in large parts of Europe during the 1920s and '30s led to a spectacular increase in the use of the death penalty. In 1931 capital punishment was restored in Italy, where there had been no executions for civil offences for many years. In Germany, where death sentences had been quite frequent under the Weimar Republic but had seldom been carried out, there was a drastic increase in the proportion of the condemned who were actually executed: the proportion leapt from 6% in 1932 to 82% in 1933. The scaffold was now a symbol of firm government, traditional values, and a rejection of the sentimental tolerance of Weimar days.[63]

In the years immediately following World War II the gallows and the guillotine thus became symbols of Fascism. In this fourth phase of the debate, abolition meant laws which respected life, and a legal system which deserved the respect of the citizen. In Germany this point was made repeatedly in the debates of 1949, when abolition of the death penalty was written into the Basic Law of the Federal Republic. The parliamentary representative who first proposed this inclusion declared that it would 'signal quite fundamentally the turning away of the German people from every system based on violence, and its abhorrence at the abundance of death sentences carried out during the past fifteen years'.[64] Referring to the example of various other European

---

61 Mackey, *Voices against Death*, xxxii–vi.
62 Mrs Lewis Donaldson, *Christ and Capital Punishment* (London, n.d.).
63 Evans, *Rituals of Retribution*, 624–50, 899, 915–16.
64 Düsing, *Abschaffung*, 250, 257–60, 279, 293, 294–5.

countries, he insisted that capital punishment had no place in a state based on the rule of law. In this fourth phase, abolition was also enacted in Austria (1950), and written into the Italian Constitution (1947). Meanwhile the British House of Commons voted in 1948 to suspend the death penalty, but it was overruled by the House of Lords.[65]

* * *

The fifth phase, lasting from the later 1950s into the 1970s, saw an end to executions in the United Kingdom, Canada, Spain, and several more American states, and from 1967 to 1977 there were no executions anywhere in the United States. Many American abolitionists believed that their cause had finally triumphed. The last execution in Ireland took place in 1954 and in France in 1977, though formal abolition in those countries came later.[66] Abolition was now part of the optimistic spirit of the era, with its faith in social science and in progressive change through rational planning. Statistical evidence seemed to have conclusively refuted the claim that the death penalty was a deterrent, and scientific penology appeared to provide more effective tools for reform of the criminal. In Britain, support for the death penalty was now associated with what was termed 'the hang 'em, flog 'em brigade' who, as well as being disqualified by their advanced years, were seen as unamenable to rational argument.

Abolitionism was an idea whose time had finally come even in those countries where public support for capital punishment had in the past been strongest. In the United States, support for the death penalty as reflected in public opinion polls was steadily dropping between 1953 and 1965, by when it was below fifty per cent. In Britain, the abolitionist cause won new support in the later 1950s as a result of a series of controversial executions, most notably that of Timothy Evans who, subsequent evidence suggested, was probably innocent.[67]

By the 1960s there was general support for abolition on the part of the main Protestant Churches. There had been a remarkably speedy change of front on the part of the leaders of the Church of England. In 1948, when the House of Lords debated the issue, the bishops of

[65] Bailey, 'Shadow of the Gallows'.

[66] Hodgkinson and Rutherford, *Capital Punishment*, 204–6.

[67] Phoebe C. Ellsworth and Samuel R. Gross, 'Hardening of the Attitudes: American Views on the Death Penalty,' in Bedau, ed., *Death Penalty*, 90–115, 108–9; Christoph, *Capital Punishment and British Politics*, 96–192, 4–7; for typical perceptions by a leading Labour politician of the supporters of capital and corporal punishment, see Roy Jenkins, *A Life at the Centre* (London, 1991), 180, 199–201, 397–8.

Winchester and Truro were strongly in favour of the death penalty, while the archbishop of Canterbury, Geoffrey Fisher, gave more modified support, with only the bishop of Chichester, George Bell, being clearly opposed. In 1956, all the bishops who spoke in the Lords' debate favoured suspension and only one voted for retention of the death penalty while eight voted against. By 1965 ten bishops voted for the suspension of the death penalty and none against, while in 1969 nineteen bishops voted for permanent abolition and only one against.[68]

Meanwhile, the leadership of the Roman Catholic Church, which until the 1950s had accepted the principle of the death penalty, while often favouring leniency in practice, was going through a similar conversion.[69] Abolition of the death penalty no longer ranked as a radical cause supported mainly by political and religious outsiders. In western Europe, and indeed in North America too, there was now a consensus of 'respectable' opinion in its favour. Public opinion was another matter, however. The case of the death penalty is a remarkable example of elite opinion diverging radically from that of the general public. In the United Kingdom, a public opinion poll in 1969 found 85% in favour of hanging, and in the United States support for capital punishment was also rising from the later 1960s onwards.[70]

Capital punishment continued to be practised by the Communist governments in eastern Europe, with only East Germany, in 1987, stepping out of line. The sixth and most recent wave of abolitions in Europe, therefore, followed the fall of Communism. Croatia, Czechoslovakia and Hungary all abolished the death penalty in 1990, Slovenia in 1991, and in Poland, where there had been no executions since the end of Communist rule, the death penalty was suspended in 1995. Here, as in South Africa, where capital punishment was abolished in 1995, the gallows had become a symbol of tyranny. In some other formerly Communist states, where executions continued to be numerous in the 1990s, a new factor was the attitude of the Council of Europe, for which abolition of the death penalty had become a touchstone of 'civilization' and a necessary part of any application for membership.[71]

The situation was very different in the United States, where in 1972 the Supreme Court had ruled that the death penalty as then adminis-

68 Potter, *Hanging in Judgment*, 153–203.
69 Megivern, *Death Penalty*, 282–98.
70 Potter, *Hanging in Judgment*, 202; Ellsworth and Gross, 'Hardening of the Attitudes', 96.
71 Evans, *Rituals of Retribution*, 805–71; Hodgkinson, *Capital Punishment*, 206–8, 215–41.

tered was unconstitutional. Supported by a rising tide of restorationist public opinion, many states passed new statutes designed to make death sentencing less arbitrary and discriminatory. In 1976, the Supreme Court ruled that the death penalty was not as such a 'cruel and unusual punishment': it was constitutional provided that various criteria were met. The way was open for the resumption of executions in 1977 and, since then, several hundred men and women have been electrocuted, gassed, hanged, shot or lethally injected, the majority of them in a small number of southern states, most notably Texas.[72] 'The rope, the chair and the needle', to borrow the title of a history of capital punishment in Texas, for long associated with the power of the state and of the ruling elite, had now become symbols of a populist crusade.[73]

Most priests, ministers and rabbis, like most academics, the editors of the more prestigious newspapers, and indeed many prominent politicians, were opposed to the death penalty. By the 1980 and '90s the Roman Catholic bishops were among the most vocal critics, and in some states they mounted energetic though mostly unsuccessful campaigns against the resumption of executions. In Iowa, where attempts to restore the death penalty failed, both supporters and opponents of the death penalty credited the Churches with having played the leading part in defeating these attempts. Religion has become an important part of the American debate again, because the fundamentalist Churches are mostly supporters of the executions which the other Churches deplore.[74]

However, religious arguments have been less significant in underpinning support for the death penalty than those concepts of individual rights which in Europe have been used to stamp the death penalty as an indefensible form of barbarism. In Europe the argument that the death penalty contravenes 'human rights' has become a powerful rhetorical

---

[72] Ibid., 45–76. The literature on the restoration of capital punishment in the USA is vast. See especially the volumes edited by Hugo Adam Bedau and entitled *The Death Penalty in America*, of which the first edition appeared in 1964 and the most recent in 1997. An excellent study of the opposition is Herbert H. Haines, *Against Capital Punishment: the Anti-Death Penalty Movement in America, 1972–1994* (New York, 1996).

[73] James W. Marquart, Sheldon Ekland-Olson and Jonathan R. Sorensen, *The Rope, the Chair and the Needle: Capital Punishment in Texas, 1923–1990* (Austin, TX, 1994).

[74] Haines, *Against the Death Penalty*, 104–6; Megivern, *Death Penalty*, 357–78; *Des Moines Register*, 26 January, 2 March, 5 March 1995. I am very grateful to Martin Ryan of the Iowa Civil Liberties Union for sending me copies of newspaper articles on the attempts to restore the death penalty in Iowa between 1995 and 1997. These suggested that whereas Catholic, 'mainline' Protestant and Jewish opponents of the death penalty were very active and vocal, those churches which supported the death penalty generally saw it as a low-priority issue.

tool. In the United States the concept of 'victim's rights' has become the strongest weapon in the hands of those demanding the death sentence. The 'deadliest D.A.', Philadelphia's Lynne Abraham, who demands the death penalty more often than any other District Attorney in the United States, cheerfully admits that it is not a deterrent. She demands the death penalty because it provides satisfaction to the victim's family and gives ordinary people a feeling that something is being done about crime: 'We are so overwhelmed by cruelty and barbarism, and most people feel the legal system doesn't work. We feel our lives are not in our own hands'.[75]

* * *

Throughout this history the role of Christianity has been ambiguous. Christians have been divided, and at most points religious arguments have played a significant part on both sides of the debate. At least three kinds of factor have influenced the stance of particular Churches or of groups within them: their theology; their relationship to the state and to secular elites; and the logic of their position on other issues.

To begin with theology: support for the death penalty has tended to be particularly strong within those branches of Protestantism which regard all parts of the Bible as equally authoritative, and believe that all should be interpreted literally. Thus, in the early and middle years of the nineteenth century, this was the position adopted by many Presbyterian and Congregationalist ministers in the United States, who believed that the authority of the Scriptures was at stake in the controversy over the death penalty, and that in particular Gen. 9: 6 was binding on Christians. This is the position taken by many evangelicals in the United States at the present day.[76] On this issue, as on a number of others, a major catalyst of change in the latter part of the nineteenth century was a shift in methods of biblical interpretation which led to literalist approaches being defined as 'fundamentalist'.

Various authors have also shown that thinking about divine punishment helps to shape thinking about human punishment. The theologian Timothy Gorringe, in a wide-ranging overview of writings on the Atonement from the eleventh century to the twentieth, has argued that

---

[75] Austin Sarat, *When the State Kills: Capital Punishment and the American Condition* (Princeton, NJ, 2001), 33–59; Tina Rosenberg, 'The deadliest D.A.', in Bedau, ed., *Death Penalty*, 319–32, 321.

[76] H. Wayne House, 'The New Testament and Moral Arguments for Capital Punishment', in Bedau, ed., *Death Penalty*, 415–28.

harsh approaches to the treatment of crime have been underpinned by penal theories of the Atonement, while the advocacy in the nineteenth century of alternative versions of the Atonement prepared the way for penal strategies which emphasized reform rather than retribution.[77] The historian Randall McGowen, drawing mainly on sermons in eighteenth- and nineteenth-century England, suggests that views on punishment in the present world correlate with views on punishment in the next world. Thus, those preachers who believed in an everlasting hell tended also to favour a stringent application of the death penalty, while those who modified in greater or lesser degree the traditional teaching on hell also wanted to modify or even abolish the death penalty.[78] For the Quakers, who were probably the most consistently opposed to the death penalty of any Christian denomination, it was effectively an article of faith that even the worst criminals were capable of responding to 'that of God' within them.[79]

Even more important, probably, has been the relationship of various branches of Christianity to state and society. Rejection of the death penalty was not an invention of the Enlightenment. At most stages of Christian history, from Tertullian, via the Waldensians and Wycliffites, to the Quaker John Bellers at the end of the seventeenth century, there have been those who saw Christianity and capital punishment as incompatible.[80] But most of the critics were either writing before the era of 'Christendom', or they were members of groups deemed heretical by the Christian authorities of their day.

Established clergies, on the other hand, have tended to identify with the existing political and social order and to take an active part in its defence. Similar attitudes have also been found in Churches which had been formally disestablished but still aspired to act as the Church of the nation. Support for the death penalty was often part of the resulting mentality. For instance, in 1945, when special courts had been set up in the Netherlands to try those accused of collaboration and the death penalty had been re-introduced, the general synod of the Dutch Reformed Church in a pastoral letter justified this step by referring to

---

[77] Timothy Gorringe, *God's Just Vengeance: Crime, Violence and the Rhetoric of Salvation* (Cambridge, 1996).

[78] Randall McGowen, 'The Changing Face of God's Justice: the Debate over Divine and Human Justice in Eighteenth-Century England,' *Criminal Justice History* 9 (1988), 63–98.

[79] Speech by Quaker peer, Lord Darwen, *Parliamentary Debates (Lords)*, 5th series, 198 (1955–6), 725.

[80] Megivern, *Death Penalty*, provides an overview of the range of Christian teaching from the Fathers to the present day.

Romans 13: the government 'bears not the sword in vain', and 'Justice is higher than a person's life'.[81]

In England in 1901, a campaigner against the death penalty wrote to various public figures asking for their views. All of the Anglican and Roman Catholic bishops who replied declared their support for the death penalty, as did all of the judges, whereas all of those Nonconformist ministers who were consulted declared their opposition.[82] The conversion of the established clergy to the abolitionist cause in the 1950s and '60s was part of a wider conversion of those in public positions, including the academic and legal professions, civil servants, prison governors, and even a substantial minority of Conservative MPs. Anglican bishops, who supported abolition in 1956, were a little ahead of the judiciary on this question, but by 1969 most of the Law Lords were voting for abolition too.

On the other hand, the Nonconformist tradition of opposition to the death penalty goes back far beyond the time when it became fashionable. In 1931 the annual assembly of the Congregational Union passed a motion declaring the death penalty to be 'an antiquated form of punishment inconsistent with the Christian belief in mercy, redemption and the value of the human personality', and in the following year the Free Church Council also called for abolition. By the 1950s support for abolition by free church leaders and by their journals was overwhelming. A 'big names' petition organized by the National Campaign for the Abolition of Capital Punishment in 1956 was notable not only for the large number of church representatives among the signatories, but also for the fact that the majority of those came from the Free Churches.[83]

In some cases, the stance of a particular denomination appears to have developed as a logical consequence of its stance on a different issue. A striking recent example has been the conversion of the Roman Catholic Church in the United States to the abolitionist cause, which has mainly taken place since the 1960s, and which developed especially rapidly in the later 1970s. Here a major factor seems to have been the Church's opposition to abortion and the realization that this would make more sense in the context of a consistent 'pro-life' position.[84] The

81 *Documenten Nederlandse Hervormde Kerk*, 1945–55 (The Hague, 1956), 8–13.

82 Josiah Oldfield, *The Penalty of Death, or The Problem of Capital Punishment* (London, 1901), xii–xxi.

83 Potter, *Hanging in Judgment*, 135–7, 172, 178; Christoph, *Capital Punishment*, 167, n. 64.

84 Megivern, *Death Penalty*, 354–5, 376–8.

background to this was the growing demand for legalization in the 1960s and '70s, culminating in the Supreme Court ruling of 1973 that abortion was constitutional. This gave opposition to abortion a central place in Catholic thinking which it did not previously have.

So long as support for the death penalty was part of the conventional wisdom both among elites and among the mass of the people, religious minorities of all kinds, whether Christian, Jewish or secularist, could provide an alternative environment within which independent thinking was possible. In those countries where religious life in the nineteenth century and the first half of the twentieth was dominated by a powerful Roman Catholic or Lutheran Church, closely linked with the state or with conservative political forces, secularists had a major part in the abolitionist movement. In religiously pluralistic societies, religious minorities have had an important role. Most often, successful abolitionist movements have been able to gather support from a variety of sources, including both secularists and those who opposed the death penalty on religious grounds.

In the case of the United Kingdom religious arguments have generally been more important to the abolitionist than to the retentionist cause. This balance may be partly because the latter have often been so confident that their position is that of all reasonable people that they have felt under no compulsion to marshal all the arguments at their disposal: heavy reliance on the claim that capital punishment is a deterrent has seemed to make other arguments unnecessary. Thus in the evidence given to the Capital Punishment Commission in 1864–5 religious arguments were used by a high proportion of those who opposed the death penalty, but by few of its defenders, and three of the four clergymen who gave evidence were among the opponents. Again, in 1930, the Select Committee of the House of Commons, which recommended suspension of the death penalty, gave considerable attention to what were termed 'Scriptural Considerations', as well as quoting in its Report St Augustine, William Temple, then archbishop of York, and other theologians.[85] In the Parliamentary debates of 1948 and 1956, in spite of the support for hanging given on the former occasion by the bishops of Winchester and Truro, religious arguments still played a bigger part on the abolitionist side.

A rare insight into British popular thinking is provided by the Mass

---

[85] *Report from the Select Committee on Capital Punishment*, par. 284–97. They argued that the whole spirit of the Gospel favours reclamation rather than retribution.

Observation survey of 1956, carried out at a time when Parliament was about to debate suspension of the death penalty.[86] 49% approved of capital punishment, 18% disapproved, and 25% said that they had not made up their minds; 34% approved and 45% disapproved of the proposed suspension of the death penalty, with the remainder either saying they did not know, or refusing to come down clearly on one side or the other. There was not a large difference between those of different religious affiliations, but Catholics, Nonconformists, Jews and those with no religious affiliation all showed above average support for suspension, whereas members of the two national Churches showed below average support.[87] Although Catholics emerged as the group most favourable to suspension, the official position of their Church in the 1950s was still supportive of the death penalty.[88]

It may be surmised that the position of British Catholics was less influenced by the official teaching of their Church (of which many were in any case probably unaware), than by the fact that most were of Irish descent and thus heirs to ancestral memories of the hangings of Fenians and Republicans and the shooting of the leaders of the Easter Rising. It may have been for similar reasons that O'Connell 'The Liberator' was an outspoken abolitionist in the 1840s.[89] The fact that social location and collective experiences have decisive influence on perceptions of executions can also be illustrated by an American example. Black Americans are considerably less likely to support the death penalty than white Americans, although blacks are at greater risk of being murder victims. This is because of the long association between the death penalty and racial oppression, which goes back to the days of lynch law, and beyond that to slavery.[90]

The questionnaires used in the Mass Observation poll of 1956 provided spaces for respondents to explain their answers. Although about 80% of those questioned claimed membership of a religious denomination, relatively few made explicit reference to the Bible or to their understanding of Christianity in justifying their attitude to hanging. In a sample of 565, only eighteen did so; of these, thirteen were opposed to the death penalty, three were in favour, and two didn't

86 I wish to thank the Trustees of the Mass Observation Archive, University of Sussex, for permission to read and quote from documents in the archive.
87 Christoph, *Capital Punishment*, 116–23.
88 See above, n. 69.
89 Megivern, *Death Penalty*, 229–39.
90 Marquart, Ekland-Olson and Sorensen, *The Rope, the Chair and the Needle*, 17–24, 191.

know. None at all gave explicitly atheist or agnostic reasons for their position. In fact, non-church-goers supported or opposed the death penalty for similar reasons as church-goers.

Among supporters of the death penalty three lines of argument were predominant: first, the claim that the numbers of murders would increase if hanging were stopped; secondly, the 'life for life' principle; and thirdly, references to particularly atrocious recent crimes with the comment that hanging was the only way of dealing with the culprits – though sometimes with the added comment that hanging would actually be too good for them. The principle of retribution found support across all classes and age-groups, among supporters of all political parties, and among adherents of all religions and none. Again and again respondents declared 'An eye for an eye is what I say', or stated that murderers 'deserved' to hang.[91]

Opponents of the death penalty most often simply referred to it as 'barbarous' or 'what they used to do in the dark ages',[92] but some also claimed that it was not a deterrent, and a considerable number referred to apparent miscarriages of justice, such as the Evans case. Each of these arguments found supporters from church-goers and non-church-goers, and from members of different denominations; but membership of a religious minority of whatever kind made it more likely that a person would question the conventional wisdom.

* * *

It will be clear from what has already been said that Evans underestimates the diversity of Christian responses to capital punishment and overstates the significance of secularism or secularization as factors favouring abolition. Some of Potter's arguments are also questionable. He overstates the part played by the Church of England, and especially the bishops, both in defence of the death penalty and in its abolition.

[91] This statement was made by a fifty-six-year-old housewife, Chesterfield, Church of England. Other examples are those of a fifty-year-old woman, receptionist, Greenock, Church of Scotland, who said: 'In the Bible it says a life for a life'; a thirty-three-year-old man, upholsterer, Coventry, non-church-goer, who said: 'It is a *just* punishment and people should be made to pay for their crimes.' All references from the Mass Observation Archive, University of Sussex Library, TC72/4.

[92] For example, a forty-two-year-old man, a solicitor from Rugby, non-church-goer, said: 'I've always felt it was a disgusting state of affairs'; a forty-four-year-old Roman Catholic man, an electrical engineer from Salford, said: 'It's cruel and uncivilised – it's barbaric'; a French polisher from Eccles, non-church-goer, forty-one, commented: 'Barbaric and out of date'; a forty-seven-year-old woman typist from Huyton, Nonconformist, stated: 'I've always been against taking life in any shape or form': ibid.

Throughout the period from 1808, when proposals to restrict the number of capital offences were first debated in Parliament, until 1965, when executions were ended, supporters of the death penalty rested their case mainly on the claim that it was a deterrent. When confronted with religious arguments against the death penalty they tended to be dismissive or uncomprehending, as with the Conservative MP who got into an argument with the abolitionist Revd Glanville Murray during his evidence to the Select Committee in 1930.[93]

Supporters of the death penalty were certainly pleased to find the bishops on their side, but when the bishops began to jump ship, few of them followed. In 1948, Archbishop Fisher's enthusiastic support for an American-style degrees of murder system failed to win over the House of Lords, and, in 1956, when the bishops were strongly in favour of suspending the death penalty, the Lords still voted by a large majority to keep it.

The main role in the abolition of the death penalty in Britain was played by the Labour Party which, through most of its history, has drawn support disproportionately from religious minorities of all kinds. An analysis of voting by MPs in 1956 showed that Nonconformists, Catholics, Jews, and atheists or agnostics were all much more likely to oppose hanging than were Anglicans or those whose religious affiliation was unknown.[94] So far as the general public is concerned, neither religious and moral arguments nor cold statistics have so far succeeded in changing majority opinion.

This fact leads to one final thought. Most historians of the death penalty have themselves been abolitionists and the Europeans among them – though not, of course, the Americans – have been inclined to see the ending of capital punishment as an inevitable, if all too frequently delayed, result of progress. Yet as long as the majority of the population is unconvinced by the abolitionist case, this hard-won achievement must remain to some degree precarious. If, as I have suggested, the symbolic meanings attached to the death penalty have counted for more than the arguments, a change in context could lead to rapid changes in either direction in the status of capital punishment.

The strongest practical argument for doing without the death penalty is that abolition works. Executions have been ended in most parts of Europe for several decades now, and in some countries for over

---

[93] Potter, *Hanging in Judgment*, 133.
[94] Peter G. Richards, *Parliament and Conscience* (London, 1970), 182–4.

a century, without any of the dire results that many predicted. However, as the American example shows, if a rising crime rate were to go hand in hand with a swing to the right in politics, capital punishment could quickly become an issue again.

In Britain, at least, the ideological basis for present-day abolitionism is fragile. If, as I have suggested, abolition here was achieved by a coalition of forces in which the most important elements were Socialists and dissenting Christians, the decline of support both for Socialism and for most forms of Christianity during the latter part of the twentieth century must be potentially problematic. The case against the death penalty as it is made today rests too much either on merely rhetorical claims that executions are 'barbaric' and 'medieval', or else on concepts of individual human rights, which immediately run into trouble as soon as one person's rights conflict with someone else's – as is shown by the success of the American victims' rights movement.

Quakers, with their faith that there is 'that of God' even in those who have committed the worst crimes, and Catholics, with their pro-life stance, base their opposition to capital punishment within a consistent set of more general principles. Yet these are very much minority positions. Up to the 1950s defenders of the death penalty were content to use lazy arguments, assuming that all reasonable people agreed with them. Maybe abolitionists are now making the same mistake.

University of Birmingham

BRITISH ARMY CHAPLAINS AND CAPITAL COURTS-MARTIAL IN THE FIRST WORLD WAR

by MICHAEL SNAPE

O F all the dark legends which have arisen out of the British experience of the First World War, perhaps none is more compelling than the fate of more than three hundred British, Dominion and Colonial soldiers who were tried and executed for military offences during the course of the conflict. Controversial at the time, these executions were the subject of much debate and official scrutiny in the inter-war period and, even today, the subject continues to have a bitter and painful resonance. Led by the Shot at Dawn Campaign,[1] pressure for the rehabilitation of these men continues and the case for a millennium pardon was marked in June 2001 by the opening of an emotive memorial to them at the National Memorial Arboretum near Lichfield. However, this paper is not concerned with the justice of the proceedings which led to the deaths of these men.[2] Whether due legal process was followed or whether those executed were suffering from shell shock are difficult and probably unanswerable questions which I will leave to legal and to military historians. Instead of investigating the circumstances of the condemned, this paper turns the spotlight onto the circumstances and attitudes of men whose presence at military executions was as inevitable as that of the prisoner or the firing squad; namely, the commissioned chaplains of the British army.

---

[1] Cf. the website www.shotatdawn.org.uk for more information (consulted 6 December 2002). For an appraisal of the Shot at Dawn campaign, see B. Bond, *The Unquiet Western Front: Britain's Role in Literature and History* (Cambridge, 2002), 82–4.

[2] For more general discussions of the military and legal issues surrounding these executions see Cathryn Corns and John Hughes-Wilson, *Blindfold and Alone: British Military Executions in the Great War* (London, 2001); William Moore, *The Thin Yellow Line* (London, 1974, repr. 1999); Anthony Babington, *For the Sake of Example: Capital Courts-Martial 1914–1920* (London, 1983; 2nd edn, 1993); Julian Putkowski and Julian Sykes, *Shot at Dawn: Executions in World War One by Authority of the British Army Act* (Barnsley, 1989; 2nd edn, London, 1992); Leonard Sellers, *For God's Sake Shoot Straight: the Story of the Court Martial and Execution of Temporary Sub-Lieutenant Edwin Leopold Arthur Dyett, Nelson Battalion, 63rd (RN) Division during the First World War* (London, 1995); Gerard Oram, *Worthless Men: Race, Eugenics and the Death Penalty in the British Army during the First World War* (London, 1998).

Although generally overlooked by historians, one of the many ways in which British army chaplains throughout the First World War demonstrated their identification with the army as an institution and with the aspirations and objectives of its commanders was in their largely uncritical attitude towards the system of military justice which led to nearly three hundred British soldiers being 'shot at dawn'. In addition to indicating tacit approval of extreme means of maintaining discipline, this attitude also reflected the attitude of many if not most British churchmen towards capital punishment *per se*. In a survey of ecclesiastical opinion on the death penalty which was carried out by the Society for the Abolition of Capital Punishment in 1900, all episcopal respondents supported the right of the state to inflict the ultimate sanction, a position which was justified in the case of murderers by reference to Gen. 9: 6.[3] However, only fifteen of the 291 soldiers from British units who were executed between 4 August 1914 and 31 March 1920 were executed for murder; the great majority (some 240) being shot either wholly or in part for the military offence of desertion, the rest being executed for cowardice, sleeping at their post, mutiny or striking a superior officer.[4] The qualitative difference between wilful murder and offences which could lead to the death penalty under the Army Act was obvious to many contemporaries. So too, it might be added, was the rate at which these executions were carried out, their number exceeding the total of executions for murder in England and Wales for the twenty-year period 1900–19.[5] The fact that the clergy either openly or tacitly endorsed the death penalty in both cases naturally invited criticism. As one ex-officer wrote of Private James Crozier of the 9th Royal Irish Rifles, who was executed for desertion in February 1916,

> In the eyes of God, of course, he had committed no specific sin demanding repentance; therefore the Chaplain's task was easy . . . why the culprit had to make his peace with God when the only trouble he had at the time was with the Commander-in-Chief of the British Armies in France, I do not know.[6]

---

[3] Harry Potter, *Hanging in Judgment: Religion and the Death Penalty in England* (London, 1993), 107.
[4] The War Office, *Statistics of the Military Effort of the British Empire during the Great War 1914–1920* (London, 1992), 649.
[5] *Royal Commission on Capital Punishment 1949–53, Report: Presented to Parliament by Command of Her Majesty, September 1953*, ed. Ernest Arthur Gowers (London, 1953, 2nd edn., 1965), Appendix 3.
[6] F. P. Crozier, *The Men I Killed* (London, 1937, repr. Bath, 1969), 51, 219.

For reasons such as these, the infliction of the death penalty for offences under the Army Act provoked a large measure of controversy among the ordinary soldiers of the British Expeditionary Force (BEF). According to one Roman Catholic chaplain, many soldiers were 'altogether opposed to the death sentence', these feelings being especially strong among the volunteers of Lord Kitchener's vast New Army.[7] In addition to stoking debate, the death penalty also caused considerable resentment in those units which were affected by its application. In part, this could be the consequence of a certain sympathy for the condemned, especially in cases where the proceedings of their court-martial were thought to be unfair. This was certainly a factor in the reaction of the 2nd Scots Guards to the execution of Private Isaac Reid, who was shot at Laventie in April 1915. In the wake of his death, 'all sentimentalised the poor private soldier and made a hero out of him', Reid being rumoured to have been the victim of a malevolent sergeant-major, an inept personal defence and a nervous disorder which the army would later officially recognize as shell shock.[8]

However, this resentment was also a product of the element of collective punishment which executions were known to symbolize. Given the mechanisms whereby the sentences of courts-martial were confirmed (death sentences being passed up the chain of command until they were confirmed or commuted by the Commander-in-Chief whose decision was then relayed downwards for promulgation),[9] a significant factor in determining whether a man should be shot was the perceived condition of his unit. Indeed, it was not unknown for commanding officers to lobby for the confirmation of death sentences because of problems of discipline and morale among their own men.[10]

As the duke of Wellington memorably put it, military punishments were essentially 'for the sake of example', with the punishment of offenders being useful 'only in the cases where the prevalence of any crime, or the evils resulting from it, are likely to be injurious to the public interest'.[11] Consequently, the exemplary nature of military executions in the First World War sometimes involved troops being

---

[7] R. H. J. Steuart, *March, Kind Comrade* (London, 1931), 94–5.

[8] S. Graham, *A Private in the Guards* (London, 1919; 2nd edn, 1928), 159–61; M. Brown, *Tommy Goes To War* (London, 1986), 128.

[9] Corns and Hughes-Wilson, *Blindfold and Alone*, 85–104; J. Peaty, 'Capital Courts-Martial during the Great War', in Brian Bond *et al.*, eds, *'Look to Your Front': Studies in the First World War by The British Commission for Military History* (Staplehurst, 1999), 89–104, 92, 98.

[10] Babington, *For the Sake of Example*, 59–60; Crozier, *The Men I Killed*, 50.

[11] Babington, *For the Sake of Example*, vi.

paraded to witness the fate of the condemned.[12] Even when executions were of a more private nature, firing parties were usually drawn from the prisoner's own unit, with details numbering as many as eighteen men.[13] In any event, news of these executions was widely and purposefully circulated in the form of the army's General Routine Orders 'to encourage others not to commit the same offence'.[14]

Despite the public manner in which Private Reid met his end, the whole of the 2nd Scots Guards being paraded to behold the salutary spectacle,[15] the number of British soldiers who actually witnessed a military execution was, relatively speaking, extremely small. In fact, the 291 British soldiers who died in this way represented a mere 0.005 per cent of the 5.7 million men who served in the British army during the First World War. If the number of soldiers who witnessed their fate was inevitably small, the same factors also conspired to ensure that the chances of an individual army chaplain being called upon to minister to a man about to die in this manner were remote to say the least. In fact, the chaplains who ministered to those who were actually 'shot at dawn' comprised only a tiny fraction of the total number of chaplains who served in the army between 1914 and 1918. Whereas 291 soldiers from British units were executed during the course of the war, there were nearly 3,500 chaplains serving with the British army by November 1918, with many hundreds more having served twelve-month or even shorter contracts since the beginning of the war.

If the number of wartime chaplains therefore vastly exceeded the number of British executions under the Army Act, a padre's chances of being called upon to prepare a man to die in this fashion were further reduced by three other factors. Firstly, although 2,690 death sentences were passed on British soldiers by courts-martial between 4 August 1914 and 31 March 1920, the overwhelming majority – over 89 per cent in fact – were commuted at the eleventh hour.[16] Under these circumstances, the number of chaplains who ministered to men about to suffer the extreme penalty was greatly exceeded by those who visited prisoners whose sentences were ultimately commuted. Secondly, there was a marked tendency for this difficult ministry to devolve upon more experienced chaplains. Julian Bickersteth, for example, attended two

12 Ibid., 59–60.
13 Ibid., 57–8.
14 Corns and Hughes-Wilson, *Blindfold and Alone*, 103.
15 Graham, *A Private*, 161–2.
16 War Office, *Statistics*, 649; Peaty, 'Capital Courts-Martial', 92.

condemned men of the 56th (1st London) Division in July and December 1917. Similarly, the Revd Leonard Martin Andrews, an Anglican chaplain in the 3rd Division, attended his first prisoner in November 1916 and maintained that he also attended a second before being badly wounded at Arras in 1917.[17] If only a select group of Anglican chaplains tended to assume this responsibility, the same was also true of other denominations, with several Roman Catholic padres claiming in 1919 to have prepared more than one prisoner for execution.[18] Thirdly, if very few chaplains were ever likely to undertake this role, their numbers were also limited by the wishes of the condemned, for, whilst a chaplain was a stock figure at military executions, it was left to the individual prisoner to decide whether he wished to make use of his services beforehand.[19] Nevertheless, despite its rarity, chaplains were aware that this summons was a definite possibility. As an eventuality that he had 'sometimes envisaged' but never expected to encounter, when Fr R. H. J. Steuart was asked by his senior divisional chaplain to attend a deserter who was to be shot the following morning, he admitted to feeling a distinct 'thrill of repugnance'.[20]

* * *

For the handful of chaplains who had dealings with soldiers about to be executed, their situation was awkward to say the least. This awkwardness stemmed from their official status as part of the military hierarchy and from their conscious identification as the soldier's friend, the latter being shaped by their status as ministers of religion, by the spiritual and practical help which they rendered to the wounded and by their role as providers of entertainment and of various other creature-comforts to the troops. Indeed, the fact that chaplains were viewed as potential allies by the other ranks is demonstrated by their being occasionally called upon to act as 'prisoner's friend' at courts-martial. Significantly, instruction on how to play the part of soldier's advocate on these occasions was a feature of the curriculum of the BEF's chaplains' school which was belatedly opened at St Omer in 1917. Indeed, Michael Adler, the BEF's senior Jewish chaplain, not only acted as prisoner's friend for

---

[17] In fact, another soldier of the 3rd Division was shot in the intervening period. See Putkowski and Sykes, *Shot at Dawn: Executions,* 134, 294.

[18] *The Bickersteth Diaries 1914–1918,* ed. John Bickersteth (London, 1996), 189–94, 224–25; *Catholic Soldiers by Sixty Chaplains and Many Others,* ed. C. Plater (London and New York, 1919), 124–8.

[19] Babington, *For the Sake of Example,* 58–9.

[20] Steuart, *March, Kind Comrade,* 95–6.

Jewish soldiers at courts-martial but also sought legal advice from Jewish lawyers who were serving in the army.[21]

If chaplains could find themselves uncomfortably sandwiched between the requirements of military justice and their responsibility to individual soldiers, it should also be noted that military executions highlighted the limits of the chaplain's ability to influence soldiers' morale. Undoubtedly, on the Western Front at least, the promotion of discipline and morale became central to the chaplain's brief after January 1916. Seen from this perspective, the execution of a soldier after this date indicated that brutal coercion had had to be used where more subtle and positive means of encouraging discipline and morale had palpably failed. In this regard, it is worth noting that the execution of Private Alfred Ansted of the 4th Royal Fusiliers occurred shortly after the Revd Noel Mellish had won the first chaplain's VC of the war whilst serving with the same battalion. Clearly, Mellish's example in selflessly recovering wounded whilst under heavy fire had failed to have a salutary influence on all.

* * *

Another sobering fact from the chaplain's point of view was that those who faced the firing squad were often persistent offenders. Significantly, 91 of the 324 British, Dominion and Colonial soldiers executed under the Army Act during the First World War were already under suspended sentences from earlier courts-martial and forty of these had already had the death sentence passed upon them.[22] Although some of these may have been suffering from nervous disorders, others appear to have been shady characters and even habitual criminals who had brought their delinquent habits into the army. For R. H. J. Steuart, the prisoner whom he attended on the night of 10 March 1916 remained an elusive quantity. According to Steuart, Corporal C. Lewis of the 12th Highland Light Infantry was 'a native of one of the bilingual Dominions of the Empire', although between his arrest for desertion and his trial Lewis maintained that he was an American. Whether a Canadian or an American, Lewis was apprehended in civilian clothes after deserting in January 1916, just before his battalion was due to return to the trenches. Although his civilian apparel, his previous absences and

---

[21] Imperial War Museum, Department of Documents, 77/106/1, Revd M. W. Murray, note dated 20 October 1920; M. Adler, *British Jewry Book of Honour* (London, 1922; repr. Aldershot, 1997), 45.

[22] War Office, *Statistics*, 649.

his capacity for dissembling certainly indicated a determined attempt to desert, Lewis told Steuart that 'his one desire, which rapidly became an obsession, was to join the French Army, in which he believed that he would find himself at home'.[23]

If Lewis had the air of an inveterate confidence trickster, in July 1917 Julian Bickersteth was called upon to attend Private Walter Yeoman of the 1/12th Royal Fusiliers, a soldier who had been imprisoned twice in civilian life and who had deserted several times since joining the army – twice before he had even left England.[24] According to Bickersteth, Yeoman had been brought over to France 'under close arrest'. Within the space of weeks, he was court-martialled for desertion and sentenced to death, a sentence which was subsequently commuted. His desertion during the battle of Arras proved to be the final straw. Significantly, although Bickersteth assumed that such reluctance could only be that of a conscript, Yeoman was a volunteer who had joined the army in 1915.[25]

Naturally enough, chaplains had very little in common with such men. Besides being clergymen and officers (and it must be borne in mind that only three of the British soldiers executed in the First World War *were* officers), both Bickersteth and Martin Andrews were exceptionally brave individuals, each of them earning a Military Cross during their service on the Western Front. If they were very different in background, rank and temperament to the men whom they attended, they were also without any formal training for the role which was thrust upon them. In the pre-war civilian context, ministering to the condemned was viewed as a highly specialized role which was best left to prison chaplains or to exemplary pastors such as Bishop Edward King, who often worked for the salvation of the condemned in Lincoln gaol.[26]

By the late Victorian period, the role of the clergyman in this situation was seen as being to nurture feelings of repentance on the part of the prisoner and to enable him (or her) to become reconciled to the Almighty. This process was naturally facilitated by the growing period between sentencing and execution which occurred in the aftermath of the Capital Punishment Amendment Act of 1868. Unsurprisingly, given sedulous clerical attention over a period of weeks, many prisoners

23 Steuart, *March, Kind Comrade*, 97–9.
24 *Bickersteth Diaries*, 189–91.
25 Ibid., 189–90; Putkowski and Sykes, *Shot at Dawn: Executions*, 178.
26 Potter, *Hanging in Judgment*, 112–13.

proved responsive to the call for repentance.[27] Circumstances were rather different, however, for army chaplains, few of whom could have had any experience of ministering to the condemned in civilian life. Significantly, death sentences were very often promulgated only days or even hours before the sentence was carried out. Hence, the chaplain usually had very little time to discuss spiritual matters with the prisoner. Perhaps because of this time scale, it was the salvation of the prisoner's soul rather than the justice of his sentence which preoccupied the chaplain.

Chaplains tended to approach prisoners and to recall their experiences in the light of existing assumptions as to the role of the clergyman in relation to the condemned. Quite simply, what was required was to ensure that the prisoner died a good death. Although chaplains' accounts indicate that visiting the condemned was taken seriously,[28] they also imply that this ministry became urgent only when death sentences were finally promulgated and when prisoners realized that their time had come. It is perhaps indicative of the background and temperament of some prisoners that denominational ties were very loosely felt until their death sentences were actually confirmed. As one Roman Catholic chaplain recalled, one prisoner converted to Catholicism only twelve hours prior to his execution. Although he had been visited by a Protestant chaplain prior to that point, the prisoner received conditional baptism and his First (and last) Holy Communion a matter of hours before his death. In a similar case, a prisoner who had been educated at a Catholic school only divulged his real denomination after a senior Anglican chaplain had been visiting him for a fortnight.[29]

Once confronted with the condemned, chaplains had to bring them to a state of readiness for the culmination of their ordeal. Although this readiness was essentially spiritual, it was not exclusively so. Bickersteth tried to give Private Yeoman rum to drink minutes before his execution.[30] Moreover, on the eve of the execution of Private Ansted, Martin Andrews not only confirmed the news of his impending death to the prisoner but also brought two pills which he had been given 'to put in his tea' and 'which would make him sleep better'.[31] Although Martin

---

[27] Ibid.

[28] *Catholic Soldiers*, 124; *Bickersteth Diaries*, 190.

[29] *Catholic Soldiers*, 125–8. For the case of a Jewish prisoner recorded as an Anglican, see Adler, *British Jewry*, 45.

[30] *Bickersteth Diaries*, 194.

[31] Imperial War Museum, Sound Archive, 4770/1, Canon L. Martin Andrews.

Andrews made no overt attempt to engage in a spiritual discussion with Ansted, and thus confined his role to that of confidant and companion, Julian Bickersteth was more pro-active and more successful in his dealings with Private Yeoman.

As Bickersteth recalled, the problem was stark enough: 'Time goes on. I know that he must sleep, if possible, during the hours of darkness, so my time is short. How can I reach his soul?' After failing to elicit a response by reading a passage of Scripture, Bickersteth's suggestion that Yeoman choose a hymn for him to read from an army prayer book met with the proposal that they should sing 'Rock of Ages' together. Seizing on 'the straw' which had presented itself, in three hours which testified to the power of Sunday schools and hymnody in shaping the religious outlook even of an ex-convict from the East End of London, Bickersteth and Yeoman sang hymn after hymn from two different hymn books, the prisoner declining to sing the same hymn twice, whilst failing to appreciate the pathos of such hymns as 'Abide with me' and 'God be with us till we meet again'. As dawn broke and the firing party made ready, they said the Lord's Prayer together, a prayer which Yeoman 'knew quite well and was proud of knowing'. Nevertheless, after the brief march to the place of execution, it was to hymnody again that Yeoman turned for solace. After Yeoman was handcuffed, blindfolded and tied to the stake, Bickersteth whispered in his ear, 'Safe in the arms of Jesus', to which Yeoman 'quite clearly' replied 'Safe in the arms of Jesus'.[32]

Thankfully, Bickersteth's next condemned prisoner proved more receptive to more conventional methods of approach. Private Henry Williams of the 1/9th Royal Fusiliers was executed on 28 December 1917 for desertion, although his refusal to obey orders during a German attack the previous month seemed more akin to cowardice in the face of the enemy.[33] Although already under a suspended prison sentence for desertion, Bickersteth saw in Williams only a misfortunate victim of the war. As Bickersteth wrote wearily on the day after the execution:

> The last twenty-four hours have furnished me with some severe tests of physical and mental endurance. Once again it has been my duty to spend the last hours on earth with a condemned prisoner . . . I have, I hope, learnt much from the simple heroism of this mere lad of nineteen, who has been out here at the Front since

[32] *Bickersteth Diaries*, 193.
[33] Putkowski and Sykes, *Shot at Dawn: Executions*, 224.

1914. . . . It was my privilege to comfort and help him all I could, to hear his first and last confession, to administer the Holy Communion and to stand by his side till the very end.[34]

Besides strengthening Williams with the sacraments, Bickersteth received the prisoner's personal possessions for subsequent disposal and once again discovered the value of English hymnody, reading the hymn 'Just as I am without one plea!' to Williams 'just before the end'.[35]

Certainly, there is more than a dash of the hagiographical in Bickersteth's account of the death of Private Williams. In addition to partaking in the idealization of the victim (which, as we have seen in the case of the 2nd Scots Guards, was a common reaction among soldiers who knew the condemned), Bickersteth's account implied a spiritually purposive element in the otherwise tragic proceedings. If Williams died bathed in an aureole glow, Bickersteth was also apparently convinced that his death was not in vain.[36] As a chaplain whose Anglo-Catholic sympathies grew stronger as the war progressed, Bickersteth was betraying here elements of a theology which was already explicit in Roman Catholicism.

Roman Catholic penitential theology had traditionally held that personal suffering could be offered up in atonement for one's sins, and this teaching was certainly impressed upon Catholic soldiers during the First World War.[37] Seen from this perspective, the exemplary piety and patient resignation of a condemned Catholic prisoner could transcend the merely admirable and attain the heights of the spiritually sublime.[38] Indeed, there does appear to have been a marked tendency in Roman Catholic circles to see their co-religionists who were 'shot at dawn' as valuable exemplars of the Faith. Significantly, Fr Charles Plater's *Catholic Soldiers*, a book which was published in 1919 and which was intended to complement the better-known *Army and Religion* report which was published the same year, contained a whole chapter on those Catholics who were shot at dawn. As one Catholic reviewer put it:

---

[34] *Bickersteth Diaries*, 224.

[35] Ibid., 225.

[36] Ibid.

[37] 'A Chaplain', *For the Front: Prayers and Considerations for Catholic Soldiers* (Market Weighton, 1918), 31–2.

[38] See, for example, Fr Benedict Williamson's account of the last hours and execution of Private Patrick Murphy of the Machine Gun Corps on 12 September 1918 in B. Williamson, *'Happy Days' in France and Flanders with the 47th and 49th Divisions* (London, 1921), 157–60.

there is one chapter in the Catholic report which is, as the soldier would say, 'a fair knock-out.' That is the chapter on 'Facing a Death Sentence.' We are not surprised to learn that Catholics, like other people, occasionally ran away or struck their officers (There is no attempt made in the book to show that R.C.'s had any marked superiority in the natural virtues.) But where, outside the Catholic Church, could you find that *in every case* religion proved the one strong, tranquillizing, consoling force to men about to be shot in cold blood by their own companions. Small wonder that an officer present at one of these scenes ejaculated, 'Good God, yours is the religion to die in.'[39]

Whatever personal sympathy chaplains may have evinced for the condemned prisoners to whom they ministered, there is no indication in any of the accounts which have informed this paper that they felt that the system of military justice which condemned them was inherently flawed, notwithstanding the resentment which capital sentences could engender in the army and the recurrent questions which they raised in the House of Commons.[40] In fact, during the war years, it is very clear that the Churches as a body were uninterested in the justice of executions under the Army Act. In Charles Plater's *Catholic Soldiers*, executions were of note only in so far as they produced exemplars of the Faith. In David Cairns's *Army and Religion* report they were ignored altogether. Furthermore, although chaplains readily acted as prisoners' friends, no case has come to light during the course of this research of any chaplain condemning a capital sentence passed by a court-martial.

Indeed, although chaplains freely admitted the unpleasantness of military executions, even in the post-war years there were still those who were prepared to defend them. Notwithstanding the growing public mood of misgiving which led to inquiries by four successive committees in the 1920s and 1930s and the drastic curtailment of capital military offences by the Army and Air Force Bills of 1928 and 1930, in 1931 Fr R. H. J. Steuart wrote that, in the case of the military executions of 1914–18, one had to think 'soldier-wise' and 'not as a county-court lawyer'. As for Corporal Lewis, whom he had attended back in March 1916, although he had died bravely, Steuart's verdict was that he had simply paid 'the just penalty of his offence'.[41]

---

[39] *The Tablet*, 14 February 1920, 210. Spellings and punctuation as printed.
[40] Babington, *For the Sake of Example*, 82–95, 175–87.
[41] Steuart, *March, Kind Comrade*, 99, 103.

The same views appear to have been widely shared in clerical quarters. F. P. Crozier, for example, the officer who played the leading role in the execution of his namesake, Private James Crozier, in February 1916, was appalled to find that a clerical friend regarded the whole case as unexceptionable: 'Undoubtedly this comes under the heading of "render unto Ceasar"', his friend explained, 'It was the law of the land'.[42] Much to Crozier's chagrin, what most clergy seemed to find objectionable about the circumstances of this execution was that the prisoner was given the opportunity to get drunk beforehand.[43] In sum, therefore, chaplains' attitudes towards capital courts-martial reflected the general attitudes of their Churches towards capital punishment *per se*. Moreover, in the context of the chaplains' broader relationship to military authority and their responsiveness to the perceived needs of the time, their attitude towards capital courts-martial was yet another illustration of their general conformity to the military culture in which they found themselves.

University of Birmingham

---

[42] Crozier, *The Men I Killed*, 228.
[43] Ibid., 219. For a further account of the trial and execution of Private James Crozier, see F. P. Crozier, *A Brass Hat in No Man's Land* (London, 1930), 81–4.

FROM RESISTANCE TO NATIONAL RECONCILIATION: THE RESPONSE AND ROLE OF THE ECUMENICAL CHURCH IN SOUTH AFRICA

by JOHN W. DE GRUCHY

SCATTERED through the history of the Christian Church are seminal moments that have shaped the future course of Christianity whether for good or ill. When later historians of Christianity will write about the twentieth century, I anticipate that they will refer to the role of the Churches in Nazi Germany and apartheid South Africa as paradigmatic both in terms of success and failure. They might also refer to the role of the Christian Church in the transition to democracy in both countries in similar terms. In what follows I will offer some reflections on the South African side of the story, briefly tracing the response and role of what I have termed the 'Ecumenical Church' in South Africa to African resistance, democratic transition and national reconciliation.

Given the character of the Church and the many forms of Christianity in South Africa, my focus on the Ecumenical Church narrows the discourse down sufficiently to be able to speak meaningfully. By Ecumenical Church I mean collectively those Churches (mainly the Anglican, Congregational, Methodist, Presbyterian, Lutheran, Roman Catholic, African Initiated, and Dutch Reformed Mission Church) who found, without being unanimous on all matters, common cause in the struggle against apartheid. This was expressed institutionally through their membership in the South African Council of Churches (SACC), and regional ecumenical organizations. By way of contrast, the Dutch Reformed Churches, and many more conservative evangelical and Pentecostal Churches, either supported apartheid or refused to oppose it, standing critically apart or aloof from the ecumenical movement. Indicative of this tension is the fact that, for periods of time at the height of the church struggle, the SACC was led by a Pentecostal and a Dutch Reformed Church minister, neither of whose own Churches were members. But the description 'Ecumenical Church' provides us with at least one manageable indicator, whatever its shortcomings. Even so, I have not attempted a comprehensive survey of the Ecumenical Church's role, but only highlighted certain key elements.

In discussions such as this, there is always the problem of deciding who represents the Church. Are we thinking primarily of church leaders, theologians, synods, and conference statements? Or is our focus on individuals, or on parishes and congregations? Is the role of the Church to be understood in terms of its corporate actions, clearly identified as 'church activity', or is the Church also dispersed in every sector, every profession, and every group in the broader society? Within the South African context, as in many others, it is very difficult to separate out these various senses of what it means to be Church/what the Church is simply because the Church in its various manifestations is so deeply engrained in the social life of the nation. At times it will be clear that I have leadership in mind, at other times my use of the term Church will be more inclusive.

During the past ten years I have been engaged in a research project on 'Christianity and the Social History of South Africa'. The project has attempted to trace the role that Christianity has played in shaping South African society since the beginning of European colonization some three hundred and fifty years ago. Of the many issues that emerge in this study, two are of particular significance for the task at hand. The first is the extent to which Christianity has penetrated African society, redefining its values and social structures, and shaping its response to politics. But this process has not been one-way, for Christianity itself has become increasingly Africanized. The second is the emergence of the Ecumenical Church in South Africa and its relation to African political aspirations. While denominational Christianity was divisive within African society, Christian allegiance brought about through Christian missions became a unifying factor, helping to make the birth of the African National Congress (ANC) possible. Thus colonial missionary Christianity and the birth and development of the ecumenical movement in South Africa not only went hand in hand, but they also developed in tandem with African nationalism. But this, too, has not been a one-way process, for African nationalism has itself been a challenge to the Ecumenical Church in the struggle against colonialism and apartheid, and now in the task of national reconstruction.

* * *

The first South African Nobel Peace Prize winner, Chief Albert Luthuli, who received the award in 1961, was a product of mission education and a devout Christian, but he was also President of the ANC and an ardent opponent of apartheid. Towards the end of his autobiography, *Let my People Go!*, he wrote these words:

From the beginning our history has been one of ascending unities, the breaking of tribal, racial and creedal barriers. The past cannot hope to have a life sustained by itself, wrenched from the whole. There remains for us the building of a new land, a home for men who are black, white, brown, from the ruins of the old narrow groups, a synthesis of the rich cultural strains we have inherited.[1]

Luthuli went on to speak of the way in which Africans had suffered oppression at the hands of European colonialism and yet, despite this, sought peace and concord rather than vengeance. But Luthuli expressed the fear that the outstretched hand he and others offered to the apartheid regime would be rejected and the struggle would have to continue and possibly intensify.

Luthuli's concern for a just peace without vengeance, and therefore of the need for non-violent resistance, can be traced back to the very foundation of the ANC in 1912. There were two reasons for this stance. The first was strategic. Born out of the ashes of repeated bloody attempts to repulse colonialism by military means, it was inconceivable that white domination could be challenged by a further recourse to arms. The second was moral. The ANC leadership was deeply influenced by Christian and democratic values. Even though this ethos was not shared by all African nationalists, it became the dominant one, and was generally endorsed by the Ecumenical Church.

Despite Luthuli's claims, the ANC decided to embark on the armed struggle against the apartheid regime in the early 1960s. This decision posed a particularly difficult challenge to the Ecumenical Church, even though the reasons and moral conditions for the adoption of the armed struggle were part of the Christian just war tradition to which the Churches were committed, as their espousal of the British cause in the South African War had proved.

The reasons for the turn to the armed struggle were set out by another product of Christian missionary education and ANC leader, Nelson Mandela, in his historic 'Speech from the Dock' during his treason trial in 1963. Mandela recounted how the ANC had attempted by peaceful means to change the situation, but had continually been rebuffed. Peaceful resistance had met with increasing force and violent repression. Mandela then came to the decisive point:

---

[1] Albert Luthuli, *Let My People Go!* (London, 1962), 231.

It was only when all else failed, when all channels of peaceful protest were barred to us that the decision was taken to embark on violent forms of political struggle. . . . We did so not because we desired such a course, but solely because the government had left us with no other choice.[2]

So it was that on 16 December 1961, an auspicious date in South Africa's political calendar,[3] the ANC decided the time had come 'to hit back by all means in our power in defence of our people, our future, and our freedom'. In line with that corporate strategic decision, Mandela felt 'morally obliged to do what he did'.[4]

One of the remarkable aspects about the ANC decision to resort to armed resistance was the extent to which its leadership went to ensure that acts of violence were, to quote Mandela, 'properly controlled'. Hence their insistence that these were only to be undertaken by the military wing of the ANC, *Umkhonto we Sizwe* ('Spear of the Nation'). There was an acute awareness of the dangers of an all-out civil war that would lead to a spiral of violence and the destruction of South Africa rather than the birth of a non-racial, just democratic order. The decision to engage in violent resistance was thus strategically far-sighted, taking account of long-term consequences. The armed struggle was a peace-making strategy, a means towards the greater good of a non-racial democratic society, a last resort made necessary by violent repression.

Less than a year after Mandela's speech from the dock, Z. K. Matthews, another distinguished ANC leader, but also a leading Christian ecumenist, addressed a conference convened by the World Council of Churches (WCC) to consider the role of the Ecumenical Church in the struggle for justice in southern Africa. This conference, held in Zambia, was a watershed in the history of the ecumenical movement because it prepared the way for the launching of the Programme to Combat Racism five years later. The significance of Matthew's speech, entitled 'The Road from Nonviolence to Violence', was the fact that he took the decision of the ANC to resort to the armed struggle and turned it into a challenge for the Church:

[2] Nelson Mandela, 'Second Court Statement, 1964', in idem, *The Struggle is My Life* (London, 1990), 160.

[3] The day on which Boer trekkers routed the Zulu army at the Battle of Blood River in 1838. This event was later regarded as the formative moment in the rise of Afrikaner Nationalism, and celebrated as the 'Day of the Vow'.

[4] Mandela, 'Second Court Statement, 1964', 160.

When the flower of African youth represented by men such as Mandela or Dr. Alexander are being sentenced to long terms of imprisonment during peace time, for fighting for their legitimate rights in what they believe to be the only ways open to them, can we say that the Christian thing to do is to advise them to acquiesce in their present situation and wait, Micawber-like, for something to turn up?[5]

This statement powerfully summed up the challenge then facing the Ecumenical Church both in South Africa and world-wide at that critical historical moment. Mandela's challenge to the apartheid regime in particular, and more generally to white South Africa, was now specifically aimed by Matthews at the Church itself. How the Churches responded to this challenge would determine their role in the church struggle in South Africa that was then unfolding.

At about the same time, the South African member Churches of the WCC, meeting together at the Cottesloe Consultation, rejected apartheid and committed themselves to new initiatives in working for reconciliation.[6] The Cottesloe Consultation signalled the beginning of the church struggle against apartheid led by the SACC and the Christian Institute under the leadership of Beyers Naude.[7] At the heart of this struggle was a theology of reconciliation that fundamentally challenged both the politics and theology of racial separation. This theology was most clearly and fully expounded in *The Message to the People of South Africa* published by the SACC in 1968, that categorically rejected apartheid as a false gospel.[8] The *Message* gave confessional direction to the church struggle, yet it also proved to be divisive within the Churches, a phenomenon that was to grow in intensity amongst the white membership as each new phase in the struggle unfolded.

Such a divisive influence became particularly acute when the WCC 'Programme to Combat Racism' was launched in the early 1970s, with its unequivocal support for the liberation movements. Despite the

---

[5] Thomas G. Karis and Gail M. Gerhart, eds, *From Protest to Challenge: a Documentary History of African Politics in South Africa, 1882–1990*, vol. 5: *Nadir and Resurgence, 1964–1979* (Pretoria, 1997), 356.

[6] *Cottesloe Consultation: the Report of the Consultation among South African Member Churches of the World Council of Churches, 7–14 Dec. 1960 at Cottesloe, Johannesburg*, ed. Leslie A. Hewson (Johannesburg, 1961).

[7] John W. de Gruchy, *The Church Struggle in South Africa* (Grand Rapids, MI, 1979), 62–8, 103–14.

[8] Ibid., 115ff.

careful way in which the WCC stated its case, namely that it was not supporting violence, the underwriting of the liberation movements meant tacit support for the armed struggle. Severe tensions within the Ecumenical Church in South Africa resulted in several schisms and divisions, as well as in the distancing of some Churches from the SACC. Nonetheless, the Ecumenical Churches did not withdraw from the WCC, despite being pressured to do so by the government and many of their white members. Rather, the Churches responded to comparable pressure from the black majority within their constituency which ensured that they remained, however uncomfortably, on the side of the struggle. Nevertheless, it must be said that they were often glad to let the SACC bear the brunt of the task of liberation and the penalties that accrued at the hands of the state.

The rise of the Black Consciousness Movement, Black Theology and the Soweto Uprising in 1976, all had considerable impact on the Ecumenical Church. Many of the Black Consciousness leaders were members of the Ecumenical Churches and some were engaged in teaching theology to its students. The escalating war in Namibia and Angola and the armed struggle likewise had a direct impact. Increasing numbers of black young people, many of whom were members of the Church, went into exile and joined the military wings of the ANC and Pan Africanist Congress (PAC).

In response, some white Christians advocated the path of conscientious objection to military service as their way of expressing solidarity. This choice did not necessarily imply pacifism on their part, but could be a tacit recognition of the justice of the liberation struggle and a refusal to fight on behalf of an unjust order. Also implicit was a growing sense of the illegitimacy of the apartheid regime. The extent to which this trend was recognized by the apartheid authorities can be seen in the extent to which they meted out punishment to those supporting conscientious objection. But the conscientious objection debate also opened up a further cleavage within the Ecumenical Church. For some it did imply an espousal of pacifism and therefore an opposition in principle to the armed struggle, even if support for the liberation struggle was otherwise endorsed; but for others, as indicated, it was intended to be a way of identifying with the armed struggle as a just cause.

Another response to the armed struggle, led largely by Archbishop Desmond Tutu, was that of advocating comprehensive sanctions against South Africa. The argument here was that while the Churches could not endorse the armed struggle as such, they could encourage economic and other measures that would bring the government to its knees and thus pave the way for a negotiated end to apartheid. But even this issue was divisive within the Ecumenical Churches, splitting them largely along racial lines.

Resistance to apartheid escalated during the 1980s. As international economic and political sanctions tightened and resistance inside the country became increasingly militant, so the government embarked on its strategy of destroying all agents of what it perceived to be the 'total onslaught' of Communism. This was the context within which the *Kairos Document* was drafted. Recognizing that the basic difference between 'Christians in South Africa was not primarily denominational or confessional, but political and economic', the *Kairos Document* perceived that the Church itself was a site of the struggle. Thus the *Kairos Document* not only attacked the 'state theology' of those who gave their support to apartheid, but also opposed what it named the 'church theology' of the mainline multi-racial Ecumenical Churches, accusing them of promoting cheap reconciliation.[9] By contrast, the *Kairos Document* called for direct Christian participation in the struggle, including acts of civil disobedience in resistance to government tyranny.

Heated controversy around the meaning of reconciliation ensued within the Churches as state repression against Christian activists associated with the *Kairos Document* intensified.[10] Even Churches and church leaders who had rejected apartheid and who were engaged in the struggle to end it were unhappy about the way in which 'church theology' and reconciliation were, in their terms, caricatured and criticized. There was, at the same time, even sharper criticism of the *Kairos Document* emanating from a circle of black theologians who remained faithful to the more radical concerns of the Black Consciousness Movement. For them, the discourse of reconciliation was controlled by the 'ruling class' rather than by those who were alienated from whites, from the land, from the means of production, and thus

---

[9] Catholic Institute for International Relations and British Council of Churches, eds, *The Kairos Document: a Theological Comment on the Political Crisis in South Africa* (London, 1986), art. 3.1, 9.
[10] See the discussion in the *Journal of Theology for Southern Africa* 58 (March 1987); John W. de Gruchy, 'The Struggle for Justice and the Ministry of Reconciliation', in Klaus Nürnberger and John Tooke, eds, *The Cost of Reconciliation in South Africa* (Cape Town, 1988), 166–80.

from power. If reconciliation was to mean anything significant for the poor and oppressed, it had to reverse this alienation.

Precisely at this time, while still in prison, Nelson Mandela began secret talks with the National Party leadership in order to explore the possibility of negotiations.[11] In doing so, he set in motion a new process of possible reconciliation between white and black. The fact that Mandela initiated the talks, and the way in which he entered into them, indicates that he was committed to pursuing the path of reconciliation as an integral part of the process of achieving the goal of liberation. It had become abundantly clear to him that there was no alternative other than a protracted civil war, in which neither the state nor the liberation movement had the capacity to achieve a decisive victory. The prolonging of such a vicious stalemate could only spell disaster for the country. Just as the turn to the armed struggle had been determined both by strategic and moral considerations, so its termination was based on political realism and a moral commitment to the common good.

However miraculous it might have appeared, South Africa's transition to democracy eventually came about through a process of tough negotiation. Political analysts and historians will long debate precisely what social and other forces finally brought an end to apartheid. However, it seems self-evident that the changes were not brought about by any single factor, but were the result of a combination of all the elements of the struggle. One contribution to the process was undoubtedly made by the Ecumenical Church which acted, in many respects, as the midwife of transition, monitoring the process and nurturing the moral values required for the transformation.[12] But how are we to assess the more general role of the Ecumenical Churches in the struggle against apartheid, and how do they see their role and responsibility in this new era of national reconstruction and reconciliation?

* * *

The final clause of the Interim Constitution, approved late in 1993, was entitled 'On National Unity and Reconciliation'. This clause paved the way for the Truth and Reconciliation Commission (TRC), speaking as it did of the need for understanding not revenge, reparation not retalia-

---

[11] The remarkable story of these talks is told in Nelson Mandela, *Long Walk to Freedom: the Autobiography of Nelson Mandela* (Johannesburg, 1994), 506–11.

[12] John W. de Gruchy, *Christianity and Democracy: a Theology for a Just World Order* (Cambridge, 1995), 205–24.

tion, *ubuntu* not victimization. Unlike the Nuremberg Trials after the Second World War, the TRC was not established by foreign powers for the sake of punishing war criminals, but was constituted by South Africans for the sake of dealing with the past in a way that would bring healing and reconciliation. As the SACC said,

> The Commission for Truth and Reconciliation is not another Nuremberg. It turns its back on any desire for revenge. It represents an extraordinary act of generosity by a people who only insist that the truth, the whole truth and nothing but the truth be told. The space is thereby created where the deeper processes of forgiveness, confession, repentance, reparation and reconciliation can take place.[13]

Indicative of the urgency of initiating the process of reconciliation, the establishment of the TRC was approved during the first session of the new South African parliament, on Friday 21 October 1994. Its mandate was to provide a record of gross human rights violations committed by both the upholders of apartheid and the liberation movements; to identify the victims and their fate; to recommend possible measures of reparation; to process applications for amnesty and indemnity; and to make recommendations with regard to measures necessary to prevent future gross human rights violations.

Although the Ecumenical Church cannot take credit for the establishment of the TRC, elements within it played an important role in preparing the way and shaping its character. The SACC had previously called on its constituency to acknowledge and confess its own guilt for apartheid and its failure to overcome it. These topics were addressed at the SACC Soweto Conference on 'Confessing Guilt' (1989), and became major themes at the Rustenburg Conference (1991), and the Cape Town Consultation of the WCC member Churches in South Africa (1995). There were, moreover, regular calls by the SACC and its member Churches for national repentance and reconciliation, and several key people involved in the formulation of the TRC proposals for the government were Christian theologians. In short, the Ecumenical Church helped shape the consciousness within which the idea of the TRC was nurtured and, in doing so, contributed some of the key insights.

The work of the TRC began in February 1996 under the chairman-

---

13 *The Truth Will Set You Free*, SACC Brochure (1995), 24.

ship of Desmond Tutu. A large number of the commissioners were also prominent church leaders. The TRC was, as one cabinet minister put it, a 'civic sacrament'. In making that observation, Kadar Asmal, who is not a Christian, presumably had in mind the sacrament of penance or reconciliation within the Christian tradition.[14] All the elements we associate with that sacrament were present in one form or another in the TRC process, from confession of sin and guilt, through absolution and amnesty, to penance or reparation. The TRC was, in fact, more a national confessional than a court of law. Much of the discussion raised issues similar to those discussed at this conference, concerning discipline, penance, forgiveness, restitution, both in the early Church and at other times. Indeed, critics of the TRC complained that its language and conceptualization were too theological, indeed, too Christian, and that its mode of operation sometimes resembled more a pastoral counselling chamber presided over by a father confessor than a court of law chaired by a judge.

During the course of the TRC it became obvious that apartheid was not only something that had been pursued by the National Party Government and its agencies, but that there were many other groups in the country that had supported the policy and its implementation, or at least benefited from it. Some might not have done so enthusiastically, or without criticism and protest, but others were integral to the workings of apartheid. Accordingly, the TRC asked these sectors, which included for example the medical profession and the banking sector, to present their case. Amongst those invited were also the Churches and other faith communities.

At the TRC hearings devoted to the 'Faith Communities', held in East London in November 1997, we were reminded of the very ambiguous role that the Churches had played during the apartheid years.[15] Some gave legitimation to apartheid, notably the Dutch Reformed Church, others tried to be neutral, like many of the evangelical and Pentecostal denominations, and yet others, in varying ways, tried to oppose apartheid, like the Ecumenical Churches within the SACC. But

[14] Kadar Asmal, Louise Asmal and Ronald Suresh Roberts, *Reconciliation through Truth: a Reckoning of Apartheid's Criminal Governance* (Cape Town, 1996), 49.
[15] See James C. Cochrane, John W. de Gruchy and Stephen Martin, eds, *Facing the Truth: South African Faith Communities and the Truth & Reconciliation Commission* (Cape Town, 1999); for a personal account by one of the TRC Commissioners and a Nederduitse Gereformeerde Kerk (NGK, i.e. the Dutch Reformed Church) theologian, see Piet Meiring, *Chronicle of the Truth Commission: a Journey through the Past and Present – into the Future of South Africa* (Vanderbijlpark, 1999), 265ff.

none came off with an unblemished record: all were guilty in varying ways and to varying degrees. Whatever their criticisms of the ideology of apartheid and its implementation, they had not done as much as they should have to combat it. Church leaders confessed that too many of their members had connived with apartheid, and some had been amongst those who had perpetrated atrocious crimes. Hence a major emphasis in their statements was that of penitence for past failure, and a commitment to work for national reconciliation and justice in the future.

At the same time it was acknowledged that certain Churches, church leaders, and many Christians had played major roles in the liberation struggle. Indeed, in so far as the majority of Christians in South Africa are black, many of the victims of apartheid were Christian, and many local church communities suffered at the hands of the regime. This connection between the victims and Christianity was often evident during the TRC, when those present, encouraged by Desmond Tutu, sang hymns or offered prayers – a matter of some concern to those of others faiths who were also present. But the representations made to the TRC highlight the extent to which, more than any other faith community, the Christian Churches represent the broad spectrum of South African society. Victims, benefactors and perpetrators were together members of the Churches, an indication both of the failure of the Church to be a community of reconciliation, but also of its potential to help bring about national reconciliation in this post-apartheid period.

The work of the TRC is now over, though the jury is still out on whether or not it succeeded in achieving its goals. Many in South Africa believe that it has, in fact, largely failed. Or, to put it differently, that South Africa has failed to make the most of the opportunity granted by the work of the TRC, for surely the TRC itself cannot be held solely responsible for whatever its failures may be. But no verdict is yet possible.

Perhaps above all else there is a question mark over whether or not South Africa is a more reconciled nation as a result of the TRC's work. South Africans are well aware that whatever the TRC has done to promote national reconciliation, it could not and did not fulfil the hopes of all those who long for justice and peace in South Africa. That challenge will be with us for generations. From this perspective, the work of the TRC must be understood as a catalyst within the process of reconciliation, a means to an end, even though, in some instances, it was also an end in itself. But national reconciliation is a huge project, a project which in many ways reflects the biblical understanding of reconciliation as the restoration of justice in society.[16]

Despite the TRC we remain, in President Thabo Mbeki's words, 'two nations, the one white and relatively prosperous, and the other black and poor'.[17] Such rhetoric highlights reality, even if it requires qualification, for the social reality of South Africa is always more complex than can be captured in trenchant phrases no matter how true. But we must not miss Mbeki's point. His comment was a call to action, for the future of South Africa depends on how past enmity and present alienation can be overcome and on how the 'two nations' find each other in order to build a new nation on a moral foundation that can endure. Central to that call to action is the need to restore justice, without which national reconciliation would be meaningless.

The biblical concept of reconciliation is closely connected to the notion of restorative justice. This aspect is of fundamental importance in considering the scope of Christian witness and the task of the Church in South Africa. It is also the understanding of justice that predominated within the vision and work of the TRC. While it is impossible to redress all the wrongs that have been perpetrated against the victims of colonial injustice and apartheid, reparation does mean that concrete steps have to be taken which will lead to a more equitable and just society. The transformation of education, health services and every other aspect of public life in such a way that justice and equity is achieved is essential if justice is to be a reality. Justice, in other words, is more than maintaining 'law and order' or pursuing any 'due process'; both of these are important, but limited in scope and open to abuse. Restorative justice has to do with reparation, the collective form of doing penance.

There has been much criticism of the failure of the government to provide reparation to victims recommended by the TRC. Indeed, the record of governments worldwide in implementing the recommendations of truth commissions, not least the TRC, has not been good.[18] There are several reasons for this failure. One is a lack of political will and commitment. Related to it is the fact that present governments

---

[16] See the discussion in John W. de Gruchy, *Reconciliation: Restoring Justice* (London, 2002).

[17] This description was given by President Thabo Mbeki in his address on the occasion of the opening of Parliament in 1998.

[18] Priscilla B. Hayner, *Unspeakable Truths: Confronting State Terror and Atrocity* (New York, 2001), 169.

have to pay for the sins and faults of previous regimes. But usually the main reason is the lack of resources and, even where this is not an insurmountable problem, new governments often lack the practical capacity to implement recommendations. So, yet again, victims of past oppression can become victims of good intentions, but no delivery, on promises.

The restoration of justice as reparation is invariably inseparable from the question of land distribution and property rights. Negative reaction to what happened in Zimbabwe during 2001–2, when the Mugabe government engaged in its controversial policy of land redistribution, should not obfuscate the issue that lies behind the social upheaval that occurred. Black alienation in southern Africa was, in the first instance, not that from white people, but alienation from land, cattle, and labour.[19] The redistribution of land is not easy to achieve after so long a period of colonialism and apartheid, but far-reaching steps must be taken. The redistribution of wealth is never easy or without pain, but it is vital, and those who were privileged in the past need to accept this responsibility as a liberating and healing opportunity. It is not simply a matter of the government trying to make reparation, but of those who are privileged, in this case, the beneficiaries of colonialism and apartheid. This is why the objectives of the worldwide Jubilee movement, or the South African campaign 'Homes for All' and many other similar programmes are so important.

* * *

During the struggle years, the SACC, as agent of the Ecumenical Church, received enormous support from the international community. Comparatively little came from South African sources. With the changes, international support began to dry up, forcing the SACC to reduce its staff and programmes and to reconsider its role in society. This, we might say, was part of the process of normalization that affected many sectors in post-apartheid South Africa, and it might explain in part the observation that the Ecumenical Church seemed to be less engaged in the political arena than before. This type of criticism was levelled at the Churches, not least by the new government leadership. Indeed, it was said that the Churches appeared as if they were putting all their energy into their own institutional needs, rather than

---

[19] Itumeleng J. Mosala, 'The Meaning of Reconciliation: a Black Perspective', *Journal of Theology for Southern Africa* 59 (June 1987), 22.

social ones. I would argue, however, that the Churches, even during the struggle years, focused as much on institutional needs as they did on combating apartheid. Moreover, those in the Churches who were actively engaged in the struggle as church *representatives* were always relatively few in number. I suspect that this situation remains the case now in the task of national reconciliation and the restoration of justice.

Nonetheless, at the 'Faith Communities' hearings of the TRC in 1997, there was general consensus that the Churches, and not just the Ecumenical ones, had to play a major role in this process. Several major themes and proposed commitments emerged in this regard. The first was a willingness to engage in the public task of reconciliation and not simply regard the matter as an internal church affair. Their understanding of reconciliation promoted interpersonal relations more than reconciliation as restoring social justice. A second was to make use of their resources. For example, some Churches who own large tracts of land obtained for mission work from chiefs during the colonial period are engaged in redistribution programmes. A third was in terms of liturgical practice. During the struggle years, liturgies of resistance as well as confession emerged that were important in raising the consciousness of congregations. Similar liturgies were now needed that focused more specifically on reconciliation in all its dimensions. A fourth was speaking out prophetically on issues such as poverty. Finally, a fifth was a commitment to becoming more engaged in the moral reconstruction of the nation. Of course, whether the Churches will do what they pledged remains to be seen, though there are some indications on the part of some that this is happening.

Although there is growing consensus in the Churches that they have to become involved in national reconciliation and reconstruction, there is admittedly no consensus on some of the burning issues of the day. Sections of the Church strongly defend traditional cultural norms, or religiously conservative values, whilst others are open to, and supportive of, the remarkably progressive values of the new South African constitution. There is, likewise, a range of positions adopted on economic policy and the like. In other words, while the terms of the church struggle in South Africa have shifted away from those that were defined in the past by colonialism and apartheid, the struggle continues around a new set of issues. This is where the cleavage is now taking place, much along the same lines as before, with the Ecumenical Church generally being more progressive, yet not undivided.

Of course, many of the problems confronting us today were already present before the transition to democracy occurred, and the social role of the Church in caring for social victims has always been important. But much of the social energy of the Ecumenical Church went into the struggle against apartheid, and many of the more traditional social roles of the Church were subsumed within that broader agenda. The transition to democratic rule meant that the energy and resources used in the struggle against apartheid could be concentrated more on serving the broader needs of society, and especially the new challenges that were emerging, such as the HIV/AIDS pandemic. So, if the liberation struggle set the agenda previously, now the agenda for the Churches is being set by a multiplicity of urgent problems that are requiring a knowledge and expertise that is not always available to the Churches. Moreover, this action has to be carried out in the context of a rapidly changing church scene and a very different relationship to the state. No longer was it a case of confronting an unjust and illegitimate regime in the name of Christ, but of seeking to live and witness in a democratic society alongside other faith communities and in critical solidarity with government.

The face and character of the Church in South Africa is changing rapidly. Nowhere is this transformation more apparent than in the burgeoning independent, charismatic and Pentecostal Churches, adding a new dimension to the already complex mosaic of African indigenous Churches and the historic Pentecostal ones. But new and unexpected social forces are changing the face of Christianity and the Church in South Africa since the transition to democracy even more. For example, the arrival of many central and West African Christian refugees has led to the founding of a growing number of Francophone church congregations. In the church where I worship, which has until recently been overwhelmingly white and middle-class, we now have a remarkable cultural mix, which includes a growing number of refugees from Central Africa. The church also accommodates a Mandarin-speaking Chinese Congregation comprised largely of new immigrants. Gone are the days when we can speak simply in terms of mainline or mainstream Churches as representative of Christianity. Indeed, even the composition of the Ecumenical Church itself has changed significantly.

Another important factor is the shift from a 'Christendom' situation, in which Christianity played a hegemonic role during the colonial and apartheid periods, to one in which other religious faiths and traditions are becoming significant players in terms of shaping public policy.

Christianity might still be the dominant tradition by far, but its influence is certainly different from what it was previously. Thus, the issues facing South Africa now have to be tackled in a way that takes religious pluralism seriously.

There can be no doubt that the role of the Church within a democratic environment must be different to that which it played within the context of totalitarian apartheid society with a particular Christian ethos. After the ANC was banned and during the years of struggle, the Ecumenical Church assumed a political role by default. Now, instead, the ANC is in power and many of those who played an important role within the Ecumenical Church are part of the new government and its agencies. So the relationship between the Ecumenical Church and the state has become far more complex, and as problematic as it is promising. This relationship is one that will take time to settle, and it may be even never finally resolved. Certainly, the Ecumenical Churches are partners with the government in a way that was never true before.

Yet there is also a sense in which the two bodies are recognizing that this partnership can come at some cost to their witness. For when liberation movements aligned to the Churches become the new power, the Churches have to be especially wary that they do not surrender their prophetic and critical role. Indeed, their task is not only to respond to the agenda set by the government, but to be the voice of conscience and thus be at the forefront of setting the agenda for the government. But however we assess this new situation, we certainly are at a different point in history from that when Luthuli, Mandela and Mathews challenged the Churches to become involved in the liberation struggle.

University of Cape Town